Hawaiian Birdlife

Hawaiian Birdlife

SECOND EDITION

Andrew J. Berger

THE UNIVERSITY PRESS OF HAWAII

HONOLULU

Library of Congress Cataloging in Publication Data

Berger, Andrew John, 1915–
   Hawaiian birdlife.

   Bibliography: p.
   1. Birds—Hawaii.   I.   Title.
QL684.H3P47   1981   598.29969   80–26332
ISBN 0-8248-0742-1

To

ALFRED M. BAILEY

EDWIN H. BRYAN, JR.

ALEXANDER WETMORE

Contents

Preface

A great deal has been learned about Hawaiian birds since the manuscript for the first edition was completed in 1970: a new endemic genus has been discovered on Maui and many new exotic species have become established. Much more effort also has been expended on the study of Hawaiian birds and their habitats, especially since the passage of the Rare and Endangered Species Law in 1973. When I first arrived in Hawaii on February 1, 1964, there were no representatives of the U.S. Fish and Wildlife Service in the state. Now more than a score of federal wildlife personnel work full-time in Hawaii; even the U.S. Forestry Service hired an ornithologist, although I have seen no evidence of a change in forestry philosophy.

I am indebted to many friends and colleagues who shared their information with me and granted permission to use their photographs; acknowledgement is given in the legends for these photographs. Those not so acknowledged were taken by me. John W. Beardsley generously identified insects for me.

Special thanks are due Sue Monden and Barbara Downs for painting the original color plates and Sally Oshiro for her meticulous typing of the manuscript. My daughter Diana devoted many tedious hours to proofreading with me.

Honolulu, Hawaii   ANDREW J. BERGER
October 1980

Preface
to First Edition

More than twenty-five years have passed since the publication of George Munro's *Birds of Hawaii,* and there is a need for an up-to-date book on the birds of the Hawaiian Islands, if for no other reason than to chronicle the continual desecration of the unique Hawaiian forests and their animal life.

I have received considerable pleasure from the creativity involved in writing this book. Part of the pleasure resulted from the memories of notable field trips in Hawaii between 1964 and 1970. I recall the feeling of freedom and well-being when sitting atop Miller's Peak on Nihoa, scanning the endless blue Pacific on a nearly cloudless day, and then of looking down the steep slopes at the many thousands of seabirds and at Gene Kridler netting Nihoa Finches. I remember exhilarating days and nights on Laysan—of swatting flies on the beach as Nelson Rice and I talked of many things; of the night that Ron Walker and I donned headlamps in order to search for roosting Laysan Finches. There was the cold January day I saw my first Crested Honeycreeper on the northeast slope of Haleakala—a day when the rain fell continuously in sheets; when the fog was so thick we could scarcely see across tiny Lake Wai Anapanapa; when the temperature did not rise above 45°F; and when John Maciolek, Dave Kawate, Joe Medeiros, and I were so cold we could hardly eat our lunch. I remember clearly the first trek into the Alakai Swamp country with Mike Ord, Ron Walker, and Warren King. Rarely in any part of the world have I seen such a beautiful, awe-inspiring, pristine area as the Alakai; the bulldozer cannot reach it, but exotic plants could destroy it. My admiration for the crew of the Bureau of Commercial Fisheries' ship the *Charles H. Gilbert* has not waned one bit since they skillfully got us and our equipment on and off Nihoa Island during the summer of 1966; these men did not bat an eye as they were bounced about in their skiff, surrounded by churning white water in

Adams Bay, as we pulled all our gear ashore by ropes from mid-morning until late afternoon.

I also remember days and nights, however, when my emotions ranged from frustration to depression and to disgust as I recalled my repeated, futile efforts to find certain Hawaiian birds after reading of Hawaii as it was in the 1890s. That the Hawaiian biota should have been raped, ravaged, and devastated during the nineteenth century was regrettable even though understandable, but that this rape has continued not only into the twentieth century but even into the eighth decade of that century is a sad commentary on man as an animal species. Man is, indeed, a disease on the planet earth.

Few people realize how ignorant we are to this day about the basic facts of the breeding biology of the endemic Hawaiian birds. There are historical reasons, of course. The nineteenth century was a period of discovering new birds and of describing and naming them. Some of the early collectors also were plagued by tragedy. William Anderson, the surgeon-naturalist on Captain Cook's last voyage, died on August 1, 1778, and most of the specimens collected on Cook's voyages have been lost. To be sure, William Ellis, an "assistant surgeon," painted 12 species of Hawaiian birds and John Webber painted 7, but apparently only seven of these works have ever been published (Medway 1981). Ellis' watercolor paintings are described as having "considerable charm and delicacy."

Andrew Bloxam made collections during the visit of H.M.S. *Blonde* in 1824 and 1825, but his collection also was lost. There was a published natural history report of the voyage, but Alfred Newton wrote that "an appendix there indeed is, but one utterly unworthy of its reputed author, for the book was edited by a lady who had nothing but a few of his notes to guide her, and though assisted, as it is stated, by 'the gentleman connected with that department in the British Museum' the Appendix is a disgrace to all concerned, since, so far from advancing the knowledge of the subject, it introduced so much confusion as to mislead many subsequent writers'' (Henshaw 1902:74). Similarly, the American naturalist J. K. Townsend collected in Hawaii in 1835, but Henshaw remarked that ''our gain in knowledge of the avifauna of the islands resulting from the visits of these three investigators was comparatively little. Nothing was published by the investigators themselves,'' and, therefore, published material dealt almost exclusively with technical descriptions of the birds, with little or no reliable information on distribution, behavior, or breeding habits. Indeed, the labels on most of the specimens gave the region of collection simply as the ''Sandwich Islands,'' typically with no other information.

Perhaps the most significant of the early collections was made by Charles Pickering and Titian Peale, who visited the islands during 1840 with the United States Exploring Expedition. However, nearly all of the specimens were lost in the wreck of one of their ships. Moreover, ''of the original report upon the mammals and birds by Peale, nearly all the copies were destroyed by fire.'' There must be an interesting story to explain why John Cassin published a revised edition of Peale's work ten years later.

The first important list of Hawaiian birds was published by Sanford B. Dole in 1869 (corrected and republished in 1879); it covered about half of the species found in the islands.

British colonial servants and army physicians made significant studies of the flora and fauna in many faraway places during the nineteenth century. How unfortunate it is that none of the early missionaries in Hawaii, such as William Ellis, C. S. Stewart, and Titus Coan, apparently had any interest in the birdlife. Each man wrote about his experiences in Hawaii, including trips to the Kilauea volcano, but birds were ignored in the writing. The highly respected Hawaiian scholar David Malo (born on Hawaii about 1793) did leave a written record (*Hawaiian Antiquities,* or *Moolelo Hawaii*) telling much of Hawaiian history and culture. Malo's book was translated from Hawaiian into English by Nathaniel B. Emerson in 1898 and was published by the Bernice P. Bishop Museum in 1951. In his biographical sketch of Malo, Emerson wrote that ''such good use did Malo make of his opportunities that he came to be universally regarded as the great authority and repository of Hawaiian lore.'' Malo wrote that the Hawaiians ate the following species of birds: Newell's Shearwater, Dark-rumped Petrel, Bulwer's Petrel, Hawaiian Stilt, Golden Plover, Bristle-thighed Curlew, Coot, Hawaiian Rail, Crow, Elepaio, Oo, Mamo, Iiwi, Amakihi, and Akialoa. Nevertheless, it is

clear from reading Malo's comments on the endemic forest birds that he had little or no personal knowledge of them because there are many errors in his descriptions.

In his *Sandwich Island Notes,* Bates (1854) mentioned only one bird (Apapane) by name. Similarly, I was also greatly disappointed in reading Isabella L. Bird's *Six Months in the Sandwich Islands* to learn that she apparently found the birds not worth writing about. She was a skilled horsewoman, and covered Hawaii in 1873 as few if any foreigners have ever done. She described the ferns and other plants repeatedly and at great length, but had hardly a word for the birds. What I cannot comprehend is how such an observant woman, traveling alone with a Hawaiian guide and living in the homes of the Hawaiian people, could have shown no interest in the islands' remarkable birds, but this is part of the historic reason for our ignorance of Hawaiian birds.

The modern era of Hawaiian ornithology began in 1887, when Scott Wilson, an Englishman, began his work in Hawaii, and all of the important work done in Hawaii from that time to the turn of the century was done because of the interest in the Hawaiian avifauna by the English. Lord Walter Rothschild sent Henry Palmer to collect in the Hawaiian Islands from December 1890 to August 1893; George C. Munro was one of Palmer's assistants. The Royal Society and the British Association for the Advancement of Science sent R. C. L. Perkins to Hawaii in 1892. Perkins, an entomologist, was a keen field observer, and it is to him primarily that the first knowledge of the habits of the birds is attributed. He studied the land fauna for ten years. Despite the highly significant contributions made by Perkins, Henshaw could justifiably write in 1902: ''Notwithstanding the important contributions of the English naturalists, there is still offered an inviting field for future study and investigation. . . . Of the nests and eggs of Hawaiian birds we know next to nothing.''

Henshaw added that he had prepared his list of Hawaiian birds ''chiefly with the hope that the meagerness of our knowledge respecting this subject may thereby be made more apparent, and thus that island observers may be stimulated to enter this very interesting and fruitful field—a field, too, which it would seem should appeal particularly to the pride and interest of the residents of the islands.'' He wrote in vain.

As long ago as the turn of the century, Henshaw (1902:71–73) also bemoaned the lack of interest of the Hawaiians in the birdlife.

The impression seems to be general that in olden times the natives were extensively acquainted with Hawaiian birds, which is true, and that even the present day natives are very well posted on the subject; the latter is by no means the case. . . . In the olden days when it was an important part of their duty for the priests to watch the motions of certain birds and listen to their songs that by this means they might learn the will of the Gods, and when the bird-catcher plied his calling that the feather tribute might not be wanting to pay the taxes imposed by the chiefs, then we may be sure bird-lore was well-nigh universal.

The bird-catchers, especially, must have been thoroughly familiar not only with the haunts of all the feathered kind, but with their songs and their habits.

But taxes are no longer payable in feathers; no longer does the bird-catcher ply his calling; the priest no more reads auguries from the songs of birds; the old days have gone forever, and with the old days and the old conditions have gone the greater part of Hawaiian bird-lore.

Now in the eighth decade of the twentieth century—when overpopulation and pollution of the environment threaten the very existence of mankind—presidents, governors, and legislators may listen to scientists, but it has not long been so. When George C. Munro made his pleas and his predictions, few listened, and he was by no means the first to make such pleas.

Writing in the *Ibis* in 1890, Scott Wilson said:

I have gone at some length into this question, as, by so doing, I may draw it to the attention of the Hawaiian Government, as well as that of the large land-owners, and their combined action cannot be too soon brought into effect if the entire disforestation of the Hawaiian Archipelago is to be prevented. It would be a disgraceful thing if such a Garden of Eden should be bereft of its birds, more especially as I am convinced that these islands have a great future before them as the great health-resort for the inhabitants of San Francisco flying from its unhealthy and treacherous climate, to say nothing of the vast number of tourists who will flock, in yearly-increasing numbers, to see the volcanic wonders of Hawaii, from all quarters of the globe. All these visitors may be expected to take an intelligent interest in the avifauna of the islands they visit or make their home, and on their behalf I appeal to the land-owners and to the Legislature of Hawaii to unite in protecting their country's birds. I would suggest that not only should forestlands be fenced in so far as practicable, but that *no* exotic birds should be introduced. Several species of Hawaiian birds, which were to be found in Cook's time, and others which were obtained even so late as 1840, have become extinct, and it would not be rash to say that ere another century has elapsed but few native species will remain.

To be sure, not all the ''sophisticated'' modern visitors ''take an intelligent interest in the avifauna of the islands,'' but vast numbers of tourists we do have, and there are all too few remaining virgin forests and native birds for those visitors who have an interest in nature.

Twenty years remain of the 100-year period mentioned by Wilson in 1890, and many more Hawaiian birds have become extinct since then. It is now reasonable to expect that Wilson's predictions will, indeed, come true unless there is an immediate change in attitude among the state's elected officials toward the value of our endemic flora and fauna.

In the interest of truth, it also seems appropriate to dispense with the widespread myth that the Hawaiians were conservationists. They were neither better nor worse than peoples in other parts of the world (see Stonehouse 1962b), but work to preserve the endemic birds they undoubtedly did not do. When Captain Cook discovered Kauai on January 20, 1778, among the articles brought to barter were ''great numbers of skins of small red birds [*Vestiaria coccinea*] which were often tied up in bunches of 20 or more, or had a small wooden skewer run through their nostrils'' (Stresemann 1950:78). Many other examples of the use of birds as food and for their feathers are given in the present book.

Figures 1 and 2 are included to aid the reader in understanding the ornithological terms used in describing plumage patterns, and especially those which provide distinctive ''field marks'' for identifying birds in the wild.

I am pleased to acknowledge the excellent cooperation of a number of people in the preparation of the text and illustrations, and I express my sincere appreciation to them:

To Dr. Roland W. Force, director of the Bernice P. Bishop Museum, for permission to use the color plate from the fine paper by Frank Richardson and John Bowles, and for his kindness in allowing me to borrow study skins from the museum's collection. To Edwin H. Bryan, Jr., Curator of Collections at the museum, for generously allowing me to use a draft manuscript of his revised *Check List and Summary of Hawaiian Birds.* To Miss Margaret Titcomb, Museum Librarian, for providing photographs from the Tanager Expedition and from Rothschild's unpublished work.

To the following people for providing photographs, either for use in the book or in preparation of the original paintings: Norman Carlson, Sherwin Carlquist, C. Robert Eddinger, Warren B. King, Eugene Kridler, David L. Olsen, W. Michael Ord, John L. Sincock, Herman T. Spieth, P. Quentin Tomich, Richard C. Tongg, Lewis Wayne Walker, Ronald L. Walker, and William O. Wirtz II. I am especially grateful to Alfred M. Bailey for providing photographs taken by him and by Walter K. Fisher on Laysan Island in 1902 and 1912–1913. Acknowledgment is given in the legend for each of the photographs; those not so acknowledged were taken by me.

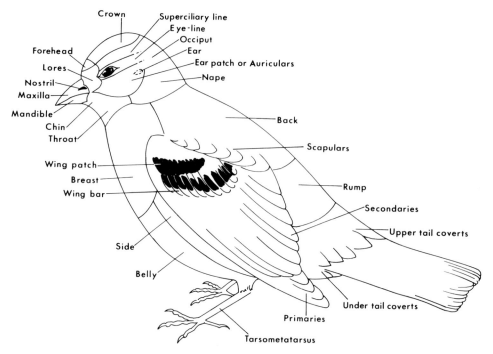

FIGURE 1. The topography of a bird.

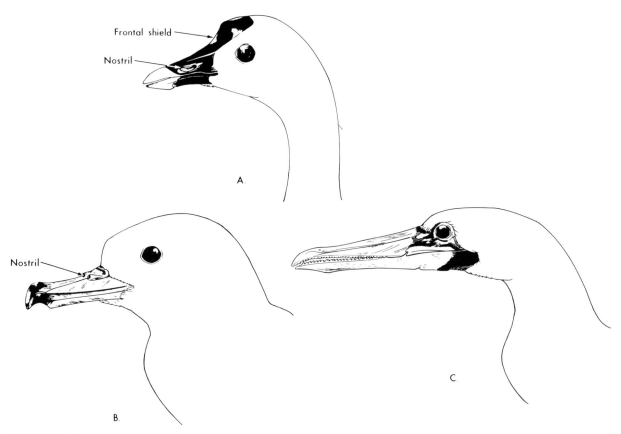

FIGURE 2. Special features of the heads of three birds: *A,* Gallinule; *B,* Wedge-tailed Shearwater; *C,* Red-footed Booby, in which species there are no external nostrils.

To Charles H. Lamoureux and William J. Hoe for analyzing the plant constituents of several bird nests. To Allen Y. Miyahara, Frank H. Haramoto, and Frank J. Radovsky for identifying bird parasites and diseases.

To Eugene Kridler, manager of the Hawaiian Islands National Wildlife Refuge, for his kindness in inviting me to accompany him on two expeditions to the Leeward Islands, for making it possible for me to raise Nihoa Finches in captivity, and for providing unpublished data on migrant species.

To Ronald L. Walker and David H. Woodside, of the State Division of Fish and Game, who were most generous in providing me unpublished material on both game birds and nongame species, as well as for being congenial and highly competent field companions for trips from Hawaii to Midway Atoll.

To Mrs. Virginia C. Cone who, in addition to giving valuable assistance in proofreading at each stage of book production, was deeply concerned about the fate of the endemic Hawaiian birds, was inspired by the skylark, and was continually insistent that the Common Mynah was a good introduction to Hawaii.

To Miss Sue Monden, who displayed great interest in painting the original color plates from fresh plant materials and bird skins, and, for several species of honeycreepers, from birds that C. Robert Eddinger and I raised in captivity.

To Miss Linda N. Tanaka and Mrs. Sally S. Oshiro for their meticulous typing of the manuscript.

A grant from the Research Administration of the University of Hawaii and, later, National Science Foundation Grant GB-5613 provided the necessary funds for interisland travel for my studies of Hawaiian birds.

Honolulu, Hawaii
October 1970

ANDREW J. BERGER

Hawaiian Birdlife

CHAPTER ONE

The Hawaiian Islands:
A Bird's-eye View

The Hawaiian Islands are entirely volcanic in origin. The islands themselves are simply the very tall peaks of a series of volcanic mountains in the Hawaiian Ridge, a mostly submarine mountain range which stretches along the floor of the central Pacific Ocean. The phrase "very tall peaks" deserves some elaboration. Mauna Kea (White Mountain, so-called because it is nearly always snow-capped throughout the winter and spring months) on the island of Hawaii rises 13,796 feet above sea level; Mauna Loa (Long Mountain), on the same island, reaches an elevation of 13,680 feet. The floor of the ocean around Hawaii, however, is as much as 18,000 feet below sea level, which means that these two mountains rise more than 30,000 feet above their base on the ocean floor, and thus are higher than Mount Everest in the Himalayas.

The Hawaiian chain of islands extends for a distance of some 1,900 statute miles (1,660 nautical miles) from the island of Hawaii in the southeast to Kure Atoll in the northwest (fig. 3). The islands in the southeast are younger, and the two active volcanoes, Mauna Loa and Kilauea, on Hawaii still erupt periodically to pour forth their molten lava. Sometimes the lava flows all the way to the ocean, as it did at Kapoho in 1960 and at Kealakomo in 1971, resulting in an increase in the size of the island.

Geologists believe that the island of Oahu, on which Honolulu is located, first made its appearance above the surface of the ocean about 10 million years ago. The islands in the Leeward chain are much older. Deep drilling through the reef at Midway Atoll, for example, suggests that the former volcanic island there was "at least partially truncated by wave action prior to the Miocene," or more than 20 million years ago (Ladd, Tracey, and Gross 1967). How large these ancient islands were is, of course, unknown, but it may be significant that a total area of about 5,000 square miles, which includes the entire Leeward chain, lies within the 100-fathom (600-foot) contour. This does suggest that what now are atolls and low sandy islands are the mere remnants of once high islands. And, indeed, Nihoa and Necker islands, La Pérouse Rock, and Gardner Pinnacles still consist of exposed volcanic rock.

Because of their present condition, which reflects their age and geological history, we refer to the "high" Hawaiian islands and the "low" islands. The high islands are all of those in the main chain of inhabited islands (Hawaii to Kauai and Niihau) and the uninhabited Nihoa and Necker islands. The low islands (and atolls) extend from French Frigate Shoals to Kure Atoll. All of the islands lying northwest of Kauai also are referred to as the Leeward Islands. The National Board of Geographical Names now calls these the Northwestern Hawaiian Islands. All except Midway Atoll and Kure Atoll form the Hawaiian Islands National Wildlife Refuge, which was established by President Theodore Roosevelt in 1909.

Mother Nature and the sea are inexorable. No sooner is an island formed (either by volcanic eruption or by a violent uplift of some part of the earth as in eons past) than the pounding sea begins its erosive action against that island. The coral reefs that more or less encircle some oceanic islands aid in protecting them because the surf breaks hardest at the outer edges of the reef so that a gentler surf reaches the island itself. Nevertheless, the inevitable erosion of the sandy beaches and the rocky shores continues, sometimes gently, at other times violently as the result of storms or tidal waves.

Wind and water erosion also play a role in "eating away" the land. These natural processes are greatly accelerated after man disturbs the balance of nature by destroying forests or other protective vegetation. It has been estimated, for example, that as much as 15 feet of topsoil and its substrate have been lost from some areas on many of the islands since they were discovered by Caucasians.

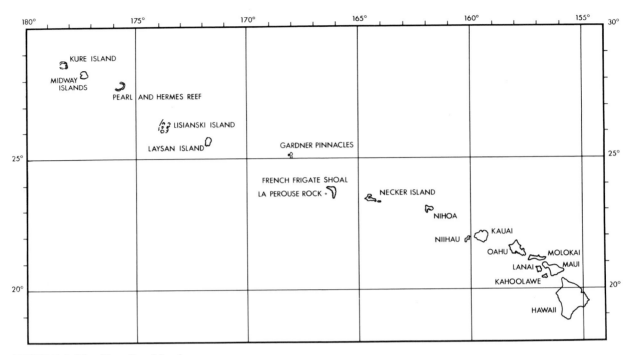

FIGURE 3. The Hawaiian Islands.

DISCOVERY OF THE SANDWICH ISLANDS

Captain James Cook, commanding two British exploring sloops (the *Discovery* and the *Resolution*), discovered Kauai and Niihau in January 1778, and during the following year, Maui and Hawaii. The group of islands was named the Sandwich Islands in honor of the Earl of Sandwich. Captain Cook was killed by the Hawaiians at Kealakekua Bay, Hawaii, on February 14, 1779. The islands were not visited again by Westerners until May 1786, at which time Captain Nathaniel Portlock and Captain George Dixon made anchorage between Diamond Head and Koko Head on Oahu, and La Pérouse anchored off the leeward coast of Maui.

The various islands, atolls, and reefs in the Leeward chain were discovered during the period of time between 1786 (French Frigate Shoals) and 1859 (Midway Atoll), either in the course of deliberate exploration or, at times, when ships were wrecked on the uncharted reefs. Many are the tales of death and survival and of heroism and some treachery associated with these shipwrecks. Some of these stories are told in the books by E. H. Bryan, Jr. (1942, 1954).

SOME DISTINGUISHING FEATURES

Hawaii is the only state that lies within the tropics, as well as the only one composed of relatively small islands completely surrounded by the vast Pacific Ocean. Hawaii's location, its high mountains, and the prevailing trade winds account for the unusual weather conditions and ecosystems found in Hawaii.

Mt. Waialeale, a mountain 5,148 feet high on Kauai, probably is the wettest area on earth. The average annual rainfall there is about 490 inches, and it has exceeded 600 inches (over 50 feet!). By contrast, some areas on the leeward coasts have an annual rainfall of less than 10 inches, and at Kawaihae Bay on Hawaii, less than 7 inches. The change in rainfall over short distances also is remarkable. The gradient or increase in rainfall is 118 inches per mile over a 2.5-mile line in the Mt. Waialeale region, and a gradient exceeding 25 inches per mile is common.

Prominent in determining weather conditions in Hawaii are the prevailing northeast trade winds, even though these winds do not blow uniformly throughout the year. Over a recent 10-year period, trade winds (north-northeast to east) were recorded 50 percent of the time in January and 93 percent of the time in August.

The combination of trade winds and high mountains produces a temperature inversion that separates a lower moist layer and a higher and drier area of air. This layering ordinarily restricts cloud development to a zone below the inversion level (fig. 4). One finds, therefore, that the clouds typically develop on the windward slopes of the mountains between 5,000 and 7,000 feet, and that the regions of highest rainfall on Maui and Hawaii are located at elevations between 2,000 and 4,000 feet. There the annual rainfall aver-

FIGURE 4. The Hamakua Coast of Hawaii Island, with the typical low-lying clouds (the "cloud belt") on the slopes of Mauna Kea. The cultivated land on the lower slopes is planted to sugarcane. The Greater Amakihi was found along this coast at elevations as low as 500 feet before the ohia forests were destroyed.

ages about 300 inches, and located there are the native rain forests.

Temperature patterns also vary tremendously. In Honolulu the range in average temperature between the warmest (78.4° F) and coldest (71.9° F) months is only 6.5° F. The average daily range in temperature below 5,000 feet on the main islands is between 8° and 20° F. Conditions are entirely different at higher elevations. At Pohakuloa (elevation 6,500 feet) on the Saddle Road of Hawaii, the difference between the maximum and minimum monthly temperatures varies from about 41° to 62° F, and averages about 51° F. Furthermore, during all but one or two months of the year, nighttime temperatures at Pohakuloa drop below 32° F. Much lower temperatures occur at higher elevations on Mauna Loa and Mauna Kea on Hawaii and on Haleakala, Maui. Both Mauna Loa and Mauna Kea are usually snow-capped for several months during the late winter and spring, and snow sometimes falls on Haleakala (highest elevation 10,023 feet).

Consequently, one finds a wide variety of ecological habitats or ecosystems in Hawaii: tropical rain forests, deserts, alpine and subalpine regions, and many intermediate types, as well as barren lava flows. Moreover, a fresh lava flow in the intermediate elevations in the rain forest belt on the windward slopes of the island of Hawaii may be revegetated in less than 100 years (for example, an 1881 lava flow, and, to a lesser extent, an 1855 flow at a higher elevation; fig. 5). By contrast, an 1843 flow in a dry area at approximately 6,600 feet elevation is still barren of vegetation (fig. 6).

Another feature that distinguishes the Hawaiian Archipelago is its great distance from any continental land mass. Honolulu is more than 2,000 miles from Los Angeles. Midway Atoll, near the western extremity of the archipelago, is even farther from Japan.

Because of these great distances, not many plants or animals reached the Hawaiian Islands. Those that did, however, found few, if any, competitors. There were many ecological niches to fill, and hence we find that many plants and animals that are endemic, or found no other place in the world, evolved throughout the islands. The fact is that Hawaiian plants, snails, insects, and birds demonstrate the processes of organic evolution to a much finer, and more striking, degree than do those of the much more publicized Galápagos Islands. Charles Darwin, unfortunately, did not have the opportunity to visit the Hawaiian Islands. He did suspect, however, that these islands would be of great interest to the biologist, for he wrote that he "would subscribe £50 to any collector to go there and work at the islands. . . . I think it is the most isolated group in the world, and the islands themselves well isolated from each other" (Darwin 1903, vol. 1:459). Had Dar-

FIGURE 5. An 1855 lava flow along the Saddle Road, Hawaii. October 4, 1969.

FIGURE 6. The 1843 lava flow from Mauna Loa; Mauna Kea lies in the background. December 17, 1967.

win been able to visit Hawaii, perhaps the rape of the Hawaiian environment would not have continued into the eighth decade of the twentieth century.

The Leeward Islands, in particular, provided ideal nesting sites for hundreds of thousands of seabirds because no mammalian competitors or predators had reached these islands before the coming of man. The islands were safe places for the green sea turtle *(Chelonia mydas)* to lay its eggs, and for the Hawaiian monk seal *(Monachus schauinslandi)* to bask in the sun with its pups. Five unique kinds of birds also evolved on Laysan Island, and two kinds, on Nihoa Island.

EXPLOITATION BY MAN

All of the lower animals have been considered fair game for man throughout the centuries. The general philosophy has been that the beasts, the birds, and the fishes were put on the earth solely for man's use. Interest in ecology, the study of the interrelations of animals and their environment, is a twentieth-century development. The full realization that man, too, is a part of nature, and that the total world environment is his environment also is not yet sufficiently widespread.

A knowledge of the great changes in the Hawaiian environment caused by man and by the foreign plants and animals he has introduced is essential to an understanding of the present status of the native Hawaiian plants and animals.

Introduced Mammals

Hawaii's only endemic land mammal is the hoary bat *(Lasiurus cinereus semotus)*. There are no endemic amphibians or land reptiles (see McKeown 1978). The Polynesians, it is thought, first came to the Hawaiian Islands sometime between A.D. 500 and 750. These ancestors of the Hawaiian people brought with them Jungle Fowl, pigs, dogs, and, undoubtedly, the Polynesian rat *(Rattus exulans)*. The people, and the plants and animals they brought with them, certainly had an effect on the native plants and animals (especially birds), which had never known such competitors or predators. What kind of new balance was established between the Hawaiians and their environment during the centuries following the first colonization of the islands will never be known.

The serious degradation of the Hawaiian environment (as well as of the Hawaiians) began in earnest within a few years after the arrival of Captain Cook and his successors. To be sure, the devastation that followed was not intentional; the ship captains' real concern was that they would be able to obtain quantities of meat on future visits to the islands. Between 1778 and 1803, cattle, horses, sheep, goats, and English pigs were given their freedom on the islands.

When, in 1794, Captain George Vancouver for the second time brought cattle to the island of Hawaii, he induced King Kamehameha to proclaim a ten-year *kapu* (taboo) on the cattle and other introduced European mammals to prevent the common people from hunting them. The cattle, as well as sheep, were driven from Kealakekua Bay to the Waimea plain, "a great tract of luxuriant vegetation," where the animals were allowed to roam unrestricted. In his journal, Vancouver wrote that observance of the ten-year *kapu* "cannot fail to render the extirpation of these animals a task not easily to be accomplished." He was correct, and it was reported that wild cattle still could not be killed without permission as late as 1818.

The feral animals multiplied rapidly in the absence of their usual diseases and predators and in a land with a year-round equable climate. As the populations increased, the mammals moved farther into the virgin forests, slowly destroying many of them by trampling ground cover and by feeding on the understory plants, including seedlings of the native trees. C. S. Judd (1927) spoke of the years from 1815 to 1921 as the "cattle period in Hawaiian forestry." Writing about Oahu in 1919, H. L. Lyon (1919), said that "cattle have been the greatest factor in pushing the forests back to their present narrow limits, and at certain vital points cattle are still allowed to penetrate the remaining forests." L. W. Bryan (1947) reported that more than 10,000 introduced mammals (cattle, goats, pigs, etc.) were killed *every year* from 1921 to 1946 in the forest reserves alone on the island of Hawaii. The last feral cattle and horses were not exterminated from Mauna Kea until the 1930s, and feral cattle are still found on some of the islands (Tomich 1969).

Feral goats, as well, have played an important role in destroying the native vegetation. Nearly 174,000 goat skins were exported from Hawaii from 1885 to June 1900 (Yocum 1967). Goats also have long been hunted for food in Hawaii, but they still plague the land, especially on Kauai and in Haleakala National Park, Maui.

An intensive effort to eradicate goats from Hawaii Volcanoes National Park was initiated in the late 1960s. Part of the strategy involved the construction of goat exclosures in 1969. Two years later, in the Kau desert, one such exclosure had a rich new plant cover and a previously unknown endemic leguminous plant, *Canavalia kauensis* (St. John 1972; fig. 7).

In some other places, the vegetated areas destroyed by the feral cattle, horses, sheep, and goats are irreclaimable because the topsoil, as well as the forests, is gone. This situation is particularly evident at the 10,000-foot elevation on Mauna Kea, where a few tree skeletons in a barren, rock-strewn waste attest to a former forest. The tree line of the mamani (*Sophora chrysophylla*) and naio (*Myoporum sandwicense*) forest there is now 500 or more feet lower, and still is receding because of the excess population of feral sheep (fig. 8).

Unfortunately for the endemic biota of Hawaii, other mammals have been introduced, primarily to provide game for hunters: axis deer (*Axis axis*), 1868; mouflon sheep (*Ovis musimon*), 1954; pronghorn (*Antilocapra americana*), 1959; mule deer (*Odocoileus hemionus*), 1961. Tuberculosis was discovered in axis deer on Molokai in 1970 at a time when great pressures were being exerted to introduce this species to the island of Hawaii.

The destruction of the native vegetation by introduced mammals was disastrous for native birds primarily because their habitat was destroyed. Pigs also destroy the nests of ground-nesting birds. Other introduced mammals were predators on birds. The rat population of the islands was augmented by two other species that reached the islands from ships that came to Hawaii: the roof rat (*Rattus rattus*) and the Norway rat (*Rattus norvegicus*).

The roof rat was responsible for the extinction of the populations of the Laysan Rail (*Porzana palmeri*) and the Laysan Finch (*Telespyza cantans*) that had built up on Midway Atoll after these species were transplanted there by man. The roof rat eats both the eggs and nestlings of tree-nesting honeycreepers on the main islands.

Kepler (1967) reported that Polynesian rats destroyed the eggs of the smaller seabirds and actually ate into the backs of incubating Laysan Albatrosses on Green Island in Kure Atoll. He observed more than twenty rats feeding on a single albatross one night; the bird was dead the following morning. How and when the Polynesian rat reached Kure Atoll apparently is unknown, but a dense population was found there by the members of the Tanager Expedition in 1923.

The small Indian mongoose (*Herpestes auropunctatus*) was first brought to Hawaii in 1883, and released along the Hamakua Coast of Hawaii Island in the hope that this species would prey upon the rats and other pests that were causing damage to sugarcane. Needless to say, as in Jamaica and other parts of the world, the mongooses did not solve the rat problem.

The mongoose has, however, been an important predator on the native duck and goose and on intro-

FIGURE 7. Two views of the Kukalauula goat exclosure at Hawaii Volcanoes National Park. The upper photograph was taken during March 1971; the lower, during March 1979, approximately two years following the removal of the goats from this area. Courtesy of Donald W. Reeser.

duced game birds. On May 24, 1964, Paul Breese, W. M. Ord, Ian MacPhail, and I watched a mongoose kill a duck-sized Red-footed Booby *(Sula sula)* nestling in its tree nest on Ulupau Head, Oahu. The mongoose is thought to be responsible for the great reduction in numbers of some species of nesting seabirds (a shearwater and two species of petrels) on the main islands. It is interesting to note that Kauai, the only one of the main islands on which the mongoose was not intentionally introduced and had not been seen until 1975, is the only island which still has all of the endemic birds known to have occurred there since 1778. If the species does become established there, the result could be the extinction of ground-nesting birds.

FIGURE 8. Rock-strewn waste on Mauna Kea; elevation about 10,000 feet. Three trees are visible on the horizon. February 6, 1970.

Feather Hunters, Rabbits, and the Leeward Islands

The first exploitation of the birds of the Leeward Islands apparently was conducted by Japanese feather hunters who killed hundreds of thousands of seabirds. More than 300,000 birds are said to have been killed on Laysan Island in a period of less than six months during 1909. It is certain that over a million were killed on other Pacific islands, such as Lisianski, Midway, and Marcus (fig. 9).

As a result of the great outcry against this slaughter and its relation to the millinery trade, Theodore Roosevelt established the Hawaiian Islands Bird Reservation in 1909. All of the Leeward Islands except Midway Atoll were included. The name later was changed to the Hawaiian Islands National Wildlife Refuge. This action, however, did not immediately halt the decimation of the seabird populations. More than two tons of feathers were collected by the Japanese, with the approval of Captain Max Schlemmer, between April 1909 and January 1910. Moreover, an earlier ill-considered act already had doomed certain unique land birds to extinction.

The excrement of seabirds, known as guano, is rich in phosphates and ammonium compounds. Large deposits of this excellent fertilizer were discovered on a number of Pacific islands prior to 1850, and claims to more than forty-five islands were made in an Act of Congress in 1856.

On March 29, 1890, the Hawaiian Kingdom leased Laysan Island to the North Pacific Phosphate and Fertilizer Company for a period of twenty years. The guano mining became unprofitable by 1904, and the company shipped its last load of guano in May of that year. The company sold all rights to Laysan, except the buildings, to Captain Schlemmer, and gave him an agent's commission. Schlemmer continued to ship some guano (his last load in 1910), but he also intended to make a coconut plantation on the island. In 1903 and 1904 he introduced three breeds of rabbits (as well as guinea pigs) to the island, in part to add variety to his diet, but, it has been said, also with the idea of starting a rabbit canning business. Schlemmer returned to Laysan Island for the last time in 1915 and was rescued from it on December 2 of that year.

Nothing came of the canning business, but, in the complete absence of their natural predators and dis-

FIGURE 9. Dr. Alfred M. Bailey on Laysan Island in December 1912, "showing the sparse population of albatrosses after a raid by Japanese poachers" during 1909 and 1910. Part of Dr. Bailey's job was to shoot rabbits. Photograph by George Willett, courtesy of Alfred M. Bailey.

eases, the rabbits multiplied, as rabbits are known to do. In only twenty years, the rabbits had destroyed virtually all the vegetation on Laysan Island (figs. 10, 11). After he visited Laysan as a member of the Tanager Expedition in 1923, Alexander Wetmore (1925) wrote: "On every hand extended a barren waste of sand. Two coconut palms, a stunted hau tree and an ironwood or two, planted by former inhabitants, were the only bits of green that greeted the eye. Other vegetation had vanished. The desolateness of the scene was so depressing that unconsciously we talked in undertones. From all appearances, Laysan might have been some desert, with the gleaming lake below merely a mirage." (Fig. 12.)

In that short period of time, the Laysan Millerbird

(Acrocephalus f. familiaris) became extinct; and two other species of unique Laysan birds became doomed to extinction: the Laysan Rail and the Laysan Apapane *(Himatione sanguinea freethii).*

The Laysan Apapane belonged to the endemic family of Hawaiian honeycreepers (family Drepanididae), which was once widespread on the main islands in the chain. The Tanager Expedition found only three of these birds inhabiting the sandy waste in 1923, and they were killed during a three-day gale that "enveloped everything in a cloud of swirling sand." This species apparently has the unenviable distinction of being the only songbird to have become extinct when man was present to document the precise time.

As is characteristic of many rails that managed to

FIGURE 10. Laysan Island in the 1890s. The birds are Laysan Albatrosses and Bonin Petrels. Courtesy of the Bernice P. Bishop Museum.

FIGURE 11. ''Laysan Island in 1913 showing destruction of scaevola and other vegetation by rabbits—a desert of dead shrubs and drifting sand.'' Most of the birds are frigatebirds. Courtesy of Alfred M. Bailey.

FIGURE 12. Laysan Island in 1923, as one looks south toward the camp of the Tanager Expedition. Courtesy of the Bernice P. Bishop Museum.

reach oceanic islands, the Laysan Rail had developed through evolution a flightless condition. The birds ate insects, the flesh from the carcasses of other birds, and the eggs of some of the smaller seabirds, such as terns and petrels. They were hardy enough to have survived the long sea voyage to England in the 1890s. They could not, however, survive indefinitely the continuing decrease in food and cover, and the members of the Tanager Expedition could find only two survivors in 1923; these died before the island was visited again. It was estimated that about 2,000 rails still occupied the island as late as 1915, before Captain Schlemmer left Laysan to the rabbits and returned to Honolulu.

Despite its fate on Laysan, the Laysan Rail could have been saved from extinction without great effort because a pair of rails had been introduced to Midway in 1891. A large population of rails had grown there by the turn of the century and still existed in 1939. That was not a time when government officials were inclined to heed the pleas of ornithologists, however, and transportation could not be obtained to transfer rails back to Laysan or to other islands. With the onset of World War II, rats gained access to the two islands (Sand and Eastern) at Midway Atoll from naval ships, and the last rails were seen in June of 1944. Hence a species became extinct needlessly.

Enlightened Modern Man

George C. Munro, who observed Hawaiian birds for over half a century, wrote (1944:68): "Since civilization came to the Hawaiian Islands the experience of the native perching birds has been tragic. Early voyagers found the birds plentiful on Oahu. In the eighteen nineties the birds of Oahu were much reduced and some were extinct or almost so. They were then still numerous on the other islands. Later this reduction was experienced on the other islands in turn. My conclusions after the survey (1936–1937) were that 25 species had a fair chance of survival while 30 species were gone or likely to become entirely extinct."

Other ornithologists, botanists, and early foresters had decried the destruction of the unique Hawaiian forests and the consequent extinction of birds, snails, and other animals (e.g., Knudsen 1909; Cooke 1949; Warner 1960, 1961). One might expect that the pleas of these writers would have been heeded, especially following World War II. Such, however, was not the case.

To be sure, the devastation of the native forests by cattle and other mammals became so serious that reforestation was at last considered. But it was the fear of financial loss and not the threat to the native biota that was the stimulus for this decision. Sugarcane had become a profitable agricultural crop during the last half of the nineteenth century. In most places in Hawaii, however, sugarcane must be irrigated. The planters recognized that the damage to the forests had been so great that they were no longer adequately protecting the watersheds, and in 1882 the Hawaiian government appropriated $12,000 for tree planting.

The first forest reserve was established in 1903. A conference was held to determine a suitable governmental policy for the reserves. The policy, as proposed to the governor in a letter from the Territorial forester in October 1904, was:

First: For the continued welfare and development of the agricultural interests of this Territory, on which the prosperity of the country depends, it is essential that an ample water supply be assured.

Second: To accomplish this end through the protection of the watersheds and the conservation of the rainfall, forest reserves are necessary and essential.

Third: The forest reserves should include all land which cannot be economically used for purposes other than forest, as well as such other areas as are needed to protect the water supply for permanent existing industries.

One finds, therefore, that the first trained biologists to work in the Territory of Hawaii were foresters. Their concern was to reforest the barren mountain ridges and slopes, such as those of the Koolau Mountain Range, that both bound and form residential areas of Honolulu.

There was no concern for the endemic biota. The human population of the islands was small, and so there was no fear of an inadequate supply of fresh water. The inhabitants of oceanic islands are completely dependent upon rain for a supply of fresh water, and, obviously, the demand for fresh water is greater as the population increases. Despite very heavy annual rainfall on windward slopes, much of the water is lost as it runs off the land and into the sea, carrying soil with it.

The understandable objective seventy-five years ago was to cover the barren areas with vegetation as rapidly as possible. Little was known about the ecology of the native flora and little effort was expended in reforesting with native plants. Instead, hundreds of species of exotic trees were planted in the hope that some would find climatic conditions in Hawaii suitable for rapid growth. L. W. Bryan (1947) reported that 1,057 different species of plants were tried in arboreta on the island of Hawaii during the period 1921–1946. Needless to say, many satisfactory species were found, and the efforts to protect the watersheds were largely successful; and since then very little thought has been given

either to understanding or to preserving the native flora and fauna, the native ecosystems. St. John (1973) lists more than 4,600 species of exotic flowering plants in the Hawaiian Islands, three times the number of endemic species.

As late as the 1950s, the State Division of Forestry was burning valuable native koa *(Acacia koa)* forests in order to plant foreign pine trees, not as watershed protection but presumably for a timber industry that did not exist, and which still does not exist in any substantial way. In the 1960s the native forests and their animal life were further abused by defoliation experiments (with Agent Orange), chemical herbicide tests, military nerve-gas experiments, and bulldozing.

Although there were already many square miles of cutover native forest areas that could have been replanted profitably, the foresters continued in 1969 and 1970 to bulldoze virgin ohia *(Metrosideros collina)* and treefern *(Cibotium* sp.) ecosystems, the products of evolutionary processes occurring over hundreds of thousands of years. Once destroyed, these ecosystems can never be recreated by man (fig. 13, 14).

In view of the rape of the Hawaiian environment by man and beast alike, albeit for a period of less than 200 years, the surprising thing is not that many endemic plants and animals have become extinct but that even more species have not passed into oblivion.

HOW DO BIRDS EVOLVE?

A neophyte bird watcher on the mainland United States recognizes that robins, sparrows, and crows are different *kinds* of birds. Similarly, in Hawaii it is obvious that mynas, doves, and cardinals are different kinds, or different species, of birds. At this level of discrimination, a bird species may be defined as a population of similar individuals occupying a definite geographical range and normally breeding among themselves and not with individuals of other species. A species is not an individual bird, but, rather, a population of similar individuals. The members of a species are similar, but not identical, in appearance; there is considerable individual variation in appearance and in structure among the individuals just as there is individual variation among the members of a human family or a race of humans. Again, each species of bird is reproductively isolated from other, closely related species, and closely related species are usually geographically isolated from each other.

Most of the individual variation occurring among the individuals of a population of a species is inherited through the genes received from the parents. Depending in part on the size of population of breeding individuals concerned, there may be a tremendous number of gene combinations possible because of the potential

FIGURE 13. One example of destruction of a virgin ohia-treefern forest by the State Division of Forestry on the advice of the U.S. Forest Service Institute of Pacific Islands Forestry in Honolulu. Near the Stainback Highway, Hawaii. February 19, 1966.

mating of different individuals within that population. However, despite the variety of gene combinations possible, the characteristics produced—whether of feather pattern or physiological process—usually fall within the limits of normal variation for that species.

There is another concept that must be understood before we discuss Hawaiian birds: that of the subspecies. The Song Sparrow (*Zonotrichia melodia*) of North America provides an excellent example. The Song Sparrow has an extensive breeding range, from the Aleutian Islands and Newfoundland southward into Mexico and most of the United States. If one examines specimens collected throughout the entire breeding range, one is impressed by differences in size and in intensity of coloration (fig. 15). There is no doubt that all are Song Sparrows, but the differences between some of the specimens are so striking that populations from different parts of the overall range are called subspecies or *geographical races*. These races are identified by adding a third, or subspecific, name to the generic and species name: for example, *Zonotrichia melodia sanaka* for a race in the Aleutian Islands. In all, 31 different sub-

species of Song Sparrow are recognized in the American Ornithologists' Union Check-List. These subspecies are recognized because, although each is more or less morphologically distinct from the other, it is assumed that reproductive isolating mechanisms have not yet evolved—that is, interbreeding among birds from any of the populations would result in the production of fertile eggs.

At times, as the result of natural causes, changes or *mutations* occur in the genes. The characteristics produced by the mutations are hereditary, and they may be either beneficial or harmful to the individuals having them. If a mutation is in some way beneficial, the offspring possessing it may be able to compete more successfully, or they may be more adaptable to changing environmental conditions, and thus will have more descendants. With the passing of time, other mutations occur in the population. The theory of *geographical speciation* postulates that new species arise because of gene changes that effect reproductive isolating mechanisms when subspecies are geographically isolated for long periods of time. Reproductive isolating mechanisms

FIGURE 14. Road bulldozed through the Laupahoehoe Forest Reserve, Hawaii. October 3, 1969. This was just the beginning for a commercial logging venture that was designed to make souvenirs for tourists.

may be the result of different breeding seasons, of sexual dimorphism (where the plumage pattern of the male is strikingly different from that of the female), or of various kinds of species-specific signal characters (song, courtship display, etc.).

Extensive speciation from a common ancestral population is referred to as *divergence* or *adaptive radiation*. As a simple explanation of this process, we may assume that at least a pair of birds from a single population invaded each of two islands, and that the birds remained on their respective islands. We may assume also that gene mutations occurred over a period of time and that the mutations in the population on island A were different from those in the population on island B. The two populations became more and more dissimilar in external appearance (as well as physiologically), and reproductive isolating mechanisms evolved. We would then have two new species, both unlike the parent or ancestral species from which the original invasion had come. Let us further assume that on one occasion some individuals of species A invaded island B. Species A and B now could live on island B without competing

with each other because each had become adapted to a particular habitat, ecological niche, or feeding habit. With the further passage of time and additional mutations, ecological isolating mechanisms might evolve in the population of species A on island B so that we would have a third species, distinct from its sister species still living on island A.

By means of this process of speciation when populations are geographically isolated, each habitat might, theoretically, become populated with a different species, each of which had evolved from a single parent species. However, these daughter species, might be so unlike each other and the parent species that the relationships among them would not be apparent. According to present thinking, the Hawaiian honeycreepers (family Drepanididae) fit this theory in that, by definition, if the birds belong to a single family, all are presumed to have evolved from a single ancestral species. The differences in bill development among the honeycreepers are so striking, however, that when some of the birds were first described in the nineteenth century, they were placed in several different families.

FIGURE 15. Some geographical races of the Song Sparrow. *From top: Zonotrichia melodia sanaka,* Aleutian Islands, Alaska; *Z. m. caurina,* southeastern Alaska; *Z. m. samuelis,* Vallejo, California; *Z. m. montana,* Chiricahua Mountains, Arizona; *Z. m. saltonis,* Oak Creek, Arizona; *Z. m. mexicana,* Lerma, Mexico.

The Endemic Birds

Of the land and freshwater birds in Hawaii, 20 genera, 44 species, and 32 subspecies belonging to 11 different bird families are peculiar to the Hawaiian Islands. Included among these is the Hawaiian honeycreeper family with its 16 genera, 28 species, and 18 subspecies. Three subspecies of seabirds can be added to the list of birds found only in the Hawaiian Islands: Newell's Shearwater, Dark-rumped Petrel, and Hawaiian Storm Petrel. The seabirds, however, have a wide range over the Pacific Ocean during the non-breeding season, and therefore, are not pertinent to the discussion of the land and freshwater birds, all of which are non-migratory in the usual sense of that word.

It should be noted that only the species and subspecies—that is, populations of birds—exist in nature.

Genera, families, and higher taxonomic categories have been created by man in an attempt to reach a better understanding of relationships among the more than 8,600 species of birds in the world. In evolutionary (or phylogenetic) relationships, the species placed in one genus are assumed to be much closer to each other than to the species assigned to other genera in that particular family. The accuracy of a system of classification, therefore, depends on how successful the taxonomist has been in finding clues to the true genetic relationships among the birds.

Students of Hawaiian birds have concluded that all of the endemic genera, species, and subspecies evolved from 15 original ancestral species. (Figure 16 shows the postulated origins for these ancestral species.) Such figures are misleading, however, in that they depict only generalizations based on what ornithologists believe to be the closest relatives to Hawaiian birds in continental areas. Three bird families that have endemic Hawaiian genera, for example, are exclusively, or predominately, Old World in distribution: Old World warblers (Sylviidae), Old World flycatchers (Muscicapidae), and honeyeaters (Meliphagidae). Most of the other families that contain Hawaiian forms have representatives in both North America and Asia.

Moreover, a map does not explain how the ancestors of modern Hawaiian birds reached the islands. The annual migratory paths of North American and Asian birds, with the exception of certain ducks and shorebirds, do not pass through or even come near the Hawaiian Islands. And yet, from the number of unusual "stragglers" that reach Hawaii from North America and Asia, it is obvious that birds are not infrequently "blown" to Hawaii by storms or high winds. Even so, it is difficult to understand how the ancestors of the Millerbird, a tiny bird less than 6 inches in total length, managed to find their way to Laysan and Nihoa islands. In this instance, one might assume that the ancestors of this Old World warbler reached Midway or other islands when they were still large high islands. Over a period of time, the birds could have "island-hopped" to the areas where they are now found.

It is clear, as well, that invasion by a single male bird or an unfertilized female would not have resulted in the establishment of a new population. Even if several birds reached a given island at one time, it is reasonable to assume that other accidental invasions could have occurred later. In fact, in terms of present estimates of the ages of the Hawaiian Islands, only one successful invasion every 300,000 or more years would have been required for the establishment of the 15 bird ancestors mentioned above.

There also are intriguing problems about the distribution of Hawaiian birds since 1778. The Elepaio, for

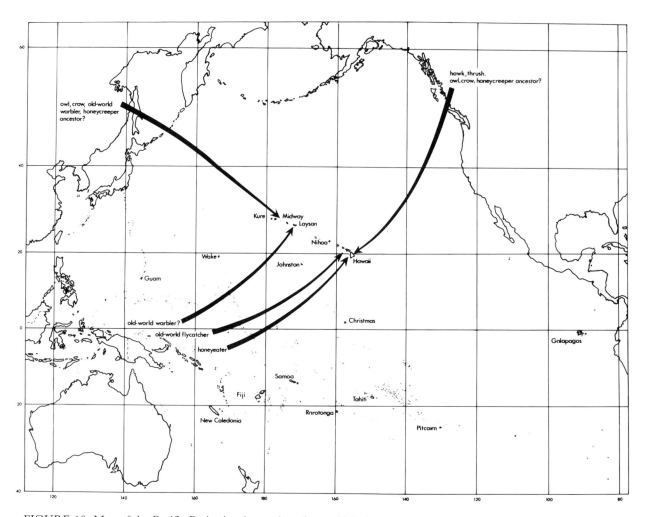

FIGURE 16. Map of the Pacific Basin showing regions from which the ancestors of endemic Hawaiian birds are presumed to have originated.

example, occurs only on Kauai, Oahu, and Hawaii. There is no evidence to suggest that this species ever inhabited Molokai, Lanai, or Maui, which at one time in their geological history were one large island.

One other factor should be mentioned. Speciation is extensive, and sometimes rapid, in certain animals; in others, it is very slow. Among the honeycreepers, the Apapane is an example of a stable species. There has been no visible differentiation among the populations inhabiting all of the main islands in the chain; the islands are inhabited by a single subspecies. A second subspecies evolved on Laysan Island. A single species of Iiwi occupies all of the main islands. By contrast, there are four subspecies of Akepa *(Loxops coccineus)*.

The Causes of Extinction

If one considers periods of geological time, a number of reasons can be suggested for the extinction of animals. These include overspecialization (as in the case

of dinosaurs), changing climatic conditions (as during the Ice Ages), competition with more adaptable forms, the evolution of higher animals, and, in recent times, the greed of man.

Although we are dealing with a much shorter period of time in Hawaii, little factual information is available to explain the extinction of so many birds. Several causes have been proposed: decimation of some species by the Hawaiians, who used feathers (especially red and yellow) for capes and other appurtenances (including fly whisks) of the kings, introduction of the mongoose, destruction of the birds' habitats, competition from introduced birds, and diseases brought in with introduced birds. All may have played a role, but it seems certain that no single factor was responsible for the extinction of some species or races and for the great reduction in numbers of others.

Published reports are contradictory as to the fate of birds caught for their feathers for royal use. Some writers state that those birds with tuffs of yellow feathers were released after their feathers were plucked. It also has been suggested, however, that because of the protein-poor diet of the Hawaiians, the birds were eaten. Therefore, it may or may not be significant that the only known surviving species of Oo (*Moho braccatus;* on Kauai) has fewer yellow feathers than any of the other three species (page 106).

A large number of the different species of honeycreepers were not discovered and described until the 1890s. Consequently, no meaningful comparative data exist for the period between 1778 and 1890. The Kioea, a remarkable member of the honeyeater family, was first collected on Hawaii in 1840 by the Pickering and Peale expedition. Munro (1944:88) said that several specimens were collected about 1859, but that the species had not been seen since then. One honeycreeper *(Ciridops anna),* first collected about 1859, was not described until 1879; a single bird obtained from natives in the early 1890s apparently was the last of the species ever reported. The mongoose, introduced in 1883, can hardly have been responsible for the demise of these species.

There can be little doubt, however, that the roof rat has been a serious predator on tree-nesting birds in Hawaii. Atkinson (1977) presented clear arguments to suggest that this rat did not reach the Hawaiian Islands until "after 1840, probably between 1870 and 1880." He pointed out that 58 percent of the kinds of Hawaiian forest birds became extinct or were greatly reduced in numbers between 1892 and 1930. Most of these species or subspecies became extinct on Oahu first, where it is presumed that the roof rats first landed. Decimation of the bird populations on the other islands followed the introduction of the rats, whose populations undoubtedly exploded within a few years. We now know that the roof rat eats the eggs, nestlings, and sometimes even the adult birds that are caught while incubating. While studying birds in the Kilauea Forest Reserve on Hawaii in 1971, I found four deserted Apapane nests that had been built on the upper surface of tree fern fronds. Two of the nests contained large numbers of wing and tail feathers of adult Apapane; one nest held bones and feathers of a large nestling. Moreover, the roof rat population reaches its highest densities in rain forests; it also occurs from near sea level to elevations greater than 8,000 feet (Radovsky et al., 1975).

Destruction of native forests in itself may not have caused the extinction of any species of endemic bird during the nineteenth century, but it certainly was responsible for the great reduction in numbers of individuals. All available evidence suggests that most of the endemic land birds are almost completely dependent upon the native ecosystems in which they evolved. Upon destruction of the forests, therefore, the birds either had to move or die. Early visitors to Hawaii reported red birds in the lowlands almost to sea level, but the bird collectors of the 1890s found no native land birds on Niihau, the first of the islands where goats were introduced by Captain Cook in 1778. It seems reasonable to assume that Niihau originally had many of the bird species now found on Kauai. Later introductions of sheep and cattle resulted in the destruction of nearly all of the native vegetation on Niihau. The forests and other lowland vegetation on the other islands also were destroyed many years ago, and it is unusual now to find native forest birds much below 3,000 feet elevation on any island (exceptions are the Elepaio, Hawaii Thrush, and Amakihi).

No studies have yet been made to determine the possible adverse effects of competition between introduced species and native land birds. Several species of exotics have penetrated the native forests and coexist there with the native birds. The Japanese White-eye (*Zosterops japonicus),* in particular, has been a remarkably successful introduction. Although not introduced to Oahu until 1929 and to Hawaii in 1937, the White-eye is now found on all of the main islands, from sea level to tree line, and in both very wet and very dry habitats. I believe it to be the most abundant land bird in the Hawaiian Islands. These birds do not compete for nesting sites with the endemic birds, but whether or not they are serious competitors for food is unknown.

One of the most plausible and "logical" explanations of extinction of native birds is the introduction of foreign diseases to which the native birds had little or no immunity. I have alluded earlier to the "degradation" of the Hawaiian people after the arrival of Caucasians. Many thousands of Hawaiians died from diseases that are relatively mild for Europeans, such as measles and chicken pox, because the previously isolated Hawaiians had no natural immunity to them. Nevertheless, although introduced bird diseases may very well have played an important role in the extinction of native birds, there are no reliable data yet available on this subject. Nor is it clear why some species (for example, Akialoa, Nukupuu, Ou) should have been so much more susceptible to the postulated diseases than others (Apapane, Amakihi, Iiwi). Moreover, in the 1890s, the Palila was "extremely numerous" above 4,000 feet elevation (an elevation presumably above the haunts of the mosquitoes) both in North Kona and on Mauna Kea. The disappearance of the Palila in North Kona can hardly be attributed to disease alone, inasmuch as these birds are still found on Mauna Kea.

Many bird diseases, of course, require some agent

or vector to spread them. Bird malaria is an example. Mosquitoes were lacking in the Hawaiian insect fauna until about 1826. Probably in that year, the night-biting mosquito (*Culex quinquefasciatus*) was introduced to Lahaina, Maui, from one or more ships from Mexico (Hardy 1960:18). In addition to being a potential vector for two serious human diseases (Japanese B-type encephalitis and filariasis), this mosquito transmits heartworm in dogs, and it may be important in transmitting fowl pox, pigeon pox, bird malaria, and *Haemaproteus*.

Two species of day-biting mosquitoes (*Aedes aegypti* and *A. albopictus*) found their way to Hawaii at a much later date, but little seems to have been known about them until the 1890s. Neither species has been suggested as a threat to the native birds, although *Aedes aegypti* is a vector for dengue fever and yellow fever in humans. Another immigrant mosquito (*Aedes vexans nocturnus*) apparently became established on Oahu and Kauai in 1962 (Joyce and Nakagawa 1963), but very little is known about its present distribution in Hawaii. It has been incriminated as a vector of Japanese B-type encephalitis on Guam. All introduced bird diseases and some of the mosquitoes are a potential threat to the remaining endemic forest birds, and some of the mosquitoes pose a potential public health problem.

In general, mosquitoes have been reported at elevations below 2,000 feet. A thorough study of mosquitoes in Hawaii remains to be completed, however; they have been found at much higher elevations, especially in water troughs for cattle. An observer in 1969 found mosquito larvae in puddles at the edge of a road recently bulldozed through the near-virgin Laupahoehoe Forest Reserve on Hawaii.

The majority of species of honeycreepers with the most highly specialized bills are either extinct or very rare. So little is known about these species, however, that one cannot assert with any confidence that extinction (or great reduction in numbers) resulted from overspecialization of bill structure and feeding habits, from destruction of suitable habitat, or from a combination of factors.

Another factor is pertinent to an understanding of the historic distribution of endemic land birds on the Leeward Islands. During the exceptionally high seas in early December 1969, Tern Island in French Frigate Shoals was covered by 3 to 4 feet of water, and waves as high as 50 feet are said to have broken over the surrounding reefs. The personnel of the Coast Guard Loran station there were rescued by helicopter from the roof of a building. The inundation of East Island (also in French Frigate Shoals) was reported as the result of hurricanes in 1946 and 1950, when a Loran station was located there. Most of the other islets in the

Leeward chain are also low enough to be swamped during exceptionally severe weather, but firsthand reports are lacking.

Obviously, the periodic inundation of the low, sandy islands of the Leeward group would preclude the permanent establishment on them of populations of flightless rails, weak-flying and sedentary ducks, and land birds. Therefore, one finds that only the higher Laysan Island (and perhaps Lisianski Island) was suitable for the establishment and evolution of such birds. Except for its small size and the fact that it was inhabited by Polynesians or Hawaiians in years long forgotten, there seems to be no other reason than chance that Necker Island did not support at least one kind of land bird.

Whatever the causes of extinction of endemic Hawaiian birds, 26 species or subspecies are known or believed to be extinct, and an additional 36 are considered endangered or threatened.

Although man has greatly accelerated its rate during the past two centuries, extinction is a normal part of evolution. Species evolve, live their alloted time, and become extinct. The first Hawaiian fossilized bird was found in a tunnel under 75 feet of lava on Hawaii in 1926. The bones belonged to those of a goose (*Geochen rhuax*) that was larger than the Nene (*Branta sandvicensis*) but not closely related to it (Wetmore 1943); the age of the fossil is unknown.

In 1971, however, Joan Aidem found fossil goose bones on Molokai that were about 25,000 years old (Stearns 1973). This goose (*Thambetochen chauliodous*) was flightless and, again, larger than the Nene but not closely related to it (Olson and Wetmore 1976). Many other fossil bones have been found on Molokai, Maui, Oahu, and Kauai since 1971. Among these are a flightless ibis, a flightless rail, a hawk, an owl, and a crow-like bird. When all of the fossils are studied, we will have a new insight into ancient birdlife in Hawaii and, perhaps, a better understanding of the relationships of the present endemic birds.

Adaptability of Hawaiian Birds

I have already mentioned that all available evidence suggests that endemic Hawaiian birds are so dependent upon the ecosystem in which they evolved that they are not very adaptable, and, therefore, are very susceptible to changes in their environment. However, the Laysan Duck, the Laysan Finch, and the Elepaio have been able to adapt to drastic changes in the environment, although it is doubtful if the two Laysan forms could have survived much longer if man had not intervened.

Hence, more surprising than the extinction of three species of Laysan birds in the short period between

FIGURE 17. Three of the seven Laysan Ducks found by Alfred M. Bailey during December 1912. Courtesy of Alfred M. Bailey.

1903 and 1923 is the fact that two other nonmigratory, endemic birds were able to survive the devastation of the vegetation, which is required as cover for breeding activities. And, indeed, the populations of both species were dangerously low. Alexander Wetmore counted 20 Laysan Ducks and several dozen Laysan Finches in 1923 (fig. 17).

The water in the long, shallow lake near the middle of Laysan Island is much saltier than seawater. It is, nevertheless, eminently suitable for myriads of brine shrimp *(Artemia)* and the larvae of a dipteran fly *(Neoscatella)*. The Laysan Duck is an insectivorous species, and its survival during critical years must have been possible because of the availability of the flies that swarm along the edges of the lake and the flies and other insects that infest the carcasses of dead sea birds. They could also feed on the crustaceans in the tidal pools on the periphery of the island.

The Laysan Finch has omnivorous feeding habits, and there can be little doubt that this species survived because of its predilection for the eggs of other birds, particularly those of several species of terns. It may well have hastened the extinction of the Millerbird and the Laysan Apapane, as well.

One of the objectives of the Tanager Expedition was to exterminate the last of the rabbits on Laysan Island. This goal apparently was reached, and both the vegetation and the birds made a remarkable recovery after 1923 (fig. 18). Censuses conducted by personnel of the U.S. Fish and Wildlife Service have indicated populations of Laysan Ducks as high as 600 birds and about 10,000 Laysan Finches.

Although the Apapane is undoubtedly the most common species of living honeycreeper, the Amakihi *(Hemignathus virens)* and the Akiapolaau *(Hemignathus wilsoni)* are far more adaptable in that both are found not only in the rain forests (with the Apapane) but also in the dry mamani-naio forest on Mauna Kea. However, the Amakihi is an abundant species whereas the Akiapolaau is an endangered one.

The best example of true adaptability to changing environmental conditions on the main islands is that of the Elepaio *(Chasiempis sandwichensis)* on Oahu. Little virgin forest remains on this island, and not only is the Elepaio thriving in the mixed forests of native and introduced vegetation but small populations inhabit the introduced forest near the head of Manoa Valley, in Moanalua Valley, and in North Halawa Valley. Although studies have not been made, the fact that the Elepaio is successful in these lowland habitats suggests

FIGURE 18. Scaevola thickets and the single ironwood tree on Laysan Island. March 1966. *From left to right:* Nelson Rice, Ronald L. Walker, Eugene Kridler, Andrew J. Berger. The two refuge signs had just been erected. Courtesy of Eugene Kridler.

that this race has developed at least a partial immunity to avian malaria and other mosquito-transmitted bird diseases present in the valleys.

Future Prospects for Endemic Birds

The passage of the Endangered Species Act (Public Law 93-205) by Congress during December 1973 has been beneficial, to a degree, for conservation in Hawaii: the U.S. Forest Service no longer decimates virgin forests by bulldozing. Moreover, the Hawaii Legislature passed its own endangered species law (Act 65) in 1975. In it the Department of Land and Natural Resources is directed to "carry out programs for the conservation, management, and protection of such species and their associated ecosystems. . . . The governor or his authorized representative shall also encourage other State and federal agencies to utilize their authorities in furtherance of the purposes of this section by carrying out programs for the protection of endangered species and by taking such action as may be necessary to insure that actions authorized, funded, or carried out by them do not jeopardize the continued existence of endangered species." Unfortunately, as of 1980 no department of the State government has ever followed the dictates of the law, and the Department of

Land and Natural Resources has ignored the recommendations of its own personnel in the Division of Fish and Game.

A much more concerted effort is still needed to aid the recovery of disturbed forest areas. This means initiating a serious program to control the spread of introduced weed pests, as well as to control the populations of feral sheep, goats, pigs, and axis deer. Detailed studies of the biology and ecology of the forest birds also are needed, as are related studies on bird diseases.

Pond and marsh birds are in even greater immediate danger because of the demand for residential and tourist areas, which already has resulted in the drainage of essential habitat. The populations of these species are dangerously small, from which any of the species might not be able to recover in the event of a serious epidemic or other disaster.

Warner (1963) pointed out a continuing threat to the islands comprising the Hawaiian Islands National Wildlife Refuge: "Hawaii has many times in the past experienced the pressures induced by the hushed phrases of 'secret' and 'national defense' when a military project was planned. Often the activity following therefrom had little immediate relation to either secrecy or national defense." Trespass by military person-

FIGURE 19. The military came and left—all of their junk behind. East Island, French Frigate Shoals, Hawaiian Islands National Wildlife Refuge. March 1966.

nel has occurred repeatedly on many of the islands, including Nihoa, over the years since Warner wrote (fig. 19). During the late 1970s, the State government applied further pressures to permit commercial fishing in the waters surrounding the Leeward Islands. A Japanese fishing vessel became stranded on the reef at Laysan Island in 1968. The concern with such wrecks is that rats could reach the islands, and their and other predators' accidental introduction to Nihoa Island or to Laysan Island would doom the endemic birds that still inhabit those islands, as well as pose a serious threat to many of the nesting seabirds.

BIRD HABITATS IN HAWAII

Because of the wide range of climatic conditions in the Hawaiian Islands, there are many kinds of habitats or areas with different weather patterns and their associated types of vegetation. No single bird species is found in all of these areas, and some are confined to a single type of habitat. Consequently, as in any other part of the world, one must know the kind of habitat needed by a particular species in order to find that species. Peculiarities of habitat requirements will be discussed in the accounts of individual species, but certain general background information should be helpful.

In general, native species are more narrow in their habitat requirements than are introduced species. The wide range of habitats occupied by White-eyes already has been mentioned. Similarly, the Common Indian Myna (*Acridotheres tristis*) is an adaptable species; it is more abundant in lowland cities and towns, but also is found in the mountains, usually, but not always, associated with man and his activities. Small flocks of Common Mynas are encountered at elevations of 8,000 feet or higher on Mauna Kea, in Haleakala Crater on Maui, and in the forests around Kokee State Park and along trails leading toward the Alakai Swamp on Kauai.

Only one species of bird is known to nest above the tree line (in the subalpine zone and possibly also the alpine zone) of Mauna Loa and Mauna Kea: the Hawaiian Dark-rumped Petrel (*Pterodroma phaeopygia sandwichensis*). However, little definite information is available on the present or past nesting habits of seabirds on the main islands. The Dark-rumped Petrel and Newell's Shearwater (*Puffinus puffinus newelli*) are thought formerly to have nested on all of the main islands. As far as is known, Newell's Shearwater now nests only on Kauai. The nests and eggs of Harcourt's Storm Petrel (*Oceanodroma castro cryptoleucura*) have

FIGURE 20. An open, grazed kiawe forest near Kukuipahu, Hawaii, at an elevation of approximately 150 feet. August 8, 1974. This area provides habitat for the Hawaiian Owl and for introduced gamebirds and song birds.

never been found; but, inasmuch as this race is found only in the Hawaiian Islands, it is assumed that it nests in remote areas on Kauai.

Mynas and wintering Golden Plover *(Pluvialis dominica)* occasionally are seen on completely barren lava flows, but these are areas utilized by birds of passage only. The Hawaiian Goose or Nene spends much of its time on open lava flows, particularly on those on which patches of suitable vegetation are found.

Of endemic land birds, only the Pueo or Hawaiian Owl *(Asio flammeus)* is found regularly in the lowland, dry areas, and these are regions with almost no native vegetation. All other birds seen in the haole koa *(Leucaena glauca)* and the kiawe or mesquite *(Prosopis pallida)* thickets (sometimes almost impenetrable ''jungles'') in the semidesert areas are introduced species: Doves, Cardinals, Mockingbirds, White-eyes, Ricebirds, and various gamebirds (fig. 20).

Most of the marsh and pond areas in Hawaii are (or were) located at low elevations, although all too many of these have been destroyed in the interests of housing developments and tourist resorts. The native coot, gallinule, stilt, and night heron are completely dependent on such wetland areas. Some of these species also make use of water reservoirs, both in water reserves and in agricultural areas. The cessation of rice growing and the great reduction in taro farming also have reduced suitable habitat for the marsh birds.

Large numbers of native land birds are to be found only in the wet native forests, although three species are common in the relatively dry mamani-naio forest on Mauna Kea. In part because of the extensive destruction of native forests, therefore, there are large areas of scrub and introduced vegetation where no native land birds can be expected, with the exception of the Pueo and, on Hawaii, the Hawaiian Hawk *(Buteo solitarius)* or the even rarer Hawaiian Crow *(Corvus tropicus)*.

In addition to the absence of native land birds over large areas in Hawaii, there is another interesting, as well as frustrating, feature about the distribution of the birds: some ecological niches are virtually devoid of native birds.

No native land bird inhabits the forest floor. The long-extinct rail on Hawaii did so, but almost nothing is known about either the habits or the ecological distribution of this small rail.

Most of the honeycreepers inhabit the canopy or upper reaches of the wet ohia forests (fig. 21). Consequently, one may spend a great deal of time amidst the tall ohia trees without seeing a native bird in the luxuriant growth of tree ferns, often 15 feet high, and other

FIGURE 21. Ohia-treefern forest in the Waikamoi Stream area, Maui; elevation 4,000 feet. October 15, 1965. This is veritable paradise for endemic plants and animals.

plants and vines of the understory. Sometimes Creepers *(Oreomystis)* do feed in the understory, as does the Anianiau *(Hemignathus parvus)* on Kauai, but both species also spend time well up in the trees. Even the native thrushes, especially the males, spend much of their time in the taller trees. The Elepaio seems to be the only native bird that habitually moves about the forests from ground level to the tops of the taller trees.

The mamani-naio forest on Mauna Kea is a relatively dry and open parkland type of forest in which most of the trees are low to moderate (less than 50 feet) in height. Here, too, the Elepaio moves from dead branches on the ground to the treetops. I also have watched the rare Akiapolaau here, foraging near the ground on the trunks or branches of both living and dead trees. However, the only ground-inhabiting birds in the area are the introduced game birds and the Skylark *(Alauda arvensis)*.

Finally, because of the destruction of so much native vegetation, there are many forests in Hawaii where one can expect to hear only the calls and songs of introduced birds. Moreover, there are some forests that, at times, appear to be completely devoid of birdlife. I have walked through such forests, hearing only the sounds of my own footsteps. Upon stopping to listen, only two sounds would reach my ears: water dripping from leaves to the ground or onto other leaves and the monotonous calls of a single species of insect. In some of these forests one occasionally encounters fallen tree trunks four feet or more in diameter, reminders of the magnificent native forests that once existed.

CHAPTER TWO

Indigenous Birds

By "indigenous birds" we mean those birds that are native to a given region, in this case the Hawaiian Islands, but whose total range of distribution includes a much wider geographical area. Included among these indigenous Hawaiian birds are many oceanic species or seabirds, the Black-crowned Night Heron, and a number of migratory species that spend the nonbreeding season in the Hawaiian Islands. The migratory species are listed in Appendix A.

THE OCEANIC BIRDS

The term "oceanic birds" is not a precise one, nor does it imply a closely related group belonging to a single family or order of birds. It refers rather to certain members of several families and orders that have become adapted to a similar mode of life. Three general groups have been defined on ecological considerations, although the first group seems to be included primarily to make a "complete" system of classification: inshore, offshore, and pelagic birds.

Inshore species are forms that, in general, keep in sight of the coast or offshore islands: they are not, strictly speaking, oceanic birds. Basically, they are continental forms. These include most species of cormorants, marine ducks, and gulls. Gulls are so characteristic of the coastal areas of North America, Europe, and Asia, that the newcomer to Pacific islands is immediately struck by their absence.

Offshore species also are associated with continents, and they are most abundant in those regions that have an extensive continental shelf. These species are primarily fish-eating birds. Examples are gannets (family Sulidae), tropicbirds (Phaethontidae), and auks (Alcidae). Offshore species are, by our traditional definition, oceanic birds because they share a common feature with the pelagic species: they come to land only during the breeding season.

Pelagic species spend their time over the open ocean except when they return to their nesting islands. Many of these species have a long life span, and the young do not reach breeding age for several years (about nine years in the Royal Albatross, *Diomedea epomophora*). Many of these immature, nonbreeding birds may remain at sea throughout the year. The larger birds typically soar and sail only a short distance above the waves and swells because wind conditions are often such that the lift required for their flight pattern may be obtained only from the updraft created on the windward side of waves.

In addition to fishes, oceanic birds feed on squid and a wide variety of Crustacea and other animal life found in the plankton near the surface of the water. Mixed flocks of oceanic birds serve a valuable function because they can find schools of fish more effectively than any means yet devised by man. It is for this reason that one may see commercial fishermen scanning the endless ocean with binoculars, searching for flocks of seabirds.

The entire order of tube-nosed swimmers (Procellariiformes) consists of true oceanic or pelagic birds. The four families of this order contain the albatrosses, shearwaters, petrels, storm petrels, and diving petrels. Some of the storm petrels and diving petrels are tiny birds (5.5 to 6.5 inches in total length) that weigh only slightly more than a common House Sparrow *(Passer domesticus)*. By contrast, some families of the order Pelecaniformes contain pelagic species, whereas others contain offshore, inshore, or continental species.

As mentioned previously, most gulls are inshore or continental birds, but the gull, tern, and noddy family (Laridae) does contain many oceanic species. Furthermore, there are two species of gulls *(Larus tridactylus* and *Larus brevirostris)* that are pelagic during the nonbreeding season; they are then found in north temperate and arctic waters.

Following are the orders and families of birds containing oceanic species that nest on the Hawaiian Islands:

A. Order Procellariiformes
  1. Family Diomedeidae (albatrosses or goo-ney birds)
     a. Black-footed Albatross *(Diomedea nigripes)*
     b. Laysan Albatross *(Diomedea immutabilis)*
  2. Family Procellariidae (shearwaters, petrels, fulmars)
     a. Wedge-tailed Shearwater *(Puffinus pacificus chlororhynchus)*
     b. Christmas Shearwater *(Puffinus nativitatus)*
     c. Newell's Shearwater *(Puffinus puffinus newelli)*
     d. Dark-rumped Petrel *(Pterodroma phaeopygia sandwichensis)*
     e. Bonin Petrel *(Pterodroma hypoleuca hypoleuca)*
     f. Bulwer's Petrel *(Bulweria bulwerii)*
  3. Family Hydrobatidae (storm petrels)
     a. Harcourt's Storm Petrel *(Oceanodroma castro cryptoleucura)*
     b. Sooty Storm Petrel *(Oceanodroma tristrami)*
B. Order Pelecaniformes
  1. Family Phaethontidae (tropicbirds)
     a. White-tailed Tropicbird *(Phaethon lepturus dorotheae)*
     b. Red-tailed Tropicbird *(Phaethon rubricauda rothschildi)*
  2. Family Sulidae (boobies and gannets)
     a. Blue-faced or Masked Booby *(Sula dactylatra personata)*
     b. Brown Booby *(Sula leucogaster plotus)*
     c. Red-footed Booby *(Sula sula rubripes)*
  3. Family Fregatidae (frigatebirds)
     a. Great Frigatebird *(Fregata minor palmerstoni)*
C. Order Charadriiformes
  1. Family Laridae (gulls, terns, and noddies)
     a. Sooty Tern *(Sterna fuscata oahuensis)*
     b. Gray-backed Tern *(Sterna lunata)*
     c. Blue-gray Noddy *(Procelsterna cerulea saxatilis)*
     d. Common or Brown Noddy *(Anous stolidus pileatus)*
     e. White-capped or Black Noddy *(Anous tenuirostris)*
     f. White Tern *(Gygis alba)*

THE PELAGIC BIRDS ON LAND

The pelagic species have been characterized as spending their nonbreeding time on the open ocean. They obtain their food from the ocean, and some of them rest and sleep on its surface. From time to time, some of them provide a meal for a shark or other predaceous fish. Most of the pelagic species exist in such large numbers, however, that the death of some birds as part of the larger food chain constitutes no threat to the success of the species.

It was pointed out earlier that some pelagic species have a very long life span (30 years or longer), and that immature birds may spend a year or more at sea. The most critical stage in the life cycle of the oceanic birds occurs when they must come to land to build their nests and lay their eggs. As long as each nesting season produces a reasonable number of replacements, the overall population will remain more or less the same over periods of time, even though there will be annual variations in relative success in the breeding season. Some years will be better than others.

In the primeval state of the Hawaiian Islands, there were no mammalian predators of either the land birds or the seabirds. This is not to say that there was then no mortality during the nesting season. Some eggs, then as now, were infertile. There were variations in climatic factors, including storms or excessively hot weather. Young, flightless birds surely had accidents, such as falling off ledges into the water or onto the rocks far below. But over very long periods of time, the reproductive potential of each species had evolved to compensate for all those factors in the environment that were likely to cause mortality of eggs, young, and adults. However, no bird species can change its breeding potential to adapt to the rapid, devastating changes that can be wrought by man and by the exotic animals, especially mammals, that man introduces to foreign environments. What, then, do we know about the past, as well as the present, status of the oceanic birds that nest on the Hawaiian Islands?

THE MAIN ISLANDS

All too little is known about the numbers, or even the species, of oceanic birds that nested on the inhabited islands during the nineteenth century and before. At least two species are believed to have nested on the cliffs of all the main islands.

Most of the Dark-rumped Petrels now nest on the walls of Haleakala Crater on Maui. James W. Larson estimated a minimum breeding population of 400 pairs there in 1966. This species nested on Mauna Kea and Mauna Loa in the 1960s, and a small population was discovered on Lanai in 1976.

Although it is possible that Harcourt's Storm Petrel once inhabited several of the high Hawaiian islands, there apparently exists no definite information. Munro (1944) knew of "no record of the nest or egg having been seen," and Richardson and Bowles (1964) commented simply that the breeding grounds were unknown.

In contrast to the shearwater and the two species of petrels, which may have nested on the main islands for many thousands of years, the Red-footed Booby has established breeding colonies on two of the islands in recent years: near the Kilauea Lighthouse on Kauai and on the Kaneohe Marine Base on Oahu. The Wedge-tailed Shearwater also nests on Kauai (for example, Kilauea Lighthouse, Na Pali coast).

Nothing seems to be known about the original birdlife of Niihau. Captain Cook left goats on Niihau on February 2, 1778, and Captain Vancouver added others in 1794. Later introductions of sheep and cattle completed the elimination of the native vegetation before the 1890s, and none of the ornithologists of that period found any nesting native land birds. "There is no native forest of any sort left on the island" (Fisher 1951). Mongooses were never introduced, but pigs, rats, and feral cats are common. Unfortunately, no ornithologist has been able to visit this privately owned island since 1947.

THE OFFSHORE ISLANDS

A number of small islands lying a mile or less offshore of the main islands are important breeding areas for seabirds (fig. 22). The larger and better known of these small islands lie off Niihau (Lehua Island), Kauai (Mokuaeae Island), and Oahu (Moku Manu, Manana or Rabbit Island, and some fifteen smaller islands). A number of very small islets lie off the coasts of Molokai and Maui. These islands are located off the north and east, or windward, coasts of the main islands, and many of them are very difficult or impossible to reach during much of the year (fig. 23).

Lehua Island, just off the north shore of Niihau, contains 291 acres and has a maximum elevation of 710 feet. Rabbits were abundant on the island in the past, but Caum (1936) found considerable vegetation on the island in 1931, and he reported eight species of seabirds plus the introduced Skylark on the island: Black-footed Albatross, Wedge-tailed Shearwater, Red-tailed Tropicbird, Blue-faced Booby, Brown Booby, Great Frigatebird, Brown Noddy, Black Noddy. Fisher (1951) found several species in 1947 not seen by Caum: Christmas Shearwater, Sooty Tern, Red-footed Booby, and the Barred Dove.

Richardson (1963) found species in 1960 not reported by Caum and Fisher: Bulwer's Petrel, House Sparrow, American Cardinal, and the House Finch. He did not, however, find the Skylark. Richardson wrote that "cactus has now entirely disappeared from Lehua, and perhaps with it the Skylark."

Although Caum had found Lehua Island overrun

FIGURE 22. Wedge-tailed Shearwaters on Popoia Islet off the windward coast of Oahu prior to the egg-laying period. April 22, 1964. Moku Manu (*right*) and Mokapu Peninsula are seen in the distance.

FIGURE 23. Part of the windward face of Moku Manu. This State bird reservation is inaccessible during much of the year, in part because the island has no beaches. Eleven species of seabirds were present on this island on August 7, 1970.

with rabbits in 1931 and 1932, Richardson found, thirty-one years later, only a "moderate" number of rabbits. He found a dead rat, however, and evidence that rats were killing adult Bulwer's Petrels. Lehua Island is owned by the State, and Richardson recommended that the island be set aside as a bird reservation and that the rats and rabbits be eradicated. However, no steps have been taken to eradicate these mammals.

Kaula Island is a small (approximately 125 acres), crescent-shaped remnant of a once larger island located 23 miles west-southwest of Niihau. The first landing by scientists was made in 1932, when H. S. Palmer and E. L. Caum visited the island in company with a work crew installing a light. Caum (1936) recorded 15 species of seabirds. The island was next visited by Navy and State Fish and Game personnel in 1971. The southeast tip of Kaula has long been used as a bombing target by the military services and civilian pressures to

halt the bombing increased during the 1970s. As a result, two expeditions visited Kaula in 1976 and again in 1978. I joined the party on August 21 and 22, 1978 at the request of Gerald E. Swedberg, the Navy Natural Resources Specialist. Ronald L. Walker of the State Division of Fish and Game supervised the field work. We found that populations were lower in the small impact area, but there was no evidence that birds had been killed by bombs. Seabirds have different breeding seasons, so that not all species have been found on each of the five expeditions since 1971. However, 17 species of seabirds now nest on Kaula Island, the maximum estimated population of 139,285 being recorded on March 7, 1978 (table 1). Of special interest was the presence of 6 species of exotic birds on September 14 and 15, 1976: Barn Owl, Japanese White-eye, Mockingbird, Ricebird, House Finch, and Cardinal. Forty House Finches and 20 Ricebirds were counted on those dates. During August 1978, we found 1 Barn Owl and

TABLE 1

Breeding Seabirds of Kaula Island

Black-footed Albatross	Red-footed Booby
Laysan Albatross	Great Frigatebird
Wedge-tailed Shearwater	Sooty Tern
Christmas Shearwater	Gray-backed Tern
Bulwer's Petrel	Blue-gray Noddy
White-tailed Tropicbird	Brown Noddy
Red-tailed Tropicbird	Black Noddy
Masked Booby	White Tern
Brown Booby	

20 House Finches. These exotic birds presumably reached Kaula from Niihau. We saw Polynesian rats both during the daytime and at night.

Little is known about the birdlife of Mokuaeae Island. Richardson and Bowles (1964) found only two breeding species (Wedge-tailed Shearwater and Red-footed Booby) during their visit to the island on July 12, 1960.

Munro (1944:43) wrote that there were very few or no seabirds on Manana Island at the turn of the twentieth century. Richardson and Fisher (1950:288) suggested that "the Hawaiians may well have killed off the birds for food before this time. The more recent reappearance and increase in numbers and species of the birds may reflect the disappearance of many of the old Hawaiians and their customs, and the protection of the birds." By contrast, the much longer canoe trip to Moku Manu, "the rough channel, and the uncertainty of being able to get on the island must have combined to keep even the old Hawaiians away much of the time."

E. H. Bryan (1935) visited Manana Island during August 1934. He wrote: "The dominant bird on the island, present in thousands, in all stages from hatching eggs to adult, was the noio or noddy tern, *Anous stolidus* (Linn.). It is curious that this is the only tern on Manana Island, while ten miles away, on Moku Manu, the sooty tern, *Sterna fuliginosa* Gmel. is the dominant bird, living in equally large numbers, with the noddy absent."

Richardson and Fisher (1950) reported that the Sooty Tern first appeared on Manana Island in 1947, when "apparently only five to ten eggs were laid." They estimated the population to be about 2,000 birds in 1948; at that time there were about 7,000 Brown Noddies. By 1971, however, the nesting populations had increased to 100,000 Sooty Terns and 30,000 Brown Noddies (Brown 1973). Wedge-tailed Shearwaters (*Puffinus pacificus*) and Bulwer's Petrel (*Bulweria bulwerii*) also nest on Manana Island (fig. 24).

European rabbits (*Oryctolagus cuniculus*) were introduced to Manana Island about 1890; several hundred

were killed each year during the early 1900s. Dixon (1973), however, found that rabbits used only about 30 acres of the island and had a density of less than two rabbits per acre. He believed that 152 young were born during 1972. Most of the mortality occurs from May to September, which is the period of summer drought. Tomich, Wilson, and Lamoureux (1968) thought that rabbits probably had destroyed certain plant species early in this century, but that, by keeping some of the vegetation under control, the rabbits now may maintain more favorable nesting conditions for the terns. Brown (1974) watched rabbits break the eggs of Brown Noddies. In one instance, a rabbit charged an incubating noddy and knocked the bird off its egg; the rabbit then pushed the egg downslope with the upper surface of its nose.

There are no rats on Manana Island, but the house mouse does survive there. The Black-crowned Night Heron is a predator on downy chicks of the seabirds and at least one crab (*Grapsis* sp.) probably preys on young Bulwer's Petrel chicks.

Moku Manu (bird island) is a double island, the eroded remnant of a tuff cone of the Honolulu volcanic series that lies just north of Ulupau Head on the windward side of Oahu. There is no beach and access to the island is impossible much of the year. Richardson and Fisher (1950) listed 10 species of nesting seabirds during the late 1940s, including the first nesting record on the island for the Laysan Albatross (Fisher 1948b). With personnel of the State Division of Fish and Game, I visited Moku Manu on August 8, 1970. We found 11 species (table 2). Richardson and Fisher reported a population of 1,000 Great Frigatebirds on Moku Manu "from May through the fall" of 1948. We estimated that at least 500 birds were soaring over the island during our visit in 1970. Robert Shallenberger had found the first Frigatebird nest on Moku Manu on July 17, 1970. Why a large breeding popula-

TABLE 2

Breeding Seabirds on Moku Manu and Manana Island

Moku Manu	
Laysan Albatross	Red-footed Booby
Wedge-tailed Shearwater	Great Frigatebird (1970)
Christmas Shearwater	Sooty Tern
Bulwer's Petrel	Gray-backed Tern
Masked Booby	Brown Noddy
Brown Booby	Black Noddy

Manana Island
Wedge-tailed Shearwater
Bulwer's Petrel
Red-tailed Tropicbird (1967 and 1978)
Sooty Tern
Brown Noddy

FIGURE 24. Looking east across the crater of Manana (Rabbit) Island. June 12, 1970. The predominant vegetation is sourgrass *(Trichachne insularis)*, wild tobacco *(Nicotiana tabacum)*, and coconut palm *(Cocos nucifera)*. Here large numbers of Wedge-tailed Shearwaters excavate their nesting burrows under the grass tussocks, and rabbits manage to eke out an existence.

tion has not become established on Moku Manu is unknown.

Kahoolawe and Molokini are two small islands off the southwest coast of Maui. Neither island is suitable now for native land birds, and nothing is known about their ornithological history. The rainfall on Kahoolawe (aptly referred to as the island of dust) is said to vary from 10 to 25 inches per year. As long ago as 1779, Captain James King wrote that Kahoolawe "is destitute of wood and the soil seems to be sandy and barren," and in 1825 Arago said that the island "will forever be uninhabited because life there is impossible." It is said that goats were first taken to Kahoolawe by a Maui chief in 1793. R. C. Wylie started a sheep ranch on the island in 1858. From then until 1910, seven different lessees attempted to ranch sheep and cattle; all were unsuccessful. In 1913 Joseph Rock wrote that "most of the land on this island has no soil, all having

been blown into the sea by the wind, after it had been robbed of its vegetation by cattle, sheep, and goats, with which the island was overstocked. The result is that there is nothing left but pure hard-pan, several feet thickness of soil having been blown away. Even now on a windy day the island is not visible, as it is enshrouded in a cloud of red dirt." Some 13,000 goats were removed from the island in a two-year span, 1920 –1921, but goats still plague the island. The Federal Government reclaimed Kahoolawe by Executive Order in 1953 and assigned it to the U.S. Navy, which uses a part of the island as a bombing target, both aerial and ship-to-shore. I spent August 3 and 4, 1978 on Kahoolawe with Gerald E. Swedberg of the navy and John L. Sincock and Darrel Herbst of the U.S. Fish and Wildlife Service. As on Kaula Island, we were accompanied by a member of the Explosive Ordinance Disposal Unit, whose job was to guide us around unexploded ordinance in the ground. The island is, indeed, a desolate place with vast areas of barren hardpan; goats continue to destroy kiawe and other introduced plants. There are no endemic birds and but a few introduced species.

THE LEEWARD ISLANDS

The islands and atolls of the Leeward chain extend for a distance of about 1,200 miles from Nihoa to Kure Atoll.

Nihoa

Approximately 125 miles northwest of the inhabited islands of Niihau and Kauai lies Nihoa Island, the first of the islands included in the Hawaiian Islands National Wildlife Refuge. Nihoa is a mere volcanic remnant of a once high island, and now consists of but 156 acres. There is very little level ground on the entire island inasmuch as it rises from the sea to a height of about 895 feet at Miller's Peak. On the east, west, and north sides there are sheer cliffs as much as 800 feet in height (fig. 25). The only approaches to the island, therefore, lie on the south side. Even here, wave-washed ledges of volcanic rock, from 10 to 50 feet in width, usually make landing hazardous or, during much of the year, impossible. Bluffs 50 to 100 feet high rise abruptly behind the ledges, although there are several accessible approaches to the higher ground.

The ledges are reported to lie 4 to 10 feet above mean sea level—but they can be approached only when there is a very calm sea. The U.S. Fish Commission steamer *Albatross* spent nearly six months along the Leeward Island chain in 1902. The ship anchored off Nihoa for two days in June and again for four days in August, but the scientists were unable to get ashore either time. Walter K. Fisher (1906) wrote that "although a landing might possibly have been made with considerable risk when we first arrived, the problem of

FIGURE 25. Looking east toward Tanager Peak from atop Miller's Peak, showing the vertical north face of Nihoa Island. August 1, 1966.

leaving the island proved scarcely reassuring, so that we had to be content with again observing the birds from a distance.''

The personnel of the Vanderbilt Nihoa Expedition spent nine days on the island in 1940. George Vanderbilt wrote that ''it is an interesting fact that, out of all the time spent on Nihoa, the only days when a landing could possibly have been effected were the day that the expedition arrived and the day that the *Navigator* returned to take them off'' (Vanderbilt and de Schauensee 1941).

There is one small sandy beach in the westernmost cove of Adams Bay, but the currents are so treacherous there most of the time that it is not a safe landing area. The sandy beach does look inviting, and more than one small boat has been swamped in attempting to reach it. The large numbers of sharks in the waters of Adams Bay make it inadvisable to attempt to swim to shore.

Nihoa was discovered by a Captain Douglas in 1789, but the first modern landing on the island was made in 1822. It then was learned that early Polynesians had inhabited Nihoa, and the remains of many house sites, altars, and cultivation terraces were found (E. H. Bryan, Jr. 1942). It has been estimated that the cultivated terraces might have produced as much as 48 tons of sweet potatoes in a year, and that the island may have supported a population between 150 and 200 people.

Princess Liliuokalani, Sereno E. Bishop, Sanford B. Dole, and a party of nearly 200 other people made an excursion, partly for pleasure and partly for study, from Kauai to Nihoa in the steamer *Iwalani* in 1885. The entire group had to make a hasty departure from the island, however, after one of the party accidentally set fire to the dry vegetation. The vegetation on the island is dry for a period of time each year; the annual rainfall is estimated to be between 20 and 30 inches, or about the same as estimated over the open ocean in this region.

I had the great pleasure in 1966 of making two trips to the Leeward Islands with Eugene Kridler, the refuge manager. We lay offshore of Nihoa for most of two days in March, but the surf made landing unthinkable. We reached Nihoa again on the Bureau of Commercial Fisheries ship the *Charles H. Gilbert* early in the morning of July 28. We had been anchored for some time when I awoke at 4:00 A.M. and went on deck. I noticed that the bright deck lights had attracted a large number of medium-sized fish as well as a dozen three- to four-foot sharks that were chasing the smaller fish right up to the sides of the ship.

After considerable observation of the surf and the

several possible landing sites, our party of four jumped onto the ledge at the easternmost landing area in Adams Bay about 8:15 A.M. However, by the time we had gotten two five-gallon cans of fresh water, some C-rations, and a small amount of equipment on the ledge, the surf had increased so much that we had to move our supplies to higher ground. We placed them in a shallow cave, and took shelter there during a short rain squall. The *Gilbert* pulled off to the lee of the island to await the passing of the squall. Afterwards the surf was much too high to reach our original landing area, so we carried our supplies over a ridge to our proposed campsite, located on a very small, flat area near the bottom of Miller's Gulch, some 40 feet above the rock ledge at the ''preferred'' landing site near the middle of Adams Bay. By this time, the surf was breaking 25 feet above the ledge.

Just before sunset, the winds increased so much that we feared that our tent would blow away. We used bags of cement (brought ashore to erect a refuge sign) to reinforce the tent ropes and pegs. We thought at first that this very strong wind was out of the south, but we learned later that the winds had been out of the east and northeast during our stay on the island, and that these strong trade winds were being accelerated by the contours of the east and south sides of the island, to be funneled up Miller's Gulch at a very high speed (fig. 26). By comparison, it may be mentioned that the winds sometimes are so strong near the summit of the Pali Highway on Oahu that warnings are issued for drivers of small cars to avoid that road because small cars have, on occasion, been blown over by the wind.

Despite its almost sheer walls on three sides and its total extent of but 156 acres, Nihoa supports a breeding population of half a million seabirds of 17 species (Clapp et al. 1977). These are the same species as those found on Kaula Island except that the Sooty Storm Petrel nests on Nihoa and the White-tailed Tropicbird does not. Based on sample plots and banding adult birds at night, we estimated a population of Bulwer's Petrels as high as 250,000 during July and August 1966. Some 3,000 White Terns inhabit the island, being especially abundant along the slopes of the Devil's Slide and the cliffs along the north face of the island. The first Wedge-tailed Shearwater young that we found hatched between 8:00 A.M. and 6:00 P.M. on August 1. The adults had been incubating their single egg only 15 feet from our tent.

Red-footed and Masked boobies had nests with eggs or young of virtually all ages, from newly hatched to large young with only traces of their white natal down. Immature Brown Boobies already were on the wing. Black-footed and Laysan albatrosses had completed

FIGURE 26. Miller's Gulch and Miller's Peak, Nihoa Island. July 29, 1966.

their nesting cycle by August. Among the more conspicuous birds during the daylight hours were the hundreds of large immature Frigatebirds in their nests, which were scattered widely over the shrubby slopes.

Nihoa is also noted for its two endemic land birds. The Nihoa Finch *(Telespyza ultima)* was named *ultima* in 1917 because W. A. Bryan concluded that it would be the last new Hawaiian bird to be discovered. In 1923, however, Alexander Wetmore discovered and named the Nihoa Millerbird *(Acrocephalus familiaris kingi)*, closely related to the then-already-extinct Laysan Millerbird.

The Ruddy Turnstone is a common winter visitor to Nihoa, and three other shorebirds occur as uncommon migrants: Golden Plover, Bristle-thighed Curlew, and Wandering Tattler. The Herring Gull, Pintail, and the Mockingbird have been recorded as vagrants.

Necker Island

This is a narrow ridge of volcanic rock, with an estimated area of 41 acres, and that was discovered by Comte de La Pérouse on November 4, 1786. He named the island in honor of the French minister of finance under Louis XVI. The existence of Necker Island apparently was unknown to the Hawaiians at that time. In the employ of John Turnbull, two Hawai-

ians landed on Necker in December 1802, and reported a "range of stones, placed with some regularity in the manner of a wall, and about three feet high" (E. H. Bryan, Jr. 1942). It was not until 1894, however, that a group under Captain J. A. King landed on Necker in order to annex it in the name of the Hawaiian government. Photographs were taken and fragments of six stone images were collected. Landing on Necker is impossible during much of the year.

The history and biology of Necker Island are discussed by Clapp and Kridler (1977). More than 200,000 seabirds of at least 15 species nest on the island, and the Sooty Storm Petrel and Christmas Shearwater may nest there. Five species of migrant shorebirds have been seen (Appendix A), as have two vagrants, Glaucous-winged Gull (1923) and the Mockingbird (1967).

French Frigate Shoals

The crescent-shaped reef of French Frigate Shoals was discovered by La Pérouse about 1:30 A.M. on November 6, 1786, when he, as well as sailors on the second ship under his command, sighted breakers only two cable-lengths ahead of their ships. They immediately "hauled on the larboard" and escaped the reefs. La Pérouse surveyed the shoal the following day and named it Basse des Frégates Francaises.

The curving reef is about 19 miles from one end to the other and 7 miles wide in the middle. When I visited the reef in 1966, sharks were abundant throughout the lagoon.

A series of islets is found in the shallow lagoon, but the number has changed from time to time. Captain N. C. Brooks of the Hawaiian bark *Gambia* reported five large coral islets in 1859. There were still five islands in 1912 and 1913, but 11 were counted in 1914 (Elschner 1915). The Tanager Expedition found 13 small islets in 1923. Whale and Skate islands, shown as separate islands on the Tanager Expedition map, have since become joined into one long, narrow piece of land. Within the southern part of the reef there were two barren sand islands named Gin and Little Gin. During our visit in 1966 we found three sand islands there. La Pérouse Pinnacle is a volcanic remnant about 122 feet high and 730 feet long.

Tern Island, the best known of the little islands in French Frigate Shoals, was the location of a Coast Guard Loran station until 1979. It is not yet suitable as a nesting area for many birds as many of the birds that did come to the island were killed or crippled by flying into guy wires.

On March 11, 1967, Eugene Kridler released 27 banded Nihoa Finches (6 males and 22 females) on Tern Island and 10 birds on East Island. A severe wind and rain storm occurred that night and only 2 females were found on East Island the following day; none were found on subsequent visits. Only 3 of the finches were found on Tern Island during December 1967. These birds nested in 1968 and 1969, but all later disappeared.

Whale-Skate and East islands, however, both provide nesting sites for many thousands of seabirds. We spent the night of March 22, 1966, on Whale-Skate Island. The Laysan and Black-footed albatrosses already had large downy young. Some Frigatebirds were sitting on empty nests; others were already incubating their single large white egg. Sooty Terns were just coming back to the island to begin their breeding activities, and we found one egg. On East Island, however, we estimated that there were 19,000 Sooty Tern nests, each with a single egg.

We counted 274 Laysan Albatross chicks and 547 Black-footed Albatross chicks on East Island. Other nesting birds included Brown Noddies, Red-footed Boobies, Masked Boobies, and Red-tailed Tropicbirds. We also counted 6 Golden Plover and 137 Ruddy Turnstones. Both are migratory species that spend the winter months in the Hawaiian Islands.

We also had the opportunity to spend a few hours checking Gin and Little Gin islands, both of them sand islands totally devoid of any vegetation, as well as a third unnamed island, new since the visit of the *Tanager*. On Little Gin (now larger than Gin Island), we found 262 Black-footed Albatross chicks, 65 adult Brown Noddies, 4 Masked Boobies, and 6 monk seals sunning on the sand.

Amerson (1971) discussed the history and biology of French Frigate Shoals. He reported on 18 species of resident seabirds, 5 migrant shorebirds, and 20 species of vagrants or accidental visitors.

Laysan Island

The island was called Moller Island by Captain Stanikowitch, who discovered it on March 12, 1828, and named the island after his ship. The evidence of earlier discovery and the origin of its present name are discussed by Ely and Clapp (1973).

Laysan, located 790 miles northwest of Honolulu, is a coral island with no volcanic rock exposed. Patches of beach rock are found near the shore, and beautiful reefs and lagoons surround part of the island. Sharks also abound. The island is a little over one mile in width and somewhat less than two miles in length. In the central area is a shallow lake of very high salinity. A small pond containing fresh water was found south of the lagoon during the early years of this century. However, the pond had already become filled with sand by 1923, as a result of the destruction of the vegetation by the rabbits mentioned previously, and no one has been able to find potable water since that time.

The beaches on three sides rise to maximum heights of between 30 and 40 feet before sloping downward to the lake. The rim on the south is only about 10 feet above sea level. Occasional bands of dead vegetation suggest that winter storms carry the surf over the lower portions of the island and inward to the lake.

The vegetation on Laysan made a remarkable recovery after the last rabbits were exterminated in 1923. Analyses were made of the vegetation during the period 1959–1961 (Lamoureux 1963). Aerial photographs taken in 1961 are very similar to those made in 1949, indicating that this recovery took less than twenty-six years. Although the unique *Pritchardia* palm, the Laysan sandalwood, and a native shrub of the genus *Achyranthes* became extinct, many of the native plants now cover a large portion of the island. Among the more important plants for the birds are *Scaevola*, a bunchgrass (*Eragrostis variabilis*), two species of morning glory (*Ipomoea indica* and *Ipomoea pes-caprae*), a member of the four-o'clock family (*Boerhavia diffusa*), and akulikuli (*Sesuvium portulacastrum*). One small patch of a sedge (*Cyperus pennatiformis*) still persists.

The dense stands of beach naupaka (*Scaevola*) are concentrated along the rim of the island, beginning only a short distance above the beach. The plant occurs both in scattered patches and in long strips, especially on the west side of the island. The highly branched shrubs grow to a height of four or five feet, and provide ideal nest sites for the Frigatebirds and the Black Noddies. The Red-tailed Tropicbird lays its single large egg on the ground under the cover provided by the plants.

Laysan Island is the most important breeding area for the Black-footed and Laysan albatrosses. For the most part, both species nest in the open on the barren sand, both on the periphery of the island and in similar areas around parts of the lake. However, there are so many birds that many also are to be found in the sandy areas in the bunchgrass association, as well as along the margins of the clumps of *Scaevola* and other vegetation.

The Laysan Duck inhabits primarily two mixed plant associations which grow concentrically around the lake. The dominant plants are *Boerhavia, Ipomoea, Tribulus,* and *Sesuvium* (fig. 27). Most of these are creeping plants, but they form very dense mats as much as 18 inches in height. Some native and introduced shrubs are also scattered irregularly throughout. The combination provides dense cover in which the ducks rest and nest. During daylight hours, one can walk over considerable expanses of this habitat and encounter only a few ducks. The birds are much more active from dusk to dawn.

FIGURE 27. Laysan Ducks are well camouflaged in the *Boerhavia-Ipomoea-Tribulus* plant association on Laysan Island. The Laysan Albatrosses are conspicuous everywhere. March 30, 1966.

The abundant Laysan Finch is found in all plant associations on the island, although this species is especially partial to the bunchgrass association (fig. 28). The thick tussocks of this grass that reach a height of over three feet provide cover, some food, and nesting sites for the birds. The individual tussocks typically are widely spaced, some in areas where only bare sand intervenes, others in areas where a low ground cover, such as morning glory, fills the spaces between the grass clumps.

There were guesses in the early years as to the number of birds on Laysan; estimates of as many as 10 million birds were made. Although such numbers may have been exaggerated, evidence suggests that there was a large decline in populations of albatrosses because of the raids of feather hunters between 1909 and 1915. Nevertheless, over half a million Laysan Albatrosses now nest on Laysan Island and the island has a total breeding population of more than three million seabirds (Ely and Clapp 1973). The 15 other nesting

species are: Bonin Petrel, Bulwer's Petrel, Wedge-tailed Shearwater, Christmas Shearwater, Sooty Storm Petrel, Red-tailed Tropicbird, Masked Booby, Brown Booby, Red-footed Booby, Great Frigatebird, Sooty Tern, Gray-backed Tern, Brown Noddy, Black Noddy, and White Tern. Five species of shorebirds are regular winter visitors and 30 species of accidentals have been observed on Laysan Island.

Lisianski Island

This island, lying about 115 miles west of Laysan, was discovered on October 15, 1805, when a Russian exploring ship under the command of Captain Urey Lisianski grounded on one of its reefs. Later exploring visits (in 1857, 1859, and 1891) provided the information that, in addition to fine beaches, much of the island was covered with coarse grass, creeping plants, and low shrubs, and that fresh water could be obtained by digging 5 feet down in a central former-lagoon basin. Birds, the Hawaiian monk seal, and the green sea

FIGURE 28. Bunchgrass association, Laysan Island. March 26, 1966. Adult and young Laysan Albatrosses are visible on the sand, and the lake is seen in the distance.

turtle were said to be abundant. The island, approximately one mile long and one-half mile wide was a favorite for Japanese feather hunters. See Clapp and Wirtz (1975) for a fascinating discussion of the history and biology of the island.

Lisianski Island was included in the 1890 lease to the North Pacific Phosphate and Fertilizer company, but it is doubtful that any guano was shipped from the island. Rabbits were introduced to Lisianski Island at an unknown time; Clapp and Wirtz wrote that rabbits could have been introduced by Japanese feather gatherers or by Max Schlemmer at "almost anytime between 1904 and 1909."

Elschner (1915) gave the following description of the island in 1912:

Save for the presence of many thousands of sea birds, the island presents such a dreary and desolate appearance as has never confronted me, even on my travels over the deserts of North Africa and Syria. Walking over this island is extremely difficult on account of the many holes in which the birds nest. Without doubt the avi-fauna is poorer in species than on Laysan Island. The rabbits introduced have just exterminated the flora, probably never very luxuriant, with the exception of the tobacco; it is almost impossible to realize the complete extermination of the vegetation; now the rest of these rabbits (we found many dead but very few living ones) will have to submit to starvation. Certainly a terrible fate for a once large population of these poor doomed animals!

It was reported that before 1915 the rabbits had destroyed all of the vegetation except for a patch of introduced tobacco and two morning glory plants, and that the rabbits themselves had died out. Alexander Wetmore (1925) wrote that the bleached and weathered bones of the rabbits "strewed the sands" in 1923. He added that "a few roots of grass and of pigweed had grown sufficiently deep to escape the incessant search of the starving four-legged pests and, with the final disappearance of the mammals, had begun a battle against the forces of wind and sand to recover the island."

The vegetation has recovered since that time. *Scaevola, Boerhavia,* bunchgrass, and morning glory now cover large areas of the island. Several ironwood (*Casuarina*) trees provide nesting sites. The three most common nesting seabirds are the Bonin Petrel with an estimated population of one million birds, the Sooty Tern, 1,700,000, and the Wedge-tailed Shearwater, 500,000. Twelve other seabirds nest in much smaller numbers. The Laysan Rail was liberated on the island in 1913 but disappeared between 1916 and 1923. The wintering shorebirds and accidental visitors are listed by Clapp and Wirtz (1975).

Pearl and Hermes Reef

This atoll was discovered on the night of April 26, 1822, when two English whaling ships, the *Pearl* and the *Hermes,* both grounded on the reef about 10 miles apart.

The reef encloses a lagoon (as much as 100 feet deep) about 17 miles long and 10 miles wide. The number of islets and sand bars changes considerably from time to time. Captain N. C. Brooks reported 12 small islands in 1858; a chart made in 1867 by Captain William Reynolds shows only 2 islands; Bryan (1942) shows 6. In recent years, there have been 9 islands, although Seal and Kittery islands joined to form a single island about 1978. Kittery existed only as a small sandbar in 1923. Galtstoff (1933) had reported noticeable changes in the configuration of sand bars and in the appearance of new bars after only two days of moderately stormy weather.

Four of the islands (Grass, North, Seal, and Southeast) have established vegetation, and 25 species of vascular plants have been recorded, including one endemic species *(Sicyos caumii).* A total of 17 seabird species nest on the islands; the breeding population is approximately 200,000 birds. Southeast Island (about 34 acres) is the largest of the group and has the greatest variety of seabirds, including a small group of Brown Boobies (fig. 29). Five species of migrant shorebirds and 13 accidental visitors have been observed on the islands. The Hawaiian Monk Seal is a common resident breeder on most of the islands, with a total estimated population of 195 in 1963. Rabbits were introduced to Southeast Island before 1916 and were exterminated in 1928 (Amerson et al. 1974).

Personnel of the Smithsonian Institution's Pacific Ocean Biological Survey banded 31,661 birds of 22 species at Pearl and Hermes Reef from 1963 to 1968. More than 200 birds were recaptured later at points on other islands of the Hawaiian chain, from Johnston Atoll, Wake Island, Ellice Islands, Philippine Islands,

FIGURE 29. Southeast Island, Pearl and Hermes Reef. April 1, 1966. Most of the birds are Laysan Albatrosses and Great Frigatebirds.

and Japan. Another 70 birds of 12 species that were banded in other areas (including Johnston Atoll, Wake Island, and the Pribilof Islands) have been recaptured at Pearl and Hermes Reef (see Ruddy Turnstone in Appendix A).

Captain William Anderson transplanted seven pairs of Laysan Rails from Midway Atoll to Pearl and Hermes Reef during June 1929. All birds died before 1930. Fourteen Laysan Ducks were captured on Laysan Island and released on Southeast Island on March 21, 1967, by personnel of the U.S. Fish and Wildlife Service. The first two ducks released flew out to sea and were not seen again. The remaining birds were wing-clipped before release. One unsuccessful nest was found later that year, but none of the ducks were found in 1968. On March 21, 1967, 110 Laysan Finches were released on Southeast Island. Since that time, nests with eggs or young have been found in February, March, April, and May. Seventeen active nests were found during May 1969, and it is thought that 110 young were produced by the end of 1969. The population as of 1979 was thought to be about 100 birds, which included those that had moved to Grass and North islands. It may be noted that the late Alexander Wetmore did not approve of such transplanting of endemic species.

Midway Atoll

Captain N. C. Brooks of the *Gambia* discovered Midway Atoll on July 8, 1859. The nearly circular coral reef is approximately 5 miles in diameter. Its two islands, Sand and Eastern, lie near the southern rim of the atoll.

Under orders of the Secretary of the Navy, Captain William Reynolds of the U.S.S. *Lackawanna* took formal possession of the atoll on August 28, 1867. This action is presumed to have resulted from pressure exerted by the Pacific Mail Steamship Company (Bryan 1942). Three years later, the United States Congress appropriated $50,000 in order to prepare a ship channel through the reef and into the lagoon, but little progress was made. Finally on April 29, 1903, the Commercial Pacific Cable Company took possession of Sand Island, which was said then to be a ''barren waste of ground coral.'' In 1908, Daniel Morrison became superintendent of this relay station for the submarine cable between North America and Asia. ''Stormproof concrete buildings, water towers, and an ice plant were erected. Supplies were carried on the company's sailing ship, the *Florence Ward,* commanded by Captain George Piltz, four times each year from Hawaii, and approximately 150 tons of soil for the gardens were transported each trip for more than a decade. Grass from the California mainland was planted in clumps to help in holding the sand in place, and hundreds of ironwood trees were planted to give protection from the glowing sun. [Fig. 30.] In a short time the cable people had a little green oasis in a desert of sand.'' (Bailey and Niedrach 1951)

Sand Island became a stopover for Pan American Airways in 1935, and a hotel and other facilities were built. Late in 1936, the Hawaiian Sugar Planters' Association assigned Fred C. Hadden to Midway to arrange for fumigation of all eastbound airplanes. His recorded observations for the following five years (Hadden 1941) are important for our knowledge of the birds before the rats reached Sand and Eastern islands.

A detachment of marines occupied Midway from January 1903 until the spring of 1908 ''to protect property and guard the cable employees from marauders who might visit the islands to kill the sea birds'' (Bailey 1956). On September 29, 1940, a Midway Detachment of 177 officers and men began installing the defenses of Midway; and on February 14, 1941, by Executive order, the atoll was declared a national defense area. In less than five years, introduced rats caused the extinction of the populations of Laysan Rail and Laysan Finch on Midway.

Many thousands of albatrosses and other seabirds were killed on the Midway Islands during the construction of military facilities during World War II (Fisher and Baldwin 1946; Fisher 1949). Many other birds were deliberately destroyed in an attempt to reduce the number of collisions of aircraft with birds, and still other birds have been killed by flying into antennas and guy wires (Fisher 1966a, 1966b; Robbins 1966).

''In 1964–1965 these towering obstacles killed more than 3,000 mature Laysan albatrosses and thereby nullified the reproductive contribution by the total of 30,000 pairs of albatrosses that nested that year on Midway Atoll's Eastern Island.'' The antenna site was abandoned in 1967, and the towers were blasted to the ground: ''The snarled masses of cables, wires, tubes, and lengths of formed steel serve man still, but now as unsightly anti-erosion devices along the southeastern shore of the island. Theirs was an ignominious fate for, as plastic explosives blew apart the supporting guy wires, the towers crumpled into shapeless masses that bulldozers later shoved toward the sea, trailing copper wires and aluminum tubing like eviscerated entrails.'' (Fisher 1970)

A great deal has been written about the albatross populations on the two islands of Midway Atoll but very little about the other seabirds or the introduced Canary (*Serinus canaria;* see Bailey 1956). James P. Ludwig and Steven I. Apfelbaum worked at Midway during February 1979. Ludwig told me that Red-tailed Tropicbirds seemed less numerous than in 1963. Roof

FIGURE 30. Ironwood trees on Sand Island, Midway Atoll. April 2, 1966. A White Tern is incubating its egg in the crotch of the large tree on the left.

rats are a serious problem on the islands: they not only eat the eggs and small young of seabirds and attack incubating adults but also have done severe damage to the *Scaevola* plants. The introduced ironwood trees also continue to spread, thus impinging on the open sandy breeding sites of the albatrosses.

Kure Atoll

Kure Atoll (also called Ocean Island) probably was visited by a Spanish vessel in 1799 but the first definite description was made by Captain Benjamin Morrell, Jr., during July 1825. The island was "rediscovered" on July 9, 1837, when the British ship *Gledstanes,* under the command of a Captain Brown, was wrecked on the reef. Captain Brown and his men built a schooner from the wreckage, and he and eight companions left the island in December, and finally reached Honolulu. Another ship returned to rescue those stranded on the island. Other ships have been wrecked on the reef at Kure, one in 1842, another in 1870 (Woodward 1972).

Kure is the northwesternmost atoll in the Hawaiian Archipelago, lying 49 nautical miles west of Midway, 1,175 miles northwest of Honolulu, and about 2,165 miles east of Tokyo. The roughly circular reef is about 6 miles in maximum diameter and about 15 miles in circumference. Green Island is the largest (1.4 miles long and 0.37 miles wide) of three islands, and presently the only permanent land. The island has a dense growth of *Scaevola taccada* surrounding an open area containing a number of low plants *(Eragrostis, Boerhavia, Tribulus,* and *Solanum).*

Kure was a part of the Hawaiian Islands National Wildlife Refuge until World War II, when the island was taken over by the military. Rather than returning the island to the Bureau of Sport Fisheries and Wildlife after the war, however, the military gave it to the State of Hawaii, and it is now a part of the City and County of Honolulu!

A Coast Guard Loran station has been in operation since 1960. Udvardy (1961b) described early efforts to "improve" Green Island for the albatrosses by bulldozing runways through the vegetation, in an attempt to compensate for the slaughter of albatrosses at Midway. At the time of his visit in 1961, however, a third of Green Island had been converted into an airstrip, and buildings and an aerial tower (625 feet high) had been erected.

Woodward (1972) discussed the history and biology of Kure Atoll. The island supports a maximum population of about 74,000 seabirds of 15 species. The Sooty Tern is the most abundant species (25,000); oddly the Black Noddy has not been found to nest on Kure. The Polynesian rat is the most important factor affecting nesting success on the island. The rats eat the eggs of the seabirds and also have been seen to prey upon the adults of 10 species, ranging in size from the Laysan Albatross to the White Tern. Winter storms and unusually high tides also sometimes destroy albatross nests. Five species of shorebirds are common winter visitants and 45 other species have been recorded as rare or accidental migrants.

NESTING HABITS OF SEABIRDS

It is generally inadvisable to use the words *always* and *never* when writing about birds and other animals because one usually finds exceptions to broad generalizations. Nevertheless, it is possible to make some general statements about the nesting behavior of those seabirds that nest on the Hawaiian Islands.

Certain species apparently always lay their eggs on the ground, either with or without using nesting material. These include the Black-footed and Laysan albatrosses, Christmas Shearwater, Red-tailed Tropicbird, Masked Booby, Brown Booby, Sooty Tern, Gray-backed Tern, and Blue-gray Noddy.

Other species usually excavate nesting burrows in the sand or other substrate, or nest in natural cavities in the rocks (although sometimes and in some areas certain individuals lay their eggs on the surface of the ground, either in the open or under shrubby vegetation): Wedge-tailed Shearwater, Newell's Shearwater, Dark-rumped Petrel, Bonin Petrel, Bulwer's Petrel, and, presumably, Harcourt's Storm Petrel.

Those of another group almost invariably build their nests in some kind of vegetation; the nest may be only a foot above ground level or it may be high up in a tree. Such species include the Red-footed Booby, the Great Frigatebird, and the Black Noddy.

The White-tailed Tropicbird typically lays its single egg on a rocky ledge in cliffs, but there is one record of a tree nest on Midway.

On most of the Leeward Islands, the White Tern lays its single egg on a rock, but on Midway this tern frequently lays its egg on a branch, on a broken stub, or in a crotch of an ironwood tree, as well as on flat roofs of buildings (fig. 31).

FIGURE 31. White Tern brooding its chick on the roof of the Bachelor Officers' Quarters Midway Atoll. April 3, 1966.

Many seabirds lay plain or unmarked white or whitish eggs: albatrosses, shearwaters, petrels, boobies, and frigatebirds. By contrast, tropicbirds, terns, and noddies lay colored eggs whose background color varies from white to pinkish white and light brown and is overlain by irregular markings (tan, brown, purple), which usually are concentrated around the larger end of the egg. There is considerable variation in the precise color pattern of the eggs laid by different females, and even among the eggs laid by the same female if there is more than one egg in a clutch. In general, however, one can recognize the species from the size, shape, and markings of the egg. The eggs of most species are smooth with a dull surface, but those of boobies are noted for their outer chalky layer.

Most albatrosses, shearwaters, petrels, tropicbirds, and terns lay a single egg. Red-footed Boobies lay a single egg, whereas the Masked and Brown boobies usually lay two eggs to a clutch.

The Hawaiian Islands extend from about 19° to 29° of latitude north of the equator. The summer sun is exceedingly hot, especially on dry offshore islands and on the volcanic or coral islands in the Leeward chain. The nesting adults encounter the problem of excessive heat and solar radiation not only for themselves but also for the eggs or newly hatched young. Rather than incubating its egg, therefore, the bird at the nest may have to stand over the egg, or nestling, in order to provide shade for it.

Birds do not have sweat glands, and both adults and young birds dissipate excess heat by evaporative cooling, which is accomplished either by panting or by gular fluttering—that is, by rapidly vibrating the throat and floor of the mouth, thus speeding up blood flow and loss of heat through the membranes in the floor of the mouth and gular (throat) area. Gular flutter occurs in most pelecaniform birds (pelicans, boobies, cormorants, anhingas, frigatebirds), as well as in a number of unrelated groups (herons, doves, roadrunners, owls, nightjars, colies, and many gallinaceous species).

Another characteristic of seabirds, although only indirectly related to nesting habits, is of interest in understanding how these birds are adapted to their environment. Fresh water is unavailable on most of the islands where seabirds nest, and not only do these birds not need fresh water but Frings and Frings (1959) discovered that captive Black-footed and Laysan albatrosses died unless they were fed adequate amounts of salt. These birds have special salt glands, located above the eyes, that secrete a fluid having a higher salt concentration than that in sea water, thereby leaving a net gain of water for the birds. The salt secretion drains to the tip of the bill, and head-shaking movements discard it.

Black-footed Albatross
Diomedea nigripes
(Color plate 1)

This is a dark brown gooney bird with a small white area at the base of the bill and below the eye, dark chestnut-colored bill, and black feet. The Black-footed Albatross is a large species with an average weight of 7 to 8 pounds and a wingspan of between 6 and 7 feet. The males are slightly larger and heavier than the females. When studying birds at night with a headlamp on East Island of French Frigate Shoals, I noticed that both the Black-footed and the Laysan albatrosses have a silvery-white eyeshine when viewed from close range. The Black-footed Albatross is noted for following ships and eating all kinds of garbage. One writer referred to it as a "feathered pig."

The Black-footed Albatross is a North Pacific species whose nonbreeding wanderings over the ocean are not completely known. It is now thought to nest almost exclusively on the Leeward Hawaiian Islands, where it has been found on all the islands except Gardner Pinnacles. It formerly nested on Wake, Johnston, Marcus, and several other islands in the Pacific. The total breeding population during 1957–1958 was estimated to be about 110,000, and the total population of the species about 300,000.

Black-footed Albatrosses are thought not to breed until they are at least 5 years old, and very few of the birds return to the nesting islands before they are 3 years old. Most of the pairs mate for life (Rice and Kenyon 1962b), and the birds return to the same small breeding territory year after year. Both Robbins (1966) and Wilson (1975) reported Black-footed Albatrosses that lived to be 27 years old. Nonbreeding birds on land long have been called "unemployed" birds, but Fisher and Fisher (1969:175) prefer the term "walker."

The albatrosses have very elaborate courtship displays, accompanied by several vocalizations (e.g., *whinny, whine, moo, double-call, yammer*) and *bill snapping* and *clappering*. These displays are described and illustrated by Rice and Kenyon.

Both adults work on the nest, which consists of a depression in the sand surrounded by a rim of packed sand (sometimes also including twigs and leaves) several inches high. The Black-footed Albatross tends to nest in more exposed areas (e.g., windblown beaches) than does the Laysan Albatross, which often nests along the edges of clumps of *Scaevola* or other plants.

A single egg is laid about 20 days after the female returns to the island. If the egg is destroyed, very rarely, if ever, is a second egg laid during that breeding season. Fisher (1969) found the average measurements of 172 Black-footed Albatross eggs to be: length 108 mm, width 70 mm. The average weight of 24 newly laid eggs was 304 g.

The eggs are dull white with a somewhat rough and chalky surface. The first eggs are laid on Midway during November. Unlike most land birds, the albatrosses lay their eggs at any time of the day or night. Following egg laying, the female usually incubates for 3 or 4 days, after which time she is relieved by the male. The male then incubates continuously for an average period of 18.2 days before he is relieved by the female. Each bird takes its turn at incubation about three times before the egg hatches. In the study by Rice and Kenyon, the incubation period for 75 nests varied from 63 to 68 days.

At hatching time, it takes the chick from 48 to 132 hours to break out of the egg. The adults take turns guarding the young chicks for periods averaging 19 days, and varying from 12.5 to 40.5 days for different pairs. The chicks are fed by regurgitation, and for several days the only food the young receive is stomach oil; later the primary diet is squid. The chicks are fed daily when very young, but later only about every third day. The parents do not recognize their own chicks until they are about 10 days old, but after that they will feed only their own chick. The average nestling or flightless period is about 140 days, and the young birds are fed by the adults until able to fly. The young birds exercise their wings and later make practice flights. They leave Midway during June for their independent life at sea. One chick banded on Sand Island, Midway Atoll, on March 2, 1966, was caught on a baited hook off the northwestern coast of Baja California on December 11 the same year (Hubbs 1968).

A generally mild climate prevails on Midway and the other Leeward Islands during the first half of the nesting season (November–February), and both the eggs and the young chicks are shielded by the adults so that "the effective environment of the egg or hatchling is actually a dry, shaded chamber kept at about 36° C" (Howell and Bartholomew 1961a:195). As the season progresses, however, both adults and the growing young are subjected to intense solar radiation and the consequent very high ground temperature and heat stress. The adults obtain relief by panting rapidly with their bills open, thus exposing the moist lining of the mouth and throat, both of which also are lowered and distended; this process is, as noted before, evaporative cooling. The juvenile birds also pant, but they have a second mechanism for dissipating excess heat. The webs of their feet are highly vascularized, and the young birds often sit on their heels with the webbed feet held in the air where the temperature is lower than that of the ground. Because of the rapid circulation of the blood through the feet, the young birds are able to lose heat through them. While assuming this posture, the young bird typically sits with its back to the sun, thus placing its feet in the shade of its own body. The larger juveniles also may seek the shade of nearby plants if available.

Laysan Albatross
Diomedea immutabilis
(Color plate 2)

The Laysan Albatross is a white bird with a blackish back, tail, and upper surface of wings. Most of the lining or undersurface of the wings is white, but there are black to brownish feathers around the edges in an irregular pattern. The bill is dark; the legs and feet are pinkish to flesh colored. The Laysan Albatross is a trimmer bird than the Black-footed Albatross: its total length (31 to 32 inches) is greater than that of the Black-foot (27 to 29 inches), but its average weight is less (5 to 7 pounds as compared with 7 to 8 pounds); the Laysan Albatross also has a slightly shorter wingspan. Both in size and in length of the beak, the male Laysan Albatross averages larger than the female.

Fisher (1967) discussed changes in body weight during the breeding season. He found that both adults lose 24 percent of their weight between the onset of incubation (November or December) and mid-May, "the end of the intensive stage of chick care," by which time the nestlings have reached their maximum weight. Both adults then regain weight in the interval between mid-May and the end of the breeding season, so that the net loss in body weight during the nesting cycle is 12 percent for males and approximately 9 percent for females.

Distribution, former breeding range, and present breeding range of the Laysan Albatross are essentially the same as those of the Black-footed Albatross (Fisher 1972). The Laysan Albatross, however, has been found breeding on all of the Leeward Islands, as well as on Niihau and Moku Manu (figs. 10, 27). The first recorded nesting on Moku Manu was of a single young bird found there during February 1947 (Fisher 1948b). The first nesting on Kauai occurred near Kilauea Point during 1977 (Zeillemaker and Ralph 1977). Byrd and Telfer (1979) saw as many as 22 albatrosses in this area in 1978, as well as 10 birds at the U.S. Navy Pacific Missile Range Facility at Barking Sands. Two eggs were laid at Kilauea Point and one on nearby

Mokuaeae Islet; however, no young were raised. Seven of the 10 birds at Barking Sands were killed by dogs.

Rice and Kenyon (1962a) estimated the total breeding population of Laysan Albatrosses in 1958 to be 560,000 and the total population of the species to be between 1,300,000 and 2,100,000 birds. Fisher (1966c) estimated a breeding population of 88,300 on Eastern Island and 92,000 on Sand Island, Midway Atoll, during December 1962.

Although nearly 25 percent first nest from their fifth to seventh years, many Laysan Albatrosses do not breed until they are eight or nine years old; at least 10 percent do not breed until after their ninth year (Fisher and Fisher 1969; Fisher, 1975b). Fisher (1975a, 1975c) has shown by studying previously banded birds that some Laysan Albatrosses live as long as 42 years; 24 percent of his sample lived 25 years or longer. This albatross has a breeding life expectancy of 16 to 18 years.

Courtship behavior is very similar to that of the Black-footed Albatross, although Rice and Kenyon noted two differences. When *clappering,* "the bill is repeatedly opened and closed so rapidly that the lower mandible is blurred." When engaged in this behavior, the pair of Laysan Albatrosses face each other, whereas the Black-footed Albatrosses hold their heads side by side. During the *scapular action,* the bird places its bill near the bend of the wing and clappers lightly; the Black-footed Albatross fans both wings simultaneously, but the Laysan Albatross fans only one wing in this display. Fisher (1972) discussed interbreeding of the two species.

Both the male and female form the nest depression, and, while sitting in it, they use their bills to scrape sand, leaves, and other debris to form the rim of the nest. The birds add to the nest rim throughout the incubation period and the guard stage of the young, and they are especially active during rain storms. A single dull white egg with a slightly rough shell is laid. Fisher (1969) found the average length of 28 eggs to be 108.2 mm; the average width, 68.1 mm. Laysan Albatrosses lay their eggs about one week later than do the Black-footed Albatrosses: the mean date for Black-footed Albatrosses on Midway during the period of 1956 to 1958 was November 21 (range: November 8 to 30); for the Laysan Albatross, November 30 (range: November 15 to December 16). Eggs are laid at night and during the daylight hours.

Fisher (1968, 1969) also reported that 97 percent of more than 3,000 eggs were laid between November 20 and December 10. He found that experienced females laid earlier (median date, November 29) than females laying for the first time (median date, December 4). He reported that Laysan Albatrosses are capable of

laying an egg and rearing a chick each year. He also presented data which seem to substantiate his conclusions that the Laysan Albatross never lays more than one egg a year; that if two eggs are found in a nest it means that two birds have laid in the same nest; and, further, that "two eggs occur only when nest desertion or interference has exposed the first egg."

The female remains on the nest no more than 3 or 4 days after laying the egg. The male then incubates continuously for an average of 22.6 days before being relieved by the female. In a study of 95 nests, Rice and Kenyon found the incubation period to vary from 62.5 to 68.0 days and to average 64.44 days, or a full day shorter than the mean (65.57 days) for the Black-footed Albatross.

After the first crack appears in the egg shell, 2.0 to 6.0 days may be required for the Laysan Albatross chick to cut through the shell and escape from it (fig. 32). The guard stage, before the chicks are left alone, for 95 Laysan Albatross chicks varied from 12 to 24.5 days. As is true of the Black-footed Albatross, the Laysan Albatrosses appear not to recognize their own young until they are about 10 days old. The average nestling period for the Laysan Albatross chick is 165 days, or about 25 days longer than for Black-footed Albatross chicks. The young Laysan Albatrosses become independent and leave the island in August; the Black-footed Albatrosses leave in July.

The following information was obtained from the experimental work of Rice and Kenyon (1962b) and of Bartholomew and Howell (1964). It was shown that

FIGURE 32. A Laysan Albatross "talking" to its egg as the hatching bird begins to utter its callnotes even before the egg is pipped. Courtesy of Harvey I. Fisher and the editor of *The Living Bird.*

both Black-footed and Laysan albatrosses can incubate only one egg, inasmuch as the incubation patch in each species is large enough to cover only a single egg. When a second egg was added to a nest, the incubating bird usually pushed it out; if the egg was left in the nest, it did not receive enough heat for development. If an adult sat first on one egg and then on the other, neither received enough heat to hatch. Both species incubated foreign objects placed in the nest: "one or two domestic fowl eggs, albatross eggs painted partly or completely red, incandescent light bulbs both smaller and larger than albatross eggs, an empty beer can, a small brick, and a red glass signal light cover."

In another experiment, the egg was removed from the nest and placed about 12 inches away; the adult was then released about 6 feet from the nest. In every case, the Laysan Albatrosses immediately returned to incubate on the empty nest; they did not leave the empty nest, nor did they attempt to roll the egg back into it. Three of the Black-footed Albatrosses, which were assumed to be in a later stage of incubation, returned to incubate the empty nest, whereas 10 birds sat on the egg outside the nest.

When chicks less than three days old were placed a short distance outside the nests, the 10 Laysan Albatrosses used in the experiment all returned to the nest, although half of the birds first stopped briefly at the chick before settling on the empty nest. Among the Black-footed Albatrosses, 11 returned to the nest and 3 returned to brood the chick.

Rice and Kenyon determined that "a clutch of one is the optimum that produces the highest number of fledged chicks per nesting pair." They added to the nests second chicks of an age that the adults would accept as foster chicks. At 15 of the nests, both chicks died; a single young survived at one nest; 2 chicks survived until May 21 at two nests, but 2 of the young were so emaciated that their survival to fledging was doubtful. Hence, no more than 3 chicks survived out of a total of 36; 12 young (66 percent) would be expected to survive from 18 undisturbed nests containing 1 young each.

During 1957, Kenyon and Rice (1958) tested the homing ability of 18 nesting Laysan Albatrosses on Midway Atoll. The birds were transported by air to various points in the Pacific. Five of them which were transported to Kwajalein Atoll, which is outside the known range of the species, returned to their nests. Only 4 of the 18 birds failed to return to Midway, and one of these was found injured in British Columbia. The fastest return (from Whidby Island, Washington) was made by a bird that flew the 3,200 statute miles in 10.1 days, or at an average speed of 317 miles per day. The longest return was made by a bird released at Sangley Point, Philippine Islands, 4,120 miles from Midway; during its 32.1-day return flight, this bird averaged 128 miles per day.

Fisher (1973) found appreciable residues of DDT, PCBs, mercury, and other chemical pollutants in the fat of both Black-footed and Laysan albatrosses that had been killed accidentally at Midway Atoll in 1969, thus demonstrating the pollution of the North Pacific Ocean. Eggshell weight in these species, however, did not show any decrease between 1910 and 1969, a reflection of the low level of DDT in the fat of these birds.

Wedge-tailed Shearwater
Puffinus pacificus chlororhynchus
(Color Plate 3)

This is a medium-sized shearwater, averaging 17 inches from bill-tip to the tip of the wedge-shaped tail, and having a wingspread of 38 inches. It has a long, slate-colored bill and flesh-colored legs. There are two color phases. The feathers of the dark-phase birds are almost entirely dark sooty brown; nearly all birds seen south of 10° north latitude are dark-phase birds. Light-phase birds, which have white underparts, predominate in the Hawaiian Islands: 97 percent of the birds of this species, on the main Hawaiian islands and 99 percent, on the Leeward Islands. King (1974) reports that the Hawaiian light-phase birds "probably migrate south to the Equatorial Countercurrent and then east to the coast of Middle America during their nonbreeding season. Molt takes place during the nonbreeding season and is nearly completed when the birds return to the central Pacific to breed." This race of the Wedge-tailed Shearwater has a pale orange eyeshine when seen at night with a headlamp.

The Wedge-tailed Shearwater nests on islands throughout nearly the entire tropical Pacific Ocean as well as in the Indian Ocean. This subspecies nests on all of the Leeward Islands, on offshore islands, on Kauai, and probably on Niihau. King estimated a total population of 332,300 Wedge-tailed Shearwaters for the Leeward Islands and 70,000 for the islets offshore of the main Hawaiian islands (fig. 22). Zeillemaker (1975) reported a maximum of 4,000 shearwaters at the Kilauea Point nesting ground on Kauai during May 1975. During 1978, 350 nesting burrows contained eggs. Byrd (1979) discovered that 21 percent of these eggs were pecked by Common Mynas, and he saw mynas eating shearwater eggs five times; signs of egg predation also were found in 12 of 18 shearwater colonies on Kauai. Shearwaters have attempted to nest at Black Point (Oahu) several times but cats, dogs, and/or mongooses have killed both adults and nestlings. I found only three dead adult birds there on May 8, 1974.

Some adults return to their breeding islands as early as March, but egg laying does not occur until June and July. The adults excavate burrows in sand or suitable soil, or, where this is not available, they lay their eggs in natural crevices. On Midway the birds commonly nest on the surface in natural depressions in sand, usually in partial shade, rarely completely in the open. On Nihoa and Rabbit islands, I have seen the birds nesting under tussocks of grass. Banding studies have revealed that pairs remain mated for at least several years and that they return to the same nesting islands year after year.

During the daytime before the egg is laid, the two adults often sit together quietly at or near the nest site. Beginning shortly after dusk, the adults emit a wide variety of moans, groans, and wails as do many of the other shearwaters and petrels. Because of these weird calls, which continue throughout most of the night, these species often are referred to as moaning birds.

One white egg forms the clutch. However, as with many other species of ground-nesting seabirds, the egg often becomes stained by extraneous materials from the incubating bird's feathers or by chemicals in the ground. Both adults share the incubation duties, and both have an incubation patch. The mate often sits near the incubating bird. The incubation period apparently is unknown, but the eggs hatch in August. The young hatch with a full coat of pale grayish-brown down; the bill is bluish black (fig. 33). The chicks are fed by regurgitation. The adults leave the nesting islands about two weeks before the young are ready to fly, usually in November, with the result that the young are independent from that time.

FIGURE 33. A Wedge-tailed Shearwater chick; Rabbit Island. September 5, 1971.

Howell and Bartholomew (1961b) studied temperature regulation in Wedge-tailed Shearwaters on Midway Atoll, where this species nests, sometimes with no protection from the sun's rays, on the surface of the ground. Like other shearwaters and petrels, the Wedge-tailed Shearwater is active primarily at night. Nevertheless, the investigators found that the mean daytime body temperature (39.5° C) of the birds on Midway was significantly higher than the mean night-time temperature (37.7° C), which presumably reflects the stress placed on these birds during the day as they incubate in open sites on the surface of the ground. It was also learned that the temperature within incubated eggs in very early stages of incubation (no visible embryo yet present) averaged 3.5° C lower than that of the incubation patch (mean temperature 37.8° C). Eggs exposed to full sun had temperatures over 6° C higher (40.2° C) than incubated eggs (mean 34.3° C), and essentially the same as ground temperature. Howell and Bartholomew noted that the parents with nests in the open sun left the nests from midmorning to mid-afternoon, presumably because the heat was too great for the adults, leaving the eggs exposed to the sun during that period. Black-bulb temperatures above 45° C often were recorded, and Howell and Bartholomew doubted that any of the fully exposed shearwater nests were successful.

Christmas Shearwater
Puffinus nativitatus
(Color plate 4)

This species is slightly smaller than the Wedge-tailed Shearwater, averaging 15 inches in length and having a wingspan of 32 inches. The plumage is uniformly sooty brown to black; the bill is black; the legs are dark brown. The tail is short and rounded. Its wingbeats are said to be faster and stiffer than those of the Wedge-tailed Shearwater.

This species breeds on the Hawaiian, Line, Phoenix, Henderson, Ducie, Tuamotu, and Austral islands; it bred formerly on Wake, Marcus, and Bonin islands. In Hawaii it nests on Moku Manu, Lehua, and most of the Leeward Islands. Very little seems to be known about this species, however. Personnel of the Pacific Ocean Biological Survey Program have estimated a population of only about 10,000 birds in the Leeward Islands. Apparently no census has been conducted on Moku Manu.

The Christmas Shearwater is rarely active during the daytime; it also is noted for its nocturnal moaning cries.

A single white egg is laid on the ground in a simple scrape among, or under, rocks or plants. The first adults arrive in March. Eggs are laid from early April to July, and the young become independent from late August to November.

Both adults have an incubation patch and both share in incubation, one bird often sitting near its mate on the nest. The incubation and nestling periods apparently have not been determined. The newly hatched chick is covered by a thick layer of sooty black down.

Howell and Bartholomew (1961b) discovered that the nighttime body temperature (mean 38.6° C) of the adults was slightly, but not significantly, higher than the daytime temperature (38.1° C). Small downy chicks have incompletely developed temperature control mechanisms. If left in the direct sun, the birds begin to pant within 10 minutes, and will die of heat stress within about 75 minutes. Hence, both eggs and young chicks must be shielded from the sun by the adults if lethal high temperatures are to be avoided. The temperature-regulation mechanism improves with age, and the older downy chicks can maintain a temperature between 42° and 43° C even when exposed to the direct sun.

Newell's Shearwater
Puffinus puffinus newelli
(Color plate 5)

This species has black upperparts and white underparts. Total length is 12 to 14 inches; wingspan is 30 to 35 inches. These are stout shearwaters with short wings and short, rounded tails. Their flight is characterized by rapid, stiff wingbeats followed by a short glide on outstretched wings. This race, which is restricted to the Hawaiian Islands, was first described in 1900. It is now classified as a threatened species by the U.S. Fish and Wildlife Service.

Munro (1944) thought this species formerly to be a common nesting bird on Hawaii, Maui, Molokai, Kauai, and "probably on other small islands also." He wrote that "it used to nest in the Waipio Valley, Hawaii, and the natives used it for food." Munro suggested that the birds on Hawaii, Maui, and Molokai probably were exterminated by mongooses, but rats, feral cats, and dogs may have played a role. A small population may still nest on windward Hawaii.

King and Gould (1967) summarized all available records of Newell's Shearwater, and stated that no birds had been reported from Maui since 1894, and none from Molokai since 1908. They concluded that "Kauai is now the primary and possibly unique breeding locality of Newell's Shearwater. We believe its population to be at least in the low thousands and base our estimate on the numbers recorded at various locations around Kauai in addition to the numbers encountered at sea, especially within 100 miles of Kauai." They noted that up to that time the nesting

burrows, eggs, and downy young had never been described.

During July 1967, Sincock and Swedberg (1969) observed a nesting colony in the Makaleha Mountains on Kauai at an elevation of about 1,500 feet (fig. 34). The nesting sites were located along a "precipitous, knifelike ridge" that the authors could reach only by jumping from a hovering helicopter. By contrast, Munro wrote, presumably basing his conclusions on conversations with old-timers, that this shearwater formerly had "nested in burrows at the foot of cliffs near the sea at from 500 to 1,000 feet elevation."

Sincock and Swedberg reported that during late July the first adults returned from the sea at 8:00 P.M., a few minutes after dark. "The birds called almost continuously as they flew in circles over the area. The nasal calling was loud and sounded like a combination of jackass braying and crow calling." After further observations, the authors noted that "calling and flight activity continued almost without interruption on cloudy, rainy nights, but subsided on clear nights about 22:30." Calling then "increased at 03:40 and continued until 05:25 when it abruptly ceased just before dawn." They estimated a population of at least 500 birds at this nesting colony.

The egg is white. A deserted egg measured 61 × 36 mm. The down of a bird estimated to be eight days old was medium gray on the head, back, and rump; white on the chin, throat, and abdomen; and whitish to very pale gray on the breast (fig. 35). The bill was slate gray; the eyes were black; the inner surface of each leg was pink, but the outer surface was gray. The incubation and nestling periods remain unknown.

The first Newell's Shearwaters arrive on Kauai in April, but the bulk of the population returns in May. King and Gould postulated that "egg-laying probably takes place at the beginning of June." From their observations, Sincock and Swedberg presumed that "most hatching occurred between mid-July and the first week of August" in 1967. "The second peak in numbers, observed at sea near Kauai in August, probably corresponds to the period of intermittent nest attentiveness, beginning one or two weeks after the eggs hatch, during which adults return to burrows only to feed their chicks" (King and Gould 1967).

Most of the adults leave the nesting grounds for unknown winter feeding areas by the beginning of October. The chicks fledge in October and November, and it is during this period that Newell's Shearwaters are noted for "raining down" on highways, parks, football fields, and buildings. More than 390 downed birds were found in the Lihue area in 1978. Birds often are found on the ground on Oahu in the fall, but it remains unknown whether there are nesting colonies on this is-

FIGURE 34. Nesting site of Newell's Shearwater in the Makaleha Mountains, Kauai. July 1967. Courtesy of John L. Sincock.

land or whether the downed birds came from Kauai. The birds are attracted to lights and sometimes they are killed on Kauai and Oahu in collisions with automobiles and lighted towers. Birds that land on the ground are unable to take off again. Telfer (1979) reported that 861 of 867 shearwaters found on the ground on Kauai during the fall of 1978 were fledglings. More than 200 other birds were found dead on highways. Uninjured birds can be launched by tossing them into the air, preferably during daylight hours.

Mr. Sincock told me that he believed there to be "nesting at several other places on Kauai, including several other sites in the Makaleha Mountains, one in the extreme upper reaches of the Hanalei River, one site in the Haupu range, one above Kahili Mountain Park, and at least three sites in the Waimea Canyon. Most of the suspected nesting sites are between 1,500 and 2,000 feet elevation, and are covered with uluhe fern *(Dicranopterus linearis).*"

If the mongoose becomes established on Kauai, the future of Newell's Shearwater would be very uncertain.

Dark-rumped Petrel
Pterodroma phaeopygia sandwichensis
(Color plate 6)

This is one of the gadfly petrels, averaging 16 inches in length and having a wingspan of 36 inches. Except for a white forehead, the upperparts are dark gray; the underparts are white; the under surface of the wings is white with conspicuous dark margins. The tail is short and wedgeshaped. Munro said that the Hawaiian race formerly nested on all of the main islands except Niihau. A second race breeds on the Galapagos Islands.

Munro (1944:26) wrote that: "the natives used the old birds as well as the young for food, netting them as they flew to the mountains in the evening. The young birds were considered a delicacy, kapu to the common people and reserved for the chiefs. The old birds were probably not kapu as their flavor was so strong that they could not be eaten till they had been salted for a considerable time." McCoy and Gould (1977) wrote of finding the remains of Dark-rumped Petrels in rock

FIGURE 35. The first Newell's Shearwater chick discovered by John L. Sincock and Gerald Swedberg; Makaleha Mountains, Kauai. August 4, 1967. Courtesy of John L. Sincock.

shelters at more than 12,000 feet on Mauna Kea that had been used by Hawaiians in their search for basaltic material used in making adzes.

Munro suggested that the Hawaiians probably extirpated this species from Oahu, and that "the mongoose has killed it out on Hawaii, Maui, and Molokai." He added that "pigs and cats accounted for it on Lanai." However, Hirai (1978a) discovered a colony on Lanai in 1976. The petrels were found at an elevation of 2,800 feet along the Munro Trail.

Specimens were collected at the breeding ground in the mountains of Molokai in 1907, but the species was rarely reported as having been seen again until November 1948, at which time a bird was caught alive at Kilauea Crater on Hawaii. One immature bird was found in a reservoir on Maui in October 1953, and five dead birds were found between 9,000 and 10,000 feet elevation on Mauna Kea in 1954; several of the Mauna Kea birds were presumed to have been killed by feral cats. In June 1954, an adult on its egg was found in Haleakala Crater (Richardson and Woodside 1954). Winston E. Banko found four occupied nesting burrows on Mauna Loa in 1968, and in 1970, he found birds at Kanakaleonui on Mauna Kea.

Munro reported that this species nested "in holes under the roots of trees and stones at elevations of from 1,500 to 5,000 feet." The nesting sites discovered recently, however, have been located at much higher elevations where burrows are dug either under old, lichen-covered lava (on Hawaii) or in soil or ash deposits overlain by bedrock lava (Maui).

James W. Larson made a study of the Dark-rumped Petrels in Haleakala Crater during 1965 and 1966. The minimum total number of adults there was estimated to be 800. All known breeding sites in the crater

occupied an area of only three square miles. Nesting burrows were found between 7,200 and 9,600 feet elevation. Burrows were from 4 to 15 feet in length.

A few birds returned to the breeding ground as early as March 1, 1966. They occupied burrows for short periods of time, but then left and did not return for one or two months. One pair, banded in 1965, returned to the same burrow in 1966. Each female lays a single white egg with a semiglossy finish. Three eggs measured: 45 × 64, 46 × 66, and 46 × 67 mm. The egg-laying period for the entire colony was thought to cover a short period in mid-May (approximately May 9 to 16). The nest is a slight depression at the end of the burrow, with a skimpy collection of twigs and feathers. Usually the adults take turns incubating for 3- to 5-day periods, but an individual may incubate as long as 12 days. Larson determined the incubation period to be between 50 and 55 days.

Newly hatched chicks have a covering of long charcoal-gray down. Feathers begin to develop at three weeks, but they do not show beyond the down until the chicks are six to seven weeks old. The young are fed at night, typically within two hours after sunset. They are fed partially digested food by regurgitation. The identifiable contents of the stomach of one adult were parts of two small fish, two squid, and a stomatopod crustacean. During their first six weeks, the young are fed every one or two days; after that, about once a week. The young are not fed at all during the last two or three weeks before they leave the nest. One chick, 110 days old, had reached the adult size of 16 inches in length and had a wingspan of 36 inches. The young leave the nest when about 115 days old. All young left their burrows between October 18 and November 2.

Larson considered the roof rat to be the primary predator on nestling Dark-rumped Petrels in Haleakala. It was believed that 7 of 18 nests were destroyed by rats during the two-year period of his study, and the predation undoubtedly would have been higher if rats had not been trapped and poisoned in one study area during 1966. Later, Buxbaum (1973) wrote that rats were the primary predator of the Haleakala petrels. Mongooses and feral dogs and cats probably would be a serious threat to nesting birds at lower elevations and on Hawaii.

Fledgling Dark-rumped Petrels also are attracted to, and become disoriented by, lights in Wailuku and Kahului, and many young birds are injured, killed, or "beached" each year during October and November. The late H. Eddie Smith told me that the average weight of eight grounded birds was 409.5 g (range 319.9 to 484.5). He force-fed fish to the birds; five of the birds later flew off toward the ocean when released, but three of the birds died.

Harris (1970) studied the Galápagos race of the Dark-rumped Petrel. His study, made in dense vegetation in the moist highlands of Santa Cruz, showed that eggs were laid between June 16 and August 10, and the last chicks left the beginning of January. Birds molted while away from the Galápagos outside the breeding season. The breeding biology was similar to that of many Procellariiformes, with long incubation (50–54 days) and fledging (about 110 days) periods and incubation spells (about 12 days). Young were fed about one night in two. Nesting success was extremely low, with only four young fledged out of a minimum of 67 eggs laid, due almost certainly to black rats *(Rattus rattus)*. This finding, associated with losses of adults and agricultural encroachments on the breeding area, causes concern for the future of the species.

Bonin Petrel
Pterodroma hypoleuca hypoleuca
(Color plate 7)

This small gadfly petrel averages 12 inches in length and has a wingspan of 25 to 28 inches. The head and back are gray; the back of neck, tail, and upper surface of wings are black; the forehead and underparts are white. The under surface of the wings is white with prominent dark margins.

The breeding range of the Bonin Petrel includes the Hawaiian Leeward Islands; the Bonin Islands; and the Volcano Islands. Very little is known about its non-breeding distribution.

The largest population (1,000,000 birds) breeds on Lisianski Island; there are about 200,000 birds on Laysan Island. Of the islands at French Frigate Shoals, only Tern Island supports a breeding population (500 to 1,000 birds). About 1,000 birds nest on the four vegetated islets of Pearl and Hermes Reef. The devastation caused by Polynesian rats on Kure Atoll has been mentioned previously; and although some 2,500 Bonin Petrels breed on the atoll, no young were raised during the four-year period of 1964–1968. Poison for the rats was placed in several areas during 1969 and 80 petrels were fledged that year (Woodward 1972). This situation demonstrates clearly the tragedy that results when mammalian predators are introduced to islands. The Bonin Petrel does not occur on Nihoa or Necker islands.

The adults return to the islands in August and copulation once was observed in September, but the first eggs are not laid until January. The adults excavate burrows (5 to 8 feet in length) in the sand; they typically turn either to the right or left after a few feet. The nest cavity at the end of the burrow is lined with grasses and leaves. Occasionally, the birds nest on the surface of the ground under dense vegetation, and eggs

have been found under an overturned basket and under a pile of boxes.

Egg-laying continues into March and possibly April. There appears to be a difference in timing of egg-laying among the populations on Laysan and Lisianski islands. The first eggs hatch by late February, but most eggs hatch during March and April. Some birds fledge by early May; nearly all leave their nesting grounds by late June or early July. Both young and adult birds are absent from the island for about two months after the young fledge. The incubation period is said to be 48 or 49 days.

On Laysan Island, especially, the Bonin Petrel and the Wedge-tailed Shearwater occupy the same habitat: sandy areas that support clumps of bunchgrass and/or morning glory. The shearwaters, however, do not begin to excavate their burrows until the petrels already have well-grown chicks. On Lisianski Island the population is so large that the birds nest under *Scaevola* bushes, in *Boerhavia-Eragrostis,* and in sand-bunchgrass associations (Clapp and Wirtz 1975).

Howell and Bartholomew (1961b) studied temperature regulation of this species on Midway Atoll. Because the Bonin Petrel is exclusively nocturnal and nests in deep burrows, it is not subjected to heat stress as are those species that nest on the surface of the ground. Nighttime body temperatures ($39.9°$ C) averaged $1.4°$ C higher than daytime temperatures ($38.5°$ C) of incubating birds.

Bulwer's Petrel
Bulweria bulwerii
(Color plate 8)

This is a small (11 inches in length), sooty-brown petrel with buffy bars on the upper surface of the wings, a fairly long, wedge-shaped tail, and a wingspan of 23 inches. This species typically flies low over the water, rarely above the horizon.

Bulwer's Petrel breeds on the Bonin, Volcano, Phoenix, Marquesas, and Hawaiian islands. It nests on many of the offshore islands of the main Hawaiian chain, as well as on Kaula, Lehua, Nihoa, Necker, French Frigate Shoals, Gardner Pinnacles, Laysan, Pearl and Hermes Reef (Southeast Island), Lisiansky, and Midway. There are no nesting records for this species on Kure Atoll. In fact, most of the Hawaiian Bulwer's Petrels nest on Nihoa Island, which has an estimated population of 250,000 birds. For the remaining islands in the Leeward chain, the populations are: Laysan Island, 20,000; French Frigate Shoals, 500; Necker Island, 200; Southeast Island of Pearl and Hermes Reef, 15.

The adults return to the islands at night, and on the night of March 23, 1966, on East Island of French

Frigate Shoals, Eugene Kridler, Ronald L. Walker, Nelson Rice, and I donned headlamps in order to watch the incoming shearwaters and petrels. We found a single Bulwer's Petrel that night. Most adults return to the islands during April, however.

Bulwer's Petrel uses a wide variety of nest sites: holes and crevices in cliffs and rocks, or under rocks (Moku Manu, Manana Island, Nihoa, Necker); holes in water-eroded rock (Popoia Islet); under "pieces of phosphate rocks or coral" (Laysan); on the ground under *Scaevola* and other thick vegetation (Mokulua Islet, Midway); and "under a pile of turtle shells" (French Frigate Shoals).

A single white egg is laid in May or June, rarely late April. Fledging occurs as early as mid-August and as late as October. I photographed several incubating Bulwer's Petrels on Rabbit Island on July 16, 1970. I watched one young bird break out of its shell, apparently the first petrel to hatch on the island that year (fig. 36). During the period from July 26 to August 4, 1966, many of the Bulwer's Petrels on Nihoa Island were still incubating eggs, but some were brooding small downy young. There were both small and large downy young on Moku Manu on August 8, 1970. The chicks are covered with a uniform coat of black down. The incubation and nestling periods are unknown.

Frank Richardson believed that rats killed adult Bulwer's Petrels on Lehua Island, and Robert Shallenberger suspected that crabs (*Grapsus* sp.) preyed on

FIGURE 36. Newly hatched Bulwer's Petrel; Rabbit Island. July 16, 1970.

downy chicks on Rabbit Island. Munro commented that the "chicks were considered a great delicacy by the ancient Hawaiians." The oldest banded bird to be recovered was 12 years old.

Harcourt's Storm Petrel
Oceanodroma castro cryptoleucura

This is a small (8 to 9 inches in length), sooty brown to blackish petrel with white rump feathers and under tail coverts and a slightly forked tail. Wingspan is between 17 and 19 inches.

This species breeds in the eastern Atlantic Ocean (e.g., Madeira, Azores, Cape Verde Islands, St. Helena), on the Galápagos Islands, and presumably only on Kauai of the Hawaiian Islands.

Very little is known about the rare Hawaiian race of Harcourt's Storm Petrel. The nest and eggs have never been found. Immature birds were found on Hawaii and Kauai in the past. The breeding area is now assumed to be restricted to Kauai, but it is possible that this species may yet be found on Maui and Hawaii.

Sooty Storm Petrel
Oceanodroma tristrami
(Color plate 9)

This is a sooty brown petrel with light brown or buffy wing bars and a conspicuously forked tail. The birds average 10 inches from bill-tip to end of tail, and have a wingspan of approximately 22 inches. The species breeds on the Volcano and Leeward Hawaiian islands, and is thought to spend the nonbreeding season north of the islands.

This is a poorly known species. It is the least conspicuous of the petrels in Hawaii and it occurs in small localized colonies. The largest estimated population (7,500 birds) occurs on the islets of Pearl and Hermes Reef. Between 2,000 and 3,000 birds nest on Laysan Island. The species occurs in small numbers (maximum of six seen on one night) on Tern and Whale-Skate islands and on La Pérouse Pinnacle of French Frigate Shoals. A few pairs may nest on Nihoa, but there are no nesting records for Necker, Lisianski, or Kure Atoll.

On Laysan Island the birds are present from October through June; the birds spend the rest of the year at sea. The adults excavate nesting burrows about 5 inches in diameter and 2.5 feet deep; a nest is built of rootlets, weed stems, and leaves. At Pearl and Hermes Reef, the burrows most often are dug in the Bermuda grass (*Cynodon*) areas; also used are places that support *Eragrostis* grass and *Boerhavia* plants. On Laysan Island, the preferred nesting habitat is in a bunchgrass-morning glory zone around the central lagoon. Flooding in this area during the winter months may be a mortality factor for the birds (Ely and Clapp 1973; Amerson et al. 1974).

Egg laying begins by mid- or late December and continues through January; at Pearl and Hermes Reef, however, eggs have been found in mid-March. Hatching of eggs takes place by early February on Laysan, by late January at Pearl and Hermes Reef. The single egg is white and faintly spotted. Neither the incubation period nor the nestling period have been determined.

White-tailed Tropicbird
Phaethon lepturus dorotheae

Tropicbirds are mostly white birds with a highly specialized pair of inner tail feathers, called streamers, which are very narrow and greatly elongated. The streamers may be almost as long as the rest of the bird.

Adult White-tailed Tropicbirds have black eye-stripes, solid patches of black feathers on the wings and back, and small black patches along the leading edge of the proximal primary flight feathers; the bill is yellow (the species is sometimes called the Yellow-billed Tropicbird). Immature birds have dark bills. Total length, including the white streamers, is between 28 and 32 inches; wingspan varies from 35 to 38 inches.

The White-tailed Tropicbird has a wide distribution throughout the tropical Pacific but is known to breed regularly only on certain of the main islands in the Hawaiian chain: Hawaii, Maui, Lanai, Oahu, and Kauai; presumably also on Kaula Island. Tropicbirds nest on the cliffs at Waimea Falls Park on Oahu, and undoubtedly in the Koolau Mountains. They are often seen in Kilauea Crater (even during eruptions) on Hawaii and in Waimea Canyon, Kauai. There is one record of the species nesting on Midway (Bailey 1956).

A single egg is laid. It has a chalky white to creamy base-color, heavily spotted with various shades of reddish brown and reddish purple. This species typically lays its eggs on the ground in cliffs, but tree nesting is common for other races in some areas.

The newly hatched young are covered with a thick coat of down except for a small area at the base of the bill and extending backward to the eyes. The down is white except on the crown of the head and the sides of the back where it is grayish brown. The bare skin on the face is black; the bill is dark bluish; the iris of the eye is brown; the feet are black.

The breeding biology of the Hawaiian race has not been studied. In the Bermuda race, the young are brooded almost continuously for the first 10 days after hatching. Both parents feed the young by regurgitation. The chicks are fully feathered when 40 days old, although some down remains attached to the feathers. The young are not capable of sustained flight until more than 60 days of age.

Red-tailed Tropicbird
Phaethon rubricauda rothschildi
(Color plate 10)

The Red-tailed Tropicbird is a white bird with a red bill, long red tail streamers, a black eye-stripe, and inconspicuous black feathers along the leading edge of the proximal primary flight feathers. At the beginning of the breeding season, most adult birds have a roseate or pinkish tinge to the white feathers. Total length, including streamers, is between 36 and 42 inches; the wingspan is about 44 inches.

This race of the Red-tailed Tropicbird breeds on the Bonin and the Hawaiian islands. In Hawaii it most commonly is found and breeds on all the Leeward Islands. It also has been reported on Lehua and Kaula islands. Red-tailed Tropicbirds nested on Rabbit Island for the first time in 1967 and a nestling was found there during August 1978 (*Elepaio* 28:34; 39:43).

Maximum populations occur on Lisianski Island (about 4,500 birds), on Laysan Island (about 4,000), and at Kure Atoll (2,000). Smaller numbers nest on each of the other Leeward islands. Gould et al. (1974) gave a maximum population of 7,500 birds on the two islands at Midway Atoll, but there has been a reduction in this population since the early 1970s.

Ely and Clapp (1973) wrote that "there probably is no time when Red-tailed Tropicbirds are not present on Laysan Island, but very few are present in winter. Numbers apparently begin to increase in late March or April with peak numbers present from mid-May to August. The population begins to decline in September, and by late October there are few birds on the island." On Kure Atoll, nests have been found during every month of the year, although the main nesting season is from March through November. On Nihoa Island, eggs have been found from March 3 to August 25, and eggs have been found in September at French Frigate Shoals. There may, therefore, be some difference in the nesting season from island to island as well as from year to year. A single egg is laid on the ground under vegetation, in small caves, or under rock overhangs. The egg is white with small spots and finer markings in various shades of brown and purplish brown concentrated around the larger end of the egg, but also scattered irregularly over the entire surface. Considerable variation in pattern and density of markings is found among eggs laid by different females. The incubation period is about 43 days (Clapp 1972), about the same as that for the Yellow-billed Tropicbird (*Phaethon lepturus ascensionis*) of 40 to 42 days and the Red-billed Tropicbird (*Phaethon a. aetherus*) of 42 to 44 days on Ascension Island in the South Atlantic Ocean (Stonehouse 1962a).

FIGURE 37. Immature Red-tailed Tropicbird; Christmas Island (Pacific Ocean). November 6, 1971.

Red-tailed Tropicbird chicks are covered with a coat of long, fine, white down when they hatch; juvenal feathers gradually replace the down (fig. 37). For several days after hatching, the young are brooded under the parent's body, but thereafter they are brooded under one wing, which is an unusual brooding pattern apparently found only in tropicbirds and curassows. Tropicbirds do not possess large, unfeathered gular pouches, as do most of the other pelecaniform birds, and both chicks and adults resort to panting in order to dissipate excess heat. Unlike the downy chicks of most seabirds, the young Red-tailed Tropicbird is able, by vigorous panting, to prevent its temperature from rising above 42.0° C.

Among the six families of pelecaniform birds, only in the tropicbird family does the adult thrust its bill deeply into the throat of the gaping chick and disgorge the food. In the other families of the order Pelecaniformes, the adult opens its bill and the chick reaches deep into the throat to obtain the regurgitated food. Howell and Bartholomew attempted to determine the stimuli that elicit the gaping response of the chicks. They concluded that the young did not gape in response to the red bill of the adult. The bill of a young Red-tailed Tropicbird is dark gray, and there is a small area of blackish skin around its base. Howell and Bartholomew were able to elicit gaping in the chicks only by touching this bare skin.

Howell and Bartholomew (1969) reported that an empty nest scrape provided a stronger attraction for adult Red-tailed Tropicbirds than either a displaced egg or chick, but that nearly all of the adults tested retrieved (rolled back into the nest) their own eggs after the investigators had placed them about 6 inches from the nest. Half of the birds tested rolled an albatross egg (much larger than a tropicbird egg) into the nest, whereas only one tropicbird retrieved a much smaller tern egg. Only one of the tropicbirds retrieved a red plastic egg, and, within a few seconds, this bird pushed the egg out of the nest. However, if a red plastic egg was substituted for the bird's own egg in the nest, the bird usually incubated it. Adults brooding young chicks accepted substitute chicks even though they differed considerably in size and color.

Red-tailed Tropicbirds are especially conspicuous at midday as large numbers take to the air to circle over their nesting island, exchanging raucous calls with mates on the nests.

Tropicbirds are diurnal birds, and the mean daytime body temperature (39.0° C) is significantly higher than the mean nocturnal temperature (37.1° C), as measured by Howell and Bartholomew (1962a). The average temperature of birds that had just landed after a flight was 40.9° C. The internal temperature of several incubated eggs was 35.0° C, and the average foot temperature of incubating birds was only 32.0° C. Tropicbirds do not develop an incubation patch during the breeding season. The incubating bird presses the egg against its abdominal feathers, in which Howell and Bartholomew found a mean temperature of 37.0° C (adequate to maintain internal egg temperatures between 35.0° C and 36.5° C).

A nestling Red-tailed Tropicbird that was banded on Green Island of Kure Atoll on September 14, 1964, was found nesting on Tern Island, French Frigate Shoals, on June 8, 1969, at an age of less than five years. Another nestling, banded on Gardner Pinnacles on June 16, 1963, was found incubating an egg there on May 26, 1967, showing that some birds, at least, come into breeding condition at four years of age (Clapp 1972).

Avian pox virus infection of both adult and young Red-tailed Tropicbirds was reported on Sand Island (Midway Atoll) in 1963 (Locke, Wirtz, and Brown 1965). Although it is a common infection among land birds, there are few records of pox among seabirds, and this appears to be the first record for the Red-tailed Tropicbird. Pox apparently has not been reported from Laysan or Nihoa islands, but the introduction of the disease to those islands could be highly deleterious to the endemic land birds there.

Blue-faced or Masked Booby
Sula dactylatra personata
(Color plate 11)

Boobies are goose-sized seabirds with strong, long, pointed bills, distensible throat (or gular) pouches, long necks, tapering bodies ("like fat cigars"), and long pointed wings and tails. Boobies (genus *Sula*) inhabit tropical oceans; gannets (genus *Morus*) inhabit cold seas (North Atlantic, southern Africa, Australia).

Boobies and gannets feed on fish and squid, which

they obtain by diving into the water from heights of 50 feet or more. During these dives, the birds have their wings folded and their heads and necks outstretched, and they hold this posture as they plunge beneath the surface. They are also said to chase flying fish through the air. Whether caught in the air or under water, the prey is swallowed rather than carried in the bill. Boobies are harassed by frigatebirds. A frigatebird will fly at and around a booby until the booby disgorges its food, whereupon the frigatebird will grab it out of the air.

No member of the booby family develops incubation patches.

The Masked Booby is the largest of the three species of _Sula_ found in Hawaiian waters: 30 inches long, wingspan 60 inches. The fully adult bird is white with black primaries, secondaries, and tail feathers. The bill is yellow; the facial skin is dark gray to black; the legs and feet are dark grayish green; the iris of the eye is yellow. This species also has been called the White Booby.

The Masked Booby breeds throughout the tropical Pacific. It nests on all of the Hawaiian islands from Kaula and Nihoa to Midway and Kure, except La Pérouse Pinnacle, and it also has nested successfully on Moku Manu. The total population for the Leeward Islands has been estimated to be 7,000 birds.

The adults are present throughout the year, that is to say, they do not leave the nesting islands to range far over the open ocean during the nonbreeding season. Masked Boobies may nest as isolated pairs or in large colonies. Nests have been found during every month of the year on some of the islands. Interesting comparative information on the boobies of the Galápagos Islands is found in the book by Bryan Nelson (1968).

The Masked Booby lays its two white eggs on the ground. One bird is often found sitting on the sand near its incubating mate. There is no sexual dimorphism in the plumage pattern of the Masked Booby, but the sexes can be distinguished because the callnotes of the males are much higher in pitch than are those of the females. This is, of course, a reversal of the pattern found in many mammals and in a few species of birds.

Kepler (1969) studied the Masked Booby on Kure Atoll during 1964 and 1965. He found that the main egg-laying period extended from January to May, although egg laying began two weeks later in 1965 than in 1964, possibly because of winter storms. The normal clutch was two eggs (average, 1.9 eggs), but only a single young bird was reared to independence. Nevertheless, Kepler discovered that two-egg clutches were significantly more successful than one-egg clutches, and that second eggs, rather than being "wasted," gave rise to 22 percent of the chicks fledged during the two seasons. The second egg in a clutch, therefore, serves as a "buffer" against the loss of the first egg or chick.

The male and female take turns in incubation, which lasts 43 days. Incubation begins with the laying of the first egg, which requires one day longer to hatch than does the second egg laid (fig. 38). Both adults feed the young birds.

Bartholomew (1966) studied the role of behavior in temperature regulation in a colony of 350 pairs of Masked Boobies nesting on a completely barren sea cliff on Hood Island in the Galápagos Archipelago at 1°22′ south latitude. Body temperatures of adult birds averaged 40.7° C during midday and 38.3° C after dark. The adults compensated for intense solar radiation during the day by "(1) orienting with back to the sun regardless of wind direction, which shades the naked gular area and feet and allows them to act as sites of convective and conductive heat loss, (2) elevation of the scapulars and drooping of the wings, which facilitates convective heat loss from the feathered parts of the body, and (3) sustained gular flutter, which contributes to evaporative cooling."

Bartholomew found that small downy chicks are unable to regulate their body temperature and that, when the chicks are exposed to full sun, their body temperature rises to near lethal limits within 20 minutes. By the time the chicks reach a weight of 400 g, they are able to stabilize their temperature at about 42° C; the chicks then either seek shade or use the same behavioral patterns as the adults. The adults brood small chicks and stand next to large chicks and shade them. Bartholomew thought that the adults may sense the temperature of the eggs or chicks with their feet, which

FIGURE 38. Newly hatched Masked Booby; Southeast Island, Pearl and Hermes Reef. April 1, 1966. The egg tooth is conspicuous at the tip of the bill.

are kept in contact with the eggs during incubation; smaller chicks also lie on the parents' feet while being brooded.

Schreiber and Hensley (1976) studied the diets of Masked Boobies on Christmas Island and found that a dozen species of fishes constituted more than 90 percent of the weight and volume in the samples examined; squid accounting for the rest of the food eaten.

George C. Munro and his assistants banded 633 Blue-faced Boobies on Howland Island (1,650 miles southwest of Honolulu and 48 miles north of the equator) in the four-year period of 1938 through 1941. During 1963 and 1964, personnel of the Pacific Ocean Biological Survey Program recaptured four of the birds that had been banded as nestlings. These four birds varied in age from 21 years 8 months to 22 years 8 months (Clapp and Sibley 1966). Wilson (1975) told of a booby that was recaptured 25 years after it had been banded; some boobies undoubtedly live longer than that.

Brown Booby
Sula leucogaster plotus
(Color plate 12)

This is a chocolate-brown booby whose breast, belly, and part of the wing linings are white. There is a striking contrast between the dark brown of the lower neck and the white of the breast. The bill is yellow to yellowish gray; the legs and feet are green to yellowish gray. Total length averages 28 inches; wingspread, 54 inches.

This species is found throughout the tropical Pacific, rarely being seen more than 50 miles from land. It nests on the Leeward Islands, on Kaula Island, and on Moku Manu, off the coast of Oahu. The maximum estimated population of 250 birds breeds on Laysan Island; the total population for the Leeward Islands is less than 1,000 birds.

The birds remain near their breeding islands throughout the year. Nests have been found during every month of the year on some islands, but most nesting occurs from February to October. There may be differences in the nesting season from year to year, at least on some islands. A detailed study of the bird's annual cycle is needed.

The Brown Booby is not highly colonial, and a pair may nest isolated from others of the species. The birds build a nest on the ground composed of twigs, driftwood, and other debris. The usual clutch is two eggs, sometimes one or three. A chalky white outer layer covers a pale blue or bluish green shell. Male and female birds take turns in incubating the eggs. The incubation period has not been determined for the Brown Boobies in Hawaii, but elsewhere it has been

reported to be between 40 and 43 days. Both adults take care of the chicks, but it is said that not more than one chick survives the nestling period.

At hatching, the chicks are naked except for short white down in the feather tracts on the top of the head, on the back, and along the posterior margin of the wings. Within a few days the birds are covered with long white down. The eyes open on the third day. The bill is dark (sooty); the feet are yellow. Small chicks are fed an almost liquid diet of well-digested food. Later they are fed whole fish. The chicks are fully feathered and begin to make practice flights by the time they are 15 weeks old.

Immature Brown Boobies wander far over the Pacific Ocean. Nestlings banded at Kure Atoll have been recaptured at Wake Atoll, at Majuro Atoll in the Marshall Islands, at the Central Moluccas of Indonesia, and at Funafuti Atoll in the Ellice Islands. A bird banded on Howland Island on February 1, 1965 was found roosting on Green Island of Kure Atoll on June 15, 1966 and nesting there in 1968 (Woodward 1972). Brown Boobies are known to live at least 24 years (Wilson 1975).

Red-footed Booby
Sula sula rubripes
(Color plate 13)

The Red-footed Booby is the smallest of the three species found in Hawaii. It has a total length of 28 inches and a wingspan of 40 inches. Three color phases occur: light (the most common), dark, and intermediate. The plumage of light-phase birds (nearly 99% of Hawaiian birds) is white with a yellowish wash to the feathers on the head and upper neck, and with black primary and secondary flight feathers; the facial skin is pink; the bill is pale blue; and the feet are bright red. Dark-phase adults are brown with a white belly and tail. Immature birds (first and second years) have brown feathers, usually lighter on the breast and belly but often with a darker breast band; they also have dark brown bills and beige-colored feet.

This species has a wide distribution throughout the tropical Pacific. It is said that adult birds are seldom encountered more than 50 miles from land, whereas immature birds and subadults (birds in their third year) show a greater tendency to wander. The Red-footed Booby nests on nearly all of the Leeward Islands (not reported for La Pérouse Rock or Gardner's Pinnacle), Kaula Island, Moku Manu, Kauai (Kilauea Point), and Oahu (Ulupau Head of Mokapu Peninsula). The colony on Oahu is believed to have established itself in 1946.

The estimated population of birds nesting on the Leeward Islands is about 11,000; Nihoa, Laysan, and

Kure each has a population over 2,500. Where there is adequate vegetation, the Red-footed Booby nests in large colonies, for example, more than 1,000 on the Kaneohe Marine Corps Air Station on Oahu.

The Red-footed Booby nearly always builds a nest off the ground, although Alexander Wetmore found ground nesting on Laysan Island in 1923 after the rabbits had destroyed most of the vegetation there. Ely and Clapp (1973) wrote that there had been a "ten-fold increase" in the population on Laysan since that time. On Southeast Island of Pearl and Hermes Reef, the birds nest on low mats of vegetation (largely composed of *Solanum, Tribulus,* and *Sicyos*). They nest exclusively in beach naupaka plants on Lisianski; on Nihoa, in *Pritchardia* palms, as well as in low bushes.

The large nest is constructed of sticks, twigs, and branches with green leaves. It is thought that the male collects most of the material and brings it to the female who constructs the nest. "Landing calls" and "stick-shake" displays accompany the return to the nest and the nest-building activity. New material is added to the nest throughout the incubation period. Richardson (1957) reported that "eggs and young are known from all months," although there is a peak of reproduction from February through October.

A single egg is laid. The egg is white with a conspicuous, soft, chalky outer surface. Scratches (presumably made by the incubating bird's feet) occur in the chalky

layer and reveal a pale blue underlayer. The adults take turns during incubation, usually for 24-hour periods. Boobies differ from most birds in that neither adult develops an incubation patch; the egg is held under the webbed feet. The incubation period as determined for another race nesting in British Honduras averaged 44.5 days (range: 42.5 to 46 days). The newly hatched chick is nearly naked. The skin is various shades of purplish pink. Very short, white down is conspicuous on the top of the head, on the back, and along the posterior margin of the wings. A white egg tooth persists for several days on the tip of the blackish bill. Within less than three weeks the chick is almost completely covered with a thick, fluffy coat of white down (fig. 39). The pinkish feet turn to grayish white as they and the down grow.

The mean daytime body temperature (40.3° C) of adult Red-footed Boobies is significantly higher than the mean nighttime temperature (38.0° C) (Howell and Bartholomew 1962a). When incubating, the parent bird covers the egg with the webbing between the first and second toes of each foot. Howell and Bartholomew determined that the temperature within the webbing averaged 35.8° C, whereas the average internal temperature of 11 eggs was 36.0° C. They concluded that "the principal source of heat is the ventral body surface and that the feet are warmed along with the egg. The feet perhaps function more importantly in

FIGURE 39. Red-footed Booby and chick; Christmas Island (Pacific Ocean). November 5, 1971.

holding the egg in place and as a site of tactile reception contributing to the incubation response.'' These investigators also reported that chicks of all ages begin gular flutter when exposed to direct sun, and that their foot temperatures were higher than the surrounding air temperature by 4° C or more. Hence the chicks lose excess heat through their feet and through evaporative cooling resulting from gular fluttering.

Causey Whittow and his colleagues (Shallenberger et al. 1974; Whittow 1976) recorded the deep body temperature of two adult female Red-footed Boobies by feeding a ''radio-pill'' to the birds. They were able to keep their body temperature below 40° C, even when exposed to direct sunlight, by gular fluttering (at a rate of about 450 movements per minute) and by other behavioral adjustments, such as a ''head down'' posture. The highest body temperatures (41.8° C) were recorded just after the birds returned to the nest from fishing excursions over the ocean. The birds shivered during early morning hours when the air temperature was 22° C.

When disturbed at their nest, both adult and young boobies tend to regurgitate their last meal, often into the nest but sometimes on an unsuspecting intruder. By examining such regurgitated meals, Ashmole and Ashmole (1967) determined that squid (family Ommastrephidae) and flying fish (Exocoetidae) were of primary importance to the colony of Red-footed Boobies nesting on Ulupau Head, Mokapu Peninsula, Oahu. The same authors studied feeding habits of seabirds on Christmas Island (1,200 miles south of Oahu) and concluded that squid and flying fish ''are of outstanding importance in the diets of nearly all species of birds typical of the tropical Pacific.''

A number of Red-footed Boobies banded at the Ulupau Head colony on Oahu have been recaptured there when they were between 13 years 7 months and 17 years 8 months of age (Clapp and Sibley 1966). One bird that had been banded on Oahu was found incubating an egg on Kauai when the bird was at least 17 years old. Movements of birds among the Leeward Islands are discussed by Amerson (1971) and by Clapp and Wirtz (1975). Wilson (1975) analyzed returns on birds that had been banded by George Munro during the late 1940s. Single birds were recaptured 18 and 19 years and two birds 20 years after they had been banded.

Great Frigatebird
Fregata minor palmerstoni
(Color plate 14)

Frigatebirds are large, primarily black, slender birds with long, pointed and angled wings and deeply forked tails, which may be opened or closed in flight. The bill is long and strongly hooked. Females are larger than males. The birds average 43 inches in length and have a wingspread of more than 7 feet (90 inches). Males are mainly black or blackish, with a metallic purple or purplish green gloss, especially on the back and on the long scapular feathers, and with buffy wing bars across the upper surface of the wings. Males also have a highly inflatable, bare, red gular pouch. Females have white feathers on the throat and upper breast, and have red eye-rings. Immature birds have a white head, throat, and breast, typically heavily marked with a rusty color.

Their plumage is not waterproof, and frigatebirds are said never to land on the water intentionally. Hence they are considered the most aerial of all seabirds. One writer stated that frigatebirds have 25 percent more flight feathers and 40 percent more wing area than any seabird of similar body weight. Unusual specializations in internal anatomy (bones and muscles) also appear to be correlated with flight habits of the frigatebirds. In flight, the head is drawn back on the shoulders rather than outstretched.

Frigatebirds are called Man-o'-war Birds because they are notorious for harassing boobies (and sometimes shearwaters and terns) to the point that the tormented birds disgorge their food in flight, which the frigatebirds easily snatch from the air. Frigatebirds also catch fish from the surface of the water. In some parts of their range, especially, frigatebirds prey on the downy young of other seabirds as well as on newly hatched sea turtles. Frigatebirds are kept as pets by the natives on Fanning and Washington islands; and, at one time at least, the birds were used for carrying messages.

The Great Frigatebird is found throughout most of the tropical Pacific. The adults tend to remain at their nesting island throughout the year, but immature birds roam widely over the Pacific. Immature birds that were banded at French Frigate Shoals, Laysan Island, and Kure Atoll have been recovered as far away as the Marshall Islands and the Philippines. Similarly, Lesser Frigatebirds *(Fregata ariel)* have been reported more than 4,000 miles from their nest sites (King 1967; Sibley and Clapp 1967).

The Great Frigatebird nests on most of the Leeward islands, not on La Pérouse Rock or Gardner Pinnacles and only on Whale-Skate Island of French Frigate Shoals. The frigatebird population of the Leeward Islands has been estimated to be approximately 26,000; of these, 8,000 occur on Laysan Island, and 10,000 on Nihoa Island.

These birds have been resident on Moku Manu for many years, but they were never known to nest there until 1970, when Robert Shallenberger found a single

FIGURE 40. A large nestling frigatebird in its nest; Christmas Island (Pacific Ocean). November 6, 1971.

nest with a young bird about a month old on July 17. Paul Breese, Norman Carlson, Ronald L. Walker, David H. Woodside, and I visited Moku Manu on August 8. We estimated a minimum of 500 frigatebirds in flight over the island at one time, but we found only the single nest previously reported by Shallenberger. Frigatebirds frequently are seen flying and soaring along the coasts and over the valleys of Oahu.

Frigatebirds build relatively frail, flat nests of twigs and branches in bushes (such as *Scaevola*), where available. On French Frigate Shoals and Pearl and Hermes Reef they also build their nests on the ground or on prostrate vegetation such as *Tribulus,* which also may be used as nest material. The birds may begin nest construction as early as December, although the onset of breeding apparently varies from year to year and, presumably, from island to island. Eggs are laid from January to June. The first young have been found in March; most young fledge by October, but two young birds were found on Necker Island on December 20, 1953.

Male frigatebirds inflate their bright red gular pouches during the courtship period and early stages of incubation. The females are said to collect most of the nesting material, whereas the males build the nest. Frigatebirds may rob twig-carrying boobies or they may steal material from other birds' nests. A single

white egg is laid. Both adults share incubation duties, and the egg is attended by one member of the pair at all times. During incubation, the gular pouches of the males may be either fully inflated or deflated.

The length of the incubation and nestling periods apparently has never been reported for the Hawaiian birds. An incubation period of 40 days has been cited for other races or species. (Fig. 40.)

A frigatebird banded as an adult on Jarvis Island (located at 0°23′ south latitude in the Line Islands) in 1939 was recaptured in 1968. It must have been nearly 34 years old, inasmuch as it is thought that this species does not begin to breed until five years of age (Clapp and Hackman 1969).

Of interest is the discovery of two new species of sarcoptiform mites from the skin of the gular pouch of a courting adult male Great Frigatebird on Lisianski Island (Fain and Amerson 1968). The mites were not visible on the outer surface of the skin but were readily seen on the inner surface. The adults of these mites are presumed to live in the nests of the birds.

Sooty Tern
Sterna fuscata oahuensis
(Color plate 15)

Relative to gulls, terns and noddies are small, slim, and graceful birds with long, slender, pointed wings.

Their graceful flight is achieved by continuous wing-beats; only occasionally do they resort to soaring. They also hover in midair, often before plummeting to the surface of the water to seize their prey, which they grasp with their pointed bills. Of the 17 species of terns and noddies that have been recorded in tropical Pacific waters, 6 species nest on the Hawaiian Islands.

The Sooty Tern is said to be the most pelagic of the tropical terns. Experiments conducted many years ago revealed that Sooty Terns tended to become water-logged within half an hour. The consensus is that they probably rarely alight on the water for more than a few minutes at a time, and that some birds may spend months on the wing without resting on land or water.

Adult (the sexes are alike) Sooty Terns are very in-appropriately named. They are very attractive birds with black upperparts, except for a white forehead. The white ends at the level of the eyes, and a black stripe passes through the eye to the base of the bill and separates the white area of the forehead from that of the throat and side of the head. The underparts are white. The tail is deeply forked; the feathers are black, except for white edgings on the elongated outer tail

feathers. Bill, legs, and feet are black. Sooty Terns are medium-sized birds, averaging 16 inches in total length and having a wingspan of 34 inches.

The Sooty Tern undoubtedly is the most abundant of all seabirds in the tropical Pacific Ocean. It is highly colonial during the breeding season, and colonies may contain more than a million birds. This tern has been reported as a nesting bird on all island groups in the Pacific except for the New Hebrides and the Solomon Islands. In Hawaii it nests on Moku Manu, Manana Island, and on all of the Leeward Islands except La Pé-rouse Rock and Tern Island of French Frigate Shoals (figs. 41, 42). In June 1942, when the Navy began construction for the Loran station, the Sooty Tern nested by the "tens of thousands" on Tern Island. An estimated 4,200,000 Sooty Terns nest on the Leeward Islands, the largest populations being found on Laysan Island (2,000,000) and Lisianski Island (1,700,000). Ronald L. Walker estimated a population of 130,000 on Kaula Island in early March 1978. About 100,000 birds nest on Manana Island (Brown 1973).

This species is a very important member of the mixed flocks of seabirds upon which fishermen depend

FIGURE 41. Manana Island as seen from Oahu. June 12, 1970. Compare with Figure 24.

FIGURE 42. A small part of the Sooty Tern and Brown Noddy breeding colony on Manana Island. July 4, 1971.

for finding schools of fish. Both it and the Wedge-tailed Shearwater have been observed feeding at sea at night (Gould 1967).

In many parts of its range, the Sooty Tern is called the Wideawake Tern because of its incessant, screeching, nerve-racking calls, which are given both day and night. Although small flocks of terns sometimes return to their nesting islands during daylight, they more commonly return at night. In speaking of his experiences on Midway, Hadden (1941) wrote:

The first flock appears some evening in March or April, usually about sundown. Their cries fill the air long before they can be seen. They come in and fly around and around in a great whirlwind-like formation but do not come down to the ground for a month or more. Sometimes they go away for a few weeks and then return again. All night they circle and scream over the Island. Early the next morning they again go out to sea for fish. In the evening they are back again. Day after day they repeat this performance, returning a little earlier every afternoon until finally after five or six weeks, they continue to fly over the Island both day and night. Then they begin to light on the ground, at first only for a few moments, and then finally after another week they settle down more or less permanently, rising only when disturbed. However, they keep up their incessant screaming long after the egg-laying period has passed.

On most of the Hawaiian Islands, Sooty Terns are absent from late October through December or January, but there are differences from island to island as well as from year to year. For example, on Nihoa Island (with a population of about 100,000 nesting birds) egg laying has taken place in February and March in most years, except in 1967–1968, when it took place in December and January. In certain years (e.g., 1900, 1937, 1938, 1940, 1946, 1947) on Moku Manu, "adults arrive, if ever entirely gone, in about October, and commence a late fall and winter breeding cycle that overlaps or replaces the spring and summer cycle" (Richardson 1957). During the period of 1946–1948, Sooty Terns began to lay eggs on Rabbit Island in April, "nearly six months later than on Moku Manu" (Richardson and Fisher 1950). However, there is no accurate information on the nesting season of birds on Moku Manu since the 1940s so that we do not know whether the birds are still on a winter breeding cycle. Brown (1973) made a detailed study of the terns on Rabbit Island during 1971 and 1972. Sooty Terns first appeared over the island on February 27, 1971, and January 23, 1972; the first eggs were laid on March 20, 1971, and April 15, 1972; the first eggs hatched on April 29, 1971, and May 14, 1972; the first young fledged on June 17, 1971, and July 7, 1972. Brown suggested that the Sooty Terns that colonized Rabbit Island came from other Pacific Islands where the birds had a spring breeding cycle. He also reported that the terns feed almost exclusively over schools of tuna and that "there is an excellent correlation between the sooty tern chick-raising period on Manana, and the time of greatest abundance of both skipjack tuna, which they feed over, and the fish *Decapterus,* which they eat."

It has been known for some time that the Sooty Terns on Ascension Island (8° south latitude in the Atlantic Ocean) have a breeding season that begins every nine and a half months. Hence, the first eggs were laid in January during the first breeding period in 1958, and the first eggs were laid in November during the second breeding period of that same year (Ashmole 1963). Ashmole concluded that "the length of the interval (9½ months) between the start of laying in successive breeding periods appears to be determined by the time required for breeding activities, a complete moult, and an assembly and courtship period during which social stimulation is probably important."

Ashmole (1965, 1968) also studied Sooty Terns on Christmas Island (about 2° N, 157° W, in the Pacific Ocean). By studying banded birds, he learned that pairs of terns that are successful in raising their chicks to fledging nest at twelve-month intervals, whereas pairs that fail to raise a chick return to nest six months later.

The Sooty Tern lays one egg (Brown 1975a). The ground color varies from white to creamish buff. There is great variation in the markings: some eggs have relatively fine, brownish to reddish brown spots scattered over most of the surface; others have large splotches of burnt sienna brown (concentrated at the larger end of the egg or over more than half of the shell) and smaller pale purple blotches irregularly scattered over the shell. Eggs on Rabbit Island average 5.10 cm by 3.59 cm in length and width, 34.2 g in weight, and 32.1 cc in volume (Brown 1973).

Both sexes develop incubation patches. Most of the eggs are laid between noon and 4:00 P.M. Ashmole (1963) wrote that 91 percent of the eggs on Ascension Island were laid between noon and 6:00 P.M. Typically, the female incubates for about three hours after laying the egg, after which time the male covers the egg. The pair then take turns incubating, a period varying from 1 to 11 days for each parent. About 84 percent of the changeovers take place at night (between 7:00 P.M. and 7:00 A.M.). The incubation period varies from 28 to 31 days and the males incubate about 59 percent of the time. Most of the eggs hatch between 8:00 A.M. and 4:00 P.M. It may take the chick four days to break out of its shell.

The fully covered downy young have a variegated pattern of black, light brown, and white. The newly hatched chicks average 25.7 g in weight. They are unable to walk until at least three or four days old. The adults brood the chicks until they are at least eight days old. When not being brooded, the young seek shelter (among rocks, under tussocks of grass, etc.) near the nest. The young Sooty Tern solicits food by biting the side of the parent's bill repeatedly. This allows the chick to "scissor" between the parent's mandibles and grasp food that the parent regurgitates. At the same time, the chick utters a "chip-chip-chip" call. The adults return from fishing trips to feed the young an average of once a day. After they are more than 30 days old, the young usually are fed at night, most often between 10:00 and 11:00 P.M. (Brown 1975d). Such a chick may be fed as little as 9 g or as much as 46 g during a single feeding.

Sooty Tern chicks can survive for at least three days without being fed, which may happen if a chick hatches during the middle of an attentive period of the adult. In such an instance, the chick receives its first meal when the other parent returns to the nest from the ocean. Ashmole also found great variation in the rate of development of different chicks. He noted that "the capacity of young Wideawakes to survive for long periods on relatively little food, while growing hardly at all, but to accept large quantities of food when it is available, is clearly an adaptation to an environment in which the food supply is precarious."

In his thorough study of Sooty Terns on Rabbit Island, Brown learned that the birds ate about half squid and half fish by weight. Four families of fishes were represented in the diet, but the Carangidae (genus *Decapterus*) were the most important. The terns fledge when about 57 days old; they then usually leave the island during the day and return at about dusk to be fed late at night by their parents.

As soon as adults recognize their own chick, they peck any foreign chick that passes close enough to the nest. Young chicks rarely stray during the period they are being brooded but may do so if there is a general disturbance in the colony. Ashmole commented that "any person walking through the colony certainly caused heavy abnormal mortality among chicks only a few days old."

Ashmole found heavy predation by frigatebirds at one colony. There were 228 eggs in one area of about 90 square yards. As these eggs hatched, in late January and early February, three-fourths of the chicks were taken in their first 24 hours of life. A frigatebird swoops low over the ground and very deftly stretches its head and neck downward to snatch up a chick in passing.

Brown (1973) wrote that the breeding success of Sooty Terns on Rabbit Island for 1971 and 1972 was between 35 and 40 percent; that is, only 35 to 40 percent of the eggs laid produced flying young. Storms often cause heavy loss of eggs, and Brown found some 300 eggs that had been washed down the slope from their nest sites on April 21, 1971. Rabbit predation on Sooty Tern eggs already has been mentioned. Large holes in eggs probably were made by Ruddy Turnstones. The ghost crab *(Ocypode ceratophthalamus)* is thought to be a scavenger of deserted eggs. Brown saw a Black-crowned Night Heron with a Sooty Tern chick in its bill, and he found the remains of other chicks in pellets at a rookery containing 15 heron nests at Sea Life Park. A Barn Owl also preyed on chicks during the two years. Fisher (1948b) wrote of Common Mynas pecking open the eggs of Sooty Terns.

Howell and Bartholomew (1962b) studied temperature regulation in Sooty Terns on Midway Atoll. They found the daytime body temperatures of incubating adults to average more than 1° C higher than those of adults incubating at night, a fact presumed to be a result of the intense solar radiation during daylight hours. The mean daytime incubation patch temperature (39.6° C) was much higher than the temperatures of incubated eggs or of brooded, newly hatched chicks. It is essential that the adults cover both eggs and young chicks on sunny days because both would be killed by the intense solar heat of summer. If put in the shade, newly hatched chicks, whose down is still wet, and chicks several days old resort to shivering, which increases heat production. If placed in the sun, they begin vigorous panting. As the chicks grow, their temperature-regulating mechanisms improve in efficiency and the young birds also seek shade.

"Even before they are able to walk well, hatchlings will crawl into any patch of available shade if they are experimentally placed in the open sun. The closest available shade is normally the shade of their own parent standing over the nest site, but very young chicks do not seem to discriminate between adult birds, and if displaced they may seek shade under the wrong one. Such chicks may be severely pecked until they find their own parent. Older chicks can find sufficient shade among low, herbaceous plants or various objects causing irregularities in the surface of the sand" (Howell and Bartholomew 1962b:104; see also MacMillen et al. 1977).

Longevities of more than 26 years have been reported for two Sooty Terns banded on Howland Island in 1938 (Clapp and Sibley 1966); Wilson (1975) told of one bird, 28 years old.

A high incidence (29 percent) of parasitism by nasal mites (Rhinonyssidae) of five-month-old Sooty Terns

on Johnston Atoll has been reported, and the first published record of ticks *(Ornithodoros capensis)* parasitizing nasal cavities of birds pertains to Sooty Terns nesting on Laysan Island (Amerson 1966, 1967).

Gray-backed Tern
Sterna lunata
(Color plate 16)

This attractive tern has a black cap and a black eye-stripe running forward to the base of the black bill, which separates the white of the forehead and superciliary (above the eye) region from the white of the chin and throat. The nape of the neck and the underparts also are white. The wings, back, rump, and deeply forked tail are gray. The feet are black. Gray-backed Terns average 14 inches in length and 29 inches in wingspan. This species also has been called the Spectacled Tern and the Bridled Tern; the latter common name, however, has been used for *Sterna anaethetus.*

The Gray-backed Tern nests on the Phoenix, Line, Tuamotu, Fiji, Wake, and Hawaiian islands. In Hawaii it nests on Moku Manu, Kaula, and all of the Leeward Islands (total of 80,900 birds), including La Pérouse Pinnacle (1,000 birds) and Gardner Pinnacle (4,000 birds). The largest population (40,000) nests on Laysan Island.

There are some differences from island to island, but the adults usually return to the islands in January or February, although Bailey (1956) found them common on Laysan in late December 1912. Eggs have been found from mid-March to July. A single egg forms the clutch; the yolk is red, like that in the Sooty Tern (Van Tyne and Berger 1976). Eggs may be laid on the bare sand; under beach naupaka or other plants; or, on Nihoa especially, on ledges in cliffs or depressions in the lava rocks. Some birds make a lining of small pieces of coral or rock. The eggs exhibit considerable variation in color and markings. The background color may be white, creamy white, or grayish white. The highly variable markings are scattered irregularly over the surface; they are not concentrated around the larger end of the egg, as is common for the eggs of many species. Most of the eggs I have seen contained irregularly shaped pale purple splotches and brownish red, tawny, or orange-brown markings of different sizes—some small, others large. Some eggs have pale purple and blackish brown markings.

The incubation and nestling periods appear to be unknown. Newly hatched chicks are covered with a coat of grayish down. After the juvenile feathers grow in, the top of head and back are grayish brown with some white-tipped feathers; the wings are gray and white; the underparts are white.

Munro (1944:61) wrote of frigatebirds trying to

catch young Gray-backed Terns on Howland Island in 1938: "When we were banding them a chick disgorged a 4-inch squid in an open space and a frigate dipped down and secured it. They were dipping at the disturbed chicks but did not catch any while we were there."

Alexander Wetmore reported that Ruddy Turnstones and Bristle-thighed Curlews ate the eggs of Gray-backed Terns on Laysan in 1923 at a time when there was virtually no vegetation left on the island. The terns often lay their eggs in the open on the sandy beaches of Laysan, and these eggs sometimes are destroyed by high surf.

The primary diet of the Gray-backed Tern consists of fishes and squid, occasionally crustaceans and insects; but Clapp (1976) wrote of terns on Enderbury Island on the central Pacific Ocean that ate lizards *(Cryptoblepharus boutoni)*.

Blue-gray Noddy
Procelsterna cerulea saxatilis
(Color plate 17)

This is a small, beautiful, bluish gray tern with a partial white eye-ring, a short, slender black bill, and a shallow forked tail. The feet are black with lemon-yellow webs (Mayr 1945:27). Two color phases occur, the light-phase birds having paler underparts and face. Length from bill-tip to tip of tail averages 10 inches; wingspan averages 18 inches. Wingbeats are constant and fairly rapid. W. K. Fisher described the birds from Necker Island as a new species in 1903; it later was relegated to subspecific status. It formerly was called the Necker Island Tern and the Blue-gray Fairy Ternlet.

Blue-gray Noddies nest throughout the central and southern Pacific, but they are said to be absent from the islands in the western Pacific. This species is reported as being abundant offshore from its breeding islands throughout the year and seldom is seen far at sea. It has been found nesting on Kaula, Nihoa, Necker, La Pérouse Pinnacle (but none of the other islets of French Frigate Shoals), and Gardner Pinnacle, but not on any of the other islands lying to the northwest of it.

Very little is known about the breeding biology of the Blue-gray Noddy. Birds are present throughout the year on Necker and Nihoa islands, and on Nihoa the birds are said to nest throughout the year. Eggs have been found from March through September on Necker Island. In writing about Necker Island, W. K. Fisher (1906) said that "the single egg is laid in a shallow bowl-like cavity or recess in the rock with no nest, but occasionally a few stray quills and rubbish scattered about." The female also lays her eggs in holes in cliffs and rocks on Necker and Nihoa islands. I found that

FIGURE 43. An egg of the Blue-gray Noddy; Christmas Island (Pacific Ocean). November 15, 1971.

they lay on the bare sand, generally under cover of low vegetation, on Christmas Island (Pacific Ocean). The ground color of the shell is dull creamy white. The eggs are sparsely marked with roundish, rod-shaped, and irregular small spots, light brown, grayish, faint purple, or bluish gray in color (fig. 43). The yolk is yellow.

According to Fisher, the newly hatched chick has a white crown, very pale buff sides and back of neck, white-tipped brownish gray down on the wings and back, and pure white on the under surface of the body. The bill is blackish; the feet greenish gray. Neither the incubation period nor the nestling period have been determined.

Brown Noddy
Anous stolidus pileatus
(Color plate 18)

Also called the Common Noddy, this is a dark brown tern with a prominent white to grayish white forehead and crown. The bill, tarsi, and feet are black. The tail is long and wedge shaped. Average length is 16 inches; average wingspan, 33 inches. The birds have strong, steady wingbeats, and occasionally they soar on motionless wings. The Common Noddy flies closer to the surface of the water than do the three terns already discussed, and it can swim in the ocean.

The Brown Noddy has been reported as a breeding bird on all island groups in the tropical Pacific except the Kermadec Islands. It is said to be abundant only within 50 miles of its breeding or roosting islands. Common Noddies have been found nesting on all of the Leeward Hawaiian islands, Kaula, Mokolea Rock, Moku Manu, and Manana Island, as well as on a number of the small offshore islands of the main chain. The breeding population on the Leeward Islands has been estimated at about 139,000 birds, the largest numbers having been found on Necker Island

(50,000), Laysan Island (30,000), Nihoa Island (20,000), and Lisianski Island (15,000). Some 30,000 birds nest on Manana Island (Brown 1973).

Munro (1944:63) wrote: "During the Rothschild expedition, 1890 to 1893, and during Perkins' collecting period, 1892 to 1902, I never heard of sea birds on islands off the coast of Oahu. They had probably been exterminated by the ancient Hawaiians and have gradually worked their way back."

Richardson (1957) summarized the great variation in breeding seasons of the Brown Noddy in different parts of the Pacific Ocean. In Hawaii as well, there is considerable variation. On Nihoa, Necker, and at Pearl and Hermes Reef, eggs or young may be found nearly every month of the year, although on each island the maximum nesting takes place during a more restricted period: Nihoa, December to August, Necker, April to December, Pearl and Hermes Reef, usually March to September. A detailed study of these populations would be very instructive.

Brown Noddies roost on Rabbit Island year-around, although only a few birds use the island during most of February. Brown (1973) wrote that "at least a thousand brown noddies roost on the island during all other months of the year." Both Sooty Terns and Brown Noddies stand in groups, or "nightclubs," at night, prior to the egg-laying period. Both species also perform aerial courtship flights, which may take the pair 1,000 or more feet above the ocean; the birds then descend rapidly, leveling off before reaching the water.

During 1947–1948, Brown Noddies laid eggs on Rabbit Island in March and April (Richardson and Fisher 1950). By 1956, at least, the egg-laying period had shifted to mid-May or June. In 1971 a few birds laid eggs during July and early August (Brown 1973). Brown's fine study was made possible because he camped on Rabbit Island from June 1 to August 17, 1971, and from March 10 to August 20, 1972, so that he lived with the birds 24 hours each day. Much of the following information is taken from his thesis.

Pre-copulatory behavior includes preening of the female by the male, "choaking" by the female, and usually by courtship feeding. In choaking, a bird (either male or female) gapes, shakes its head from side to side, and makes a croaking sound. The male then steps onto the female's back and the birds press their cloacal lips together. Copulation lasts an average of 5.5 minutes, which is a long time for birds; it lasts an average of 1 minute for the Sooty Tern. Post-copulatory behavior consists primarily of preening and courtship feeding.

In Hawaii most Brown Noddies lay their eggs on bare ground, on rock ledges, and on both flat and steep slopes. Individual birds may make no nest, a small nest, or a fairly bulky one. Nesting materials may include sticks, weed stems, feathers, straw, bones, pebbles, sea urchin shells, rope, crayons, and other debris. On Green Island of Kure Atoll, about 6 percent of the birds build nests in *Scaevola* or other plants, as they do on other Pacific islands.

Females lay a single egg. The background color of the shell may be white, pinkish white, or buff. The markings of small spots and dots are sparsely scattered over the entire shell, occasionally concentrated at the large end; most are light brown or reddish brown in color, but there is a wide variety of shades and patterns. Brown wrote that "an experienced observer, however, can nearly always distinguish the two kinds of eggs by their luster, which is glossy in the sooty tern and dull in the brown noddy." The yolk of the Brown Noddy egg is yellow; it is red to orange in the Sooty Tern. This is an interesting, and unexplained, difference because the two species eat the same foods.

Brown Noddy eggs average 5.28 cm in length (range 4.9–5.9), 3.6 cm in width (3.5–3.8); they average 36.3 g in weight, and have an average volume of 34.1 cc. The eggs on Rabbit Island are about 2 g heavier than the Sooty Tern eggs there. Brown Noddies lay their eggs both during the daytime and at night, whereas 97 percent of Sooty Tern eggs are laid between noon and 8:00 p.m. Both the male and female noddy incubate the eggs, each bird spending an average of one day on the egg; about 60 percent of the changeovers take place between 8:00 p.m. and midnight. The incubation period averages 36 days, the range being from 34 days 16 hours to 37 days 12 hours.

Brown Noddy chicks are notable because of the striking difference in the color of their natal down, which varies from pure black to pure white (fig. 44). Brown found that 51 percent of 502 chicks were black (from pure black to sooty), 22 percent were gray, and 27 percent were white (dirty white to pure white). Brown wrote that "Dorward and Ashmole (1963) reviewed the color phases of brown noddy chicks reported from several oceanic islands, but they were not able to explain the differing proportions of color phases on the different islands; I cannot explain them either." Brown found no relationship between color phase and survivorship of the noddy chicks. Bill and feet are black in both color phases, and both phases develop the same juvenile plumage, which is similar to the adult except that the white is whiter and less extensive in the young birds. Brown Noddy chicks can walk when just over a day old, and they grow more rapidly than Sooty Tern chicks. The noddies fledge when an average of 42.5 days old, but there is a post-fledging period of 100 days or longer when the young are still fed by the adults.

Brown found that about 44 percent of the Brown

FIGURE 44. A recently hatched, black-phase Brown Noddy chick; Manana Island. July 3, 1971.

Noddy eggs laid before June 11, 1971, produced fledged young and that no nests were successful after that date. Only 16.5 percent of the eggs laid in 1972 produced fledged young. He attributed much of the loss to predation by Black-crowned Night Herons, especially after mid-June. "The heron chicks [at Sea Life Park] hatched from mid-June through July 10th. This means that these chicks began to hatch around a month after the sooty tern chicks began hatching; the heron chicks hatched more or less simultaneously with brown noddy chick hatching." More than 40 percent of the mortality of noddy chicks was attributed to heron predation in 1972.

Woodward (1972) reported that from 42.9 to 57.4 percent of noddy eggs were successful during the five years from 1964 through 1968 on Kure Atoll. There rats preyed heavily on both eggs and young birds. Frigatebirds have been reported to prey on noddy chicks in other areas (e.g., the Dry Tortugas).

Wilson (1975) told of a banded Brown Noddy that was recaptured 24 years after being banded, and Brown (1975c), of one that was 25 years old.

Black Noddy
Anous tenuirostris
(Color plate 19)

This tern is known also as the White-capped Noddy, Lesser Noddy, Hawaiian Noddy, and Hawaiian Tern.

The Hawaiian name is Noio. Two color phases occur. Light-phase birds have conspicuous white caps, dark gray-brown backs and abdomens, pale gray rumps, and dark gray tails; there is a gradual change from the white of the cap to the gray-brown back feathers. Dark-phase birds are sooty black except for the white cap. The large, pointed bill is black; the tail is slightly forked. The tarsi and webbed feet are yellowish orange. These small noddies have an average length of 14 inches and a wingspan of 28 inches. Their flight is described as being "more fluttery," with faster wing-beats, than that of the Brown Noddy. The wings are said to look broader, giving the birds a less graceful appearance.

This noddy breeds on most of the island groups in the tropical Pacific. The Black Noddy nests on most of the Leeward Islands including Gardner Pinnacle; but, only on La Pérouse Pinnacle of French Frigate Shoals (the birds roost on Trig and Whale-Skate islands, however). The total population for the Leeward Islands has been estimated to be roughly about 31,000 birds. On Nihoa Island, for example, "virtually nothing is known of the population size since these birds occur primarily on the nearly inaccessible north cliff face, and to a lesser extent on the eastern and western cliff faces" (Clapp, Kridler, and Fleet 1977). This noddy also nests on Lehua Island, Kaula Island, Moku Manu, Mokolea Rock, and along the coasts of Hawaii, Maui, Lanai, and Kauai. This species is said to be abundant only within 50 miles of the breeding or roosting islands. There is considerable movement of birds from one island to another throughout the Hawaiian chain.

A thorough study of the annual cycle of the Black Noddy is needed. On Necker Island and on the North and Southeast islands of Pearl and Hermes Reef, nesting has been reported during every month of the year. On Lisianski Island, eggs are laid from January through June; on Kure Atoll, the birds usually are absent from late December to mid-March. On Laysan Island, the birds are present throughout the year, but the primary nesting season is from November through July.

Black Noddies build a substantial nest of grasses, twigs, leaves, and, sometimes, seaweed. The nests are placed in shrubs, trees, on rock ledges, in clefts in rock, or holes in cliffs. The birds nest on branches of ironwood trees on Laysan and Lisianski islands and on Midway (fig. 45). Others nest in beach naupaka, *Pluchea,* and clumps of bunchgrass, and even in coconut trees on Laysan Island (Ely and Clapp 1973). Nests measured by Clapp and Wirtz (1975) varied from 6 to 13 inches wide (mean 7.5 inches) and from 2.5 to 6 inches deep (mean 4.4 inches). Nests built in

FIGURE 45. This lone ironwood tree on Laysan Island provides nesting sites for many Black Noddies. March 26, 1966.

beach naupaka were placed 18 to 32 inches above the ground; those in ironwood trees, from 21 inches to 10 feet above the ground. On Midway Atoll, however, nests are placed at much greater heights above the ground.

A single egg with a white background is laid. The eggs are sparsely marked with irregularly shaped spots and blotches of very pale violet to reddish brown. The newly hatched chicks are covered with black down except for a white head. The white area extends from the base of the bill backward over the crown, from which an arm of white passes forward under the eye. Bill, tarsi, and feet are black. The white egg tooth is very conspicuous at the tip of the upper mandible, as is true for the other species of terns and noddies.

The following information is taken from a paper by Rahn et al. (1976). Black Noddy eggs average 4.49 cm in length, 3.15 cm in width, and 23.7 g in weight. Egg temperatures reach 37.4° C during incubation. The incubation period is 35 days, during which time the eggs lose about 14 percent of their water. The same authors give comparable information for the Sooty Tern, Brown Noddy, and White Tern. The breeding

biology of the Black Noddy on Ascension Island is discussed by Ashmole (1962) and by Cullen and Ashmole (1963).

White Tern
Gygis alba rothschildi
(Color plate 20)

Named the White Tern by early writers, this species has more recently been called the Fairy Tern in Hawaiian literature. The latter common name, however, has long been used for *Sterna nereis* of the Australian region.

The White Tern has snow-white plumage except for a ring of black feathers around each dark eye; the iris is dark blue. The bill is black, changing to blue at the base. The tail is slightly forked. The feet are black or bluish with yellow webs. The birds average 10 inches in length; the wingspan is 28 inches. The flight has been described as being light and ethereal with slow effortless wingbeats, but with an overall pattern of erratic fluttering. The birds are inquisitive and often hover just over one's head, especially during the breeding season.

The birds dive to the surface of the water after fish, but they do not submerge. It is said that the White Tern catches small fishes as they leap out of the water. The birds carry them crosswise in the bill, and they have been known to return to their chicks with as many as 12 small fishes held this way. The minnows are expertly manipulated by the adult's bill and tongue, and are fed to the chick one by one. Ashmole (1968b) thought that White Terns specialize in fishing largely at dawn at Christmas Island and that, like the other Hawaiian terns, they catch their prey (fishes and squid) within a few centimeters above or below the surface of the ocean after the prey is frightened to the surface by schools of tuna and other predatory fish.

White Terns breed on most of the islands in the tropical Pacific region except for the Bismarck Archipelago and the Solomon Islands, where the species is a migrant. The White Tern is known to breed on Kaula and on nearly all of the islands in the Leeward Chain. At French Frigate Shoals, however, the birds nest only on La Pérouse Pinnacle and on Tern Island; they are known to nest only on Southeast Island of Pearl and Hermes Reef. The estimated population for the Leeward Islands is about 10,000; the majority of the birds occur at French Frigate Shoals (3,700 birds), Nihoa (3,000), and Laysan (1,500). By contrast, no more than a dozen birds form the breeding population on Kure Atoll and on Southeast Island of Pearl and Hermes Reef.

The first observation of the White Tern nesting on any of the main Hawaiian islands was made in 1961, when a pair with an egg was found at Koko Head, Oahu, on July 15 by Ord (1961). He also saw 16 adults in the air at one time. Ord and I found an immature tern capable of flight in the same area on July 4, 1965; and Henry Yuen found two downy chicks there in 1968 (July 21, August 13) and an egg in 1969 (June 3). We now know that White Terns lay eggs on Oahu at least from March 6 (1977, at Fort DeRussy) to October 6 (1970, Kapiolani Park). I have seen eggs or young each month from March to October; and on November 16, 1976, I watched three terns fly in from the ocean to roost in the tall ironwood trees at the City nursery opposite Kapiolani Park. There is one record of an egg in Kahala (August 14, 1972). White Terns raised a nestling in a tree in the courtyard of the Fernhurst YWCA on Wilder Avenue during September 1980.

On Laysan Island and Necker Island, eggs and young can be found during every month of the year. Most nesting occurs from March through August on Lisianski Island, from March to November or December on Gardner Pinnacles, and from April to June on Kure Atoll.

The White Tern builds no nest and is well known for its propensity for laying its single egg on a horizontal branch, or in the crotch, of any suitable tree or shrub in the habitat. On Midway and Lisianski, it nests in one of the introduced ironwoods; on Oahu, in ironwoods and kiawe. The egg found by Ord at Koko Head in 1961 had been laid on a kiawe branch about 15 feet above the ground; the first chick found by Yuen in 1968 was on a kiawe branch approximately 60 feet above ground in the same area.

On volcanic remnants such as Nihoa and Necker islands, the terns lay their eggs on rocky ledges. On Laysan they commonly deposit their eggs on low blocks of coral or beach rock; rarely directly on the ground.

On Midway I have seen adults incubating eggs and brooding young chicks at the very edge of the flat roofs of the Bachelor Officers' Quarters, and one bird incubated an egg on the stub of a 5-inch-diameter ironwood tree that had been broken off about 30 feet above the ground (fig. 31). Terns sometimes lay their eggs in the abandoned nest of a Black Noddy.

The eggs of the White Tern are more perfectly elliptical in shape than those of other Hawaiian terns, being relatively blunt at both ends. They also are beautifully marked (fig. 46). The ground color varies from grayish white to creamy white. There is great individual variation in the amount and pattern of the markings, although most contain irregular splotches, specks, lines, scrolls, and scrawls. All of the eggs I have seen contain markings of at least two colors, one pale, the other dark. The markings are scattered over the entire surface of the shell: on some, these markings are concentrated around one end of the egg; in others, they are not. The most common of the pale colors seems to be grayish purple; the dark color varies from light brown to reddish brown to deep chocolate brown.

Numerous experiments have been conducted to determine whether or not seabirds can recognize their own eggs, and in general, the finding has been that they do not. Alfred M. Bailey (1956) wrote of substituting a piece of rounded coral for a White Tern egg and of then watching an adult return to the nest site and immediately settle down to "incubate" the piece of coral.

Thomas R. Howell determined the usual incubation period of White Terns on Midway Atoll to be 35 days. Incubation begins as soon as the egg is laid, and the egg is covered almost continuously during the entire incubation period, as the adults take turns on the egg. After hatching, the young tern remains at or very near the nest site for 42 to 48 days before it can fly (Woodward 1972). Murakami noted that the chick that she studied in Honolulu made "several circular flight patterns within and around" the nesting tree when the

FIGURE 46. An egg of a White Tern at the site where it will be incubated; Christmas Island (Pacific Ocean). November 15, 1971.

bird was about 50 days old. In writing about White Terns on Christmas Island, Ashmole (1968a) said that "the rearing of a chick occupies about five months, not counting the preliminaries to laying but including just over one month for incubation and about four months during which the chick is dependent"; he thought it possible that chicks sometimes become independent when only about three months old. Ashmole also reported that a female White Tern will lay a replacement egg if the first egg or chick is destroyed. This is the only known seabird in Hawaii with this behavior pattern; if an egg or young of the other species is destroyed, the birds will not nest again until the following breeding season.

A careful analysis of a large number of chicks has not been made, but there seems to be considerable variation in the color and pattern of newly hatched young (fig. 47). I have seen the following combinations, and others undoubtedly occur. Some are completely white; some are white with one or two black streaks (or spots) on the top of the head; others have pinkish buff to very light tan-colored down with small patches or bars of black on the back (occiput) of the head, and with a

black line or streak extending downward behind the eye (a postocular line). The bill and toes are bluish black; the webs of the toes are flesh colored to light tan. The feet and toes are well developed and have long, sharp claws, a necessity for enabling the chick to hold on to rocks or bare branches. The iris is blue to black.

Of 164 adult and nestling White Terns banded on several islands at French Frigate Shoals, only seven returns have been recorded. An adult banded on Tern Island on August 4, 1965, was found dead on Johnston Island (516 miles to the south) on February 14, 1967. Another adult that was banded on Johnston Island was recovered on Tern Island on July 6, 1966 (Amerson 1971).

Black-crowned Night Heron
Nycticorax nycticorax hoactli
(Color plate 21)

Herons, bitterns, and egrets (family Ardeidae) are long-necked, long-winged, and long-legged birds that inhabit marshes, swamps, lakes, or rivers. They eat fish, frogs, snakes, mice, insects, crayfish, and a wide variety of other aquatic life. Herons and egrets nest in

FIGURE 47. A White Tern chick in the remains of a noddy nest where the adult tern laid her egg; Christmas Island (Pacific Ocean). November 15, 1971.

colonies, often several species together; bitterns tend to nest as isolated pairs or in very loose colonies in such areas as cattail marshes. The members of this family are noted for their elaborate courtship and postnuptial displays. Two species are found in Hawaii: the Black-crowned Night Heron and the Cattle Egret, an introduced species.

The Black-crowned Night Heron (Hawaiian name, Aukuu) is considered indigenous rather than endemic (see gallinule and coot) because the Hawaiian birds have not been recognized as subspecifically distinct in plumage characters from the American continental birds. This subspecies has a very large breeding range, extending from Washington and Oregon, south to northern Chile and south-central Argentina. However, the future of this species in Hawaii is dependent on the preservation of suitable wetland habitat.

The male and female are alike in breeding plumage. The top of the head, the back, and the scapular feathers are a glossy greenish black; the forehead, throat, sides of head, and underparts are white, the latter often tinged with pale bluish green, lilac, or cream; the rump, wings, and tail are ashy gray to bluish gray; the iris of the eye is red; the large, heavy bill is black; the legs and feet are yellow. Three (usually) highly modified, long, narrow, white feathers (nuptial plumes) grow backward from the occipital region of the head.

Total length of adults (North American specimens) is between 23 and 26 inches; wingspread, 43 to 45 inches.

Immature birds are grayish brown above, spotted and streaked with whitish and rusty hues; mainly whitish below, streaked with brownish and grayish; the bill is variable in color; the iris is yellow.

The Black-crowned Night Heron inhabits all of the main Hawaiian islands. The State Division of Fish and Game conducts an annual January census of Hawaiian waterbirds. Comparative data for 1978 and 1979 are given in Table 3. The figures given for Maui demonstrate the critical importance of both Kanaha and Kealia ponds because the birds fly from one to the other, presumably in accordance with the availability of food. This heron has strayed at least once to Midway Atoll and once to Kure Atoll (Bryan and Greenway 1944; Clapp and Woodward 1968).

The heron inhabits marshes, ponds, streams, reservoirs, and lagoons, where it feeds primarily on aquatic insects, fish, frogs, and mice. Although it is generally known that owls regurgitate (through the mouth) compact pellets containing hair, feathers, and bones of the rodents or birds that they have eaten, it is less generally known that herons also regurgitate such pellets. Predation by herons on Sooty Terns and Brown Noddies on Rabbit Island was mentioned previously.

Unfortunately, we still await a detailed study of the biology of the Black-crowned Night Heron in Hawaii. Robert Shallenberger found 15 nests in kiawe trees at Sea Life Park during June and July 1970; hatching of eggs took place primarily between June 7 and July 10. I found only one active nest (with two eggs and a small chick) in this heronry on July 16.

In North America, the female of this subspecies builds a bulky nest of twigs and sticks, which the male usually collects. The eggs are pale greenish blue. Clutch size of mainland birds varies from three to five eggs.

The young are hatched with a coat of grayish down except for a small white crest on top of the head; the bill is grayish; the iris is grayish olive; the legs and feet are buffy brown; and the skin is flesh colored to pinkish buff.

TABLE 3
Annual January Black-crowned Night Heron Censuses

	1978	1979
Oahu	153	81
Kauai	53	20
Maui		
Kanaha Pond	1	70
Kealia Pond	138	53
Reservoirs	28	18

CHAPTER THREE

Endemic Birds

We have defined "endemic" birds as those that are peculiar to a particular region and, therefore, that are found nowhere else in the world. The endemic Hawaiian birds include 20 genera, 44 species, and 32 subspecies belonging to 11 bird families. Of these, 16 genera, 28 species, and 18 subspecies form the unique family of Hawaiian honeycreepers (Drepanididae). This chapter deals with all of these in phylogenetic sequence, that is, starting with those orders of birds that are considered to be older in evolutionary terms.

ORDER ANSERIFORMES
FAMILY ANATIDAE
(DUCKS, GEESE, AND SWANS)
Nene or Hawaiian Goose
Branta sandvicensis
(Color plate 22)

The Nene, the state bird of Hawaii, is an attractive, medium-sized, heavily barred, gray-brown goose with a black face, head, and nape of the neck. The highly specialized, buff-colored feathers of the cheek and neck grow in a pattern that produces deep furrows. The bill and feet are black. The sexes are alike in plumage pattern. The birds vary from 22 to 28 inches in length. Captive male Nene weigh about 15 percent more than females. Males average 5 pounds; females, about 4 pounds 6 ounces. The weight in both sexes fluctuates throughout the year, and both are heavier during the breeding season.

The Nene is endemic to the island of Hawaii. Although many of the early writers reported that it occurred on Maui, it is debatable whether or not the Nene formerly nested on that island. In any case, the Nene has the smallest range of any species of goose.

Baldwin (1945a) pieced together available information on the Nene from 1789 to 1944. He estimated the maximum population of Nene during the latter part of the eighteenth century to be about 25,000 birds. Re-duction in this population began shortly after the islands were discovered, and progressed rapidly between 1850 and 1900. Baldwin believed the reduction to be due to a number of man's activities: "hunting with firearms, probable increase in capture of live birds and eggs, flushing and frightening of birds from nests and foraging grounds, sandalwood gathering in uplands, ranching developments and activities, and building of beach resort homes and of military roads in uplands." It should be noted that hunting was particularly devastating to the Nene because the open season was scheduled during the breeding season, a situation apparently resulting from ignorance of the winter breeding cycle of this species, although H. W. Henshaw had called attention to this problem as early as 1904.

Indirectly, man caused the reduction of populations with the introduction of goats, sheep, cattle, horses, pigs, dogs, cats, and mongooses. Not only are the eggs and young goslings easy prey for mongooses, pigs, and feral dogs and cats, but the adults molt all of their flight feathers over a short period of time and then are flightless for four to six weeks until the new flight feathers grow in. Baldwin thought that the total population of wild Nene was about 50 birds in the early 1940s.

Charles and Elizabeth Schwartz (1949) spent eighteen months of intensive field work in Hawaii during 1946 and 1947 and did not find any wild Nene. They wrote that "this wildfowl is the next Hawaiian, if not world, species facing imminent extinction," and they proposed that the most practical way of saving the Nene was to "secure breeding stock from captive birds and propagate this species as intensively as possible." They also recommended that "an immediate study should be undertaken of this bird's life history and means of survival." By 1952 the wild population was estimated to be less than 30 birds. Almost nothing was then known about the breeding biology or ecology of the Nene, although Baldwin (1947b) had studied the food habits of this vegetarian (greens, fruits, and seeds) goose.

A Nene Restoration Project began with a $6,000 appropriation from the Territory of Hawaii in 1949, using a pair of captive Nene obtained from Herbert Shipman of Hawaii. This project was designed to study the ecology of the wild N•ne as well as to rear birds in captivity for later release. However, the field study was not approved by the Board of Agriculture and Forestry at that time. In 1956, William H. Elder obtained funds from several sources and made an extensive field study of the Nene from September 1956 to September 1957 (Elder and Woodside 1958). His findings, plus the production of 36 Nene in captivity during the period 1949 to 1957, led to the passage of a bill in the U.S. Congress in 1958 providing the U.S. Fish and Wildlife Service with $15,000 per year for a five-year period for the study and management of the Nene. At the end of the initial five-year period, the newly named Bureau of Sport Fisheries and Wildlife was authorized to continue the annual expenditure of $15,000 for the project,

and this sum was increased to $25,000 per year in 1968.

Mr. Shipman also sent two Nene to Peter Scott at the Wildfowl Trust, Slimbridge, England, in 1950, but both proved to be females; a gander was then provided. In an attempt to increase fertility in the captive flock, two additional males were sent to England from Pohakuloa (on the Saddle Road of Hawaii) in 1962; and two, in 1967. A pair of Nene was sent to England as early as 1834 (Stanley 1834). More than 600 Nene were raised at Slimbridge between 1952 and 1976.

The rearing program at Pohakuloa has been increasingly effective throughout the years, primarily through the dedicated efforts of Mr. Ah Fat Lee, and more than 1,650 birds were raised there between 1950 and 1978 (fig. 48). The first releases into the wild Nene habitat were made in 1960; 1,272 birds had been released in four sanctuaries on Hawaii by June 30, 1978 (Kear and Berger 1980).

In an effort to extend the breeding range of the Nene to Maui, 35 birds were released in the Paliku cabin area of Haleakala Crater in 1962. A total of 488 birds

FIGURE 48. Ah Fat Lee with a pair of Nene and their four downy young at Pohakuloa about 1955. Courtesy of the Hawaii Division of Fish and Game.

was liberated there between 1962 and 1978. Of these, 197 were birds raised at Slimbridge, 284 at Pohakuloa, and 7 at S. Dillon Ripley's aviaries in Connecticut. The first birds were taken into the crater in boxes carried on the backs of boy scouts and personnel of the State Division of Fish and Game; later the birds were carried by mule pack-train; in recent years, by helicopter. The program has not been a howling success: as of 1972, apparently only two young birds survived to enter the breeding population; and during the 1977–1978 nesting season only two goslings were raised to maturity (Berger 1978b).

In its native habitat on the island of Hawaii (20° N latitude), the Nene begins to nest during the early winter (November in the wild; as early as August 30 at Pohakuloa), when daylengths are decreasing. The shortest daylength at this latitude is 10.8 hours. By contrast, at the Wildfowl Trust in England (52° N), the birds usually begin to lay in February, when daylength is about 9.5 hours. Janet Kear wrote to me that, in a pen where floodlights burned until midnight in winter, "Nene moulted in January (three months early) and failed to breed at all."

Most of what we know about the breeding biology of the Nene has been learned from the captive flocks at Pohakuloa and at Slimbridge. The dates for first eggs at Pohakuloa have varied from August 30 (1974) to December 5 (1953); in England, the birds begin to lay eggs in February. A small percentage (3.2 percent) of female Nene lay eggs near the end of their first year of life, but thus far all eggs of such females have been infertile. Almost 84 percent of the females lay during their second year, and approximately 13 percent, during their third year. Data thus far obtained indicate that the greatest period of production for a goose at Pohakuloa is between her third and fifteenth years. (A gander in the aviaries of Jean Delacour in France was 42 years old when killed during World War II.)

Fertility of eggs seems to be related primarily to the bloodline of the ganders, the age of the ganders, and the position of the egg in the clutch. Ganders are able to fertilize eggs for at least 12 years, beginning in their first year. Both fertility and hatchability of eggs were low during the early years of the program, and it was discovered that there was a high degree of infertility among the inbred ganders. Wild birds were added to the experimental flock beginning in 1960, and there followed an immediate improvement in the fertility of the eggs.

Chickens (1949–1952), Muscovy Ducks (1953–1960), and Silky Bantams (1960–1965) were used to incubate Nene eggs and to act as foster mothers for the goslings. These efforts were generally unsatisfactory, however, because many of the hens failed to develop broodiness behavior during the winter months at Pohakuloa. Consequently, hatchability of fertile eggs was low.

Experiments begun during the 1965–1966 breeding season demonstrated that hatchability was much greater when the female Nene was allowed to incubate her first clutch of eggs to hatching. As soon as they hatched, the goslings were removed to indoor brooders and the nest was destroyed. A majority of the pairs renested within eight weeks, and the female laid a second clutch of eggs and proceeded to incubate them. This method makes it possible, of course, to raise two broods for each female during a single season.

As a result of the new technique, more than 100 goslings were raised each year, beginning during the 1967–1968 breeding season. However, the work load for the two-man staff at Pohakuloa proved too heavy and the breeding stock was reduced to 32 pairs for the 1972–1973 season; it was further reduced to 5 pairs for 1979–1980, presumably in anticipation of a time when the captive breeding program might come to an end. Although there is no evidence yet to suggest that wild Nene renest, two geese at Pohakuloa laid second clutches of eggs after rearing a brood of goslings during 1979, which was the first time that the goslings of the first brood were not taken from the goose.

Clutch size usually varies from 3 to 5 eggs; the average of 182 clutches was 4.26 eggs over a four-year period at Pohakuloa. Eleven 6-egg clutches have been recorded at Pohakuloa, and several more at Slimbridge. A 6-egg clutch at Pohakuloa in 1970 was fertile and 6 goslings hatched successfully.

The eggs are immaculate, creamy white, and average 3.36 inches in length and 2.35 inches in width (fig. 49). The incubation period varies between 29 and 31 days, but usually is 30 days. The newly hatched young are covered with a full coat of down: light gray below, darker above, and with a light-colored V on the forehead and a dark ear patch. Like the downy young of other precocial species, the young Nene is able to run about as soon as its down dries. However, it is unable to fly until between 10 and 12 weeks old, which, indeed, is a long period of time to escape predation by mongooses, rats, feral pigs, cats, and dogs. Studies of color-marked Nene have revealed that the birds have a marked homing instinct and that they commonly return to the same area to nest in successive years (Walker 1969). Homing also has been demonstrated by pen-reared Nene that returned to Pohakuloa after having been released on Mauna Loa as well as on Maui.

In the nesting season (approximately October through March), Nene are restricted to Mauna Loa and Hualalai. During the summer months, however, the birds feed on the lava flows of Mauna Loa during

FIGURE 49. Nest and eggs of the Nene; the nest is lined with the goose's own down feathers. Photographed at an elevation of about 6,500 feet on Mauna Loa. January 9, 1973.

the day but fly across the Saddle Road in the evening to roost on the lower slopes of Mauna Kea. The primary flyway crosses the Saddle Road between the 17- and 21-mile markers, the distances being measured from Hilo.

The Nene is a highly specialized goose, adapted for living in a rugged habitat of lava flows far from any standing or running water. Among the more noticeable anatomical specializations for this terrestrial life is a reduction in the webbing between the toes (Miller 1937; Humphrey 1958). The birds spend most of their time on sparsely vegetated lava flows on Mauna Loa and Hualalai, at elevations between approximately 5,000 and 8,000 feet (fig. 50). Here the birds often build their nests on the lava, typically well concealed in clumps of vegetation; they also nest in the vegetation near the edges of kipukas. The nests are lined with the goose's own down feathers, and, if time permits, she covers the eggs with down before leaving the nest to feed or to distract a predator.

Despite the expenditure of some $350,000 of Federal money at Pohakuloa, of an estimated £5,000 (to ship 200 birds from the Wildfowl Trust to Hawaii), and of thirty years of effort, there is still no reliable information on the size of the wild Nene population. Published estimates of the population are admittedly "pie-in-the-sky" guesses, based primarily on the numbers of cap-

tive birds that have been released on Hawaii and Maui. Similarly, there are no meaningful data on the annual reproductive success of the wild population. Consequently, we still do not know if this population can be self-perpetuating.

Two reasons for this lack of information are clear. First, no biologist with training and interest in waterfowl or game management has been assigned to the field studies for more than a decade, even though Schwartz and Schwartz urged an immediate study of the life history of the Nene in its mountain habitat as long ago as 1949. Secondly, the Nene habitat, particularly on Mauna Loa, is one of the most difficult areas in the world to study. As compared with precipitous cliffs of Kauai, Maui, and parts of Hawaii, the slopes of Mauna Loa are gentle, but large areas occupied by the Nene are covered by aa lava. Travel by foot over the sharp angular blocks of lava is very slow and tiring because one has to test almost every block before taking a step forward. Thin-roofed lava tubes and crevices also make hiking dangerous.

Moreover, problems have been encountered when birds reared in captivity are placed in the release pens; these have been discussed by Berger (1978a) and by Kear and Berger (1980).

As a part of its resources management program, Volcanoes National Park initiated in 1972 a plan to de-

FIGURE 50. Nene on an aa lava flow at an elevation of about 6,200 feet on Mauna Loa. January 10, 1973.

termine if a lowland population of Nene could be established in its former habitat. Between then and November 1978, nine open-topped breeding enclosures (1 to 2 acres in extent) were constructed in various parts of the park. Placed in each enclosure was a pair, made flightless by pinioning or by clipping the primary wing feathers. The goslings, however, were free to leave and return to the pens at will. Although mortality of goslings has been high, at least 30 Nene had survived to adulthood in the park as of November 1978. Concurrent with the development of the Nene project, a concerted effort was made to exterminate wild goats from the park; as a result, much of the vegetation has recovered and provides a better habitat for the geese.

A similar program was initiated at Haleakala National Park on Maui in 1972. At that time, two small pens were built adjacent to the park headquarters building at an elevation of 7,030 feet; a release pen (30 × 30 m) also was built between Hosmer's grove and the headquarters building. Although the caged Nene were viewed daily by visitors, one pair hatched five goslings during December 1972; another pair raised four goslings the following year, after which time a third breeding pen was constructed. However, only one gosling

was raised from 17 eggs laid during the 1977–1978 breeding season. Nevertheless, these additional rearing programs give the public an opportunity to see this unique Hawaiian goose and may well aid in establishing the Nene in its former range.

Koloa or Hawaiian Duck
Anas wyvilliana
(Color plate 23)

Koloas are small brownish ducks whose plumage is mottled in shades of brown and buff. There may be very little difference in color pattern between males and females, but adult males do tend to have more brown-tipped, blackish feathers on the head and neck and a deeper brown color on the other feathers. Males also may have a patch of chestnut-colored feathers on the breast and rufous brown on the sides, and the head may have flecks or streaks of deep green, similar to the head color of the closely related Mallard *(Anas platyrhynchos)*. The speculum (a distinctly colored patch on the secondary feathers) in both sexes varies from greenish to a deep metallic purplish blue, bordered behind first by a band of black feathers and then by a band of white. A small white eye-ring may be fairly distinct, indistinct, or absent; it is never as extensive as in the Laysan Duck. Bill color is variable: olive, characteristic of adult males; yellow-orange, with dark spotting at the base of the upper mandible, or uniformly dark gray, two patterns found in adult females. Foot color also is variable: dark gray, orange-yellow, scarlet. Scarlet feet have been found only among adult males, but not all males have scarlet-colored feet (Swedberg 1967).

Total length of adult males is 19 to 20 inches; females are about 3 inches shorter. Sixteen drakes at the Pohakuloa propagation station averaged 23.6 ounces; hens averaged 3.4 ounces lighter than the drakes.

The Koloa originally was found on all of the main Hawaiian islands except Lanai and Kahoolawe. A decline in numbers of Koloa on most of the islands was noted by several writers after the turn of the present century, and by the 1950s the fate of the ducks on Oahu was in doubt. Schwartz and Schwartz (1953) wrote that "without doubt the drainage project in progress (1952) of the major marsh areas on windward Oahu will extirpate the duck from that island within the next few years." The drainage project involved the destruction of Kaelepulu pond to form "Enchanted Lake." Only on Kauai was the species to survive.

Man probably was the most serious predator of the Koloa; the birds could be hunted legally during the early 1920s, when the bag limit was 25 ducks per day. In 1939 duck hunting was prohibited for a period of

two years, and the prohibition was continued during World War II. Fortunately, duck hunting (both for the Koloa and the wintering migratory ducks) has been prohibited since that time. The decline in taro farming (from 18,922 acres in 1900 to 510 acres in 1960) and the cessation of rice growing greatly reduced suitable habitat for the Koloa, as has draining and filling of marshlands for agriculture and urban use (fig. 51).

Wild dogs are known to be serious predators, not only of ducklings but also of the adults in their flightless stage (about 6.5 weeks' duration) during the annual postnuptial molt. A number of other animals (e.g., largemouth bass, bullfrogs) have been known to kill small ducklings on Kauai, and there is one record of a Black-crowned Night Heron flying with a duckling in its bill. Wild cats, rats, and pigs also destroy nests. The role of the mongoose in the extinction of the Koloa throughout most of its former range is unknown, but it is perhaps significant to note that Kauai, the last stronghold of the Koloa, is the only main island on which the mongoose had not been introduced.

The Koloa is tolerant of a variety of climatic and ecological conditions. On Kauai the birds nest at any elevation from sea level to 3,500 feet, and where annual rainfall may be as low as 35 inches or as high as 125 inches. They are found in lowland marshes, reservoirs, taro patches, pastures, drainage ditches, and agricultural lands below 1,000 feet elevation, where disturbance by humans is common and sometimes

FIGURE 51. Waikiki duck ponds and Diamond Head about 1900. Photograph by A. Gartley, courtesy of Bernice P. Bishop Museum.

causes rapid changes in water level. They also inhabit stream and river valleys in densely wooded areas at higher elevations. The birds have a strong, rapid, usually silent flight, characteristically at low heights above the terrain. One bird was clocked at speeds of 45 to 50 miles per hour as it flew parallel to the road for more than a quarter of a mile.

The main breeding season on Kauai appears to extend from December through May, although the species apparently breeds throughout the year, inasmuch as nests or downy young have been found in every month except August.

Koloas have a nuptial flight, usually involving two or three birds. After taking flight, the birds "climb almost vertically to around one hundred feet elevation, and begin chasing in small circles. The favored suitor can be identified by his proximity to the female. The less favored male keeps a much greater distance usually from the very beginning of the flight. Occasionally, he makes a rapid dive to intercept the other or follows closely for a short time only to be driven off quickly by the favored suitor. The flight appears almost a formality. The matter seems to be largely decided before the birds take flight" (Swedberg 1967:13).

The well-concealed nests are built on the ground. Frequently they are constructed of honohono grass *(Commelina diffusa)* and are lined with varying amounts of the hen's down and breast feathers. Nests are typically between 12 and 18 inches in diameter and 4 inches deep.

The eggs are immaculate; white, buff, or light tan in color; and similar to, but smaller than, the eggs of domestic ducks. They are short-oval in shape, and, according to Munro (1944), average 2.12 by 1.29 inches in size. Clutch size is reported to vary from 2 to 10 eggs, although Swedberg believed that "two and three-egg clutches may indicate improper food or other conditions in captivity." Such small clutches reported for wild birds probably represent observations made before egg laying was complete. The mean clutch size for wild Koloa is 8.3 eggs. The incubation period in captivity has been determined to be 28 days. Koloas are capable of breeding when one year old.

Hen Koloas "sit tight" during incubation, as well as when caring for small ducklings, and they typically do not flush until an observer has approached to within 5 or 10 feet. Swedberg wrote of one hen that had allowed herself to be captured rather than abandon her brood.

The duckling is covered with a coat of light buffy yellow and chocolate brown, with the brown beginning at the base of the upper mandible and extending backward over the forehead, crown, and back of the head, and posteriorly to the rump (fig. 52). Brown down also is found on the sides and flanks, usually interspersed

FIGURE 52. Koloa family at Pohakuloa, Hawaii; the ducklings are about three weeks old. Courtesy of the Hawaii State Division of Fish and Game.

with buff-colored spots. A second brown stripe extends from the base of the bill backward through the eye to about the level of the ear opening. Swedberg's observations led him to believe that a brown spot, located below the posterior end of the eye stripe, is larger and darker in male ducklings.

The tail feathers of the juvenile plumage first make their appearance when the ducklings are three weeks old, but nine weeks elapse before the juvenile plumage is well enough developed to enable the birds to fly.

Extensive studies of food habits have not been conducted, but it is known that the Koloa feeds on a wide variety of plants (green algae, rice, several species of grasses) and animals (earthworms, dragonflies, several species of snails).

A Koloa restoration project was initiated at Pohakuloa by the State Division of Fish and Game during November 1972. Funds were provided by the Pittman-Robertson Act and the World Wildlife Fund. The program began with 21 ducks, 15 birds from Kauai, and the rest from mainland zoos. The breeding program has been very successful, with 56 ducklings raised during 1977 and 71, during 1978. A total of 293 Koloa have been released on the island of Hawaii. As of April 1979, 347 Koloa had been released on Oahu: 199 birds at Kawainui swamp; 103 at Waimea Falls Park; and 45 at Nuupia pond on the Kaneohe Marine Corps Air Station. Most releases are made during November or from January through March.

A "gentle release program" is followed, wherein the birds are caged in predator-proof pens at the release site. Usually the primary wing feathers are pulled out so that the birds cannot fly and thus injure themselves in the pen. The birds are able to adjust to their new environment as the new wing feathers are growing in. The wings of the ducks at each site are dyed a distinctive color in order to facilitate easy identification at later sightings; the birds also receive color-coded leg bands. A hen with six ducklings was seen at Waimea Falls Arboretum on March 16, 1978; the ducklings kept disappearing, however, until bullfrogs were removed from the pond. One bullfrog that I dissected contained the remains of one of the ducklings. Notes on the distribution of the Koloa on Oahu are given in the December 1978 issue of the *Elepaio*.

Lewin (1971) suggested that the release of mainland Mallards might pose "a distinct genetic threat to the endemic form through hybridization"; and, during April 1978, Ah Fat Lee placed Koloa drakes with Mallard hens and Mallard drakes with Koloa hens. He proved that the crosses were fertile and produced ducklings, thus demonstrating again the unforseen problems that can result from the indiscriminate introduction of exotic birds.

Laysan Duck
Anas laysanensis
(Color plate 24)

Because of its small size (15 to 17 inches in length), early writers called this species the Laysan Teal. It is a dark brown duck with a fairly extensive patch of white feathers surrounding the eye and extending backward to, or beyond, the auricular or ear region; the females tend to have more white on the head and neck. In some individuals the white covers a good portion of the head. Birds in first-year plumage may have very small, pale eye-rings. Males tend to have a blackish face and sometimes a greenish head. Both sexes have a bright purple-green speculum, somewhat richer in the males, bordered behind first by a band of black feathers and then by a band of white feathers. The legs and feet of males are a deeper orange than those of females. Males have a blue-green bill with black spots along the top of the upper mandible; females have a dull, brownish yellow bill with black spots along the lateral borders of the upper mandible. Fewer than 50 percent of the males have upturned upper tail coverts, a feature characteristic of the Mallard and, to a lesser extent, of the Hawaiian Duck.

Though nonmigratory, Laysan Ducks are capable of strong and fairly swift flight, but only infrequently are such flights observed. The birds exhibit a greatly reduced fear response to man, and generally seem reluctant to fly. When they do take to the air, they typically fly off only a short distance before landing again. Because of very high winds during storms, a reluctance to fly would be advantageous to any relatively sedentary species inhabiting the small island of Laysan. Warner (1963) noted that "resistance to water soaking was reduced" in these ducks and that several hours were required for complete drying of the feathers on nights when heavy showers occurred.

The Laysan Duck was reported to inhabit both Laysan Island and Lisianski Island (140 miles northwest of Laysan) in 1828, when these islands were visited by the Russian ship *Moller*. However, when Henry Palmer visited these islands for Walter Rothschild in 1891, he found no evidence of this duck on Lisianski.

The Laysan Duck was in danger of extinction during the first three decades of this century. Again, man was the agent of destruction. The birds were hunted for sport and for food during at least the early years of the guano mining company on Laysan, and, later, Japanese feather hunters used them for food. Although Theodore Roosevelt established the Hawaiian Islands National Wildlife Refuge in 1909, the area was not adequately patrolled, and Alfred M. Bailey believed there were only seven ducks left by 1912. Traveling on the Revenue Cutter *Thetis* as a member of the Biological Survey Expedition, Bailey (1956) worked on Laysan from December 22, 1912 to March 11, 1913. He described the condition of Laysan Island during that period:

The various buildings of the old guano company were in a sad state—the warehouses were disintegrating, and the headquarters bungalow had been left in a filthy condition by the departing Japanese poachers. Our first task was to make the house livable, and to clean out the cistern with the thought that we could catch a usable supply of water—a vain hope, for too many sea birds had been trapped and died there. A Japanese bath tub left by the poachers served admirably to catch water from the roof of our dwelling place.

The island was treeless, except for two coconut palms in front, and a hau tree on the side of our dwelling, and it was evident that the vegetation was fast disappearing due to the onslaught of the rabbits. There were a few stunted *Scaevola* bushes along the inner eastern slope where the man-o'-war-birds nested and extensive portulaca flats along the salt lagoon. Back of the house, and along the lagoon, were stands of wild tobacco. Formerly, as has been noted above, there were native palms, which had disappeared long before our time. On the northwest corner was a little cemetery with several graves enclosed by a disintegrating fence, and it was certain that all would soon disappear under the drifting sands.

Efforts to exterminate the rabbits at that time were unsuccessful, although Bailey and his companions killed more than 5,000 of them. Alexander Wetmore counted 20 Laysan Ducks during the visit of the Tanager Expedition of 1923. Since that time, when the last of the rabbits were killed, both the vegetation and the Laysan Duck have made a remarkable recovery. Brock (1951a, 1951b) found 33 birds in June 1950 and 39 birds in June the following year. During my visit to Laysan Island in March 1966, we donned headlights at night in order to net and band birds for the continuing studies made by personnel of the U.S. Fish and Wildlife Service.

Because of the dense vegetation inhabited by the ducks, as well as their nocturnal habits, it is virtually impossible to make an accurate count of the birds. Estimates of as many as 500 ducks were made in the 1960s, but there have been rapid and large fluctuations in the populations. As few as 25 birds were seen in 1973 and as many as 350 were counted in 1978 (Sincock and Kridler 1980). The downward trends are thought to occur, in part, because of severe winter storms, but the lowest population recorded in 1973 occurred when the water level in the lagoon was the lowest known during a nine-year period.

It is imperative for the future welfare of the Laysan Duck, as well as for the surviving honeycreeper and the tens of thousands of nesting seabirds, that predators such as rats, cats, dogs, and pest insects and plants (which alter the ecology of the island) be prevented from gaining access to Laysan Island, a warning first expressed by Walter Fisher (1906:800). Therefore, when a Japanese fishing vessel was wrecked on the reef at Laysan Island in 1970, the possibility of rats getting onto the island caused great concern; fortunately, none did so. Nevertheless, Sincock and Kridler recommended that all commercial fishing be prohibited within the refuge waters.

Laysan Ducks are most active at night, especially between sundown and about midnight. Then they search for the larvae of lepidopterous insects, which are particularly common among the clumps of *Boerhavia* plants. Warner (1963) found the cutworm larva of a noctuid moth (*Agrotis* sp.) to be a favorite food item during the spring and summer months. The ducks also feed on the larvae and pupae of flies and beetles which are common around the carcasses of seabirds, on the myriads of flies of the dipteran genus *Neoscatella* near the edge of the highly saline lake, as well as on crustaceans and other inhabitants of shallow tide pools. The birds seek shelter in the vegetation during the heat of the day.

Although Laysan Ducks use fresh water when it is available, they are adapted to survive without it. It is assumed that the birds obtain most of the water they require from the larvae they eat. It seems probable that this duck actually is adapted to drink seawater and to excrete the excess salts through its nasal salt gland, as do the seabirds. Udvardy (1963) wrote that the mean body temperature of the ducks was 40.6° C.

Pictures of the eggs and newly hatched young of the Laysan Duck were taken many years ago (figs. 53, 54), but the breeding biology has not been studied thoroughly. Nests are constructed on the ground in patches of a sedge, under chenopodium bushes, in morning glory plants, and under clumps of beach naupaka. Warner reported one observation of copulation during which he noted neither precopulatory nor postcopulatory display. The clutch apparently varies from 4 to 6 pale greenish eggs. Fisher found a nest with 6 eggs on May 18, 1902; 3 of the eggs had hatched by the following morning. Warner found a nest with 4 eggs on July 1, 1957, and David H. Woodside found another nest with 4 eggs on July 3, 1957. Eugene Kridler found a nest under construction on March 10, 1964. Warner and Woodside also saw 10 separate broods of young ducks between June 25 and July 3, 1957; the broods varied from 1 to 6 ducklings and averaged 3 birds per brood (Sincock and Kridler 1980). From these records we can conclude that the Laysan Duck has a breeding season lasting at least from late February into July.

There appear to be no detailed descriptions of the

FIGURE 53. Nest and eggs of the Laysan Duck. May 1902. Photograph by Walter K. Fisher, courtesy of Alfred M. Bailey.

newly hatched ducklings. The down is said to be darker in color than that of the Hawaiian Duck.

The first efforts to ensure the survival of the Laysan Duck were made in 1957, when 8 birds were brought from Laysan to the Honolulu Zoo. An additional 36 ducks were captured in 1958 and returned to Honolulu for acclimatization. Birds were then sent to a number of zoos and aviaries (Warner 1963). A pair of Laysan Ducks kept at the Pohakuloa propagation project hatched 4 of 7 eggs during the summer of 1977, the first successful nesting of this pair in nine years. The adults and their offspring were paired in 1978, but the three pairs of birds produced only 4 ducklings; as with the Nene earlier, inbreeding caused a high rate of infertility. Hence, during August 1978, 7 wild birds from Laysan were added to the breeding flock. These birds produced 14 ducklings during the 1979 breeding season.

The U.S. Fish and Wildlife Service transplanted 12 Laysan Ducks from Laysan to Southeast Island of Pearl and Hermes Reef on March 21, 1967. The first 2 ducks that were released flew out to sea and were not seen again; consequently, the remaining birds were wing clipped so that they would be unable to fly until after the annual molt and new wing feathers grew in. Eugene Kridler found a nest with 6 eggs there on July 4, 1967; only 2 ducks were found on September 27, and these had disappeared before the next visit to the island.

Warner had written in 1963: "I am compelled to stress more strongly the conviction that our success in preserving the bird under artificial conditions must not be a justification for relaxing vigilance in the protection of the wild population on Laysan Island. Any wild species loses much of its identity, its aesthetic value, and its ecologic significance when divorced from the habitat instrumental to its evolution."

One can agree with Warner's sentiments but also with Sincock and Kridler (1980), who wrote that there are some who believe that there is "a certain sanctity to having a wild, undisturbed, unmanaged, natural population of animals that takes precedence over the very extinction of such animals if the population must be 'managed' in order to preserve it. As wildlife managers, we disagree with that attitude, and only wish that Bryan's recommendations in 1911 for transplanting some of the species that later became extinct at Laysan Island had been carried out while there was still time.

FIGURE 54. Eggs and newly hatched ducklings of the Laysan Duck. May 1902. Photograph by Walter K. Fisher, who focused his camera on the fly sitting on one of the eggs. Courtesy of Alfred M. Bailey.

The Laysan rail might be with us today had some been returned to Laysan Island before the life of the species ran out at Midway in the early 1940s.''

ORDER FALCONIFORMES

FAMILY ACCIPITRIDAE

(HAWKS, KITES, EAGLES,
AND OLD WORLD VULTURES)

The Accipitridae contains 205 species of diurnal birds of prey, or flesh eaters, which are distributed throughout the land and coastal areas of the world except Antarctica. The members of this family range from 10 to 14 inches in length (Sharp-shinned Hawk, *Accipiter striatus*) to powerful and majestic birds 38 inches long (Harpy Eagle, *Harpia harpyja*), and some Old World vultures are even bigger. Only one member of this large family reached the Hawaiian Islands and, ac-

cording to all available evidence, it has always inhabited the island of Hawaii only.

The Io or Hawaiian Hawk
Buteo solitarius
(Color plate 25)

The Io has two color phases. Dark-phase birds have dark brown plumage both above and below. Light-phase birds have dark upperparts and light buff underparts, frequently streaked with darker feathers. The feet and legs are yellowish in both sexes and in both color phases. As is characteristic of birds of prey, the females are larger than the males. Overall length of females is given as 16 to 18 inches; of adult males, as 15.5 inches.

Buteo hawks are large, heavy-set birds with broad wings and broad, relatively short, rounded tails. They habitually soar in wide circles, often at considerable heights above the ground. However, a soaring bird seen on Hawaii is not necessarily an Io because the diurnal Pueo also soars.

The Io is found on the slopes of Mauna Loa, on both the windward and Kona coasts, and less commonly on Mauna Kea. I saw three hawks over a distance of three miles along the road near the Dillingham Ranch at Puuwaawaa on August 8, 1969, and I have seen hawks near Hilo.

In reporting on a two-year study of the hawk in Hawaii Volcanoes National Park, Morrison (1969) concluded that the "Hawaiian Hawk is likely to be found *anywhere* in the park below about 8500 feet where woody vegetation exists. The barren sections of the park are apparently not part of the normal hawk range. The hawk does not show a preference for any specific vegetation type within the park."

In comparing his data on hawk observations for the period 1938 to 1949 with those of Morrison, Baldwin (1969a) concluded that the hawk probably had increased in numbers in Volcanoes National Park. Nevertheless, 62 sightings of hawks over a period of two years does not suggest a large population, and the Hawaiian Hawk has been placed on the list of endangered species. The total population has been estimated by personnel of the U.S. Fish and Wildlife Service to be in the low hundreds. The chief reasons for the decline in numbers of this interesting and beneficial bird are believed to be shooting by uninformed people who consider all hawks to be "chicken hawks," and by the drastic alteration of the environment by man and the animals he has introduced.

Our ignorance of the basic biology of the endemic birds is truly incredible. Very few nests of this species have been found and, consequently, little is known of the breeding habits. W. A. Bryan (1906) apparently was the first to describe and publish a photograph of the nest of the Hawaiian Hawk. The nest, containing two well-feathered young, was collected from an ohia tree "some distance" from Pahala during early October 1902. The young were killed and stuffed. Bryan described the nest as follows:

It is composed of sticks a little more than a quarter of an inch thick and twelve inches in length, which appear to have been gathered from the ground. These are all loosely piled in the upright fork without an attempt at giving the structure form until the bowl of the nest is reached, when they take on a more systematic arrangement to conform to the shape required for a nest. Into this pile of sticks the Io has introduced the stems and fronds of ferns, and of them it has made a loose floor or lining for the nest. The structure measured over 18 inches from out to out across the top, was 15 inches

high, with the hollow depression some three inches in depth. No trace of egg shells could be found about the nest, hence the color and form of the eggs remain unknown.

The few nests reported since that time indicate a nesting season lasting from May to October. H. Eddie Smith observed a pair in copulation in the Kilauea Forest Reserve on June 9, 1974, and found a nest in an ohia tree with "several young birds" that day (*Elepaio* 35:21). Shallenberger (1977) described a nest in a koa tree that contained one large nestling on August 11, 1976. The female of this pair was a light-phased bird, the male was the dark phase. Two pellets regurgitated by the adult birds were ⅜ by ⅝ and 1 × 1.5 inches in dimensions. By dissecting the pellets and by watching the adults bring food to the nest, Shallenberger learned that the adults were preying on wild turkey chicks, a nestling House Finch, and other unidentified passerine birds; he found no evidence that the hawks were bringing rodents to the nestling at this nest, but he did see another hawk with a rat in its talons.

Ernest Pung and boy scouts at the Honokaia boy scout camp found an Io nest about 20 feet from the ground in a eucalyptus (*Eucalyptus robusta*) tree during June 1973. There were three chicks in the nest by early July, but two of these later disappeared. An average of "six to eight rodents was brought in daily, plus an occasional frog and smaller bird" for the single nestling. The young bird left the nest at the end of the eighth week after hatching (*Honolulu Star-Bulletin,* September 20, 1973, page B-12).

Although I have found no detailed descriptions of the eggs, clutch size is said to be two or three eggs. Walker (1969) mentioned a nest with a "single light blue egg" found by Harry Fergerstrom during May 1961. The nest was built in a mamani tree at an elevation of about 6,000 feet on Mauna Kea. Winston Banko and George Schattauer visited a nest in the Kaapuna area of South Kona on June 17, 1969. The nest contained a single egg, which apparently was deserted, and Banko sent the egg to the Patuxent Wildlife Research Center for chemical analysis. Traces of DDT and of polychlorinated biphenyls were found in the egg.

In writing of his experience as an assistant to Henry Palmer in the 1890s, Munro (1944) said that the "birds we killed were gorged with mice, rats, spiders, hawkmoths and caterpillars." One stomach contained the remains of a Ricebird. Baldwin wrote of a hawk that had just killed a Common Myna; and of watching another hawk, soaring about 100 feet above the ground, that had suddenly glided downward and seized a dragonfly out of the air.

Tomich (1971b) told of the food found in the stomachs of two hawks that had been found dead. One stomach contained two adult praying mantises *(Tenodera angustipennis),* part of one Barred Dove, one whole house mouse and part of a second. The second hawk had eaten a crayfish *(Procambarrus clarkii),* an introduced species.

Like other hawks, the Hawaiian Hawk utters shrill, high-pitched screams, described by some as sounding like *kee-oh!* or *i-o!* Shallenberger mentioned a second call that was "more abrupt and pure in tone" than the scream. He referred to the food calls of the chick as being "high-pitched and throaty."

Dr. Robert L. Pyle told of the possible relationship between a volcanic eruption at Kilauea Volcano on Hawaii and the presumed sighting of a Hawaiian Hawk on Oahu during 1977. On September 25, a new phase of continuous strong activity began. "At this time, the normal easterly trade winds had been replaced by generally light winds from the south. By the 28th, on the date of the observation of the buteo, volcanic dust was already discernible in the air over Oahu. Two days later, a statewide air stagnation alert was issued—a very rare event in Hawaii." Pyle concluded that "one might hypothesize that an 'Io could have been driven from its home range by the sudden burst of volcanic activity on September 25, and might have drifted with the volcanic dust on the abnormal southerly winds until it reached Oahu, some 380 kilometers (235 miles) to the northwest" *(Elepaio* 38:67).

ORDER GRUIFORMES

FAMILY RALLIDAE

(RAILS, CRAKES, COOTS, AND GALLINULES)

This family contains small- to medium-sized, running, wading, and swimming birds, most of which inhabit marshes, ponds, and lakes, and a few that live in drier regions (forests or plains). Some are chicken-like in appearance and are called swamp hens, marsh hens, mud hens, or moor hens in different parts of the world. Rails with short, conical bills are called crakes in Europe. Coots and gallinules have been described as rails that are specialized for life in a particular habitat of more open water. Rails have narrow bodies ("thin as a rail") and are especially adapted for running rapidly through dense marsh grasses and other underbrush. Rails are relatively weak fliers, although continental forms often make long migratory flights, usually at night. Rails also are noted for having reached oceanic islands where they evolved into flightless birds. At least four members of the rail family reached the Hawaiian Islands. Two are now extinct, and the other two are endangered.

Laysan Rail

Porzana (Porzanula) palmeri

(Color plate 35)

This species had a historical life of 116 years. It was discovered in 1828 and it almost certainly became extinct in 1944. Sailors on the Russian ship *Moller* reported seeing this bird on Laysan and the same or a very similar species on Lisianski Island in 1828. No birds were collected, however, and the first specimens were obtained on Laysan by Henry Palmer of the Rothschild expedition in 1891. At that time, no rail was found on Lisianski.

The Laysan Rail was one of the smaller members of the family, being about 150 mm (6 inches) in length. The birds were flightless and had small rounded wings 54 mm long; the tail also was very short (25.4 mm, or about 1 inch). The number of primary flight feathers had become reduced from 10 to 8. The legs and feet were well developed. The straight, stout bill was 18 mm long. The bill and feet were green; the iris was ruby red. The feathers of the back were pale brown but had strongly contrasting russet-brown to chocolate-colored shafts; the scapular feathers, flanks, and sides were sandy brown; the top of the head was pale brown with dark streaks; the sides of the head, a line over each eye, and the throat were slate-gray; and the breast was mousy gray (fig. 55).

Baldwin (1945b, 1947a) summarized the known information about the Laysan Rail acquired from published sources and by talking with several people who had seen live rails, either on Laysan or Midway.

Laysan Rails were active, swift, and restless. They were agile when running over the sand between grass tussocks, but they also walked mouselike through the vegetation and in and out of burrows dug in the sand by petrels and shearwaters. The rails also were fearless. T. M. Blackman noted that the birds would come to bathe in a pan of fresh water only three feet from where he was sitting. Hadden (1941:40) wrote: "If you make no swift or sudden movement, but sit real still they will come right up to you and run around and between your feet, looking for flies." They came into buildings in search of flies, moths, or scraps of meat. Several authors have commented on how easy it was to net the birds. Walter Fisher (1906:801) wrote: "We caught all our specimens with an ordinary dip net. Usually it was merely necessary to place the net on the ground edgewise, when presently a rail would make its appearance and proceed to examine the new phenomenon at close range. Sometimes they would fairly walk into the net."

The rails were omnivorous, although the bulk of their diet apparently consisted of animal matter: flies,

FIGURE 55. Laysan Rail on Laysan Island. December 1912. Photograph by Alfred M. Bailey, courtesy of Alfred M. Bailey.

maggots, moths, caterpillars, beetles, earwigs, and spiders. They also ate decaying flesh from the carcasses of seabirds, as well as the maggots of the blowflies (family Sarcophagidae) and dermestid beetles (family Dermestidae) that hatched in the carcasses. At a certain stage, the maggots emerged from the carcasses to crawl into the sand to pupate. At these times, the rails would dig up the maggots and pupae by flipping the sand sidewise with their beaks. The rails were fast enough to snatch flies from midair. A small part of their diet consisted of seeds and green plant materials.

Laysan Rails also were noted for eating the eggs of the smaller terns and petrels. Writing in his diary in 1891, Henry Palmer said: "While out this morning both my assistant [George C. Munro] and I saw a little rail break and eat an egg. We had disturbed from its nest a noddy *(Anous)*. Immediately the rail ran up and began to strike at the egg shell with its bill, but the egg being large and hard he was quite a long time before making a hole. The rail would jump high into the air, and come down with all its force on the egg, until it accomplished the task, which once done the egg was soon emptied." Although the rails sometimes broke open eggs, they are said usually to have waited until Laysan Finches broke through the shells with their more powerful bills and then to have chased the finches away to eat the egg contents.

Bailey (1956:89) also wrote about the tameness of the rails and their taste for eggs: "During late December [1912] when the heavy rain flooded out the albatrosses' nests, Willett and I salvaged many of the eggs. We would sit upon the sand, and blow the eggs, and several rails were sure to be on hand to feed upon the contents. They would climb over our outstretched legs in their eagerness for food." In mid-February of 1913, Bailey began to capture rails to transplant to Lisianski and Midway: "It proved easy, for we merely took a little box and a six-inch stick to hold up one side of it. A chicken-egg—which the rails could not break—was placed for bait, and when half a dozen birds were inside, jumping off the ground to give more force to the beaks' strike on the egg, we merely pulled the string. We caught more than one hundred [rails]."

The Laysan Rail had several callnotes. Wild birds "rattled," their throats swollen and their bills opened slightly. Walter Fisher (1906) saw two rails "approach each other with feathers erect and when close together begin rattling in each other's face. Then they suddenly ceased and slunk away in opposite directions." Writing of captive birds, Frohawk (1892) said that they chirp incessantly during the day, uttering from "one to three soft, short, and clear notes; but soon after dark they all, as if by one given signal, strike up a most peculiar chorus, which lasts but a few seconds, and then all remain silent. I can only compare the sound to a handful or two of marbles being thrown on a glass roof and then descending in a succession of bounds, striking and restriking the glass at each ricochet."

In writing of a male and female on Midway, T. M. Blackman (quoted by Baldwin 1947a) reported that "they sat several minutes close together, close to main stem of a bush on the shady side and in turn held their heads down close to the ground while the other picked among the feathers at the top of head and back of neck." This kind of behavior is now referred to as mutual preening.

The breeding season on Laysan apparently lasted from April through July, although none of the early expeditions visited Laysan during the period from July through November. The nests were built on or close to the ground in juncus thickets and grass tussocks on Laysan, and under *Scaevola* and other plants on Midway. The nests appear to have been roofed over, with an entrance on one side. Nests with eggs were found during May and June on Laysan, but downy young were seen on Midway in March (figs. 56, 57).

Baldwin (1947a) pointed out that about a dozen clutches seem to have been recorded on Laysan, "and of them about two-thirds consisted of three eggs and the rest of two." Walter Donaghho, however, found a

FIGURE 56. Nest and eggs of the Laysan Rail, Laysan Island. May 10, 1902. Photograph by Walter K. Fisher, courtesy of Alfred M. Bailey.

nest on Sand Island of Midway Atoll with 4 eggs on June 20, 1941. W. A. Bryan (Dill and Bryan 1912) said that he saw one pair of rails "with a flock of five young following them," but there is no way of knowing whether all five were the offspring of that pair. Nevertheless, clutch size of the Laysan Rail was considerably smaller than that of Mainland rails, which commonly lay 6 to 10 eggs in a clutch.

The eggs of the Laysan Rail were described as "bluntly ovate," meaning that they were not distinctly pointed at one end, as is characteristic for most bird eggs. Fisher gave the following description: "The ground color is a pale olive buff, closely spotted with pale clay color or raw sienna, and faint lilac gray. The maculations are distributed fairly evenly over the egg, but in some specimens seem more crowded at the broader end. The clay color is brightest and seems to predominate. . . . None of our specimens present the

creamy buff ground-color mentioned by Rothschild, or figured in his 'Avifauna of Laysan.' "

The incubation and fledgling periods were never determined. The newly hatched chick had a complete covering of black down; the legs and feet were black; the bill was yellow. Hadden (1941) said that by the time they were five days old the chicks were able to run as fast as the adults, and that the two- to three-day-old chick "looks like a black velvet marble rolling along the ground. Its little feet and legs are so small and move so fast that they can hardly be seen."

Palmer made no estimate of the rail population when he visited Laysan Island in 1891. It remained for Dill and Bryan (1912) to estimate that there are "about 2,000 rails on the island." Bailey, who worked on Laysan Island from late December 1912 to March 11, 1913, reported that the vegetation was rapidly being destroyed by the hordes of rabbits. The island was next

FIGURE 57. Laysan Rail on its nest. May 1902. Photograph by Walter K. Fisher, courtesy of Alfred M. Bailey.

visited by Alexander Wetmore and other personnel of the Tanager Expedition in 1923, twenty years after the rabbits and guinea pigs had been released. We have already quoted (chap. 1) Wetmore's description of Laysan as then being a "barren waste of sand." He could find only two rails; there were none when the island was visited again in 1936.

The Laysan Rail may have been transplanted to Eastern Island of Midway Atoll as early as 1887 (Baldwin 1945b), and it is known that a pair was released there on July 13, 1891. Bailey and Willett collected "more than one hundred" rails on Laysan and liberated them on Lisianski Island and Eastern Island in March 1913. Bailey wrote that the birds released on Lisianski Island probably did not survive long because "the vegetation was disappearing due to the ravages of rabbits," which had been introduced about the same time that Captain Schlemmer took them to Laysan Island. A Captain Anderson took seven pairs of rails from Midway and released them on one of the small islands at Pearl and Hermes Reef in 1929 (Fisher and Baldwin 1945). However, that was an ill-advised site for release because the islands in that reef are too low,

and, when George Kaufmann visited Pearl and Hermes Reef in 1930 he found neither rails nor any live vegetation, presumably because storms had inundated the island. Biologists now realize that a good understanding of a bird's ecological requirements must be had before a potentially good release site can be selected. For any animal, these include provision for adequate food, shelter, and safe breeding places.

Eastern Island in Midway Atoll obviously filled all of the needs of the Laysan Rail; by 1905 the rails were said to be almost as common on Eastern Island as they were on Laysan. In 1910 employees of the cable company released rails on Sand Island, in part because the birds ate caterpillars and insects from the vegetation. An estimate (probably greatly exaggerated) was made of 5,000 rails on the two islands at Midway in 1922. T. M. Blackman found rails numerous on both islands in 1939 and 1940. In 1943, however, roof rats of two color phases got onto both islands from navy ships (at the time, these were listed as 80 percent roof rats and 20 percent "black rats"). The last rails were seen on Sand Island on November 15, 1943; the last on Eastern Island, probably in June 1944. Fisher and Baldwin searched for rails on both islands for eleven days in May 1945 and felt certain that the species was then extinct.

Hawaiian Rail
Porzana (Pennula) sandwichensis
(Color plate 36)

So few specimens were collected and so little was written about the flightless rail that was obtained on Captain Cook's last voyage that confusion long existed as to whether one or two species of rails inhabited the island of Hawaii. Munro (1944) mentioned two: the Hawaiian Rail and the "Spotted Hawaiian Rail." Stresemann (1950:80–81) and Greenway (1958:236) explained the confusion and the synonymy in names, and suggested that the paler coloration of one specimen might have represented the immature plumage of a single species. Greenway gave the following descriptions of the two forms:

Dark form: Top of the head brown with a faint grayish tinge, lores fulvescent, ear coverts gray, cheeks deeper reddish brown (vinous). Back dark reddish chocolate, the lower back with darker centers to the feathers. Throat and breast reddish brown shading to grayish chocolate on the belly, flanks, and under tail coverts.

Paler form: Black spots on feathers of the back more apparent, giving a mottled appearance.

Perkins (1903:453–454) and Munro (1944:51) believed that the Moho, as the Hawaiians called the rail, had once inhabited Molokai and perhaps other of the main islands; but the only evidence for this belief is a statement made by Perkins: "It certainly inhabited Molokai, and the late R. Meyer, when I stayed with him in 1893, assured me that when he first came to that island (some 30 or 40 years before) it was well known to the natives, and they even offered to catch specimens for him. Unfortunately at that time he took no great interest in the matter," and, consequently, no specimens were ever collected from Molokai or any other island except Hawaii.

Perkins wrote that "the Moho frequented the open country below the continuous forest, and the open country covered with scrub that lies within the forest belt. Its last home on Hawaii appears to have been the rather open country which lies just outside the heavily timbered part of the Olaa district on the smooth or pahoehoe lava, and the country between the same heavy forests and the crater of Kilauea." However, the Hawaiian Rail presumably was already extinct before Perkins came to Hawaii. The last rails were collected about 1864, and the last were seen about 1884. The nest, eggs, and young were never described.

The causes of extinction of this small (about 5.5 inches in total length), flightless rail are unknown, but it seems certain that rats, dogs, and cats played a large role in the extermination of this unique species. Perkins wrote that "in olden times the Moho and the small native rat . . . shared the distinction of providing sport for the chiefs, who hunted them with bow and arrow." The rail presumably was close to extinction when the mongoose was introduced to Hawaii in 1883.

Hawaiian Gallinule
Gallinula chloropus sandvicensis

The Alae ula is a subspecies of the Common Gallinule of North America and Eurasia. The Hawaiian birds are nonmigratory and have been inhabitants of the islands for an unknown length of time.

Munro (1944:52) wrote that "this bird, according to tradition, is one of the great benefactors of the Hawaiian people. Fire was unknown to the people, hence they could neither cook their food nor warm themselves during the cold weather. The bird took pity on them and, flying to the home of the gods, stole a blazing brand and carried it back to earth. On this return flight its formerly white forehead was scorched by the flames; hence its name *alae,* signifying a burnt forehead. The descendants of this valiant bird all bear the red mark of honor."

The adults (sexes look alike) are slate-gray birds, darker on the head and neck and lighter on the back, breast, and sides. White feathers under the tail and along the flanks are conspicuous field marks. The gallinule has a short, mostly red, chickenlike bill (the tip of the bill is light green to yellowish). The red of the bill continues upward over the forehead in a red to scarlet-vermilion frontal shield (a hard, featherless area). The tarsi and toes are green to yellow-green; there is a scarlet "garter" surrounding the tibia. Hawaiian birds are much darker and blacker (less bluish gray) and have less white in the plumage than the North American subspecies. Juvenile birds are dusky olive-brown to grayish brown and have a pale yellow or brown bill.

Gallinules are birds of freshwater ponds, marshes, irrigation ditches, reservoirs, taro patches, and, formerly, rice fields. The birds require relatively dense marginal vegetation, and they are far more secretive than coots, seldom being seen on deeper, more open bodies of water, although the birds swim well. They "pump" their heads and necks when swimming.

Gallinules eat "algae, aquatic insects, and molluscs of which there is an abundance in all range except where the periodic poisoning operations by sugar-cane plantations may affect the supply" (Schwartz and Schwartz 1949).

These birds formerly were found on all of the main

islands except Niihau and Lanai. They are now apparently limited to Kauai and Oahu. Attempts to reestablish the species on Hawaii and Maui appear to have been unsuccessful.

Writing in the early 1940s, Munro could say that "a small colony of these birds frequent and breed in the open lagoon and marshy ground close to the Moana Park, in Honolulu. The coot and migratory birds also come there. The lagoon would make an interesting addition to the park with its reedy margin and feathered inhabitants." Repeated draining and filling of wetland areas throughout the islands has continued, and the gallinule is an endangered species. Because of their secretive habits, we do not know precisely how many birds still survive. The following were recorded during the annual waterbird census conducted by state and federal biologists in January 1978 and 1979: Oahu, 28 birds (1978), 155 (1979); Kauai, 81 (1978), 79 (1979). These figures, indeed, indicate a dangerously low population of gallinules in the state. When Charles and Elizabeth Schwartz worked in Hawaii during the late 1940s, gallinules also occurred on Maui and Molokai. Low populations of any bird species are in danger because of the disastrous effects of an inadequate gene pool and because of the possibility of some unusual mortality factor. For example, during January 1975, there was an outbreak of waterfowl botulism at the Lihue Plantation settling basin on Kauai. Fortunately, few birds were infected by this fatal agent at that time.

The U.S. Fish and Wildlife Service now manages refuges on Kauai and Oahu. Hanalei and Huleia National Wildlife Refuges are on Kauai; on Oahu the James Campbell National Wildlife Refuge contains Kii pond and Punamano pond near Kahuku, and the Pearl Harbor National Wildlife Refuge consists of two areas, the Waipa Refuge near Pearl City and the Honouliuli Refuge near West Loch (*Elepaio* 37:125; 38:61). These refuges are of critical importance for the survival of the gallinule and other Hawaiian waterbirds.

In addition to the destruction of the birds' essential habitat in the name of "progress," mongooses, rats, and cats are serious predators of the birds. Gallinules are protected by both state and federal laws, but they are shot illegally, particularly on Kauai.

The gallinule builds its nest of reeds and other aquatic vegetation. Like its continental relatives, the bird is thought to lay large clutches of eggs, but there is a dearth of information about the breeding habits of the Hawaiian birds. Munro said that "the egg is light brown, thinly covered with small dark brown spots thicker at larger end, ovoid, 1.75 × 1.25 inches."

A pair of gallinules with 4 large young and 9 other birds were seen in the Kaelepulu Canal, Kailua, on January 13, 1977; two pairs raised chicks during April and May 1978 in "the flooded pasture along Hamakua Drive in Kailua," and 4 chicks and 14 adults and immature birds were seen there during July (*Elepaio* 39:62). Robert J. Shallenberger studied a nest at the Honouliuli pond at West Loch during 1974. The nest was built in a clump of cattails where the water was about 3 feet deep. The nest held 7 eggs on February 13; 6 of the eggs hatched on March 1, whereupon the chicks hid in the cattails. Shallenberger watched the brood feed on sedges near the edge of the pond, and he saw the adult gallinules chase coots away from the young by charging with their heads lowered and outstretched (*Elepaio* 35:19). Thomas Telfer saw 5 downy gallinule chicks at the Ahukini Reservoir on Kauai on November 29, 1977. Gallinules apparently nest throughout the year in Hawaii, but there may be an increase in nesting from March to August.

The newly hatched gallinule chick has black down on the wings and body; the feathers of the throat have whitish, curled tips; the top of the head is scantily covered with black, hairlike down. The bill is bright red. The chicks are precocial and are able to swim within a few hours after hatching, and then leave the nest. The young chicks are fed by the adults and stay with them for several weeks.

Hawaiian Coot
(*Fulica americana alai*)
(Color plate 26)

The coot, Alae keokeo in Hawaiian, is a subspecies of the American Coot, which has a breeding range extending from Canada, south to Panama. The Hawaiian birds are nonmigratory and, like the gallinule, have been permanent residents in the islands for an unknown period of time.

Coots (the sexes look alike) are dark slate-gray birds with white under tail coverts. The head feathers may be slightly glossy, exhibiting dark bluish or greenish reflections at close range but appearing black from a distance. The bill and frontal shield are white. Hawaiian birds are smaller, darker in color, and have a more slender bill and a larger frontal shield than North American birds. Both Palmer and Munro mentioned specimens from the 1890s that had a chocolate-brown frontal shield, and said that the Hawaiians called them *alae awi*. Juvenile birds are brownish and have a smaller yellowish brown frontal shield that gradually turns white. Coots differ from gallinules in having lobed toes. They also are more ducklike in appearance.

Large winter concentrations of coots occur in some habitats, but Udvardy (1960b) concluded that these were not the result of an influx of migrant birds from North America (see also *Elepaio* 38:73).

The coot occurs on all of the main islands except Lanai. The total population, however, is far lower than it was thirty years ago. As many as a thousand coots were seen on Kaelepulu pond in Kailua during the 1940s; unfortunately, Kaelepulu pond was dredged to make Enchanted Lake, where there is little suitable habitat for the waterbirds. More than 800 coots were seen on the Menehune Fish pond on Kauai in 1969. From 453 (1973) to 2,360 (1975) coots were counted during the annual waterbird censuses conducted by the Division of Fish and Game between 1969 and 1978; but only 424 coots were recorded on all the islands during January 1979, as compared with more than 1,100 birds in 1978.

The reasons for the decline of coot populations are similar to those for the gallinule: elimination of ponds and marshes and predation by mongooses, feral cats and dogs, and by large-mouthed bass, bullfrogs, and Black-crowned Night Herons on downy young. The coot was on the gamebird list until 1939, and birds still are killed illegally, sometimes by taro farmers. Herbicide and pesticide residues probably are polluting the habitat of the waterbirds. "Poisoning operations by sugar plantations for the control of filamentous algae clogging the drainage ditches and eradication of vegetative growth and insects along the margins of irrigation ditches may have an adverse effect upon coots by destroying much of their food and harming them directly if they consume the poisoned food" (Schwartz and Schwartz 1949).

Coots occupy the same general areas as gallinules, but they prefer more open water and are often found on brackish water. They obtain food by hunting near the surface, and also by diving. Like the gallinule, the coot pumps its head and neck back and forth when swimming. When taking off from the surface of the water, the coot "skitters" or paddles its feet along the surface.

Coots build large, floating nests of aquatic vegetation, hence their need for deeper water. The nests may be anchored to vegetation and rise and fall with changes in water level. Coots apparently nest throughout the year in Hawaii.

Schwartz and Schwartz (1952) reported finding 48 nests on Kaelepulu Pond, Oahu, on May 14, 1947. Three were under construction, 15 held eggs, and 30 were old nests. Most of the nests were located in the open water but near the outer margin of the aquatic vegetation surrounding the pond. These plants were bulrush (*Scirpus validus*), a submerged grass (*Paspalum vaginatum*), and beach akulikuli (*Batis martina*). One nest, 2 feet in maximum diameter, consisted of a partially floating platform of bulrushes; the nest bowl was 6 inches in diameter and 2 inches deep; the rim of the nest was about 3 inches above the water. A second nest was composed primarily of grass but was strengthened with bulrush stems; still other nests were built exclusively of beach akulikuli or of combinations of it and bulrush. Some nests had a landing stage on one side which the adults used in entering and leaving the nest. The clutches in the 15 nests on May 14 varied from 4 to 10 eggs and averaged 6.1 eggs. Coots sometimes build resting platforms ("false nests") close to an active nest.

Two full-grown juvenile coots and a pair with two newly hatched chicks were seen at the Honouliuli refuge on Oahu on March 14, 1976 (*Elepaio* 36:138). Olsen (1971) found five nests at Kii pond, near Kahuku, on April 29, 1971: two nests were being built, one had 3 eggs, one, 5 eggs, and one nest held 3 eggs and 2 newly hatched chicks. Coleman (1978) reported that five pairs of coots were nesting at the Kakahaia National Wildlife Refuge on Molokai during 1977 and 1978; five nests were still active on January 24, 1978. Warren B. King found a nest with 4 eggs at Kanaha pond, Maui, on September 1, 1970. Joseph Medeiros and Edwin Andrade of the Division of Fish and Game found 46 coot nests at Kanaha and Kealia ponds, Maui, during April and May 1976; they reported an 83.7 percent hatchability for 43 eggs. Very few coots remain on Kauai during the spring months of the year, and it is assumed that most of the birds fly to Niihau to nest.

Seven eggs measured by the Schwartzes averaged 47.7 mm by 34.5 mm. They described the color as light buffy tan, speckled with tiny flecks of dark brown or tan. The incubation period apparently has not been determined for the Hawaiian birds.

The newly hatched chicks are covered with black down except on the head, neck, and throat, where the down is reddish orange. The down is short or absent on the forehead and crown, giving the bird a bald-headed appearance. The bill is red to orange-red, tipped with black. Like gallinule chicks, the young are able to swim shortly after they hatch and their down has dried.

ORDER CHARADRIIFORMES
FAMILY RECURVIROSTRIDAE
(STILTS AND AVOCETS)

The members of this family are slender birds with long slender bills and very long legs. The family name describes the bill of the avocet, which is curved upward (recurved) toward the tip. The Ibisbill (*Ibidorhyncha struthersii*), which nests at elevations of 10,000 feet and higher in the Himalayas, has a bill that curves downward (decurved). The bills of stilts are straight. Stilts are wading birds and they usually probe into mud for their food; whereas, avocets sweep their bills back and forth through the water in search of food.

Hawaiian Stilt
Himantopus mexicanus knudseni
(Color plate 27)

The Hawaiian Stilt, or Aeo, is a race of the Black-necked Stilt that is found on both the east and west coasts of the mainland United States and south to Brazil, Peru, and the Galápagos Islands (Hamilton 1975). Adult males are glossy black above; females have a dull brownish back. Both sexes have a white forehead and underparts; the tail is pale gray; the eye is red. The legs vary from light to dark pink. Juvenile birds have salt-and-pepper tipped feathers on the back of the neck, pale pink legs, and brown eyes. The Hawaiian race differs from continental races in having the black extending lower on the forehead as well as around to the sides of the neck (sometimes to the front of the neck), and by having a longer bill, tarsus, and tail. The gray tail feathers also tend to be tipped with black. The birds average about 16 inches in length.

The stilt is endemic to the islands of Niihau, Kauai, Oahu, Molokai, Maui, and Hawaii. Studies of color-marked birds have proven that stilts fly from one island to another, especially between Niihau and Kauai.

The stilt was considered a game bird until 1941, and it still is sometimes shot illegally. The birds also are subject to predation by mongooses and feral dogs and cats. However, a major reason for the decline of this species has been the drainage of marshes and other wetland areas. Kanaha Pond on Maui is of prime importance to the stilt because it appears to be protected by a State Regulation (1978). However, the County of Maui built a sewage treatment plant adjacent to the pond with an injection system that environmentalists believe will pollute the waters of this spring-fed pond. The establishment of an undefiled refuge at Kealia Pond, also on Maui, is essential for the preservation of the waterbirds because the birds use both areas at different times of the year and under different conditions.

The United States military services have done far more than the State government to provide essential habitat for the endangered waterbirds. The refuges at Pearl Harbor already have been mentioned. In addition, the Nuupia ponds at the Kaneohe Bay Marine Corps Air Station have been improved for the benefit of the stilt and other birds. The station received the Secretary of Defense's Environmental Quality Award for its conservation program in 1976; in 1978, the Secretary of the Navy's Environmental Protection Award.

The estimated summer stilt population on all of the islands from 1969 to 1978 has varied from 857 in 1971 to 1,477 in 1976. Only 523 birds were counted during January 1979, however. This low population parallels the low population for the Hawaiian Coot, but no explanation is available.

The breeding season of the Hawaiian Stilt may extend from mid-February into August. Robert J. Shallenberger found 4 recently hatched chicks on the Kaneohe Marine Corps Air Station on March 10, 1974. Most nests have been found during April, May, and June. Richard A. Coleman found a nest with 4 eggs at the James Campbell National Wildlife Refuge on Oahu on June 29, 1978. Warren B. King found a nest at Kanaha pond, Maui, in which the eggs hatched between June 26 and 30, 1970. I found 3 nests, each with 4 eggs, at Kanaha pond on May 23, 1974, and 1 nest with 4 eggs on July 5, 1972; the previous day, I had seen a nest with 2 eggs and 2 newly hatched chicks. Joseph Medeiros and Edwin Andrade found 20 stilt nests at Kanaha pond during May 1976: 12 of the nests had been built on the islands that had been constructed for nesting; they found several nests with 5 eggs, one more than the typical clutch; there is a record of a nest with 7 eggs. Personnel of the Division of Fish and Game found 32 nests with eggs at the Nuupia ponds on Oahu during May 1977. Unusually heavy rains on May 12 raised the water level so much that 12 nests were flooded; some eggs were found to have puncture marks that suggested predation by mongooses. Both events are frequent causes of stilt nest failure. Richard A. Coleman found the first floating nest of the stilt near Kahuku on May 16, 1978; the nest was built exclusively of water hyssop, *Bacopa monnieria* (*Elepaio* 39:42).

The nest of the stilt is a simple "scrape" made on the ground in sparsely vegetated areas by the birds themselves; small stones, bits of wood, and other debris often are added to form a partial lining. The normal clutch is 4 eggs. The eggs have a smoke-gray ground color, heavily marked with blackish brown spots, splotches, and lines scattered irregularly over the surface and not concentrated around the larger end of the egg. The eggs are beautifully camouflaged, and it is difficult to locate the nests even when the adults indicate by their loud, persistent alarm calls and distraction behavior that a nest is nearby (fig. 58).

The incubation period varies between 24 and 26 days (Berger 1967). The newly hatched young are covered with a coat of variegated brown, buff, and black down, which makes them very difficult to find when they leave the nest (fig. 59). The white egg tooth is conspicuous near the tip of the upper mandible. The precocial young are able to run about as soon as their down has dried, and within a few hours they character-

FIGURE 58. Eggs of the Hawaiian Stilt. The egg in the lower right is "pipped," and the young bird is in the process of breaking out of the shell. Kaneohe Marine Corps Air Station, Oahu. May 27, 1964.

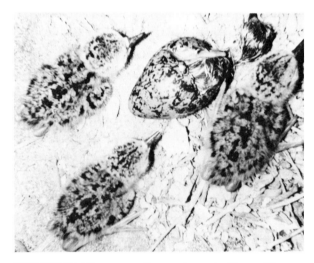

FIGURE 59. The same stilt nest shown in Figure 58, but 23 hours later. The hatching chick is resting; a few minutes later it had cleared itself of the shell.

istically leave the nest to hide in surrounding vegetation when disturbed. When the disturbance has ended, the young return to the nest, where they are brooded by one of the adults. The adults do not feed the young birds but do lead them to suitable feeding areas. Four young stilts studied by Warren King at Kanaha Pond, Maui, first flew on August 14, 1970, when between 51 and 54 days old.

Allen and Lum (1972) described the resting and foraging behavior of stilts at Paiko Lagoon. Stilts are known to eat aquatic insects and their larvae (e.g., waterboatman, *Trichocorixa*, shore flies, *Ephydra*), polychaete worms, crabs, and small fishes. On Kauai Robert Broshears found that stilts preferred ponds with a high concentration of the larvae of a midge (*Chironomous hawaiiensis*) and an unidentified tubificid oligochaete.

ORDER STRIGIFORMES
FAMILY STRIGIDAE
(TYPICAL OWLS)

The 132 species of living owls are placed in two families. The Barn Owl, which has a heart-shaped facial disc of feathers, is placed in the family Tytonidae (page 181). All other owls, which have rounded faces, are members of the Strigidae. Most owls are nocturnal in habits, and most have highly specialized feathers which give them an almost noiseless flight. Owls also are noted for their loud and often weird nighttime calls. Females usually are larger than the males.

Pueo or Short-eared Owl
Asio flammeus sandwichensis
(Color plate 28)

Throughout the world and throughout the ages, owls have been regarded with fear and superstition, often as birds of ill omen, and, by some, as deities to be worshiped. The Pueo is no exception, and it was worshiped by the ancient Hawaiians. Human sacrifices were offered to certain owl gods with the belief that the corpses would be transformed into owls. An owl god of Kauai was said to call together all of the other owls of that island and to drive the Menehune from a valley near Pu'u-pueo or owl hill. The god Kane might appear as an owl and turn aside the weapons of enemies. Even in defeat, the flight of an owl might show the vanquished where to hide, "protected by the wings of an owl." Owls also served as family protectors. Another owl god on Maui was said to be able to bring back to life the souls of those wandering about on the plains.

The sexes are alike in plumage pattern: brownish to buffy white, heavily streaked with brown on both the upper parts and the lower parts. The eyes are yellow. The legs are feathered down to the toes. The birds are from 13 to 17 inches in length, the females being larger.

The Pueo is a permanent resident on all of the main islands, and is found from sea level up to at least 8,000 feet elevation. It is found in open grassland (e.g., the grazing land along the western part of the Saddle Road on Hawaii), in forested areas, and often in towns. This species appears to be tolerant of wide climatic extremes, inhabiting relatively dry areas (the mamaninaio forest on Mauna Kea) and very wet areas (the

Kokee region of Kauai). Short-eared Owls (probably of the subspecies *flammeus*) have been seen on Green Island, Kure Atoll (Clapp and Woodward 1968), and on Tern Island, French Frigate Shoals, by Eugene Kridler on December 7, 1967, and December 3, 1970.

The Pueo differs from most continental owls in that it is diurnal, as well as crepuscular and nocturnal, in habits. Andrew Bloxam found a nest of young owls "in a tuft of long thick grass on Ford Island" (then called Rabbit Island) in Pearl Harbor on May 17, 1825. He wrote that the owls "are very numerous here and are constantly flying about all day, and not like those in England, which come out only at dusk."

The Pueo is noted for its frequent soaring at considerable heights above the ground, a behavior pattern that sometimes leads to mistaken identity so that people report seeing a Hawaiian Hawk where none occur. The owls also fly closer to the ground and hover before diving to the ground after prey, which usually consists of mice or rats. Owls swallow small prey whole, and later regurgitate pellets containing the hair and bones. Richardson and Bowles (1964) examined pellets found on Kauai and reported that they contained the remains of three Hawaiian rats and one house mouse. I have not examined a large number of pellets, but those I have contained only rodent remains. Tomich (1971b) found the usual food of the Pueo to consist of house mice and Polynesian rats, although one owl had killed a larger roof rat. Four Pueo pellets measured, in length and thickness, 29 × 17, 42 × 22, 55 × 24, and 57 × 24 mm.

When perched in trees during the daytime, owls not infrequently are "mobbed" by mixed groups of passerine birds. In reference to this behavior, Perkins (1903:448) said the small birds would flock around an owl "with much chattering, but always keeping at a respectful distance." Richardson and Bowles (1964) observed this behavior in both Apapane and White-eyes on Kauai. About 8:00 A.M. in Kailua Kona on August 8, 1969, my attention was drawn to a Pueo, perched about 25 feet above the ground in a large mesquite tree, by the alarm notes being given by three American Cardinals and several White-eyes. The owl, perched on a bare branch in plain sight, ignored the birds for ten minutes or so, and then flew off.

Little is known about the breeding biology of the Pueo. The nest is built on the ground and the nearly round eggs are white (fig. 60). Derral Herbst photographed a nest with 6 eggs near the Pole Line trail on Kauai on December 15, 1972. Nests containing young have been found on March 6 (1905), May 17 (1825), May 23 (1907), and November 20 (1901), suggesting that this owl may nest throughout the year. On Kauai, Richardson and Bowles found a fully-grown owl, not quite able to fly, on August 4, 1960. Owls begin to incubate with the laying of the first egg, and that egg hatches first; hence, there is a conspicuous difference in size among the young.

ORDER PASSERIFORMES

Of the approximately 8,600 species of birds in the world, more than half (5,100) belong to the order Passeriformes. These passerine birds also are called perching birds and songbirds. They have unwebbed feet, admirably suited for perching on branches; three toes point forward and one (the big toe or hallux) points backward. All have altricial young, meaning that they are helpless and naked, or nearly so, when they hatch, so that they require parental care for some time. This period of dependence on the parents for food and, when very young, for warmth, lasts about one month in many species, but considerably longer in others. Even after they leave the nest, the young must be fed by the parents for a time before the young begin to pick up food for themselves.

Although fossils of the earliest bird have been found in slate of the Jurassic period (about 150 million years old), fossils of passerine birds are known only from the Tertiary period (about 40 million years ago) and later. Since that time, passerine birds have evolved both more rapidly and more successfully than have the older bird groups. As a result, the anatomical differences among passerine families are less pronounced than among the families of non-passerine orders, and this is particularly true among the members of the suborder Passeres which contains over 4,000 species and which constitutes the groups of "true songbirds" or "true oscines." Taxonomists around the world differ in their interpretation of the true relationships among these birds, and this difference of opinion expresses itself in the different systems of classification that have been formulated. The reader is reminded that only the species and their subspecies, or populations of birds, occur in nature. The genera, families, and higher categories are concepts man uses to attempt to indicate true phylogenetic relationships in accordance with the knowledge available.

Hence, one finds that two different groups of birds are considered to be the highest or most advanced among the passerine birds. European ornithologists, in general, place the crows and other presumably closely related families at the apex of the passerine family tree. This interpretation is based on research that suggests that these birds have larger brains relative to body size, and, therefore, that these birds are more intelligent than other birds. American taxonomists generally place at the apex the seed-eating finches and several other families that together are known as the nine-

FIGURE 60. Nest and eggs of the Pueo; Kauai. December 15, 1972. Courtesy of Derral Herbst.

primaried passerines. As the name suggests, these families possess only nine functional primary flight feathers in contrast to ten primaries in the other families. These nine-primaried families are considered by many ornithologists to exhibit the greatest and the most recent adaptive radiation, and, therefore, to "represent the main stream of songbird evolution."

Among the endemic Hawaiian birds, six passerine families are represented.

FAMILY CORVIDAE
(CROWS, JAYS, AND MAGPIES)
Alala or Hawaiian Crow
Corvus tropicus
(Color plate 29)

Among the 100 species of the Corvidae are the biggest-bodied of the passerine birds, the largest being 26

inches from bill-tip to tip of tail. Only one representative of this family reached the Hawaiian Islands, and it is now on the verge of extinction.

The Alala differs from North American crows in being a duller black in color and in having especially the wings tinged with brown. The feathers of the throat are stiff, with hairlike webs and grayish shafts. The bill and feet are black except that the ventral surface of the toes is "greyish flesh-colour." The iris is dark brown, although Rothschild said that Palmer collected a female with a dark blue iris. Total length is given as 18 to 20 inches.

The Hawaiian Crow is endemic to the island of Hawaii only, early writers stating that they found it only in the Kona and Kau districts of that island. They are reported to have nested within a few miles of the Volcano House. Peale (1848:107) wrote that his specimens were collected "a few miles inland from the village of Kaawaloa, celebrated as being the spot where the renowned Captain Cook was killed."

Writing of his experiences in the 1890s, Perkins (1903:372) said that the crow was extremely numerous in the wet belt of the Kona district, "especially inhabiting the open park-like country between the lava-flows, where dense masses of clinging Ieie *(Freycinetia)* invested the scattered trees. In these it nested freely, and numerous nests containing young were found in the summer months. At this time it was extremely tame and would often follow the intruder for a considerable distance, repeatedly uttering its harsh cries, thereby often attracting others from a distance, perhaps to the number of a dozen, the whole assemblage raising a deafening clamour. Here also it found abundant food in the large red fruit of the Ieie, which in this district attained unusual size."

They also ate ohelo *(Vaccinium calycinum)*, poho *(Physalis)*, and other berries and fruits; and early writers referred to their eating the flesh from dead horses, sheep, and cattle. Tomich (1971a) found a pair of nesting crows eating the fruit of lama *(Diospyros ferrea)*, which they often brought to the nest during incubation. Jon Giffin saw wild crows eat hoawa seeds, ohia leaf buds, and the fruits or berries of pilo, banana poka, mamake, lobelia, pukiawe, and olapa.

The decrease in the population of the crow was noted before the turn of the present century, and Perkins wrote that "the cause of the restricted range of the Alala is an unsolved enigma and to me inexplicable." He added that "the deficiency of our knowledge of the conditions of the avifauna at a time when the country was still largely unchanged is much to be regretted, since the older explorers could so easily have supplied this, either from their own observations or on information derived from the native bird-catchers."

Baldwin (1969b) summarized the continuing decline of the population from 1938 to 1949. He heard as many as a dozen crows on the west flank of Hualalai at an elevation of about 4,000 feet in 1949. The habitat was a very rough aa lava flow with ungrazed and, therefore, relatively undisturbed native vegetation (e.g., ohia, *Clermontia*). He also found crows at elevations of 3,750 feet and higher in the vicinity of Poohohoo cinder cone near Puuwaawaa (where the rainfall is approximately 30 inches per year) and at the summit of Hualalai (8,250 feet).

The reasons for the great decline in numbers of the Hawaiian Crow are not conclusive. Munro wrote that "the Hawaiians snared the crow and used the black feathers for kahilis and for dressing idols." He also noted that farmers "made war on it" in the 1890s, and

shooting is believed to be one of the chief reasons for the decline. The effect of the great alteration of the environment on the decline of the species is unknown, as is the possible effect of avian malaria and bird pox. The possibility of pesticide contamination exists.

Working on the Rare and Endangered Species Program on Hawaii, Winston Banko obtained two fledgling crows on Hualalai in 1970: one, on June 18, the other, on June 19. Although both young birds were out of the nest, neither could fly well. Both birds had growths on the head, and the blood of one bird revealed a moderate number of malarial parasites.

Despite the fact that Perkins said that "numerous nests containing young were found in the summer months," very little is known about the breeding biology of the Hawaiian Crow. The birds build a nest of twigs and sticks, lined by finer plant materials. Munro (1944:71) wrote that "there seems to be no record of eggs or chicks."

Tomich (1967, 1971a) found a nest under construction in an ohia tree at an elevation of about 2,300 feet in the Puuanahulu Game Management Area near Puuwaawaa on March 26, 1964. This is a dry area (annual rainfall about 24 inches) where the land is covered by an undated flow of very rough aa lava in which there are some kipukas of an earlier pahoehoe flow. Ohia and lama are the dominant trees in this open forest. Fountain grass *(Pennisetum setaceum)*, an aggressive African tussock grass introduced about 1920, forms a solid ground cover on the pahoehoe kipukas and grows on about half of the aa flow (fig. 61). This grass dies annually, provides its own fuel, and "hence promotes its own increase through fires that destroy other species." Consequently, fires (1960, 1969) have "seriously reduced the acreage of endemic forest available to the crows by killing segments sufficiently undergrown by the grass." Tomich also found four nests from earlier years, two of which were located in fire-killed ohia trees.

The 1964 nest was built 27 feet from the ground near the top of an ohia tree. Most of the nest was constructed of branched twigs of ohia (80 percent) and lama trees (20 percent), which the birds broke off the trees near the nest. The average length of these twigs was 12.5 inches. The lining of the nest was made primarily of stems and blades of fountain grass. The diameter of the nest varied from about 17.5 to 19 inches; total depth was 9.5 inches; diameter of the nest cup varied from about 7.5 to 8.0 inches, and its depth was 2.75 inches.

A clutch of 5 eggs was laid during early April, but one of the eggs had been broken by April 12. Tomich wrote that "no two eggs were of the exact same color;

FIGURE 61. Nesting area of the Hawaiian Crow, near Puuwaawaa, Hawaii. April 12, 1964. The substrate is very rough aa lava; the dominant trees are ohia and lama; the grass is introduced fountain grass. Courtesy of P. Quentin Tomich.

however, three had a pale greenish-blue ground color and were heavily splotched with brown. The fourth had a paler ground color of grayish-blue, but generally heavier blotching than the others. In addition to the blotching, which was concentrated near the larger ends of the eggs, there were relatively dense flecks and a few spots, generally in black.'' In length and width the eggs measured: 42.7 × 29.0, 44.9 × 30.5, 46.2 × 30.2, and 46.4 × 29.1 mm (fig. 62).

The nest was observed for five hours on approximately the eighth day of incubation. The adults took turns incubating the eggs, and the eggs were left un-

covered for only short periods of time. The nonincubating bird spent much of its time perched on the rim of the nest, often preening its feathers for several minutes at a time. The birds practiced mutual billing and one bird sometimes preened the head feathers of its mate. Only rarely did both birds leave the nest and forage for food. The crows were not seen more than 0.4 of a mile from the nest, and Tomich felt it likely that they did not go much beyond that distance. They often fed within sight of the nest.

Although the crows were still incubating on April 26, Tomich discovered that the nest then held only one

FIGURE 62. Four crow eggs from a nest found by
P. Quentin Tomich. April 12, 1964. Courtesy of
P. Quentin Tomich.

egg, which was heavily stained with yolk from other eggs. This egg weighed 15.6 g; it contained no embryo, and Tomich concluded that the egg had been infertile. He postulated that the breakage of four of the eggs might have been "attributable to the softness of egg shells which could not withstand the usual pressures during the turning of the eggs and in incubation," or that roof rats might have eaten the eggs.

Tomich collected the nest, and analysis showed that "in the approximately 21 days that elapsed between completion of the nest and its collection, at least 11 genera of arthropods had come to use it for foraging, for temporary refuge, or for rearing of young."

Tomich contrasted the usually coarse and raucous *caw* of the American Crow with the "generally mellow and musical" *cawk* of the Hawaiian Crow. Its call "sounds as if it were produced from a pair of reed pipes of different tones, but has a trace of a harsh final inflection." At other times the call is a wild *ca-wák* or *caw-áwk,* which may denote sudden alarm. While selecting nesting materials in trees near the nest, the pair studied by Tomich uttered low, guttural *cawk* calls. He also heard a low *churk* call given by a bird some distance from the nest at the time its mate was incubating the eggs.

Other nests of the crow have been found during the past decade, but, because of the tendency for the adults to desert nests, the contents have not been checked during the incubation period. The wild population is estimated to contain less than 50 birds. Jon Giffin of the State Division of Fish and Game found 5 nests during April and May 1977 that were located at elevations varying from 3,500 to 5,050 feet on the Palani, Hualalai, and McCandless ranches. He found 6 nests during April 1978 at elevations between 4,800 and 5,450 feet. He was able to band several of the fledglings, and he saved 6 young birds, taking them to Pohakuloa, during those two years. Howard F. Sakai (Sakai and Ralph 1980b) made observations at nests of three pairs of crows in the Honaunau Forest Reserve between May 2 and June 23, 1978. One of the nests was built about 50 feet from the ground in a kolea (*Myrsine* sp.) tree; all previous nests had been built in ohia trees. Only 1 of 4 nests was successful in producing young.

Plans for initiating a captive rearing program at Pohakuloa were made during February 1976, at which time a pen 12 × 25 × 50 feet was constructed. Three captive crows that had been kept at Volcanoes National Park were transferred to Pohakuloa in March. A pair of these birds built nests during 1976, 1977, and 1978, but no young were reared. However, the State did not devote the effort necessary to carry on a successful breeding program with these crows. Three juvenile birds were added to the breeding flock in 1977 and three others in 1978. Barbara Churchill Lee began donating her time (and money) to the crow-rearing project in January 1977. Since then she has made more observations on crow behavior than anyone else. Among many other things, she has seen the crows catch House Sparrows and house mice that have gotten into the pens, thus showing that the Hawaiian Crow, like its continental relatives, is omnivorous. The captive crows at Pohakuloa have contracted bird pox; and one adult died from an infection with *Clostridium,* a bacterium found in moist soil. The captive crows have weighed from 19 to 27 ounces over a period of time. An elaborate, nutritious diet has been developed by Mr. and Mrs. Lee. They learned that the juvenile birds have a streaked red and black palate, a reddish tongue, and red at the junction of the upper and lower mandibles. As time passes, these areas change to black. The mild temperatures of Honolulu are not found in the mountains of Hawaii, and the maximum and minimum temperatures at Pohakuloa for December 1978 were 90° and 20°F.

FAMILY TURDIDAE
(THRUSHES, ROBINS, BLUEBIRDS, AND SOLITAIRES)

This is one of the larger families of passerine birds containing some 300 species. It has representatives throughout the world except in extreme latitudes, some oceanic islands, and New Zealand (although two species have been introduced there). This family contains some of the finest singers among birds; the European Nightingale for one has been celebrated by many poets. The thrushes are closely related to several other families but differ from them in that the juvenal plumage generally is unlike that of the adults, and the young birds typically have spotted or scaled breasts. Thrushes also typically have unscaled or "booted" tarsi. Some species, however, are not "typical," which accounts for the fact that the number of species of thrushes is variously given as from 303 to 306. Some authors prefer to consider the thrushes, the Old World flycatchers (Muscicapidae), and the Old World warblers (Sylviidae) as subfamilies of one gigantic family containing over a thousand species, or about one-eighth of all birds.

Sometime in the distant past, ancestral thrushes reached the Hawaiian Islands. Here they evolved into two species and several subspecies.

Omao or Hawaiian Thrush
Phaeornis obscurus
(Color plate 49)

The Omao developed races on all of the main islands except Maui. These were described as separate species in the 1890s, but they are now considered to be subspecies or races of one species. A number of Hawaiian names have been given; some of them were applied to the birds of a given island, whereas others were used for the birds on several islands. These names were Amaui, Kamao, Kamau, Olomau, and Omao (Munro 1944).

The Oahu race *(P. obscurus oahensis)* became extinct sometime after 1825. Greenway (1958:387) wrote that "exactly when it was extirpated is not known . . . nor are there any specimens in museums, for although Bloxam collected a few [1825] they were lost."

The Lanai race *(P. obscurus lanaiensis)* is extinct. Munro (1944:74) wrote: "From 1911 to 1923 this bird was under my observation as I frequently rode the bridle trails to the forest. It was at that time a common bird and its call notes could be heard constantly, especially in the north and south ends of the small Lanai forest. It declined from 1923 when the population of Lanai increased and the town of Lanai City was built. . . . I watched its decline till 1931. The few times I have been through the Lanai forest since 1931 the thrushes' call notes have been conspicuously absent." Little now remains of that native forest. The nest, eggs, and nestlings were never described.

The large (more than 8 inches in length) Molokai race *(P. obscurus rutha)* persists in very small numbers.

Scott et al. (1977) saw two birds a half mile east of Puu Wahaulu at an elevation of 4,460 feet during July 1975. All of the collectors of the 1890s found this thrush common on Molokai, and W. A. Bryan (1908) said that he collected 20 birds there in 1907. Prior to that time, the same species was considered to inhabit both Lanai and Molokai, but, on the basis of his new specimens, Bryan described the Molokai bird as a new species (now subspecies). No nest with eggs or young was ever described for the Molokai race.

Molokai very appropriately has been called a "biological disaster area." Very little remains of its endemic forests and birds. In the early days after Captain Cook's discovery of the islands, cattle and goats began destroying the forests. Eight axis deer, gifts to Kamehameha V, were released on the king's private lands on Molokai in January 1868. The herd had increased to an estimated 1,000 animals within twenty years, and the deer continued the destruction of forests originally opened up by cattle. Beginning in 1900, imported professional hunters are said to have killed between 3,000 and 4,000 animals in a two-year period, but the deer continue to ravage the land to this day.

A herd of 12 deer was transplanted to Lanai in 1920, apparently on the recommendation of George C. Munro, who later said that that was the greatest mistake he ever made *(Elepaio* 31:15).

The Kauai race, also called the Large Kauai Thrush *(P. obscurus myadestina),* was said to be the most common forest bird on Kauai in the 1890s. Munro (1944: 77) wrote that it was found from "near sea level on the north side and outer edges of the forest to the mountain tops." By 1928 the birds had disappeared from the "outside forests." The Kauai Thrush is now confined to the Alakai Swamp. For more than a decade, John L. Sincock, a U.S. Fish and Wildlife Service biologist, has explored the Alakai more extensively than anyone else ever has; he estimates a total thrush population of less than 200 birds.

Kauai Omao are described as being dull hair-brown above, tinged with olive, especially on the back; the wing quills are deep brown. The under surface is light smoky gray and "somewhat mottled in appearance," lighter on the throat and becoming white on the belly. The bill is black; the tarsi and toes are brown, but the ventral surface of the toes is pale yellow. The birds are nearly 8 inches in length (Rothschild 1893–1900).

Richardson and Bowles (1964) collected an Omao on August 16, 1960, and found that the stomach contained primarily lapalapa berries and their seeds plus parts of one insect. They described the song as usually being "a series of flute-like notes, but it was sometimes more like that of the exotic Melodious Laughing-thrush although shorter and repeated.'' The nest, eggs, and nestlings have never been described.

The Hawaii Omao *(P. obscurus obscurus)* is 7 to 8 inches long; it is darker in color than the Kauai Omao, being dusky olive brown above and ashy gray below, and has a narrower bill. Immature birds of all races are spotted brown and buff, the feathers on the lower parts being buffy white and broadly bordered with blackish brown (Rothschild).

Writing after six years' residence on Hawaii, Henshaw (in Thrum's Annual for 1902:78) said that the Omao ''is found abundantly all over the island of Hawaii; but only in the denser forests above one thousand feet.'' It now is unusual to find the thrush much below 3,000 feet. I have found them at 2,500 feet in the Laupahoehoe Forest Reserve on the Hamakua Coast; unfortunately, this virgin forest was opened to commercial logging by the Hawaii State Department of Land and Natural Resources in late 1969. I also have seen the thrush in the magnificent and very rugged Puna Forest Reserve where the birds occur as low as 1,000 feet elevation.

The Hawaii Omao is still fairly common in suitable habitat above 3,000 feet elevation. Preferred habitat now appears to be near-virgin ohia forests in regions of high annual rainfall. I have found it most common along the eastern part of the Saddle Road, which ascends from Hilo into the high ''saddle'' land between Mauna Kea and Mauna Loa; along the Kulani Prison road on the eastern slope of Mauna Loa; at the Thurston Lava tube in Hawaii Volcanoes National Park, as well as in the cutover pasture land of the Keauhou ranch adjacent to the Park. The thrush occurs sparingly in forests of the Kona coast.

Annual rainfall at Volcanoes National Park Headquarters is 100 inches. The part of the Saddle Road area that lies between elevations of about 2,000 and 4,000 feet boasts the highest rainfall, 300 inches, the result of the combination of prevailing northeast trade winds and Hawaii's two large mountains. This is the rain forest. The rainfall decreases above 4,000 feet elevation—about 100 inches annually at 6,000 feet—but is still ample for some distance to encourage the revegetation of lava flows and the growth of treeferns and other moisture-loving plants.

A number of eruptions from the north flank of Mauna Loa have poured lava across the region of the present Saddle Road during the past 125 years. The amount of vegetation on these several lava flows varies primarily with the amount of rainfall in the area, which is in turn directly related to the elevation. Where the rainfall is adequate, the revegetation of lava flows by lichens, ferns—including treeferns—and ohia trees

takes place in a relatively short time, and a passable native forest may develop in less than 100 years (e.g., on the 1881 flow).

Molten lava flows like water, seeking the lowest level. It flows around hills and mounds of older lava, thus leaving ''islands,'' called kipukas, which may be heavily forested (fig. 63). Because of a succession of eruptions from different vents in a rift zone, therefore, kipukas may be bounded by lava flows of different ages and in different stages of revegetation. Kipukas are good places to search for endemic plants and animals.

It is difficult to work in typical thrush habitat on the windward coast of Hawaii because a dense growth of mosses, vines, and treeferns so conceals gaping holes and crevices in the lava substrate that it is necessary to watch every step taken. In many areas it is necessary to move slowly and carefully along slippery and rotting tree trunks that have fallen in profusion across lava ravines 10 to 15 feet deep. I often followed the thrushes into the luxuriant vegetation because of its intrinsic beauty and because I always anticipated finding a nest on the next trip.

Because the nest and eggs of the Omao had never been described and because there was not enough information in the literature to base even a remote guess as to the breeding season of the thrush, I decided, in December 1967, to visit known habitats periodically in order to learn something about the breeding season. During the winter months, I discovered that singing thrushes were fairly well scattered over the very rough but relatively open lava flows where the ohia trees were only 15 to 25 feet tall. I thought that if the thrushes did, in fact, build their nests in ohia trees (as Henshaw had predicted), the finding of one in these low trees would be an easy matter. Although I spent many hours, often rainy hours, climbing slowly over lava flows with series of ravines 20 or 30 feet deep, where I had to test each lichen-covered block of aa lava to make sure that it would not roll or tip, I found no nests, and, as the season progressed, I could not even find females or pairs of birds. To be sure, when I found the first thrush nest after nearly six months of searching, it was not on a lava flow at all but in the depths of a dense kipuka.

The kipuka was, in part, an elevated area bounded on the western, or upslope, side by a lava flow less than 100 years old, on which the scattered ohia trees were of moderate height. On its eastern, or downslope, side, the land fell away steeply into a craterlike depression. Both the crater and the elevated portion of the kipuka supported a dense tropical vegetation, of which ohia was the dominant tree. In addition to a variety of mosses, liverworts, and ferns, other plants included kolea *(Myrsine* sp.), pukiawe *(Styphelia tameiameiae),*

FIGURE 63. A kipuka surrounded by an 1855 lava flow near the Saddle Road, Hawaii. Two pairs of thrushes occupied this kipuka when the picture was taken on October 4, 1969.

lapalapa (*Cheirodendron* sp.), kanawao *(Brussaisia arguta),* pilo (*Heydyotis* sp.), ohelo (*Vaccinium calycinum* and *V. reticulatum*), pioi *(Smilax sandwichensis),* and treeferns (*Cibotium* sp.).

I found that first thrush nest on May 11, 1968. The nest was built 4.3 feet from the ground near the top of the trunk of a treefern, and it was supported, in part, by the bases of both dead and living fronds (fig. 64). The dead leaflets of one dried frond had been molded around the exterior, thus serving to camouflage the nest. The rim of the nest had a maximum thickness of one inch; the outside diameter at the rim was 4 inches; the inside diameters of the nest cup were 2.75 inches from side to side and 2.25 inches from front to back. The nest cup was 3 inches deep in back and only one inch deep in front (Berger 1969c).

The bulk of the nest, both the body and the lining, was constructed of unidentified rootlets and strips of bark. Woven primarily into the outer wall of the nest were a variety of mosses *(Taxithelium mundulum, Leocobryum solfatare* var. *hawaiiense, Pseudosymblepharis mauiensis),* liverworts (*Lophocolea* sp., *Bazzania* sp., *Herberta* sp.), and ferns (*Xiphopteris saffordii, Sphaerocionium obtusum, Grammitis hookeri, Cibotium glaucum),* as well as one ohelo *(Vaccinium reticulatum)* seedling, one pukiawe seedling, and several parts of leaves of an unidentified grass or sedge.

When I found the nest at 12:45 P.M., it contained one egg, which had a grayish white background heavily covered with small, irregularly shaped, reddish brown markings distributed over the entire surface of the egg. Not until I had photographed the egg and picked it up did I discover that it was pipped. The bill of the young bird sometimes protruded through a hole about 0.25 inch in diameter in the shell.

A nest I found in the same region on June 23, 1971, held two small nestlings with black down and a bright yellow mouth lining (fig. 65). This nest was built 5 feet 8 inches from the ground on a branch of a pukiawe shrub. I flushed a roof rat from a hollow in the top of a treefern nearby; the nest was empty on my next visit.

I found a nest with 2 eggs in the Kilauea Forest Reserve on March 15, 1972. This nest was built about 6 feet from the ground on the side of the trunk of a treefern. I conducted censuses of the birds in this magnificent forest during 1972 and found a very high density of thrushes, numbering about one pair per acre.

J. Michael Scott of the U.S. Fish and Wildlife Service organized intensive surveys of the Kau and Hamakua forests during the summers of 1976 and 1977. During this time, four Hawaiian Thrush nests were discovered in cavities of trees, a completely unexpected finding. John F. Walters also found a thrush nest in a shallow cavity on June 4, 1978. This nest "was located about 5 m off the ground in a 'ohi'a perhaps 30–40 cm in diameter. The cavity was more of a shelf in a concavity formed where a branch appeared to have split out of the trunk. A small, bushy shoot partially concealed the cavity." Walters took photographs of the adult bird on the nest but did not determine the contents of the nest (*Elepaio* 39:75).

A surprising feature about the distribution of the thrush on Hawaii is that the birds occur not only in the rain forests but also in subalpine scrub and above tree line, birds having been heard almost to an elevation of 10,000 feet on Mauna Loa. At elevations below 8,500 feet, one finds ohelo, kukainene *(Coprosma ernodeoides)*, pukiawe, and aalii *(Dodonaea viscosa)*. Also present is a light-colored lichen that grows luxuriantly on the blocks of lava that thrushes use as perches and where accumulations of their droppings occur. Thane K. Pratt examined nearly 100 thrush droppings from this habitat and found that they contained 82 ohelo berry seeds, 48 pukiawe pits, 18 kukainene seeds, and 49 had insect remains of bugs, wasps, and beetles. Both adult

FIGURE 64. Hawaiian Thrush nest found on May 11, 1968, showing how the nest was molded around the bases of living fern fronds.

FIGURE 65. Nest with two nestlings of the Hawaiian Thrush; Saddle Road, Hawaii. June 23, 1971.

and juvenile thrushes have been seen in this habitat above tree line but we do not know if the birds are permanent residents or are birds of passage during certain periods of the year.

Very little is known about the relationship between singing and the breeding season for Hawaiian birds. They definitely do not follow the pattern of North American passerines. I have heard thrushes sing nearly every month of the year, although the songs may be very infrequent during August and September. There seems to be a resurgence of song in October, particularly whisper songs, given from a concealed perch in the interior of a shrub, thicket, or tree; but I have also heard whisper songs in January and February. From December onward, the birds typically sing from exposed perches, usually from an exposed branch or the top of a tall dead tree. They also have a flight song. For this, a bird flies from an exposed perch 50 or more feet above the ground, singing during its slightly arched upward flight; at the end of the upswing, the bird may stop singing and dive quickly downward into the forest or may sing during the downward flight as well, stopping only an instant before it lands. Although I have often watched thrushes, I have never seen them circle "widely about" flooding the air with their notes, as described by Henshaw. The thrushes also have several poorly understood callnotes. They have a short, harsh alarm note and a hoarse, meow-like note.

The Omao is well known for "quivering" its wings when perched, a behavior pattern characteristic of the species and not a response to any of the external stimuli suggested by various early writers. As is true for most passerine birds, the Omao scratches its head over the wing, a method called indirect head scratching by ornithologists.

Munro reported that the thrushes' food is largely fruit, berries, insects, and caterpillars, as well as the fleshy flower bracts of the ieie vine. I have watched them eat the berries of the ohelo and the lapalapa, and, on one occasion, I watched a thrush fly from a branch and, in full flight, pick off a lapalapa berry.

Puaiohi or Small Kauai Thrush
Phaeornis palmeri
(Color plate 37)

The Puaiohi has dark brown upperparts, darker on the head; grayish underparts, becoming white on the abdomen; a white eye-ring or white superciliary line; and flesh-colored legs, in contrast to the dark brown legs of the Omao (fig. 66). The Puaiohi also is a smaller bird, averaging 7 inches in length, and it has a longer and narrower bill than the Omao. The immature birds are said to be more heavily spotted than the immature Omao.

FIGURE 66. Small Kauai Thrush after it had been removed from a mist net prior to banding with a U.S. Fish and Wildlife Service band; near the Koaie Stream, Kauai. May 29, 1966.

This species is confined to Kauai. Henry Palmer collected the first specimen at Halemanu in 1891. The skin of the specimen was later badly damaged by rats, and Rothschild sent Palmer back to Kauai for more specimens in 1893. At that time he collected only two immature birds, and Rothschild wrote that "these birds must be very rare, as they were only found at Halemanu." Perkins also wrote that it is "by far the rarest and most local of the Hawaiian thrushes . . . and after spending three weeks in specially studying this bird, I came to the conclusion that in this locality the larger was at least one hundred times more numerous than the smaller species."

The Small Kauai Thrush is now known to inhabit only the ohia forests in the Alakai Swamp region. John L. Sincock believes the total population to be less than 100 birds. Both this thrush and the Hawaiian Thrush appear not to tolerate many changes in the environment. Hence, the further spread of exotic plants into the depths of the Alakai Swamp must be prevented if the native birds are to survive; population levels of goats and pigs also must be controlled.

The Small Kauai Thrush was thought to be extinct until Richardson and Bowles (1964) collected 2 specimens and saw at least 15 more during the summer of 1960.

[The Puaiohi] chiefly frequents the underbrush and smaller-sized forest trees, rarely perching at any great height from the ground. It may be seen flying with a straight swift flight beneath the lower branches of these trees, sometimes alighting on a dead twig at a height of not more than three feet from the ground. More rarely it actually settles on the ground, and in one shot in this situation I found a small terrestrial species of land shell. When it alights on a really large tree it is usually on the lower branches, excepting only when about to sing, on which occasions it will perch on the topmost branches of one of the tallest trees in the vicinity. (Perkins 1903:377)

The stomachs of birds collected by Palmer contained weevils, spiders, and caterpillars. The food of two birds collected by Richardson and Bowles in 1960 was primarily the fruit of the lapalapa, "and the gizzards and intestines were stained purple by the juice of these berries." They also found the remains of several species of insects.

Perkins wrote that the song of the Puaiohi is entirely different from that of the Omao, consisting of a "simple trill." However, Pratt (1979) said that "the Puaiohi's song is wheezy and high pitched, rather resembling the squeaking of a metal wheel in need of lubrication." According to Perkins, this thrush also has a flight song.

Nothing is known of the nesting habits of this thrush. However, Jack Throp netted an immature Puaiohi in the Alakai Swamp in 1965 and took the bird to the Honolulu Zoo. The bird adapted rapidly to captivity. No indication of sex was shown, however, until the spring of 1968, when a broken egg was found on the aviary floor. In 1969, Mr. Throp put a male Slate-backed Solitaire or Clarino *(Myadestes unicolor),* a Mexican Thrush, in the aviary with the Puaiohi. During June 1969, the Puaiohi laid 2 eggs in a finch basket-type nest, but the nest proved unsuitable and the eggs were soon abandoned. The female laid several eggs at a later date (fig. 67).

FIGURE 67. Three eggs laid by a captive Small Kauai Thrush.

Three eggs that Mr. Throp gave to me had length and width measurements as follows: 25.1 × 18.25, 28.0 × 18.9, and 29.8 × 17.95 mm. The ground color of these eggs varied from very pale greenish blue to pale grayish green. Large reddish brown splotches and smaller spots were scattered irregularly over the entire surface of the shells but were especially concentrated around the larger ends of the eggs.

FAMILY SYLVIIDAE
(OLD WORLD WARBLERS, KINGLETS, AND NEW WORLD GNATCATCHERS)

This family is a catchall group consisting of, according to different authorities, 395 or more species, and is the largest of all the bird families. Most of the species are small and have dull-colored or nondescript plumage, small thin bills, and weak legs and feet. The sexes are usually alike in plumage pattern. Most are excellent singers, and most are insectivorous. They have 10 functional primaries in contrast to the 9 found in the New World wood-warblers and the Hawaiian honeycreepers. Taxonomists group these species into either three or four subfamilies. Only one representative of this very large family reached the Hawaiian Islands.

Laysan Millerbird
Acrocephalus familiaris familiaris
(Color plate 38)

The Laysan Millerbird became extinct between 1913 and 1923 because of the destruction of the habitat by rabbits. How the ancestors of this small bird (about 5.5 inches in total length) managed to reach Laysan and Nihoa is, of course, unknown. Because of their Old World affinities, however, it is assumed that they came from Asia and "island-hopped" to reach Laysan and Nihoa islands. The first specimens were collected by Palmer and Munro in 1891.

The Laysan Millerbird was gray-brown above and buffy white below; it had a white superciliary line. It was named because of its taste for moths, called millers.

W. K. Fisher (1906) said that the Millerbird "is one of the most abundant of the four strictly land birds peculiar to Laysan. In the cool of the morning or in late afternoon it is seen to best advantage, for then it is very active and at times musical." The birds were described as fearless. Fisher photographed a bird at the nest while sitting only a few feet from it. Their diet apparently consisted exclusively of insects and their larvae.

Fisher found two nests "placed in the middle of a large bunch of grass about 2 feet from the ground." The nests were constructed of dried grass stems and blades, fine rootlets, and lined partly with white albatross feathers (fig. 68). He found considerable differ-

FIGURE 68. Laysan Millerbird at its nest. May 1902. Photograph by Walter K. Fisher, courtesy of Alfred M. Bailey.

ence in the markings among five eggs. The ground color varied from very pale olive-buff through greenish white to almost pure white. The markings on one egg consisted of olive blotches and spots of various intensities crowded at the blunt end, and very tiny lines and specks were scattered all over the shell.

Bailey (1956:117) also found the Millerbird abundant during the early part of 1913. He found them "regular visitors to our table at meal times and to our workshops throughout the day, and so tame that if we remained quiet they would land upon our head. They searched in crannies for millers and caterpillars, their favorite food, and we often saw them over the portulaca flats bordering the lagoon. They were always extremely busy. It is probable that we were the last to see this species in life, for the bird had become extinct by the time Wetmore visited Laysan in 1923."

Nihoa Millerbird
Acrocephalus familiaris kingi

The Nihoa Millerbird was discovered by Alexander Wetmore (1924) during the Tanager Expedition in 1923. He described it as being similar to the Laysan Millerbird "but throat, breast, and abdomen paler, nearly white; auricular region darker; markings about eye not yellowish; upper surface much darker; bill heavier, averaging slightly longer; tarsus heavier, slightly longer." The upper mandible is blackish; the lower mandible is pale gray, darker toward the tip. The tarsi are medium gray; the toes are blackish gray. Total length is 5.38 inches. A specimen collected in June 1969 was growing new tail feathers.

The darker plumage of the Nihoa race presumably reflects an adaptation to the dark volcanic substrate that forms Nihoa, in contrast to the light sand and coral of Laysan Island.

The birds are secretive in habits, usually staying in the dense, knee-high cover afforded by the woody-stemmed goosefoot *(Chenopodium sandwicheum)* and ilima *(Sida fallax),* which grow on the steep slopes of the island. The birds were singing during our visit to Nihoa in late July and early August of 1966. The somewhat metallic and bubbling songs do not carry far, however, largely due to the pounding surf below and the piercing calls of the thousands of terns flying over the island.

The first active nest of this species was found by David B. Marshall on June 10, 1962. The nest held a "single, brown-splotched, pale blue egg" (Marshall 1964). C. Robert Eddinger found the second nest on August 25, 1968; the two white eggs had spots of varying sizes and colors from sepia brown to black; they measured 15.1 × 20.0 and 15.4 × 20.0 mm. John L. Sincock found a nest with two small young on May 30, 1969, and another nest with a fully feathered nestling on June 2. Karl Kenyon observed a short-tailed fledgling on March 7, 1968. These records suggest a nesting season lasting from March through August. Of the nests found to date, two have been built in *Sida;* all of the rest, in *Chenopodium;* all have been between 1.0 and 1.5 feet above the ground.

We found 6 old nests but no active ones, on August 1, 1966, and we saw no evidence that the birds were nesting. Our main concern that day, however, was to census the birds. The old nests averaged about 3 by 4 inches in maximum diameter and were composed primarily of strips and pieces of grass stems and blades, with varying amounts of rootlets. All of the nests contained some feathers of other species of birds, white being the predominant color used. One nest contained the dried skeleton of a nestling. The newly hatched nestling has not been described, nor is anything else known about the breeding cycle.

Millerbirds presumably are exclusively insectivorous.

Inasmuch as Nihoa contains but 156 acres, both the Nihoa Millerbird and the Nihoa Finch have one of the smallest distributions of any bird species. Accurate censusing is extremely difficult because of the dense habitat and the secretive nature of the birds. Personnel of the U.S. Fish and Wildlife Service have estimated populations varying from 165 (1975) to 625 (1967) birds. The lowest populations were found during very dry periods on the island (Sincock and Kridler 1980).

The species is considered endangered because of its limited distribution, and it is imperative that potential predators and foreign plants be prevented from gaining access to the island. The greatest danger of accidental introductions in all the islands in the Hawaiian Islands National Wildlife Refuge lies in the almost complete disregard by military personnel and others for the purpose of the refuge.

FAMILY MUSCICAPIDAE
(OLD WORLD FLYCATCHERS)

This family, too, is very large, containing over 300 species. They are found throughout the Old World and eastward in the Pacific to the Marquesas and the Ha-

waiian Islands. There are no representatives in North or South America. As with the Sylviidae, taxonomists disagree on the placement of many species, so that the number of species included in the family varies according to the system followed.

These flycatchers are nearly exclusively insectivorous, feeding upon insects and spiders. Typically, they fly from exposed perches to capture the prey in mid-air, but, at times, also from the ground; they also forage among leaves and branches. In plumage they are extremely diverse in color. The family Muscicapidae is divided into four subfamilies: typical flycatchers, monarchs, fantails, and whistlers.

Elepaio
Chasiempis sandwichensis
(Color plate 40)

At least one ancestral population reached the Hawaiian Islands via Micronesia or Polynesia and evolved to the extent that it is recognized as a genus unique to Hawaii. The genus *Chasiempis* is believed to be most closely related to the genus *Monarcha* and to be of Melanesian origin.

The Elepaio has a puzzling distribution in that distinct races developed on Kauai, Oahu, and Hawaii, but there is no evidence that the species ever inhabited Niihau, Molokai, Lanai, or Maui. The three subspecies are brown- or gray-backed birds with lighter underparts and a long blackish tail; all races have prominent black rictal bristles (stiff, hairlike feathers at the corners of the mouth). Each differs from the other two subspecies in several ways, and there is considerable variation in the juvenal plumage. Because these plumage differences were not understood, some early writers described as many as five different species. Pratt (1979) proposed that there are five subspecies, three on the island of Hawaii alone. However, he also described integration between the three Hawaiian subspecies, as well as overlap in some of the characters he analyzed. He added that the Elepaio "on the island of Hawai'i provides the only clear expression of Gloger's Rule among Hawaiian birds." Gloger's Rule states that there is an increase in melanin (black pigment) with an increase in humidity; it also predicts an increase in yellowish or reddish brown pigmentation in regions of high temperature and aridity. Pratt noted that the darker plumage of his proposed *C. s. ridgwayi* "appears to be caused not only by an increase in melanins but also by an increase in red pigments. Indeed, *C. s. ridgwayi* is the reddest of the three subspecies." Gloger's Rule does not seem to apply for the Elepaio on Hawaii; I recognize one subspecies for the Hawaii group.

The Elepaio is noted for frequently carrying its tail

cocked upward at a nearly ninety-degree angle, and, largely because of this behavior, a number of early writers said that the Elepaio exhibited "wren-like behavior." I have never been impressed that the Elepaio's behavior is much like that of North American wrens. The Elepaio scratches its head indirectly (that is, over the wing).

The Elepaio was important in Hawaiian folklore. Perkins (1893) gave the following as told to him by a native woman in Kona: "Of all the birds the most celebrated in ancient times was the *Elepaio,* and for this reason. When the old natives used to go up into the forest to get wood for their canoes, when they had felled their tree the *Elepaio* would come down to it. If it began to peck it was a bad sign, as the wood was no good, being unsound; if, on the contrary, without pecking, it called out 'Ona ka ia,' 'Sweet the fish,' the timber was sound."

The Kauai race *(C. sandwichensis sclateri)* has a dark gray head, back, and wings, two white wing bars, white upper tail coverts, and a blackish brown tail, the outer feathers tipped with white. Underparts are whitish tinged with buff, especially on the throat, breast, and sides of body. The plumage is variable, however, and some males are bright red-brown. Immature birds are brownish to rufous above and lighter below; they lack the white rump of the adults. Total length is about 5.5 inches.

The Kauai Elepaio is common in the ohia forests of Kokee State Park and in the Alakai Swamp. Richardson and Bowles found the species as high as 4,500 feet west of Mt. Waialeale. They also found it at 450 feet elevation in Hanakoa Valley, where the birds were inhabiting a mixed forest of Java plum *(Eugenia cuminii),* kukui *(Aleurites moluccana),* and coffee *(Coffea* sp.).

Available data suggest a breeding season for the Kauai Elepaio beginning in March and ending in June. C. Robert Eddinger found nests under construction on March 22 and 29 and April 1 and 6, 1970; he found nests under construction on April 16 and 20, 1969. On March 23, 1970, he found a nest with two eggs, the earliest date yet recorded. Sheila C. Frings, Eddinger, and I found five nests at Kokee State Park on April 21 and 22, 1967. Two nests were under construction, one held one egg, and two nests held two eggs each on April 22. Eddinger and I found a nest about 25 feet from the ground on a slender branch of an ohia on May 19, 1968; an adult was incubating or brooding, but there was no way to check the nest. On May 29, 1966, I found two recently fledged young near the Koiae Stream in the Alakai Swamp. The two birds were perched side by side on a branch near the top of a 35-foot ohia tree, and were being fed by both adults.

On May 30 I found another nest with two well-feathered nestlings. This nest that was near the end of a slender branch was built about 12 feet above the ground in an olapa *(Cheirodendron)* tree. Eddinger found one nest in olapa and another in hoawa, *Pittosporum acuminatum,* but most of the Kauai nests were built in ohia.

Clutch size was two eggs in each of eight Kauai nests; in one, it was three eggs. Two eggs measured 20.4 × 15.2 and 20.5 × 15.18 mm. Eddinger determined the incubation period at three nests to be 18 days.

The skin of the newly hatched Elepaio is dull gray-pink; down on the head, back, and wings is smoky black; the gape is a dull cream color; the eyes are closed (figs. 69, 70). On the day of hatching, four nestlings weighed 2.2, 2.2, 2.6, and 2.8 g, respectively. The birds reached a maximum weight of 10.5 g at 13 days of age. The weight of one 14-day-old nestling had dropped to 10.0 g. Body temperature of one-day-old nestlings was 90° F; 11-day-old nestlings maintained a body temperature of 98° F when the air temperature was 60° F; one nestling had a body temperature of 101° F when 13 days old. The nestling period at one nest was 16 days. Two 11-day-old nestlings died in the nest, apparently from exposure to heavy rain throughout the night; the birds' wing feathers were about two-thirds unsheathed, and it seems likely that the young were not brooded at night despite the rain.

The Oahu race *(C. sandwichensis gayi)* is dark olive-

FIGURE 69. Nest, egg, and 24-hour-old nestling Kauai Elepaio. May 10, 1970. Courtesy of C. Robert Eddinger.

FIGURE 70. Two 7-day-old Kauai Elepaio (note the developing wing quills). April 15, 1970. Courtesy of C. Robert Eddinger.

brown above, except for two white wing bars and a white rump. The throat is black; the rest of the underparts (including the chin) are white, sometimes tinged slightly with buff; the bill is black. Both the male and the female have a black throat. In most cases, Frings (1968) "could not distinguish males in adult plumage from females in adult plumage." Immature birds lack the white rump and black throat and have a rufous color on the head and neck.

The Oahu Elepaio is still common in the mixed forests of the island, and a small population is resident in the lowland introduced forest near the head of Manoa Valley and in Moanalua and North Halawa valleys. It occurs at elevations as low as 255 feet in Moanalua Valley. Although not as common as reported during the early 1900s, the Elepaio has been able to adapt to man-made changes in the environment as no other endemic land bird has been able to do.

S. C. Frings (1968) found that the Oahu Elepaio defended an average territory of 4.9 acres in the Manoa Valley habitat. She reported that the most prominent feature of courtship was sexual chasing, accompanied by excited chatter and, usually, song. The female selects the nest site, usually in an upright fork, less commonly on a lateral branch among several supporting branches. Both sexes take part in building the nest, but the female does more than the male. The average height above ground of 32 nests was 25 feet; the lowest nest was 8.5 feet from the ground; the highest was estimated to be 50 feet. The small cup-shaped nests are

very neat and compact and contain large amounts of spider web, which aids in holding the plant materials together. Frings watched an Elepaio fly into a spider's web so that strands of the web were caught on the beak and the rictal bristles. The bird then applied the web to the nest with a wiping motion of the head. The average measurements of 11 nests were: outside diameter, 2.8 inches; total height, 3.0 inches; diameter of nest cup, 1.9 inches; depth of nest cup, 1.6 inches. Outside dimensions vary much more widely than do the inside dimensions of the nest cup.

Most of the nest is built within one week; lichen, fine lining material, and spider's web are added during the second week; the first egg is laid about 14 days after the nest is started. The eggs have a white background covered with reddish brown spots, which are concentrated at the larger end of the egg. Eggs usually are laid before 8:00 A.M., at approximately 24-hour intervals. The clutch size was two eggs in 15 nests and three eggs in 1 nest.

The parents take turns in incubating the eggs and in brooding the nestlings. The eggs usually are uncovered for less than 30 seconds when one parent relieves the other at the nest. Males frequently sing briefly while incubating and brooding; females rarely sing from the nest. The male sometimes feeds the incubating female (courtship feeding).

Two common variations of the primary song are *e-le-pa-i-o* and *two-whee-oo*. Frings found the Oahu Elepaio to be "invariably the first bird to sing in the morning and the last to sing in the evening." A morning song period begins before 6:00 A.M. and lasts up to 45 minutes. An evening song period begins about 6:30 P.M. and lasts about 20 minutes. The most persistent singing occurs during the first week of nest building, when both sexes, but especially the male, sing throughout the day; at other times, singing is intermittent during the day. Only infrequently do the birds sing during incubation, and then only for short periods of time. Singing increases again after the eggs hatch, and, after the young leave the nest, the frequency approaches that of the courtship period.

Other vocalizations are a *chip,* a *chatter,* and a *rasping cry.* A chip is a relatively soft note used during feeding as a signal when one bird replaces the other on the nest, and sometimes, apparently, as a mild alarm note. The harsh chatter is used as a prelude to singing, as a scolding alarm note, as a food-begging call, and also by the female when she is ready for copulation. The rasping cry is given by older nestlings or fledglings when disturbed, or by the adults when young in the nest are threatened.

Frings found the breeding season in Manoa Valley

to extend from mid-January to mid-June (the season differs on the other islands for as yet unanalyzed reasons). She reported only a 13 percent nesting success of 27 nests containing 53 eggs, a very low figure for a passerine bird. She attributed the high mortality to the fact that all of the birds built their nests in slender-stemmed trees in an area where, especially in March, high winds and extremely heavy rains occur. The greatest mortality occurred when the nests held eggs (34 of the 53 eggs were destroyed because of heavy wind or, probably in a few instances, by rats). Her study area was predominantly introduced forest (fiddlewood, *Citharexylum spinosum;* guava, *Psidium guava;* Java plum, *Eugenia cuminii;* and kukui, *Aleurites moluccana*), interspersed with grassy clearings. Stands of introduced *Eucalyptus* sp. and paperbark (*Melaleuca leucadendron)* were totally unsuitable for nesting for the Elepaio. Java plum (13 nests), fiddlewood (7 nests), guava (5 nests), and kukui (4 nests) were the preferred nesting trees in this habitat. Males, at least, breed at an age of less than one year and while still in the immature plumage stage.

The Hawaii race *(C. s. sandwichensis)* has the most striking plumage pattern of the three subspecies. Pratt (1979:31) said that the adult birds "are basically brown birds boldly patterned with white wing-bars, rump, and tail tip, a pale breast and belly more or less streaked with rufous-chestnut, and a pale eyebrow that varies from deep rufous-chestnut to pure white. The throat feathers of males are black, more or less tipped with white. The white tips wear away between molts, and thus some very worn specimens appear entirely black throated. In females the throat is often entirely white, and at most only a small area of black in the chin is present. . . . Immatures of both sexes are plain gray-brown or dull reddish brown above, white below, and lack the white wing-bars, rump, and tail tip of the adults." The bill and feet are black to slaty blue. Because of the extent of variation that he found in male plumage, Pratt recognized three subspecies on Hawaii: *ridgwayi* on most of the windward coast; *bryani* on Mauna Kea; and *sandwichensis* on the Kona coast (fig. 71). Total length of the Hawaii Elepaio is about 5.25 inches. Charles van Riper (1974b) saw an albinistic Elepaio on Mauna Kea on July 23, 1973.

The Elepaio is a common species in the ohia rain forests on the windward slopes of both Mauna Kea (Hamakua coast) and Mauna Loa (Saddle Road area southeastward in the forests around Kulani Prison to Volcanoes National Park). I have seen the Elepaio in forests above 3,000 feet elevation in North Kona and at an elevation of 1,700 feet at Manuka State Park.

The Elepaio also is a common and characteristic species in the mamani-naio forests on Mauna Kea. The

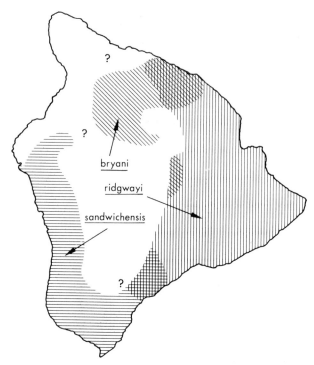

FIGURE 71. Approximate distributions of the three subspecies of the Elepaio on the island of Hawaii as proposed by Pratt. Areas where the Elepaio occurs but which were not represented by specimens are indicated by question marks. Cross-hatching indicates intergradation between the adjacent populations. Courtesy of H. Douglas Pratt, Jr.

Elepaio, the Amakihi, and the Akiapolaau appear to be the only native passerine species that are found both in the rain forests and in the relatively dry mamani-naio forest.

Little is known about the breeding biology of the Hawaii Elepaio. On the Kaohe Game Management Area on Mauna Kea, I have seen sexual chasing in the third week of January, but the earliest active nest I have found was under construction on April 14, 1967 (fig. 72). I have found several nests on such small, brittle branches of the mamani that it was not possible to check the nest contents. I saw an Elepaio feeding a fledgling on July 6, 1968.

The first published photographs of the nest and eggs (of the Hawaii race) and of nestlings (of the Kauai race) of the Elepaio are in a paper by Berger (1969b). Van Riper (1977) discussed Elepaio nests on Mauna Kea that incorporated wool from feral sheep.

FAMILY MELIPHAGIDAE
(HONEYEATERS)

This Old World family has 160 species whose center of abundance is Australia and New Guinea, although the

FIGURE 72. Nest and two eggs of the Hawaii Elepaio in a mamani tree; Kaohe Game Management Area, Mauna Kea, Hawaii. April 30, 1967.

range includes New Zealand, the Solomon Islands, Micronesia, Polynesia, and Hawaii. A genus of doubtful affinities but included in the family is found in South Africa. Two genera and five species were found in Hawaii, but all except one of the species are now thought to be extinct.

The four species of the genus *Moho* had patches of bright yellow feathers, which the Hawaiians prized, using them for their feather capes and headdresses. The role that the Hawaiians played in leading to the extinction of the several species of the Oo, also called Ooaa, is unknown, but it may be significant that the sole known surviving species (on Kauai) has fewer yellow feathers than any of the other species. The evidence also suggests that the Oo, like nearly all of the other endemic Hawaiian land birds, was intolerant of any extensive changes in the environment. Also suspect are several species of rats as predators of the eggs and young of tree-nesting birds because some species of rats are agile climbers and have been seen in tall trees and in treeferns in the ohia forests.

Because the Caucasians who lived in Hawaii in close relationship with the Hawaiian people from the 1820s until the 1890s wrote so little about birds, and about the Hawaiians' use of birds, most of what is known was recorded during the latter decade (Brigham 1899). Apparently by that time, most of what was told to the foreigners by the Hawaiians was, in a real sense, hearsay, in that the stories told presumably had been passed down from generation to generation. By the 1890s, many decades had passed since the kings' birdcatchers

had plied their skills. Consequently, conflicting accounts appear in the literature. Hence, it would seem wise to follow Emerson's (1895) advice: "One old birdcatcher aroused my incredulity by the surprising tale, which I recommend the readers of this article to take with as many grains of salt as are necessary for the catching of a bird. . . ."

Emerson wrote as follows about the use of feathers by the Hawaiians:

The plumage-birds, like everything else in Hawaii, were the property of the *alii* of the land, and as such were protected by *tabu;* at least that was the case in the reign of Kamehameha I, and for some time before. The choicest of the feathers found their way into the possession of the kings and chiefs, being largely used in payment of the annual tribute, or land tax, that was levied on each *ahupuaa.*

As perquisites of royalty, they were made up into full length cloaks to be worn only by the kings and highest chiefs. Besides these there were capes, *kipuka,* to adorn the shoulders of the lesser chiefs and the king's chosen warriors, called *hulumanu,* not to mention helmets, *mahiole,* a most showy head-covering. The supply needed to meet this demand was great, without reckoning the number consumed in the fabrication of *lei* and the numerous imposing *kahili* that surrounded Hawaiian royalty on every occasion of state.

It is, therefore, no surprise when we learn that in the economic system of ancient Hawaii a higher valuation was set upon bird-feathers (those of the *mamo* and *o-o*) than upon any other species of property, the next rank being occupied by whale-tooth, a jetsam-ivory called *palaoa pae,* monopolized as a perquisite of the king.

While the plumage-birds were of such diminutive size and so difficult of capture that it would not have been profitable to hunt them for food, they were in reality such delicacies for the table, that the hunters were quite willing to use them in that way.

And, in truth, it is difficult to see what better disposition could have been made of them in many cases. In the case of the *mamo, i-iwi, akakani, o-u* and *amakihi* the extent of skin-surface left bare after stripping the plumage from the bird was so considerable that it would have been an act of cruelty, if not of destruction, to have set it loose in such a condition. It was entirely different with the *o-o.* In its case the injury done was trifling and constituted no bar to its being immediately released.

In writing of the Hawaii Oo, Wilson (1890a:178) said: "It is doubtful whether in ancient days it was from the yellow feathers that grow beneath its wings, or from the still more beautiful yellow feathers of the now extinct *Drepanis pacifica* . . . that the state robes of kings and chiefs were wrought." The fact that the Mamo *(Drepanis)* was nearly extinct in 1890 (and was thought to be so by Wilson) while the Oo was still fairly common in some habitats would suggest that the Mamo feathers were preferred, and that only after that species became rare were the Oo feathers used. After he returned to England, however, Wilson examined feather cloaks in the British Museum and concluded that they were made primarily of the wing-tuft feathers of the Oo, with the more beautiful feathers of the Mamo introduced, "though in small quantities only."

In either case, it has been estimated that feathers from about 80,000 Mamo were required to complete the feather cloak of Kamehameha I. Wilson estimated that "two hundred birds must have been sacrificed" for one small lei that he purchased for $50. Munro saw a kahili made from the central tail feathers of the Hawaii Oo.

Henshaw (1903) remarked that it must not be overlooked "that the brilliant shining black body feathers of the o-o were also in great demand for making cloaks and, as remarked by Prof. Brigham, the bird could hardly survive the loss of nearly its entire plumage. It may well be, therefore, that the old bird catchers were not wholly unacquainted with the good qualities of the flesh of the o-o, which is said to be most excellent eating." In fact, Wilson (in Wilson and Evans 1890–1899) said that "the O-O is esteemed a great delicacy by the natives, and used formerly to be eaten by them, fried in its own fat." Wilson had an opportunity to confirm the excellence of the meat when his cook prepared for dinner a specimen he had collected.

Emerson wrote: "The *mamo, i-iwi* and such birds as were destined to be eaten after being plucked, were, as soon as caught, killed by pressure over the thorax and then wrapped in the outer dried parchment of the banana stalk, and packed in the hunting bag. The *o-o* and birds destined to be released were secured in cages."

To be sure, Kamehameha I is reputed to have said, "The feathers belong to me, but the birds themselves belong to my heirs." There is, of course, no way of knowing how faithfully his bird catchers followed the King's admonition (if indeed he gave it) to release the birds after their feathers had been plucked, but it seems highly doubtful that the practice was followed after his reign. Moreover, as has been stressed by several authors, release of a plucked bird was not a guarantee that the bird would survive. The extent of the area from which the feathers were plucked would be one critical factor because the birds retain their body heat by fluffing their feathers, and this protection would have been needed nightly during the long, cold, and rain-drenched nights even at elevations of only 4,000 feet. It is now known, as well, that passerine birds sometimes die of shock merely as a result of being handled, although this is not a common occurrence. I once watched a Kauai Omao die in the hands of the bird bander after the thrush had been removed from a mist net. The bird was not injured in any way; it died simply from the stress of being caught and handled.

Kauai Oo
Moho braccatus
(Color plate 37)

The Kauai Oo, which for many years was thought to be extinct, was rediscovered by Richardson and Bowles (1964) in 1960 in the depths of the Alakai Swamp region. They collected one specimen and saw or heard 12 more. The birds were found in the undisturbed native ohia forest between elevations of 3,750 and 4,250 feet. They preferred the thick forest habitat, and more birds were seen or heard in high canyons than on the forested ridges. The birds foraged in both ohia and lapalapa trees, and they were observed to eat lapalapa berries. The stomach of the specimen collected contained remains of spiders, insects (beetles and hemiptera), and insect larva, and three small snails.

The Oo were curious and sometimes came from distances of more than a hundred yards in response to imitations of their calls, a characteristic also reported for the other species. The variable calls were described as "typically loud, mellow whistles," the most common of which was transcribed as *whip-poor-weeo.* Other calls included *ah-o* and "slurred, liquid, double notes."

The specimen collected by Richardson and Bowles on July 21 was a male with very small testes and presumably was in a postbreeding condition; it also had molted several tail feathers. Palmer and Munro collected immature birds in May (1891). The first nest of any species of Oo was discovered in the Alakai Swamp by John L. Sincock on May 31, 1971. He told me that the birds were nesting in a cavity about 40 feet above the ground in a very tall, dead ohia tree. With the aid of a rope and tree saddle, Sincock reached the nesting cavity on June 10 and learned that it held two nestlings. The primary and secondary wing feathers were about 0.38 inch long and were gray in color; down on the head was gray; down on the ventral feather tracts of the neck, breast, and abdomen was cinnamon. The bill was very wide and had bright yellow margins. Although Sincock could barely squeeze his hand through the entrance cavity, he reported that the cavity itself was nearly a foot in diameter and that the entire floor of the cavity was covered with dead plant materials.

Sincock also found Oo nests in a cavity about 25 feet above the ground in an ohia tree in 1972 and 1973. He reported that when there were young in the nests in 1971, 1972, and 1973, "both parents were continually searching for insects and arthropods, particularly in the moss-covered tree trunks, and carrying their prey into the nest cavity every few minutes. Often as one adult entered the cavity the other adult would emerge. Both nest cavities had openings toward the west, which would afford some protection from the predominantly northeast wind.''

The Kauai Oo has a black head, wings, and tail, smoky brown lower back, and a brown rump and upper tail coverts. The bend of the wing and the under wing coverts are white. The feathers of the throat are black with a subterminal bar of white, giving the throat a scaled or barred appearance. The abdomen is dark smoky brown; the under tail coverts are rufous brown. The feathers of the legs are golden yellow (black in immature birds). Brownish feathers in the axillary (armpit) region are small and inconspicuous. Bill and feet are black, except the soles of the toes, which are pale yellow. The iris is yellowish white. Total length is between 7.5 and 8.5 inches; early collectors called it the dwarf Oo.

There seems little doubt that this species is on the verge of extinction. Sincock saw one bird during July 1978, and he thinks that there may be no more than a dozen surviving Oo.

Oahu Oo
Moho apicalis

The Oahu Oo is thought to have become extinct within a short period after 1837 (Greenway 1958:423). This was a striking black, brown, white, and yellow bird about 12 inches in length. Most of the plumage was sooty black, but the tail was brown with large patches of white. The two central tail feathers lacked the white tips, were narrower than the others, and tapered to end as upturned hairlike points. The sides and under tail coverts were yellow. The under wing coverts were white.

Molokai Oo
Moho bishopi

The Molokai Oo was last reported in 1904. Munro and W. A. Bryan failed to find it in 1907, and it has not been reliably reported since then. This also was a large (about 12 inches), primarily black bird, but with elongated golden yellow ear coverts, axillary tufts, and under tail coverts; the black tail had a narrow fringe of white. The bill and feet were black. The iris was dark brown.

Writing of his experiences in the 1890s, Perkins (1903:442) said of the Molokai Oo:

[It is] seen numerously in the Ohia trees, when these are in flower, but this is clearly because its favorite lobelia nectar is unattainable. Thus on one of my visits to Molokai of about a score of Oo that I watched while they were feeding, at a time when the Ohias and lobelias were both in flower, one only was seen to visit the former, though these were attractive enough to other birds. This Oo also visits the flowers of the banana in some of the deep gulches and valleys, and is said to also eat the fruit. To insect food, when the nectar of the lobelias is abundant, it pays little attention. Thus of ten shot at the lobelias and dissected not one contained a trace of insect food, although these were secured on different days and at very different times of day. On the other hand, the one mentioned above as visiting the Ohia flowers at this season contained a considerable amount of insect food.

Hawaii Oo
Moho nobilis
(Color plate 39)

The Hawaii Oo, which was first collected during Captain Cook's third voyage to the Pacific, was aptly named. Emerson (1895) referred to it as "the prince, or king, of Hawaiian plumage-birds." It was the largest of the four species of Oo: males being between 12 and 13 inches in length; the females were smaller, 9 to 9.5 inches in length. The head, body, wings, and central pair of tail feathers were glossy black; the central tail feathers were elongated and twisted at their tips; the other tail feathers had varying amounts of white and/or yellow in the basal portion. The bright yellow axillary feathers were greatly elongated, and, according to Rothschild, in some specimens they seem to "part naturally into two tufts." The under tail coverts also were bright yellow. The bill and feet were black. The iris was reddish brown.

Perkins (1893:109) had the following to say about the Oo in Kona: "In the lower forest the Oo . . . was a common bird, frequenting, as is well known, the lofty *lehua*-trees, especially when growing on the rough lava. Save its antipathy to the red birds *(Vestiaria),* its habits are difficult to observe, as it usually keeps very high up in the trees." Munro (1944:86) wrote that they were common "above Kaawaloa" in 1891 and 1892, but that they had disappeared there by 1894, apparently due in part to the "influx of coffee farmers."

Later, Perkins (1903:441) wrote that the Molokai Oo and the Hawaii Oo "no longer occupy extensive tracts of country, where once they were very plentiful. Neither of these species thrives in forests opened up by cattle, and as a rule they sooner or later entirely desert these, so that the area of forest land suitable for them has for years been diminishing."

Henshaw (1903:85–86) also reported that the Oo had been "widespread throughout the lower as well as the middle forest." He added that "the districts of Olaa and Puna are today almost absolutely tenantless of this beautiful bird, where formerly there were multitudes. As late as 1898 more than one thousand individuals of this species were shot by the lei hunters in the heavily wooded district north of the Wailuku River, where their presence had probably been overlooked."

Henshaw (1903:89), who knew the Hawaii Oo well, wrote that he "saw a single adult male o-o in the forest tract northeast of Olinda [Maui], at an elevation of about 4,500 feet" on June 9, 1901, and, although he was "positive as to its identification as one of the members of this genus," no one else before or since has reported an Oo on Maui. Henshaw thought that the bird he saw might have been a Molokai Oo. The Hawaii Oo is presumed to have become extinct sometime after the turn of the present century.

Rothschild wrote that Palmer collected most of his specimens at about 2,000 feet elevation. Most of the collectors of the 1890s reported the vertical range to be from about 1,200 to 4,000 feet, but they were told that the species was found at least as high as 6,000 feet at certain times of the year.

Both Wilson and Perkins considered the Hawaii Oo to be the most timid and wary of all the forest birds, typically feeding in the tallest trees. The birds sometimes foraged in the understory, however, feeding on lobelias, ohia lehua, the ieie vine, and, occasionally, mamani. Perkins called attention to the predilection of the Molokai Oo for lobelia nectar, but both it and the Hawaii Oo also ate caterpillars and insects. Perkins watched the Hawaii birds eat the red fruit of the ieie vine, and observed them foraging in the foliage of koa trees. Perkins (1903:444–445) wrote that the birds "are easily kept alive in captivity, and will live for a considerable time on the juice of the sugar-cane, and probably for the natural term of their lives if freely supplied with their favourite nectar-producing flowers. They were habitually kept thus by the old native birdcatchers to serve as decoys, as also were some of the Drepanididae, and are said to have become tame and reconciled to confinement." Munro (1944:86) wrote that "a small lot of 3 males and 2 females were received alive by the Gay and Robinson family in 1892 and released at Makaweli, Kauai. They survived for a time but eventually disappeared."

The Hawaii Oo was described as being aggressive, especially toward the Iiwi. The Oo displayed its yellow axillary tufts and under tail coverts when attacking other species, and probably also during courtship displays. The birds were found in pairs during the breeding season but in family groups or flocks the rest of the year.

Titian Peale (1848:171) wrote that "in voice and manners," the Hawaii Oo had some resemblance to the Baltimore Oriole (*Icterus galbula*) of North America.

Palmer referred to a "short song with but little melody, a 'kind of squeaking noise.'" Perkins said that "the cry of the Oo is unlike that of any native bird, and no one who has once heard it and identified it can ever again be in doubt as to the bird that utters it. This cry is usually dissyllabic, as represented by the bird's name, but sometimes may be represented by only a single sound. It varies somewhat, especially in loudness and clearness, according to the season, and is either uttered once or repeated." He found the birds mostly silent during the hotter hours of clear days, but vociferous in wet or foggy weather. The Oo also had a distinct song, "though it is extremely rarely heard, never uttered so far as I know from the tall Ohias, but always from some thick bush of the undergrowth." Perkins heard the song "only once or twice, even where the bird was very abundant."

Kioea
Chaetoptila angustipluma
(Color plate 41)

The Kioea was a large bird about 13.5 inches in length. Its color pattern was unlike that of any other Hawaiian bird: a black face mask, greenish brown wings and tail, and a heavily streaked pattern of brown and white feathers on the head, upper back, and underparts. The bill was long and slightly downcurved. The feet and legs were strong. Rothschild presented a colored plate of the Kioea, and Greenway (1958:426), a pen-and-ink drawing.

The type specimen was collected by the Pickering and Peale expedition in 1840 on the island of Hawaii, the only known range of the species. According to Munro (1944:88) several additional specimens were collected by Mills about 1859. The species apparently has not been seen since that time.

Cassin (1858:169) bemoaned the fact that but a single specimen was available to him for description. Peale (1848:148), who was one of the few persons to see this species in the field, commented: "This rare species was obtained on the Island of Hawaii. It is very active, and graceful in its motions, frequents the woody districts, and is disposed to be musical, having most of the habits of a *Meliphaga;* they are generally found about those trees which are in flower." Just so much and no more seems to be known about this interesting bird.

FAMILY DREPANIDIDAE
(HAWAIIAN HONEYCREEPERS)

This is Hawaii's unique bird family. This family exhibits among its numerous species the most striking example of adaptive radiation (especially in bill shape) from an assumed single ancestral species of any bird family in the world. Specimens of a few species were acquired by members of the expedition during Captain Cook's visits to the Hawaiian Islands, but many of the species were not collected and described until the 1890s; the Nihoa Finch was described in 1917, *Melamprospos,* in 1974. In all, 16 genera, 28 species, and 18 subspecies are now recognized. Of these, approximately 40 percent are either extinct or are believed to be extinct and many more are threatened with extinction (Fisher, Simon, and Vincent 1969). The family name formerly was spelled Drepaniidae.

Postulated causes of extinction of Hawaiian birds were discussed in chapter 1. After comparing Baldwin's data on relative abundance of birds in Volcanoes National Park in the 1940s with his censuses made from 1959 through 1961, Dunmire (1962) reported that the White-eye had shown a striking increase in numbers whereas native birds seemed "to be declining in numbers in some parts of the park and holding their own in others." He added that "the decline is probably due in part to increased competition by more versatile exotic forms, but there may be other unassessed deleterious factors involved." As mentioned earlier, however, no studies of the interrelations of introduced species with endemic species have been conducted as yet.

That this remarkable family of birds has not been studied more intensively can be attributed in part to the fact that Charles Darwin visited the Galápagos Islands and not the Hawaiian Islands. Darwin, however, believed that the Hawaiian Islands had a unique flora and fauna, as suggested on page 4. It seems certain that Rothschild and others sent collectors to Hawaii in the 1880s and 1890s as a result of Darwin's publications on evolution. After Perkins left Hawaii, however, ornithologists demonstrated an amazing disinterest in the Hawaiian avifauna for a period of some 40 years. There were no significant contributions to our understanding of the honeycreepers until the publication of the theses by Amadon (1950) and Baldwin (1953).

Henry Palmer, sent to Hawaii by Lord Rothschild, was primarily a bird collector. Although trained as an entomologist, R. C. L. Perkins (1901, 1903) was a keen field biologist who wrote extensively on the habits and behavior of Hawaiian birds. In 1901 he wrote that two groups of Hawaiian drepanine birds exist, "indicating either two distinct original immigrants or, more probably, very early divergence from one ancestor in two directions."

Perkins' two subdivisions were the melanodrepanine, or black, and chlorodrepanine, or green, sections. The members of the melanodrepanine group

(subfamily Drepanidinae) exhibit little or no sexual dimorphism in adult plumage; the adults have white on the wings or upper parts of the body; the immature birds have partly black or dull-colored plumage; all except *Palmeria* have truncate apices of the primary feathers; and the skin in all is "comparatively thick, and sometimes extremely tough and thick." Perkins also noted that all of the species known to him in the field have a peculiar noisy flight, "so that the sound caused by their wings, when they fly freely, can be heard at a long distance."

In the chlorodrepanine group (subfamily Psittirostrinae), the primaries are never truncate; the young are invariably clothed to a large extent in green or olivaceous plumage, which also is characteristic of the adult female; and, in most species, there is sexual dimorphism in plumage, although in some it is slight.

It might be noted here that the name "finch" was given to certain species by taxonomists in the 1890s because they thought that the large-billed birds belonged to the finch family (Fringillidae). This interpretation was based exclusively on the superficial resemblance in bill shape and size.

The noted German anatomist Hans Gadow (in Wilson and Evans 1890–1899) had suggested that the closest relation to the Hawaiian honeycreepers was the American neotropical family Coerebidae, also called honeycreepers. Beecher (1951) later concluded that the Coerebidae was, in fact, "an artificial group composed of nectar-adapted warblers and nectar-adapted tanagers that have become convergently similar due to similar diet." Primarily because of Gadow's remarks, Amadon (1950:233, 253) and others have postulated an American origin for the ancestors of the Hawaiian honeycreepers.

The Hawaiian honeycreepers have one important characteristic in common with a number of American bird families: they have but 9 functional primary flight feathers; whereas most of the other passerine bird families have 10 functional primaries.

Sushkin (1929) suggested that the honeycreepers had evolved from cardueline finches. Many species of these finches inhabit the Northern Hemisphere, and the family is presumed to have originated in Eurasia; some species are noted for their erratic wanderings; about 32 species are now found in North and South America. Life history studies have been conducted on only a small number of the more than 120 species in the subfamily Carduelinae, but those species studied share an uncommon trait among passerine birds in that the adults allow the fecal sacs of the nestlings to accumulate on the nest (page 223). Van Riper (1978b) has found this also to be the case with the Palila. Cardueline finches feed their young by regurgitation, a behavior also found in the Palila, in my captive Nihoa Finches, and, according to van Riper, in the Hawaii Amakihi.

A great deal has been learned about the physiology and internal anatomy of honeycreepers during the past decade. Bock (1972), Richards and Bock (1973), Mac-Millen (1974), Raikow (1974, 1976, 1977a,b, 1978), Sibley (1970), authors who have studied them, also conclude that the ancestor of the honeycreepers was a cardueline finch; they differ, however, in what they believe was the nature of the founding population. Richards and Bock proposed that the ancestral population consisted of birds similar to *Ciridops anna* (page 153); Raikow (1977b) believed that *Psittirostra* is "the most primitive genus, little modified from the founder"; Pratt (1979:96), in writing about *Telespyza,* said that "they may not only resemble the ancestral honeycreeper closely, but may even represent a direct line of descent from it." There is little doubt that previous systems of classification—based almost entirely on museum study skins—have been inadequate for depicting the relationships among the honeycreepers. Additional information is needed, but I agree with Pratt who recognizes three subgroups rather than two as proposed by Perkins and other twentieth-century writers. Pratt, however, considers the honeycreepers to be a subfamily of the Fringillidae and, therefore, he calls his subgroups tribes. I maintain the family Drepanididae, with three subfamilies: Psittirostrinae, Hemignathinae, and Drepanidinae (Van Tyne and Berger 1976). I agree that the overwhelming evidence points to a Cardueline ancestry for the Hawaiian honeycreepers, and I think that a neotropical origin for the ancestral forms (as has long been proposed) is entirely wrong; an Asian origin is far more likely.

Recent students of this family have concluded that the honeycreepers do constitute a true monophyletic family, derived from a single ancestral founding species. It should be emphasized, however, that the nests, eggs, and newly hatched young still have not been described for many of the species and subspecies (Scott et al. 1980). No explanation has been offered for the differences in yolk color: orange in the Apapane and Iiwi; yellow in the Nihoa Finch, Amakihi, Anianiau, and Akepa. The internal anatomy of most species is also not known. It is doubtful that *Melamprosops* is a honeycreeper. The arrangement of genera and species proposed here certainly will be modified when more information is available.

C. Robert Eddinger (1970b) was the first to determine the incubation and nestling periods for any species of the honeycreepers. Incubation periods for four species were either 13 or 14 days. Nestling periods varied from 15 to 17 days for the Apapane, 17 to 19 for the Anianiau, 17 to 20 for the Amakihi, and 21 to 22 for the Iiwi. These are long nestling periods for the members of the higher families of passerine birds. At the same time, the nestlings have a strong instinct to leave the nest prematurely when disturbed. They climb from the nest and flutter or fall to the ground at an age when they cannot fly and when they undoubtedly are unable to withstand the cold and wet nights on the ground. The adaptive value of this behavior is difficult to conceive of. I first noted this trait in the Hawaii Amakihi, and Eddinger discovered the same phenomenon in the species he studied on Kauai. For example, the normal nestling period for the Iiwi is either 21 or 22 days. Eddinger found, however, that some of the nestlings will jump from the nest when only 12 days old and that nearly all nestlings will leave the nest if disturbed when they are 14 days of age. The young birds can fly well when they leave the nest at the end of the full nestling period.

All species of honeycreepers thus far observed to scratch their heads have done so indirectly, that is, by lowering a wing and raising the foot over the wing to reach the head: Laysan Finch, Nihoa Finch, Amakihi, Anianiau, Creeper, Akepa, Palila, Apapane, and Iiwi. This is not an unexpected behavior pattern, however, inasmuch as very few passerine birds scratch their heads directly, or under the wing (Van Tyne and Berger 1976).

Members of the honeycreeper family inhabited all of the main Hawaiian islands, and two species were found on certain of the Leeward Islands in historic times. The tragic remnant population of three individuals of the Laysan Honeycreeper (also incorrectly called the Laysan "Honeyeater"), a race of the Apapane, became extinct in 1923.

Unfortunately, all of the highly specialized honeycreepers have become extinct on Oahu, Molokai, and Lanai, as have most of those on Hawaii. Kauai is the only island that still has all of the endemic birds known to have occurred there in historic times. Most of these are confined to the Alakai Swamp region, and many are now rare. The outer, windward, east and northeast slopes of Haleakala also have provided a haven where some unique Hawaiian birds have survived. These are areas which have not been much disturbed by wild cattle, nor have they been desecrated by foresters and ranchers.

Our knowledge of the biology of the honeycreepers is still sparse. Except for the Laysan Honeycreeper, the nests, eggs, and newly hatched young were never described for any of the extinct species. I found the first nest with eggs of the Palila in 1968; the first nests of the

Akepa and the Creeper were found by C. Robert Eddinger in 1969. The first incubation periods for this family also were determined by Eddinger in 1969.

Subfamily Psittirostrinae
Laysan Finch
Telespyza cantans

In the first edition of this book, I followed Amadon's (1950) system of classification and used the name *Psittirostra c. cantans* for this honeycreeper. Banks and Laybourne (1977) presented cogent reasons for placing the Leeward island birds in a separate genus.

Males in breeding plumage have a bright yellow head, throat, and breast; the abdomen is white; the under tail coverts are white but with a tinge of pale yellow. The upper back is greenish yellow broadly streaked with black; the lower back and upper tail coverts are soft medium gray. The tail feathers are brownish but they are edged with greenish yellow. The primaries are black edged with greenish yellow; the secondaries also are black but have much larger areas of yellow. The heavy finchlike bill is pale bluish gray to horn colored. Females are brownish streaked with black above, with traces of a greenish yellow tinge; yellowish on the upper breast and dirty white on the abdomen and under tail coverts, streaked with brown, especially on the breast. Immature birds of both sexes lack the bright yellow of the adult male, and they are heavily streaked with black or brown both above and below. Overall length is between 6 and 6.5 inches.

The Laysan Finch was first described in 1890 by Scott B. Wilson (1890b), who erroneously said that it inhabited Midway Atoll. Wilson saw several birds in cages in Honolulu and was able to buy one. "With considerable trouble and some good luck (the bird escaped twice into the car during the railway-journey across Canada)," he succeeded in getting the bird alive to England.

Wilson tells us how the birds happened to be in Honolulu. About March 1888, "a small schooner named the 'Mary Böhm' arrived in the Hawaiian Islands from Japan, off the coasts of which country it had been engaged in a fishing venture." The schooner had encountered several mishaps on its return voyage and stopped at one or more of the Leeward Islands. The finches were not collected on Midway, and there is some doubt as to whether they were collected on Laysan Island or Nihoa Island. Although probably the latter, there is the possibility that birds were collected from both islands. In either case, the finch "was so tame that it could be easily taken by the hand, and about sixty specimens were captured."

Henry Palmer and George C. Munro were the first to collect the birds on Laysan Island (June 16 to 27, 1891). Palmer wrote in his diary for June 18 that "Mr. Freeth has just told me his little boy caught one of the Finches this morning and then got an egg and offered it to it; the bird broke and ate the egg while being held in the boy's hand. This would give you an idea how tame all the birds are here."

From the skins that Palmer sent to Rothschild, he described two species: *"Telespiza cantans,"* Laysan Finch, and *"Telespiza flavissima,"* Yellow Laysan Finch. The former, however, were birds in immature plumage (W. K. Fisher 1906).

Fisher (1906) notes: "One can not walk anywhere without encountering them singly or in little flocks, diligently searching for food among the bushes, or out in the open. When disturbed they eye the intruder with interest or half in doubt and utter their low, mellow, linnet-like call. They do not fly far, but prefer to alight soon, and run along the ground, or elude pursuit by suddenly crouching under a grass tussock. . . . The 'finches' were common in the vicinity of the house, and hopped about the piazza in a very familiar way. While I was preparing specimens one came several times and lit on a table within a few feet and explored my belongings."

Bailey (1956) also encountered the Laysan Finches "everywhere over the island" during his visit from December 1912 to March 1913. The destruction of the vegetation on Laysan Island by rabbits between 1903 and 1923 has already been discussed. In 1923 "a few dozen Laysan Finches still sang their sprightly songs about the buildings or hopped among the rocks near the lagoon" (Wetmore 1925:103). It was undoubtedly because of its omnivorous feeding habits that the Laysan Finch managed to survive the destruction of the vegetation. During the extended breeding season of the seabirds, the finches break the eggs of the several species of nesting terns and petrels and eat their contents; when still available, they probably also ate the eggs of the Laysan Rail, the Laysan Millerbird, and the Laysan Honeycreeper.

During March 1966, I watched Laysan Finches catch insects and eat seeds and flower buds, as well as the eggs of the Brown Noddy. Earlier visitors to Laysan had reported seeing the finches eating the eggs of the Gray-backed Tern and the Brown Noddy, and it seems probable that the finches eat any egg that they can crack. They also are said to feed from the carcasses of dead seabirds, and to eat the soft parts of grass stems and the tender shoots of shrubs. Bailey wrote that the Laysan Finches on Eastern Island of Midway Atoll "nipped the buds of the hibiscus, and were destructive to the eggs of the canaries and Fairy Terns."

After the last of the rabbits were killed, both the vegetation and the birds made a rapid recovery, and an estimate of at least 1,000 Laysan Finches was made during the visit of the Zaca expedition in 1938. Brock (1951b) estimated a population of approximately 5,000 in 1951. The population now fluctuates drastically from year to year (7,500 in July 1974, but 14,800 during August 1975), but the species appears in no danger so long as predators are kept off of the island.

Eugene Kridler released 108 Laysan Finches on Southeast Island of Pearl and Hermes Reef on March 21, 1967 (Sincock and Kridler 1980). Some of these birds began to nest less than two months later. The estimated population on Southeast Island since 1970 has varied from 182 (April 1970) to 730 (March 1973). Finches also have spread to Grass, North, and Seal-Kittery islands of Pearl and Hermes Reef.

The Laysan Finch also was introduced on Midway Island in 1891 and again about 1905. Bailey (1956: 124) wrote, however, that "the disappearance of the finches and the [Laysan] rails was very rapid when rats overran the islands during the war years, and few if any existed on Midway after 1944."

The Laysan Finch is found in all plant associations on Laysan Island, although this species is especially partial to the bunchgrass association (page 34). The thick tussocks of this grass reach a height of over three feet, and provide cover, food, and nesting sites for the birds. The individual tussocks typically are widely spaced, some in areas where only bare sand intervenes, others in areas where a low ground cover, such as morning glory, fills the spaces between the grass clumps.

The song of the Laysan Finch is loud, melodious, and canarylike, even to the inclusion of trills. Call-notes, of which there are several, also are melodious, some resembling those of the canary; other, slurred notes resemble those of the Palila but often are longer. The alarm note is a harsh *cheruup*.

The breeding season of the Laysan Finch has not been determined precisely, and there may be annual variations. Bailey reported that "nesting starts in February and we saw birds carrying nesting material into crannies in the piles of phosphate rock, and into the bunches of clump grass. Willett found an early nest with one egg among rocks on February 11, and the next was in a similar site on March 3 and on March 10 another with three eggs was located in bunch grass." Fisher found nests with eggs in May (1902; fig. 73), and Palmer and Munro found a nest with one egg and two nestlings in June (1891). Ely and Clapp (1973) wrote that "although eggs may occasionally be laid in February and March, other observations and collections suggest that most egg laying occurs from late

April through May and June and that most young have fledged by the end of July or early August. Young have been seen in the nest as late as mid-September (1964) but evidently few nests are active in this month, or in the following months until the beginning of another breeding season." We did not find any active nests during the last week of March 1966, nor were any found by Eugene Kridler in March 1968 and 1969.

Nests are built almost exclusively in clumps of bunchgrass, usually in "the dense portions of the grass clumps where the old blades had fallen down and where new green blades overhung." Nests have been found from 4 to 17 inches above the ground. Crossin (Ely and Clapp 1973:256) wrote that, "in all finished nests, dead grass blades and stems were interwoven among the rootlets and the entire structure was composed of these plant portions. There was essentially no cup lining, the entire cup being constructed of smaller and finer grass blades and rootlets. The finished structure is compact and the surrounding grass blades allow the nest to remain in place for long periods."

The clutch varies from 2 to 4 eggs, 3 eggs being most commonly found. The incubation and nestling periods for wild birds have not been determined.

I accompanied Eugene Kridler, the refuge manager, to Laysan Island in 1966, a time when he had been authorized to bring live Laysan Finches to Honolulu. As was true for earlier observers, we found the birds very tame, and we had no difficulty in catching a large number of them with butterfly nets. Most of the birds were released after being banded as part of a long-term study of this species. We discovered that the captive birds were very hardy and that they readily ate lettuce and a number of fruits, such as papaya and apple, that were entirely foreign to their natural diet. Upon arrival in Honolulu, 19 birds were turned over to Mr. Jack Throp, Director of the Honolulu Zoo, and 10 pairs were sent to Dr. Harrison B. Tordoff at the University of Michigan.

Throp (1970) discussed the diet of his 19 captive Laysan Finches and described several types of artificial nests he used in order to induce the birds to breed in captivity. Some pairs did so when suitable grass tussocks were provided in their cages. One pair of birds hatched 3 eggs and raised 1 nestling to independence in 1966. Throp reported the incubation period at this nest to be 16 days. A second pair raised 2 young, and a third pair raised a single young bird to independence in 1967. Before the end of 1967, however, infections had killed all but 4 of the 23 birds (19 wild birds plus the 4 raised in captivity). The last male died in 1969, leaving only 3 females, one of which was a captive-raised bird.

Throp wrote that he never saw his captive Laysan

FIGURE 73. Female Laysan Finch at its nest; Laysan Island. May 1902. Photograph by Walter K. Fisher, courtesy of Alfred M. Bailey.

Finches drink water even though it was available at all times. This is in marked contrast to my captive Nihoa Finches.

Professor Tordoff told me that the female of one of his pairs of Laysan Finches skipped at least three days between the laying of the second and the third eggs in the clutch. In this nest, two of the eggs hatched 16 days after the second egg was laid. He wrote that "the incubation period for the third egg could not have been over 14 days, and might have been as short as 12 days."

Nihoa Finch
Telespyza ultima
(Color plate 43)

In 1917, this honeycreeper was named "ultima" by W. A. Bryan (1917) because he thought it would be the last endemic Hawaiian bird to be discovered. In 1923, however, Alexander Wetmore visited Nihoa and discovered the Nihoa Millerbird. Bryan described the Nihoa Finch as closely resembling the Laysan Finch in color "but smaller in all dimensions." His figures for the length of four specimens varied from 5.5 to 5.65 inches, and he commented that the "Nihoa birds are in reality a somewhat dwarfed form of the Laysan species." I found three Bishop Museum specimens to vary from 5.06 to 5.63 inches.

"In adult males the head, neck, and back are Pyrite Yellow, with a broad Gray band between the neck and mid-back. The lower back and rump are Gray. The throat and breast and secondary edgings are between lemon chrome and Aniline Yellow, and the flanks are Smoke Gray. Adult females differ less from the first winter birds than do males. The head and back feathers are edged with Pyrite Yellow and streaked with Fuscous Black. The back is also streaked as in the first winter birds. The sides of the head are Pyrite Yellow. The throat, breast, and edgings of the secondaries are Wax Yellow, and the flanks are Drab Gray. The yellow on the breast does not extend as far posteriorly on the female as on the male. The abdomen in both sexes is whitish" (Banks and Laybourne 1977:345). These authors also stated that Nihoa Finches acquire their fully adult plumage before they are one year old, whereas the fully adult plumage of the Laysan Finch is not acquired until the birds are three years old. Juvenile birds of both sexes are heavily streaked with black, both on the back and on the breast. The weights of six of my captive birds varied from 21 (male) to 28 (female) g.

Population estimates have varied widely, from a low of about 1,300 birds in 1973 to highs of about 6,600 in 1968 and 6,000 in 1975. The causes of these fluctuations are unknown. The survival of the species depends upon maintenance of the native vegetation and the prevention of the introduction of rats and other mammalian predators to this 156-acre island.

Like the Laysan Finch, the Nihoa Finch has omnivorous tastes. In addition to insects, seeds, and flower buds, the Nihoa Finch eats the eggs of the smaller seabirds, especially those of the Brown Noddy (fig. 74). I watched several birds break the shell of a Noddy egg by pecking it. The Noddies do not build a nest but simply lay their single egg on the ground, or, on Nihoa, often on a rock. Several times I watched the finches peck at the under side of an egg. This pecking caused the egg to roll and soon to fall to a rock a foot or so below, whereupon the shell cracked. Several finches would immediately fly to the egg and begin to eat its contents. On one occasion, I counted 20 finches within 30 feet of a single broken egg. Several birds would hop around the egg, engaging in frequent fights as first one bird and then another would have an opportunity to eat. Once I was able to approach within 3 feet of where finches were eating an egg. Whether or not the Nihoa Finches also destroy the eggs in each others' nests or eat the eggs of the Millerbird apparently has not been determined. Vanderbilt and de Schauensee said that the stomachs of several specimens "contained a gelatinous yellow substance (probably yolk of egg), minute black seeds and microscopic pebbles."

Frank Richardson (1954) watched the birds eating the small, green flower heads of *Chenopodium sandwicheum,* and one bird "picking out the still partly green seeds of *Portulaca caumii,* a plant endemic to the island."

Little has been written of the nesting habits of the Nihoa Finch. Vanderbilt and de Schauensee spent nine days on Nihoa during August 1940. They wrote that "the birds were not nesting, but two old nests were found in a small volcanic crevass." We found no evidence of nesting in early August 1966. Richardson (1954) found two old nests in December 1953, one of which was "in a rocky recess near the base of a cliff." On March 18, 1954, he found in this same cliff nest a young bird "not quite fledged," meaning a nestling; this, apparently, is the first record of the nesting of the Nihoa Finch.

Eugene Kridler and John L. Sincock have found eggs and young (from newly hatched to fully feathered) during March; they found 13 nests on March 7, 1968, containing a total of 10 eggs and 28 nestlings. Some nests had 4 nestlings. The nests were made of grass and feathers of frigatebirds and boobies. All of the nests were built in holes in cliff outcroppings at elevations from 100 to nearly 850 feet. Kridler and Sincock believe that "nesting occurs during the winter and spring, with a peak in March."

FIGURE 74. Nihoa Finches at a Brown Noddy egg; Nihoa Island. August 1, 1966.

In June of 1969, personnel of the U.S. Fish and Wildlife Service brought some Nihoa Finches to Honolulu for me to raise in captivity in an effort to learn more about the behavior and breeding habits of these honeycreepers. The birds adjusted immediately to captivity in a cage, approximately 4 × 6 × 8 feet in dimensions, into which I had placed branches, a number of large grass tussocks, and cement building blocks. The carrying box, with the door in its roof open, was placed in the larger cage, but none of the finches emerged. Consequently, we had to remove the birds one at a time and release them in the cage. The birds flew to nearby branches, displaying no wildness whatsoever. Within 5 minutes after all of the birds had been released, some of them went to the food dishes and five birds began to take water baths in the pan provided. Two of the birds began to sing within 10 minutes after being released from their confined quarters in the carrying box. Several hours later, I noticed that five of the birds were resting in holes in the cement blocks.

The staple diet for the birds was parakeet seed, but I tried many other foods until I learned their preferences. During the first few weeks that I had the birds, I recorded that they much preferred fruit, which was, at that time, a ground-up mixture of apple, papaya, avocado, and banana. Later, I simply put the separate fruits in the cage, and added mango, slices of orange or grapefruit, and, occasionally, raisins and prunes, which they also ate. During the early weeks, I gave them dishes of commercial "Mockingbird food" and "mynah food," both separately and mixed with baby cereal, but discovered that they did not eat much of this mixture. After some six weeks, I concluded that the preferred diet was mixed bird seed, lettuce, orange, and papaya, plus chicken egg.

I first placed a chicken egg in the cage four days after receiving the birds. One of the finches immediately flew to the egg and soon was followed by three more. Frequent flights occurred and only one bird pecked at the egg at a time; however, none of the birds was able to crack the shell. The following morning I made a small hole in the shell, whereupon a finch flew to the egg and began to peck at the ragged edge of the shell. Three birds were soon eating shell and yolk at the same time. Thereafter, I cracked the shells before putting eggs into the cage. As time went on, the birds ate more of the shell than they did of the yolk.

We had a stock of standard half-pint milk bottles containing cultures of fruit flies, which we had been feeding to other species of honeycreepers. I placed several bottles in the Nihoa Finch cage, placing the bottles on their sides. Each day I noticed one or more finches reaching into the necks of the bottles to eat flies, larvae, or pupae. On several occasions, I watched a finch crawl all the way into a bottle and eat from the medium at the bottom, where it must have been eating either pupae or larvae. Once I thought that surely the bird was stuck in the bottle, but then it managed to turn around and come out. To avoid mortality due to birds getting stuck in bottles during my absence, I stood the bottles on their bottoms so that the birds could easily catch the flies that emerged. However, just one day later, I found that a finch had entered an upright bottle and, of necessity, was "standing on its head" as it ate from the medium in the bottom of the bottle. The bird extricated itself without much difficulty, but thereafter I placed the bottles on their sides again.

Except during infrequent periods of rain on Nihoa, there is almost no place for the birds to take water baths. In captivity, however, four or five birds invariably flew to the water pan to bathe as soon as I had given them fresh water. Very rarely was there any fighting at the water pan. The birds drank fresh water daily in captivity. The drinking habits of the birds on Nihoa have not been studied, but they have been observed to drink from water seeps located under rock overhangs in the main canyons.

The roosting habits of the captive birds also were interesting. Only one or two of ten birds in the big cage would spend the night on the branches; all of the others roosted either in the cement blocks or in the grass tussocks.

All but two of my birds seemed to be in female or immature plumage when received on June 11. The birds were very heavily marked with black on the head, back, and wings, and they were streaked, some very heavily, with black on the throat, breast, and abdomen. The birds began their annual molt during late June or early July. Several birds on July 13 had new outer tail feathers only about half the length of the others, and by the end of the month nearly all of the birds had tails of irregular shape because of the shorter incoming feathers. The molt did not appear to be complete until late September or early October, although it may have been slower than in wild birds.

By July 15, seven of twelve birds were singing. They continued to sing throughout the fall and winter, although the males were more persistent in singing than the females. The loud, melodious, advertising song has a distinct canarylike quality, containing trills, whistles, and warbles. Two of the callnotes also are melodious or "sweet." One is a two-syllabled, upslurred note. The other consists of three syllables of which the first is upslurred and the last two downslurred. Both seem to be location notes. The alarm or distress callnote is a loud, harsh *chip.*

The advertising song, used both in courtship of the female and, apparently, to intimidate other males, often is accompanied by a display. While singing, the male holds his wings horizontally away from the body; sometimes he also sways slowly to the right and the left, and he may move short distances along the perch.

On September 30, 1969, I asked C. R. Eddinger, my research assistant, to bring in some fresh clumps of grass. The ones I had put in the cage in June had died, and the birds had chewed at least a foot off the ends of

each tussock. In the process of removing the old tussocks, we discovered two partially completed nests, one in a tussock and one in a cement block. During the following month, there was continued singing and occasional sexual chasing. Even though this somewhat gregarious species seemed to do very well in the cage, I felt that there probably were too many birds to permit actual nesting.

Space was limited, but, on November 14, we built another cage approximately 2.5 × 3 × 7 feet in dimensions on one end of a work bench in my laboratory. We added branches, a large grass tussock, one 6-inch-diameter elbow pipe, and one cement block, placing a slab on the top so as to leave just enough space for the birds to enter into the secluded areas in each half of the block. We then transferred a male and a female to the new cage. At first the birds hid in the dense grass, but within five minutes both birds were perched high on the branches and the male was singing.

The roosting habits of this pair were very interesting. Until the female built a nest and laid a clutch of eggs, she perched at night on one of the highest branches in the cage, whereas the male slept in the tussock of grass. After the female began incubating and spent the night on the nest, the male roosted on one of the highest perches in the cage.

The birds in both cages often broke off pieces of grass and "mouthed" them for short periods of time before dropping them, and by December 20 the female in the smaller cage had begun to build a nest in the pipe. A few days later, however, she was carrying nesting material into both sides of the cement block, finally finishing one of the nests by early January.

I first observed soliciting behavior by the female on December 27. She had taken a water bath and was preening on a branch below the male when she began to utter soft callnotes. She later interrupted her preening activities to chase the male. A short time later she continued to add grass to her final nest. By the end of the month she courted the male many times each day. Typically she flew to a branch below the male, began giving soft soliciting notes, crouched slightly, and quivered her wings. When the male flew, she would follow and repeat the soliciting behavior. Sometimes the male fed her.

I first observed the male mount the female on January 5, 1970; on one occasion, copulation did not take place, but it seemed to occur during several other mountings that day and on the following days. The first egg was laid on the morning of January 8; the third egg of the clutch was laid on January 10. The female perched on a branch on the nights following the laying of each of the eggs, but she had begun incubating very early on January 11. When she left the nest, apparently in response to the male's callnotes, at 11:15 A.M., I was greatly disturbed to find only two eggs, one of which had a little dried yolk on the shell. Either the male or the female had eaten one of the eggs early that same morning.

From that time on, however, the female incubated most of the time, leaving the nest only for periods of one or two minutes to feed. In response to her soliciting behavior, very often the male fed her after she left the nest. Usually the female perched slightly below the male but sometimes nearly on the same level. He would stand high on his legs, arch his head and neck upward, and then reach down to feed the female. Once when she came off the nest and solicited, the male fed her five times in rapid succession, hopped away, returned, fed her again, hopped away a second time, and then returned to feed her. Pumping movements of the male's head and neck suggested that he was feeding her by regurgitation. Only rarely did I see the male enter the cement block, where he probably fed the incubating female.

The male sang frequently throughout the day (as well as at night when the lights were on in my office) while the female was incubating, and he repeatedly flew down to the cement slab to look in on the female. He would give a special callnote when I entered the room, apparently to alert the female, although she invariably remained on the nest.

There was a marked change in the female's callnotes after she began to incubate. The soft, twittering notes she had used when soliciting, as well as prior to the start of incubation, were replaced by a loud persistent begging note. She also fluttered her wings more rapidly so that the behavior was very similar to the food-begging pattern of recently fledged birds. A second marked change occurred after incubation had been underway for 5 or 6 days: the female was completely quiet when on the nest, and typically gave few or no callnotes when off the nest.

The female continued to incubate the two eggs day and night, and one of the eggs hatched after 15 days and 9 hours of incubation (fig. 75). The egg hatched

FIGURE 75. Nihoa Finch that has just hatched in a nest of captive Nihoa Finches. January 26, 1970.

between 8:00 A.M. and 9:00 A.M. on January 26. The egg shell was still in the nest at 9:00 A.M. At 9:10 the female left the nest with half of the shell and began to eat it; but most of the shell dropped into the grass below, and the female returned to the nest. The other egg did not hatch.

In order to supplement the diet, I added foods processed for babies (protein cereal, egg yolk, carrots) and the larvae of the Oriental fruit fly. However, the adult finches ate very little of any of these items, and apparently fed none to the nestling. The female brooded and fed the nestling, but its growth was not normal after the first few days, and the nestling died when a little more than 12 days old.

The female began remodeling the old nest the day after the nestling died. Two days later, the female began soliciting again; the male fed her, and then mounted her for copulation. The female laid an egg in the remodeled nest on February 17, 9 days after the nestling had died. The female was on the nest at 7:45 A.M. She left the nest at 8:20, and I discovered that most of the upper portion of the shell had been eaten and the white and yellow yolk were conspicuous in the bottom portion of the shell. By 10:20, all of the shell had been eaten or carried away and there was only a small wet area in the bottom of the nest.

The eggs were always laid before 8:00 A.M., and I did not find any eggs in the nest during the following 3 days; I assumed that the female had laid but a single egg in this second clutch. Nine days after that egg was laid, she laid the first egg in a third clutch of three eggs on February 26 (fig. 76). She incubated these until March 10, on which date there were only two eggs in the nest at 7:45 A.M.; one had been eaten. Nevertheless, she continued to incubate these eggs until March 15, by which date I thought that one or both eggs might hatch, and, when I checked the nest, it looked as though one of the eggs was pipped. When I picked up the egg, however, I learned that the embryo was dead; it seemed more likely that the female had begun to eat the shell rather than that the embryo had cracked the shell. I replaced the egg with its dead embryo in the nest, and the female immediately returned to the nest. That afternoon, however, the nest held only one egg; the female had removed the other and dropped it somewhere in the grass where I did not see it. Six days later, I found the head, neck, and a small part of the body of the embryo in the water pan. The female continued to incubate or stand on the rim of the nest for 2 days after she had removed the dead embryo, but she then deserted the nest.

The unhatched eggs from the first and third clutches measured 15.7 × 21.2 and 16.0 × 21.45 mm, respectively. This female Nihoa Finch laid a minimum of 19

FIGURE 76. Two clutches of eggs of one of my captive Nihoa Finches: *top*, March 27, 1970; *bottom*, March 1, 1970.

eggs between January 8 and July 27, 1970, but 10 of these were laid on top of a cement block or on the floor of the cage and then were eaten. She laid one infertile egg in a nest on December 17, and continued to incubate this egg for 24 days, after which time she ate the egg.

Another female in the large cage had raised one fledgling to independence by July 1, 1971, and had then been incubating a second clutch of two eggs since June 18. At that time, there were three females (all with nests) and two males in the cage, but I never saw either of the males feed the young bird. However, at another nest in which one of two eggs hatched on June 26, both the female and her mate fed the young bird

FIGURE 77. Sixteen-day-old Nihoa Finch that was raised in captivity. July 12, 1971.

(by regurgitation) when it was a nestling, as well as after it left the nest on July 19 (fig. 77). I watched one of the immature birds sing when approximately 65 days old. The finches nested from March to June in 1972 and from March to May and in September and November 1973. Some of these birds lived much longer than wild passerine birds usually do: three birds died at 6 years of age, one at 7 years and 10 months, and one bird at 9 years and 4 months.

Eugene Kridler of the U.S. Fish and Wildlife Service transplanted 42 Nihoa Finches to French Frigate Shoals on March 10, 1967; of these, 32 were released on Tern Island and 10 on East Island. The birds on East Island were never seen again. Kridler found nests inside of concrete blocks on Tern Island in 1968; however, no more than 6 birds have been seen in recent years.

Ou

Psittirostra psittacea

(Color plate 46)

The Ou is a parrot-billed, yellow-headed bird with an olive-green back tinged with yellow. The wings and tail are blackish brown and edged with olive-green; the chin and throat are bright yellow; the rest of the underparts shade from olive-green to whitish on the abdomen and under tail coverts. Total length is about 7 inches. The bill is pale colored; the curved upper mandible hangs over the lower mandible.

A single species once inhabited Kauai, Oahu, Molokai, Lanai, Maui, and Hawaii. It is extinct on Oahu, Molokai, and Lanai. Maui is not even listed as part of the former range in many books, and the species has not been seen there for many years. The Ou now oc-

curs in widely separated areas on the windward coast of Hawaii in the Hamakua, Puna, and Kau districts. It is thought to be the rarest of the honeycreepers on Hawaii.

The Ou is most common in the Alakai Swamp region of Kauai, where John L. Sincock estimates a population "in the low hundreds." There, he told me, the birds are found only in the ohia rain forest at elevations between 3,500 and 4,250 feet. The birds frequently perch in the tops of dead ohia trees and in the uppermost clusters of leaves in lapalapa trees.

The causes of extinction on some islands and the great reduction in numbers on others are unknown. Certain diseases may have played a role at low elevations, as has been suggested by nearly all authors writing about the honeycreepers (e.g., Warner 1968), but there seems to be no evidence that the necessary vectors were present at the higher elevations to transmit the diseases. Nor is there any evidence to suggest why the Ou and many other species became so reduced in numbers whereas other species—Apapane, Iiwi, Amakihi, Palila, Anianiau—did not. Wilson and Evans (1890–1899) wrote: "Necklaces, 'leis,' used sometimes to be made from the bright green plumage of the back and underparts of this bird, but they were commonly used in combinations with the black feathers of *Acrulocercus nobilis* and the scarlet feathers of *Vestiaria coccinea*. I saw a wreath thus made at Olaa in the district of Puna, which I attempted to purchase, but the native wanted a higher price than I was inclined to give."

Perkins (1903:433) saw a pair of Ou, which he did not collect, on Oahu in March 1893. He wrote:

Since that year, although I have spent much time in the forests of Oahu, I have never seen or even heard another individual, though the song of the Ou and its callnote are audible at a considerable distance, and cannot be mistaken for those of any other bird. Why the Ou should have become extinct on Oahu and remain abundant in far more restricted forests on Molokai and Lanai is by no means clear, but with regard to the former island it may be noted that now over extensive areas it is often difficult to find a single red Ieie fruit, which the foreign rats have not more or less eaten and befouled, and they may thus have indirectly brought about the extinction of the Ou, even if in times of scarcity of the fruit they do not actually prey on the bird itself. That the Ou is easily caught is proved by the number of times that, when on Lanai, I found the remains of those that had been killed by cats, and twice I shot these vermin while in the act of devouring this very bird.

Munro wrote that the Ou and other honeycreepers were holding their own, or even increasing, on Lanai in 1923, but he considered the Ou extinct there by 1932.

W. A. Bryan (1908:168) collected 16 Ou, "of both

sexes, adult and immature," on Molokai during the period from April 15 to June 15, 1907, and he referred to the almost 100 specimens of the Ou then in the collection of the Bishop Museum. He wrote that "the Ou was met with at all the stations visited in the forest area, in a ratio of about one to twenty, as compared with the Amakihi. Hence it is not, relatively speaking, the abundant species its size and song would seem to make it. . . . The Halawa forest makes an ideal home for this Ieie-loving bird." When the Ou became extinct on Molokai is unknown, but it was gone before 1948 (Richardson 1949).

In writing about middle Kona on Hawaii in 1892, Perkins said that the Ou was "in countless numbers throughout the wet-belt," and that many strayed up into the dry and higher forest at the end of the fruiting season of the ieie and "occupied the haunts of their ally the Palila." They also moved "downwards below the range of *Freycinetia*, especially frequenting the clumps of Kukui trees, but many of these returned in the evening from these isolated clumps to the shelter of the continuous forest at a higher elevation." He noted that the Ou was both scarce and wary in forests that had been opened up by cattle.

Perkins (1903:389) wrote that the Apapane, Iiwi, and Ou "are all birds which take extensive flights, often at a great height in the air, and frequently form small companies in these flights. If we stand on the main ridge of some of the islands the birds may be seen passing high overhead from leeward to windward or vice versa. All freely traverse open country, in passing from one feeding-ground to another. Consequently when storms arise they are extremely likely to be carried across the channels between the islands, and no doubt this often happens." By contrast, Creepers, Akepas, Nukupuus, and Akialoas "do not take these extensive flights, but keep closely to the forest, very rarely—and most of them never—venturing into the open."

Perkins (1903:434) gave the best description of the feeding habits of the Ou.

Although the large female inflorescence of the *Freycinetia* is the chief food of the Ou, yet it also sometimes feeds on the male flowers, as well as on parts of the pretty red leaf-bracts which surround these. It also in a lesser degree eats the fruits of several other trees, and in forests above the range of the Ieie is very partial to the berries of some of the arborescent Lobeliaceae, and more especially to the large yellow ones of some species of *Clermontia*. In scattering the seeds of these, which like those of some other trees pass undigested through the alimentary canal, the Ou like the thrush is of great benefit to the forest, the more so on account of its wide-ranging habits. The fruit of the introduced guava, which has run wild and spread so widely over the lower parts of the mountains, is greatly appreciated by this bird, nor does it disdain other foreign fruits, which the white man has brought with him. Sometimes the stomach is entirely filled with green vegetable matter, apparently young leaves in a finely divided state. In some localities the bird pays great attention to the red flowers of the Ohia, and I have repeatedly noticed, both on Lanai and Kauai, that it visits these one after another on the tops of the tallest trees, thrusting its head amongst the numerous stamens. Specimens shot while so engaged contained only much finely divided green vegetable matter, so far as could be distinguished, but I suspect that the exposed nectar of the flowers was really the attraction, although it could not be detected amongst the green stuff with which the stomach was quite filled. Like several other birds of the family, the Ou may not yet have entirely lost the nectar-eating habit, the structure of its tongue being such that it might easily obtain nectar from the Ohia flowers, as *Oreomyza* does on rare occasions. Certainly the birds that were shot while visiting the flowers contained no insect food whatever. The Ou feeds its young very largely with caterpillars, especially those of Geometridae, and at times, when frequenting the forests of lofty Koa trees, itself partakes of hardly any other food. It generally seeks these in the bushy tops of the very tallest trees and is not always by any means easy to get sight of, even when it is in reality quite numerous. When crammed with this food decomposition sets in very soon after death, more quickly in fact than when it is on vegetarian diet, and the skin over the posterior ventral half of the body should be opened and pushed back soon after death, or most of the feathers of the belly will slough off.

Perkins also noted that "on another occasion large numbers of Ou wandered upwards above the wet-belt to feed on the swarms of looper caterpillars that were defoliating the Koa. . . . A similar incursion for the same purpose was noticed in the Koa forests above Kilauea in Kau both in 1895 and 1896 in the summer months." The Ou also were accompanied by large numbers of the Hawaii Thrush.

Perkins wrote that the Ou

has a rather sweet song, which at times reminds one somewhat of a canary, but is much inferior to a first-class songster of that species. Three or four very distinct and penetrating whistled notes form the beginning of its full song, and are highly characteristic. It sings very freely in the early morning hours, especially just before the nesting season, and when singing delights to perch on the loftiest dead branch that it can find. Sometimes it sings as it flies, and when a small company are on the wing together they not infrequently sing in concert, as they sometimes do at other times, and in a very pleasing manner. The call of the Ou is a rather long note, so whistled as generally to appear of an enquiring nature. To this it will readily respond again and again, and may by this means be brought close to the observer. In foggy weather especially, the birds are continually uttering this call, and often from this single note they break into their full song.

The nest and eggs of the Ou have never been described. Rothschild reported that "from the end of March to the middle of May females were procured with greatly enlarged ovaries." Perkins wrote: "In the middle forest of Kona in June, I observed great numbers of the young, some scarcely able to fly, but neither eggs nor nest. These young were frequenting the dense masses of Ieie, with which the great Ohia trees growing on the roughest lava-flows were covered, and no doubt the nests are built either in the tangled climbers or the trees themselves. In some parts of the islands no doubt the nests might be found without much trouble by anyone who devoted special attention to the matter, but certainly not in localities like the one above mentioned."

Palila
Loxioides bailleui
(Color plate 40)

The Palila is superficially similar to the Ou, being a large-billed, large-headed bird with a golden-yellow head and throat but with a gray back; the abdomen is grayish white; the lores are blackish. The bill of the Palila is dark, rather than light, in color and it is not hooked or parrot-billed. Amadon (1950) wrote that this attractive species is quite similar to the Laysan and Nihoa finches, "but it is never streaked with black." The female's "throat and breast are duller, while the crown is only slightly yellowish." Overall length is between 6.0 and 6.5 inches.

The Palila is endemic to the island of Hawaii. In the 1890s, Palmer (in Rothschild 1893–1900:198) found it "in the Kona and Hamakua districts, between elevations of 4000 and 6000 feet, . . . and in the Hilo district, on the slopes of Mauna Kea, they were seen even higher, at about 7000 feet."

In 1892 Perkins (1903:435–436) found it

extremely numerous in the Mamani belt of the middle and North Kona district, from rather below 4000 ft. to at least 6000 ft. above the sea. In this region it nested in the Mamani trees, and here I saw many young in all stages from those scarcely able to fly to nearly mature examples, but was not able to find any nest containing eggs. Some years later I revisited this spot in the winter and early spring months, when I found the adult bird in splendid plumage, but no immature examples. A few miles from the volcano of Kilauea the Mamani grows quite freely, and I was surprised to find none of the bird in that locality, since it much resembles its haunts in the Kona district.

The food of the Palila is to a very large extent derived from the Mamani trees, on the seeds of which it chiefly feeds. I have frequently seen it cut off a pod and hold it down on a branch with its claws in order to extract the seeds, as Wilson has already described. It feeds its young on caterpillars, and is itself at some seasons most partial to such food, a considerable variety of these being found in its stomach. Amongst these caterpillars is that of a conspicuous yellow, green, and black species of Pyralid, which it finds on the Mamani, and which is sometimes eaten so freely as to exclude all other food. It may be noted that this caterpillar possesses the so-called "warning colours" in the highest degree, and theoretically should be inedible, yet it is actually chosen in a locality which abounds in the protectively coloured Geometrid caterpillars.

The Palila has a distinctly whistled callnote which is easily imitated, and to an imitation of which it will readily respond. When answering the callnote often sounds of an enquiring or inquisitive nature, just as is the case with that of the Ou. It has too a distinct song, which is pleasing, but less so than that of the latter. Like the Ou it is of a sociable disposition, and frequently four or five or more adults in the perfection of plumage were seen in company during the winter months, while birds in immature plumage are nearly always accompanied by their parents long after leaving the nest.

Numerous in its special haunts, tame, and in foggy weather constantly uttering its callnote, the Palila of the more local birds is one of the easiest to observe or collect.

Despite its much wider distribution in the past, the Palila is now found only in the mamani-naio forests on Mauna Kea. Only rarely do the birds descend as low as 6,500 feet, but they are common from 7,000 feet upwards to tree line, which now ends at approximately 9,300 feet, varying somewhat around the mountain. The birds were found to occupy only about 25 percent of the forest by van Riper and his co-workers (1978). During January, the nonbreeding season, the birds were concentrated near tree line, and no birds were found below an elevation of about 8,600 feet, presumably because of a better food supply at the higher elevations. These fluctuations in distribution of populations throughout the year are very marked. On a few occasions, I have tramped through the open parkland forest for several hours without seeing or hearing a Palila, which typically gives melodious callnotes while feeding, even at those times of year when songs are not heard; whereas at other times of the year they are very common.

The Palila feeds on the dry, brown seed pods as well as on green pods of the mamani. From the larger pods, 4 to 5 inches long, a bird may eat only a single seed before dropping the pod to the ground. I watched one bird feeding on green seed pods, and, after the bird flew to another part of the tree, found 18 seed pods on the ground below its previous perch; from none to 3 seeds had been eaten from these 18 pods. Most of the birds I have watched held the seed pods with one foot, rather than two, as reported by Ord. The Palila also eats mamani flowers. Munro said that he had watched the birds eating the poha fruit and the seeds of naio.

Wilson (in Wilson and Evans 1890–1899) wrote that, as far as he knew, the Palila "has no song, but merely a very clear whistle-like note, which, when often repeated, is held by the natives to be a sign of approaching rain." The Palila has several callnotes, a whisper song, and a louder advertising song, but I have never heard it utter anything like a "wolf whistle," as has been recorded in the literature. Most of the Palila's notes and songs are melodious ("sweet" seems highly appropriate) and canarylike, but it has one call that reminded me of the song of the Olive-sided Flycatcher *(Nuttallornis borealis)*. The most common callnote, an upslurred, two-syllabled call, seems to be a location note, given back and forth as several birds are feeding in the same or adjacent trees. A longer warbling call is given under the same circumstances. Palila also sometimes sing while flying.

I was the first to find an active nest of the Palila on July 6, 1968, at an elevation of about 7,000 feet in the Kaohe Game Management Area. Although only 15.3 feet above the ground in a mamani tree, the nest was placed in a small branch so near the top of the tree that I could not climb high enough to look into the nest, but I could reach into it. I knew as soon as I picked up one of the two eggs, however, that they were too large to belong to any of the species whose nests I had already found in the study area; and as I held the egg carefully in my finger tips, I heard a bird fly into the tree behind me. The bird was a female Palila. The bird began to give its callnote, and a male answered from a short distance away. The male did not, however, come to the vicinity of the nest. I climbed down the tree and moved off a short distance, whereupon the female returned to the nest to incubate the eggs.

I returned to the study area on July 15. No Palila was singing, nor did I hear any callnotes. Nevertheless, I discovered that the Palila nest contained one egg and one nestling less than 24 hours old; as I was examining the nest, a female Palila again flew into a nearby tree and began to give her alarm notes.

This Palila's nest was irregular in shape, being about 5 inches by 7 inches in maximum outside diameters. The nest rim varied from about 1 to 1.25 inches in thickness. The nest cup itself varied from 2.25 to 2.5 inches in diameter, and was about 1.25 inches in depth.

The bulk of the body of the nest was composed of unidentifiable grass leaves, stems, and roots, with large dead mamani twigs woven into and around the exterior of the nest. Among these larger twigs there were mamani leaflets, fine strips of bark, and several dead flower stalks of a composite. The nest was lined with lichen.

The ground color of the eggs was white (fig. 78). Reddish brown markings formed a dense cap around the larger end of each egg and lighter markings were scattered thinly and irregularly over the remaining surface. The two eggs were virtually identical in coloration and in pattern.

The skin of the newly hatched nestling was a bright reddish orange in color. The lining of the oral cavity was only slightly redder than the general skin color. Long black down feathers in discrete tracts were conspicuous on the top of the head, back, and thighs.

I saw one stub-tailed fledgling on July 6, 1968, and saw three full-tailed fledglings with two adults on July 15, 1967.

On June 13, 1966, I watched a pair of Palila feeding in a mamani tree for nearly an hour. Near the end of that period, the female suddenly began to flutter her wings, whereupon the male fed her. Before he had finished, a second male flew into the tree and was immediately chased by the first male.

Van Riper (1978b) studied the Palila for several years (1971–1975). He found 26 active nests: 15 were placed on horizontal branches, 7 were in lateral forks, and 4 in terminal forks of the tree. The female builds most of the nest, although the male helps during the early stages. The time required to complete a nest varied from 7 to 20 days. He found that the average measurements of 26 nests were: width, 5.75 inches; height, 3.12; depth of the nest cup, 1.5. Six nests averaged 74.1 g in weight and varied from 41 to 105 g.

FIGURE 78. Egg and newly hatched nestling of the Palila. Kaohe Game Management Area, Hawaii. July 15, 1968.

The interval between completing the nest and laying the first egg varied from 1 or 2 days (most nests) to 20 days (for one nest). The eggs were laid before 8:00 A.M.; the clutch size in 11 nests was two eggs. The average width and length of eight eggs was 16.8 and 25.0 mm. Van Riper recorded incubation periods of 21, 23, 24, and 27 days, which are very long periods for passerine birds. The female alone incubates the eggs and broods the newly hatched young. The young are fed by regurgitation by both adults. The adults eat insects, especially during the breeding season, but van Riper was unable to learn whether the nestling food included insects; we assume that it does. The adults remove the fecal sacs voided by the nestlings until they are four days old, and the sacs begin to accumulate on the rim of the nest (fig. 79). Van Riper wrote that "by day 22, the nest, limbs of the tree, and ground below were covered with dried fecal material." The eyes begin to open when the nestlings are about 5 days old; preening of the sheathed feathers begins at about 10 days; and the nestlings begin to flap their wings when 21 days old. The bill is yellow at hatching, gradually changing to orange and then to black by the time that the young are 12 or 13 days old. The young leave the nest when between 21 and 25 days old, at which time the young fly strongly, usually to a nearby tree. Twelve young birds fledged from a total of 23 eggs, giving a reproductive success of 52.2 percent.

Because the Palila is one of the few surviving finch-billed honeycreepers on the main Hawaiian islands, it seems appropriate to emphasize again that the continued survival of this species is entirely dependent upon the continued maintenance of the mamani-naio forest on Mauna Kea. This "continued maintenance" is dependent upon a complete halt to any further bulldozing of the forest and to planting of exotic plants (including game bird foods), as well as upon the extermination of the feral sheep and goats, which continue to destroy this forest (figs. 80, 81).

Lesser Koa Finch
Rhodacanthis flaviceps
(Color plate 42)

Henshaw called this species the Yellow-headed Koa Finch. Rothschild (1893–1900:205) described it as follows:

Adult male. Head and neck dull golden yellow; back and upper wing-coverts greenish olive, shading into bright olive-green on the rump and upper tail-coverts; wings and tail

FIGURE 79. Two 20-day-old nestling Palila. July 11, 1972. Courtesy of Charles van Riper III.

FIGURE 80. The dying forest of the Mauna Kea Game Management Area, Hawaii. December 19, 1967. This is the only extensive mamani-naio forest in the state; it is the habitat of the Palila, Akiapolaau, Amakihi, and Elepaio.

FIGURE 81. Tree line in the Mauna Kea Game Management Area, elevation approximately 9,300 feet. February 6, 1970. Feral sheep and goats destroy all of the vegetation that they can reach, and the goats sometimes even climb leaning trees to get at the leaves. Consequently, the tree line continues to recede down the mountain. The forest once extended to about 10,000 feet. Compare with Figure 8.

dark-brown, the feathers externally margined with green. Chin, throat, and upper breast dark wax-yellow; abdomen and under tail-coverts yellowish green. Total length about 7.5 inches according to Palmer's measuring in the flesh, but only 6 inches in skin; wing 3.8 to 3.85, tail 2.5, culmen 0.7 to 0.72, tarsus 0.95 to 1.

Adult female. Underparts of a yellowish green, much paler than in the male; above similar to the male, but the head greenish olive like the back, only a yellow wash on the forehead. The female is also a little smaller than the male, the wing measures only 3.6 to 3.7 inches.

Young males closely resemble the adult females, but they are paler beneath and indistinctly spotted or clouded on the breast.

From September 30 to October 16, 1891, Palmer and Munro collected several specimens of this species in the same habitat where they had found the Greater Koa Finch. Neither Wilson nor Perkins found this species during their field work; however, nor has the species ever been seen again.

Perkins (1893:437) wrote:

In 1892 in a longer stay in exactly the same locality, I saw several score of the larger bird, and in two subsequent visits, the latter of which was made for the special purpose of investigating this matter, certainly some hundreds were examined with the naked eye or glasses, as the case required. On none of these occasions did I see a single one of the yellow-headed bird, nor did I hear any song or callnote that could be referred to a species unknown to me. It is possible, and in my opinion even probable, that the yellow-headed specimens secured by Mr. Rothschild's collectors were strays from some unknown locality, and only by chance occupied the range of the red-headed bird.

Consequently, Perkins and others doubted that *flaviceps* was a valid species, and it was suggested that the birds in question might be hybrids or that they might merely have been immature birds. After examining eight specimens, however, Amadon (1950) concluded that *flaviceps* "is a perfectly distinct species. If a hybrid, the parents would presumably be *Psittirostra palmeri* and *P. psittacea. P. flaviceps,* however, is not intermediate in size but is a little smaller even than *psittacea.* The bills of these two species are so different that one would certainly not expect a hybrid to have a bill precisely like that of *P. palmeri.* To postulate any other species, such as *Psittirostra bailleui* or *P. kona,* or members of another genus, as parents of hybrids involves still more difficulties." In summary, Amadon said that "the strikingly smaller size and the distinct coloration of the adult male of *flaviceps,* together with the presence of both adults and immatures among the known specimens, indicate that it is a good species."

Inasmuch as Palmer and Munro did not realize that they were collecting two different species, nothing was

recorded about the habits of the Lesser Koa Finch, nor were the nests and eggs ever described.

Greater Koa Finch
Rhodacanthis palmeri
(Color plate 44)

This species was called the Orange Koa Finch by Henshaw. The adult male has a rich reddish orange head and throat; the upper breast is a dull reddish orange, changing to dull orange-yellow on the abdomen and to pale yellow on the under tail coverts. The back is greenish olive, washed with orange, especially on the rump. The wings and tail are blackish brown, the feathers being margined with yellow on their outer vanes. The grayish olive axillaries and under wing coverts also are washed with orange. Perkins noted that "unfortunately the golden sheen of the orange-reddish crown partially loses its lustre after skinning, and never again does the brightness of the freshly-killed bird return."

The adult female is olive-green above with yellow on the forehead and yellow-green on the rump and upper tail coverts. The throat and sides of the body are yellowish olive-green; the breast and middle of the abdomen are ashy white washed with green.

Immature males resemble the females, "but the feathers of the throat, breast, and abdomen are spotted and clouded with dusky, thus giving these parts a very different aspect" (Rothschild 1893–1900:203).

This is one of the largest species in the honeycreeper family, although some measurements in the literature are misleading. Munro (1944:127), for example, gives the total-length measurement of two males as 9 inches. In the preface to his book, however, Munro points out that "without knowing the system by which these measurements were taken they can be considered only as approximate, especially in small perching birds. A bird measured in the flesh by contour from tip of bill to end of tail, as practiced by the Rothschild expedition, may differ considerably from the measurement in a straight line from tip of bill to end of tail as used by some other authors" (and by virtually everyone today). Munro also pointed out that when measurements are taken from a dried museum skin, "much depends on the system of preparing and filling it"; this is immediately evident to anyone who has examined a drawer of museum study skins. Rothschild, also aware of this problem, described the Greater Koa Finch as having a total length of "about 8¾ inches according to Palmer's measurings in the flesh, but only 7 to 7.5 in skins." I found that a male specimen of the Greater Koa Finch in the Bishop Museum measured 7.0 inches "in a straight line." An adult female measured 6.75 inches.

Rothschild (1892, 1893–1900), who named this species for his collector Henry Palmer, said that Palmer collected the first specimen of this species on September 28, 1891. The bird was collected at Puulehua on the Greenwell ranch at an elevation of 5,000 feet. He collected five more birds on October 5, also on the slopes of Mauna Loa, and one or more on November 20. The latter birds were collected in the koa forests on a dairy ranch called "Honaunau," owned by "a Mr. Johnston"; Palmer thought that the dairy was located "about 6000 feet above the sea and some twenty miles to the south of Pulehua." He presumably collected the Greater Koa Finch at an elevation greater than 6,000 feet because he mentioned riding "at least to 9000 feet," and seeing a crow at about 8,000 feet elevation. This was the first day he had seen the Greater Koa Finch in this part of the country. Palmer recorded in his diary: "When going down we had a rough time. We lost our way and had to ride across a big lava-field, and when we came into the track again it became pitch dark and none of us escaped without bruised and half-skinned legs, while one of Mr. Johnston's men fell and injured his arm very badly. It was indeed the worst riding I ever experienced."

Rothschild wrote that the Greater Koa Finch was "by no means rare in the Kona and Hilo districts of Hawaii," but he must have been in error in including the Hilo district. Perkins wrote that it was to be found in the Kona district and "in Kau in the Koa woods some miles above Kilauea," and I have found no evidence that it was ever collected elsewhere.

Only Perkins (1903:437) recorded much about the habits of the Greater Koa Finch. He wrote that the bird's plumage was at its best in the winter time, "and at this season the bird in life must be counted one of the most beautiful of Hawaiian species." He continued:

Although spending most of its time in the tops of the loftiest Koa trees, *Rhodacanthis* occasionally visits the lesser trees, especially those already mentioned, chiefly for the sake of the caterpillars that feed upon them. Like the Palila, it sometimes devours large quantities of gaudily coloured species, as well as the more sombre brown or green looper caterpillars. Its chief food is however the green pod of the Koa tree, which it swallows in large-sized pieces, and its blue beak is often stained with green juice and fragments of the pods. The development of the abdominal part of the body is large, possibly in accordance with the coarse fragments that it swallows, and in this it differs markedly from *Chloridops,* which feeds on the delicate embryos of the bastard sandal, and has the abdominal parts much less developed.

The song, if such it can be called, for apparently it serves also as a mere call, is entirely different from that of any other native bird. It consists of four, five, or even six whistled notes, of which the latter ones are much prolonged. It frequently differs somewhat as whistled by different individu-

als, and also is sometimes distinctly varied, when repeated by the same bird. Although the notes are not loud, they are very clear, and are very easily imitated, and the bird responds most freely to an imitation. Were it not for this fact *Rhodacanthis,* when keeping to the leafy crowns of tall Koa trees, as it often does, would be most difficult to get sight of. Not only is the male attracted by this means, but the female likewise comes, perhaps not less often than the male, but even when called into the tree, beneath which the observer stands, it is often difficult to locate her. In misty weather they are particularly ready to answer, and I have called as many as seven adult males and two females into one large tree at the same time.

The green-plumaged young, which greatly resemble the female, are fed partly on large fragments of Koa pods, such as their parents eat, both sexes being assiduous in feeding them. At this time the adult female can easily be obtained, but the plumage of neither adult bird is now comparable with its condition in the winter months.

When thoroughly scared the female sometimes gives utterance to a deep single note, which is repeated at frequent intervals with varying intensity, so as to have a ventriloquial effect, and make it extremely difficult to locate the bird. The young male soon acquires the full song of the adult, sometimes even before the crown of the head begins to assume the plumage of maturity and while the skull is still of soft consistency.

I have seen the male bird come down to the ground for building material and carry this to the top of one of the tallest Koa trees, and in this situation, in the locality frequented by the bird, certain largish nests which became visible later, when the trees were stripped by caterpillars, I have no doubt were built by *Rhodacanthis.*

The eggs and nestlings were never described.

The Greater Koa Finch was first collected in 1891, and apparently was last collected about 1896. Henshaw did not find it, and there appear to be no reliable records of this species having been seen since the 1890s.

Kona Grosbeak
Chloridops kona
(Color plate 44)

Perkins and Henshaw erroneously called this species the Palila, but apparently neither this species nor the two Koa Finches had a Hawaiian name.

Scott Wilson (1888) collected a single specimen of the Kona Grosbeak "in the district of Kona" at an elevation of 5,000 feet on June 21, 1887. He described it as a new genus, *Chloridops.* Palmer later found the species "not rare at Pulehua, Nawina, and Honaunau, Kona, within a range of from 15 to 20 miles, and at all altitudes from 3500 to 5500 feet, but he did not meet with it elsewhere."

Rothschild (1893–1900:209) described the Kona Grosbeak as follows:

Adult male. Bright olive-green above and below, paler and washed with buff on the vent, more olive on the under tail-coverts. Lores dusky. Quills dusky blackish, paler towards the base of the inner webs, margined with bright olive-green on the outer webs. Under wing-coverts brownish buff, washed with olive-greenish. Rectrices dusky brown, edged outwardly with olive-green. Iris dark hazel. Maxilla horn-grey; mandible grey, much lighter at base. Legs and toes dark brown, almost blackish, not pale as in the figure in "Aves Hawaiienses" *(H. C. Palmer)*. Total length, as measured in the flesh by the collector, 6½ to 7½ inches, but hardly 6 inches in skin; wing 3.45 to 3.55, tail 2.2 to 2.35, culmen 0.8 to 0.85, bill from gape to tip 0.75 to 0.8, height of bill at base 7.3 to 7.6, width of maxilla at base 3.56, width of mandible at base 0.57, tarsus 0.8 to 0.9. [A specimen in the Bishop Museum measures 5.75 inches.]

Quite a number of specimens differ materially from the above described specimens, which undoubtedly are the adult males. They are smaller, the wing measuring only 3.25 to 3.4, and are much lighter and pale yellow on the abdomen. These birds are apparently younger specimens. They cannot belong to a different species, because there are specimens intermediate between them and the darker-bellied form, and as the majority of them are marked as females they probably are the females, and some that are marked males are evidently young.

Perkins (1903:439) had the following to say about the Kona Grosbeak:

In this monotypic genus the gross development of the skull and beak surpasses that of any other Drepanid, and is carried to such an extent that in skinning the bird it is impossible to withdraw the skull through the skin of the neck.

Chloridops is found in the same localities in the Kona district as *Rhodacanthis,* but so far as known to me its range is more restricted, all the specimens seen being noted within an area of about four square miles, and even within this area the bird appeared local. There is no apparent reason why new localities should not be found for it, but it certainly is absent from extensive areas which appear to be admirably adapted to it. Within the area that it inhabits it cannot be considered other than a rare bird, and on the most favourable and exceptional days I have never seen more than 6 or 8 specimens, as paired or solitary individuals. It may be exclusively and diligently sought for a whole day, or for several successive days, without a single example being seen or heard, even when one is acquainted with its favourite haunts and habits. . . .

Usually it is a dull, sluggish and solitary bird and spends nearly its whole time in feeding, mostly in silence,—unlike others of its allies, which at intervals interrupt their search for food to utter cheery song or callnote. For the greater part of the year its food consists almost entirely of the embryos of the Naeo or bastard sandal *(Myoporum),* although I have known it to occasionally take a caterpillar. As the dried fruit of the Naeo is excessively hard, it is probable that nothing short of extremely powerful jaws of *Chloridops* and their great

muscles would be able to crack these. In cracking them a sound is produced, which is audible at some distance, and as it is incessant when the bird is feeding, by far the most easy way to get sight of this, is to listen attentively for the sound. The flycatcher when taking an insect on the wing frequently produces a somewhat similar snap with its beak, but the two sounds can always be distinguished. The somewhat sombre green plumage of *Chloridops* conceals it well amongst the foliage, so that, but for the snapping sound that it produces, it would probably be the most difficult to collect of all the forest birds, that are not on the very verge of extinction. It very rarely visits any other tree than the Naeo, but I have once seen it in the true sandal, the fruit of which it also possibly eats.

Palmer described a callnote as "a low prolonged 'cheep', not at all loud, and apparently not to be heard at any greater distance than the cracking of the berries." He also described "a low chirping noise" when the bird was in flight, and a song "consisting of several whistling notes, not very loud but clear."

Rothschild reports that "Palmer once (October 12th) shot as many as a dozen on a big lava-flow, and six of them during five minutes within a distance of fifty yards. On another lava-flow about 200 feet or so lower down Palmer did not obtain one, although the Aaka-trees were there just as plentiful and just as full of seed."

How many birds Palmer collected I do not know, but it may have been because of his collecting that Perkins never saw more than six or eight birds in a day when he observed the species in 1892 and 1894. If so, and if the range of the species at that time was as limited as believed, the Kona Grosbeak must already have been uncommon to rare when it was discovered.

Munro (1944:131) wrote that the Kona Grosbeak "seldom strayed from the more recent aa or clinker lava flows. These areas were covered with medium-sized trees and little undergrowth. In working over this rough, jagged loose rock we wore out a pair of shoes in a very short time."

The nests, eggs, and nestlings were never described. The Kona Grosbeak and the two species of Koa Finch provide a real puzzle. The three species were discovered and described between 1888 and 1892, all in the same habitat on the Kona Coast. There appear to be no reliable records of any one of these species having been seen since about 1896.

Maui Parrotbill
Pseudonestor xanthophrys
(Color plate 45)

This is a small (5.5 inches long), olive-green honeycreeper with a golden yellow superciliary line, a short tail, and a large, hooked, parrotlike bill. The wing and tail feathers are brown, but the outer web of each has a border of olive-green. The throat, breast, abdomen, and under tail coverts are yellow, washed with olive on the sides of the body. The upper mandible is deep, compressed from side to side, and markedly decurved, greatly overhanging the straight, heavy, lower mandible. The curve of the upper mandible (the culmen) is about half the length of the tail! Females are smaller than males.

Henry Palmer first collected the Maui Parrotbill in 1892. Perkins and Henshaw later collected specimens. They believed it to be restricted in range "to a small portion of the forest on the north-west slope of Haleakala, at an elevation of 4000–5000 ft." Perkins frequently saw it with the Maui Nukupuu, and he once "killed both birds at a single shot."

Perkins (1903:431) said that the Maui Parrotbill "is extremely partial to the Koa tree, and at most seasons obtains its food almost entirely from these. This food consists for a great part of the larvae, pupae and immature beetles of the native Cerambycidae, but more especially of *Clytarlus pennatus* and *modestus*, enormous quantities of which it destroys. It also visits other trees occasionally, especially some kinds of *Pelea*, whence it obtains the larvae of *Plagithmysus*, leaving remarkable scars on the tree as a token of its visit. It feeds its young partly on these and partly on looper caterpillars, but they very soon learn to extract the beetle larvae for themselves."

He described their foraging habits in more detail by stating that "in opening out the burrows of the *Clytarli* it often wrenches and pulls in a very similar manner [to the Nukupuu]; it frequently clings to the under-side of a branch and by stretching its neck raises its head above it, before laying hold of the upper surface with its beak. It is in this position that it bears most resemblance to a diminutive parrot, but the size and shape of the beak greatly increase the resemblance. The twigs and smaller branches of the Koa, in which the *Clytarli* are found, are never rotten, but generally even drier and harder than the healthy, growing wood, and require enormous strength to open them. To perform this, the branch is gripped by the curved upper mandible and the lower one opposed to it, and the burrow of the larva is exposed, either by the act of closing the beak or by wrenching with it, the somewhat slender tongue assisting in extracting the prey."

Perkins described the callnote as a loud *kee-wit*, and he said that the song resembled that of the Nukupuu, "a short, vigorous trill, at its best fully as loud as that of the" Akiapolaau of Hawaii. He also noted that the Parrotbill sometimes sings while in flight.

The first sighting of this species in the twentieth century apparently was of two birds seen by Lawrence P. Richards on December 4, 1950. He collected one bird a short distance northwest of Puu Alaea at an elevation of 6,400 feet on the north slope of Haleakala (Richards and Baldwin 1953).

The Maui Parrotbill was not reported again until August 29, 1967, the last day of the Kipahulu Valley expedition, when a single bird was seen at an elevation of approximately 6,500 feet (Banko 1968). Banko points out that this sighting of the Maui Parrotbill and those of the Maui Nukupuu not only extend considerably the upper range of these two species but also reveal that both species are inhabitants of the ohia forest, which is the dominant forest from 4,000 to 6,700 feet. Here the birds have been observed feeding on ohia, oheohe (*Tetraplasandra*), hoawa (*Pittosporum*), kolea (*Myrsine*), olomea (*Perrottetia*), kanawao (*Broussaisia*), and akala (*Rubus hawaiiensis*). The Parrotbill is rare in these forests.

The nest, eggs, and newly hatched young have never been described. Perkins once found an empty nest, about 25 feet from the ground in a koa tree, which he assumed to be the nest of the Maui Parrotbill because he observed two adults and two young birds, just able to fly, in this tree for several days. Henshaw (1903:79) said that he had found adults in June feeding young out of the nest.

Subfamily Hemignathinae
Amakihi
Hemignathus virens
(Color plate 40)

The second most common living honeycreeper, the Amakihi is found on all of the main islands. The four subspecies are distributed as follows: *H. virens stejnegeri*, Kauai; *H. v. chloris*, Oahu; *H. v. wilsoni*, Maui, Molokai, and Lanai; *H. v. virens*, Hawaii. All are small (averaging 4.5 inches in length), yellowish-green birds. The several races differ primarily in the amount of bright yellow on the underparts of the male, although the bill of the Kauai subspecies is considerably larger than those of the others. The lores (the area from the base of the bill to the eye) are black or brownish black. In the Hawaii race, the black may extend as a narrow line above the eye and continue for a short distance behind it so that, in company with the black eye, the black streak is conspicuous as a field mark. The brownish black lores of the Kauai form are much smaller, and Kauai males have a pale yellow superciliary line.

The Amakihi is rare (possibly extinct) on Lanai; it is uncommon on Molokai and Oahu as compared to its abundance on Hawaii, Maui, and Kauai.

The Amakihi is a characteristic bird of the ohia forests on all of the islands. Palmer wrote (in Rothschild 1893–1900) that the Hawaii Amakihi "ranges from 1000 feet above the sea to the uppermost forest regions, about 10,000." Perkins found the species abundant in the higher forests in Kona but noted that it also "ranges down in some numbers even as low as 1400 or 1500 feet." Richardson and Bowles (1964) found the Kauai Amakihi to be a "moderately common resident of native forest above approximately 1,500 feet." They also commented that "like the elepaio, the amakihi seems able to tolerate some vegetational or other human disturbances of the native forest."

In very few areas have I found the Amakihi at elevations as low as 2,800 feet on Hawaii and Maui, although there are some notable exceptions; much more intensive study is needed of the present distribution of many of the honeycreepers. On May 27, 1970, I heard at least four Amakihi singing in the Malama-Ki Forest Reserve (Hawaii) at an elevation of only 250 feet. I saw adults with two fledglings at the Naulu picnic area (elevation 1,600 feet) along the Chain of Craters road on August 4, 1969. Amakihi are fairly common at Manuka State Park on the Kona Coast at an elevation of 1,700 feet. They have been seen at 1,800 feet in Kipahulu Valley, Maui; at 900 feet in the South Kona District of Hawaii; and at the Makiki nursery in Honolulu.

The Hawaii Amakihi is found in the wettest rain forests and in the relatively dry mamani-naio forest on Mauna Kea, as well as on Hualalai mountain. It occurs at the tree-line ecosystem at about 8,000 feet on Mauna Loa and to about 9,000 feet on Mauna Kea. Common in the ohia rain forests on the northeast slope of Haleakala and at Hosmer's Grove is the Maui race inhabiting the mixed forest of native trees and introduced pines; it occurs in low numbers in the West Maui mountains.

Baldwin (1953) studied the food habits of three species of honeycreepers at Volcanoes National Park. He found that the Amakihi uses less nectar and more insect food than the Apapane and the Iiwi, but that the Amakihi, unlike the other two species, also drinks the juices from fruits. The two most important flowers for nectar for the Amakihi are those of ohia and of mamani, but it also has been observed to feed from the flowers of koa *(Acacia koa)*, sandalwood *(Santalum paniculatum)*, maile *(Alyxia olivaeformis)*, ieie *(Freycinetia arborea)*, forest palm *(Pritchardia* sp.*)*, lobeliads, and bananas. It also feeds from the flowers of a number of introduced plants: lantana *(Lantana camara)*, fuchsia *(Fuchsia magellanica)*, honeysuckle *(Lonicera japonica)*, gosmore *(Hypochaeris radicata)*, and air plant *(Bryophyl-*

lum calycinum). I have seen the Kauai race feeding from the flowers of lilikoi or passionfruit *(Passiflora* sp.*)*, the Maui race feeding from fuchsia, and the Hawaii race feeding from koniza *(Erigeron)*. Eddinger has seen the Kauai Amakihi, Anianiau, Apapane, and Iiwi feeding from the blossoms of Methley plum *(Prunus cerasifera* x *salicina)* trees; and the first two species, at flowers of the introduced blackberry, as well as pecking at the yellow fruits of the lilikoi.

Baldwin noted that, when feeding from the air plant, the Amakihi pierces the base of the tubular calyx and corolla rather than inserts its bill into the flower. Baldwin saw Amakihi pierce the fruits of the Jerusalem cherry *(Solanum pseudo-capsicum)* and drink the juice. Perkins had watched the Kauai race drink juice from the red berries of akia *(Wilkstroemia* sp.*)* and the berries of poha or Peruvian groundcherry *(Physalis peruviana)*.

MacMillen (1974) reported that the upper thermal limit for the Apapane and the Iiwi was greater than 40° C, whereas that of the Amakihi was 35° C. The Amakihi typically forages at lower levels than the other two species and, therefore, competes with them for nectar less frequently. Carpenter and MacMillen (1979) wrote: "However, we do not know whether the lack of high temperature tolerance is a cause or an evolutionary result of preference for low levels in the canopy. Alternative explanations may be 1) edible insects may be more abundant lower in the canopy and therefore more attractive to the relatively more insectivorous *L. virens*, or 2) predation by the hawk *(Buteo solitarius)* or diurnal owl *(Asio flammeus)* may select for the green *L. virens* to occupy areas with a high foliage (green) to flower (red) ratio and the two red species to occupy areas with a high flower to foliage ratio."

In regard to animal food, Baldwin found that 33 percent of the bird stomachs he examined contained spiders, although the number of individual spiders was low as compared with the number of caterpillars that had been eaten. Nine orders of insects were represented in the stomach contents; of these orders, the most abundant were the Homoptera (75 percent occurrence) and Lepidoptera (71 percent). Flies (Diptera) were found in only 6 percent of the stomachs; snails were found in none.

Eddinger and I have raised several species of honeycreepers in captivity: Hawaii and Kauai Amakihi, Anianiau, Kauai Creeper, Apapane, and Nihoa Finch. All but the Nihoa Finches were hand-raised from the nestling stage, and these hand-raised birds remain very tame. They usually fly to the wire of the cage when one walks up to it, and probe under one's fingernail with their bills. The Apapane typically explores the end of a finger with its tongue, whereas an

Amakihi gapes or opens its mandible with noticeable force, as the birds undoubtedly do when exploring crevices in bark or when piercing fruit or flowers with their bills. One captive Kauai Amakihi lived for nine years (Berger 1980).

Although the Amakihi was described scientifically in 1782, there are no detailed statements in the early literature about the nesting of this very common species. W. A. Bryan (1905b) described a single nest and its three eggs of the Hawaii Amakihi which had been collected by a friend in the Hamakua district of Hawaii on May 3, 1905. Bryan commented that the eggs "are much paler in color" than those figured by Newton (1897), but that the eggs illustrated by Rothschild (1893–1900) "are very satisfactory figures." Bryan added that the nest shown by Rothschild "lacks character" and that the nest and eggs in the work by Wilson and Evans (1890–1899) "are both misleading." A color photograph of the nest and eggs of the Hawaii Amakihi was first published in 1969 (Berger 1969a).

Munro (1944:103) wrote that on April 13, 1913 he found only one nest on Lanai. He shook the tree and "two or three young birds flew out of the nest." Insofar as I have been able to determine, only one additional active Amakihi nest was mentioned in the literature during the period from 1905 to 1964.

The Kaohe Game Management Area and the contiguous Mauna Kea Game Management Area contain about 10,000 acres of mamani and naio (*Myoporum sandwicense*) forest on the southern and western slopes of Mauna Kea (fig. 82). The two areas extend from an elevation of about 6,500 to 10,000 feet. The present tree line, however, ends at about 9,300 feet, and feral sheep are rapidly destroying the vegetation there, thus preventing regeneration and lowering the timber line even farther. Not only does this region support a very high population of Amakihi, but it is also the only known breeding ground for the Palila; the Akiapolaau also inhabits this forest. This also is the last extensive remaining mamani-naio forest in Hawaii. Nevertheless, the State Department of Land and Natural Resources bulldozed 200 acres during the summer of 1969 in order to "open up" the land to make it better habitat for pheasants (fig. 83). An additional 200 acres were "selectively treated" for the same reason in 1970.

In contrast with the windward slopes of the mountains, the mamani-naio area is a dry, open, parkland type of forest. Annual rainfall during the five-year period 1965–1969 varied from 13.87 to 40.9 inches (1965, 26.9 inches; 1966, 15.6; 1967, 30.69; 1968, 40.9; 1969, 13.87).

I made my first trip to the mamani-naio forest on May 20, 1966. I have found exposed Amakihi nests, but many are very well concealed, some being visible from only one angle on the ground. The birds also often build their nests so near the tips of small and brittle

FIGURE 82. Kaohe Game Management Area on the slopes of Mauna Kea, Hawaii. Snow-capped Mauna Loa (13,680 feet) lies in the background, and clouds hang in the saddle area between the two mountains. December 19, 1967.

FIGURE 83. "Habitat enrichment" for pheasants; part of the 400 acres of mamani-naio forest that were bulldozed in the Kaohe Game Management Area. August 5, 1969.

branches that it is impossible to reach the nests to check their contents. I have found 85 active Amakihi nests in this area. Of these, 74 were built in mamani and 11 in naio. The average measured height above ground of 60 of the nests was 13.6 feet, ranging from 7.4 to 20.2 feet. I estimated the height of several nests I could not reach to be at least 25 feet above the ground. I found a number of deserted nests, which are not included in the above figures, and one old nest was built just 4.8 feet from the ground in aalii.

One nest that Dr. Charles H. Lamoureux analyzed for me was composed primarily of mamani (including leaflets, petiole and rachis of leafstalks, and one seed pod), runners of a grass, and the whole plants of the lichen *Usnea*. There also were a few bits of thistledown (the pappus of *Cirsium lanceolatum*) and a few feathers.

Charles van Riper (1978b) studied the Amakihi in the dry forest on Mauna Kea from late 1970 through 1975. He reported that only the female builds the nest, averaging 10 days to complete it. Some of the birds, at least, are double-brooded. The female begins a second

nest about 22 days after the young fledge from the first nest, but an interval as short as 7 days or as long as 35 days may elapse before the second nest is built. However, if a nest is destroyed, the female begins a new nest within 6 days (range 1 to 9 days). Van Riper found the average clutch size of 125 nests to be 2.54 eggs; he found only two four-egg clutches. In my earlier study in this area, I found clutches of two eggs (9 nests), three eggs (32 nests), and four eggs (2 nests); the four-egg clutches were found during March 1967 and 1969 (figs. 84, 85). The average measurements of 90 eggs were: 13.9 mm (range 12.6 to 15.0) × 19.0 mm (range 15.8 to 21.7). Only the female incubates the eggs, the average period being 14.1 days, but varying in different nests from 12 to 16 days. The young are fed by both parents and the male also courtship feeds the female during the nestling period; both adults also eat the fecal sacs of the nestlings. The young remained in the nest for periods varying from 15 to 21 days, averaging 16.8 days. At the time that they hatch, nestling Hawaii Amakihi have flesh-pink skin and gray

FIGURE 84. Nest and three eggs of the Hawaii Amakihi; Kaohe Game Management Area. December 8, 1966.

down along the major feather tracts; the bill is yellowish and the palate is rose red; the eyes are closed—they open when the young are between 5 and 7 days of age. (Figs. 86, 87.)

One of the strange things I have observed about the Amakihi is that the young scramble out of the nest prematurely when disturbed. They flutter or fall to the ground at an age when they undoubtedly would be unable to withstand the cold nights at elevations above 6,500 feet.

A high percentage of the Amakihi nests in the mamani-naio forest are unsuccessful in producing young. In some the eggs disappear, in others the young are taken, and in a number of instances I have found the entire nest gone when I returned on a subsequent visit. Amakihis and House Finches often remove nesting material from deserted nests, and undoubtedly they sometimes completely dismantle old nests. Infrequent but very strong winds and drenching rains probably knock some nests from the trees. Van Riper found that only 34.7 percent of the eggs laid produced young that left the nest. He reported that the mortality result-

FIGURE 85. Nest and three eggs of the Hawaii Amakihi; Kaohe Game Management Area. March 29, 1969. Compare with Figure 84 for differences in pattern and density of egg markings and in nest structure.

ed mostly from desertion of nests shortly after the eggs were laid; this happened usually either during the early or the late part of the breeding season. About 11 percent of the eggs laid failed to hatch; he thought that many of these were eggs in three-egg clutches and that the embryos in the first egg laid were killed by freezing temperatures because the female did not cover the eggs at night until the second egg was laid.

Young birds often die in the nest. On April 13, 1967, a female was brooding two young that were 3 to 4 days old in nest number 36, but when I next visited the nest on April 30, I found the nestlings dead. A nest with three eggs on May 26, 1968, held three dead nestlings on June 15. A nest with three small nestlings on November 4, 1966, had only one dead young covered with maggots on November 20. After further development, these were identified as larvae of the blowfly *Eucaliphora lilae.*

The discovery that the breeding season of the Hawaii Amakihi on Mauna Kea often begins by mid- or late-October was a complete surprise. I found five nests on November 3 and 4, 1966. Two nests were being built, two held eggs, and one nest contained three nestlings estimated to be 3 or 4 days old. In view of an incubation period of about 14 days, the latter nest indicates that that pair of birds started nest construction by mid-October. I found four nests under construction during the first week of November 1967; three of these held eggs when next visited on November 16. Similarly, I found three nests on November 8 and 9, 1968; two looked complete but were empty; the third nest held

three eggs. By contrast, the 1969–1970 breeding season was much later than during the previous three seasons, and I found no active nests either on November 4 or December 4, 1969. I do not understand why van Riper found only one successful December nest (December 27, 1974) and none in November during the five-year-period of 1971–1975.

Not only do the birds often begin to nest in late fall, but the nesting season is a long one. Amakihi were still feeding fledglings in mid-May 1967. One nest held one egg and two small young on June 15, 1968, and fledglings giving food calls and following adults were seen on July 15 that year. I did not visit the study area during May, June, and July, 1969, but I saw a fledgling on August 5, 1969.

The Amakihi is adapted to wide temperature fluctuations at elevations between 6,500 and 9,000 feet on Mauna Kea. The monthly difference between maximum and minimum recorded temperatures at Pohakuloa (elevation 6,500 feet) varied from 41° F to 62° F during the four-year period 1966–1969, and averaged 51° F. The maximum temperature recorded was 88° F; the minimum was 20° F. During very few months of the year does the nighttime temperature not fall to freezing or below; and during only one month in the four-year period was the temperature not below 37° F. The maximum temperature during October 1966 was 78° F; the minimum was 31° F. It was in this month that at least one pair of Amakihi built their nest and incubated a clutch of three eggs, which hatched on or about November 1. Other Amakihi that nest during

FIGURE 86. Three nestling Amakihi; Kaohe Game Management Area. December 7, 1966.

FIGURE 87. Two fully feathered nestling Hawaii Amakihi; Kaohe Game Management Area. December 23, 1966.

the winter months are, of course, exposed to even colder nights. During the winter months ice crystals often persist until noon in shady areas. The high and low temperatures during January 1979 were 90° and 20° F.

Apparently I was the first to find a nest with eggs of the Kauai Amakihi—on June 22, 1968 (fig. 88). This nest was built 13.8 feet from the ground in an ohia at Kokee State Park; the female was incubating four eggs. On February 23, 1964, I observed copulation between a pair of Amakihi near the Koiae Stream. The female crouched, quivered her wings rapidly, and gave a soliciting callnote before and during copulation. Within a few seconds after dismounting, the male fed the female.

Eddinger (1970b) later made a study of the Kauai Amakihi. The first egg of the first complete clutch (three eggs) was laid on March 3, 1970. Eddinger found an active but inaccessible nest on June 21, 1969, and a nest with one egg on June 23, 1970; the clutch of three eggs was completed on June 25; this nest held three nestlings in pin feathers on July 22.

Sexual chasing is common, beginning at the onset of the breeding season and continuing until nest construction begins. The male defines and defends a territory by flying to a series of four or five singing perches around the nest. The defended territory is surprisingly small: for example, a circle with a radius of only 18 feet for one pair. Other Amakihi are immediately chased out of the territory, usually by the male, but other species are tolerated within the territory unless they approach to within a few feet of the nest. The female takes part in territory defense only when an intruder approaches the nest.

All nests thus far found on Kauai have been built in ohia trees. The average height above ground of 23 nests was 18.5 feet; the range was 12.3 to 27.15 feet. Eggs are laid before 8:00 A.M. and at 24-hour intervals. Clutch size was two eggs in 2 nests, three eggs in 12 nests, and four eggs in 5 nests; in 1 nest, apparently only one egg. The eggs have a whitish background with irregularly shaped markings scattered over the entire surface but concentrated at the larger end of the egg. The irregular markings exhibit considerable variation in pattern and in color (tan, chocolate brown, reddish brown). The average measurements of 16 eggs were 18.8 × 24.1 mm; extremes were 17.7 × 26.0, 19.0 × 23.9, and 19.0 × 21.8 mm.

Eddinger found that the female begins to incubate with the laying of the last egg in the clutch. The incubating bird does not call or sing from the nest. When disturbed the bird flies off without giving any alarm notes. Courtship feeding is common during the incubation period, but the male does not feed the female on the nest. She flies to the male, solicits food, and is then fed by him. The incubation period at each of seven nests was 14 days. All eggs hatch within half a day, usually before noon.

At hatching, Kauai Amakihi nestlings have pinkish yellow skin and fine, light gray or dirty white down on the head, back, and wings. The gape is rose pink and the corners of the mouth are pale yellow. The nestlings weigh about 1.0 g at hatching. They weigh between 14.5 and 17.0 g at 16 days of age (fig. 89). The cloacal temperature of two-day-old nestlings was 78° F; the temperature increased daily and was 101° F when the nestlings were 14 and 16 days old.

The nestling period varied from 17 to 20 days (one nest, 17 days; one nest, 18 days; eight nests, 19 days; one nest, 20 days). The young usually will not remain in the nest if disturbed after day 14 or 15. If undisturbed during the nestling period, the young are able to fly well when they first leave the nest.

Of 63 eggs laid in 25 nests, 56 eggs (88 percent) hatched and 51 (80.9 percent) nestlings survived to the fledgling stage.

I found feather mites of the family Proctophyllodidae on an Amakihi collected near Olinda, Maui, in 1965, and mites of the genus *Ornithonyssus* on a nestling Amakihi taken at an elevation of about 7,300 feet in the Kaohe Game Management Area on Mauna Kea on April 17, 1969. M. Lee Goff found mites (family Syringophilidae) in the quills of Amakihi, Palila, Elepaio, and Japanese White-eye on Hawaii in 1979. This

FIGURE 88. Nest and four eggs of the Kauai Amakihi; Kokee State Park. June 22, 1968.

FIGURE 89. Two 15-day-old Kauai Amakihi. Kokee State Park, Kauai. May 21, 1969. Even at this age the greater development of the bill of the Kauai Amakihi is evident; compare with Figure 87. Courtesy of C. Robert Eddinger.

was the first report of these parasites for endemic Hawaiian birds.

Differences in the songs of the races on the several islands appear to be minor in nature, although a thorough comparative study has not yet been made. Amakihi often sing in flight, as well as when perched. During February 1966, I watched a male on Oahu fly from an ohia tree for nearly 100 yards over a valley. There was a gentle upswing near the end of the flight, and the bird began to sing, actually tipping its head upward and backward as it sang; then the bird dove in arching flight downward to the top of a tall ohia in the valley.

I have observed courtship feeding between pairs of Amakihi on several occasions. As was mentioned before, during the courtship the female crouches, quivers her wings, and gives a soliciting call, not unlike that given by young birds when begging for food. Eddinger (1970b) observed courtship feeding prior to and during nest construction, but found it most often during the incubation period.

In writing about a nest he found on Lanai in 1913, Munro (1944:103) said that "a female amakihi approached and by scolding and fluttering about tried to lure me from the nest." This type of distraction behavior, however, apparently occurs only after the young have left the nest. I have never encountered it during the incubation or nestling periods. On one occasion, a male gave a shrill alarm note at a nest under construc-

tion, but there was no distraction behavior. It has been my experience on both Hawaii and Kauai that when a female is flushed from a nest containing eggs, she flies off swiftly for some distance or darts quickly into nearby thick vegetation, giving no alarm notes whatever. In fact, when I first began to study Hawaiian birds, I often had to return to a nest several times before I could make a positive identification as to the species whose nest I had found. Eddinger has had the same experience. However, after the eggs hatch and the young are several days old, the adults do often stay in the nest tree and give alarm notes when disturbed.

As I was checking the contents of a nest I had just found on March 14, 1967, a female Amakihi flew into the nest tree and hopped from branch to branch as close as two feet from me; she uttered no callnotes. Dr. Konrad Lorenz, who was standing a short distance away, reported that as I was climbing down the tree, the Amakihi performed displacement preening behavior and after-bathing wing shaking, although the bird had not taken a bath; at no time did she give any alarm notes. The nest held four eggs.

Anianiau or Lesser Amakihi
Hemignathus parvus
(Color plate 37)

The Anianiau is endemic to Kauai, and is fairly common in the Kokee and Alakai Swamp regions of the island.

This is one of the smallest species of honeycreeper, varying from about 4.0 to 4.25 inches in total length. Rothschild said that the females are slightly smaller than the males. The males are bright yellowish green above and bright yellow below. The female is similar but often has less bright yellow feathers on the throat and breast and is more greenish yellow above. The bill is relatively small and only slightly decurved. The iris is brown. The bill is brownish except that the basal portion of the lower mandible is pearly gray. Immature birds are greenish gray above and light gray below.

The Anianiau inhabits the rain forests where ohia is the dominant tree. Over 600 inches (50 feet!) of rainfall have been recorded in a single year on Mt. Waialeale only a few miles from the Kokee region where most of what is known about this species has been learned. In these areas, the Anianiau is more numerous than the Amakihi (fig. 90).

Although the Anianiau often feeds in the crowns of the trees, it also forages in the understory. Sometimes it feeds, like a creeper, on bark and dead twigs. We have seen the birds feeding from the flowers of the introduced passionfruit and from the blossoms of Methley plum. Two stomachs analyzed by Richardson and

FIGURE 90. Nesting habitat of the Anianiau, Amakihi, Apapane, Iiwi, Akepa, and Creeper at Kokee State Park, Kauai. May 18, 1968. The photograph was taken near the Kalalau lookout.

Bowles contained parts of insects (including beetles), insect larvae, a spider, and several small seeds.

During the nonbreeding season, the Anianiau gives a simple, sweet, unslurred callnote, *ps-seet,* but it also has a loud territorial or advertising song as well as a whisper song.

Eddinger (1970b) studied the breeding biology of the Anianiau in the Kokee area. He found that sexual chasing begins early in the breeding season and continues until nest building is under way. He also witnessed a more elaborate courtship display in which the male, while holding his wings away from the sides of his body, hopped along a branch in a bobbing manner in front of the female. During this performance, the male gave his loud territorial song as well as a whisper song. The female responded by chasing the male from the tree, but he simply circled around the tree and lit near her again. This pattern was repeated 14 times, after

which the male sang from a perch and then flew away, whereupon the female followed him. Courtship feeding is common at this time and throughout the incubation period. I observed courtship feeding near the Koaie Stream in the Alakai Swamp on February 23, 1964; Eddinger observed sexual chasing during late February at Kokee.

Data obtained thus far indicate a nesting season extending from about the middle of February until the end of June with slight differences from year to year. Nesting began earlier in 1964 and 1970 than in 1968 and 1969. During January, February, and March, nighttime temperatures sometimes drop to 39° F or below. Daytime temperatures usually reach the low 70s.

All nests found to date have been built in ohia trees. The nests are built in terminal crowns or within thick clumps of small branches growing from the main trunk of a tree, so that the nests are very well concealed (fig.

91). The average height above ground of 24 nests found by Berger, Eddinger, and Frings (1969) was 20.03 feet; the lowest nest was 10 feet 11 inches from the ground, and the highest measured nest was 31 feet 1 inch from the ground.

One nest analyzed by Charles H. Lamoureux and William J. Hoe was composed primarily of unidentifiable fine plant fibers. Woven among these but primarily in the outer wall of the nest, were thin flat strips 4 to 5 mm wide, probably strips of bark; these strips were a dark reddish brown on one side and a much lighter tan color on the other side. Also embedded in the outer wall of the nest were several dead branchlets of pukiawe. The outer surface of the nest was covered by a layer of lichens (*Usnea* sp.). In addition to these nest materials, seven species of mosses and one liverwort were found woven among the other constituents of the nest: *Acroporium fusco-flavum, Aerobryopsis longissima, Campylopus purpureoflavescens, Homaliodendron flabellatum, Leucobryum gracile, Macromitrium owahiense, Thuidium plicatum,* and *Bazzania* sp. (a liverwort).

Nest dimensions for eight Anianiau nests varied considerably. Rim thickness varied from 0.25 to 1.25 inches (average, 1 inch); the outside diameter, from 2.5 to 4.25 inches (average, 3.5 inches). Measurement from the top rim to the bottom of the nest varied from 2.5 to 3.5 inches (average, 3 inches). The inside diameter of the nest cup varied from 1.5 to 2.5 inches (average, 2 inches); depth of the nest cup, from 1.25 to 1.5 inches (average, 1.33 inches).

The Anianiau sometimes uses material from a deserted Anianiau nest or from nests of other species, either deserted nests or those from previous years. A deserted or old nest may be completely disassembled and carried away.

The eggs have a whitish background with irregularly shaped markings that vary in color from tan to reddish brown (figs. 92, 93). The eggs of different females exhibit considerable variation in color, amount, and pattern of the spotting. In 28 nests, the clutch was two eggs in 3 nests, three eggs in 21 nests, and four eggs in 4 nests. The eggs are laid before 8:00 A.M. daily until the clutch is complete. Eddinger found complete sets of eggs laid in March, April, May, and June (one clutch).

FIGURE 91. Terminal branch of an ohia tree containing an Anianiau nest, 1967. The arrow points to the nest.

FIGURE 92. Anianiau nest with three eggs. April 15, 1968.

FIGURE 94. Three 2-day-old Anianiau. May 6, 1969. Courtesy of C. Robert Eddinger.

FIGURE 93. Anianiau nest with four eggs. April 26, 1968. Note the difference in markings on these eggs and on those shown in Figure 92.

The average measurements of 21 Anianiau eggs were 18.0 × 22.1 mm. The longest egg measured 18.2 × 22.9 mm; the shortest, 17.9 × 20.0; the widest, 18.8 × 22.0; the narrowest, 15.0 × 22.8. Berger, Eddinger, and Frings (1969), however, reported two eggs that measured 13.1 × 17.6 mm and 13.5 × 17.9 mm.

The Anianiau begins incubation with the laying of the last egg in the clutch; only the female incubates. The male actively defends the territory around the nest tree against other Anianiau but ignores other species that often feed in the nest tree. The male apparently does not feed the female on the nest; the female leaves the nest and flies to the male and solicits food in the same manner as a fledgling. After being fed by the male, the female either returns to the nest or forages for food for herself. The incubation period at each of eight nests was 14 days.

When it hatches, the nestling Anianiau has a light pink skin with smoky black down on the head, back, and wings. It has a bright pink gape with a pale yellow margin at the corners of the mouth. Eddinger found that the young weighed between 1.0 and 1.5 g at hatching. Their weight increased daily until they were 10 days old, at which time they weighed between 9.0 and 11.0 g; all nestlings showed a decrease in weight on the eleventh day. Both adults feed the nestlings and remove their fecal sacs (figs. 94, 95).

The nestling period was 17 days in one nest, 18 days in ten nests, and 19 days in one nest. When they leave the nest, the young are able to fly well from tree to tree. However, Eddinger found that he could not weigh the nestlings after they were 11 days old because then they would not remain in the nest even though they were not yet far enough along in development to fly or to survive outside the nest. Cloacal temperatures increased slowly from 85° F in one-day-old birds to 93° F in nine-day-old birds.

Only 5 percent of 80 eggs laid failed to hatch, but 22.5 percent of the eggs laid were destroyed or deserted; 82.7 percent of the eggs that hatched produced nestlings that survived to fly from the nest.

FIGURE 95. Three 8-day-old Anianiau. May 23, 1969. Courtesy of C. Robert Eddinger.

Dr. Frank Haramoto identified feather mites (family Analgidae, genus *Megninia*) from one Anianiau examined.

Eddinger hand-raised three nestling Anianiau during the summer of 1970. We kept these birds in a large aviary on the Manoa campus of the University of Hawaii. One bird died at an age of 3.5 years, another when 7 years old, and the third bird when more than 9.5 years old. Many passerines in the wild have a life span of only 2 or 3 years.

Greater Amakihi
Hemignathus sagittirostris
(Color plate 49)

The Greater Amakihi had a very short known history. The species was first collected near the Wailuku River on Hawaii in 1892. It was rediscovered by Perkins in 1895, but has not been observed since early in the present century. The early collecting sites probably were near the upper limits of the present sugarcane fields. There are, however, extensive cloud forests along the Hamakua Coast of Hawaii where this species may still survive (fig. 4).

Five specimens of the Greater Amakihi in the Bishop Museum measured between 5.0 and 5.56 inches in length. The upper parts were bright olive-green, being a brighter yellow on the forehead, sides of the head, and the upper tail coverts. The throat, breast, and abdomen were yellowish olive-green. The wings were blackish brown, with the flight feathers margined with yellowish green. The under surface of the wings was ashy colored except that the margin of the wing was yellowish. The mandibles were black or blackish brown, becoming bluish to slate colored at the base. The iris was hazel with a reddish tinge. Fully adult males and females apparently were indistinguishable in plumage.

Henry Palmer discovered this species on April 23, 1892. He wrote (in Rothschild 1893–1900):

When marching along the slopes of Mauna Kea, above Hilo, and not far from Wailuku, through old forest of Ohia, here and there intermixed with the Koa, and much enjoying the beautiful contrast of the thousands of bright crimson-coloured flowers of the lofty Ohias, which were frequented by numerous birds of the common Hawaiian species, I heard a strange note coming from an Ohia tree that I had just passed. At the first moment I thought it might be an Akialoa's note, but on hearing it again was convinced I had never heard it before. I soon saw the bird among the leaves, but before I could fire it flew into the tree just above my head, where it began to call again, as if calling its mate, until I shot it. On picking it up I saw it was quite new to me, and I hope it may be so to science. Its call-note might be described as a high clear 'chirrup' uttered three or four times in quick succession at short intervals. After waiting a few minutes its mate came up, but was shy and escaped me. I waited on the spot for about an hour, but none came back: on returning to my camp, however, I was fortunate enough to shoot another specimen, to which I was attracted by its cry, and I think I heard two or three more which I could not get; but so many birds of various kinds were singing among the flowering trees that it was very difficult to distinguish their various notes from a distance.

Palmer collected but four specimens of this new species, and Rothschild wrote that it was observed only at elevations of about 500 to 1,500 feet above Hilo and "all within a radius of a few miles." Perkins did not know where Palmer collected his birds but found the species along the Wailuku River in December 1895. Perkins considered it one of the most local of all the honeycreepers because "it has so far only been found in the forests behind Hilo on Hawaii on either side of the Wailuku River, at an elevation of from 1200–3000 ft. above the sea." Henshaw collected a number of specimens (now in the Museum of Comparative Zoology at Harvard and at the Bishop Museum) between January 27 and March 21, 1900, along the Kaiwiki Stream north of the Wailuku River, and A. M. Woolcott collected in the same area in 1901. Henshaw gave the range of the Greater Amakihi as between 2,000 and 4,000 feet.

Perkins (1903:412–413) is the only writer to give a firsthand report of the behavior and feeding habits of the Greater Amakihi. Rothschild had established the genus *Viridonia* for this species, hence Perkins' reference to that genus; the Amakihi was at that time placed in the genus *Chlorodrepanis*.

Were it not for its distinct song and call note, this bird might easily be passed unnoticed, unless one were specially searching for it, on account of its general similarity to the other very abundant species which it resembles. I find on reference to my notes that I paid three visits to the locality for *Viridonia*, each of them during the winter months, and on each about two weeks were spent in camp deep in the forest. During my first visit I saw but two specimens and obtained only one of these, but became acquainted both with the song and call note. For the whole two weeks it rained continuously throughout each day, which made collecting both disagreeable and difficult, and exactly similar weather was experienced during my second trip. On the latter however, in the course of a long march on one morning I saw as many as twelve of these birds, all single individuals or pairs, there being no young visible at this season. Six of these I shot at and killed and with no prospect of fairer weather I was content to return to Hilo. My third visit was entirely given up to entomological work, and the weather was as delightful as it had been abominable before, not a drop of rain falling during my fortnight's camping. On this occasion I noticed several individuals of *Viridonia* almost every day, most of them in pairs, and in certain spots the same birds, no doubt, were seen many times, but I collected none of these, since all were in fully adult plumage like those already procured.

Nearly all the *Viridonia* seen by me were in the Ohia trees or more often in the dense masses of Ieie clothing the trunks of these trees, whence they were obtaining their food. In the eight examples that I dissected I found the small forest crickets of the genus *Paratrigonidium* to form a large part of this food in each case. Some of these crickets are specially attached to the Ieie and some live beneath the loose bark of large Ohias, while others are only found on certain ferns, which on more than one occasion I noticed *Viridonia* visiting, no doubt in search of these insects. Caterpillars and spiders were also taken from the bird's stomach as well as a common carabid beetle, which lives at the base of the Ieie leaves, where these are closely attached to the stem. For obtaining the latter and the crickets which live in the same situation, the strong beak of *Viridonia* is well adapted. Once only I saw one feeding at the flower of the Ohia, and although I was unable to procure this for examination, I have little doubt that it was feeding on nectar, since its tongue is still unchanged from the form exhibited by that of the most persistent nectar-eaters. As in some species of *Oreomyza*, *Loxops* and *Heterorhynchus* the habit of feeding on nectar probably survives as a rare occurrence, the typical form of the tongue being fully preserved, since it assists in obtaining some of these insects which form a large part of the bird's food, and not because nectar is of much importance as an article of diet.

The song of *Viridonia* is, as might have been expected, very similar to that of its near ally *Chlorodrepanis;* indeed it would be difficult to distinguish between them were it not that the former whistles two or three distinct additional notes after completing the Chlorodrepanid trill. Many times my attention was called to the presence of *Viridonia*, when I was engaged in insect-collecting, by its song, and but for this it would certainly have been passed unnoticed. It has also a

soft cry as a call or alarm note, which somewhat resembles that of *Drepanis*, and by imitating this it can sometimes be called even within a few feet of the observer.

The natives of the present day have no name for *Viridonia*, although those to whom I have shown it, have always recognised it as distinct from any other bird. As far as I can judge, it is one which would have been unlikely to have been caught by the means adopted by the old bird-hunters, and even had it been caught its dull plumage would have been of little value, as the easily caught and extremely abundant Amakihi furnished feathers of a similar or superior quality.

Henshaw called this bird the Green Solitaire, but the name is inappropriate for several reasons.

Akialoa
Hemignathus obscurus

Subspecies of the Akialoa formerly inhabited Oahu, Lanai, and Hawaii. The races on Oahu (*Hemignathus obscurus ellisianus*) and Lanai (*H. o. lanaiensis*) are certainly extinct, and the Hawaii race (*H. o. obscurus*) is presumed to be extinct. All were yellowish or greenish birds; the quills of the wing and tail were brown.

The Akialoas (curvebills) had greatly elongated, decurved (sicklelike) bills in which the lower mandible was at least four-fifths the length of the upper mandible. In the Oahu race, the bill accounted for 1.75 inches of the bird's total length of 7 inches; the tail also was 1.75 inches long. Perkins (1903:423) wrote: "I am quite satisfied that the different kinds of Akialoa are all still largely nectar-eaters, although possibly on the way to become entirely insectivorous." He found that the several subspecies fed at ohia flowers and that they were "partial to the nectar of some kinds of arborescent Lobeliaceae (called Haha and Oha-wai by the natives), especially to those with large corollas, while to certain kinds they pay no attention at all, however profusely they may be in flower." The stomachs of three specimens collected by Palmer on Lanai, however, were "full of beetles and other insects," although he also saw the birds feed from the flowers of the haha.

The Oahu Akialoa was last collected in 1837. Perkins thought that he saw a pair in 1892; neither Wilson nor Palmer found this bird, and there are no reliable reports for the twentieth century.

Palmer collected several specimens of the Lanai Akialoa, but, only a short time later, Perkins could find but a single male in his search on the island. Munro, who worked and collected on Lanai for twenty years, did not see a single bird that he could identify as an Akialoa.

Although Wilson (Wilson and Evans 1890–1899) reported that the Hawaii Akialoa occupied "the lower forest-zone from about 1100 to 2500 feet," Palmer

(Rothschild 1893–1900) "found them common in the district of Kona, on the south-west side of the island, at altitudes of about 2000 to 6000 feet. . . . They were comparatively numerous in Hamakua district, northeast, between 2000 and 5000 feet. Numbers were seen in Hilo district above Hilo, at heights of 1400 to 3000 feet, and a few in the upper parts of Puna district on the east side." Perkins' observations were similar: "It was common in Kona in 1892 and 1894, not only in the denser forest but also in the open parts at all elevations, abundant in Kau district in the Koa woods three to four miles from Kilauea, numerous in the heart of the virgin forest of Mauna Kea, north of the Wailuku river, as also in the Kohala mountains. In Olaa it was less common, at least at 1500 to 2000 ft., where I chiefly observed it; and here the magnificent virgin forest has now been cut down for the purpose of planting coffee and sugar-cane."

Nevertheless, it is possible that the Hawaii Akialoa still survives in small numbers, and the following observations of Perkins (1903:423–424) may be useful.

In the large Koa trees of open woods in Kona from 2000–3000 ft. above the sea the Akialoa could be traced by its audible tapping on the bark, the sound resembling that produced by the strokes of the beak of the Nukupuu, except that it was less loud. In the excessively wet forests of windward Hawaii it was sometimes seen on the stems of the tree-ferns, or amongst the masses of climbing Ieie *(Freycinetia arborea)*, exploring with its long beak in the first case the cavities of the stems of old fronds, broken off close to the caudex, and in the second the bases of the stiff clasping leaves and the débris found there, in both of which situations insects habitually harbour. In most of the higher forests where the rainfall is less, the Akialoa is mostly attached to the Koa, though it visits the lesser trees, Mamani, Naeo and stunted Olapa, and on Kauai comes even to the ground in the Ohia forests, when, no doubt, it is in search of fragments of lava, such as are sometimes found in its stomach.

The species of *Hemignathus* are fond of spiders, which they chiefly obtain on or beneath lichen-covered bark, and of many insects, which hide beneath the bark of trees, or actually live on this or the wood beneath. Amongst these are Geometrid caterpillars which secrete themselves by day; wood- and bark-eating Gelechiid larvae or such as feed in the rubbish which collects in the forks of trees or at the bases of the leaves of certain plants; beetles in the mature state, such as arboreal species of Carabidae rarely, the small metallic weevils of the genus *Oodemas* (favourite food also of the Nukupuu) very freely in many localities, Anobiidae in some districts; larvae of the latter and of Cossonidae, and others. In addition to these in the Kauai bird were found specimens of the small native cockroach and of certain remarkable crickets (Prognathogryllides), quite peculiar to the islands. For obtaining such insect food the long, slender, curved beak and brush-tongue is as admirably adapted as it is for extracting the hidden nectar in the long curved tubular corolla of the Lobeliaceae. To a small extent the Akialoa feeds on leaf-frequenting insects . . . picking off caterpillars, or even making a dart at some more active form.

Several times, both on Kauai and Hawaii, I have killed a specimen when feeding woodpecker- or creeper-like on the surface of a tree-trunk, and it has remained suspended from the tree by its beak alone, this organ at the moment of death having been thrust into some crevice or insect burrow, which it was probing for food. I have seen *Heterorhynchus wilsoni* suspended by the curved maxilla alone in similar fashion.

The song of *Hemignathus* is a short, vigorous trill, recalling that of both *Heterorhynchus* and *Chlorodrepanis*, but distinct from either. It has a louder and deeper call or alarm note than the latter, and this too is easily recognizable. Both the Kauai and Hawaii bird sing quite freely at certain times and places, and it is remarkable that when feeding on the nectar of flowers they are more lavish of this song than at other times. In this connection it may be noticed that of the *Oreomyzae* the two nectar-eating species alone have been heard to sing, the song being as rare as the nectar-eating habit, and it would appear possible that in these genera such a diet is a stimulus to song.

I once saw the nest of *Hemignathus obscurus*. It was built towards the extremity of one of the largest spreading branches of a Koa, placed above a fork and well concealed. It contained only one young one, and that already able to fly, while a second one was seen sitting on the branch outside the nest, with the old birds. The nest itself so far as I could get sight of it appeared to be quite similar in form to that of *Chlorodrepanis*, but was better concealed amongst the lichens covering the branch, and these appeared to have been partly used in its construction. This nest was found at the end of June, and in the same district (Kona) many young birds were noticed at the time being fed by the parents.

If the Hawaii Akialoa is, indeed, extinct, this is all we shall ever know of the habits and behavior of this bird.

Kauai Akialoa
Hemignathus procerus
(Color plate 37)

This highly specialized honeycreeper with its extremely long and strongly decurved bill was long feared to be extinct but was rediscovered in the Alakai Swamp region in 1960 by Richardson and Bowles (1964). The species may now be extinct, however, because John L. Sincock has not seen this unusual bird in more than 400 days of observations throughout the Kauai forests since 1967.

The overall length of the Kauai Akialoa is about 7.75 inches, which includes a bill from 2.2 to 2.6 inches long. Adult males are bright olive-yellow above, the top of the head being spotted or "scaled" with brown;

they have a bright yellow superciliary stripe. The chin, breast, and sides of the body are olive-yellow; whereas the abdomen is bright canary-yellow. Females are greenish olive-gray above and yellow to olive-green below; they also have a yellowish superciliary line. Both sexes have a black loral area. The bill of the female is considerably shorter than that of the male (Rothschild). Pratt (1979) saw no basis for considering the Kauai Akialoa to be a separate species, and suggested that it be a fourth subspecies of the *obscurus* group.

Rothschild (1893–1900:85) published the following notes made by Munro and (?) Palmer during January through April of 1891:

This bird is much more common and enjoys a wider range than the Nukupuu (*Heterorhynchus hanapepe*, Wils.), which bird it much resembles in habits. It seems to inhabit the whole forest-region of Kauai; its food consists of insects, their eggs and larvae, and we have also seen them sucking honey from the Lehua flowers. Above Makaweli in January and February we found it less common than at other places we visited: there they were mostly on the Koa trees, these being the most suitable hunting-ground for them in this locality. . . .

At Kaholuamano in the latter end of February and beginning of March they were more common, generally, in company with the Akikiki (*Oreomyza bairdi*), feeding on the Lehua trees, the pairs keeping more together. In one instance I shot a female, and the male stopped in the top of the tree calling desperately. I fired at him without effect, and so intent was he in looking for his mate that he immediately returned and was brought down by another shot. At Halemanu, towards the end of March, we found them as plentiful as at the latter place; but the Akikiki not being so common, the Akialoa (*Hemignathus procerus*) were more often found apart from them; here we first heard the Akialoa sing, although it was some time before we knew for certain it was the bird whose sweet note we heard every day; once I heard one sing while flying from one tree to another. Near Hanalei in April we found these birds not uncommon, generally in pairs, chasing each other about or singing in the tops of the trees. Their chirp seemed different here; Mr. Palmer likens both the chirp and song to that of the canary. We watched a pair singing together one day; the smaller and duller bird (probably the female) seemed to have fewer notes than the other.

Females that I dissected here (in April) had the ovaries enlarged, which, with before-mentioned notes on the subject, would denote the approach of the breeding season. I have seen these birds from the branches in the tops to the roots of the trees, probing into holes and under the bark, where they find a harvest of cockroaches' eggs, beetles, and grubs; on one occasion I saw one alight on the ground and insert its long bill amongst mats of dead leaves and bits of wood; have also seen them collecting insects from the bases of the leaves of the halapipi tree; have not often seen them feeding on nectar. In feeding they do not seem to depend much on sight; have never noticed them to *look* into a crevice, as the O-o,

before inserting their bill. I saw one send its bill at full length into a hole in a tree; have seen them work about one spot for some minutes, but have not noticed them break off any portions of bark or wood. Like the Nukupuu, it is an active bird, but can be easily approached within gunshot with ordinary caution. They have a strong smell when killed; and some, shot at Makaweli, had sores on their feet like the other birds in that locality at that time.

Rothschild added that "these swellings on the feet, which were so bad that in some cases the affected birds had lost one or more claws and toes, were also observed in many other birds in Oahu and Hawaii during the rainy season in wet places. . . ." Perkins and others had commented on the large swellings often seen on the feet and heads of the birds.

Bryan and Seale (1901) collected four specimens in 1900 and "saw a number of others." They commented that a young male collected on April 27 "is in a plumage that would make February and March the probable nesting season." The eye of the immature bird was dark hazel; the feet were gray; and the bill was dusky grayish. They saw no Akialoa below 3,500 feet. The nest and eggs have not been described.

Richardson and Bowles saw only two birds during their field work in the summer of 1960. Both were seen in the high, forested ridge country (elevation 4,000 feet) "within a mile southeast of the upper Koaie River Cabin." One bird was foraging on "the moss, lichen, and fern-covered trunk of a large ohia." A specimen collected on July 20 was a female in post-breeding condition. Its stomach contained the remains of several beetles and beetle larvae as well as one sprouting seed.

Ord (1967) described the callnote as "not unlike that of the Housefinch, though louder." He described the song as being "short and soft, similar to the trill of the 'Amakihi."

Nukupuu
Hemignathus lucidus
(Color plate 45)

The strongly decurved bill of the Nukupuu is unique among birds in that the lower mandible is only about half as long as the upper mandible. Subspecies were distributed as follows: *Hemignathus lucidus hanepepe*, Kauai; *H. l. lucidus*, Oahu; *H. l. affinis*, Maui. The Oahu race is extinct; the Maui race was rediscovered in 1967; and the Kauai race is rare, inhabiting the depths of the Alakai Swamp.

The males of the Kauai and Maui subspecies are similar in plumage pattern. The head, throat, and breast are bright yellow; both have black lores connected by a black line or band across the forehead. The back of the Kauai bird is yellow olive-green, whereas

PLATE 1. Black-footed Albatrosses on Whale-Skate Island, French Frigate Shoals. March 22, 1966.

PLATE 2. Laysan Albatross feeding its chick; Laysan Island. March 30, 1966.

PLATE 3. Wedge-tailed Shearwater prior to egg laying at nesting site on Popoia Islet. April 22, 1964.

PLATE 4. Christmas Shearwater on Laysan Island. March 1969. Courtesy of David L. Olsen.

PLATE 5. Newell's Shearwater at Kilauea Point, Kauai. May 5, 1965. Courtesy of Warren B. King.

PLATE 6. Dark-rumped Petrel at Haleakala Crater, Maui. May 1964. Courtesy of Warren B. King.

PLATE 7. Bonin Petrel on Lisianski Island. Courtesy of William O. Wirtz, II.

PLATE 8. Bulwer's Petrel brooding a newly hatched nestling; part of the egg shell can be seen in front of the bird. Rabbit Island. July 16, 1970.

PLATE 10. Red-tailed Tropicbird incubating; Laysan Island. March 30, 1966.

PLATE 9. Sooty Storm Petrel on Green Island, Kure Atoll. January 1964. Courtesy of Warren B. King.

PLATE 11. Masked Booby and its two eggs on Whale-Skate Island, French Frigate Shoals. March 22, 1966.

PLATE 12. Brown Booby and its chick on Moku Manu. August 8, 1970.

PLATE 13. Incubating Red-footed Booby threatening the photographer; Ulupau Crater, Oahu. March 8, 1964.

PLATE 14. Incubating male Great Frigatebird with his gular pouch inflated; Laysan Island. March 27, 1966.

PLATE 15. Sooty Tern standing over its egg; East Island, French Frigate Shoals. March 23, 1966.

PLATE 16. Gray-backed Tern on Southeast Island, Pearl and Hermes Reef. June 1970. Courtesy of Eugene Kridler.

PLATE 17. Blue-gray Noddy; Nihoa Island. March 1965. Courtesy of Eugene Kridler.

PLATE 18. Brown Noddy and its egg on Rabbit Island. June 12, 1970.

PLATE 19. Black Noddy incubating on its nest in an ironwood tree; Sand Island, Midway Atoll. April 3, 1966.

PLATE 20. White Tern incubating its single egg on the top of an ironwood stub; Sand Island, Midway Atoll. April 5, 1966.

PLATE 21. Black-crowned Night Heron. Courtesy of W. Michael Ord.

PLATE 22. Nene on Mauna Loa, Hawaii. These pen-reared birds have been color banded for precise identification when seen in the field. Courtesy of Norman Carlson.

PLATE 23. A pair of Koloa. Courtesy of Eugene Kridler.

PLATE 24. Two Laysan Ducks. Courtesy of Eugene Kridler.

PLATE 25. Light phased Hawaiian Hawk. Courtesy of Norman Carlson.

PLATE 26. Hawaiian Coot. Courtesy of Eugene Kridler.

PLATE 27. Hawaiian Stilts at Makalawena Marsh, Hawaii. Courtesy of Norman Carlson.

PLATE 28. Pueo in a characteristic pose on a fence post along the Saddle Road, Hawaii. Courtesy of Warren B. King.

PLATE 29. Hawaiian Crow at its nest. April 24, 1964. Courtesy of P. Quentin Tomich.

PLATE 30. The author taking a Startech photograph of an Amakihi nest in the Mauna Kea Game Management Area, Hawaii. December 22, 1966.

PLATE 31. Two nestling Kauai Creepers. Kokee State Park, Kauai. May 22, 1970. Courtesy of C. Robert Eddinger.

PLATE 33. Nest and eggs of the Iiwi; Kokee State Park, Kauai. March 7, 1970. Courtesy of C. Robert Eddinger.

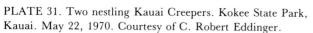

PLATE 32. Laysan Apapane. A water-color painting made from a motion picture taken by the late Donald Dickey of one of the last three surviving honeycreepers three days before the species became extinct in 1923. Courtesy of Alfred M. Bailey.

PLATE 34. An immature Cattle Egret; Kaneohe Marine Corps Air Station, Oahu. October 5, 1970. Courtesy of David L. Olsen.

PLATE 35. Laysan Rails and their chicks. From Rothschild (1893–1900).

PLATE 36. Hawaiian Rails. From Rothschild (1893–1900).

PLATE 37. Four unique bird species of Kauai. *Top*, Anianiau; *left*, Kauai Oo; *right*, Small Kauai Thrush; *bottom*, Kauai Akialoa. From *A Survey of the Birds of Kauai, Hawaii*, by Frank Richardson and John Bowles. Courtesy of the Bernice P. Bishop Museum.

PLATE 38. Laysan Millerbird. From Rothschild (1893–1900).

PLATE 39. Hawaii Oo. From Rothschild (1893–1900).

PLATE 40. Birds of the mamani-naio forest on Mauna Kea. *Top,* Hawaii Amakihi feeding from a mamani flower; *right center,* Palila working on a mamani seedpod; *left center,* Hawaii Elepaio perched on a branch of naio; *bottom,* Akiapolaau. Also shown are the endemic prickly poppy *(Argemone glauca)* and the introduced (from Africa) yellow stinking everlasting *(Helichrysum foetidum)*.

PLATE 41. Kioea. From Rothschild (1893–1900).

PLATE 42. Lesser Koa Finch. From Rothschild (1893–1900).

PLATE 43. Nihoa Finches. The female (lower) is eating shell from the egg of a Brown Noddy. The plant with the yellow flowers is ilima *(Sida fallax)*; the plant on the left is goosefoot *(Chenopodium sandwicheum)*.

PLATE 44. Birds of the island of Hawaii that are presumed to be extinct. *Top,* male and female Greater Koa Finches perched in a koa tree; *left center,* Kona Grosbeak perched in a naio tree; *right center,* Hawaii Mamo; *bottom,* Ula-Ai-Hawane in an endemic palm, *Pritchardia affinis.*

PLATE 45. Some birds of the ohia-koa forests on the outer, windward slopes of Haleakala Crater, Maui. *Top,* Maui Nukupuu; *left center,* Crested Honeycreeper; *right center,* Maui Parrotbill with a larva in its bill and perched on a dead branch of a koa tree (an adult cerambycid beetle, *Plagithmythus,* sp., is shown on the branch); *bottom,* Iiwi feeding from a flower of *Clermontia arborescens* (based on figure in Spieth 1966).

PLATE 46. Some birds of Kauai and Molokai. *Top,* Ou; *left center,* immature Apapane at an ohia blossom; *right center,* Kauai Akepa; *bottom left,* Kauai Creeper; *bottom right,* Molokai Creeper.

PLATE 47. Black Mamo. From Rothschild (1893–1900).

PLATE 48. Male (above) and female Greater Necklaced Laughing-thrushes. The tree is *Cassia surattensis,* introduced from southeastern Asia; the common name is kolomona, the Hawaiian word for Solomon.

PLATE 49. Some birds of the ohia forests of the Hamakua Coast, Hawaii. *Top left,* Hawaii Thrush; *top right,* Apapane; *left center,* male Hawaii Akepa; *right center,* Greater Amakihi with a cone-headed katydid (*Banza* sp.) in its bill; *lower left,* immature Hawaii Thrush perched on a branch of *Cheirodendron; lower right,* Hawaii Creeper.

PLATE 50. The Poouli perched on a kolea tree (*Myrsine* sp.). A painting by H. Douglas Pratt, courtesy of H. Douglas Pratt.

PLATE 51. *Top left,* Lace-necked Dove (the vine with green fruits is passion fruit, *Passiflora* sp.); *top right,* Japanese White-eye feeding a fledgling perched on haole koa *(Leucaena glauca); lower left,* Skylark; *center,* Western Meadowlark; *lower right,* Barred Dove.

PLATE 52. *Top left,* Guam Cave Swiftlet; *top right,* Red-billed Blue Magpie perched on a fish-poison tree *(Barringtonia asiatica); left center,* Red-billed Leiothrix perched on guava *(Psidium* sp.); *right center,* Red-whiskered Bulbul; *bottom,* Red-vented Bulbul perched on a chenille plant *(Acalypha hispida).* The magpie was painted three-fourths natural size; the other birds, natural size.

PLATE 53. *Top*, White-throated Laughing-thrush perched on kukui or candlenut tree *(Aleurites moluccana); upper left*, Varied Tit on fiddlewood *(Citharexylum spinosum); upper right*, Melodious Laughing-thrush on ironwood *(Casuarina equisetifolia)* and maile pilau *(Paederia foetida); center*, Japanese Bush Warbler on alaea or lipstick tree *(Bixa orellana); bottom left*, Shama on bark and taro vine *(Scindapsus aureus); bottom right*, Magpie-robin on pikake hohono *(Clerodendrum philippinum)*.

PLATE 54. *Top,* Mockingbird perched in a banyan tree (*Ficus* sp.); *left center,* Red-crested Cardinal; *upper right,* House Finch; *lower left,* female Cardinal; *lower right,* Hill Myna in a monkeypod tree *(Samanea saman)* and a Common Myna with a worm in its bill.

PLATE 55. *Top,* male and female Red-cheeked Cordon-bleu; *left,* male and female Cordon-bleu; *bottom,* male and female Blue-headed Cordon-bleu. The tree is cotton-leaved jatropa *(Jatropa gossypifolia),* a tropical American species.

PLATE 56. Two Lavender Fire-finches. The plant is oleander *(Nerium indicum)*.

PLATE 57. Orange-cheeked Waxbills (above) on aloe (*Aloe* sp.), an African genus; and Red-eared Waxbills on prickly pear cactus (*Opuntia* sp.), an American cactus.

PLATE 58. Red Munias in tree tobacco *(Nicotiana glauca)*, a shrub native to Argentina and Uruguay.

PLATE 59. Warbling Silverbills on a branch of kou *(Cordia subcordata).*

PLATE 60. Pin-tailed Whydahs: *upper right,* male in breeding plumage; *lower left,* male in nonbreeding plumage; *lower right,* female; *upper left,* immature male. The plant is Christmasberry *(Schinus terebinthifolius).*

Susan G Monden

PLATE 61. Adult and immature Ricebirds near nest in a kiawe tree *(Prosopis pallida)*, a Peruvian species. The wasps are *Polistes exclamens,* a pugnacious introduced species accountable for a high percentage of wasp stings in Hawaii.

PLATE 62. A Tri-colored Mannikin (top) on a branch of balsam apple. *(Momordica balsamina)*, native to Africa and Asia; an adult Black-headed Mannikin on a branch of Indian pluchea or fleabane *(Pluchea indica)*; and an immature Black-headed Mannikin on a grass stem (below).

PLATE 63. Java Sparrows in a wiliwili tree *(Erythrina sandwichensis)*, a native Hawaiian tree.

PLATE 64. Female (above) and two male Saffron Finches in an Indian banyan tree (*Ficus benghalensis*).

PLATE 65. Male (above) and female Yellow-faced Grassquits perched in an octopus tree (*Brassaia actinophylla*).

PLATE 66. Female (above) and male (middle) Yellow-billed Cardinals; male Red-capped Cardinal (below). The plant is jacaranda (*Jacaranda acutifolia*).

PLATE 67. Gray Canaries (above) on a dead branch of a kiawe tree, and Yellow-fronted Canaries on an African pencil tree *(Euphorbia tirucalli)*.

that of the Maui bird is grayish olive-green. The abdomen and under tail coverts of the Kauai bird are whitish; those of the Maui bird are yellow. The adult male of the Oahu Nukupuu was olive-green above, "darker and more olive on the back, lighter and more green on the head, wing, and tail-coverts" (Rothschild). Females are smaller and duller in color than males, especially those of the Kauai race which are olive-gray with a greenish tinge above and dusky white to grayish below, being washed with yellow only on the chin and upper throat. Total length of the birds varies from about 4.5 to 5.6 inches. The tail is very short, and Perkins wrote that the perfect climbing movements and extremely short tail at once betray the Nukupuu "when its beak is not visible to the collector, and its voice is not heard."

The Oahu Nukupuu was not found by Perkins or other collectors in the 1890s. Feral cattle had largely denuded the Koolau Mountains in the vicinity of Honolulu, as is depicted by Perkins' (1903:426) comparison of the region as late as 1837 with its condition in the 1890s:

From such information as I have been able to gather from native or other sources it occurred in some numbers at least until about 1860, and frequented what must now be considered as the lower belt of continuous forest, its range in fact being apparently that of the Koa tree. Over the greater part of Oahu the Koa fails long before the main ridge of the mountains is reached, and an examination of the lower edge of the existing forest shows that a large, and probably much the larger part of the Koa belt has now been destroyed. If the bird was really restricted to this lower forest I should consider its total extinction as almost certain. The specimens obtained by Deppe and Townsend in 1837 were from Nuuanu valley, at no great elevation above the sea and were said to frequent the flowers of the banana. No doubt at that time the valley was densely forested for the greater part of its length, since Bloxam records that in 1825 he visited its head by a narrow path through a dense and shady forest. Lying as it does immediately behind the city of Honolulu this fine valley is now practically denuded of its forest and largely filled with unsightly guava scrub; and the cliffs on either side, which to Bloxam appeared bare in comparison with the valley itself, now alone retain their native vegetation. Of late years some attempt has been made to reforest the head of the valley, but the exotic trees now planted are a poor substitute for the many rare and beautiful native species, which once flourished there; nor is it likely that any reforesting will bring back the birds which the American and Prussian naturalists found so plentifully some sixty-five years ago.

Perkins found the Kauai Nukupuu "by no means a common bird, and its range is rather restricted. It is found on the high plateau of that island, but only over a limited portion, whence came the original specimens obtained by Wilson. At lower elevations (from 2000–3000 ft.) it can be obtained in the forests forming part of the Hanapepe water-shed, on the west side of the main river. Here it can always be met with in certain favoured spots frequenting the Koa trees."

Munro (1944:117) wrote that he "took a specimen in December 1898, and two more on May 6, 1899, all males," and that he doubted that the Kauai Nukupuu had been seen since that time. Richardson and Bowles, however, saw two birds on August 16, 1961, in the same area where they observed the Akialoa. Two or three birds were seen in the same region by W. Michael Ord in September 1964.

Perkins (1903:427) found the Maui Nukupuu (which he called *Heterorhynchus affinis*) to have a very restricted range:

on the north-west slope of Haleakala, where it is chiefly found about a mile below the upper edge of the forest at an elevation of 4000–4500 ft. above the sea. Here it is often found in company with *Pseudonestor*, which would, however, appear to stray both above and below the range of *Heteroryhynchus*. It is rather more numerous in individuals than the Kauai species, since on some occasions a dozen or more adults have been observed on a single day, while rarely have we seen half that number of *H. hanapepe*, even when well accustomed to their habits and favourite haunts. Of course of either species a greater number may perhaps be noticed in a day's hunting at a time when the young are still following the parents, but on the other hand it is quite possible to search very diligently for a whole day on either island and not get a glimpse of either species.

It seems reasonable to conclude that both the Kauai and Maui Nukupuu were uncommon even in the 1890s. Winston E. Banko saw three Nukupuu on August 24, 1967, during the Kipahulu Valley expedition, and a fourth bird was seen by George Morrison on September 11, 1967. These birds were observed at elevations between approximately 5,650 and 6,550 feet, which extends considerably the range defined by Perkins. Banko (1968) points out that this upward extension of the range also places the Nukupuu "in a forest dominated by ohia rather than by koa." John L. Sincock watched Kauai birds feeding among the stamens of ohia flowers.

Because it is now known that both the Maui and the Kauai Nukupuus still survive, albeit in greatly reduced numbers, it is pertinent to record some of the early reports on their habits and behavior. It should be noted, however, that Perkins, Rothschild, and Munro considered each of the subspecies of Nukupuu and the Akiapolaau of Hawaii to be distinct species of the same genus (*"Heterorhynchus"*). Some care is required, therefore, in interpreting the early literature in order to be sure that one understands which birds are being discussed.

As pointed out previously, Perkins appears to have been the most perceptive observer of the habits of Hawaiian birds. He wrote (1903:428–429):

In their manner of feeding both the Maui and Kauai species [of Nukupuu] greatly resemble *H. wilsoni* [the Akiapolaau], but they are, though very active, less vigorous in their movements, when hunting their prey. Both hammer on the surface of trunk or branch and produce a tapping sound, audible at a distance, but it is generally much less loud than that of the Hawaii bird. They moreover entirely agree with one another in all of their habits. *H. affinis* on rare occasions sucks the nectar of the flowers of the Ohia, and *H. hanapepe* is said, on native authority, by Wilson to eat bananas and oranges, which no doubt means visits the flowers for nectar. So the natives say of many birds that they "eat lehua" i.e. obtain nectar from these flowers. As already mentioned, the Oahu species had a similar partiality for the banana flowers. Of all the species of *Heterorhynchus* the insect and other animal food consists to a large extent of spiders, which live exposed on the surface of branches or amongst the lichens which cover these; of caterpillars of Tineidae which live in dead wood, such as *Thyrcopa*, those that live within cases being swallowed case and all, and of larvae of some wood-boring beetles. Looper caterpillars, of such species as hide by day beneath the bark, are frequently eaten, and even those which live exposed upon the foliage, during their periodical swarming. But considering the various species of *Heterorhynchus*, as examined in all localities and at all seasons, their favourite food would appear to be the small brassy weevils of the genus *Oodemas*, a form not less peculiar than the birds themselves. In many localities these beetles invariably form a considerable portion of the contents of the stomach. As these beetles as well as a large proportion of the larvae eaten by *Heterorhynchus* feed solely on wood absolutely dead, these birds have not by any means so great an economic value in the forest as might be supposed, in fact the large number of spiders that they kill largely discounts their services as eaters of looper caterpillars. Though they habitually frequent trees infested with the native Cerambycid beetles they appear to trouble these rarely or not at all, either as larvae or as adult beetles. For this reason *H. affinis,* feeding side by side, as it sometimes does, with *Pseudonestor,* and constantly frequenting the same trees, enters but little into competition with this species, which is constantly on the hunt for these larvae. Strongly built as is *Heterorhynchus* it probably requires the much stouter beak and huge muscles of the allied genus, to open the burrows and extract the grubs of these beetles with sufficient expedition to make them a profitable food. All the species of *Heterorhynchus* are of a sociable disposition, so that when feeding they often join or are joined by several other kinds of birds. This fact makes it far easier to obtain the rarer species. . . .

All the species of *Heterorhynchus* occasionally come down to the ground in quest of fragments of lava, which are no doubt swallowed for the purpose of grinding up the extremely hard

brassy weevils, already mentioned as being a favourite food. Although I have frequently observed this habit in all the *Heterorhynchi* from dissections of the body, yet only twice, once on Hawaii and once on Kauai, have I seen the bird on the ground in the act of swallowing these pieces of lava. In each case the bird was standing on one of the narrow paths made by the cattle through the underbrush and trodden bare by these.

The song of the three species is very similar and is a short, loud trill. It is loudest in the Hawaii bird, but otherwise like that of the others.

Because of Perkins' thorough knowledge of both the insects and the birds, his commentaries on the feeding habits of the various species of honeycreepers are both reliable and instructive, and they suggest that the highly specialized species of birds may have been important in controlling populations of forest insects.

The nests, eggs, and newly hatched young have never been described for any of the subspecies of Nukupuu.

Akiapolaau
Hemignathus wilsoni
(Color plate 40)

The Akiapolaau is very similar to the Nukupuu except for its bill. The upper mandible is strongly decurved but the lower mandible is straight, robust, and only about half as long as the upper mandible; the upper mandible is much more slender and delicate than the lower one. The birds are bright olive-green above, often yellow on the head; the lower parts are bright yellow. The lores are black. Sometimes females are paler than the males and, according to Rothschild, have shorter bills than the males. Overall length is between 5.5 and 5.75 inches.

Until one learns the callnotes and songs of the Akiapolaau, it is not always easy to distinguish it from the Amakihi in the field despite the Akiapolaau's unique bill. Male Hawaii Amakihis often have bright yellow plumage like that of the Akiapolaau, and the size difference is not obvious when the two species are flitting rapidly about in the dense foliage of the mamani. The Akiapolaau does appear to have a larger head, and the head is slightly different in shape than that of the Amakihi. The Akiapolaau's habit of feeding on the trunks and larger branches is usually diagnostic. Positive identification usually depends on finding a bird that will perch quietly long enough so that one can get a clear look at the bill.

The Akiapolaau is endemic to the island of Hawaii. Perkins (1903:427) wrote that

[it] is not only widely distributed over that island, but is abundant in localities differing greatly in their climates. In

the middle Kona district this *Heterorhynchus* [Akiapolaau] was numerous in the forests of mixed Koa Mamani and Naeo from 3500 ft. upwards. Below this elevation it was not seen, its range being almost exactly identical with that of the underbrush of the bastard sandal (Naeo), the fine Koa trees below this elevation, and situated well within the wet-belt, having no attraction for the bird. This is the more curious when one considers that it is very much at home in the Koa trees of the Hilo forest with its excessive rain-fall, where I found it commonly from 1500 ft. upwards. A few miles from the volcano in Kau it can be observed to great advantage at close range, as it is particularly fond of the stunted bushy Koa trees, that are occasionally met with in those woods. These it habitually frequents in company with the Akialoa (*Hemignathus*) and several other birds, and numbers can be seen on any favourable day. It is also found in the Mamani woods of the Waimea district.

Perkins found none of the honeycreepers more interesting in their habits than the Nukupuu and the Akiapolaau:

Their climbing movements are more perfect than those of other birds, and they creep over the tree-trunks either upwards or downwards with equal ease, and hunt both along the upper and under surface of the branches. On the 11th of July, 1892, in the high forest of Kona I first had the opportunity of watching one of these birds [Akiapolaau] in pursuit of food, and as I was able to examine all its actions for a long time and at a very short distance, both with the naked eye and with field-glasses, I have little to add to the account then written, after similar observations on many other individuals. The bird in question was an adult male in fine plumage, and when first seen was about 10 yards off, but showed no fear when I approached it much more closely. It was visiting one after another a number of fallen tree-trunks, large but smooth-barked examples of *Acacia koa*. Along each of these it proceeded from one end to the other, peering now over the right side of the trunk and now over the left, so that in a single journey it searched both sides of the tree without retracing its steps. The upper mandible is thrust into small holes or cracks in the wood, while the point of the lower presses on the surface of the bark, and in this manner the burrows of wood-boring insects are opened out. So too it thrusts its upper beak under loose pieces of bark, resting the lower one on the surface, and breaks off fragments of the bark, under which its food is concealed. The upper mandible, though so slender as to be slightly flexible, is very strong, and this flexibility of the beak aided by the extreme flexibility and strength of the neck no doubt greatly assists the bird in exploring and opening out the burrows. In extracting and capturing its prey it also employs the thin brush-tongue, which can be extended to the length of the upper mandible. At frequent intervals it gives several blows to the trunk, the sound of which can be heard at a considerable distance. These blows are dealt with great vigour and with the beak wide agape, so that the point of both mandibles comes in contact with the surface at the same time. On one occasion I watched one lying on a branch of the mamani and basking for a time in the hot sun. Now and then it would lazily turn its head and peck at the bark without otherwise changing its position. Suddenly it started up and began to feed in earnest, dealing blows on the bark with savage energy. Into these blows it throws its whole weight, swinging backwards from the thighs to renew its stroke. In some cases these blows, if not for the purpose of driving out hidden insects, at least have that result, for several times I saw the bird after a stroke make a sudden dart, sometimes even taking an insect on the wing. Though less powerful than those of some other allied birds, the muscles of the head are unusually developed, as indeed are those of the legs, neck and other parts of the body, and the whole bird is of remarkably compact and sturdy build. Not infrequently it lays hold of a projecting piece of bark or the stump of some small broken branch, and shaking its head from side to side and pulling in all directions, endeavours to tear it out. If unsuccessful in the attempt, it will alternate this treatment with a shower of blows from the points of its gaping bill, till either the stump gives way or the labourer is convinced of the futility of further efforts.

In commenting on Perkins' description of the feeding habits, Munro (1944:119) wrote: "Perkins states that it strikes with the points of both mandibles at the same time. I watched them very closely, but without a glass, and was sure that the bird held the upper mandible out of the way and struck only with the lower which is stiff and strong and fitted for digging into the rotten bark and wood." My observations agree with those of Munro. I have watched foraging Akiapolaau on several occasions, sometimes at such close range that field glasses could not be used. The birds pounded the dead tree with their lower mandibles only, then picked up the food with both. It is correct to say that the Akiapolaau has woodpeckerlike feeding habits, pounding its lower mandible into dead branches and tree trunks in its search for grubs and insects. I have seen them forage only a few feet above the ground. The feeding habits of one bird I watched reminded me of that of the Brown Creeper (*Certhia familiaris*), which begins at the bottom of a tree trunk and works upward in a spiral path along the trunk.

Both Perkins and Palmer found the Akiapolaau common in the Kona district, and Palmer found it above Hilo (as low as 1,400 feet) and in the Hamakua district (from "2000 to 5000 or 6000 feet"). Palmer believed the Akiapolaau to be found in all the upland forests. Perkins, however, said that the Akiapolaau "has little or no liking" for ohia trees. He added that it never eats nectar.

Richards and Baldwin (1953) presented data on birds seen between elevations of 4,150 and 5,500 feet in Volcanoes National Park from 1938 to 1946, and reported it to be "rather common locally" between 3,900 and 7,750 feet on the eastern slope of Mauna

Loa and on the northeastern slope of Mauna Kea during the period of 1948 to 1950.

I first saw the Akiapolaau at an elevation of about 6,800 feet in the mamani-naio forest on Mauna Kea on June 13, 1966; two days later I saw two males and a female in the same area (fig. 96). During 71 days of field work in the Kaohe and Mauna Kea Game Management areas from June 11, 1966, to February 7, 1970, I saw one or more Akiapolaau on 21 days. On several occasions I saw two birds together that behaved like mated pairs. Two of the presumed females were just as brightly colored as the males, but other females were duller than the males.

I heard males sing during the winter months (November–January) as well as during the summer (April–July). Males have at least two primary songs and a whisper song. One of the primary songs is a loud, short (three-syllabled), melodious trill, much louder than a similar song of the Palila. The other also is loud but longer, and has a more warbling character. The whisper song is much softer, longer, and more elaborate than either of the primary songs.

On December 7, 1966, I watched a pair perched about 15 feet apart and only 4 feet from the ground on large dead branches of a mamani tree. The male faced the female and sang several times while rapidly quivering his wings over his back. I have watched males singing both one of the primary songs and the whisper song from dead and living branches only 4 to 6 feet above the ground; the primary songs also are given from the tops of trees, sometimes while the bird is perched on a bare exposed branch, at other times concealed among the foliage. In my experience, song periods rarely lasted more than five minutes, after which time the bird might be silent for several minutes to a half hour or more. Some birds sang only two or three times and

FIGURE 96. Habitat of the Akiapolaau in the Kaohe Game Management Area on Mauna Kea at an elevation of approximately 7,350 feet. December 22, 1966. The author's daughter is standing in one of the numerous eroded gullies, which are largely the result of destruction of ground cover by cattle (in the past) and by pigs, goats, and sheep (both in the past and at present).

then were silent. There were other days when I saw one or more Akiapolaau but did not hear a single song or callnote. To me, the callnote is very similar to that of the Amakihi but much more melodious.

January 31, 1968, was typical of many days in the mamani-naio forest on the southwestern slopes of Mauna Kea. The day dawned bright and clear. High scattered clouds had appeared by late morning, and by 12:30 P.M. there was a dense fog and light rain. I found a pair of Akiapolaau in the area where I had watched a male sing the day before. The female was feeding from the larger branches of a naio. The male began feeding near the bottom of the trunk of a dead mamani tree and worked his way upward, stopping to sing occasionally. After reaching the top of the trunk, the male sang again and flew off a short distance and then was quiet for about five minutes. On this day, the male sang from one to three songs and then was quiet for several minutes to ten minutes. Unfortunately, the State Division of Fish and Game bulldozed 200 acres that included this Akiapolaau habitat during the summer of 1969.

During 1972 I discovered the Akiapolaau during my census work in the magnificent ohia-treefern-koa habitat of the Kilauea Forest Reserve and in the adjacent cut-over pastureland of the Keauhou Ranch. Since that time, J. Michael Scott has censused all of the major forest habitats on Hawaii. He found the Akiapolaau in the rain forests of the windward coast, in the mamani-naio forest of Mauna Kea, and in two widely separated areas in south Kona; he did not find it in Volcanoes National Park. The small isolated populations of the Akiapolaau (and of other species of honeycreepers) would seem to be especially endangered because we have no evidence of the movement of individuals from one area to another.

A nest under construction was found in the Kilauea Forest Reserve on January 18, 1973, but it apparently was deserted before eggs were laid. The nest was built in a lateral fork of an ohia tree about 40 feet from the ground. The nest, eggs, and nestlings have not been described. William A. Bryan (1905c, 1905d) had a habit of describing old nests that were sent to him from friends on Hawaii. Among the common species of honeycreepers, however, the birds not only feed in trees containing active nests of other individuals but they also steal nesting material from active nests of the same or of a different species. Consequently, to identify a nest (either active or deserted) as that of a particular species because a bird was seen to fly out of the tree is likely to lead to a misidentification of the nest. In his thesis, Eddinger (1970b) remarked that he found it reliable to identify a nest only if he saw a bird adding material to the nest, incubating eggs, or feeding young in the nest.

Kauai Creeper
Oreomystis bairdi
(Color plate 46)

The Hawaiian name for this species is Akikiki. The adults are brownish gray above and white to creamy white below. They have short, pointed and downcurved bills. Total length is about 4.5 inches.

Rothschild considered the unfeathered operculum over the nostrils, the different wing formula, and the much straighter bill of the Creepers, as compared with the Amakihis, to justify a separate genus for the Creepers. Amadon, however, included the Creepers in the genus *Loxops*. Raikow (1977b) and Pratt (1979) presented additional evidence to support Rothschild's conclusion.

This species is fairly common in the Alakai Swamp and the Kokee State Park region of Kauai. The birds are primarily insectivorous, typically foraging while creeping over trunks and branches of trees. They have a simple song consisting of descending trills; they give a quiet *chip* callnote.

Very little is known about the biology of the Kauai Creeper. C. Robert Eddinger found the first nest of the Kauai Creeper on April 19, 1969 (fig. 97). Both adults were working on the nest, which, however, was deserted after one egg was laid. It measured 18.3 × 23.3 mm. This nest was built 26.5 feet above the ground in the terminal cluster of leaves of an ohia tree with a basal circumference of 39 inches. Eddinger found another nest on April 26, 1970. Although this

FIGURE 97. Nest of the Kauai Creeper; Kokee State Park. May 14, 1969. Courtesy of C. Robert Eddinger.

FIGURE 98. A hand-raised Kauai Creeper at four months of age; September 20, 1970.

nest was inaccessible, he was able to climb to within 10 feet of it. The behavior of this female Creeper was unlike that we have found in any other species of honeycreeper in that she refused to leave the nest regardless of how much Eddinger shook the tree. He was still trying to make a positive identification of the bird on May 9. He touched the bird on the head with a long stick, assuming she would fly off to a neighboring tree, but she merely crouched deeper in the nest. Finally, Eddinger decided to collect the nest on May 20. He wired a plastic bag to a pole, held it under the nest, and dislodged it with a second pole, while holding onto the tree with his feet and legs. The nest held two nestlings with brownish green feathers on the back and wings; their wing feathers were white to cream colored; and there was a considerable amount of long, white down sticking up between the feathers on the head over each eye and on the back. The lining of the mouth was bright pink; the edges of the mandibles were bright yellow. The legs and feet were pinkish gray. The nestlings showed no fear response and immediately gaped for food (color plate 31; fig. 98).

Hawaii Creeper
Oreomystis mana
(Color plate 49)

Munro said that no Hawaiian name was known for this species. Hawaii Creepers are a drab olive green above; below they are dull white washed with olive green on the flanks and breast. The throat is always white and contrasts with the greenish tones of the breast in adults.

Immatures are much paler below, with less contrast between the throat and breast, and they usually have a prominent yellowish-white superciliary line. The iris is dark hazel; the legs and feet are dark brown. Total length varies from about 4.25 to 5.12 inches. Some Amakihi are just as drab in color but they never have the contrasting white throat. Moreover, the black lores of the Amakihi give it a masked appearance; the adult creeper has a broad black or dark gray mask that extends behind the eye, which gives the bird a wide-eyed or black-eye appearance. The bill of the creeper is only slightly curved and is brownish white; it appears pale at a distance and never looks bluish at the base; the bill of the Amakihi is more strongly decurved and it looks black at a distance, and at close range reveals a pale blue area at the base of the lower mandible.

J. Michael Scott described the Hawaii Creeper's song as a quavering, descending trill, frequently being very soft. It is most easily confused with the song of the Akepa, which, however, is "loose and lackadaisical and is not so stereotyped, often changing pattern from one song to the next. The song of the 'Amakihi is a slower and choppier trill, with the individual notes more distinct than in either the 'Akepa's or the creeper's song." The creeper's common callnote is a soft *sweet*, but family groups utter a loud, distinctive chatter of wheezy notes in short series (*whit-whit . . . whi-whi-whit*) reminiscent of the calls of the Pygmy Nuthatch (*Sitta pygmaea*) of western North America. The callnote of the Akepa is "a high-pitched, two-note whistled cheedlee," entirely unlike that of the creeper. Scott found that foraging behavior was an unreliable method for distinguishing between creepers and other birds.

Although Perkins found the Hawaii Creeper to be an abundant species, "generally distributed over the large island," its distribution was puzzling even at that time. He wrote (1903:414):

Thus in the middle Kona district, though extremely common at an elevation of about 3500 ft. and upwards, it was altogether wanting in the lower forest, its range coinciding exactly with that of *Heterorhynchus* in the same locality. Seeing that the lower forest with its magnificent Koa trees seemed admirably adapted for both species, I at first supposed that the climatic conditions of this region, with its comparatively heavy rainfall, were unsuitable, but subsequently both were found in company in great abundance in the lower forests of the windward side of the island, where the rainfall far exceeds that of the wettest belt in the Kona district. In the dry upper woods of Kona and Kau, as well as the lower rain-soaked forest of Hilo district, *O. mana* is extremely common, yet the climatic conditions are as different as can well be imagined for so small an area of distribution. In a considerable extent of the Puna forest the bird is likewise absent, but here the Koa is also wanting, and for this tree it has a decided predilection in other localities.

The present distribution of the Hawaii Creeper does not bode well for its survival. Widely separated populations occur on Hualalai, in South Kona, and on the windward coast of Hawaii; J. Michael Scott told me that he knew of no reliable records of this species in Volcanoes National Park in recent years.

Perkins wrote that all of the subspecies of the creeper are very much alike in habits, "a large part, and in some species nearly the whole, of their food being obtained from the trunks and limbs of the forest trees and bushes." He found all to be expert at climbing, working either upwards or downwards on trunks and along both the upper and under sides of horizontal branches. He found the Hawaii Creeper to be "extremely partial" to large koa trees and to the smaller mamani trees. On Kauai, where koa was sparse, the birds foraged on ohia and other trees in the forest. He noted that all of the races "come down to the base of the trunks and sometimes even to the ground itself, and some habitually hunt in the masses of creeping ferns, as well as on the fronds and stems of those which form large trunks." Their feeding behavior on large branches has been likened to that of nuthatches. Perkins reported that the food consists almost entirely of animal matter (caterpillars, spiders, beetles, moths, myriapods, slugs), and only occasionally do the birds eat nectar from ohia and other flowers. They obtain larvae both on the foliage and under bark or in dead wood. Perkins also noted that "the Oahuan species has the knack of obtaining one of the most remarkable of the Hawaiian Carabid beetles in quantities, to judge from the remains found in the bird's stomach, yet for the entomologist it is difficult to obtain even a single specimen. I have little doubt that it obtains these from the interior of dead branches of lofty Koa trees, practically inaccessible to the insect collector, since they are generally found in those shot when feeding in this situation."

Perkins wrote, presumably about the Hawaii Creeper: "I have several times found the nest of *Oreomyza*, never with eggs, but once with a single young one hardly able to fly and still retaining a little of the down. It was placed in an Ohia tree at a height of about 20 ft. and resembled the nest of *Chlorodrepanis*, for which, but for the presence of the young, it might have been mistaken."

J. Michael Scott watched a pair of creepers carrying nesting material to a crevice between loose bark and the trunk of a dead ohia tree on February 8, 1975. This inaccessible nest was about 35 feet from the ground and it was abandoned three days after its discovery (Scott et al. 1980). Howard F. Sakai also found a nest under construction on January 3, 1978; this nest was placed in a fork of a horizontal dead branch of a koa

tree about 42 feet from the ground, and both adults took part in nest construction. The nest branch was covered with a mat of lichen, and Sakai watched the birds bring lichen, twigs, and spider webs to the nest. During one period of observation, the birds visited the nest 23 times in 99 minutes, but spent less than 6 minutes in actual work on the nest. This nest was abandoned two days later (Sakai and Ralph 1980a).

Maui and Lanai Creeper
Paroreomyza montana

Pratt (1979:156) expressed doubt that the birds in the genus *Paroreomyza* actually are honeycreepers. He wrote: "They lack both the musty odor and the truncate base of the tongue. Their vocalizations are unique in the subfamily, as are such behavior patterns as predator mobbing. These facts suggest that, if these birds are drepanidines at all, they diverged very early from the ancestral stock, perhaps even before the ancestor of most modern thin-billed genera diverged from the finches." Pratt proposed that these birds be called by their Hawaiian name *Alauahio,* but this name has not been used for the past hundred years, and I see no justification for reintroducing it. Moreover, so little is known about the three species in this genus that I have elected to maintain the traditional name in this book.

Perkins found the Lanai Creeper (*P. m. montana*) "ubiquitous throughout the Lanai forest from 2000 ft. to the actual highest point of the island" in the 1890s. It now is extinct. Adult males were bright yellow on the forehead and the underparts and yellowish green on the upperparts; females had the same color pattern but were somewhat paler. The nest and eggs were never found.

The Maui Creeper (*P. m. newtoni*) is a common species in the rain forests on the northeast slope of Haleakala Crater. The birds eat insects (sometimes by flycatching) and nectar; I watched a bird feed on *Cyrtandra* on July 9, 1966. Pratt called the Maui Creeper an "active, sprightly bird" that "virtually never clings close to the bark of a tree but rather sits upright, usually with the tarsi clearly exposed." He thought its behavior like that of a Black and White Warbler and not like that of a nuthatch, and he found the most frequent foraging sites to be among leaves rather than along large branches.

I agree with Henshaw who reported that the Maui Creeper has a single, distinctive *chip* note like that of the Song Sparrow which apparently is used both as a location note and as an alarm note.

Pratt wrote that the songs are varied "and in overall quality and pattern are unlike any other drepanidine songs I have heard." He described the song as "a monotonously repeated but lively *whurdy-wheesy-whurdy-*

check, the last syllable being identical to the callnote. This song is apparently used in territory establishment. During aggressive encounters, the birds utter a more varied song that eventually grades into a loud version of the more stereotyped advertising song given by the victor.'' The birds also have a courtship flight song.

Henshaw (1902) saw adults and fledglings during June, but the first nest was not found until 1971, when van Riper (1972) found a nest near Lake Wai Anapanapa on March 15. The nest was built in an ohia tree 14.5 feet from the ground and was composed of leaves and leaf skeletons, covered on the outside with moss and lined with fine plant fibers; however, the nest was empty. Grant Merritt and Charles Whittle found a nest with two eggs in the Hana Forest Reserve at an elevation of 6,900 feet on July 4, 1973; this nest was built 10 feet from the ground in a kolea tree. Unfortunately, this nest was deserted; but, the following day, Tonnie Casey watched the female take material from the nest, and she found a new nest on July 8. This nest was placed at the end of a lateral branch of an ohia tree about 15 feet from the ground. The two eggs in this nest hatched before 9:15 A.M. on July 30. Casey described the nestlings as having a dark pinkish red mouth color. The male fed the female both on the nest and away from it; both adults fed the nestlings by regurgitation. Although it is very unusual for a passerine bird to desert a nest containing young, the female did so when the young were four days old.

Molokai Creeper
Paroreomyza flammea
(Color plate 46)

Males of the Molokai Creeper were described by Rothschild as being ''deep scarlet-vermilion'' above but more ''flame-scarlet'' on the forehead, rump, and upper tail coverts; they are ''altogether of a brilliant flame-scarlet'' below. The females are ''dark olive-brown, washed with orange'' above and buffy white below, often with a trace of bright orange on the throat. The bill is nearly straight although the upper margin of the maxilla is curved. Nasal setae (bristles) are absent, but nasal operculae are well developed.

Perkins found these birds to be common on both the leeward and windward sides of Molokai during the 1890s. This striking species may now be extinct. Pekelo (1963a) saw three birds in 1962, but Scott et al. (1977) did not find it during intensive field surveys.

W. A. Bryan (1908:166) mentioned three ''fairly well identified nests'' he found on Molokai in 1907. One nest he collected was under construction; he noted that ''the old bird was seen carrying the moss of which the exterior is composed.'' The other two were old

nests, one of which he assumed to be a creeper nest because he saw a pair and three immature birds in the same tree; however, the nest might just as well have been that of several other species. A nest with eggs or young of the Molokai Creeper has never been described.

Oahu Creeper
Paroreomyza maculata

Adult males of this species are olive green above and golden yellow below. Females and immature birds are gray to grayish green above and yellowish white below. The plumage is so similar to that of the Oahu Amakihi that other characters must be used to distinguish between the two. Wing bars usually are present in female and immature creepers and they may be present in female and immature Amakihi; they are absent in the adult male of both species. Oahu Creepers have prominent, though pale, superciliary lines above the eyes. A dark stripe extends from the lores to behind the eye in the creeper; only the lores are black in the Amakihi. The bill of the creeper is straight; that of the Amakihi is decurved. The upper mandible typically is brown and the lower mandible is dull yellow in the creeper; the bill of the Amakihi is black except for a pale blue base of the lower mandible. Shallenberger and Pratt (1978) discussed differences in feeding behavior and vocalizations in the two species.

In the 1890s, Perkins found the Creeper abundant on all of the islands except Oahu, where it was still to be found in both the Waianae and Koolau ranges, except that it seemed to ''have entirely disappeared from the mountains in the immediate neighbourhood of Honolulu.'' It now is a rare species. Shallenberger and Pratt found only three creepers during nearly three months of intensive field work in 1978.

Bryan (1905a:241) collected an incomplete nest of the Oahu Creeper on January 29, 1901, and he reported that Alvin Seale collected a nest with two eggs, as well as both adults, the following day. The eggs were described as having a creamy white background ''into which is worked the pale brown under-markings. Over these are sprinkled the redder brown spots which form an ill-defined wreath about the larger end, though they are thinly scattered all over the surface.'' The two eggs measured 0.58 × 0.80 inch and 0.60 × 0.78 inch.

Akepa
Loxops coccineus
(Color plates 46, 49)

This species differentiated into subspecies on Kauai *(Loxops coccineus caeruleirostris),* Oahu *(L. c. rufus),* Maui *(L. c. ochraceus),* and Hawaii *(L. c. coccineus).* Pratt

(1979:129) suggested that the Kauai Akepa be considered as a separate species *(L. caeruleirostris)*.

Akepas are small birds 4 to 5 inches in length. Unlike other honeycreepers, they have short, conical bills in which the tips of the two mandibles are twisted slightly in opposite directions *(Loxops,* meaning "twisted face"). This character, however, is not observable in the field. The tail is longer and more deeply notched than in the Amakihi and Creeper.

The sexes are alike in the Kauai race. The crown and underparts are yellow (in some birds very bright); the back and wings are olive-green; black lores are conspicuous in the field. Sexual dimorphism in plumage is pronounced in the other races. The Hawaii male is bright red-orange to ruby colored; the female is greenish above and yellow below. The Maui males are said to vary from brownish orange to dull yellow; the females are yellowish green, similar to the Hawaii female but said to be less yellow. Nothing is known about the sequence of plumage changes from nestling to adult for any of the subspecies.

As for the common name, Perkins (1903:418) wrote:

The various species of *Loxops* are amongst the most active of native birds and their name Akepa, signifying "sprightly," "turning this way and that," is singularly appropriate. This name is applied by well-informed natives of the present day to both the species inhabiting Maui and Hawaii, and Bloxam gave the same name for the Oahuan form three-quarters of a century ago. For the Kauai species Scott Wilson gives the name Ou holowai, but in various parts of that island I have been assured by natives that the true name is Akekee. If the latter, as I suspect, be correct, it is very appropriately applied, and would indicate that the natives had observed a noticeable generic character of *Loxops,* namely the abnormally bent mandible. It is true that Andrews says the Akekee is "a small brown bird resembling the wren, found on Waialeale Kauai," which could only refer to the flycatcher (and of which Wilson's Apekepeke might perhaps be a corruption); but as he is sometimes clearly in error in the remarks on birds made in his dictionary, and some extremely well-known species are altogether omitted, I am disposed to accept this name as correctly applied to the *Loxops* by living natives, who showed themselves well acquainted with other birds of the same island. It is certainly strange if the 'Elepaio' *(Chasiempis),* a bird so famous in song and legend, was given a distinct name on Kauai alone, for though the Kauai form is specifically quite distinct, in its voice, habits and superficial appearance it agrees with those on the other islands. On the other hand the *Loxops* of Kauai is a bird which, when adult, is of very distinctive appearance and highly characteristic of the avifauna of Waialeale.

Again, we must rely primarily on Perkins for information on distribution and habits of the Akepas. He wrote that the Akepa of Hawaii "is very widely distributed on that island, and in parts of the Kona district, in Kau, Hilo and the Kohala mountains is abundant. It is extremely partial to the Koa forests, but is found in localities where there are none of these trees, as in the forest between Kilauea and Keauhou (in Puna) and elsewhere. *L. ochracea* on Maui is also often seen in the Koa trees but more often in the Ohia, which latter are the favourite feeding ground of *L. caeruleirostris* on Kauai."

Wilson, however, wrote that he obtained only five specimens during eight months of collecting on Hawaii in 1877 (in Wilson and Evans 1890–1899). He collected two specimens at Puulehua, elevation 5,000 feet on the Kona coast; another was obtained "about three miles from the Volcano House, on the Keauhou road"; one, "in the forest on Puukapu near Waimea"; and the fifth, "within a few miles of Mana, the Hon. Samuel Parker's residence." All were obtained at elevations between 3,000 and 5,000 feet.

Palmer (in Rothschild) said that the Hawaii Akepa was to be found in "the higher regions from between 5000 to 7000 feet, although one was occasionally shot not higher than about 3000 feet. It frequents chiefly old lava-flows, where the Aaka [*naio*]-flowers are plentiful." Palmer also found the Akepa common in the Kohala Mountains at 4,000 feet elevation, and he also observed the species in Puna, near Hilo, and in the Hamakua region.

The Oahu Akepa is extinct. The Kauai Akepa appears to be the most common of the surviving forms, especially in the Alakai Swamp region, less commonly at Kokee State Park.

Eddinger (1972) discovered the first nest of the Kauai Akepa on March 9, 1969. The nest, placed 30.5 feet from the ground in a nonblooming ohia tree, was being built by both the male and the female. On one occasion, the male brought nesting material and the female took the material and added it to the nest cup. Between 8:30 and 10:30 A.M. on March 11, the male and female each added material to the nest eight times. During the absence of both birds, an Apapane flew to the nest and removed nesting material from it. On another day, an Apapane flew to the nest while both Akepas were present. The male chased the Apapane from the nest and through several nearby trees; but less than 15 minutes later, while both Akepas were absent, an Apapane flew to the nest again and took more material. The Akepas were still adding material to the nest on March 18, but later it was deserted, probably after one egg was laid; Eddinger found half an egg shell on a branch about a foot below the nest.

The male sometimes sang from a neighboring tree as the female worked on the nest. The song was a high trill, higher in pitch and shorter in duration than the song of the Anianiau; the male also uttered whisper songs not unlike those of the Amakihi.

Eddinger also observed courtship feeding, once on a branch near the nest and another time on a branch only three feet from the ground. The female crouched slightly, depressed and quivered her wings, and gave a rapid soliciting call.

Eddinger also found three Kauai Akepa nests in 1970 (March 26, March 29, April 11): two were inaccessible and all three were unsuccessful. The lining of one nest was pulled up over two eggs, and the adults deserted it. Two eggs measured 13.1 × 16.6 and 13.3 × 16.6 mm, respectively. The egg shells were white with dark brown speckles covering the entire surface but concentrated around the larger end of the egg.

The Kauai Akepa nests were composed largely of moss. One nest was lined with fine grasses, and another, with thin strips of soft bark.

Perkins collected a female of the Maui Akepa on April 4, 1894. This species apparently was not reported again until Amy B. H. Greenwell saw three small orange birds "in an *Acacia koa* growing in a gulch at an elevation between 2000 and 3000 feet between Kipapa and Nakaaha areas, Hana District, on the south slope of Haleakala Volcano" (Richards and Baldwin 1953). The Akepa now persists in unknown numbers in the rain forests on the northeast slope of Haleakala Crater (Scott and Sincock 1977).

Richards and Baldwin (1953) reported sightings of the Akepa at several locations on Hawaii during the period from 1938 to 1950. It was "fairly common at Keawewai, 6800 feet, Kau District" in 1938. One or more birds were seen on several occasions in 1941, 1943, 1948, and 1950 at elevations between 2,000 and 6,800 feet. Akepas were observed in Volcanoes National Park (Kau District), in the South Hilo District, and on the north slope of Hualalai Volcano at an elevation of 4,350 feet. I saw single male Akepas at an elevation of approximately 4,500 feet on the Stainback highway on July 11, 1966, and one at an elevation of 7,500 feet in the mamani-naio forest in the Mauna Kea Game Management area on February 6, 1970; the latter bird being a transient in that habitat. Because of intensive censuses organized by J. Michael Scott, we now know that the Akepa occurs in moderate numbers in widely separated habitats: Hualalai, a small area in middle Kona, and in scattered areas on the windward slopes of Mauna Kea and Mauna Loa.

John L. Sincock (Scott et al. 1979) found the first nest of the Hawaii Akepa on May 12, 1976, when he flushed a female from a cavity in an ohia tree at an elevation of about 6,100 feet in the Kau forest reserve.

The cavity was located about three feet from the ground and the entrance was about 2 by 5 inches in dimensions. The nest held three dull white eggs with brown spots circling the larger end. Two of the eggs hatched by May 28. The nestlings had pinkish skin and very fine medium gray down on the head, back, and wings; the gape was reddish pink and the corners of the mouth were light yellow; the feet also were yellow. Between dawn and dark on June 7, the female came to the nest 35 times and the male, 33 times to feed the young birds and to remove their fecal sacs. The nest was composed of tightly woven aerial rootlets of ohia, grass, and some fern fragments; it measured 10 cm in outside diameter, 8 cm in inside diameter, and was 3 cm deep.

Like the Amakihis, the Akepas seek their food primarily from the leaves and twigs of trees rather than from the trunks and larger branches, as is characteristic of the creepers. Perkins found that the Akepas feed largely on caterpillars and spiders, occasionally drinking the nectar from ohia and other flowers. Perkins felt that there was no doubt that the Akepas are "of high value in the forests," destroying quantities of insects which "are well concealed and obtained only to a comparatively small extent, or not at all, by the other native birds. For many of these hidden larvae, they compete rather with the native wasps than with other birds."

Gadow (in Wilson and Evans 1890–1899), who had never seen live Akepas, had proposed that the slight twisting at the tips of the mandibles was due to the fact that the birds "twist open seeds and cracks of bark in search of food." Munro believed that the mandibles are adapted for removing scale insects from the leaves of trees. Perkins said that the crossed mandibles are "without the least doubt for the extraction of insects living hidden in the leaf-buds of certain forest trees. These buds may not inaptly be compared to the pine cones from which *Loxias* procures its food, although their much softer substance by no means requires the more powerful implements of the crossbill. . . . the bill of *Loxops* is also useful in opening out the Koa phyllodes, when fastened together by certain caterpillars, or by some spiders (of which it is extremely fond) which thus conceal their nests."

Perkins (1903:420) said that the full song of each of the subspecies of Akepa "is a short trill, nearly or quite identical in all. The adult female of *L. coccinea* [on Hawaii] sings more musically, but still more softly, than the male. Her song is generally uttered from the dense cover of some tree of the underbrush, the notes sometimes being repeated at such short intervals as to form a practically continuous song lasting for some minutes. The call note is a simple 'keewit,' much less loud than the otherwise similar call of some other species [of honeycreepers].''

Subfamily Drepanidinae
Ula-Ai-Hawane
Ciridops anna
(Color plate 44)

Only five specimens of this bird were collected, the first about 1859. However, the species was not described until 1879. Palmer and Munro obtained one specimen from natives in the early 1890s, the last of this species ever reported. This bird was collected "near the headwaters of Awini on Mt. Kohala, Hawaii."

The tail, flight feathers, scapulars, and breast were black; the feathers of the crown also were black but tipped with gray to buff, forming a buffy band across the nape of the neck. The wing coverts, back, rump, and middle of the abdomen were bright red; the lower abdomen and under tail coverts were brownish buff. Some of the specimens, at least, were unsexed, and it is not known whether the sexes were alike in plumage. Total length is given as 4.25 inches by Wilson and Munro, but 5.5 inches, by Dole (1879), who first described this species. A mounted specimen in the Bernice P. Bishop Museum measures 5.13 inches.

The common name is said to mean "the red bird that feeds on the hawane" palm: *Ula* (red) -*Ai* (to eat) -*Hawane* (the Hawane palm), as given by Wilson.

Perkins (1903:405) wrote that the Ula-Ai-Hawane was "formerly widely distributed on the island of Hawaii, to which it was restricted, and known to have inhabited both the Kona and Hilo districts as well as the Kohala mountains. . . . It seems to have been found only in the neighbourhood of the Loulu palms (*Pritchardia*), the blossoms of which as well as the unripe fruit supplied it with food. The palms themselves seem to have been always of sparse or local distribution, and still exist singly or in scattered clumps in the dense forests above Hilo, where I have often observed them, as well as in the Kohala mountains and the Kona district."

There are no firsthand reports of the behavior of this bird in the field, and the nest and eggs were never described.

Iiwi
Vestiaria coccinea
(Color plate 45)

The Iiwi is a brilliant orange-red bird with primarily black wings and tail; there is some white on the inner vanes of the proximal secondary flight feathers. It has a very long, deeply curved, salmon-colored to pinkish red bill; the legs are orange. The sexes are alike. Total length is between 5.5 and 5.75 inches.

Immature birds are greenish yellow to brownish yellow, most of the feathers having blackish spots at their tips; wing and tail feathers are black. The bill is light brownish gray, but the lower mandible or maxilla has yellow margins; tarsi and feet are brownish pink. The red feathers of the adult usually grow in on the head and breast first.

Perkins (1903:404) wrote:

The yellow black-spotted young follow the parents sometimes till they are far advanced in their red plumage, but they very early learn to obtain nectar for themselves, even at a time when the parents are still feeding them on caterpillars. The changes that take place in the plumage from the young to the adult state are of much interest and are so great that the natives considered some of these stages to be distinct species. This is a curious error and detracts much from our opinion of their powers of observation, seeing that the birds in full plumage are constantly to be seen in company with and feeding their young. Such an error might easily be made by a museum student with insufficient material for study, but it is extraordinary how those who have seen the birds in life could be so deceived. The black markings of the plumage are sometimes very late in disappearing, and in one (the male) of two already paired, shot in the early spring months, black-tipped feathers so far remained as to form a black oblique streak for an inch or more from the shoulders on each side.

The Iiwi is the most striking in appearance of the common honeycreepers. The single species once inhabited all of the main islands. According to Munro, it became extinct on Lanai between 1923 and 1929. The Iiwi is close to extinction on Molokai and Oahu. The species is still fairly common on Kauai, Maui, and Hawaii, where, in general, the birds are found at elevations above 2,800 feet.

The Iiwi is such a conspicuous and vocal bird that more seems to have been written about it than of any other Hawaiian species, particularly about its feeding habits. Titian Peale (1848) wrote after the United States Exploring Expedition of 1838 to 1842 that "at Oahu, we found them generally about the gigantic lobelias which characterize the botany of that interesting island; they extract their food from the flowers of the lobelia for which the singularly-formed bill is admirably adapted." He added that "the red feathers of this species were usually selected for the ornamental figures on capes and robes of the ancient Hawaiians, but by reason of their abundance were not so highly valued as those of the O-O." (See also page 105.)

Wilson said that "the food of the Iiwi consists chiefly of honey, which it finds in the blossoms of the ohia and of the arborescent Lobeliaceae; no doubt it also preys on the small insects found in the flowers; but as honey will often drip from the bill of this bird, when shot, it probably constitutes its sustenance to a greater extent than that of other species.''

Perkins (1903:402–403) made a more intensive study of both the distribution and the feeding habits of the Iiwi. He wrote:

The general scarcity of birds on Oahu as compared with the other islands is noticeable, both as to the number of species and individuals, but this scarcity applies only to recent years, for the well-known ornithologist Townsend expressly states that he found birds more abundant on Oahu than on Kauai, some 65 years ago. On all the other islands the Iiwi was found to be very common from the lower forest up to the highest elevations reached by forest birds, even at those which during the summer months are subject to frequent frosts and at which in the winter the cold is really severe.

The Iiwi is a more powerful flier or at least takes longer continuous flights than most of the Drepanididae, and as its food-supply becomes deficient in one locality it readily migrates to another. In most localities there is however at all seasons a resident population, since all do not depart when these migrations take place. Some parts of the forest, absolutely devoid of native birds at most seasons, are regularly visited by the Iiwi at special times. Thus in some of the valleys of Oahu the mountain apple *(Eugenia)* forms extensive groves, below the ordinary range of forests birds. For a brief period each season numbers of the Iiwi visit the blooms of these trees, and after these fail are seen no more in the neighbourhood until the next flowering season. In the higher forests of the more lofty mountains large numbers are added to the usual stock of residents during the flowering season of the yellow-blossomed Mamani trees *(Sophora)*. In the lower forests of middle Kona many thousands of these birds could be seen in a very small area when the great Ohia trees were covered with flowers. On the nectar of these and many others the Iiwi habitually feeds, and is extremely partial to many of the native campanulate or tubular flowers, the arborescent lobelias, the bananas, some labiates, as *Phyllostegia,* the Nukuiiwi *(Strongylodon),* so called from the resemblance of its flowers to the beak of this bird, and many others. Nor does it despise garden flowers which the settlers have brought from other countries, sometimes visiting these even when at some distance from the nearest forest— nasturtium, cannas, lilies, and even roses and peach-blossoms. Nevertheless at the present time, considering the whole range of the bird, its main supply of nectar is furnished by the Ohia, which is not only the most abundant of all forest trees but can also be found in flower either at high, low, or moderate elevation in the mountains at all seasons of the year. However as I have pointed out in the introductory remarks there is little doubt that, had the Ohia existed on the islands throughout the period of the evolution of the avifauna, or at least had it existed in its present abundance, as the chief constituent of the forest, the Iiwi in its present form

would not have been developed. This development must have taken place when more or less deep tubular flowers, many of which are quite clearly very ancient components of the forest brush, yielded the main supply of nectar, for obtaining which the beak of the Iiwi is specially adapted, both in length and form. Besides the nectar of flowers, which on some occasions is the only food to be found in the stomach, this bird is especially fond of looper caterpillars, and so far as I have observed feeds its young entirely on these. It also feeds on those species of spiders which are so commonly found on the limbs of forest trees, alive or dead. When hunting amongst the leaves of large Koa and other trees it has a quick, gliding movement, noticeable also in a few of those species most closely allied to it. Its conspicuous black and scarlet plumage is particularly pleasing when seen in the densest and gloomiest forests, so generally devoid of colour and where scarcely any sunlight can penetrate. Here it frequently visits the white campanulate flowers of the underbrush, and as in such situations it is very tame all its movements can be examined with ease at a distance of two or three paces.

Spieth (1966) gave the most careful analysis of the feeding of the Iiwi at lobeliad flowers, and discussed the earlier theories of Perkins and others.

The Iiwi flies to the flower and quickly perches on the flower-bearing twig just basad of the flower pedicel. The bird then quickly swings into an *upside-down* position under its perch and simultaneously twists its body so that its head is under the open corolla, with the bill pointing upwards. It then easily and with precision slips its slender decurved beak into the corolla. The nicety of fit between the bird's head and bill and the fleshy corolla of the flower is indeed striking. . . . The entire bill and fore part of the head are thrust deeply into the corolla, reminding one of a finger slipping into a well-fitting glove. After probing into the corolla for a few seconds, the bird flies to another flower, performs its acrobatics and probing, and then on to another flower. Within a few minutes a bird will have visited and fed upon dozens of flowers. As Perkins (1903) and others have noticed, these visitations to the flowers seem to exhilarate the birds and they become visibly excited as they fly about in the tree.

Despite the observations and reports of Perkins (1903 and 1913), Bryan (1908), and Munro (1960) that the honeycreepers fed frequently on lobeliads and were presumably the major pollinators of these plants, doubts have been raised subsequently by both botanists and ornithologists, for the following reasons:

1. Numerous observers have seen the honeycreepers feeding and presumably collecting nectar from flowers of diverse plant species, especially those of the Ohia *Metrosideros collina* (Gaud.), and the Mamani, *Sophora chrysophylla,* but have not seen them feeding upon lobeliads (see Baldwin, 1953).

2. Since the lobeliads continue to exist and set seeds upon the various islands despite the extinction of many species of

honeycreepers or despite the extinction of species such as *Hemignathus* sp. from Maui where lobeliads are common, botanists have concluded that the honeycreepers are not necessary as pollinating agents for the lobeliads (Rock, 1919, p. 31; Amadon, 1950, p. 200).

It should be recalled that the *Clermontia* flowers are protandrous. When the pollen reaches maturity, the antheral sections of the staminate column are easily ruptured by any slight abrasion and the sticky pollen immediately oozes out. The staminal column of *C. arborescens* is equipped with an "upper" and a "lower" row of stiff, inwardly directed antheral hairs at the distal end of the column. Presumably these scrape pollen from the bird's head as it is retracted from the flower. The enclosed style eventually elongates and pushes out of the end of the staminal column, but this does not occur until the flower has shed its pollen. As the style elongates, the stigma brushes against the antheral hairs which have previously accumulated pollen due to the actions of the birds.

The Iiwi originally were extremely numerous and ranged throughout the forest areas of the major islands without racial variation. The unique posture that they display in feeding upon the lobeliads, which results in the decurved bill of the birds fitting with such precision into the decurved flower of the plant, would seem to indicate a long-time association between the two organisms. I observed no other birds visiting the flowers that were physically able to feed upon these particular lobeliad flowers in the manner displayed by the Iiwi. In a broader context, however, it should be noted that many of the Hawaiian honeycreepers, both small and large species, have decurved bills and, with few exceptions, the Hawaiian lobeliad species also are unique in possessing decurved flowers. Thus we can reasonably suggest that there exists a significant coadaptation between a number of species of the lobeliads and various species of the honeycreepers.

Spieth's conclusion that his observations "further support the thesis of Perkins and others that the honeycreepers serve as prime pollinators of the Hawaiian lobeliads" is important because Baldwin (1953:311), in his intensive study of the Iiwi in Volcanoes National Park, wrote that "despite the reputed preference of *Vestiaria* for feeding at flowers of the lobelias, of all the many shrubs of *Clermontia, Cyanea,* and *Lobelia* I observed in bloom on Hawaii and Maui, not one was visited by *Vestiaria* or any other drepaniid, although the birds were present and feeding in *Metrosideros* or other plants."

I visited the Kula pipeline forest (elevation 4,000 feet) on Maui with Dr. Spieth on July 8, 1966, and had the opportunity to watch several Iiwi feeding in precisely the way he described it. Several of us also observed one or more Iiwi feeding on the lobeliad *Trematolobelia macrostachys* only a short distance from Base Camp 1 (elevation 3,100 feet) in Kipahulu Valley dur-

ing the first week of August 1967. At this elevation and higher, immature Iiwi and Apapane were seen feeding in kanawao *(Broussaisia arguta).* Only rarely were adult birds of these two species seen at this plant, however; the Amakihi and the Creeper, on the other hand, were seen at it often.

Both Eddinger and I have seen the Iiwi feed from the passionfruit flowers on Kauai, and I have seen it feed from the yellow flowers of the mamani on Hawaii. An interesting observation by Baldwin was that "in spite of the long bill and tongue possessed by *Vestiaria,* this bird pierces the corollas of nasturtium and *Passiflora* to obtain nectar."

Baldwin also reported that "all the 60 or more specimens of *Vestiaria,* as well as all the large numbers of *Himatione* and *Loxops virens* that I examined, had remains of insect food in the gizzard; hence I would minimize the suggestion that this species depended wholly on nectareous food at any time." The choice of insect food by the Iiwi is more like that of the Apapane than that of the Amakihi. Stomachs of Iiwi examined by Baldwin contained adults or larvae of the following orders of insects (numbers in parentheses are percentages of stomachs in which that group was found): Lepidoptera (100), Homoptera (73), Neuroptera (60), Corrodentia (43), Hymenoptera (33), Diptera (30), Heteroptera (30), Coleoptera (27), Thysanoptera (7). Spiders were found in 30 percent of the stomachs; molluscs, in 3 percent. The majority of animal food taken by both the Apapane and the Iiwi was "probably between 2.0 and 12.0 mm, although caterpillars frequently were longer than this."

Carpenter and MacMillen (1975, 1979) wrote that the Iiwi was more nectar-dependent than the Amakihi or the Apapane and, therefore, defended a territory in flowering ohia trees, visiting the flowers in a timed sequence.

Perkins emphasized the fairly loud noise produced by the wings of the Iiwi in flight, which is "very audible even when they are high up and at a distance." He also described the song and some of the callnotes:

The song of the Iiwi is harsh, strained and discordant, the finer the condition of its plumage the more cracked as a rule does its voice become. When the birds are paired and the male is singing to his mate he can often be approached very closely, and no less from the appearance of the bird itself than from the notes does this song appear to be forced out with difficulty. When however large numbers of these birds are found in neighbouring trees mixed with other species, especially the Apapane *(Himatione),* and a regular concert is kept up, the combined effect is not unpleasant. As an alarm or call note the Iiwi gives utterance either to a rather loud unmusical squeak or a clear and distinct whistle. Both call notes and song appear to exhibit some variation in different localities.

The terms "rusty" and "creaky" also apply to the song. Munro wrote that it reminded him of "the creaking of a wheelbarrow but a little more musical."

Despite the fact that the Iiwi was collected during Captain Cook's visits to Hawaii, and was described technically as early as 1780, little has been learned about the nesting behavior of the species. Rothschild (1893–1900:155) wrote:

Palmer says: "These birds place their nests on the thin branches out of reach from the stem, so that it is *impossible* (sic!) to take eggs from them. One would have to climb the tall Ohias and to cut the branches off and let them fall."

It is to be deeply regretted that none of the collectors showed enough pluck to procure the eggs of *Vestiaria,* for it is not very likely that any such efforts to explore the ornithological treasures of the Sandwich Islands as were made within the last decade will be made in the near future.

Rothschild, however, was not a field ornithologist, nor did he ever visit Hawaii. He undoutedly would have been more sympathetic with Palmer and the others had he had a discussion with Alvin Seale (1900), who wrote:

Owing to the bubonic plague quarantine these observations, since January 3, have been restricted to the immediate vicinity of Honolulu. The difficulty of collecting in these islands, with their dense tropical jungles and knife-like mountain ridges, has been mentioned by all former collectors, and I can only add, that while I have collected in difficult places before, including the boggy tundra of Siberia, the high mountains of Alaska, the Tamerack swamps of Michigan, and the Everglades of Florida, I have found nothing that could discourage an Ornithologist so much as one of these islands.

Perkins described the nest but not the eggs: "The nest of the Iiwi is larger than that of *Chlorodrepanis,* and not of a very compact or neat appearance. It is usually placed in tall Ohia trees, but occasionally in trees of lesser growth, such as the Mamane *(Sophora).* It is built of dry stems, leaves and rootlets, and the least inartistic specimens that I have seen are formed to a considerable extent of skeletonized capsules of the Poha."

During four months (November 12, 1899, to March 20, 1900) of collecting on Oahu, Seale was able to shoot only two Iiwi. On February 27, he saw an adult Iiwi enter a nest in an ohia at 1,300 feet elevation on Waiolani Mountain. He collected the adult female and the nest, which, however, was empty. "The nest was placed about 40 feet from the ground, and was well secured in the crotch of three small branches, at the end of a big limb standing straight up for 12 feet without any lower branches. The nest was completely hidden by leaves and the yellow ohia blooms; the exterior was composed of club moss and small twigs; the inside was of moss, fern pulu, and hair-like fibres from leaves; outside it was 5–7 in diameter; inside, 3.5–2; depth, 2."

Bryan (1905a) wrote that "as yet the eggs of this species are unknown to science." He made a similar statement (1908) after his field work on Molokai. Nothing is known about the nesting of this species on Maui.

In his study in Volcanoes National Park on Hawaii, Baldwin learned that "enlargement of the testes commences in October in old adult males. Behavior characteristic of the breeding condition accompanies enlargement of the testes. Younger members of the population may not achieve enlargement until February; hence throughout the winter the population is heterogeneous in testicular condition. Testicular regression occurs between the end of May and July." He found that the annual molt of the feathers occurs between June and November with most of the population molting in August, September, and October.

Baldwin's earliest record of a fledgling was February 3 (1942); he frequently saw immature birds from February to early June. His latest record for an immature bird in greenish plumage was July 29 (1949).

I watched an Iiwi giving a courtship display at an elevation of 4,000 feet along the Saddle Road, Hawaii, on January 29, 1968. While perched near the top of a dead ohia tree, a singing male slowly fluttered his wings below the level of his body and swayed first to one side and then the other. The bird then flew to a live ohia nearby and continued to sing and flutter his wings as he hopped from branch to branch. A second bird flew into the tree and chased the male for several seconds, after which the male flew to another dead ohia tree, singing in flight.

Baldwin (1944) apparently was the first observer to find an Iiwi nest with eggs (three), but he did not describe them. He also mentioned a nest holding two nestlings: "The young *iiwi* in the nest appeared green, except for their tan bills. Not long after leaving the nest the fledglings begin to produce red feathers which show in ever enlarging patches on their bellies and elsewhere. Later the juveniles develop a yellow, black-speckled head and neck before they finally achieve their brilliant, scarlet adult plumage."

C. Robert Eddinger studied the Iiwi at Kokee State Park, from 1968 through 1970. He found that courtship feeding occurs prior to and during the nest-building stage as well as throughout the incubation period. The female solicits feeding by crouching, fluttering her wings, and uttering a fledglinglike callnote. On one occasion courtship feeding preceded copulation.

The Iiwi defends a larger territory than does the Amakihi, Anianiau, or Apapane. One territory was a circle with a radius of 57 feet surrounding the nest tree. Although both the male and the female Iiwi take part in building the nest, Eddinger never observed a male visit a nest after the female began to incubate the full clutch of eggs. During nine hours of observation at one nest, the male fed the female twelve times. Each time the male gave a single, loud callnote, whereupon the female left the nest, flew to the male, crouched, fluttered her wings, and was fed.

Although intolerant of other Iiwi, nesting birds are tolerant of other species unless they approach the Iiwi's nest. One Iiwi nest was built only 16 feet from an active Apapane nest and 64 feet from an active Anianiau nest.

The average measured height above ground of 17 Iiwi nests was 21.9 feet; the range, 13.09–29.75 feet. All of the nests were built in ohia trees.

The dimensions of seven nests varied considerably. Outside diameter varied from 3.0 to 4.5 inches (average, 3.75 inches); depth from the nest rim to the bottom of the nest, from 2.5 to 3.5 inches (average, 2.93 inches). The inside diameter of the nest cup varied from 1.75 to 2.5 inches (average, 2.13 inches); depth of the nest cup, from 1.25 to 1.5 inches. From four to six days are required to build the nest. The bulk of the nest is completed in two or three days, but another two or three days are taken to line the nest. Iiwi nests on Kauai differed from nests of the Amakihi, Anianiau, and Apapane in that they were built largely of twigs (especially of ohia) and were lined primarily with lichens. Several species of mosses were found in the nests of each of the four species, but the principal moss used by the Iiwi was *Barbella trichophora,* whereas the most common moss in the nests of the other species was *Aerobryopsis longissima.* The bodies of the nests of both the Anianiau and the Apapane were composed largely of mosses.

The first egg of the first complete set of two eggs found by Eddinger was laid on February 27 (1970). The last egg of the last complete clutch was laid on April 18 (1970).

Iiwi eggs have a whitish background overlain with irregularly shaped, dark chocolate-brown markings scattered over much of the surface of the shell but concentrated around the large end of the egg. There is considerable variation in the pattern of the markings among the eggs laid by different females. Eddinger found several clutches of eggs that were largely white, with very few markings. Two other clutches, however, consisted of eggs in which nearly half of the shell was marked with chocolate-brown. (Color plate 33.)

Clutch size was three eggs in 2 nests; two eggs in 10 nests; and, apparently, only one egg in 2 nests. The average width and length of 10 Iiwi eggs was 15.5 × 20.7 mm. The egg with the greatest length and the narrowest width measured 15.0 × 21.7 mm; the widest egg, 15.8 × 20.8 mm; the shortest egg, 15.7 × 20.0 mm.

The Iiwi begins to incubate after the last egg in the clutch has been laid. Only the female incubates; she neither sings nor gives any callnotes while on the nest. If disturbed, the female flies to a nearby tree and gives alarm calls; usually she is joined by the male. Eddinger determined the incubation period at each of seven nests to be 14 days.

Newly hatched Iiwi nestlings have bright orange-pink skin. The gape is deep rose-pink but with a tinge of orange in the center of the roof of the mouth; the margins of the bill are bright yellow; both the legs and the bill are orange-pink to yellow-orange. The bill is short and straight, and gradually changes in color and shape. Near the end of the nestling period, the bill is obviously elongated, slightly decurved, and has changed to a light horn-color. The cloacal temperature of four one-day-old nestlings averaged 76° F. Cloacal temperatures had increased to 98° F when the birds were 11 days old.

Newly hatched Iiwi have well-developed down on the top of the head, above each eye, on the lower back, on each wing, and on each thigh. About 80 percent of the down is dirty white in color; the other 20 percent is dark gray and most abundant on the head.

On the day of hatching, the average weight of six Iiwi nestlings was 2.1 g. At 13 days of age, the average weight was 19.8 g. The following day, the average weight had dropped to 19.0 g. Eddinger could not weigh the nestlings after they were 14 days of age because they would then no longer remain in the nest when replaced. Some of the nestlings jumped from the nest when 12 days old, but these would crouch down in the nest when replaced (figs. 99, 100).

Both adults feed the nestlings and carry away their fecal sacs. The nestling period at six nests was 21 days for two nests and 22 days for four nests. At this age, the young birds fly with ease from tree to tree after leaving the nest.

Total success of 22 nests was only 53.3 percent. Seven nests were deserted during construction; 5 eggs disappeared from nests or were deserted; 2 nestlings died from exposure to rain, and 7 nestlings disappeared from the nests. Hence, of 30 eggs laid, 16 nestlings survived to leave the nest.

Feather mites of the family Analgidae and predaceous mites of the family Cheyletidae (genus *Cheyletus*) on a nestling Iiwi from Kokee State Park, Kauai, were identified by Frank Radovsky.

FIGURE 99. Two 3-day-old Iiwi that died in the nest; Kokee State Park, Kauai. April 15, 1970. Courtesy of C. Robert Eddinger.

FIGURE 100. Two 12-day-old Iiwi; Kauai. April 16, 1970. Courtesy of C. Robert Eddinger.

Mamo
Drepanis pacifica
(Color plate 44)

Naturalists accompanying Captain Cook first obtained specimens of this striking yellow and black bird with its very long, decurved, black bill, in which the upper mandible was a few millimeters longer than the lower. The nostrils were large but were almost completely concealed by an overhanging operculum. The head

and most of the body feathers were black; the wing and tail feathers were chiefly brownish black, with varying amounts of the outer webs of the primaries washed with ashy white and the outer tail feathers with indistinct whitish shaft-spots near the tip. The rump, upper and lower tail coverts, thighs, legs (tibia), anterior margins of the wings, and part of the under wing coverts were bright yellow. Bill, tarsi, and toes were black, but the soles of the toes were yellow. Total length varied from about 7.5 to 8 inches.

The Mamo was endemic only to the island of Hawaii in historic times. Wilson (Wilson and Evans 1890–1899) thought it was already extinct in the late 1880s, inasmuch as he did not find the species. He wrote: "To the late Mr. J. Mills of Hilo, Hawaii, science is indebted for the preservation not only of several specimens of *Drepanis pacifica,* but also of several more species now extinct. Mr. Mills died, I regret to say, some two months after I landed on the Islands. He was an ardent naturalist, and would shut up his store and disappear in the forest for weeks together, accompanied only by natives who aided him in collecting specimens. Mr. Mills was also an accomplished artist, some of his paintings possessing great merit." Apparently, Mr. Mills left no written record of his experiences. Wilson continued:

Of this extremely rare and apparently extinct species I obtained two specimens from a collection which was formed by the late Mr. Mills of Hilo in Hawaii, some thirty years or more ago. The fact of its native name "Mamo" being the same as that used for the war-cloaks mentioned below seems to imply that they received it from this bird, and that they were originally chiefly wrought of the beautiful golden yellow feathers from its back and vent, which are much deeper in colour, as they are larger and longer, than the axillary tufts of *Acrulocercus nobilis.*

I could obtain no certain information of examples having been observed since those in the Mills collection were procured—about 1859, though while staying at Olaa in the district of Puna in Hawaii, where Mr. Mills secured them, I was assured by the natives that the bird still existed, and at the time of my visit (October) had, together with the O-O, migrated to the mountains, which is barely possible. I saw several fine wreaths, "leis," composed of its plumes in the possession of the Hon. C. R. Bishop, while since my return I have carefully examined the feather-robes in the Ethnological Collection in the British Museum, and find that in the three large war-cloaks it contains, chiefly made of the yellow feathers of *Acrulocercus nobilis,* are interspersed here and there, usually in diamond-shaped patterns, the deeper yellow feathers of the present species.

Henry Palmer was the last to obtain a specimen of the Mamo. Palmer had been "severely kicked by a horse, and therefore, not being able to do long walks in the woods, sent the old bird-catcher Ahulan with several other natives, together with his 'assistant' [Wolstenholme] into the forests on the Mauna Loa above Hilo." The group left Hilo on April 12, 1892. They continued working their way up the slope, the Hawaiians cutting a trail through the dense forest. On April 15, Wolstenholme wrote that they "struck camp at 7 A.M. and marched along the trail, where we soon came across two Lolu-palms. I watched them close on an hour, but saw no signs of Ulaaiwahane. At 3 P.M. we struck the big gulch again and followed it till 5 P.M. There is here a beautiful waterfall, but I don't appreciate it much as I am very hungry. Not seeing a good camping place, we camped here in a very narrow and uncomfortable place."

It was on April 16 that the Mamo was said to have been caught (Rothschild 1893–1900:161; in his "Résumé of Palmer's Diary," he said it was April 18). Wolstenholme recorded the events of that day:

Broke the camp up at 6 A.M. and pushed on till 4 P.M. The old bird-catcher Ahulan was leading to cut the trail, whilst Holi and myself came next, followed by the others, who were a long way behind. We had not gone more than three miles, when I heard a call from the other side of the gulch, and thought it was a native calling, but immediately afterwards a bird flew across, and I saw in a moment it was the bird we were after. I was going to follow it up to shoot it, but Ahulan begged me not to shoot as it would scare the other away, which I had heard calling a little way off. Ahulan fixed the snares and bird-lime on a haha, which growed out on a tree-fern, and which has flowers somewhat like those of a fuchsia. Ahulan fulfilled his promise and caught the Mamo! He is a beauty, and takes sugar and water eagerly and roosts on a stick in the tent. I now feel as proud as if someone had sent me two bottles of whisky up.

Wolstenholme and his party worked in this area for two or three days, but, not having seen or heard any other Mamos, they returned to Hilo with their live bird, which Palmer killed and skinned on April 21. After he was able to travel again, Palmer visited the Mamo's habitat, but neither saw nor heard this species.

H. W. Henshaw wrote to Rothschild on October 9, 1899:

Drepanis pacifica is still a living species, though unquestionably very rare. No doubt it is on the verge of speedy extinction. About a year ago last July I found what, no doubt, was a family of Mamos in the woods above Kaumana. I am sure that I saw at least three individuals, possibly four or five. The locality was a thick tangle, and a momentary glimpse of a slim, trim body as it threaded its way through the leafy tree-tops was all I could obtain. After about two or three hours I succeeded in getting a shot at one bird in the very top of a tall Ohia-tree. It was desperately wounded, and clung for a time to the branch, head downwards, when I saw the

rich yellow rump most plainly. Finally, it fell six or eight feet, recovered itself, flew round to the other side of the tree, where it was joined by a second bird, perhaps a parent or its mate, and in a moment was lost to view. I need not speak of my disappointment, which was bitter enough, for I had looked upon that bird as absolutely mine own. Of the others I saw no more, though I have repeatedly visited the locality again.

Henshaw's observations of the Mamo in July 1898 are the last of record. Despite his intensive field work in Hawaii, Perkins apparently never saw this species.

Henshaw (in Thrum's Annual for 1902) wrote, "We know next to nothing of the habits of the mamo. The birds I saw in Kaumana were very active, and evidently were in pursuit of insects which they were hunting in the very tops of the tall ohias. The birds' flight from tree to tree was not rapid, but was smooth and well sustained, and the bird on the wing reminded me of nothing so much as the cuckoo. Though I observed the birds at intervals for more than two hours, I did not hear a single note."

Palmer considered the Mamo to be "very partial to the berries of the 'Haha' or Hawaiian mistletoe, a parasitic plant with long oval leaves and bell-shaped purple flowers," but, inasmuch as he never saw the Mamo in the field, he must have based this belief on dissection of the stomach of the one specimen he obtained, or on hearsay.

In his discussion of the Mamo, Perkins (1903:398–399) wrote:

Formerly it was without doubt of wide range over the island of Hawaii since it is known to have occurred both in the leeward and windward forests as well as in the Kohala Mountains. Unlike the Oo, which after the yellow axillary feathers were plucked out, could be, and sometimes was, liberated practically uninjured, the Mamo entirely denuded of its yellow feathers would have been in a sad plight, and would almost certainly have succumbed to such rough usage. It is quite certain that up to about 20 years ago these birds still existed in some numbers in the forests of Hilo district, for at the time of great lava-flow of 1880 a considerable number were shot for the sake of the yellow feathers, as many as twelve having been obtained by a native bird-hunter in a single day. None of these were preserved as entire skins, the yellow feathers alone being saved. . . .

Very little is known as to the habits of the Mamo, and the accounts that have been handed down, and the information one can glean from the few existing natives who have seen it, do not always agree. Some speak of it as very tame, others as wild and shy, but the latter account seems generally to refer to localities where, and to a time when, it was systematically hunted. All agree as to its fondness for the nectar of the arborescent lobelias, and it was at the blossoms of these that it was usually captured. Like the allied form on Molokai it seems to have cared little for the Ohia flowers when the lobelias were in bloom. Emerson says that it was also partial to the flowers of the native fan-palms *(Pritchardia)* when in blossom, and I have myself been informed that it habitually frequented these in company with the Ula-ai-hawane *(Ciridops).* . . . We are also told by the above-named writer that the bird devoured the ripe red fruit of the Ieie, but I suspect that this may be an error from confusion with the Oo, which is well known to be partial to that food in some localities.

The call of the Mamo is a single, rather long and plaintive note, as imitated by natives who have been familiar with it, and is so generally similar to that of its relative of Molokai, as to leave no doubt as to the correctness of these imitations. It would readily respond to this call, which was regularly used to attract it to the hunter's snare.

Henshaw also discussed the extinction of this large and colorful honeycreeper:

The explanation of the extinction of this fine bird is doubtless to be found in the persecution it suffered at the hands of the natives, both in ancient and in modern times. Its feathers were more highly prized than those of any other bird, and were dedicated solely to the service of the higher chiefs. It may be doubted if the mamo was ever very abundant, nor is it likely that many of the feather mantles, even in ancient times, were made solely of the yellow feathers of the mamo. The bird was probably never numerous enough to permit of this extravagance. Still there is indubitable proof that a few such cloaks existed, and it is entirely credible that their manufacture occupied several generations, and that they were of priceless value when once made. The word mamo had several meanings according to Andrew's Dictionary, and one of them signified a yellow war-cloak covered with the yellow feathers of the mamo. Alaneo was another name for a royal robe made of the feathers of the mamo only.

It is said that the birdcatchers in Kamehameha's time, and perhaps before, were strictly enjoined not to kill any of the royal birds, but to turn their captives loose when stripped of the coveted yellow feathers. Had this injunction been strictly obeyed, the golden harvest might have been reaped indefinitely without in any wise affecting the welfare of the bird. But the forests in which the bird-catcher plied his calling was distant and deep, and it is possible that the injunction was not strictly heeded; for meat of any kind was always scarce in Hawaii and in any form was highly prized. However, the mamo was ever a wary bird and difficult to secure, and we may feel tolerably sure that the ancient system of the natives of limeing the mamo would never have caused the bird's extinction, even if the tapu against its use for food was not strictly observed. After the introduction of fire-arms into the islands and they became at all general, bird lime rapidly gave way to the quicker and more deadly shot-gun and the birds quickly met their doom. In later historic times, at least, the mamo has always been very rare.

Henshaw believed the bird to be so rare by 1899 that there was little hope that "it will ever again be seen by human eyes."

Black Mamo
Drepanis funerea
(Color plate 47)

This jet black bird, with buffy to white on the outer webs of the outer primary flight feathers, had an even longer and more pronounced decurved bill than the Mamo. The bill, too, was black, but the nasal operculum and the base of the upper mandible were yellowish. The upper mandible, from its base to its tip, was 2 inches long; the lower mandible was about 0.3 inch shorter than the upper. The tarsi and toes also were black; the soles of the toes were yellow. W. A. Bryan (1908) gave total length measurements for males as great as 9.5 inches, but he did not state how the measurements were made. Two poorly preserved specimens (collected by Bryan) in the Bishop Museum measure 7.0 and 7.5 inches, respectively. The plumage of the females was like that of the males, but the females were smaller and had shorter bills.

The Black Mamo or Perkins' Mamo was discovered on Molokai by Perkins on June 18, 1893, at an elevation of about 5,000 feet. Hawaiian names were Oo-nuku-umu and Hoa. Only Perkins (1903:401–402) gave us information on the behavior of the Black Mamo, pointing out that it took the place of the Mamo on Hawaii.

From what we know of the habits of the latter the two forms closely resemble each other in these, as well as in their cries. The Oo-nuku-umu is one of the rarer island birds and is now confined to the higher parts of the forest on Molokai, where the ground is soft and boggy. At the time when I discovered it these woods were in an absolutely natural condition, but since that time both cattle and deer have run through them and they are in most parts much less dense and less wet than they were in 1893. The bird is essentially one of the underbrush, and I never saw it alight high up in a large tree, and only very rarely was it seen at more than twelve feet from the ground. It is a true honey-sucker, and not one of those obtained by me contained animal food. In my earlier notes I supposed it to be insectivorous from the fact that I saw it exploring beneath the wet moss, which covered the tree trunks, with beak and tongue. However a specimen subsequently obtained after it had been watched at this pursuit for some minutes proved on dissection to contain no trace of insect food, and that the adult or the young after they have left the nest are insectivorous is not yet proved. As the moss coating the trees was invariably soaked with water it may be that this only was the object of its search, the more so as insects in this situation were always very scarce. No doubt nestlings will be found to be fed on caterpillars, as is customary with the other honey-sucking Drepanids, but the youngest specimens seen, which were probably about a month from the nest, entirely confined their attention to the nectar of flowers. When investigating the wet moss the tongue is darted in and out with great rapidity so as to appear like a liquid streak, the eye not being able to distinguish each separate movement. On one occasion only was the bird seen to visit the red flowers of the Ohia; the crimson Apapane *(Himatione)*, the Akohekohe *(Palmeria)*, and the Oo *(Acrulocercus)* being present with it in the same small bushy tree. With that pugnacity which is said to be equally characteristic of the Mamo, it continually drove the smaller red birds from the bush, to be itself in turn driven off by the superior strength of the Oo, but always returning after a few moments to the same flowers. Excepting the above instances, the Oo-nuku-umu entirely confined its attention to the large tubular flowers of certain arborescent lobelias. On one occasion, when engaged in entomological work, I saw three adult males of this bird in one low bush passing from flower to flower and spending only a few seconds over each. These were very tame, and I was able to watch their movements in this and neighbouring bushes for at least an hour. Even those flowers which were at a height of not more than a foot from the ground were carefully explored. The crown of the head of each of these birds was plentifully encrusted, as indeed is usually the case, with the sticky white or purplish-white pollen of the lobelias and gave them a singular appearance. Of all that I ever saw the first two specimens alone were really timid, but at the time I was proceeding carelessly and with much noise, cutting a path as I advanced. More usually they readily approach and even follow the collector, or alight on a branch at a distance of only a yard or two, moving occasionally from place to place and turning the head this way and that to make a thorough scrutiny. For this reason they are sometimes even difficult to shoot, as they keep following the collector as he retires to a suitable distance for a shot, and when they fly off at last it is for good and all. Sometimes when they have satisfied their curiosity they will sit quietly preening their feathers, when they have a very comical appearance, much stretching of the neck being necessary to enable them to reach the fore parts of the body with the tip of their long beaks; at other times they will proceed to feed quietly on the flowers of a neighbouring bush. They readily respond to an imitation of their call note, which much resembles that of the Mamo, but sometimes they utter a loud cry of extraordinary clearness, repeated at short intervals, such as I have never heard imitated by the old natives, who well knew the call of the latter. No doubt this loud cry takes the place of a true song and differs rather in degree than kind from the more gentle call note. The Oo-nuku-umu would appear to be the rarest of all the birds of which I obtained specimens. On one occasion when not prepared to collect birds I saw seven individuals in a single day, but this was quite exceptional, and when wanting a specimen I have spent a whole day or several days in its haunts, and in exclusive search for it, without seeing even a single one, and this at a time when I had become perfectly familiar with its habits.

Bryan (1908) collected three male specimens during June 1907. Museum specimens of birds are rightly needed for serious studies, but the zeal and philosophy of some collectors leave much to be desired. After shooting his first Black Mamo, Bryan exclaimed: "To my joy I found the mangled remains hanging in the tree in a thick bunch of leaves, six feet or more beyond where it had been sitting. It was, as I feared, badly mutilated. However, it was made into a very fair cabinet skin."

Munro (1944:93) wrote that "private collectors later depleted the district above Pelekunu valley where Perkins had collected. Neither Alanson Bryan nor I could find any there in 1907, but Bryan secured 3 male specimens at Moanui farther round the island to the east." Amadon (1950) said that the "Meyers family, Perkins' hosts on Molokai, collected a few others," and that the Black Mamo had not been seen since 1907. Munro found no evidence of this species during his survey in 1936.

Crested Honeycreeper
Palmeria dolei
(Color plate 45)

This strikingly plumaged honeycreeper once inhabited both Molokai and Maui. The species is extinct on Molokai (Richardson 1949), and very little is known about the birds on Maui.

The black feathers of the Crested Honeycreeper are tipped with gray on the throat and breast, with white on the ends of the wing and tail, and with orange on the rest of the body. The orange tips are large enough on the nape and the sides of the neck to form an orange collar. The feathers of the forehead are elongated and project forward to form a white, gray, or golden crest. The sexes are alike, and are 6.5 to 7 inches in length. Immature birds are dull brownish black, washed with buff or brownish pink.

Scott Wilson collected an immature bird of this species in the "district of Kula in Maui" during July 1888. Rothschild later described the adult, but placed it in the family Meliphagidae.

Perkins (1903:405-406) found the Crested Honeycreeper "locally abundant" on both Molokai and Maui, and he provided most of what is known about this species in the field:

In its habits it very closely resembles the Apapane, which is often to be found in company with it. Why the range of the larger bird should be now so restricted on the islands on which it is found, as compared with that of *Himatione*, is not manifest, but we know that on both the islands named it had formerly a far wider range than is now the case, and it is possibly more susceptible to those changes that have in recent years taken place in the forests than is the other. Woods opened by the invasion of cattle it sooner or later, as I have myself noticed, deserts, retiring to deep gulches where they cannot penetrate, and from these depths it can be called, while in the surrounding and more open forests not one can be seen or heard.

Its diet of nectar appears to be obtained almost entirely if not solely from the flowers of the Ohia, and the whitish frontal crest is sometimes filled with the entangled pollen grains from these blossoms. It is also partial to caterpillars, and not only obtains those which feed upon the foliage but also searches the dead branches of trees in dense wet woods for those which feed on this substance. When feeding on the Ohia blossoms it is aggressive to other birds, especially to the Apapane, which it drives off, but is itself similarly treated by the Oo (*Acrulocercus*).

Its call note is a simple clear whistle, very easily imitated, and by this means the bird can always be easily called in numbers in a good locality. It is uttered most often naturally on the approach of the mountain fogs, which are so frequent in the favourite localities of these birds, when they call freely to one another across the gulches. The adults, though easily called and curious, are less tame than the young, as is shown by their restless movements when they are attracted, but in dense, untrodden forests they will not infrequently approach the collector from mere curiosity, without any imitation of the call note being necessary. On one occasion I assembled no less than nine adult birds at the same time in one small Ohia tree not more than twenty feet high, and a pair of adults and several young were quite an ordinary gathering. Even when fired at and obviously touched by the shot I have been able to call this bird back into range and secure it at the second attempt.

The young follow the parents often until they have arrived at almost their full plumage, and after they have acquired their full song, but in the winter months these companies are mostly disbanded. In February and March they are generally paired and ready to nest, and are then clothed in their finest plumage. *Palmeria* has the characteristic odour of the family in a varying degree, it being as I have elsewhere noticed much more pronounced in some specimens than in others. Its song is quite distinct from that of any other bird, and when fully rendered consists of a most curious low vibrating sound, then ends with two or three sounds rapidly uttered, and sometimes omitted, which might be expressed as follows: hurr hurr—gluk gluk gluk. There is, however, no difficulty in tracing some resemblance between this song and some of the varying sounds produced by others of its allies, such as the Apapane and Iiwi. Though less lavish of its song than either of the last-named birds, yet it may often be heard, and when about to sing it will often perch on the topmost branch of a dead tree or an isolated dead branch of a living one. Its song like that of the Iiwi appears to be forced out with difficulty and lacks all beauty. It has too other cries, especially a soft note not greatly differing from that of *Drepanis*.

George Munro spent a month on Molokai in 1907 but did not see the Crested Honeycreeper; he later wrote that he never saw this species in life. William Alanson Bryan collected on Molokai for two months in 1907, shortly after Munro's trip. Bryan saw five individuals on one day and three more on another, but he was "unfortunate in not securing this species." According to Munro (1944), the Crested Honeycreeper had not been seen on Molokai since 1907.

Henshaw (in Thrum's Annual for 1902) wrote of the Crested Honeycreeper on Maui, but he gave no information—dates or places—other than to say that "it is not found much if any below an altitude of 5,000 feet." Henshaw often summarized from other authors, particularly Perkins, so that it is difficult to know which observations are his own. He did write, however, that "*Palmeria* has a call note which is as characteristic as any sound heard in the Hawaiian woods. It is a loud, clear and rather shrill whistle, somewhat like a flycatcher's call (great crested flycatcher), but perhaps best described by comparison with the well known call of Bob White. The note is easily imitated, and the birds can invariably be induced to answer, and usually can be called up close to the observer. But for this fact *Palmeria* would be indeed difficult to discover, since it is neither numerous nor generally distributed but, on the contrary, is very local, the birds seeming to dwell in small, isolated communities."

The haunts of the Crested Honeycreeper apparently were not visited again by people interested in birds until January 1942, when Gordon A. Macdonald and Harold T. Stearns saw a bird, "probably of this species, near the north rim of Kipahulu Valley, 6300 feet, Haleakala Volcano, Maui" (Richards and Baldwin 1953). Baldwin visited this area ("between Wai Anapanapa and the divide separating Kipahulu and Waihoi valleys") in November 1943 and found the Crested Honeycreeper there, as well as at an elevation of 5,800 feet one mile northwest of Puu Alaea on the north slope of Haleakala. Richards saw several birds between December 2 and 5, 1950, in an area "about five acres in extent" at elevations between 6,300 and 6,700 feet. He collected three specimens which are now in the Museum of Vertebrate Zoology at Berkeley.

The Maui Crested Honeycreeper was not reported again for 15 years. Kridler (1966) told of seeing two birds near Puu Alaea on November 16, 1965.

I saw one bird at Lake Wai Anapanapa on January 17, 1967, and several were seen during the Kipahulu Valley expedition during August 1967. These birds were seen above 6,000 feet elevation. We now know that the Crested Honeycreeper is relatively common in a restricted habitat, extending from Manawainui and Kipahulu valleys northwestward to the forests west of the Koolau Gap, at elevations between 4,200 and 7,100 feet. The nest, eggs, and nestlings have not been described.

Apapane
Himatione sanguinea sanguinea
(Color plates 46, 49)

The very attractive Apapane is the most common of the surviving species of honeycreepers. The sexes are alike in plumage, but the female averages slightly smaller in size. The wings and tail are black. Except for white feathers on the lower abdomen and under tail coverts, the body plumage is a deep crimson color. The long, slender, and slightly decurved bill is primarily bluish black, although the basal portion of the lower mandible may be straw colored. The legs are blackish. The birds average 5.25 inches in length. Immature birds are gray-brown above and buff below. All kinds of intermediate stages are seen as the immature birds begin to acquire their adult plumage. Albinistic Apapane have been seen at Volcanoes National Park.

The Apapane has not undergone any important geographical variation, and one race inhabits all six of the main islands. The Apapane is the most conspicuous of the native birds in the wet ohia forests, as well as in the koa forests and the mixed koa and ohia groves, such as along the Mauna Loa Strip Road in Volcanoes National Park and on the eastern slope of Mauna Kea. It also is common at Kokee State Park on Kauai and at Hosmer's Grove on the slopes of Haleakala Crater, Maui. Only rarely have I seen birds in the mamani-naio forest on Mauna Kea, where they are birds of passage only.

Perkins (1903:407) wrote that in Captain Cook's time, the Apapane "even visited the coast in so apparently inhospitable a locality as Kealakekua Bay, frequenting the flowers of the coco-nut palms with other forest birds." Seale, writing in 1900, said that although "the Apapane is by no means abundant it is still not uncommon in the mountains of Oahu. They are found in the ohia forests at an elevation of 1000 feet." They now usually are found above 1,500 feet. Gary Long found a dead Apapane on the snow at an elevation of about 11,000 feet on Mauna Kea during April 1976.

The Apapane is typically a bird of the crown of the forest, whether the trees are 25 or 100 feet high. The birds are gregarious during most of the year, and are conspicuous both because of their numbers and because of their calls chorused as they fly from one tree to another to feed on ohia blossoms. Their wings produce a distinctive whirring noise in flight that is audible for some distance. This phenomenon also is found in the Iiwi and the Crested Honeycreeper, and, according to Perkins, also was characteristic of the now-extinct members of the subfamily Drepanidinae.

The Apapane also makes longer and higher flights than other species. I have seen single birds and small groups of four or five flying over barren lava flows at elevations of 7,000 feet and higher on the north flank of Mauna Loa. Similarly, Baldwin saw individuals and small groups of birds in lateral flight across lava flows a mile or more in width at elevations between 7,000 and 7,500 feet in Volcanoes National Park.

Within an ohia forest itself, the birds often take off from a tall tree and fly several hundred feet above the forest canopy until lost from sight. From Puu Hulu-hulu (an old, forested, cinder-cone kipuka surrounded by lava flows of 1843 and 1935) on the Saddle Road of Hawaii, the Apapane fly at considerable heights over the barren and near-barren lava flows to some distant kipuka or forest. Nevertheless, I feel that literature that speaks of birds being blown from island to island during storms and of being lost in the fog and flying to another island engages in speculation and exaggeration.

In his study at Volcanoes National Park, Baldwin (1953) noted that seasonal movements of the Apapane were more conspicuous than those of the Amakihi. These seasonal shifts in population, however, were not uniform in his various census plots, located at elevations from 2,300 to 7,500 feet, although he did find a summer reduction "at most of the plots, probably representing dispersal." He found an increase in population at a plot located at 4,050 feet, which probably indicated "an upward movement from the lowlands in summer in correlation with the advance of flowering periods of *Metrosideros*."

At an elevation of about 4,300 feet on the Keauhou Ranch on July 20, 1972, Richard E. MacMillen, Ernest Christopher, and I watched a striking movement of Apapane and Iiwi. Beginning at 4:00 P.M., loose flocks of birds (primarily Apapane but with occasional Iiwi) were noted flying upslope from Volcanoes National Park toward the direction of the Kulani Cone. Many of the flocks contained 20 or more birds, and 300 birds were counted during the first 20 minutes of observation; we estimated that more than 600 birds flew up the slope of the mountain during one hour. Some birds flew at treetop level but others, 100 or more feet above the crown of the forest. The nesting season was over so we assumed that the birds were flying to a nocturnal roost. Not all of the Apapane leave their daytime feeding areas, however, because a small number of Apapane were seen and heard each evening in the residential area of the park. I heard the last Apapane callnote at 6:45 P.M. on July 17 and at 7:08 P.M. the following night; these birds certainly roosted in the immediate vicinity.

Carpenter and MacMillen (1979) later studied these summer roosting flights and estimated that 41,700 birds were involved during July 1974 and only 5,700 birds during August 1974. The birds went to roost earlier during the summer of 1975 than in 1974. These authors found that nectar in the ohia trees was abundant during the summer of 1975 but less available in 1974, especially during August of that year. They added that they would expect the Apapane to be relatively sedentary when nesting and when flowering of the ohia was patchy and poor throughout the forest. Under the latter condition, the birds would have to eat more insects. By contrast, "when flowering is good, then an individual could wander larger distances with less risk of failure to locate nectar." Carpenter and MacMillen also suggested that the birds were roosting in the dense ohia-koa rain forest at elevations above the usual fog belt, which "would provide the warmest and driest site nocturnally in the forested southeastern slopes of Mauna Loa."

Although usually seen feeding in ohia trees, the Apapane also gets nectar from the mamani and from introduced garden plants *(Fuchsia magallanica, Hebe salicifolia)*. Early writers said that they also fed from the flowers of the coconut palm. They undoubtedly feed from other flowers on occasion. Captive birds eat lettuce as well as fruits.

Baldwin made a thorough study of the stomach contents of 63 specimens he collected. The following insects, mites, and spiders were identified (the number in parentheses is the percentage of stomachs in which that group was found): Lepidoptera (87), Homoptera (75), Neuroptera (60; primarily larvae), Araneida (43), Hymenoptera (43), Corrodentia (41), Diptera (21), Coleoptera (17), Thysanoptera (14), Heteroptera (10), Acarina (3). Scale insects (Homoptera) are not native to Hawaii, but these insects were found in 11 percent of the stomachs examined. Spiders are an important source of food (43 percent occurrence) for the Apapane. Baldwin reported that spiders are common on the leaves and branches where the birds forage, and that they are available throughout the year. Moths (Lepidoptera) were eaten to a limited extent, but the remains of their caterpillars were found in 87 percent of the stomachs.

The Apapane is a persistent singer throughout the day during the extended breeding season, and it also sings less persistently at other times of the year.

Ward (1964) taped and analyzed Apapane songs in different localities on several islands. He described one song as "a rolling call, followed by 3 whistles, 5 chucks, a drawn-out note, and a faint squawk at the end"; this particular recording proved the song "to have greater variation in sound structure than our other Apapane recordings, and to rank with other very complicated bird songs."

Ward found so many different songs that he wrote: "we decided that the musicianship of the Apapane appears to be unsurpassed. In this article, spectrograms of six calls and ten songs, made at eight locations on three islands, illustrate these variations. There probably are so many others unrecorded that we wonder if the songs of the Apapane might possibly compete with the 'twenty basic themes in forty-seven songs' of the European Mistle Thrush *(Turdus viscivorus)*."

The Apapane also has a flight song that it gives either in straight flight or while circling the nesting tree. Sometimes a bird sweeps upward from a perch, sings in a hesitating flight, and then flies downward to a perch, giving callnotes on its way. The birds also have a *chip-churr* note, which reminds me of the similar note of the Scarlet Tanager *(Piranga olivacea)*. I have heard this note given alone and also as the first part of a four-syllabled song.

Surprisingly little has been published on the nesting of the Apapane. Neither Wilson nor Palmer found a nest with eggs. Perkins (1903:407–408) said that the Apapane nests "chiefly from March to June but sometimes as early as January, and those nests which I have seen the birds in the act of building (and they have been many) have always been placed in the thin topmost branches of tall ohia trees and quite inaccessible without special climbing appliances." Palmer did watch a pair building a nest on November 23: "It was at a great height, almost at the top of a tree, in a fork, well concealed from below, and built of moss." C. Robert Eddinger and I, however, have found about 70 Apapane nests in much smaller ohia trees, although many of the nests were still inaccessible (fig. 101). In the Kilauea Forest Reserve on the slopes of Mauna Loa on June 24, 1971, I found four Apapane nests that had been built on the top surface of drooping treefern fronds, which placed the nests between 12 and 15 feet above the ground. I have seen similar nests at Thurston lava tube and in kipukas along the Saddle Road. Van Riper (1973b) told of Apapane that built their nests in lava caves on Mauna Loa.

A great deal of intensive field work will be needed before we will have a very good understanding of the breeding season of the Apapane on the several islands and of differences that may occur from island to island. I do not know of a single record of the nest of an Apapane on Maui.

Baldwin made a detailed study of the Apapane, Amakihi, and Iiwi at Volcanoes National Park during the 1940s. His earliest record of a fledgling Apapane was February 3 (1942). He saw other recently fledged birds during February and "on through the spring and summer." The latest juvenile bird he saw that still did

FIGURE 101. Apapane nest with two eggs; Kokee, Kauai. April 26, 1968.

not show any traces of red feathers was August 16 (1941).

At elevations above 3,000 feet on the Saddle Road on Hawaii, the Apapane is the most conspicuous bird because of its singing during November and December. The earliest nest I have found there was under construction, about 14 feet from the ground in a slender ohia tree, on December 9; this nest had three eggs on December 24 (1966). Another nest contained a single broken egg on December 19 (1967). On December 21 (1965) I watched a fledgling follow an adult and beg continuously for food.

At Volcanoes National Park on January 22, 1966, I watched a singing male Apapane fly to a bare branch of an ohia tree. The bird's mate flew to the same branch, and the male immediately mounted her twice; then both birds flew off. On February 21, 1966, I observed a male's courtship behavior. While singing, the male hopped from branch to branch with his tail held upward at nearly a 90-degree angle to his body, thus displaying the white belly and under tail coverts.

Seale (1900) found five nests of the Apapane on Oahu, "but as yet no eggs." W. A. Bryan (1905a) reported on a field trip in the Waianae Mountains on Oahu from January 21 to March 9, 1901 (except for the period of February 3 to 19, "during which time terrific rain storms forced us to suspend our work and leave the mountains") and described the egg of the Apapane from "fragments of an egg shell" in a nest collected by Seale on March 27, 1900. From these fragments more than a year old, Bryan proceeded to give

the approximate size of the egg! Needless to say, his estimates were not very close to the actual measurements of the Apapane's egg, although they have been quoted in literature.

The first description of the eggs of the Apapane is that of Munro (1944:97): "Eggs, three in a clutch .69 × .5 inch, white with streaky reddish brownish spots thicker in a band round the large end." He found several nests on Lanai during 1913 and 1914. He said that the nests there were generally built in scrubby ohia trees 7 to 10 feet above the ground. He found several nests with three eggs or three nestlings, but he did not describe the nestlings.

Apapane eggs are white with irregularly shaped spots and speckles concentrated around the larger end of the egg and widely scattered very small spots on the rest of the egg. The markings on different eggs may be smoke gray, buffy brown, or reddish brown. Sixteen eggs measured by Eddinger averaged 18.4 × 24.1 mm; extremes were 18.0 × 22.6 mm and 18.7 × 25.8 mm.

Eddinger (1970b) began a study of the Apapane on Kauai in 1968. He found that the nesting season extended from February through June, with the first complete clutch of eggs being laid in late February (1970) and the last being completed on June 5 (1970). Pair formation and courtship involved singing by the male and aggression toward other males. When a male intruded, the male of a mated pair sang loudly and then flew at the intruder. The two males flew at each other with feet extended and fell downward together until they were within two or three feet of the ground, whereupon the intruder flew away. Sexual chasing is common until the start of nest construction. Eddinger first observed copulation, following sexual chasing, on February 14 (1969). The female lit on a branch about four feet from the ground, crouched, and was mounted by the male. Both birds then flew off without singing or any other type of postcoital display. On another occasion, the male sang both before and after copulation. Courtship feeding appears to be important in maintaining the pair bond. Eddinger observed courtship feeding before the nest was started, during nest construction, and throughout incubation.

All nests found on Kauai were built in ohia trees. Most of the nests were placed in the terminal crowns of the trees, and 25 were completely inaccessible. The average measured height above ground of 38 nests was 27.57 feet; the lowest was 17.5 feet from the ground; the highest, 36.5 feet from the ground. Several inaccessible nests were estimated to be more than 40 feet from the ground.

Nest dimensions varied considerably. The outside diameter varied from 2.75 to 4.75 inches; depth from the top rim to the bottom of the nest, from 2.5 to 5.25 inches. The inside diameter of the nest cup varied from 1.5 to 2.75 inches; depth of nest cup, from 1.0 to 1.75 inches.

Clutch size was four eggs in 3 nests; three eggs in 24 nests; two eggs in 10 nests; and, apparently, only one egg in 1 nest. Most of the eggs were laid before 8:00 A.M., but the last egg in two nests was not laid until 10:00 A.M. to noon. Only the female incubates, and Eddinger never observed a male at the nest from the time the nest was completed until the eggs hatched. Only rarely does the male fly into the nest tree. He establishes definite singing perches in adjacent trees, and other males are chased when they enter the territory. Other species of birds are permitted to enter the territory, but they are chased from the nest tree itself.

The female neither sings nor calls from the nest during the incubation period. If disturbed, she flies off without giving any alarm call, although she may give alarm notes from a neighboring tree. Courtship feeding is common during the incubation period, but the female leaves the nest and flies to the male, where she crouches and depresses and quivers her wings. The male's behavior changes markedly when the female is off the nest. He then gives a soft two-syllabled call, *twe-ha, twe-ha.* As soon as the female returns to the nest, he resumes his regular loud song. Eddinger determined the incubation period at each of eight nests to be 13 days.

When they hatch, nestling Apapane have flesh-colored to pink skin, with a small amount of gray down on the head, back, and wings. The eyes are closed. The mouth lining is bright pink, and the margins of the bill are cream-colored. Both adults feed the nestlings and remove their fecal sacs. The eyes open four days after hatching. Feather tracts first appear on the wings and back on the sixth day (fig. 102). By the eighth day, the feathers begin to unsheathe, and they are unsheathed when the nestlings are 14 days old (fig. 103).

It is perhaps impossible for those who have not studied the forest birds of Hawaii to appreciate the many difficulties involved. Eddinger observed an Apapane nest with young seven days old from 9:00 A.M. to noon on March 18, 1970. The minimum temperature that morning was 36° F. It rained continuously until 11:00 A.M., after which time there was an almost constant drizzle. The wind was strong and it was cold. He wrote in his field notes: "I am beginning to see why there are so few field ornithologists. You may not have to be crazy to spend three hours lying in the mud during a cold rain—but I'm sure that it helps." The female brooded the nestlings from 9:00 until 11:04 A.M., returned in two minutes and fed the nestlings,

FIGURE 102. Apapane nest with three nestlings about six days old; Kokee, Kauai. May 19, 1968.

FIGURE 103. Three Kauai Apapane that were brought to Honolulu to be raised in captivity. May 30, 1968. These are the birds shown in Figure 102.

and then left immediately and did not return to feed them again until 11:47. The male had fed the nestlings at 10:00 and 11:04 A.M. Therefore, during that three-hour observation period, the male fed the nestlings twice and the female fed them twice. From 11:04 A.M. until noon, the nestlings, and Eddinger, were exposed to a drizzling rain. At 2:00 P.M., the air temperature was 66° F. One nestling weighed 10.5 g and had a cloacal temperature of 97° F; the other nestling weighed 14.0 g and had a cloacal temperature of 98° F.

The nestlings weigh approximately 3.0 g at hatching; they weighed between 13 and 15 g on the tenth day. Eddinger found, however, that he could not weigh the nestlings after they were 11 days old because they would then not remain in the nest even though they were unable to fly. After they were 13 days old, they would jump out of the nest if the tree shook while Eddinger was climbing it, and sometimes even if he climbed a neighboring tree. When the young are undisturbed, the average nestling period is 16 days: 15 days for 2 nests, 16 days for 14 nests, and 17 days for 3 nests. At those ages, the young are able to fly well from tree to tree after leaving the nest.

Deserted nests often are dismantled by Apapane. The deserted nest may be of another Apapane or of another species of honeycreeper, and it may be a nest of the current season or of an earlier one. A deserted nest may be completely carried away within one week.

Many Apapane nests are unsuccessful. Either eggs or young may disappear from the nests, and some young die in the nests. A nest I found near the Saddle Road, Hawaii, on April 6, 1968, contained three nestlings about 9 days old and one egg. At 1:45 P.M. the following day, one of the nestlings was dead; a second died before the end of the day.

An Apapane caught in a mist net at an elevation of 6,500 feet near the Saddle Road on Hawaii on January 13, 1968, was released two days later in a large aviary at Paradise Park in Manoa Valley, Oahu. This male bird died of cranial trauma on January 19. Dr. Allen Y. Miyahara performed a thorough postmortem examination of this bird. He found no internal parasites but did find two pairs of adult feather mites and a single cutaneous mite larva. These were identified by Dr. Frank Haramoto as being feather mites of the genera *Megninia* and *Proctophyllodes;* the cutaneous mite larva belonged to the genus *Harpyrhyncus.*

Navvab Gojrati (1970) examined the blood of 27 Apapane from Kauai and Hawaii and found one bird at Volcanoes National Park infected with bird malaria (*Plasmodium relictum* or *P. cathemerium*). He also found three of nine White-eyes from the same area infected with *Plasmodium circumflexum.*

Laysan Apapane
Himatione sanguinea freethii
(Color plate 32)

This race of the Apapane was first collected by Henry Palmer during June 1891; Rothschild described it in

1892, naming it for Mr. Freeth, the manager of the guano company on Laysan during the visit of Palmer and Munro. Palmer (in Rothschild 1893–1900:x) recorded the following in his diary for June 17, 1891: "A most touching thing occurred: I caught a little red Honeyeater in the net, and when I took it out the little thing began to sing in my hand. I answered it with a whistle, which it returned and continued to do so for some minutes, not being in the least frightened."

Rothschild (1892:110) has described the Laysan Honeycreeper as somewhat resembling the Apapane of the main islands "but differs from that species in being more vermilion and not blood-red in tinge of colour, and in having the lower abdomen and under tail-coverts pale ashy brown or brownish white, and not white; besides, the bill is shorter and rather stouter in the present species." He gave the length as about 6 inches, but in his later work he changed this to about 5.5 inches. W. K. Fisher (1906) said that the bird pictured in Rothschild's book is "far too pale and gives an erroneous idea of the color of the bird." Palmer reported that the Laysan Honeycreeper was "by far the rarest of the Laysan-Island birds, though I have observed a fair number, generally in pairs." Fisher found "it by no means rare, however, for in a short walk we were always able to see plenty of them. Their bright scarlet plumage renders them especially conspicuous as they flit about amid the soft green of the chenopodium bushes, and very attractive creatures they are on such a curious island as Laysan."

Fisher found the Laysan Apapane most abundant in the interior of the island among the tall grass and low bushes bordering the lagoon. "Its favorite nesting-place is this same area, and the proximity of broad patches, acres in fact, of a prostrate succulent portulaca with yellow and a sesuvium with pink flowers has many attractions for the honey-eaters. Here they may be found throughout the day *walking* around after small insects or drinking honey from the blossoms."

Fisher also watched them eat "tiny, green, and hence protectively colored, caterpillars from *Chenopodium sandwicheum,*" as well as "a small brownish-gray moth or 'miller,' which abounds on the island to the point of distraction."

Fisher found only one nest (fig. 104). It was built about two feet from the ground in a grass tussock, and contained but a single egg. The nest was loosely made of fine grass and rootlets, lined with fine rootlets and brown down from the young albatrosses. Fisher remarked that "there are no white feathers in the lining, thus making the structure at once distinguishable from the nest of the miller-bird." Captain Schlemmer gave Fisher a honeycreeper nest that contained four eggs.

FIGURE 104. Nest and egg of the Laysan Honeycreeper; Laysan Island. May 1902. Photograph by Walter K. Fisher, courtesy of Alfred M. Bailey.

Fisher described the egg as "pure lusterless white, blotched and spotted at the large end with grayish vinaceous, and with fewer light and dark spots of Prout's brown." He gave typical egg measurements as 13.75 × 18.0 mm.

Homer Dill (Dill and Bryan 1912) worked on Laysan from April 24 to June 5, 1911. He had little to say about the Laysan Apapane but did mention that "we found a few nests, all of which contained young birds or well-incubated eggs." He estimated that there are "possibly 300 living birds of this species." He added: "There were four birds of this species that roosted on an old rope which hung across the corner in one of the sheds. Here each night we would see them huddled closely together. An occasional bird would flit into our workroom in quest of millers. . . . Among the old specimens left by the feather hunters we found several skins of the honeyeater."

Bryan had visited Laysan during 1903, and he returned for the period April 24 to 30, 1911. He wrote (Dill and Bryan 1912): "The Laysan canary, Miller bird, Laysan honey eater, and the Laysan rail, without doubt, are doomed to extermination on the isolated island on which they have maintained themselves long enough to develop into distinct species, unless something is done to preserve for them the source of their food supply." He added: "Rabbits now literally swarm over the island by thousands. The amount of damage done by them can better be imagined than told. They are exterminating first one species of plant then another. Several species that were common everywhere eight years ago have entirely gone, others are already doomed. Unless some drastic measures are resorted to within a very short time not a bush or spear of grass will be alive."

George Willett, William S. Wallace, and Alfred M. Bailey worked on Laysan Island from December 22, 1912, until March 11, 1913. Unfortunately, they were not equipped to exterminate the rabbits. Bailey (1956) does not mention finding any nests of the Laysan Apapane, but he gave the clutch as four to five eggs. Bailey does, however, include photographs taken by Walter Fisher in May 1902: one shows an adult bird perched on the rim of the nest, and a second shows the same nest with one egg.

When Willett and I arrived on Laysan December 22, 1912, and climbed the sandy shore to the little bungalow, which was to be our headquarters, the first of the native land birds to greet us was one of these brightly colored birds perched on a dead twig of the hau tree which was sheltered on the southern side of the building. It sang as though to welcome us, and possibly this first introduction was the reason the Honey-eater was our favorite bird of the atoll. They were less common than the Millerbirds and the Laysan Finches, but they were tame and we had a few constantly about the building—confiding birds, bouncing in and out of windows and doorways, searching for small insects and millers. Because of the rapidly disappearing vegetation, the birds we noted about the island were few, and were confined to patches of wild tobacco, and the few remaining clumps of *Scaevola* and bunch grass.

The tragic history of the little Honey-eater closed in 1923, when rabbits had wiped out the vegetation, and the food supply of the land birds. The last naturalists to see these birds alive were the members of the Tanager Expedition, and the late Donald Dickey was probably the last to take photographs when he secured his dramatic motion picture of a male in full song on a coral rock twig—one of three survivors of the race which was doomed to extinction in swirling dust a few days later.

And so, Wetmore (1925) wrote, "Three individuals alone of the little Honey Eater remained on our arrival; these perished during a three-day gale that enveloped everything in a cloud of swirling sand. The Millerbird had disappeared entirely, and of the Laysan Rail but two remained." (Fig. 105.)

Bryan compared conditions on Laysan Island in 1903 with those in 1911, and he made a number of recommendations "for future protection of the Reservation." In addition to emphasizing that "drastic measures" would have to be taken to eliminate the rabbits as soon as possible, he proposed that "a resident warden should then be provided who should be supplied with a small auxiliary power schooner, or a large power sampan, that would enable him to make frequent and unannounced visits at irregular intervals to all of the islands along the chain." However, no effort was made to kill the rabbits until 1923, and by then it was too late. A refuge manager finally was appointed in 1964, fifty-two years after Bryan wrote, although that warden still has not been provided with the "power schooner," nor with any other means of visiting the islands at unannounced times.

Poouli
Melamprosops phaeosoma
(Color plate 50)

This black-faced, brown-backed, buff-bellied bird was discovered at an elevation of about 6,500 feet on the northeast slope of Haleakala Crater during the summer of 1973 (Casey and Jacobi 1974). The sex apparently was not determined for either of the two specimens collected, but the birds were described as being dark grayish brown above, washed with paler cinnamon brown on the neck and back and becoming brighter on the upper tail coverts and on the outer vanes of the wing quills. A dull black mask extends across the forehead, chin, and eyes, and comes to a

FIGURE 105. Laysan Island in 1923. The last three Laysan Honeycreepers "perished during a three-day gale that enveloped everything in a cloud of swirling sand." Courtesy of the Bernice P. Bishop Museum.

point behind the eyes. The sides of the head and throat and the underparts are pale buff, washed with gray across the breast. The sides and under tail coverts are washed with dull rufous brown; the flanks are light cinnamon brown. The plumage is described as being "very dense and fluffy." The legs and feet are dark brown. The bill is black except for a shell pink area at the tip of the lower mandible; the iris is dark brown. Total lengths of the two specimens were 122 and 135 mm (4.75 and 5.25 inches), respectively. "The corneous tongue is straight and relatively thick, the anterior end being rounded and entire. The dorsal surface contains a distinct trough, shaped like a narrow spoon, being widest and deepest anteriorly and sloping upward posteriorly and ending in a narrow, shallow slit." Unfortunately, the remainder of the bird's anatomy was not studied.

The Poouli was classified as a honeycreeper and was considered to be an "offshoot of the psittirostrine genus *Loxops*," even though "*Melamprosops* may not be as closely related to *Loxops* as is *Hemignathus*." Pratt (1979:13, 99), however, doubted that *Melamprosops* was indeed a honeycreeper. He wrote, "Zoogeographic considerations make a drepanidine origin of *Melamprosops* likely, but until additional data are available the genus must be considered *incertae sedis*." I agree with Pratt, and, therefore, discuss this species last.

This species has been found above 4,500 feet elevation in the Koolau forest on the northeast slope of the crater. It frequents the understory plants in the ohia rain forest. It has creeper-like habits, searching leaves, branches, and trunks of trees. It is thought to feed largely on insects and snails. It has been seen in flocks with the Maui Creeper. The nest, eggs, and young have not been found, but fledglings have been seen in August.

CHAPTER FOUR

Introduced Birds

Mr. Taner brought from Australia an Australian Ostrich or Emu, a pair of Black Swans, a Kangaroo Rat and a pair of White Rabbits, as well as a variety of plants and shrubs, some of which are new at the Islands. The introduction of new animals, plants etc., by residents returning from their visits to other countries, is highly praiseworthy and commendable; and we hope persons visiting foreign countries and returning, will bear in mind that they may thus contribute to the general good of the islands, by the introduction of many things that will contribute to the pleasure or profit of themselves or the residents generally.

That little gem is to be found in the October 22, 1853 issue of the *Polynesian*. Reporting on the importation of 15 pairs of European Goldfinches and Chaffinches from Germany in the *Commercial Advertiser* of August 16, 1860, the writer added, "Owners of vessels leaving foreign ports for Honolulu, will confer a great favor by sending out birds, when it can be done without great expense. We need more songsters here."

Virtually nothing was known of the native birds, which by then were presumably to be found primarily in the forested regions of the higher valleys and in the mountains. As I pointed out in the Preface, the first partial list of the native Hawaiian birds was not published until 1869, and it contained no more than half of the birds to be found here. One must assume that the vast majority of foreigners who lived in Hawaii between the 1820s and the 1890s were concerned primarily either with making money or with putting clothes on the natives, and, therefore, left their compounds and settlements only when business required it. The difficult, even hazardous, walk or horseback ride to distant places must have been very distasteful, being that the virgin forests were considered a great nuisance rather than places of pristine beauty.

"Insectivorous birds of foreign importation" were protected and anyone caught killing, snaring, or trapping these birds was subject to a fine of $10 by the game laws of 1881. It was noted in *Thrum's Hawaiian Annual* for 1881, however, that the law had "so long remained a *dead letter,* that there are few who are aware even of its existence; and it would be an injustice if, at this period, any prosecution should be held under it."

Nor did the philosophy expressed in the above quotations change after Rothschild, Wilson, Evans, and Perkins made the remarkable Hawaiian birdlife known to the world in the 1890s. It continued in both official and unofficial places, and the Hui Manu was organized in Honolulu in 1930 for the express purpose of introducing more exotic "songsters." As a result, "there has been a great increase in public interest in bird introduction, and appreciable sums of money have been contributed by this organization as well as by private individuals toward the purchase of song and insectivorous birds for liberation in the islands" (Caum 1933; see also *Elepaio* 31:24–28 and Berger 1974, 1975g).

Caum listed 93 exotic birds that had been released (or had escaped from cages) in Hawaii, in addition to the Jungle Fowl, Laysan Rail, and Laysan Finch. The rail was released on the lands of the Oahu Sugar Company in 1904 "for the purpose of assisting in the destruction of the cane leafhoppers," but the birds did not establish themselves. The Laysan Finches were brought to Honolulu as cage birds, some of which escaped, but they did not survive (Wilson 1890b; Henshaw 1903).

Bryan's (1958) checklist included 95 species of introduced or escaped cage birds. The number of such foreign birds released in Hawaii is now more than 170. These cover the gamut from the Chinese Fishing Cormorant and the Guam Cave Swiftlet to a wide variety of passerine birds.

Excluding the Jungle Fowl, at least 78 kinds (species and subspecies) of potential game birds had been released in Hawaii as of 1967 (Walker 1967a). Of these, 53 were gallinaceous birds (quails, pheasants, partridges), and 20 were columbiform birds (pigeons and doves). The general philosophy seems to have been "if one species doesn't survive, let's try 10 more." Of the total of 78 kinds of game birds, only 12 had become well enough established to make possible a hunting season for them.

Lewin (1971) studied on the Puuwaawaa Ranch on the island of Hawaii in 1966 and 1967. He reported that more than 2,600 game birds belonging to 33 species had been released on this ranch during the preceding decade; he did not state whether or not any of these birds had been subjected to quarantine before being released. Of these, 13 species apparently had become established as breeding birds. Lewin and Holmes (1971) found 11 different species of worm parasites among 115 game birds examined, and they reported 13 new host records for these parasites; 4 species of parasites were recorded for the first time in Hawaii. They discovered that an introduced host species that does not survive may still prove harmful by infecting other species with its parasites. As Lewin (1971) wrote: "Exotic species pose a great threat to the native fauna of any area but especially in tropical environments that provide unusually favorable conditions for introduced species. The ultimate effects of the introduction of these exotic game birds will not be known for some time." Other introduced parasites have been discussed by Kocan and Banko (1974), Smith (1973a, 1973b), and Smith and Guest (1974).

It is impossible to give a precise listing of all species of exotic birds that have been released, or have escaped, in the Hawaiian Islands. Edward Caum stated the problem:

Early records are extremely fragmentary and scattered, and many contain no definite notation as to when a given species made its appearance in Hawaii. As early as 1855 Mr. J. W. Marsh, in an address given at the Fifth Annual Meeting of the Royal Hawaiian Agricultural Society, said that "A record of the introduction of new species [of birds] is still a desideratum." Note the word "still." His statement holds good today; after almost 80 years such a record is still a desideratum. Had it not been so at that time and for many years thereafter, the task of compiling the present data would have been considerably simplified. Unfortunately, Mr. Marsh neglected to mention any of the species he had in mind, but from contemporary newspaper accounts it is known that during the time of the Royal Hawaiian Agricultural Society, 1850 to 1867, enthusiasm for bird introduction was great.

As of 1933, Caum could write:

It has been only within the past few years that any definite records of bird introduction have been kept, and many of these are not entirely comprehensive. For instance, it is recorded that on March 5, 1921, there were imported from the Orient for Maui County 28 pheasants, 502 doves, and 3 partridges, and on June 5 of the same year 75 pigeons, 100 doves, and 100 quail, with no notation as to species or kinds. A record like this does not greatly help in a tabulation of species, and there are many reports no more definite. This is unfortunate, but where game birds were concerned such records have fulfilled the official requirements. If the particular varieties in the shipment were not specified in the accompanying papers, it was not necessary to investigate further. Of course, as there was with the non-game species the possibility that birds inimical to agriculture might be offered for introduction, species not obviously belonging in the game bird category have been closely scrutinized, within the past 15 years or so at least, and only those admitted whose potentialities for evil seemed slight.

Fifteen years later, Fisher (1948a) again raised questions about the advisability of continued introductions of foreign birds. He wrote that "if importations for transplanting and for cage purposes are to continue, a definite program of control should be set up." He proposed a control program containing seven steps, among which were maintaining permanent records and establishing strict quarantine provisions in order "to provide some protection against introducing parasites and disease."

Both Fisher and Caum were too optimistic, however. The desire to import new exotics still persists in official and unofficial circles. The lack of understanding of the full implications of such introductions is widespread. Expressing his philosophy toward new introductions, J. d'Arcy Northwood wrote in the December 1966 issue of the *Elepaio*:

The danger to native birds by this introduction is long past, most of the native birds succumbed around the turn of the century to various causes such as the introduction of predators (dogs, cats, mongoose, rats, etc.) and the destruction or interference with their habitat. The chief cause was probably the introduction of diseases to which the native birds had no immunity. As you know, the native Hawaiians suffered greatly from the exposure to such simple diseases as measles.

Now the native birds that have survived have developed some immunity and the introduction of more exotics will not affect them, unless the newcomers compete with them for food or nesting sites. This is not likely, since the natives live in the mountain forests and the exotics prefer the lowlands.

Needless to say, there are no data to substantiate the statement that the existing endemic birds have developed an immunity to introduced diseases, but there is some evidence to the contrary. Furthermore, many of the exotic species definitely do not "prefer the lowlands." And, to the best of our knowledge, about 60 percent of the endemic birds still manage to survive.

Contrary to the recommendations of both Caum and Fisher, the quarantine divisions of the Hawaii

State Department of Agriculture have destroyed past records and now keep current records on file for only five years before destroying them. There still is no permanent record.

Act 203 passed by the 1965 State legislature provided funds for a nongame bird biologist in the State Division of Fish and Game as well as funds for the importation of still more nongame species.

Moreover, private land owners have continued to release both game and nongame species for which there are no official records. Many illegal releases of cage birds have been made by presumably well-meaning but totally uninformed citizens. A surprising number of weaverfinches (family Ploceidae) have been liberated on the slopes of Diamond Head in recent years, and a number of these have become established as breeding birds (fig. 106).

There are numerous reasons for not introducing any species of animal except under the most carefully controlled conditions (Berger 1974). These include the spread of plant weed species, potential competition with endemic birds, the transmission of parasites and diseases to wild and domestic birds as well as to humans, and the destruction of native flora.

The discovery of tuberculosis in Molokai axis deer in 1970 was mentioned in chapter 1. For years, wild pigs on Hawaii have been carriers of leptospirosis and brucellosis, both of which are transmittable to man. The Department of Health has been conducting a survey of leptospirosis in rats and mongooses since 1946 (Minette 1964), and it intensified this program in 1970 to include a study of incidence among the pigs. About a hundred cases of leptospirosis in humans were diagnosed between 1950 and 1970. Brucellosis, which pro-

FIGURE 106. Kiawe and euphorbia habitat in the Na Laau Botanical Garden on the slopes of Diamond Head, with Kapiolani Park and Waikiki hotels in the background. September 11, 1970. This area supports a wide variety of introduced finches.

duces abortions in cattle and swine, causes undulant fever in humans. Trichinosis, a disease for which there is no cure in man, is found in wild pigs on most, if not all, of the islands.

Bubonic plague was first reported in Hawaii during December 1899. The history of this disease in Hawaii since then has been one of regression, although the State Department of Health recognized two endemic plague regions as of 1965: the Makawao District of Maui and the Hamakua District of Hawaii. Meyer, McNeill, and Wheeler (1965) concluded that their study proved "the continued presence of a permanent reservoir of plague in indigenous rodent and mongoose populations after a period of 65 years since the introduction of plague into Hawaii and has demonstrated that the mongoose is an excellent indicator of plague infection." Mice on Rabbit Island also harbor the plague flea *(Xenopsylla cheopis).*

More than 700 human cases of murine typhus were reported in Honolulu between 1933 and 1965, and 254 cases were reported from Kauai, Molokai, Lanai, Maui, and Hawaii. The vectors for murine typhus, as for plague, are fleas or other ectoparasites on rodents.

Little is known about the role of introduced diseases in the decimation and extinction of native birds, and of their actual and possible effects on other animals and man. Except for psittacine birds (parrots and their allies) and poultry from foreign countries, pet store birds are not subjected to any quarantine at all, even though it is common knowledge that diseases brought in by lower animals may be ones to which man is susceptible. A good example is the serious disease known as psittacosis or parrot fever. However, this bird-borne disease (also called ornithosis) is not limited to the parrot family but can be carried by nearly all birds, and Hull (1963) noted that "in the U.S.A., at least, most cases probably are now of non-psittacine origin." The State epidemiologist in Hawaii issued a warning to physicians in 1968 to be alert for ornithosis in humans and noted that the disease is present in commercial poultry as well as in both pet and wild birds.

More than 25 different diseases can be transmitted from birds to man (Hull 1963). Wild birds serve as a reservoir for a virus that causes encephalitis, a form of "sleeping sickness," in California, which spends millions of dollars annually to control the mosquitoes that transmit this disease to humans. More significantly, at least two species of mosquitoes in California are said to have become immune to all available pesticides.

Several viral and fungous diseases pose public health problems for humans in Hawaii, although these have been little studied here (see Bisseru 1967, Joyce and Nakagawa 1963, and Wallace et al. 1964). Two law

professors at the University of Michigan contracted histoplasmosis from pigeon droppings in 1973; and cryptococcosis has been demonstrated repeatedly throughout much of North America in the droppings and nests of pigeons and European Starlings *(Sturnus vulgaris).* The starling belongs to the same family as the Common Myna. Kishimoto and Baker (1969) found 11 species of fungi pathogenic to man in beach sands, soil, and bird droppings on Oahu.

The 1972 discovery of Newcastle disease in poultry flocks in California resulted in a Federal ban on the importation into the United States of all birds except under the most stringent conditions. The drastic effect that this action had on the cage-bird trade in Hawaii was described in the August 29, 1973 edition of the *Honolulu Advertiser.* The federal government spent $65,000,000 to eradicate the disease in California. The disease was brought to Hawaii via parrots from California during July 1977, and 190 birds in one pet shop had to be destroyed; on February 26, 1979, the State Department of Agriculture banned the importation of all live birds from California because of a new outbreak of Newcastle disease. Should the disease become established in Hawaii, it could virtually eliminate the poultry industry in the state.

An average of 16 new species of insects per year are accidentally brought to Hawaii (Beardsley 1962). The potential exists, therefore, for the accidental introduction of vectors that could spread new (or old) diseases to the native birds and to other animals, including cattle and man. This threat would appear to be especially ominous, as well as obvious, in view of the greatly increased air traffic between Hawaii and the entire South Pacific area. The poisonous, brown recluse spider was discovered on Oahu during 1978 after a girl was bitten on the heel: "The gash, about two inches wide and one-half inch deep, took about a month to heal." The bite can be fatal.

Similarly, the unfortunate introduction of the giant African snail *(Achatina fulica)* and the poorly planned later introductions by the State Department of Agriculture of two predator snails *(Gonaxis quadrilateralis* and *Euglandina rosea)* not only had profound adverse effects upon the endemic snails but it was learned, too late, that the introduced snails were intermediate hosts for the rat lungworm *(Angiostrongylus cantonensis).* Although a normal parasite of rats, the lungworm also can cause eosinophilic meningoencephalitis in man, and has done so in Hawaii (Alicata 1964, 1969; Char and Rosen 1967; van der Schalie 1969). A tourist took some snails to north Miami, Florida, in 1966; by 1969 the snails were infesting a 20-block area and the Florida Department of Agriculture appropriated $30,000 to begin a control program; one woman said that she had killed 200,000 snails, but to little avail.

Beginning in 1956, freshwater prawns of the genus *Macrobrachium* from Guam, Tahiti, and the Marquesas were released in Hawaiian streams, although little was known of their life history. These prawns, also known to be paratenic or transport hosts for the rat lungworm, have been very successful, and they now occur in large numbers in every inhabitable stream in Hawaii. The fate of the much smaller, endemic Hawaiian prawn (*M. grandimanus*) remains to be determined.

No way has been found of predicting in advance changes in the behavior or feeding habits of an alien animal that is turned loose in a foreign environment. For example, one of the predator snails was a lowland form (but a known tree-climber) introduced from Florida. In Hawaii, however, this snail did not remain in the lowlands to decimate the giant African snail (as was hoped) but moved up into the mountains, where it preyed on the already rare endemic snails. Anyone who thinks that he can predict the precise behavior of introduced game mammals should read Laycock's (1966, 1970) chronicle of what has occurred in other parts of the world, and Wodzicki's 1965 discussion of exotic animals in New Zealand.

It should be pointed out that there are no hummingbirds in Hawaii. The Hui Manu wanted to import hummingbirds during the 1930s but found it impractical before the days of air service to the islands. Later hummingbirds were prohibited entry because it was feared that the birds would interfere with agriculture, specifically that they would cross-pollinate pineapple. People who think that they have seen a hummingbird in Hawaii actually have seen a hawk moth or sphinx moth. At least 10 introduced species of these moths now occur in the islands. The moths have a rapid wing beat and feeding behavior very similar to that of hummingbirds.

This chapter deals with those species known to have become established as breeding birds in Hawaii, but excluding the gallinaceous birds that have been introduced solely for hunting. Both space and lack of information make this decision necessary, though the fine work of Schwartz and Schwartz (1949) on game birds in Hawaii should be followed up by a new study of the same sort. All bird species known to have been introduced, other than those discussed in this chapter, are listed in appendices B and C.

We know very little about the many species of introduced birds in Hawaii. Only four species have received any attention at all: the Red-billed Leiothrix (Fisher and Baldwin 1947), Common Myna (Eddinger 1967a), Japanese White-eye (Guest 1973a), and House

Finch (Hirai 1975). There have been no intensive studies of the distribution, breeding biology, parasites and diseases, or interrelations with endemic birds of any introduced species.

ORDER CICONIIFORMES
FAMILY ARDEIDAE
(HERONS, BITTERS, AND EGRETS)

This family is characterized on page 66.

Cattle Egret
Bubulcus ibis
(Color plate 34)

This is a small (20 inches), stocky, predominantly white heron. The legs and bill are yellowish in adult birds and greenish or blackish in immature birds. During the breeding season elsewhere, adults typically have an orange-pink bill, coral-pink legs, and a buffy tinge to the feathers on the crown of the head, back, and breast, but this plumage seems to be uncommon among birds in Hawaii.

The Cattle Egret is native to Spain, Africa, and Asia. The birds appeared in British Guiana about 1930, apparently being wind-borne from Africa, a natural colonization of the New World. By 1962 the birds were nesting in southern Canada and by 1965 the birds had reached California. (Peterson 1954, Van Tyne and Berger 1976)

The Cattle Egret was imported from Florida to Hawaii to aid "in the battle to control house flies, horn flies, and other flies that damage hides and cause lower weight gains in cattle" (Breese 1959). Most of the funds were provided by ranchers for the purchase of birds to be released on their ranches. A total of 105 birds were released on five islands between July 17 and August 24, 1959: one site each on Kauai, Molokai, and Maui, and two sites each on Oahu and Hawaii. Sixteen additional birds were maintained at the Honolulu Zoo for later release. A progress report on the dispersal of these birds was published in the *Elepaio* in January 1960. Another 22 birds were released on Oahu in July 1961, and, by that time, 26 wing-clipped birds had been given their freedom at the Honolulu Zoo. By July 1962, Alan Thistle (1962) reported that the population of Cattle Egrets on Oahu exceeded 150 birds. The population has increased dramatically since that time. During the Audubon Society Christmas count on December 17, 1972, 1,208 birds were counted on Oahu. Thomas Cajski estimated that 2,000 birds roosted and nested at the Kaneohe Marine Corps Air Station during 1978.

On the island of Hawaii, I saw one Cattle Egret at an elevation of about 900 feet along the Chain of Craters road on November 21, 1970; Dr. Charles Lamoureux saw a group of 6 to 8 birds in a pasture near South Point on January 11, 1972; and I saw 6 egrets at the Nakagawa pond near Hilo on January 16, 1972. Sixty birds were counted in the Waiakea Uka area during January 1978. Fish and Game personnel also reported 618 egrets on Kauai and 9 on Niihau between January 16 and 20, 1979. Warren B. King told me that he saw a maximum of 7 Cattle Egrets on Maui during the summer of 1970. During the summer months of 1972, however, I watched a flock of 40 egrets come to roost at Kanaha pond. However, there still has not been a detailed study of the Cattle Egret in Hawaii so that the actual population is unknown for any island.

Cattle Egrets habitually feed with cattle, horses, and water buffalo, as well as with wild grazing mammals in other parts of the world. They feed close to the mouths of the animals and often perch on their backs, eating the insects on the animals and those disturbed by their movements. The egrets also feed where cattle are absent—newly cut alfalfa fields, in plowed sugarcane and pineapple fields, along highways, and even on lawns, as at Mililani Town. Food habits in Hawaii have not been studied but it is known that the egrets eat the Louisiana red crawfish (*Procambarus clarkii*).

The first active rookery was found near Kahuku, Oahu, in 1960 by Paul Schaeffer, Ruth R. Rockafellow, and Mary Riggs (*Elepaio* 21:39–40). The rookery was in a "practically impregnable" thicket, 12 to 15 feet high, of haole koa, lantana, Christmas berry, and various vines. Three nests were found on September 25, 1960. One deserted nest contained two eggs; one nest contained one downy nestling; the third held two large young. This rookery was about 15 miles from the release site of July 1959.

W. M. Ord, Alan Thistle, and David Woodside found a large rookery in a mangrove swamp in West Loch, Pearl Harbor, during the last week of February 1963. They estimated that it contained about 60 nests, most of which held young birds. Some of the young were newly hatched, but others were large enough to fly. Nesting at this site must have begun during December 1962.

The same rookery was visited during April 1963. "The nesting area had expanded considerably over our observation in February and we estimated a minimum of 100 active nests, some with eggs, some with newly hatched infants and others with young birds hopping around the Mangrove branches outside the nests. The average was about 2 young per nest." Clutch size in India varies from 3 to 5 eggs; the average size of 80 eggs was 44.1 × 36.5 mm. The dimensions of one egg I measured were 53 × 36.5 mm.

A pair of Cattle Egrets built a nest 4 feet from the ground in a *Pluchea odorata* bush at the Honolulu Zoo in March 1963. The nest held two pale blue eggs on March 6; both eggs hatched on March 25, hence the incubation period was 19 days. By April 26, the young birds were capable of flight from one branch to another in the nest bush, and by May 2 they could fly to a monkeypod tree some 100 feet from the nest. The adult birds fed in the buffalo paddock at the zoo.

David L. Olsen told me of a heronry with some 30 active nests he visited at the Marine Corps Air Station at Kaneohe on October 5, 1970. I visited this heronry on March 10, 1979, and found 200 nests in about half of the habitat. A few nests held eggs but most had young birds, from newly hatched to nearly ready to fledge. This meager information shows a breeding season lasting at least from September through May. It seems likely that birds nest throughout the year.

I watched the roosting habits of a flock of 40 Cattle Egrets at Kanaha pond, Maui, from August 6 to 9, 1972. No birds were seen at the pond during most of the daylight hours. The birds first appeared as a close-knit flock at approximately 6:00 P.M. When I first saw the birds, they were flying about 100 feet above the ground, but, before reaching the pond, the birds descended suddenly and flew less than 10 feet above the water. The birds veered off to kiawe trees, where they perched in the lower branches. Shortly after 6:30 P.M., the birds flew in a flock, circling for several minutes over the pond at heights between 10 and 20 feet above the water before settling into the vegetation for the night. The birds left their roost between 5:55 and 6:00 A.M. each morning.

On August 5, 1976, I counted a minimum of 227 Cattle Egrets in and flying over Kawainui swamp (Oahu) toward their roosting trees at the Marine Corps Air Station. Not all of these birds had been feeding in the swamp; some came in small flocks from the Koolau mountains and either alighted in the swamp for a short period of time or continued in flight to the roost. At 6:48 P.M., two birds left the swamp; after that, I saw only one egret in the swamp. At 7:02 P.M., however, a single egret approached from the direction of the Pali highway on its way to the roost.

ORDER GALLIFORMES
FAMILY PHASIANIDAE
(PHEASANTS, QUAILS, PARTRIDGES, PEAFOWLS)
Red Jungle Fowl
Gallus gallus

This Jungle Fowl is believed to be the ancestor for all breeds of domestic chickens. The native range is from Ceylon and India eastward to Java and the area formerly called Indochina. From these regions, the birds were transplanted to all parts of the world, and there is evidence that they have been domesticated for more than 5,000 years. In fact, cock fighting was prevalent in the fifth century B.C., and it is thought that keeping the birds for cock fighting was more important in the spread of the species than was their use for meat and eggs. Centuries before the birth of Christ, therefore, the Jungle Fowl had been carried to Jerusalem, Greece, Rome, Turkey, China, and Japan; later it reached Egypt, England, and the Philippines.

The Polynesians brought Jungle Fowl with them when they settled in Hawaii. It is assumed that the birds were introduced to all of the main islands in the following years, but there appear to be no details on the distribution of this species at the time Captain Cook discovered the islands, or during most of the nineteenth century. Munro (1944) wrote that the Hawaiians "kept them for food, sacrifice and the sport of cock fighting."

Schwartz and Schwartz (1949) commented that, although little is known of the former range in Hawaii, "it included parts of the forest from 7,000 feet elevation down to sea level on all major islands." They felt that the extirpation of the species from all of the islands except Kauai was due to "excessive hunting, destruction of forested lands forming their preferred habitat, and interbreeding with domestic stock which tended to reduce their ability to survive in the wild." In the absence of information to the contrary, however, it is reasonable to assume that the introduction of the mongoose, beginning in 1883, presented the ground-nesting Jungle Fowl with a predator with which it could not cope.

Jungle Fowl are now common in the mountains of Kauai (especially in the Kokee and Alakai Swamp regions), and they are said to exist on Niihau and, in smaller numbers, on Hawaii near human habitation where the birds find some protection from rats and especially mongooses. The Schwartzes estimated a total population on Kauai of about 1,400 in 1946–1947. I know of no more recent estimate of population size.

A fresh-plumaged male is a very attractive bird, although there is considerable individual variation in coloration, presumably because of an unknown amount of interbreeding with domestic varieties introduced since Captain Cook's time. The general coloration of the males is rufous on the head, neck, and body, and the tail is green-black; in many males, the tail and top of wing are bronzy green. The comb, face, and wattles are red. Munro (1944) described two cocks collected in 1891. One had silver hackles (long slender feathers on the neck), a golden back, slate-blue underparts, and spurs on the tarsi nearly an inch long; the other had blood-red hackles and blue-black underparts and tail.

FIGURE 107. Three Jungle Fowl chicks; Kokee State Park, Kauai. April 14, 1968.

The hens are rufous on the face and breast; chestnut on the crown; striated light gold to yellow on the neck; and brown on the rest of the body, the brown feathers being streaked and vermiculated with black and/or white. The males range in size from about 27 to 30 inches long; the females, about 17 to 20 inches long.

The breeding season is said to extend from early February until late September. According to the Schwartzes, "Nests are built on the ground usually in dense thickets and consist of a shallow depression lined with dry leaves or other debris. From four to nine white to buff eggs are laid, measuring about 1¾ by 1⅜ inches. Incubation requires 21 days and is performed by the hen although the male participates in caring for the chicks." However, on April 6, 1979, Marleen G. Davis showed me three nests in trees at Waimea Arboretum. These nests had been built in crotches of monkeypod and mango trees from seven to more than 20 feet from the ground. Mrs. Davis told me that this was the customary nesting site for the jungle fowl in the arboretum. We also saw a peahen incubating in a nest built in a crotch of a monkeypod tree about 20 feet from the ground.

Eddinger (1969b) and I found three broods of downy chicks at Kokee State Park on April 14, 1968 (fig. 107).

We brought seven of the chicks back to Honolulu, where Eddinger cared for them; four of the birds were cocks and three were hens. One cock and two hens were placed in a separate aviary on August 1. One hen laid her first egg on August 21; the other, on August 23. These Jungle Fowl, therefore, matured and reached sexual maturity within four to five months after hatching. The eggs of one hen were light tan; those of the other were brown. After two nesting boxes were added to the aviary, both hens laid eggs in each box until one nest contained six eggs, the other nine. The hen was unable to incubate the clutch of nine eggs, but four eggs hatched after 22 days' incubation. One egg of the six-egg clutch hatched after 21 days' incubation, but the hen then deserted the other eggs and spent her time brooding the chick.

Jungle Fowl eat a wide variety of plant and animal matter. In one study, seeds and fruits formed 96 percent of the diet. The birds are most active in feeding in the early morning and late afternoon, at which times they are often seen along roads, trails, or other open spaces. During the rest of the day, they tend to spend their time in thickets or the denser parts of the forest, where they rest and feed casually. When weather conditions are suitable, the birds also take dust baths.

At night the Jungle Fowls roost singly, in pairs, or family groups.

Late afternoon feeding terminates in the close vicinity of the nightly roosting site which is usually a moderately-sized koa tree. The birds linger on the ground until about 15 minutes before dusk when they become restless and start to clamber or fly to low stump or limbs. From these vantage points, neighboring cocks invariably engage in bouts of lusty crowing which lasts for about 5 minutes. With the termination of this crowing, the male joins the female who has by this time worked her way upward by flying and jumping to smaller and outer limbs about 25 to 30 feet above the ground which are capable of supporting their combined weights without bending. Here they roost. (Schwartz and Schwartz 1949)

Hens with their flightless chicks, however, must roost on the ground, where they are vulnerable to mammalian predators such as mongooses, rats, and feral cats. As soon as the chicks can fly, the hens coax them up to tree roosts at dusk.

ORDER COLUMBIFORMES
FAMILY COLUMBIDAE
(PIGEONS AND DOVES)

Pigeons and doves are found throughout most of the world except for extreme northern and southern latitudes and many oceanic islands. The 289 species of this family vary in length from 6 to 33 inches. All are easily recognized as being pigeonlike or dovelike. Some are brightly colored. The members of this family are noted for feeding their young nestlings "pigeon milk," a protein- and fat-rich secretion of the parent bird's crop. Most of the species lay a clutch of two eggs, rarely one or three eggs.

The members of this family established in Hawaii are considered game birds and three are open to public hunting.

Rock Dove
Columba livia

All domestic varieties of the Common Pigeon are descendants of the European Rock Dove. Birds that escape from captivity soon revert to the wild condition. Their introduction to Hawaii has been traced back to 1796.

Schwartz and Schwartz (1949) reported that the feral pigeon was formerly very abundant on all of the islands except Kauai, and that it was widely hunted. They added that, among feral flocks in Hawaii, there is a strong tendency toward a uniformity in the feather color and pattern, closely resembling that of the wild European birds. They estimated a total population of 2,550 birds (mostly on Hawaii, but also on Lanai, Oahu, and Molokai) in 1949.

They postulated several reasons for the drastic decline in population. "The popular method of shooting birds at their common roosting and nesting sites contributed to the decline and still constitutes a serious threat. In certain places where rookeries are accessible to humans, it was and still is the custom for local residents to periodically take the squabs for food."

The Schwartzes wrote that the Rock Doves "roost and nest the year around in sheltered portions of cliffs along the sea coast, in rocky gulches, and in collapsed lava tubes up to 10,000 feet on Mauna Kea." Two white eggs form a clutch.

Analysis of 36 stomachs revealed that seeds comprised 77 percent of the diet; animal matter, 16 percent; and fruit, 7 percent. No further studies of food habits of this species have been made.

The Schwartzes found a very heavy parasitism by tapeworms, which, they reported, not only retards proper nutrition of the host but also "occludes the intestine, produces undesirable toxins, and hinders breeding." They considered the tapeworm involved to be a recent introduction to the islands, presumably brought in with some other species of exotic dove.

Navvab Gojrati (1970) found a small number of Rock Doves at the Honolulu Zoo to be infected with bird malaria, but 65 percent of 924 doves were infected with *Haemoproteus*. He also found the first *Leucocytozoon* infection reported for Hawaiian birds: 3.8 percent of the Rock Doves and 4.0 percent of 482 Lace-necked

Doves and 468 Barred Doves. He found no parasitism by malaria or *Haemoproteus* in the latter two species. *Haemoproteus* is thought to be only "slightly pathogenic," whereas some of the species of *Leucocytozoon* are known to be "markedly pathogenic," causing heavy losses among young birds. A mortality rate as high as 85 percent has been reported for young ducks in Michigan.

Kishimoto and Baker (1969) found a fungus, *Cryptococcus neoformans*, in 13 of 17 samples taken from pigeon droppings on Oahu. In man this fungus causes a chronic cerebrospinal meningitis. In writing about this disease, Hull (1963:468) said that "in all but the cutaneous form the prognosis is very grave." (See also Abou-Gabal and Atia 1978.)

Pigeon racing is popular in Hawaii, and not all birds make it back to the loft. The late Albert Tester once found a banded bird in the stomach of a tiger shark.

Lace-necked Dove
Streptopelia chinensis chinensis
(Color plate 51)

The Spotted, Lace-necked, or Chinese Dove was introduced at an early date, the exact year being unknown. This species has a wide distribution in eastern Asia: Ceylon, India, Pakistan, Nepal, Burma, southern China, and southward into the Indochinese region.

This is a large (12 inches) grayish brown dove with a rosy tinge on the upper breast feathers and a band of black with discrete white spots on the back and sides of the neck, hence the name Lace-necked Dove. Immature birds lack the black and white pattern. The legs and feet are purplish red.

In populated areas such as Honolulu, Lace-necked Doves are relatively tame and can be approached without being disturbed. In rural areas, however, they are far more wary than Barred Doves, typically flushing at a considerable distance from the intruder. They are found on all of the main islands, and are most common from sea level to 4,000 feet elevation; smaller numbers occur as high as 8,000 feet. The Lace-necked Dove inhabits areas with as little as 10 inches of annual rainfall and those where more than 100 inches of rain falls annually. Schwartz and Schwartz (1949, 1951) found the highest densities (101 to 200 birds per square mile) in relatively dry areas on Molokai.

These doves have a strong and direct flight, with rapid wing beats. The males perform an aerial display in which they fly upward at an angle from the top of a tree and then coast downward with tail spread to another perch.

The Lace-necked Dove is multiple brooded, but, in the absence of studies of banded birds, it is not known how many broods a pair may raise in a year. Schwartz

and Schwartz found that most nesting occurs between February and October, although they thought that the species might nest throughout the year in Hawaii. The birds build a characteristic dove nest—a flimsy platform of twigs and branchlets, sometimes lined with rootlets—placed from about 5 to 35 feet above the ground. Two white eggs form a clutch; the eggs are said to average 19 × 35 mm. Incubation and nestling periods apparently have not been determined.

The diet, as determined by examining crop contents of 91 doves, was found to consist of 77 percent seeds and about 23 percent fruits, with animal matter being almost negligible. Tapeworm parasitism was found to be heavy in Lace-necked Doves, however, indicating that the small amount of animal matter eaten was important in contracting the parasites. H. Edward Smith told me that he found eyeworm (*Oxyspirura mansoni*) infection in 74 percent of 532 Lace-necked Doves at the Honolulu Zoo in 1970.

Doves are classified as game birds in Hawaii, and hunters reported killing 728 Lace-necked Doves during the 1974–1975 hunting season.

Barred Dove
Geopelia striata striata
(Color plate 51)

This attractive little (8 inches in length) dove is pale brown above and soft gray below, the breast having a rosy tinge. The lower neck, back, and wings are heavily barred with black; the sides of the body (flanks) are barred with brown and buffy white. The forehead and throat tend to be bluish gray; the top of the head and back of the neck, cinnamon to tawny. The tail is relatively long, and, like that of many doves, contains large white areas on the outer feathers, which are conspicuous in flight.

Also called the Zebra Dove in its native habitat, this species has a wide distribution from the Philippines south to Malaysia and Australia. Records of introduction are scanty, but Bryan (1958) says that the species probably was introduced from Malaysia since 1922. The species is now common to abundant on all of the main islands. Schwartz and Schwartz (1949) reported densities as great as 800 birds per square mile in some areas on Oahu and Molokai in 1947.

The Schwartzes reported that the Barred Dove was common on all of the islands except Hawaii by 1936. During their studies (1946–1947), they found that the range on the several islands "occurs generally from sea level to 3,000 feet but occasionally extends up to 4,000 feet elevation." They felt that the Barred Dove probably reached the island of Hawaii from Maui unassisted by man about 1937. Ten years later, they found it "only on the Kona Coast and in a few places in North

FIGURE 108. Nest and eggs of the Barred Dove; Kawaihae, Hawaii. November 8, 1974.

Kohala," but they predicted that "in the near future this species will probably occupy all suitable range on this island below 4,000 feet." Their predictions came true, and the species is now present at even higher elevations. I found a nest with two feathered nestlings at Pohakuloa on December 8, 1966, where the elevation is 6,500 feet.

Both the Lace-necked Dove and the Barred Dove are found in urban areas and in relatively open rural areas such as pineapple and sugarcane plantations, small truck gardens, pastures, cutover forests, and relatively dry areas where the introduced haole koa and kiawe flourish. They inhabit the high saddle area between Mauna Loa and Mauna Kea, where there is a mixture of endemic and introduced plants. They are uncommon to rare in heavily forested areas, and they are found then only where there are openings or jeep trails. The Barred Dove is much more abundant than the Lace-necked Dove, but both are found in Waikiki and in the residential areas of Honolulu. The Barred Dove is especially tame in these places, commonly walking around the feet of people in open restaurants in Waikiki. They are readily attracted by seeds, and as many as 50 or more Barred Doves will congregate daily at feeding stations, even at office buildings in the middle of downtown Honolulu.

Barred Doves appear to breed throughout the year in Hawaii, although the Schwartzes reported two breeding peaks: February–April and August–October. Courtship takes place on the ground, in trees, and on the roofs of buildings. The male faces a female, lowers his head, gives cooing notes, and elevates and spreads his tail, thus displaying the white on the outer tail feathers; he then may also circle a female or follow her.

The frail nest platform is placed from about 4 to 20 or more feet above the ground; some nests are so skimpy that the eggs can be seen through the bottom of the nest. On April 25, 1976, I photographed a Barred Dove that was incubating two eggs in a nest built on the top of a clock on the ninth-floor lanai of G. H. Steventon in Waikiki.

Two white eggs form a clutch (figs. 108, 109). The incubation period has not been determined in Hawaii. The young are said to remain in the nest 14 to 16 days, and to be attended by the adults for about one week after leaving the nest.

The diet of the Barred Dove consists of 97 percent

FIGURE 109. A Barred Dove incubating two eggs in a nest built on a clock on a ninth-floor lanai of an apartment building in Waikiki. April 25, 1976.

seeds and other plant matter; the 3 percent animal matter includes several species of beetles, weevils, and wireworm larvae. The Schwartzes emphasized that the Barred Dove and the Lace-necked Dove do not compete for food even though they feed in the same fields. They commented that ''it is highly significant that only one plant occurred as more than 2 percent by volume in the diet of both birds. This one, uhaloa, occurs in great abundance throughout most dove range and is more than ample to supply the needs of both species of doves, California and Japanese quails, pigeons, and pheasants, all of which utilize it.''

As predominantly seed-eating birds, doves must have a daily supply of water. In desert areas of some parts of the world, doves fly many miles twice a day from their feeding grounds to a source of water; hunters use this fact to wait at water supplies for the birds to flock in. In dry areas in Hawaii, the doves drink from watering troughs and irrigation ditches. Like some species of gallinaceous birds, they also obtain moisture from dewdrops, which collect on leaves.

The Schwartzes found no internal parasites in Barred Doves, but H. Edward Smith told me that he found two species of intestinal roundworms and one species of tapeworm in Barred Doves at the Honolulu Zoo in 1970. Smith and Guest (1974) reported birds that were infected with Coccidia and the eyeworm *Oxyspiura mansoni*. Kocan and Banko (1974) found two Barred Doves on Hawaii that had trichomoniasis (*Trichomonas gallinae*). These authors speculated that the parasite might have been introduced to the Hawaiian Islands with a flock of homing pigeons used by the

Army Signal Corps many years ago. They wrote that ''the small area and geographic isolation of the island could result in a catastrophic effect on the columbid population if an epizootic of trichomoniasis occurred on the same scale as is frequently seen in North America.''

Hunters killed 1,197 Barred Doves during the 1974–1975 hunting season.

ORDER STRIGIFORMES
FAMILY TYTONIDAE
(BARN OWLS)

The barn owls (11 species) are found throughout most of the world, being absent as native birds from New Zealand, the Hawaiian Islands, and some other islands. The barn owls have a heart-shaped facial disc of feathers.

Barn Owl
Tyto alba pratincola

The Barn Owl is a little larger (16 to 20 inches) than the Pueo. The upperparts of the Barn Owl are golden-brown to buffy, spotted or speckled with blackish or grayish. The underparts vary from being immaculate and white to tawny or rusty and sometimes finely spotted with black. In the field, the birds appear to be plain white below. The head is large and lacks ear tufts. The eyes are black; the Pueo has yellow eyes. The tarsi and toes are less well feathered than those of the Pueo. The Pueo is largely diurnal; the Barn Owl, largely nocturnal.

The first Barn Owls were released in Hawaii in April, June, and October 1958. A total of 15 birds were imported from California by the State Department of Agriculture and released at Kukuihaele, Hawaii, in 1958. Like the mongoose much earlier, the Barn Owl was introduced in the hope that it would prey upon the abundant rats in the sugarcane fields.

From April 1959 through June 1963, 71 additional owls were imported and released at Kukuihaele, Hawaii; at Kilohana, Mana, and the Kekaha Sugar Company lands on Kauai; at Hauula, Oahu; and on the Molokai Ranch on West Molokai.

Tomich (1962) summarized information on the early releases on the Hamakua Coast of Hawaii. As of July 1962, Tomich wrote that the records show that ''from the 36 barn owls released at Kukuihaele, survivors or offspring have moved at least 24 miles toward Hilo (Laupahoehoe) and 5 miles toward Kohala (Waimanu Valley).'' Barn Owls had by that time also been reported seen near Puuwaawaa, ''some 30 miles southwest of Kukuihaele, at an elevation of about 1500 feet in dry range country.''

Tomich was aware ''of no evidence that the barn owl

is established anywhere in the islands as a breeding bird'' and he noted that the ''imported owls were not banded so they cannot be distinguished from those which may have hatched here.'' This is an example of the haphazard way in which introductions have been made in Hawaii.

Au and Swedberg (1966) summarized the status on Kauai from the first release of 18 owls at Kilohana on June 10, 1959, through June 30, 1965. Two owls had also been released in Waimea Valley on November 3, 1961; four in Mana on Kekaha Sugar Company land on May 10, 1963; and four in Kekaha on June 4, 1963. Of the 28 Barn Owls released from 1959 to 1963, 27 dead, sick, or injured owls had been recovered by June 30, 1965; a number of the birds had been killed by flying into automobiles. There were also some 35 sightings of live Barn Owls, indicating that the species was established and breeding. The recoveries of dead birds and the sightings of live birds showed that the species had spread nearly around the entire island, especially in lowland areas.

''Observations of individual birds in some instances showed apparent weakness and lethargy; which indicates the possibility that there may be predisposing factors contributing to deaths as road kills, and that there may be a great deal more mortality occurring unnoticed in areas away from the highways'' (Au and Swedberg).

Barn Owls not infrequently are found dead along highways. I found a dead owl near Kealia pond, Maui, on April 11, 1975, and another in Moanalua Valley on April 14, 1977. I have seen owls fly across the Pali highway at night, and Kirk A. Cramar brought me a bird that had flown into his car on the highway on the night of June 20, 1973. A photograph of a Barn Owl that had been trapped in the Waipahu incinerator during April 1971 appeared in the *Honolulu Star-Bulletin,* although the caption erroneously called the bird a Pueo.

Intensive studies on the distribution, feeding habits, and breeding behavior of the Barn Owl in Hawaii remain to be initiated. The known spread of the Barn Owl in Hawaii to grazing land and into forested areas suggests, however, that this species has done no more in controlling rats in the sugarcane fields than did the mongooses.

Tomich (1971b) reported his observations on the feeding habits of the Barn Owl on Hawaii from 1959 to 1970. He remarked that the Barn Owl is almost entirely nocturnal in habits. In an analysis of 104 regurgitated pellets, Tomich found that 91 pellets contained only the remains of the house mouse (from three to nine in number). Nine pellets held the remains of roof rats and house mice, and four pellets contained the bones of seven Polynesian rats and two house mice. Tomich commented that, although the Barn Owl feeds on rats when they are available, it is not likely a significant factor in their economic control.

Tomich also reported that the regurgitated food pellets of the Barn Owl are larger than those of the Pueo, and that those of the Barn Owl tend to be flattened rather than cylindrical as in the Pueo. He gave width and length measurements of five Barn Owl pellets as 28 × 67, 35 × 60, 34 × 60, 32 × 56, and 32 × 47 mm.

Only a few nests have been reported in Hawaii. John Leper found a nest with two eggs in a lava tube at South Point, Hawaii, during May 1972, and Ronald L. Walker told me of three pairs of Barn Owls on Kaula Island during his visit there from March 6 to 8, 1979; a nest with one chick was seen, the other sites were inaccessible (fig. 110). These adult owls were eating both adult and young Gray-backed and Sooty terns. During March of 1977 and 1978, I heard the calls of young Barn Owls whose nest was on the cliff above Huelani Street in Manoa Valley.

On January 24, 1969, Janet Lind Dorigan and Janath L. Moehring found a young Barn Owl about three weeks old on the ground some 20 feet below a cliff nest containing at least two other owlets. The nest, found along Highway 19 near the Kamuela airport on Hawaii, was inaccessible. Unsuccessful in interesting the police or anyone else on Hawaii in the young owlet, the two graduate students brought it back to Honolulu, where it was raised in the Department of Zoology. When given its first live mouse on February 7, the owl ate the mouse tail-first, but that evening and thereafter the owl always ate mice head-first. We often watched the owl jump from a branch to the floor just as though it were pouncing on a mouse, even when none was in the cage. After we released live mice in the cage, the owl would jump from a branch and pounce on the bare floor while watching a mouse in some other part of the cage. The owl engaged in such practice jumps for a period of several days and then often missed when it tried to catch a mouse on the floor. This particular bird was the tamest captive owl I have ever seen.

ORDER APODIFORMES
FAMILY APODIDAE
(SWIFTS AND SWIFTLETS)

Because of their very strong and swift flight, swifts have been called the most aerial of land birds. They rest only by clinging to cliffs or inner walls of caves, hollow trees, or chimneys. Their wings are long and pointed, and they capture all of their food (insects) in flight. Their bills are very small, but their gape is large. Swifts' legs are so short that the family was named Apodidae (without feet); however, their feet,

FIGURE 110. Two nestling Barn Owls in their cave nest on Kaula Island. September 9, 1976. Courtesy of C. Fred Zeillemaker.

although small, are strong. The hallux, or big toe, of the typical swift is completely reversible, so that it can be turned forward to align with the three front toes or it can be turned backward in opposition to them. The family has a worldwide distribution, being absent only from some oceanic islands, the northern latitudes of North America and Asia, and the extreme southern latitudes of South America. The 76 species vary in length from 3.5 to 9 inches.

Guam Cave Swiftlet
Aerodramus vanikorensis bartschi
(Color plate 52)

This small (4.25 inches) swiftlet sometimes has a greenish tinge to its sooty black upperparts. The rump is paler than the back. The throat is silver-gray; the abdomen is dull gray. The tail is only slightly forked.

The range of Cave and Edible-nest swiftlets includes the Philippines, India, Malaysia, Indonesia, and the Mariana Islands of Micronesia.

The nests of some species of the genus *Aerodramus* are made entirely of the birds' saliva. It is these species that provide the best nests for bird's-nest soup. The nests of the Guam species are composed largely of plant materials, with minimal amounts of saliva. In some parts of its range, *vanikorensis* is called the mossy-nest swiftlet.

Between 125 and 175 (the birds were not counted) Guam Swiftlets were released in Niu Valley, Oahu, on May 15, 1962, by David Woodside of the State Division of Fish and Game. "The birds were collected by mist net on Guam and flown to Hawaii where they were released in one large mass at about 3 P.M. All of the birds survived the trip. There was also a broken egg found in the crate. A previous sample of 12 birds had been thoroughly studied for parasites, etc., and all tests showed negative. The project was sponsored and paid for by the Hui Manu organization in Honolulu" (Bowles 1962).

Woodside also released approximately 200 swiftlets at Waimea Falls, Oahu, on January 29, 1965. Woodside later remarked that the birds "took off straight up into the air, and we haven't seen them since."

None of the birds were reported again until November 29, 1969, when Walter R. Donaghho (1970) observed six birds a little more than a mile from the end of the dirt road in North Halawa Valley. The birds were flying over a stream and over groves of eucalyptus, mango, and kukui trees. Some birds skimmed along the surface of a pool of water, drinking while in flight. On December 1, Donaghho and Woodside estimated a population of about 25 birds in the same area. The birds were not seen in the valley on some later dates, and Woodside told me that they seemed to be found there primarily when Kona (south or southwest) winds were blowing. Woodside and I failed to find the birds there on August 11, 1970.

George-Ann Davis told me that she saw two swiftlets near the summit of the Pali in Moanalua Valley on August 2, 1975. The swiftlets were next seen during June 1976 when Robert J. Shallenberger (1976) found two birds in the same area in North Halawa Valley where Donaghho had found the birds in 1969. Several birds were seen there on September 2, 1977, but none were there on December 19; old nests, however, were found in a cave in the upper part of the valley on January 16, 1978 (*Elepaio* 39:18). Two swiftlets also were seen on the Manana trail during the monthly field trip of the Hawaii Audubon Society on July 9, 1978.

ORDER PASSERIFORMES
FAMILY ALAUDIDAE
(LARKS)

Larks occur in North America, Africa, Madagascar, Eurasia, the Philippines, and southward to Australia. No native species are found in New Zealand or on Pacific oceanic islands. The 75 species of world larks vary in size from 4.75 to 9 inches in length. One species is all black, but the others have a cryptic plumage of gray, brown, and buff streaked with brown or black. Some larks are crested; some have "horns," or tufts of feathers on the head. Larks are terrestrial birds, and most have a long, straight, and sharp claw on their hind toe. They walk rather than hop on the ground.

Skylark
Alauda arvensis arvensis
(Color plate 51)

The Skylark is a nondescript bird. It is grayish brown above, the feathers being tipped with buffy white; there is a short crest on the crown of the head. The chin and throat are buffy white to yellowish white; the upper breast is rufous-buff; the lower breast, belly, and under tail coverts are buffy white. The throat has fine, dark brown streaks; the breast is strongly streaked with brownish-black. The two outer tail feathers are largely white, which shows when the birds are in flight. The birds are about 6.5 inches long.

No studies have been made of possible plumage changes in the Hawaiian birds since the species was first introduced from England in 1865. Other Skylarks were introduced from New Zealand (where they had been introduced in 1864) in 1870.

Henshaw (1904) wrote that the introduction of the Skylark to Oahu had been a "great success," and that some birds had been released on the windward side of Hawaii, "but their fate is at present unknown." He also believed the species to be found "in small numbers upon Maui." Bryan (1908) found the Skylark "common on the grass lands" of Molokai in 1907.

Fisher (1951) reported that Francis Sinclair introduced Skylarks on Niihau before 1920, "and later took some of this stock to Kauai for release there." During his visit to Niihau in August 1947, Fisher found the Skylark nowhere abundant, "but it was found everywhere except in those areas where kiawe or koa haole formed extensive, dense thickets. It occurred on all grassy areas in the sand dunes and on the plateaus, in short-weed patches in open stands of kiawe; some were even observed feeding on the steep, barren slopes of Lehua." Caum (1936) had reported earlier that the Skylark was "rather common" on Lehua Island.

Fisher wrote that it seems unlikely that the Skylark "will become a major nuisance as long as it continues to frequent open grassland; on most of the islands the area of suitable habitat is relatively small and is not in juxtaposition to truck farms. However, on the island of Kauai this species is regarded as a scourge to newly planted lettuce in the truck farming country. If the skylark should become more and more reliant on seeds of cultivated plants, or if the truck farms should expand to include part of the range of the skylark, or even extend to the edge of the range, it seems likely that the species will be on the pest list."

The Skylark is now common to abundant in suitable open habitat on Hawaii. I have seen the species at South Point (sea level) and above treeline (approximately 9,300 feet) in the Mauna Kea Game Management Area on Mauna Kea. I found Skylarks singing at the end of the Mauna Loa Strip road (6,600 feet elevation) on February 20, 1966, and at Halepohaku (9,200 feet) on the south slope of Mauna Kea on November 16, 1968. I also have seen Skylarks in Devil's Country in the saddle area between Mauna Loa and Hualalai, as well as in the saddle between Mauna Loa and Mauna Kea.

The Skylark is common on the grassy outer slopes of Haleakala Crater, Maui, and in the eastern end of the crater itself. It is common on Lanai, inhabiting grassy areas and plowed pineapple fields. C. Fred Zeillemaker wrote (May 2, 1975) that he was certain that the skylark no longer occurs on Kauai. When I came to Hawaii in 1964, skylarks could be seen regularly at Wheeler Air Force Base and in the open country of Waipio Peninsula between West Loch and Middle Loch of Pearl Harbor, but there have been very few reports of this species on Oahu during the last decade. Robert L. Pyle saw two skylarks on the Waipio Peninsula and two others near Walker Bay during 1976 (*Elepaio* 37:9).

Except for the references already cited, I have found no other information on the Skylark in Hawaii. Most of my experience with this species has been in the Kaohe and Mauna Kea Game Management areas on the southwestern slope of Mauna Kea from elevations of approximately 6,500 feet to tree line. The relatively dry, parkland type of forest there and the adjacent pasture land seem to be especially attractive to the Skylarks, and the birds are widely distributed.

Skylarks are noted for their flight song, which may last for several minutes. Their song has been described by Roger Tory Peterson as being "a high pitched, tireless torrent of runs and trills," which the males give while hovering or circling high in the air. Skylarks rarely perch in trees, and only once have I seen a male sing from a tree. I watched this bird sing on a dead stub of a mamani tree early in the morning of October 18, 1967.

On Mauna Kea, a few birds begin to sing by mid-October, but the flight songs are given intermittently then. By the first week of November, many birds give their flight songs throughout much of the day. The period of song ends before late June, and I have never heard the flight song in July or August; only rarely are songs heard in September.

I reached the Puu Laau cabin area (about 7,400 feet) at 6:25 A.M. on December 7, 1966. There was a thick cloud cover and a light rain; dawn was just breaking in the east; the air temperature was 49° F. A number of Skylarks were in full flight song at that time.

Even when the day dawns bright and clear, fog often rolls around the mountain by late morning. Such was the case on November 16, 1967, on which date the fog began to roll in about 11:00 A.M. By noon, the entire area was completely fogged in, there was a considerable amount of fog drip from the trees, and it was impossible to use field glasses. Nevertheless, several Skylarks continued to sing high in the fog. On April 6,

1968, however, the Skylarks stopped singing shortly after noon, when a dense cloud moved over the area and the fog drip changed to heavy rain, accompanied by some thunder—a rare event in Hawaii. As quickly as they had arrived, the clouds lifted at 1:35 P.M., and within minutes, two Skylarks were in the air singing again.

My data are inadequate to state the length of the nesting season on Mauna Kea. I found a recently fledged bird on February 18, 1967. The fledgling was just able to flutter along the ground. When I placed the bird in the palm of my hand, it flew off down the slope about 50 feet before alighting on the ground. The nest from which this bird fledged was built in January. I have found nests with eggs in February and March, the latest on March 30 (1969) (fig. 111). I assume that the nesting season is considerably longer than my few records indicate. None of the nests I have found have contained more than two eggs. In England the Skylark usually lays a clutch of three to five eggs, and the breeding season extends from March (rarely) until July.

The Skylark always builds its nest on the ground, often at the base of a grass tussock or other plant; on Mauna Kea, sometimes near the base of a lava stone. The eggs of the Skylark are unusual for passerine birds because of their very dark color. The eggs in one nest I found had a tawny background overlain with chestnut spots on the smaller end of the egg, and the larger end was almost uniformly dark chocolate-brown. The single egg in another nest had a grayish white background color but with a cap of chocolate-brown completely covering the larger end of the egg.

FAMILY CORVIDAE
(CROWS, JAYS, AND MAGPIES)

This family was described on page 90.

Red-billed Blue Magpie
Urocissa erythrorhyncha
(Color plate 52)

This species is native to China, the Himalayas, and southward to northern Burma and Laos. The species formerly was included in the genera *Kitta* and *Cissa* (Blake and Vaurie 1962).

The Red-billed Blue Magpie has a pigeon-sized body but a very long tail, sometimes 17 inches in length. The overall lengths of two specimens collected on Oahu was 22.5 and 23.2 inches. The head and throat are black; the abdomen and belly are white; the back is blue. A patch of white on the back of the head and the nape of the neck is produced by white-tipped black feathers. The wings are primarily blue but with small white tips on the feathers. The tail feathers are

FIGURE 111. Nest and eggs of the Skylark; Mauna Kea Game Management Area (elevation about 7,400 feet), Hawaii. March 10, 1968.

graduated, the innermost pair being the longest; all of the blue tail feathers have large white terminal patches. The bill is red; the legs and feet are orange.

Although several species of crows and magpies of the genus *Pica* are listed under the ''prohibited entry'' category by the plant quarantine branch of the Hawaii State Department of Agriculture, the genus *Urocissa* is not mentioned. Five individuals of the Red-billed Blue Magpie were sold by a Honolulu pet store to an aviculturist in 1965. These birds were kept in an outdoor aviary in Kahaluu Valley on windward Oahu until wild dogs broke through the wire of the cage in late 1965 or early 1966. Little is known about these birds after their accidental release; but by mid-1970 they had become established, and several adults and immature birds were collected in Kahana Valley, about 10 miles from the site of their release. The Division of Fish and Game tried to exterminate the population, but we do not know if they were successful.

Like many other species of jays and magpies, the Red-billed Blue Magpie tends to travel in small groups. The birds usually forage in the crowns of trees but they sometimes come to the ground to feed. Because of their large size and their liking for fruit, this species could become a serious pest in Hawaii. Stomach contents of one bird consisted of papaya seeds and pulp as well as snails.

FAMILY PARIDAE
(TITMICE)

Generally called titmice in North America and tits in the Old World, these are small birds, 3 to 8 inches in length. The family, containing 65 species, is found throughout most of the world, except in Madagascar, New Guinea, Australia, and Polynesia. None of the species are spotted, streaked, or barred. They tend to be gregarious, and are restless and active birds. They build rather bulky nests in holes in trees, walls, or rock banks. Most species lay large numbers of eggs (6 to 14) in a clutch.

Japanese or Varied Tit
Parus varius
(Color plate 53)

The male Japanese Tit or Yamagara has a predominantly black head, throat, and upper chest. The forehead, cheeks, ear coverts, and part of the abdomen are chestnut. Back, wings, and tail are bluish gray. The straight bill is blackish; the tarsi and toes are gray. Overall length is 5.25 inches. Females are said to be shorter and somewhat duller.

Eight subspecies are recognized by taxonomists. It is not known which were introduced into Hawaii. The first Japanese Tits were released on Kauai about 1890; others, both from Japan and from Germany, in 1905 and 1907. Birds from Japan were released on Oahu, Maui, and Hawaii in 1928 and 1929, and the Hui Manu brought more birds to Oahu in 1930 and 1931 (Caum 1933).

The species did not survive on Maui or Hawaii. Both Caum and Ord (1967) reported the Japanese Tit to be fairly well established in the Kokee area of Kauai; but neither Eddinger nor I ever saw it there, and C. Fred Zeillemaker wrote to me (December 6, 1976) that he was very sure that the species no longer occurs on Kauai. The birds became established in the Koolau Mountains of Oahu and brief comments about sightings of these tits during Audubon Society field trips were published in the *Elepaio*. Nothing was written about the habits and nesting behavior of this species in Hawaii, and the Oahu population probably has died out. The last reliable report for the species is of two birds seen along the Aiea Loop trail by Unoyo Kojima on February 3, 1963 (*Elepaio* 23:47).

FAMILY TIMALIIDAE
(BABBLERS, BABBLING-THRUSHES, LAUGHING-THRUSHES)

This is a large, poorly understood, predominantly Old World family containing about 280 species. It is a very diverse passerine family, with species ranging in size from 3.5 to 16 inches in length, and with species that superficially resemble wrens, thrushes, titmice, jays, thrashers, pittas, and a crow. Seven subfamilies are recognized.

The family is poorly defined on an anatomical basis, but its species have a soft, lax, or fluffy plumage. All have 10 primaries and 12 tail feathers. Unlike thrushes, immature babblers are never spotted.

The Wrentit (*Chamaea fasciata*) of the western United States is the only New World representative of this family. The many species are widespread in Africa, southern Asia, Malaysia, Papuan region, Philippines, and Australia. Some species are solitary, but many are gregarious and are known for being noisy birds that when in moving flocks, keep up a more or less continual babbling, chatter, or squeaking. Some species have rich musical songs; callnotes typically are harsh.

White-throated Laughing-thrush
Garrulax albogularis
(Color plate 53)

This species also has been called the Collared Thrush, the Brown Thrush, and the White-throated Laughing Jay Thrush. This is a large babbler, about 11.5 inches in length. The sexes are alike: olive-brown above and bright iron-red or rufous-orange below. The cheeks, throat, and breast are white, the breast being bordered below by a broad, olive-brown pectoral band. The tips of the tail feathers are white, and appear as a broad band when the bird is in flight or as the bird "brakes" just before alighting on a perch.

The White-throated Laughing-thrush is a native of the Himalayas from northern Pakistan southward into India and northward into China and Formosa; three subspecies are recognized. The species was first imported from San Francisco and released on Kauai in 1919 (Caum 1933). It was released on Oahu about 1950 (Bryan 1958).

Richardson and Bowles (1964) considered this species to be an "uncommon resident of a few lowland areas" of Kauai. They saw what they presumed to be this species in an *Albizzia* forest near Ka Loko Reservoir, and Richard E. Warner saw it near Lihue in 1959 (*Elepaio* 20:9–10). Warner wrote: "A check of Munro [*Birds of Hawaii*] after the first excitement of seeing a new species wore off produced a very similar description for the collared thrush, *Garrulax albogularis*." However, there is no illustration of this species in Munro's book and there is reason to doubt that the species ever became established on Kauai; it did not do so on Oahu. C. Fred Zeillemaker wrote (December 6, 1976) that he had "not found any evidence that the White-throated Laughing-thrush ever has been established on Kauai." Several reports on this species in the *Elepaio* are known now to be erroneous.

Greater Necklaced Laughing-thrush
Garrulax pectoralis
(Color plate 48)

This species is called the Black-gorgeted Laughing-thrush by Ali and Ripley (1972). The sexes are alike in plumage pattern: olive-brown above, with a rufous nuchal collar, and a white superciliary line; the ear coverts vary from striped black and white to entirely white or black, bordered below by a black chin stripe and behind by a black band that extends downward to form a necklace across the upper breast; the throat is buffy colored and may be bordered by white; the center of the belly is white; the tail is graduated and the feathers have white tips, which show in flight as a broad terminal band. Total length is about 12 inches. This species is very similar to the smaller (about 11 inches long) Lesser Necklaced Laughing-thrush *(Garrulax monileger);* but the latter species lacks a chin stripe between the throat and ear coverts, has a narrower necklace, a white chin and throat, yellowish brown legs and feet, and the bill is entirely dark. The bill of the Greater Necklaced Laughing-thrush is paler at the base of the lower mandible and the legs and feet are slate gray in color.

The native range of the Greater Necklaced Laughing-thrush is the Himalayas, Burma, southeastern China, Thailand, and northern Laos. There are five subspecies. Although unidentified at the time, this species has been found in the Wailua Homesteads region of Kauai since 1965 (*Elepaio* 27:90). Gerald E. Swedberg saw six birds there on March 10, 1967, and Charles G. Kaigler saw two birds near Kapaa on July 6, 1970.

C. Fred Zeillemaker wrote that this species "is now regularly encountered in the Huleia Valley (including the Huleia National Wildlife Refuge) and the Wailua Valley (including the Wailua House Lots area) of Kauai." He reported 19 birds on the Christmas count on the Huleia Refuge on January 4, 1976 (*Elepaio* 36:114). There is no information on the introduction of this species.

Gray-sided Laughing-thrush
(*Garrulax caerulatus*)

This laughing-thrush has an olive-brown crown, nape, back, rump, throat, and upper breast; crown and nape feathers may be edged with black. The lower breast, belly, and sides are gray, becoming white on the undertail coverts. The primary and secondary flight feathers are rufous except for a cinnamon-beige color on the leading edge of the primaries. A black mask covers the forehead, chin, and lores, extending through the eye. The skin around the eye is dark blue. The tail is long and rounded, rufous on the upper surface and gray on the lower surface; the three outermost tail feathers are broadly tipped with white. The bill is black with a yellowish tip; the legs are dark gray. Total length is about 10.5 inches. There are eight subspecies whose range includes the Himalayas, Assam, Burma, and southern China.

The origin of these birds is unknown. Caum (1933) reported that five birds of an unidentified laughing-thrush were released on Oahu in 1928. Sightings of an unknown bird were made in 1949, 1950, 1954, and 1960, but not until 1979 was the species identified (Taylor and Collins 1979). Two birds were seen on the Poamoho trail on February 16, 1978.

As is true for many of the other introduced birds, virtually nothing has been published on the biology of the species in their native lands. Detailed studies of the birds in Hawaii would reveal much interesting and important information.

Melodious Laughing-thrush
(*Garrulax canorus*)
(Color plate 53)

Although not a thrush at all, this babbler has been called the Chinese Thrush (the Chinese name is Hwamei) and the Spectacled Thrush. Other names used in the cage bird trade are Spectacled Jay Thrush and Melodious Jay Thrush. The birds have a prominent eyering and a bar of white feathers extending backward over the auricular region of the head. The rest of the plumage is nearly a uniform reddish brown; the sexes look alike. The bill is yellowish; the tarsi and feet are yellow to flesh colored. Length is about 9 inches.

This species is native to the Yangtze Valley, China, and southward to Laos; it also is found in Formosa. Three races are recognized.

This species was introduced as a cage bird, and "a number obtained their freedom at the time of the great fire in the Oriental quarter of Honolulu in 1900, and took to the hills behind the city" (Caum 1933). Later, birds were imported and released on Molokai, Maui, and Hawaii. Birds from Oahu were shipped to Kauai in 1918.

Richardson and Bowles (1964) classified the Melodious Laughing-thrush as a common resident on Kauai. They wrote that "the species was present from the coast to the highest forests (over 4,500 feet), and from humid forested valleys to dry, barren canyons of the southern Na Pali Coast. It seemed equally at home in many introduced plant thickets (as lantana, *Melastoma*, and blackberry) and forests (as *Albizzia*), and dense, native forest of the Alakai Swamp region. Its numbers became smaller, however, in the high, forested area, perhaps in relation to increasing amounts of rainfall."

The species is now very common in the Kokee and Alakai Swamp regions, which are characterized by very heavy annual rainfall. I found one singing Melodious Laughing-thrush in Milolii Valley on September 6, 1969, and one singing bird in Naulolo Valley the following day. Both are very dry areas.

A similar statement on distribution of this species is lacking for the other islands. Ord (1967) said that it was "abundant on Hawaii, Maui and Oahu, from 400 feet up to the tree limit."

Paul Baldwin found this species fairly common from 3,500 feet and lower in Kipahulu Valley, Maui, in December 1945, but none were seen or captured in mist nets in the month of August 1967 during the Kipahulu Valley expedition, and only one expedition member reported hearing this species. I found the species at Wai Anapanapa State Park on July 21, 1969.

I made my first trip to the Mauna Kea mamani-naio forest on May 20, 1966. I did not happen to see a Melodious Laughing-thrush in that area until July 15, 1968, although I have seen them often since then. These birds were seen at elevations between 6,700 and 8,000 feet.

This laughing-thrush is typically a shy and wary bird. It is more often heard than seen. Eisenmann (1961) wrote that "on June 19 they were singing a sweet many-phrased song, somewhat suggestive of a Mockingbird *(Mimus),* in that each phrase tended to be repeated two to three times (occasionally more) before the bird went on to a new phrase. Some phrases were composed of clear musical whistles, others were rather buzzy; often churring and chucking sounds were interspersed. A frequent phrase sounded like *cheeooeē.* A call heard was *wheereēo.*"

There are few records of the nests of the Melodious Laughing-thrush in Hawaii, but we know that the nesting season lasts at least from March through July. William H. Meinecke found a nest with three eggs in the Waianae Range, Oahu, on March 30, 1934. Richard C. Tongg told of a nest built in a pair of brogues that he had placed on an outdoor rack on Kauai during April 1966: a Shama Thrush began to build a nest in one shoe, whereupon the Melodious Laughing-thrush deserted her half-finished nest in the other *(Elepaio* 27:37). C. Robert Eddinger found a nest with three blue-green eggs near the Kalalau lookout at Kokee State Park on April 18, 1969; a fourth egg was laid after 1:45 P.M., April 19 (fig. 112). Three of the eggs measured 24.7 × 32.6 mm, 24.8 × 32.6 mm, and 25.6 × 33.7 mm. Three eggs had hatched by 9:25 A.M., May 2, and the fourth egg hatched before 11:15 that same morning, giving an incubation period of about 13.5 days. At 8:45 A.M. the following day, when the nestlings were approximately 24 hours old, two weighed 4.8 g each, one, 5.0 g, and one, 5.8 g. Unfortunately, the nest was empty on the morning of May 4. This nest was built 9.5 feet above the ground.

Eddinger found a second nest, containing three nestlings, on June 20, 1969. The following day, one of the nestlings was dead, a second appeared to be very weak, and only the third bird seemed to be normal. This nest was placed only 3 feet 2 inches from the ground.

Eddinger also found a nest with four eggs in the same area on July 21, 1970; it was built 12.25 feet from

FIGURE 112. Nest and eggs of the Melodious Laughing-thrush; Kokee State Park, Kauai. April 26, 1969. Courtesy of C. Robert Eddinger.

the ground in an ohia tree. He found a deserted nest about 8 feet from the ground in an olopua *(Osmanthus sandwicensis)* tree the following day. The nest held fragments of egg shells plus six loulu palm fruits, suggesting that the nest had been usurped by a rat.

Van Riper (1973) mentioned two nests with three eggs and four nestlings, respectively, that he found on Kauai on May 1 and 2, 1971. During 1972, on Hawaii, he found three nests: May 4 (three eggs), June 2 (three eggs), and June 15 (three nestlings). Some of the nests were built in high grass at ground level; others were built from 7 to 15 feet above the ground, two of the nests in mamani trees.

Red-billed Leiothrix
Leiothrix lutea
(Color plate 52)

Known in the cage bird trade as the Peking Nightingale and Japanese Hill Robin, the Red-billed Leiothrix is not native to either area. The species is found in northern India, the Himalayas, Burma, and southern China.

The Red-billed Leiothrix is olive-green above. The throat is yellow; the breast, yellow to orange-yellow; the abdomen and under tail coverts, yellowish green. Cheeks and side of neck may be bluish gray. The closed wing shows an edging of yellow and bright red. The bill is orange-red; there is usually a dull yellow eye-ring; sometimes a dusky green moustacial streak. The tarsi and toes are greenish. The sexes are similar. Total length is about 5.5 inches.

According to Caum (1933), this species was first imported from San Francisco for liberation on Kauai in 1918; birds from the same source were released on Oahu in 1928. Also in 1928 and 1929, birds were imported from the Orient and released on five islands: Oahu, Molokai, Maui, Hawaii, and Kauai. Fisher and Baldwin (1947), however, presented a tabulation showing that the Leiothrix was imported to Hawaii as a cage bird as early as 1911, and suggested that some of these probably escaped and became established before 1918. This study was the first to be made of an introduced nongame bird in Hawaii. By that time, the Red-billed Leiothrix was reproducing and increasing its range on Kauai, Oahu, Molokai, Maui, and Hawaii. "On Oahu the species ranges from 400 to 3,000 feet in the Koolau Range and probably goes to about 4,000 feet in the Waianae Mountains." However, there has been a drastic reduction in the Oahu population during the past decade. The Red-billed Leiothrix was one of the most common species identified on the annual Christmas count of the Audubon Society through 1967. Only 18 were counted in 1968 and none, in 1969. "Since then, it has been found on only four counts, and only one or two birds each time" (*Elepaio* 39:96). In writing about single birds seen in the Waianae Range and the Koolau Range in 1976, Alan D. Hart said that they were the only two birds he had seen during the previous four years of field work in the mountains (*Elepaio* 37:57).

The Red-billed Leiothrix was the most common bird observed in Kipahulu Valley, Maui, in August 1967, from the beginning of the forest to the area around Basecamp 1 (elevation 3,100 feet). It was the only species heard singing during the first week of August. The Leiothrix was found at all elevations to Basecamp 3 (elevation 6,500 feet), but was present in reduced numbers above about 3,300 feet.

Fisher and Baldwin noted that "on Hawaii the bird has been found chiefly at elevations ranging from near sea level (Puna district and windward Hawaii) to 7,500 feet on Mauna Loa. We may assume that the upward limit of their livable range on Hawaii is between 8,000 and 9,000 feet. However, there is no definite upper limit to the distribution in fall and early winter, when the birds band together and wander all over the island." Flocks of Leiothrix have been observed at elevations greater than 13,500 feet on Mauna Loa, and one dead bird has been found near Lake Waiau at an elevation of 13,007 feet on Mauna Kea. Birds that remain at these high elevations are soon killed by exposure and starvation. Hence, Fisher and Baldwin believed that temperature "may be a factor in limiting upward distribution."

The Red-billed Leiothrix has a wide distribution on the islands, but is least common on Oahu and on Kauai, where the species was first introduced. Richardson and Bowles considered it to be an "uncommon resident in widespread localities" on Kauai, and my own experience since 1965 confirms their observations. The bird has been seen in Kalalau Valley on the Na Pali Coast; I did not find it in Milolii Valley or Naulolo Valley on September 6 and 7, 1969. Only infrequently is it encountered in the Alakai Swamp or Kokee areas. Scott, Woodside, and Casey (1977) found the Leiothrix to be a common species in the forests of Molokai, especially at elevations above 4,000 feet.

The Red-billed Leiothrix prefers the wetter areas (both native and introduced vegetation). Fisher and Baldwin remarked that "despite the bird's proclivity for moist valleys, rainfall apparently is not the determining factor except possibly in areas having less than 40 inches a year, for yearly average of precipitation in its observed range on Oahu vary from 30 to 200 inches. On Hawaii the species is rare or absent in areas having less than 20 inches a year; this is true in the leeward districts. In the Kau district, where rainfall is 20 inches or less in much of the lowland, *Leiothrix* is rare below 3,000 feet and absent below 2,500 feet." They felt that the presence or absence of surface water might be a significant factor, but this appears not to be the case, at least in the mamani-naio forest on the south and southwestern slopes of Mauna Kea. The Red-billed Leiothrix is a common bird in the Kaohe and Mauna Kea Game Management areas (above 6,500 feet). The annual rainfall there during the period 1965–1969 varied from 15.6 inches (1966) to 40.9 inches (1968), and standing water is rare.

Fisher and Baldwin point out that "a cover of dense vegetation near the ground is the major characteristic of the habitat of Leiothrix." They "never found this species feeding, nesting, or even remaining long in the large plantings of imported ironwood *(Casuarina)* or exotic *Eucalyptus;* there is rarely any ground growth in such places." The species is found where there are suitable thickets, however, whether the dominant trees are native or introduced.

Singing is most persistent during the breeding season, but some songs may be heard throughout the year. In the nonbreeding season, when the birds may move some distance from their nesting territories, the species is noted for forming large flocks, occasionally as large as 100 birds. Such flocks may be very noisy, uttering loud choruses of harsh, chattering calls when disturbed by a man or other animal. Red-billed Leiothrix also are noisy when going to roost. I watched a flock of birds go to roost in a thick-leaved naio tree about 6:00 P.M., January 3, 1968, at Pohakuloa, Hawaii. A dense fog had rolled in about 5:00 P.M. and hung about a thousand feet above the ground. It was nearly dark by 6:00 P.M., and the birds called incessantly as first one and then another flew into the tree, where the birds continued to call, as they found suitable perches for the night. Two White-eyes, perched side by side, were already settled for the night in the same tree.

Additional information is needed on the length of the breeding season of the Red-billed Leiothrix in Hawaii. Fisher and Baldwin found active nests between March 3 and May 7 on Oahu. These nests were found at elevations of between 500 and 2,500 feet. I found a nest with two eggs near a stream bed in the upper end of Manoa Valley on June 2, 1966. The two eggs hatched late on June 8 or early on June 9, and the nestlings left the nest on June 20. Late in the afternoon that day, the two fledglings were perched side by side on a small branch of a sapling about 4 feet above the ground and 35 feet from the nest. This nestling period was about 11 days.

Fisher and Baldwin found active nests on Hawaii from early March through June. The earliest hatching they observed was March 14, the latest, June 16. My records extend this period more than a month. I found three nests with eggs in the Mauna Kea Game Management Area on June 15, 1968. These nests were located as follows: one, 1.5 feet from the ground in a thick clump of weeds; one, 4.7 feet up in aalii; one, 6.1 feet from the ground near the end of a thickly leaved, drooping branch of a large mamani tree. I also found several empty nests that had been built in naio; one of these was 15 feet from the ground. On July 7 the same year, I observed an adult carrying food, but I was unable to find a nest and concluded that the adult may have been feeding a fledgling. On Mauna Kea, I have found Leiothrix nests at elevations between 6,500 feet (Pohakuloa) and about 7,600 feet (above the Puu Laau cabin).

I found two nests (each with three eggs) in the Kilauea Forest Reserve on Hawaii on June 24, 1971, and July 23, 1970; both of these nests had been built near the ends of the drooping tree fern fronds. The latest date I know of is of a nest with two feathered young that was located 75 yards from Basecamp 1 (elevation 3,100 feet) in Kipahulu Valley, Maui, on August 5, 1967. The nest, about 5 feet from the ground, was built in a small alani *(Pelea)* tree.

Leiothrix eggs are very attractive, having a pale blue background color and reddish brown spots or splotches, which are usually concentrated as a wreath encircling the larger end of the egg; however, on some eggs the spots are irregularly scattered over nearly the entire surface of the shell (fig. 113). Three eggs in one clutch measured by Fisher and Baldwin averaged

FIGURE 113. Nest, egg, and nestling (less than 48 hours old) of the Red-billed Leiothrix; Manoa Valley, Oahu. April 10, 1966.

16.56 × 20.8 mm; four eggs in a second clutch averaged 15.47 × 20.4 mm. They found clutch size to vary from two to four eggs with an average of three; my data agree with their findings.

The incubating birds at two nests I found on Mauna Kea performed the "rodent run" distraction behavior when I flushed them from their nests containing eggs: they left the nests quickly but quietly, and ran rapidly along the ground, giving alarm notes only after they had flown into a nearby thicket.

Newly hatched nestlings have a bright reddish apricot skin, except in the areas where the blackish down covers the future feather tracts. Down feathers occur above the eye, on the head, and down the back, from the interscapular area to the oil gland. The gape is a rich orange red; the margin of the open mandibles (or rictus) is pale yellow. Three siblings studied by Fisher and Baldwin weighed 3.1, 3.0, and 3.2 g when they were one day old; at seven days of age, these three birds weighed 13.0, 13.9, and 13.5 g, respectively; only the first and third birds were in the nest at the age of 11 days, and these weighed 15.0 and 15.2 g.

Food of the Leiothrix includes both plant and animal matter. The birds eat considerable quantities of fruit: thimbleberry *(Rubus rosaefolius)*, strawberry guava *(Psidium cattleianum)*, overripe papaya, and others (Fisher and Baldwin 1947). They also eat flower petals and small new buds. Animal food includes various species of Diptera, Hymenoptera, Lepidoptera, and Mollusca.

Fisher and Baldwin were the first to demonstrate the presence of the bird malaria parasite *(Plasmodium vaughani)* in the blood of an introduced species. From blood smears of 11 Leiothrix from Hawaii, one showed

Plasmodium; this was a bird collected near Kipuka Puaulu in Volcanoes National Park.

FAMILY PYCNONOTIDAE
(BULBULS)

Bulbuls are birds of the Old World tropics. The center of abundance is in Africa and Madagascar, but the family is widely distributed throughout southern Asia, Malaysia, and the Philippines. The 109 species range in length from 5.5 to 11.25 inches. Bulbuls have highly modified, vaneless feathers growing among typical feathers on the nape of the neck. They have short necks and wings and especially long and fluffy rump feathers. Some species are crested. The plumage pattern varies widely among different species, but the sexes within a species are similar. The male in some species is larger than the female. Many have contrasting head patterns and/or brightly colored under tail coverts. Bulbuls are believed to be most closely related to the babblers, differing from them in having well-developed rictal bristles and in possessing much shorter legs. Bulbuls are largely fruit eaters, although they also eat insects; a few species drink nectar. Some bulbuls have been known to become drunk from drinking fermented juices. Bulbuls tend to be gregarious and noisy.

Red-whiskered Bulbul
Pycnonotus jocosus
(Color plate 52)

This species is native to India, Nepal, Bangladesh, Burma, and the Indo-Chinese subregion to Hong Kong and the South China coast, as well as to the Andaman and Nicobar islands. Five subspecies are recognized. This species is sometimes called the Red-eared Bulbul in the pet store trade. It has become established in Florida (Banks and Laybourne 1968).

The Red-whiskered Bulbul is brownish above and white below. It has a black head, pointed crest, and a broken "necklace" of black on the sides of the breast. A crimson patch of feathers behind the eye forms the "whiskers." The under tail coverts also are crimson; the ends of the outer tail feathers are white. The sexes are alike in color. Length is about 7 inches.

Although all species of bulbuls are classified in the "prohibited entry" list of the State Department of Agriculture, several species have been imported illegally. Two Red-whiskered Bulbuls were reported in lower Makiki Heights (Oahu) during the fall of 1965; by the fall of 1967, 24 birds were counted at one time in this area (*Elepaio* 29:35). Four birds were observed on Pacific Heights in the latter part of 1967, and seven birds were seen there during the annual Christmas Count of the Hawaii Audubon Society on December 29, 1968 (*Elepaio* 28:24; 28:70; 29:69). The species has been

very successful and by 1979 Red-whiskered Bulbuls were found from Hawaii Kai to Pearl City Heights; 77 birds were reported on the December 19, 1976 Christmas count.

The first nesting in Hawaii was reported in 1971, when a pair fledged young from two nests (April 20 and August 14) in lower Makiki Heights (*Elepaio* 32:38; Berger 1975e). We now know that the breeding season lasts at least from January into August. A nest with two fully feathered young was found on the grounds of the Unitarian Church on the Pali Highway on February 13, 1976; the birds fledged that day or the following day (*Elepaio* 39:19). I found a pair with two well-fledged young (without red whiskers) in a plumeria tree on Oahu Avenue on March 5, 1977. On April 19, 1977, a pair was constructing a nest about 12 feet from the ground in a jasmine *(Trachelospermum jasminoides)* hedge on the Manoa campus of the University of Hawaii; the third egg was laid on April 23. Two young had hatched by 3:40 P.M. on May 2 and the third egg hatched that evening, giving an incubation period of 11 days; the nestling period was 12 days (van Riper et al. 1979). I photographed a nest with three eggs at the home of Sue Gaffney on the Old Pali Road in Nuuanu Valley on May 10, 1977; this nest was built about 18 feet from the ground in a magnolia tree (fig. 114). Ohashi and Ueoka (1977) told of three nests they examined on May 4, 1977; the three nests were built in English ivy *(Hedera helix)* about 7.5 feet from the ground; the distance between the nests varied from about 9 feet to 13 feet. Each of the nests held eggs (2, 3,

FIGURE 114. Nest and eggs of the Red-whiskered Bulbul; Nuuanu Valley, Oahu. May 10, 1977.

and 3), but only one pair of bulbuls was seen at the site.

Red-whiskered Bulbul eggs have a pinkish background, heavily freckled and mottled with reddish brown or purple spots or splotches that are concentrated at the larger end of the egg; there is much variation in pattern among different eggs. The clutch is two or three eggs. Ali and Ripley (1971) give the average size of 100 eggs as 16.1 × 24.4 mm. Young bulbuls are naked at hatching; the lining of the mouth is red, changing to yellow at the midline of the palate, their eyes are still closed at three days of age.

Bulbuls eat fruits, berries, figs, flower buds, nectar, insects, and spiders. Nestlings are fed soft-bodied insects and caterpillars at first, but, as they grow older, berries and other fruits. In Hawaii adults have been seen feeding on the fruits of the date palm (*Phoenix dactylifera*), papaya (*Carica papaya*), mango (*Magnifera indica*), autograph tree (*Clusia rosea*), loquat (*Eriobotrya japonica*), avocado (*Persea americana*), octopus tree (*Brassaia actiniphylla*), and mock orange (*Murraya exotica*). They have been seen gathering nectar from coconut palms and bottle brush (*Callistemon lanceolatus*) trees.

Red-vented Bulbul
Pycnonotus cafer
(Color plate 52)

Larger (8.25 inches) than the preceding species, the Red-vented Bulbul is smoke-brown with a black head and tail, a white abdomen and rump, and crimson under tail coverts. The head is only slightly crested. The white rump and white at the tips of the tail feathers are conspicuous in flight. The seven subspecies of this bulbul are native to Pakistan, India, Ceylon, and eastward to the Indo-Chinese subregion and Java. It was introduced to the Fiji Islands where it is considered a serious pest on fruit trees and in vegetable gardens (Watling 1978). During March 1977 the U.S. Fish and Wildlife Service proposed that bulbuls be added to the list of "injurious species" that cannot be imported into the United States without a special permit; other prohibited species already found in Hawaii were the Japanese White-eye, Common Indian Myna, and Java Sparrow.

At least six Red-vented Bulbuls were seen on the Oahu Plantation at Waipahu in 1966 (*Elepaio* 27:55). By June 1967, the species had been reported near Fort Shafter, in Kailua, and at the Bellows Air Force Station at Waimanalo (*Elepaio* 28:23). I saw five birds at Waimanalo on September 27, 1970. The occurrence of the birds in such widely separated areas suggests that birds escaped or were introduced intentionally in these different places. Berger (1975e) summarized the distribution and spread of this bulbul on Oahu to 1975. This abundant species now occurs from Hanauma Bay and Koko Crater to Waipahu and Wahiawa on the leeward side of Oahu and from Waimanalo to Laie on the windward side. It will not take many years before the species is found throughout the island. The rapid increase in numbers of bulbuls is revealed by the annual Christmas counts of the Audubon Society: 212 birds were recorded in 1975; 744, on December 18, 1977.

Both species of bulbuls are noted for perching in the open on telephone wires, on the edges of building roofs, or on the topmost branches of trees, where they utter their callnotes. Both species flock during the nonbreeding season and I have seen flocks of approximately 50 Red-vented Bulbuls during mid-October. David Bremer (1977) described the behavior of some 60 bulbuls that roosted in a banyan tree on the golf course at Pearl Ridge during December 1976. The birds came to the roost between 4:55 and 6:05 P.M. during a four-day period; they left in the morning between 6:45 and 7:45. Bulbuls may be very noisy at times; in the nesting season, they tend to be less vociferous during much of the day, but during spring, I have heard both species sing before dawn. Bulbuls may be attracted to fruit placed on feeding trays; Peggy H. Hodge wrote that the birds liked papaya seeds and rind (*Elepaio* 35:92). Bulbuls are belligerent and aggressive birds and often chase other species.

The red under tail coverts are used in courtship displays. The male perches facing the female, spreads both wings, fans the tail feathers, and depresses the tail, which thus emphasizes the red color.

The breeding season of the Red-vented Bulbul is an extended one, lasting from January into October. Hodge (*Elepaio* 35:107) wrote of fledgling bulbuls being fed by adults at a bird feeder at Lanikai on January 21, 1975, and fledglings have been seen in Kailua during mid-September and in Hawaii Kai during early October (*Elepaio* 38:105). Red-vented Bulbuls were first seen on the Manoa campus of the University of Hawaii on November 1, 1971. The species is now common there, and nests were found on May 19 and July 10, 1972; May 2, 1973; April 4, 1974; March 21, 1975; and June 27, 1977. I saw fledglings on May 12 and August 25, 1972; August 31, 1976; and July 14, 1978 (Berger 1977e). Pyle (1976) wrote of a pair that nested "in June in a potted plant hanging under the eaves of a home in Kailua. Another nest, presumably built by the same pair, was built in the same place in July. Two young fledged on July 30, and one full grown chick was left dead in the nest."

Two or three eggs usually form the clutch. The eggs have a pinkish-white base color, more or less profusely blotched with purplish brown or claret and either concentrated around the larger end of the egg or scattered

FIGURE 115. Nest and eggs of the Red-vented Bulbul; Manoa campus of the University of Hawaii. May 2, 1973.

over much of the surface (fig. 115). Average measurements of 100 eggs were 15.5 × 21.1 mm (Ali and Ripley 1971). The incubation period is about 14 days. The birds typically build their nests in monkeypod trees on the university campus. (A pair in India built their nest in a room on the second floor of an apartment house [Dixit 1963].)

FAMILY MIMIDAE
(MOCKINGBIRDS, THRASHERS, AND CATBIRDS)

This is a New World family, the 30 species being distributed in both North and South America, including the West Indies and the Galápagos Islands. Four species evolved in the Galápagos. These are medium-sized to large passerines (8 to 12 inches) with longer tails and a slimmer body build than thrushes. They have been described as resembling giant wrens. All species are known for their highly developed songs. Some of the mockingbirds mimic the songs and calls of other birds, as well as other sounds. Alarm notes are very harsh. They are very active and aggressive birds. Most of the species feed on the ground.

Mockingbird
Mimus polyglottos
(Color plate 54)

The Mockingbird is a large grayish bird (much paler on the underparts), making white patches in the wings and tail conspicuous in flight. Overall length varies from 9 to 11 inches. Albinism is reported rarely in the Mockingbird; Samuel A. Grimes photographed an al-

bino at a nest in Florida; H. Eddie Smith saw an albino at La Pietra on the slopes of Diamond Head on September 2, 1973. The species has a wide distribution from southern Canada throughout the United States and into southern Mexico. The Hui Manu released birds on Oahu in 1931, 1932, and 1933, and on Maui in 1933 (*Elepaio* 21:81). There seems to be no further records of introductions, but the species is now well established on Kauai, Oahu, Molokai, Lanai, Maui, and Hawaii.

Mockingbirds have been seen on the Leeward Islands several times; Nihoa Island, August 18, 1971; Necker Island, September 15, 1966; Tern Island, French Frigate Shoals, October 19, 1960, two birds on August 4, 1965 (Clapp and Woodward 1968; Amerson 1971).

Richardson and Bowles (1964) wrote that they had heard "an unconfirmed report of the liberation of this species on Kauai, but lacking verification of this we think it is quite possible that mockingbirds have naturally spread from Oahu, where they have been established for many years, to Kauai. Prevailing easterly winds could have helped in the crossing of the 80 miles of ocean between the two islands." They listed the Mockingbird as being "uncommon locally near [the] southern coast" of Kauai in 1960. They saw one bird at Barking Sands on August 20, 1960. By March 1967, at least, the Mockingbird was fairly common in the Barking Sands area, as well as in the dry kiawe belt between Mana and Waimea. On January 28, 1969, Eddinger and I saw our first Mockingbird near the Kalalau lookout in Kokee State Park; others have been seen there since that time.

The Mockingbird has a spotty distribution on Oahu, being absent from many areas but common in others (for example, Diamond Head, Fort Shafter, Radford Terrace, and Barber's Point); there are very few reports for the windward side of Oahu. I found the species to be common in the dry, lowland areas on Molokai during August 1969. Noah K. Pekelo, Jr., had reported the Mockingbird to be "abundant" at mid- and low elevations by 1964. How the species got to Molokai is unknown. The birds also occupy most habitats on Lanai, and they have been reported on Kahoolawe (e.g., 1970, 1971, 1978).

Udvardy (1961a) was the first to report on the widespread establishment of the Mockingbird on Maui after the species' release there in 1933. During March 1959, he found the Mockingbird to be a "very common resident, with pairs occurring on every 4–5 acres of kiawe forest, in all the dry, kiawe-covered habitats that I visited, namely: the southwest foot of Mt. Haleakala, from Kakena [Makena?], near sea level, to Ulupalakua, about 2000 ft elevation; from there, along the highway toward Pulehu, between 2000–3000 ft; also in West Maui, near Papawai Point, in the kiawe along the highway, near sea level.''

I first visited Maui in 1964. I found the birds common near Makena, and also saw five or six birds in the eastern end of Haleakala Crater on the trail to Paliku cabin at an elevation of approximately 7,000 feet. Robert Carpenter, a Park naturalist at Haleakala, had reported seeing Mockingbirds along the park road at elevations as great as 9,000 feet, as well as in the crater in 1961. The species is now abundant in suitable habitat throughout Maui.

Dunmire (1961) reported that Mockingbirds, ''apparently migrants from Maui,'' were seen in the northern part of Hawaii in 1959. Hanson (1960) saw one bird near a school at Puuwaawaa in 1960. Virginia B. Cleary saw one bird near Kamuela on January 1, 1971. I found several widely scattered populations of Mockingbirds on the western slope of Kohala Mountain during 1974. The birds occurred from sea level to Kukuipahu (just south of the Upolu Point Coast Guard Station) up the slope at least to the Hawi–Kawaihae highway. I also found several pairs on the western slope, beginning about 3 miles upslope from Kawaihae. Another population inhabits the grounds of the Mauna Kea Beach hotel.

Mainland Mockingbirds are noted for imitating the songs and calls of other species of birds. A bird that I hand-raised in Michigan had in its repertoire parts of the songs and callnotes of 15 species of birds (Berger 1966). On May 30, 1972, I watched a Mockingbird perched on the top of an aerial on the roof of Hawaii Hall on the University of Hawaii campus. This bird sang notes from the Red-vented Bulbul, Common Myna, and Cardinal. From time to time, the bird flew several feet into the air while still singing, then returned to its perch. David Bremer made observations of Mockingbirds at dawn on the golf course at Pearl Ridge from December 12 to 18, 1976. One bird imitated the calls of about eight species of other birds, including the Golden Plover and Shama Thrush (*Elepaio* 37:98). A study of Mockingbird song in Hawaii is needed. I have heard the song from October to May 30, only once in July and once in August, but I have never lived where the birds are common.

A great deal has been written about a behavior characteristic of Mockingbirds known as wing-flashing. Usually performed when on the ground, wing-flashing involves extending the wings upward in ''archangel fashion,'' and thus displays the large white wing patches. The wings are extended by steps, however, the successive movements being interrupted by momentary pauses. As many as five pauses may occur before the wings are fully extended. Several theories

have been proposed to account for this behavior, but most of the evidence, especially for immature birds, suggests that it is an innate behavior triggered when the bird encounters something new in its environment (Berger 1971).

Although the Mockingbird is an abundant species on some islands, few nests have been reported. I found a nest with three eggs about seven feet from the ground in a kiawe tree near Makena, Maui on April 25, 1964 (fig. 116). Lawrence Hirai found a nest with three eggs on the Manoa campus on March 26, 1974, and Cindy Foursha showed me a nest with three eggs at Radford Terrace on May 7, 1977. The earliest date for a fledgling is March 27, 1969, when I found one bird just out of the nest on the Manoa campus.

Mockingbird eggs have a bluish green background; it may be heavily covered with reddish brown splotches irregularly scattered over the entire surface of the shell or concentrated around the larger end of the egg, the pattern varying from female to female. The down of the newly hatched young is black; the lining of the mouth is bright, egg-yolk yellow. The nestling period in one nest was 14 days.

FAMILY TURDIDAE
(THRUSHES)

This family was described on page 93.

Magpie-robin
Copsychus saularis prosthopellus
(Color plate 53)

Caum (1933) said that a pair of these birds was imported from Hong Kong and released on Kauai in 1922, and that the Hui Manu released an unknown number on Oahu in 1932. Bryan (1958), however, said that this race of the Magpie-robin was introduced to Oahu in 1950. It has been called the Dyal Thrush in Hawaii, a name presumably coined by a pet store dealer. It is a corruption of the Hindi name *Dhaiyal*. Magpie-robin is the common name used throughout the range of the species.

The species, with its 17 subspecies, has a wide distribution, including southern and southeastern China, Philippines, India, Pakistan, Burma, Thailand, Vietnam, Laos, Sumatra, Java, Bali, and other islands.

The male Magpie-robin has a glossy black head, neck, breast, back, wings, and tail; the abdomen varies from white to gray. It has a white shoulder patch and white outer tail feathers. The bill is black; the tarsi and feet are dark gray. Overall length is about 8 inches. The female has a slate-gray chin, throat, and breast; the upperparts are tinged with brown.

Very little is known about the status or distribution of this thrush. A note in the *Elepaio* for July 1961 said

FIGURE 116. Mockingbird nest in a kiawe tree near Makena, Maui. April 25, 1964.

simply that the "Dyal thrush has taken up residence along Manoa Stream." William and Mae Mull saw a bird on Tantalus in 1966. The species was not seen again until 1976, when a visitor presumably saw a Magpie-robin at the Wahiawa Botanical Garden. Another visitor reported one bird at Waimea Falls Park on January 22, 1977 (*Elepaio* 38:4). Donaghho saw one bird near the Menehune ditch in Waimea Canyon, Kauai, on August 22, 1967.

Shama
Copsychus malabaricus
(Color plate 53)

There also are 17 subspecies of the Shama. These are native to Ceylon, India, Nepal, Burma, Malaysia, Vietnam, Laos, Java, and throughout Indonesia. Shama is the Hindi name for this species. It was released on Kauai in 1931. The Hui Manu imported birds in 1940 and released them on Oahu in Nuuanu Valley and "at some homes in the 2400 block on Makiki Heights road" (Harpham 1953). Lorin Gill saw the Shama in Pauoa Flats in 1948 and in upper Manoa Valley in 1949. He saw Shamas on the Round

Top side of Tantalus, beginning in 1950. They apparently were first reported on Tantalus (elevation 1,340 feet) in 1953.

The Shama is a large, slender thrush about 9 inches in total length; some races are 11 inches. The male is glossy black on the head, throat, upper breast, back, wings, and tail (there is a purple sheen on the head, throat, and back); bright chestnut on the abdomen and under tail coverts. The rump and outer tail feathers are white. The bill is black; tarsi and feet, pinkish. The female is brown rather than black, and usually has a shorter tail.

Richardson and Bowles (1964) found the Shama a "moderately common resident locally, usually in inhabited lowland areas" on Kauai in 1960. They found it at Haena, Lihue, and Waimea, and in a mixed *Albizzia* forest, a casuarina grove, and in kiawe, "thus showing much adaptability to habitats varying widely in vegetation and aridity." They noted one thrush eating flying termites emerging at dusk, and they observed the species' characteristic habit of repeatedly raising the tail rapidly then slowly lowering it.

The Shama is common on both the windward and

leeward sides of Oahu. The birds prefer areas of lush vegetation, but they also occur on the Manoa campus of the university, at the Makiki nursery, occasionally at Kapiolani Park, the Na Laau arboretum on Diamond Head, and even in the residential areas of Kailua. Although often a shy species, typically keeping well hidden in dense vegetation, they also are inquisitive, so that they can be induced to approach an observer who imitates the bird's clear whistle-like song or callnotes. In such places as Waimea Falls Park and Paradise Park, where the birds are accustomed to people, the birds often perch on a bare branch only a few feet away. The Shama is noted for its loud, clear, and melodious songs.

Little has been written about the nesting of this species in Hawaii. Richard C. Tongg found a Shama nest built in a pair of shoes on an outside shelf of a house in Wailua Homesteads, Kauai (*Elepaio* 27:37). Mr. Tongg told me that the shoes were left directly under the eaves of the roof, and that the thrushes seemed not to be bothered by slamming of the door or by people walking in and out of the house. The nest was built during April 1966; in it the female thrush laid four eggs, three of which hatched, and at least two of the young fledged.

Mr. Tongg also told me of a pair of Shama Thrushes that built a nest during April 1970 ''in a woman's purse hung opened up under the eaves and over the side door of a house owned by my neighbor, H. Fujimoto.'' The four eggs in this nest had hatched by May 6, 1970. Several young were fledged from this nest, and the pair used the same nest for two more broods, the last leaving the nest in late July. The female laid four eggs in each of the first two clutches and five eggs in the third clutch. The male sometimes flew to the purse and looked down at the incubating female.

Nests that I have found were built in tree cavities: March 31, 1974, 4 eggs; April 20, 1976, two nests, one with 3 eggs, the other with 4; April 4, 1978, one egg and one newly-hatched young (fig. 117). In writing about an Audubon Society field trip on the Makiki Loop Trail on October 13, 1974, Erika Wilson told of a pair of Shamas that were ''staying close to a natural cavity in a tree about 50 feet above the ground.'' She saw one bird enter the cavity, but we have no evidence that the birds nest during October. On a Tantalus trail on Oahu Sue Monden found a fledgling Shama still unable to fly on July 18, 1970 (fig. 118). Frank Richardson collected a juvenile Shama on Kauai on August 24, 1950 (specimen in the Bishop Museum). The Shama also builds its nest in vines or shrubs, but there are no descriptions of such nests in Hawaii.

Shama eggs have a white or pale bluish green background, densely marked with splotches of reddish

FIGURE 117. Nest and eggs of a Shama Thrush in a tree cavity; Tantalus trail, Oahu. May 1, 1976.

FIGURE 118. A fledgling Shama Thrush; Oahu. July 20, 1970.

brown. Ali and Ripley give the average measurements of 64 eggs as 17.2 × 22.0 mm. The incubation period is unknown. Both sexes apparently incubate and feed the young. The young birds are naked at hatching; the lining of the mouth is yellow. The nestling period for four young at one nest was 12 days.

FAMILY SYLVIIDAE
(OLD WORLD WARBLERS)

This family was described on page 99.

Japanese Bush Warbler
Cettia diphone cantans
(Color plate 53)

This species was introduced to Oahu by the Territory of Hawaii Board of Agriculture and Forestry in 1929 and "several times after that by the Hui Manu and by private individuals" (Caum 1933). The Japanese Bush Warbler or Uguisu is native to Japan. Six other subspecies are found in China, Formosa, Assam, and the Philippines.

This is a small (5.5 inches) warbler with olive-brown upperparts, sometimes tinged with green; the underparts are greenish to yellowish. There is a pale yellowish area both above and below the eye. The upper mandible is slate colored; the lower mandible is paler. Tarsi and feet are flesh colored. The tail is medium long. The sexes are similar, but the female may be duller and smaller.

These are shy and secretive birds, characteristically occurring in habitats with luxuriant underbrush, so that they are heard far more often than seen. The birds have two primary songs and a high melodious rattle. One song consists of a prolonged, loud, low-pitched whistle, followed by two short, higher pitched phrases. The second song, also loud, consists of rapidly repeated notes that sound to me like *chee chee chee cha cha, chee chee chee cha cha*. The high pitched melodious rattle may follow the second song. I have heard songs from January to mid-July. After the song season has ended, the birds are very difficult to locate.

Berger (1975f) summarized the distribution and history of this species. It occurs in the Waianae Range from Peacock Flats in the north to Pa Lehua in the south. In the Koolau Range the species is found from Waialae Iki Ridge to Waimea Valley and Pupukea, as well as on the windward side of the Pali as far north as Kahuku (*Elepaio* 38:56). The birds are common at the Makiki nursery in Honolulu and in Moanalua Valley. Bush Warblers were heard on Molokai in 1979 (*Elepaio* 40:27), on Lanai in 1980 (*Elepaio* 41:77).

On April 12, 1977, I took my ornithology class on a field trip to Moanalua Valley, where we found three fledgling Bush Warblers that had left their nest earlier that morning. Cindy Foursha found the empty nest in a dense stand of false staghorn fern directly under the tree where the fledglings were perched. I returned to the valley on April 17. On that date I found a nest with three eggs (fig. 119). The eggs of this warbler are remarkable in comparison with those of most passerine

birds in that they are uniformly a bright, shiny, reddish brown in color. This nest was built in a clump of introduced grass (*Themeda gigantea*) in a dry stream bed. Unfortunately, a storm a few days later filled the stream and washed the nest away. The nests were domed, with the opening on one side. The first nest was made of various grass stems and leaves and neatly lined with finer materials. The nest was 5 inches high, 4.5 inches from front to back, and 4 inches wide. It seems likely that the Bush Warbler is double-brooded in Hawaii.

The Bush Warbler is primarily insectivorous (insects and spiders), but its diet sometimes includes fruit and nectar.

FAMILY ZOSTEROPIDAE
(WHITE-EYES AND SILVER-EYES)

The 80 species of this Old World family inhabit Africa, Madagascar, and Asia, from China, Japan, and the Philippines south to India, Burma, Malaysia, and Australia, as well as east to New Zealand and the Fiji Islands. All are small (4 to 5.5 inches), and most have a conspicuous white eye-ring. The Japanese name is Mejiro.

Japanese White-eye
Zosterops japonicus japonicus
(Color plate 51)

This race of the Japanese White-eye inhabits the main islands of Japan from Honshu to Kyushu and the islands lying between Japan and Korea. The scientific name used above follows Mayr (1967). It is possible that one or more of the other 10 subspecies of this Asian species may also have been imported to Hawaii.

The White-eye is a small (4.5 inches), olive-green bird with a conspicuous white eye-ring. In full breeding plumage, the throat is yellow, shading to buffy on the breast and white on the abdomen. Many intermediate plumages are seen, however, especially in the amount of yellow on the underparts.

Caum (1933) wrote that the Japanese White-eye was first imported from Japan in 1929 by the Territorial Board of Agriculture and Forestry and released on Oahu. There were several later importations "by the Hui Manu and by private individuals," and Caum said that, by 1933, the bird was known to be established on Oahu and "possibly on Kauai." At least 252 White-eyes were released on Hawaii during June 1937 (Berger 1975g). It seems probable that birds were released by the Hui Manu on Maui, as well, but I have been unable to obtain any records. At any rate, the Japanese White-eye now certainly is the most abundant land bird in the Hawaiian Islands. It occurs on all of the islands and is found from sea level to tree line on

FIGURE 119. Nest and three eggs of the Japanese Bush Warbler; Moanalua Valley, Oahu. April 17, 1977.

Maui and Hawaii. It occurs in very dry areas (e.g., Kawaihae, Hawaii) and very wet areas (300 or more inches of rain per year). There is virtually nowhere that one can go in Hawaii without seeing these birds.

White-eyes are very active, "nervous" birds, being almost constantly on the move as they fly—"flit" seems more appropriate—from branch to branch and tree to tree in their search for food, primarily insects but also some nectar. Except during the breeding season, White-eyes usually are seen in flocks, and these often are noisy. The birds utter a rather sweet *pseet* call-note, but they also have a somewhat harsh scolding twitter. When quiet, however, White-eyes are a nuisance to the bird watcher in the ohia forests because of the general similarity in size and color of the White-eye to the Amakihi and other greenish honeycreepers.

White-eyes have a lengthy, high-pitched song in which the phrases ascend and descend repeatedly and rapidly. The notes are too high and too rapid to be described as a warble, yet the song is not unmusical.

Richardson and Bowles (1964) reported two instances in which they observed a Pueo, perched in a tree in the daytime, being "mobbed" by White-eyes and several Apapanes. I watched several White-eyes

and three Cardinals *(Cardinalis cardinalis)* flying around a Pueo perched in a large mesquite tree in Kailua-Kona at 8:00 A.M. on August 8, 1969. Both species of small birds were giving their respective alarm notes while flying from branch to branch in the tree. The owl, however, ignored the small birds, but later flew off.

Only rarely have I observed White-eyes taking a water bath. On one occasion, however, I watched a bird fly onto the upper surface of a large wet orchid leaf and crouch against it to wet its plumage. The bird then moved to other wet leaves and leaned against them, after which it performed the usual bathing motions of shaking and preening the feathers. I was sprinkling the orchids with a hose, and the White-eye took its bath no more than 20 feet from me. I have observed both captive and wild White-eyes scratch their head over the wing.

Richardson and Bowles believed that most breeding had been completed on Kauai by late June. They found only one active nest; it contained three small young on June 20, 1960. On April 6, 1969, I found a White-eye nest under construction in the ohia forest near the Kalalau lookout on Kauai. C. Robert Eddinger followed the developments in this nest (figs. 120, 121). The third egg in the clutch was laid on April 16. The immaculate white eggs measured 12.2 × 15.8, 12.9 × 16.3, and 12.8 × 16.3 mm. Two of the eggs hatched shortly before 10:05 A.M. on April 27, giving an incubation period of approximately 11 days; the third egg did not hatch. Each of the two nestlings weighed 1.8 g when 24 hours old. When the nestlings were four days old, they weighed 5.0 and 5.2 g, but Eddinger noted that one of the nestlings was very weak, and, when he examined the nest two days later, one of the nestlings was dead. The single remaining nestling weighed 7.4 g when it was both 8 and 9 days old. The bird was well feathered at 9 days of age, and tried to jump out of the nest after being weighed. The nestling left the nest when it was between 11 and 12 days old.

Eddinger found two nests in the same area on April 21; I found two nests there on May 31, one with three eggs, the other with a single egg. The third egg in the latter nest was laid on June 2; the nest contained two small nestlings on June 17. The clutch was 3 eggs in 5 nests, 4 eggs in 1 nest.

On Oahu, some White-eyes sing during the day as early as mid-December. Early morning singing, characteristic of the breeding season, is especially noticeable beginning in February. Birds were singing at 6:30 A.M. on February 23, 1970, and one, at 6:15 A.M. (still dark) on March 15, 1979. The first eggs are laid in February; I have seen nestlings as early as March 9

(1967), and recently fledged birds as late as July 26 (1966).

Guest (1973a) studied White-eyes on the university campus for two breeding seasons. She found the first egg on February 20, 1972, on March 1, 1973; the last egg was laid on July 20, 1973. The nesting season began about two weeks later in 1973, and Guest thought that food might have been less abundant then because of a severe winter drought during 1972–1973. She reported a population of about 52 breeding pairs of White-eyes on the 84 acres of the Manoa campus of the University of Hawaii, or an average of 0.62 pairs per acre and a density of 124 birds per 100 acres.

The average size of 35 eggs was 12.6 × 16.5 mm. The newly laid egg is white or pinkish white. The clutch usually is 3 or 4 eggs, sometimes 2; the average was 3.14 eggs. I know of only one 5-egg clutch in Hawaii. The incubation period is about 11 days, the nestling period 9 to 10 days, and the fledgling period, when the young are still fed by the adults, about 20 days. Both sexes incubate the eggs, carry food to the young, remove fecal sacs from the nest, and defend the young. Guest noted that "initial pairing of juveniles probably occurs in winter flocks and the birds then remain together for at least more than one season, possibly for life."

White-eye nests typically are neat, compact structures that are attached to at least two twigs, so that the nests are semipendent. Nests measured by Guest averaged 56.2 mm in cup diameter and 41.7 mm in cup depth. The body of the nest is composed of grass, fine plant material, string, tin foil, hair, leaves, mosses, spider web, and spider cocoons, but the components vary with the habitats of the birds. The lining is of finer material, often human hair on the university campus. On two occasions, Guest found dead nestlings that had become entangled in the lining hair. White-eyes have been observed to steal nest material from active nests of the Elepaio, House Sparrow, and House Finch. On the university campus, nests were built in 42 different kinds of trees and shrubs, by far the largest number being in haole koa and banyan (45 out of a total of 119 nests). Height above ground varied from about 2 feet to more than 90 feet; average height was about 19 feet. White-eyes not infrequently build nests in trees where there are nests of other species (e.g., Common Myna, House Sparrow, House Finch, Cardinal). During April 1974, a White-eye built a nest about nine feet above a Shama nest along Manoa stream on the university campus.

White-eye chicks are naked (except for two small tufts of down over the eyes), blind, and helpless at hatching. The eyes begin to open on the fifth day after hatching. When not being fed, the nestlings spend

FIGURE 120. Two 3-day-old White-eyes and an unhatched egg; Kokee State Park, Kauai. April 30, 1969. Courtesy of C. Robert Eddinger.

FIGURE 121. Nest and three eggs of the White-eye in a kiawe tree near Makena, Maui. April 25, 1964.

most of their time sleeping, as much as 94 percent of the time when they are six days old. They begin to preen their growing feathers on the eighth day, by which time a fear reaction has developed, so that the young crouch down in the nest when disturbed. The birds will leave the nest prematurely on the ninth day if they are disturbed, on the tenth day if not. The birds are unable to fly when they leave the nest, but they are adept at climbing to the higher branches of shrubs or trees. The White eye-ring is complete when the birds are 23 days old. The success rate of 73 eggs over two years was high: 58.6 percent of the eggs produced young. Wind and rain caused most of the destruction of nests. H. Eddie Smith did see an albino mongoose kill a newly fledged bird, and Guest thought it possible that a large lizard *(Anolis)* took two young from one nest. Guest learned from studying banded birds that some pairs reared three broods in a single nesting season. One bird that she banded on February 20, 1972, was still alive in December 1976.

Guest described four callnotes (location notes, fledg-ling calls, a "chitter," and a "whine") and three kinds of song (whisper, a flight song, and the primary song). The primary or territorial song is given only by the male. A singing bout may include from 1 to 50 songs, each song averaging about 5 seconds, with an interval of 2 or 3 seconds between songs. The daily song cycle begins at dawn or earlier and lasts from 20 to 40 minutes. There is then a sharp decrease in frequency of singing throughout the rest of the day, especially when nestlings or fledglings are being fed. The White-eye long has been a favorite cage bird in Japan and the birds are used in singing competitions. The Mejiro Club of Honolulu was an active song contest club forty years ago. Guest (1973b) wrote of a White-eye that sang the song of the Cardinal so well that she would have mistaken the bird for a Cardinal if she had not been watching the bird.

Despite the abundance of the White-eye on both Maui and Hawaii, I have found very few nests in the areas I have studied. I found my first, and only, nest on Maui near Makena on April 25, 1964. This nest was built about seven feet from the ground in a mesquite tree; the clutch was three eggs.

I found two nests in ohia trees at an elevation of about 4,000 feet near the Saddle Road on Hawaii in 1968. One nest contained three eggs on March 9; the other nest had four eggs on May 12 and four well-feathered nestlings on May 25. I have spent far more time in the mamani-naio forest on Mauna Kea than in any other area on Hawaii, but I have found but a single active nest. This nest was placed about 6 feet from the ground in a naio tree at an elevation of approximately 7,500 feet; this nest contained four eggs on April 6, 1968. On June 5, 1967, I found an abandoned nest with one addled egg about 7 feet from the ground in a mamani tree in the same area. I also found a pair of White-eyes with two recently fledged young near sea level at Kapoho on March 26, 1964.

Eddinger (1967b, 1970a) described his experiences raising White-eyes in captivity. When he placed an immature White-eye approximately 56 days old in the same cage with two White-eyes about 22 days old, the older bird immediately began to feed the younger birds as soon as they begged for food. About two weeks later, he placed a recently fledged White-eye in the cage, and all three of the older birds fed the young bird until it became independent. A month later (July 26, 1966), a fifth fledgling was added to the cage. There now developed a conflict among the four older birds, but eventually all four fed the younger bird.

During April of 1968, Eddinger began to hand-raise a brood of House Finches. Again, his captive White-eyes, now mature birds, fed the young finches. As soon as they left the nest, the finches went to the White-eyes to be fed even though there was an adult House Finch in the same cage. Later the White-eyes also fed a brood of nestling House Sparrows.

An interesting behavior pattern of the captive White-eyes was their group preening. Eddinger repeatedly observed one bird preening a second bird while it was preening a third. The five birds also perched side by side when roosting for the night, and often perched close to each other during the daytime.

The captive White-eyes ate fruits (e.g., papaya, avocado) placed in the cage, and Eddinger also observed wild birds on the University campus eating the fruits of the introduced Chinese banyan *(Ficus retusa)*.

A thorough study is needed of relationships between the White-eyes and the endemic birds. Dunmire (1962) reported an "explosive increase of exotic White-eyes" in Volcanoes National Park, and a decrease in the numbers of certain honeycreepers from 1940 to 1961. We do not, however, have any information to show that the two facts are directly related. We do not know whether or not the White-eyes compete seriously for

food, or how important they may be as a reservoir of parasites detrimental to endemic birds. Navvab Gojrati (1970), however, found malarial infections in 3 out of 9 White-eyes from Volcanoes National Park. Smith and Guest (1974) found nematodes *(Microtetrameres)* and nasal mites *(Ptilonyssus)* in White-eyes studied on Diamond Head.

White-eyes are pests in parts of their range, and the California Department of Food and Agriculture recommended that their importation, transportation, or possession be prohibited in that state (Keffer et al. 1976). Kikkawa (1961) discussed the importance of ecological implications of flocking and aggressive behavior of the related White-eye *Zosterops lateralis* in New Zealand. This species colonized New Zealand from Australia without man's help before 1850. Despite their small size, White-eyes are strong flyers, and Ely (1971) reported on Japanese White-eyes that were observed on 11 different occasions far at sea between Oahu and Johnston Island; a flock of 42 birds was seen at sea on December 4, 1963. Five individuals were seen on Johnston Island, itself. Ely wrote that the sightings were made during late fall and winter, and he assumed that the birds had flown from the main islands of Hawaii.

FAMILY STURNIDAE
(STARLINGS AND MYNAS)

This is a widespread Old World family whose members are found throughout Eurasia, Africa, Malaysia, northeastern Australia, and many islands of Oceania. The 104 species range in length from 7 to 17 inches. Most are highly gregarious.

The European Starling *(Sturnus vulgaris)* was introduced in New York City in 1890; since that time, it has spread across the continent, northward into Canada and southward into Mexico. The Starling became a pest in such a short period of time that the Lacey Act of 1907 was passed, prohibiting the introduction of any other bird species in the United States until exhaustive studies have been made. Needless to say, the Act did not apply to Hawaii.

Many starlings mimic other birds, and the Indian Hill Myna is well known for its talking and its "wolf whistle" in captivity.

Common Myna
Acridotheres tristis tristis
(Color plate 54)

The Common Myna is native to Ceylon, India, Pakistan, Nepal, and contiguous regions. It has been introduced to Malaya, Natal, Seychelles, Australia, Hawaii, and many other Pacific islands.

The Myna is a stocky bird, 9 inches in length, with a

short tail. The sexes are alike in plumage color. The head and neck are black; the back is brown; the throat and upper breast are sooty, shading to brown below; the abdomen is white. Large white wing patches and the white tips of the tail feathers are conspicuous when the birds are flying. There is a bare patch of yellow skin around the eye; the bill, tarsi, and toes are yellow. Females may be slightly smaller and paler than males.

The Myna was "introduced from India in 1865 by Dr. William Hillebrand to combat the plague of army worms that was ravaging the pasture lands of the islands. It has spread and multiplied to an amazing extent; reported to be abundant in Honolulu in 1879, it is now extremely common throughout the Territory" (Caum 1933). Mynas were first found on Midway Atoll during 1974; the population had increased to several hundred by mid-1980.

The Myna is common to abundant in lowland areas of the inhabited islands, being most common in residential areas and in the vicinity of human habitation in outlying districts. I have seen it sitting on the backs of cattle at South Point, Hawaii, and the birds may be encountered at almost any elevation. It is common at Pohakuloa (6,500 feet), and I have seen small flocks in the mamani-naio forest on Mauna Kea at elevations up to at least 8,000 feet. It is found at Park Headquarters both at Volcanoes National Park and at Haleakala National Park. Richardson and Bowles (1964) found at least 35 birds roosting in fire trees behind Waialae cabin at an elevation of 3,650 feet in the Alakai Swamp region of Kauai. They also found it at sea level in Milolii Valley, a remote and arid valley on the west coast of Kauai.

More than a dozen species of myna live in India; most of these would appear to be more attractive in appearance than the Common Myna. However, some of my best friends assure me that the Common Myna was a good choice for introduction because this species is comical, clownish, charming, impertinent, and intelligent. Mynas sometimes harass dogs, cats, and mongooses by diving within a few feet of the animal while giving harsh alarm notes.

It would be difficult to improve on Caum's comments on the myna: "The mynah is a perky, self-confident, pugnacious, and noisy bird, in many of its actions and antics disconcertingly human. It is gregarious, and the large flocks that gather at roosting time are most noisy and quarrelsome. It is omnivorous in its tastes, eating house scraps, fruit, grain, insects, and grubs of all kinds. In Hawaii it has been accused of many crimes and misdemeanors, from nest-robbing down, and is popularly supposed to have been a major factor in the extinction of many of the native birds. It is most unlikely that the latter charge can properly be laid

at its door. . . . Everything considered, although it must be admitted that the mynah can be and frequently is a nuisance, an impartial observer will be forced to the conclusion that the bird's advantages to the islands are popularly decidedly underrated, while its disadvantages are overemphasized. It is without doubt of considerable value to the agriculturist."

I agree with Caum that the myna probably had little or nothing to do with the extinction of the endemic Hawaiian birds. Many mynas do, however, harbor a heavy infestation of a bird mite *(Ornithonyssus bursa)*, which also infests the nestlings and nests. After the nestlings leave the nests, the mites soon follow and often become annoying when they invade houses or offices. This is one good reason for screening ventilation holes in houses. A second reason has not been documented in Hawaii, but there is good evidence to suggest that House Sparrows and Starlings sometimes carry burning cigarettes to nests in attics in mainland homes and thus start fires (Van Tyne and Berger 1976). The sparrow and the myna might do so in Hawaii.

Both adult and nestling mynas in Honolulu, at least, are often parasitized by an eye nematode *(Oxyspirura mansoni)*. Nestlings with acute infections refuse to eat in captivity and probably die in the wild. This parasite also has been found in the chicken, Ring-necked Pheasant, Barbary Partridge, Gray Francolin, Bare-throated Francolin, California Quail, Japanese Quail, Lace-necked Dove, House Sparrow, and Red-crested Cardinal. Alicata (1969) said that there "is thus good reason to believe that wild birds serve as reservoir hosts from which infection can be acquired." The intermediate host is a roach.

Navvab Gojrati (1970) examined 73 Common Mynas and found malarial infection *(Plasmodium circumflexum)* in 4 birds, 3 from the Honolulu Zoo and 1 found at sea level on Maui. It is significant that none of the four species of *Plasmodium* found by Navvab Gojrati had been previously reported in Hawaii.

Great numbers of mynas assemble at communal roosting trees, very often large banyan or monkeypod trees. The birds begin to arrive singly and in small groups before dusk, giving their calls in flight and after they have reached the tree. A veritable din of raucous calls continues as the population builds up, until darkness falls and the birds settle for the night. In residential and business areas, where street lights shine, some calls are heard intermittently throughout the night. The birds begin to call again before daybreak, remaining in their roosting tree for some time before flying off to their daytime feeding grounds. The roosting colonies are largest during the nonbreeding season, but they are used by smaller numbers of birds throughout the year. Frings and Frings (1965) estimated roosting populations of more than 4,000 birds in two trees in Honolulu.

Mynas will build their nests in any nook or cranny that will hold a large pile of leaves, twigs, paper, and other materials. These sites include holes in trees or buildings, air-conditioners, water drainpipes, open-ended steel rafters, narrow ledges, traffic lights, palm trees, and even under engine covers of airplanes.

Eddinger (1967a) studied the breeding behavior of mynas on the university campus in 1966 and 1967. Much of the following is based on his findings.

Nest-site selection began in late February and continued into March. Of 25 active nests studied by Eddinger, 17 were on or in campus buildings. Birds may return to the same nesting site in subsequent years. Only the immediate vicinity of the nest is defended, but it is defended vigorously. Courtship display includes the presentation of nesting material by the male to the female. The male walks to a female with his wings slightly depressed and quivering while carrying a feather, cigarette butt, piece of cellophane, or other nesting material in his beak. He usually places the material in front of the female and she carries it to the nest.

In a precopulatory display, the male bows repeatedly toward the female, with the feathers on the top of his head and back of his neck being erected. The display is accompanied by "singing." If the female is receptive, she crouches and the male mounts her. Copulation may occur at any time of the day and on the ground, in a tree, or on a building. Copulation occurs from two to five months before most mynas begin nest building, and may possibly occur throughout the year, as is true of the European Starling (Berger 1971). In such instances, copulation is presumed to be a means of maintaining the pair-bond.

Both sexes take part in building the nest. Cellophane was used in the lining of each 25 nests found by Eddinger. Material is added even after the eggs have been laid. The size and shape of the nest is directly related to the available space of the nesting site. One nest was 20 inches long, 18 inches wide, and 6.5 inches high. The same nest may be used two or more times in a single season, with new material being added after a brood fledges or after the nest is unsuccessful.

Myna eggs are immaculate blue to blue-green. Clutch size in 10 nests varied from 2 to 5 eggs and averaged 3.5. The first egg in the earliest clutch was laid on March 7 (1967). In 1979, however, a nest in an air conditioner in Edmondson Hall on the campus had nestlings during the first week of February; these birds fledged on March 7–8; the fourth egg in a new clutch

was laid on March 23. I also saw a fledgling myna on the campus on March 10, 1979. The first egg in the latest clutch found by Eddinger was laid on July 25 (1966). The eggs are laid at 24-hour intervals. Incubation begins with the laying of the last egg; both adults incubate. The incubation period in each of seven nests was 13 days.

Small nestlings are brooded and fed by both adults. At night, one bird broods and the mate perches near the nest. Fecal sacs of the nestlings are carried away from the nest by the adults. The nestling period varied from 29 to 35 days, which is a very long nestling period for passerine birds. Young more than four weeks old are able to fly well when they first leave the nest (fig. 122). On August 25, 1972, I watched two adults fly with a young bird as it left its nest. The fledgling landed on the ground near me and the adults veered off, giving loud alarm notes. Mynas were still feeding large young in a nest in an air conditioner in Snyder Hall on August 23, 1969.

Eddinger found a very high mortality for both eggs and young. Only eight young fledged from 18 nests containing a total of 56 eggs. He postulated three factors that contributed to nest failure: poor selection of nest sites, unfavorable weather, and an apparent insufficiency of food for the nestlings. He found some instances in which birds laid three or more eggs in such small cavities that there was room for only one nestling to develop, the others usually dying at an early age. Other nests were built in drainpipes and became flooded; some, on windswept ledges; and others, in houses where the birds were not welcome. Some nests appeared to be deserted, even when they contained young, solely because of very heavy rains.

Eddinger learned that the yellow skin around the eyes, typical of the adults, began to appear when the young were about 125 days old, and that mynas reach sexual maturity before they are one year old. Comparative data on the nesting of the myna in India is given in the paper by Sengupta (1968).

Hill Myna
Gracula religiosa
(Color plate 54)

The 10 subspecies of the Hill Myna are found in Ceylon, India, Nepal, Bangladesh, Burma, southern China, and southward to Sumatra and Borneo. One race has been introduced to Christmas Island (Indian Ocean).

The Hill Myna is a jet black bird, with a purple and green sheen and with a white wing patch, which is conspicuous in flight. Orange-yellow wattles and patches of bare skin are found on the nape of the neck and sides

FIGURE 122. A hand-raised Common Indian Myna.

of the head. The bill and legs are yellow. These are large birds, the different races varying from 12 to 15 inches in length.

Three Hill Mynas escaped from a pet shop in 1960, and 5 more in 1961 (Donaghho 1966). These birds soon established themselves in upper Manoa Valley, but their wanderings also took them to Tantalus. I saw 12 birds at the Lyon Arboretum of the University of Hawaii during November 1965. I saw one in the Woodlawn area of Manoa Valley on October 20, 1966. Hill Mynas also have been reported at the State Forestry Division nursery in Makiki Valley, in Kahana Valley, and at Mokuleia County Park on the northwestern shore of Oahu (Walker 1967b). Four Hill Mynas were counted at the Lyon Arboretum on the 1976 Christmas count of the Audubon Society, and two were seen there in 1978. Nothing, however, has been published on their behavior in Hawaii.

This species nests in natural hollows in trees, lining the cavity with grass, leaves, and other debris. In the native range, the birds also nest in deserted woodpecker holes. The two or three eggs in a clutch have a bright blue background color marked with spots and blotches varying from chocolate to reddish brown.

FAMILY ICTERIDAE
(BLACKBIRDS, ORIOLES, TROUPIALS, MEADOWLARKS, AND COWBIRDS)

This is a New World family with 94 species. These are nine-primaried birds that are very closely related to the tanagers and cardinal-like birds. The center of abundance for the family is in tropical America, and most of the Temperate Zone species are migratory. Most are arboreal species, but the meadowlarks and the Bobolink inhabit grasslands, alfalfa fields, and pastures. In nesting habits they vary from solitary nesters to colonial species. Orioles and their allies weave elaborate nests that are suspended from branches. Several species of cowbirds do not build nests at all but lay their eggs in the nests of other species.

Western Meadowlark
Sturnella neglecta
(Color plate 51)

This species is native to western North America from British Columbia southward into Mexico and eastward to western Michigan and northwestern Ohio.

Meadowlarks are large (8 to 10 inches), "chunky" birds of open fields. The upperparts are brown streaked with black and white. A conspicuous V-shaped patch of black feathers on the bright yellow breast is diagnostic. White outer tail feathers are conspicuous when a bird flies. Meadowlarks walk when on the ground. Their flight appears labored because the short, rapid wingbeats alternate with short periods of gliding.

Western Meadowlarks were released on Kauai and Oahu in 1931. Nothing seems to have been recorded about the birds on Oahu, but they did not survive. On Kauai the birds are fairly common but highly localized, being found near Kekaha, Lihue, Kapaa, and Kilauea.

FAMILY PLOCEIDAE
(WEAVERBIRDS AND ALLIES)

There has been, within the past twenty years, a drastic change in concept as to the limits of this family, as well as to its relationship to the Fringillidae, a large group of seedeaters with an American origin. The two families contain 700 species. There still exists, therefore, considerable difference of opinion among authorities about the classification of both groups. The family Ploceidae is viewed in this book as consisting of five subfamilies, although some taxonomists prefer to give full family rank to some of these subgroups. Additional information on both families and the chief reasons for the uncertainties of the relationships are given in the books by Austin (1961:295) and by Van Tyne and Berger (1976:763).

The five subfamilies are: Estrildinae, waxbills; Bubalornithinae, buffalo weavers; Passerinae, sparrow weavers; Ploceinae, typical weavers; and Viduinae, widowweavers.

The species forming the family Ploceidae vary from 3 inches to 25.5 inches in length, the greatly elongated tails of the larger species accounting for much of their length. The Long-tailed Widow Bird (*Euplectes progne*) of Africa, for example, is nearly 2 feet long when in breeding plumage but only about 9 inches in length in the nonbreeding plumage when the tail feathers are short.

The bill is typically conical in shape; in several it is massive in structure, comparable to that of the Kona Grosbeak of the Drepanididae (page 126). There is great variation in plumage patterns, many of the species being brilliantly colored. The nestlings of all waxbills are noted for having striking patterns and colors in the roof of the mouth.

There also is a wide variation in the nesting habits, although most species tend to be colonial and only a few are solitary nesters; one small group is parasitic. Groups of 75 or more pairs of the Sociable Weaver (*Philetairus socius*) of Africa build cooperative nests as large as 25 feet long, 15 feet wide, and from 5 to 10 feet in height; each pair of birds has its own nesting chamber.

The Red-billed Quelea (*Quelea quelea*), another African species, has been described as "the most destructive bird in the world" because of its damage to crops. As many as 10 million nests of this species have been estimated in an area of some 3,000 acres. Most of the members of this family are prolific breeders, a fact which should suggest that great care be taken that these birds do not become widely established in Hawaii. The Baya or Common Weaverbird (*Ploceus philippinus*) of India and Malaya, for example, was reported in the Diamond Head area in 1965 (*Elepaio* 26:54). On October 13, 1970, Helen Y. Lind brought me two abnormal Baya nests that had fallen from a coconut tree on Maunaloa Avenue in Kaimuki; I did not find any birds or nests there the following day. During September 1971, however, I found five nests in the helmet stage of construction attached to palm fronds. The male Baya weaves a retort-shaped nest of grasses and strips of other plant leaves; polygamy is common and males usually build nests for two or three females (fig. 123). Apparently only males escaped in Honolulu, and we assume that the population has died out. This is fortunate because in India roosting flocks of this highly gregarious species typically number in the hundreds, and this species causes great damage to cereal crops (Ambedkar 1964).

SUBFAMILY ESTRILDINAE
(WAXBILLS)

This subfamily contains 107 species of small, brightly colored seedeaters that are given many names in the cage bird trade: munias, mannikins, firefinches, crimsonwings, cutthroats, cordon-bleu, grenadiers, and parrot-finches.

Waxbills are small (3 to 6 inches in length), highly gregarious birds that are native to tropical Africa,

FIGURE 123. Part of a small nesting colony of Bayas; near Baroda, India. November 17, 1964.

southern Asia, the East Indies, and Australia. All species build domed nests with a side entrance. The loosely constructed nests vary in shape (globular, pear shaped, retort shaped, etc.), and are very large for the size of the birds. The eggs are pure white, and the clutches are large (4 to 10 eggs). The young breed before they are one year old, and in captivity as many as five broods may be reared in a year. The adults do not remove the fecal sacs from the nests.

More than a dozen species of this subfamily were reported in the Diamond Head–Kapiolani Park region of Honolulu during the 1969 Christmas Count of the Hawaii Audubon Society. Several of these species were reported for the first time in 1969, but others have been found there annually since 1965. Some have become established as breeding birds; others may have but, in the absence of records, these are listed in appendix B.

Red-cheeked Cordon-bleu
Uraeginthus bengalus
(Color plate 55)

Three species of Cordon-bleu were released on the slopes of Diamond Head during the 1960s. All are Af-

rican species that are popular cage birds. The adult male Red-cheeked Cordon-bleu is pale brown on the forehead, crown, nape, and upper back; the rump, upper tail coverts, face, throat, breast, and sides of the body are a bright turquoise blue, the tail, a darker shade of blue; the wings are drab brown in color; the belly, under tail coverts, and thighs are light gray-brown; the bill is grayish or pinkish brown, the tip blackish; the legs and feet are grayish flesh color; a bright patch of crimson on the ear coverts gives the bird its name. The adult female is similar to the male, but the blue may be much paler and females lack the crimson ear patches. The eyes have a reddish tint. Males are about 4.5 inches long; females, about 4.12 inches.

The Cordon-bleu *(U. angolensis)* has a similar plumage pattern but lacks the cheek patches of the Red-cheeked Cordon-bleu. The Blue-headed Cordon-bleu *(U. cyanocephala)* is similar to the other two species except that the entire head is blue. A male that I measured was 4⅝ inches long; according to the collector, the iris was scarlet, the bill pink, and feet flesh pink in color. A female measured 4.25 inches; the iris was said to be brown, the bill purplish pink, and the feet brownish pink.

Hawaiian bird watchers were confused by the three species of Cordon-bleu so that many reports in the *Elepaio* are of doubtful value. However, Walter Donaghho first reported two pairs of Cordon-bleu at the Na Laau botanical garden on the slopes of Diamond Head on October 15, 1965 *(Elepaio* 26:54); 5 birds were found there on the Christmas count during December 1975. The Blue-headed Cordon-bleu was seen in the same area on December 29, 1969, when 12 birds were counted; one bird was seen during December 1975, but not since then on the annual Christmas counts. As many as 17 Red-cheeked Cordon-bleu were reported during the 1972 December census of the Audubon Society, but none were recorded in December 1978 *(Elepaio* 29:99). Six Cordon-bleu were reported at Koko Head on June 8, 1969 *(Elepaio* 30:18).

Each species builds a loosely constructed, domed nest with an entrance on the side. The eggs are immaculate white. Little is known about the nesting habits of these species in Africa, but the females are thought to lay a clutch of four or five eggs. The nestlings are noted for having a conspicuous pattern of dark marks on the light-colored palate or roof of the mouth. The pattern thus formed is thought to serve as a releaser or target area when the adults enter the relatively dark nest cavity to feed their young.

I found a Red-cheeked Cordon-bleu nest about nine feet from the ground in an olive tree *(Olea europa)* at La

Pietra (Oahu) on October 10, 1976. The nest held five small young at that time. On October 20, two young flew from the nest as I was climbing the tree and two others flew out before I could place my hand over the opening. The young flew strongly to nearby trees. The nest was built of fine grasses and small stems with grass heads. The nest was globular in shape, about 4 inches wide, 4 inches high, and 5 inches from front to back; there was no special lining material. The nest also had a great many dried fecal sacs in it; this is characteristic of this subfamily in which the adults do not remove fecal sacs during the latter part of the nestling period.

I watched a pair of Cordon-bleu building a nest in a kiawe tree on the slopes of Diamond Head on October 9, 1971. Unfortunately, the pair did not complete the nest. I also found a nest with three white eggs in the same area on February 15, 1972, but this nest, too, was later abandoned, and, because I did not see any adults at this nest, I did not know which of the three species it belonged to. These few records do indicate, however, that the Cordon-bleu nests during the fall and winter in Hawaii.

Smith (1973b) found an internal mite *(Sternostoma tracheacolum)* in a Cordon-bleu and in a Red-eared Waxbill that he collected on the slopes of Diamond Head; his was the first report of this parasite in Hawaii.

One or more species of the Cordon-bleu group was liberated on the Puuwaawaa ranch on Hawaii and can be seen there and in adjacent areas.

Lavender Fire Finch
Estrilda caerulescens
(Color plate 56)

This finch is native to Africa, from Senegal to northern Nigeria and southwestern Chad. The birds are gregarious and often flock with other finches. They inhabit gardens, high-grass country, and the edges of forests, but little is known about the biology of this species in its native habitat.

The plumage of the male and female is the same. The crown, neck, back, and wing coverts are pearl gray; the breast feathers are pale gray; the rump, the upper tail coverts, the two middle pairs of tail feathers, and the under tail coverts are crimson; the chin, cheeks, and throat are nearly white, sometimes faintly streaked with gray; the eye is dark brown; the bill is blue gray (sometimes crimson at the base) with a black tip; the legs and feet are slaty black.

This finch was first reported on the Christmas count on the slopes of Diamond Head in December 1965; 40 birds were seen on December 17, 1972, 34 birds on December 21, 1975, and 22 in December 1977. The Lavender Fire Finch certainly is established as a breeding bird in the Diamond Head–Kapiolani Park region. About 10 birds were seen on the Puuwaawaa ranch on Hawaii during June 1978 *(Elepaio* 39:75).

The males have an elaborate courtship dance. Holding a piece of grass in his bill, the male pumps up and down on his legs while uttering a shrill whistle that sounds to me like *wheet-whee,* the first syllable slurring upward and the second slurring downward.

Orange-cheeked Waxbill
Estrilda melpoda
(Color plate 57)

This species is native to West and Central Africa. These birds have a gray crown, brown back and wing coverts, blackish brown tail, and crimson upper tail coverts. Chin and throat are whitish; breast is pale gray; middle of abdomen is yellowish buff. The bill is orange-vermillion; the lores and eye-strip are scarlet; and the ear coverts are orange, sometimes tinged with scarlet. The sexes usually are alike, but the female may be slightly duller. Immature birds have a brown crown. Total length is 4.25 inches.

Walter Donaghho saw 8 Orange-cheeked Waxbills along the Na Laau trail on Diamond Head during October 1965, and 30 birds were counted there during the annual Christmas census of the Hawaii Audubon Society. Twenty or more birds have been counted during six censuses made since then. I saw this species in the West Beach sugarcane fields on Oahu on November 7, 1973. "At least 20, including several apparent immatures, were found in the south pond complex" at Waipio (Oahu) on May 29, 1978 *(Elepaio* 39:75).

Red-eared Waxbill
Estrilda troglodytes
(Color plate 57)

This is another African species whose range includes semiarid habitats from Senegal to Ethiopia and southward to Zaire (Congo). Males and females are alike: the upper parts are a pale gray brown with a rosy tint; a crimson band passes through the eye; the rump and upper tail coverts are black; the tail is dark brown, and the outer webs of the two outermost feathers are white or buffish-white; the chin, throat, breast, and belly are ashy colored, but the middle of the belly has a crimson patch (less noticeable in the female); the eye is reddish brown, the bill, dark red, and the legs and feet, blackish brown. Total length is about 3.25 inches. This species is also called the Common or Black-rumped Waxbill.

Like the Orange-cheeked Waxbill, this species builds its nest on the ground, typically at the base of a grass tussock or shrub. The nests are pear-shaped, with an opening on one side. The eggs are immaculate white. No nests have yet been found in Hawaii.

The Red-eared Waxbill also was first reported in the Diamond Head area in 1965. As many as 48 were recorded there during December 1975. I observed a flock of 20 to 25 birds in sugarcane fields at West Beach (Oahu) on November 7, 1973, and 15 were seen at Kuilima pond near Kahuku during November 1977 (*Elepaio* 38:105).

On February 6, 1975, I saw a flock of nine Red-eared Waxbills in a haole koa thicket just south of the Upolu Point Coast Guard Loran Station in the North Kohala district of Hawaii.

Red Munia
Amandava amandava
(Color plate 58)

Mayr, Paynter, and Traylor (1968:348) removed this species from the genus *Estrilda*. Other names for this species are the Red Avadavat and (in the pet store trade) Strawberry Finch. The three subspecies inhabit Pakistan, India, southern Nepal, Burma, Java, Bali, and adjacent regions.

Caum (1933) wrote that "it is not known with certainty just when these birds came to Hawaii, but it was probably some time between 1900 and 1910. Many were imported as cage birds during this period and it is supposed that the present population is derived from individuals escaped from captivity."

In breeding plumage the male has a crimson head, neck, and body; the body, especially, has many fine white spots. The wings, tail, and abdomen are brownish to black. Females are mostly brown above but have dull crimson upper tail coverts; the lower parts are dusky yellow-brown except for a whitish chin and throat. Males in nonbreeding plumage are like the females. Total length is between 3.75 and 4 inches.

The Red Munia has been established in the Pearl Harbor region for many years. It has now begun to increase its range on Oahu, and I saw two birds at the edge of a cane field along Makakole Road in the West Beach area on November 4, 1973. Nine males and six females were seen in Kawainui Marsh on December 6, 1977 (*Elepaio* 39:20). Nothing has been published on the breeding biology of this species in Hawaii.

Warbling Silverbill
Lonchura malabarica cantans
(Color plate 59)

The native range of this popular cage bird is the dry country in Africa from Senegal to western and southern Sudan. Another subspecies occurs from Kenya to Ethiopia, and a third, from Arabia to India. The adult male and female are alike: the upper surface is brown (with narrow blackish, scalelike shaft streaks especially on the crown), shading to grayish-brown on the back; the cheeks are brown with a sandy-rufous tinge; the chin and throat are sandy or rufous-brown, shading to buff or white on the lower throat and breast; the wing feathers are dark brown, but the under wing coverts and lining of the wing are pale cinnamon-buff; the rump and upper tail coverts are black; the tail is sepia brown, the middle tail feathers are elongated and taper to a point; the eye is black, the upper mandible is slate colored, the lower mandible is light blue, the legs and feet are pale gray. Two males collected in Hawaii measured 4.25 inches in length; one female, 4.00 inches. Immature birds are uniformly pale brown above, the rump is brown, and the central tail feathers are not elongated.

This species was first reported in Hawaii by Berger (1975b) who found a large population on the leeward slope of Kohala Mountain (Hawaii) during 1974 (fig. 124). This species later was found at Pohakuloa; flocks totalling "hundreds of birds" were seen in both North Kohala (Mahukona) and South Kohala (Waikoloa) during February 1978 (*Elepaio* 39:20). Dr. P. Quentin Tomich sent me the skin of a Warbling Silverbill that he had found dead in a water tank at an elevation of 2,200 feet in the Puuanahulu Game Management Area on May 2, 1972. It is assumed that this species was first liberated on the Puuwaawaa ranch, but no details are available. During December 1978, some 40 silverbills were found in kiawe thickets below Ulupalakua, Maui (*Elepaio* 39:89) and several were seen on Lanai during 1979 (*Elepaio* 40:119).

Silverbills build a relatively large, domed nest of grasses with an entrance on one side. A nest in Africa was described as "being composed of the upper stems of seedling grass about six inches in length, with a bedding of multitudinous white flake-like seeds and a few white feathers." I also found the nests to be lined with grass heads and feathers (fig. 125). I found nests in February, March, April, and November, which were the months that I visited Hawaii. The breeding season undoubtedly is longer than six months. Most of the nests I found were built in kiawe trees, sometimes even in a dead tree with no leaves at all. The eggs are immaculate white. Clutches of eight nests varied from 3 to 8 and averaged 5.5 eggs per nest. A nest that I found under construction on March 23, 1974, was being built directly above an active wasp nest; when completed, the entrance to the silverbill nest was located less than three inches from the wasp nest.

Like the other species of waxbills and finches, the

FIGURE 124. Nesting habitat of the Warbling Silverbill, near Kawaihae, Hawaii. April 10, 1974. The arrow points to a nest.

FIGURE 125. Nest of the Warbling Silverbill opened to show the eggs and the lining of fine grasses and grass heads. April 10, 1974.

silverbill is primarily a seed-eating bird. Hence, the tremendous populations of these birds will make impossible the growing of small grain crops on Hawaii.

Spotted Munia or Ricebird
Lonchura punctulata
(Color plate 61)

The Spotted Munia has a wide distribution in Ceylon, India, Nepal, Burma, and southward into Malaysia and the Indo-Chinese region, and in the Philippines. The species was introduced to Hawaii by Dr. William Hillebrand about 1865. Caum (1933) wrote that this species "feeds on the seeds of weeds and grasses and does considerable damage to green rice." As of 1933, Caum reported that the Ricebird was "not particularly common in districts where rice is not grown." Rice is no longer grown in Hawaii, but the Ricebird is now a common species on all of the main islands. This species also is called the Spice Bird, Spice Finch, Nutmeg Finch, and Scaly-breasted Munia.

The head, neck, and throat are chocolate brown. The back, wings, and tail are brown, often with buffy streaks. The breast, sides, and abdomen are white to buffy; all except the center of the abdomen is marked with brownish crescents. The nonbreeding plumage is duller. The sexes are essentially alike. Total length is about 4 inches.

Pekelo (1963b) described two albinistic Ricebirds, with all-white plumage, on Molokai in 1963.

Ricebirds are highly gregarious, and flocks of a hundred or more are not uncommon at certain times of the year. The birds feed largely on the seeds of grains, grasses, rushes, and weeds. They were a pest when rice was grown in Hawaii. Richardson and Bowles (1964) found them feeding in plum trees, "apparently eating the fruit." Ricebirds do not have a true song but utter rather plaintive cheeps and chirrups.

A thorough study of the behavior and biology of the Ricebird in Hawaii should be very interesting and revealing, in part because the species has never been studied intensively in its native habitat. The species seems to be highly erratic, indicated by its seasonal and annual distribution: it is present in large numbers in certain areas during one year and scarce or even absent in others. In the Kokee area of Kauai, for example, I found four nests during April and May 1967, but I found none in 1968. Eddinger found none in 1969 although he worked in the area daily from February to June.

Richardson and Bowles pointed out that Ricebirds on Kauai are "seen under extremely diverse conditions, as along the uppermost Koaie River (3,750 feet) and in dry Milolii Canyon near sea level. They were common usually in high-grass clumps along roads or by clearings in the Kokee region, and also in the grasses beside the innumerable roads of sugarcane fields. Ricebirds appear to occur in virgin forest areas rarely, except along open stream beds, . . . roads and jeep trails." Ricebirds often are found in residential areas.

On the island of Hawaii, I have found the Ricebird from sea level to at least 7,500 feet elevation on Mauna Kea. On Maui, I have seen the species at sea level and near Paliku cabin in Haleakala Crater.

I have found the Ricebird to be common in dry regions where the rainfall averages 20 inches or less annually: for example, Barking Sands, Kauai; Barbers Point, Oahu; and Makena, Maui. They occur sporadically on the Kaohe Game Management Area on Hawaii, where the annual rainfall varies from about 15 to 40 inches. By contrast, I have found the Ricebird in extremely wet areas, such as the Kokee region of Kauai, near the head of Manoa Valley on Oahu, the Waikamoi Stream area at 4,000 feet elevation on Maui, and at a similar elevation along the Saddle Road on Hawaii.

Spotted Munias nest throughout the year in Hawaii, although we do not have enough data to determine if there is any variation in the breeding season from year to year. I have found active nests in every month except August, and a nest with large young I watched on September 19, 1974, must have been built in August. One or more pairs of Ricebirds built a series of five nests in the same small mango tree in the Woodlawn area of Honolulu where I lived for a year. The first nest was built in September (1967), the fifth, in May (1968). The latter nest held five feathered nestlings on June 12.

In the dry areas, Ricebirds commonly build their nests in kiawe, whose heavy thorns discourage climbing of the trees in order to check nest contents. In the Kaohe Game Management Area on Mauna Kea, I have found the nests in aalii and in mamani. On Kauai I have found them in ohia trees. The nests commonly are built 15 to 20 feet above the ground, often higher and sometimes lower. I found one nest 5.7 feet from the ground in a mango tree and one about 5 feet up in an aalii shrub. I have seen nests in monkeypod, banyan, and kukui trees and in a mock orange bush. Peggy Kai told me of a nest she watched being built from July 31 to August 2, 1974, in a camelia tree near Volcanoes National Park.

The large, grass nests are roughly retort shaped, and often have their small entrance at the end of the slightly downward-directed neck of the nest. This configuration makes it difficult to check the contents of the nest without damaging it or its eggs. Consequently, I have not checked the contents of all the active nests I have found. I have seen nests containing from three to six eggs and others containing four or five nestlings. Several females undoubtedly were responsible for the 12 eggs that Charles van Riper, III, found in a nest on Kauai during June 1971. Sandra J. Guest and I have found roof rats several times in nests of the Spotted Munia on the university campus, and van Riper (1974a) told of rats using nests on Hawaii. Mice and other small animals often usurp bird nests in North America (Berger 1971).

Ricebirds use their old nests as dormitories for roosting after the young have fledged. I had an opportunity to observe this behavior repeatedly during the winter of 1967/1968 at the Woodlawn nests mentioned above. The nestlings left one of the nests during the third week of March. From four to six Ricebirds used this nest as a dormitory for at least a month. The birds would fly into the tree shortly after sunset, perching from 10 to 30 seconds before quickly entering the nest. On April 12, two birds flew into the tree at 6:42 P.M.; at 6:46, two more arrived. At 6:00 A.M. on April 14, one bird was perched in the top of the tree preening itself. At

6:10, four Ricebirds left the nest in rapid succession and flew off. The following day, five birds left the nest, one after the other, beginning at 6:04 A.M.

Black-headed Munia
Lonchura malacca atricapilla
(Color plate 62)

This race of the Black-headed Munia is native to northeastern India, Burma, and northwestern Yunnan. There are nine other races which have a range extending from the Philippines to Java. This species also is called the Chestnut Mannikin, Black-headed Nun, Black-hooded Nun, and Black-headed Mannikin.

Both sexes have a black head, throat, and upper breast. The rest of the plumage is tawny brown to chestnut. The bill is pale blue to horn colored. The legs and feet are gray. Immature birds lack the black hood and have a darker bill. Length is 4 inches. The nominate race *(L. m. malacca),* Southern Black-headed Munia or Tricolored Munia, has a white breast and flanks. It, too, is a popular cage bird, often called the Tricolored Nun or Three-colored Mannikin (see Appendix B).

Udvardy (1960a) first reported the successful establishment of this species as a breeding bird in Hawaii. He observed 10 adults and 15 juvenile birds near West Loch, Pearl Harbor, on April 26, 1959.

E. H. Bryan, Jr., informed Udvardy that the Black-headed Mannikin was brought to Hawaii as a cage bird between 1936 and 1941. Udvardy saw birds in two Honolulu pet shops in 1959, and was told that the birds had been imported from Calcutta, India.

The birds frequent kiawe thickets and open grassy areas along roads between sugarcane fields in the vicinity of West Loch. Udvardy watched the birds come to a waterhole about every 40 minutes during a two-hour period. An estimated 900 birds were seen in this area on March 6, 1972 (*Elepaio* 38:56).

Donaghho (1967) reported that he observed Black-headed Mannikins along the road to Palehua at the southern end of the Waianae Mountains. The species has continued to expand its range. Adults feeding young were seen at Salt Lake in 1972; I found a dozen birds, including adults and immature birds, in the West Beach area during November 1973; Virginia B. Cleary saw a flock of some 20 birds near her home in Mililani Town on February 21, 1977; one bird was collected near Laie by Delwyn Berrett.

Black-headed Munias were first seen on Kauai in 1976; Pratt (1977) saw between 40 and 50 birds in the Poipu Beach area during May 1977. R. Yorke Edwards wrote to me (January 31, 1978) of seeing a flock of 80 Black-headed Munias at the end of the road beyond the Coast Guard Station on January 10, 1978.

This munia frequents golf courses, grassy roadsides, the weedy margins of cane fields, and anywhere that grass seeds are available. The birds have the notable behavior of flushing rapidly, flying upward, and then dropping downward quickly into the cane or other vegetation, where it is impossible to see them. The nest has not been described in Hawaii.

Java Sparrow
Padda oryzivora
(Color plate 63)

This species is thought to have been endemic to Java and Bali, but it was introduced to many areas, from the Philippines to Ceylon. The male has a black head with two large, white ear or cheek spots; the belly is brownish gray to vinaceous; the rest of the plumage is pearl gray. The bill is pinkish white; the legs and feet are flesh colored. Length is 5 inches. Females tend to be smaller in size and have a smaller bill. Immature birds are mouse-gray above, the wings and tail being darker; they have buffish underparts, being grayer on the breast. The iris is reddish and the orbital skin is pink in the adult male; in the immature male, the iris is brownish gray, the orbital skin, grayish pink. This is the Paddy Ricebird and Java Ricebird in the East.

Caum (1933) wrote that this species may have been introduced to Hawaii about 1865 by Dr. William Hillebrand and that the species also may have been brought in about 1900. When released in the wild, the birds did not survive.

One Java Sparrow was seen on the grounds of the Bishop Museum, in Honolulu, on July 22, 1964, and two were seen at Fort Shafter during August 1965. Throp (1969) reported that Java Sparrows nested and raised young on Diamond Head during late 1968 or early 1969. The increase in numbers and the range expansion since that time have been phenomenal (Berger 1975d). I saw a dozen birds, including five juveniles, at the Diamond Head tennis courts on December 21, 1971. They were first seen on the university campus during January 1973; they reached upper Manoa Valley by November of 1974. Virginia B. Cleary saw one bird on Harding Avenue (near KAIM radio station) on December 21, 1974. I saw three birds on the grounds of Iolani Palace during October 1975. Peggy Kai wrote that she first saw Java Sparrows in Nuuanu Valley on December 21, 1976. A flock of more than 100 birds came to a feeder on Prospect Street (slopes of Punchbowl Crater) on September 28, 1978 (*Elepaio* 38:105).

In Hawaii the Java Sparrow begins to nest in the fall and continues throughout the winter. I have seen juvenile birds from November to April: November 24 (1973), December 2 (1976), December 10 (1974), December 22 (1971), January 11 and 22 (1979), February 23 (1977), March 16 (1974), April 14 (1976), and April 27 (1972).

Lawrence T. Hirai watched a pair of Java Sparrows carrying nesting material at Klum Gymnasium on the university campus on November 21, 1976; the nest was being built in a space between the roof and the wall of the building. Gordon Mark hand-raised a nestling Java Sparrow that had fallen out of its nest on December 10, 1976; this nest had been built in a horizontal pipe of the old engineering building on the campus. I visited this area on December 15, 1976, and heard nestlings calling from another nest that had been built in an unused electrical outlet.

SUBFAMILY VIDUINAE
(WIDOWBIRDS, WHYDAHS, AND COMBASSOUS)

This small African group contains some striking species that do not build a nest but lay their eggs in the nests of other species, usually those of waxbills and their relatives. Knowledge of these parasitic weaverbirds was summarized by Friedmann (1960). Sexual dimorphism is marked, the females tending to be brownish, whereas the males of most species are brightly colored, with very long tails during the breeding season. The nestlings are unusual in the nature of the directive marks on the palate and the tongue; some of these contrast with the background color of the palate whereas other globular structures are so highly reflective that they appear to be luminescent. Presumably these stimulate the host species to feed the young birds.

Pin-tailed Whydah
Vidua macroura
(Color plate 60)

The Pin-tailed Widowbird or Pin-tailed Whydah is native to most of Africa, from Senegal and Ethiopia southward to the Cape Province. It inhabits bushy areas and open scrub land with scattered trees, from sea level to about 7,500 feet elevation. Males have a black and white plumage, a red bill, and, during the breeding season, two pairs of very long (more than 9 inches) tail feathers. A postnuptial molt produces an eclipse plumage in which the male develops a female-like plumage of streaked brown, rufous, black, and white and with a tail only some two inches in length. Bill color changes from salmon pink to brown during the year in the female. The males perform elaborate dance-flights in their courtship of the females.

The Pin-Tailed Widowbird was first reported in the wild on Oahu by John Bowles near the Waikiki Aquarium during June of 1962. Birds were next reported during the 1969 Christmas Count of the Hawaii Audu-

bon Society when seven birds were seen. They have been seen regularly in Kapiolani Park and on the slopes of Diamond Head since that time, as many as 15 birds during December 1972 and April 1974, and 10 birds during May 1975. One male was reported at Ewa Beach on September 16, 1972, and I saw a male in breeding plumage on the university campus on July 19, 1973.

The birds have bred successfully in Hawaii, but we have no records of eggs or of the host species. I saw a male with a short tail in company with nine other birds in female and juvenile plumage on April 21, 1974, at the Waikiki Natatorium; I saw 10 birds there, all in female plumage, on March 2, 1975. The usual hosts for the Pin-tailed Whydah in Africa are thought to be waxbills and mannikins. If the Whydah is unable to change hosts here, it may well die out.

SUBFAMILY PASSERINAE
(SPARROW WEAVERS)

This is a small, Old World group with 37 species. Most of its species are highly gregarious. The Sociable Weaver, already mentioned, is a member of this group. It engages in the extreme example of cooperative nest building. A few species are solitary nesters. A number do not weave nests at all but build bulky and untidy nests. These may be built in crevices among rocks, in holes or on branches in trees, or in buildings. Song is poorly developed in most species, but the birds often are noisy, chirping and chattering loudly. The House Sparrow has been introduced into many parts of the world, and the European Tree Sparrow (*Passer montanus*) was introduced into Australia and North America (Missouri and Illinois).

House Sparrow
Passer domesticus

The House Sparrow, also called the English Sparrow, is native to Europe and northern Asia. Its range extends from Lapland to Britain and Spain; eastward through the Balkans to Russia and Siberia; southward to northern Mongolia and Manchuria. It has been introduced to North, Central, and South America, southern Africa, Australia, New Zealand, and to many islands.

The male in breeding plumage has a gray crown, white cheeks, black chin and throat or "bib," and a chestnut nape; the upperparts are brown, streaked with buff and black; the underparts are grayish white. Females and immature birds are brownish above and gray-white below; both have a dull grayish eye-stripe, and both lack the white cheeks and the black bib. Total length averages about 5.75 inches.

Johnston and Selander (1964; and Selander and Johnston 1967) studied evolution in the Hawaiian House Sparrows. They found that these birds "are very distinctive in color, being unlike specimens from English, German, and North American localities. They are characterized by a reduced value of the dark markings of the plumage, a general absence of fine streaks on the under parts, and an overall rufous-buff color which is especially intense on the breast and flanks. The legs and feet tend strongly to be pale buff in color rather than dark brown as in continental birds." They also found that the bill averages longer in the birds from Honolulu than in the continental birds.

Caum (1933) reported that nine House Sparrows were imported from New Zealand and released in Honolulu in 1871, and that "whether or not there were further importations is not known, but the species was reported to be numerous in Honolulu in 1879."

After its release in Brooklyn, New York, in 1852 and 1853, the House Sparrow multiplied and spread so rapidly that it became a serious nuisance, and many thousands of dollars were spent in attempting to control the population. This phenomenon did not occur in Hawaii, and Caum considered the House Sparrow "if anything, rather useful."

The House Sparrow is basically an associate of man. It is most common in metropolitan areas. Indeed, in very large cities, the only birds that many people ever see are House Sparrows and pigeons. The House Sparrow also is found in rural areas and in the mountains but usually only around human habitation. The species is omnivorous, eating seeds, insects and their larvae, and table scraps. House Sparrows and Barred Doves are common species in open restaurants in Waikiki and in resort areas on the other islands. A study of the food habits of Mainland sparrows revealed that the diet of the adults consists of about 96 percent vegetable matter and 4 percent animal matter, whereas the nestlings were fed more animal matter (68 percent) than plant material (32 percent). The sparrows seem to be far less aggressive in Hawaii than on the Mainland. They do not have a true song, but utter a wide variety of nonmusical chirps.

So ubiquitous is the House Sparrow that it has attracted little attention from ornithologists, either in Hawaii or on the mainland, and the annual cycle has not been studied thoroughly even in North America.

The House Sparrow is noted for building its nest in nearly any nook and cranny that is large enough, and it is readily attracted to nesting boxes on the mainland. As a weaver sparrow, however, it also builds large nests of grasses, often lined with feathers, in trees; and this seems to be a special propensity of sparrows in Hawaii. These are globular, domed nests with a side opening. In Hawaii the birds nest in the tops of palm trees, pandanus trees, and a wide variety of other species. At Pohakuloa, Hawaii, a colony nests in the naio trees around the park buildings; one nest there held three eggs on April 14, 1967. Four eggs hatched on March 5, 1972, in a nest on the university campus. I observed copulation on March 13, 1972. I have found nests with nestlings as late as August 19 (1971). At Pohakuloa, I found 12 sparrows roosting in a single naio tree on the night of July 16, 1967.

The House Sparrow in Hawaii undoubtedly is multibrooded, and as a species it may nest throughout the year, but only a concerted study will show if this is so. Mainland House Sparrows lay clutches of three to seven eggs. The background color is greenish white to brownish, often heavily covered with tan, dark brown, or black spots and splotches (fig. 126). The last egg in the clutch often has a much different pattern than the others.

Guest (1973a) once saw a House Sparrow kill nestling White-eyes and probably break the eggs in a second nest. Three of nine House Sparrows captured on Oahu were found to be infected with the malarial parasite *Plasmodium cathemerium* (Navvab Gojrati 1970). This was the first record for this species of *Plasmodium* from any Pacific island. Smith and Guest (1974) found House Sparrows parasitized by coccidia and a species of tapeworm.

FIGURE 126. Three eggs of the House Sparrow; Pohakuloa, Hawaii. April 13, 1967.

FAMILY FRINGILLIDAE
(SPARROWS, CARDINALS, AND BUNTINGS)

This large (over 400 species) family has representatives in both the Old World and the New World, but it is believed to have originated in the New World. The species have nine functional primary flight feathers, and are closely related to a number of other nine-primaried New World families, as well as to the Ploceidae. Taxonomists have included three or four subfamilies in the Fringillidae, although the latest proposed system (Mayr 1968; Howell, Paynter, and Rand 1968) contains only two. I include four subfamilies for the purposes of this book: Carduelinae, Cardinalinae, Geospizinae, and Emberizinae (Van Tyne and Berger 1976). It may be noted here that the Galápagos finches, or Darwin's finches (Geospizinae), exhibit striking adaptive radiation, and that they were important in stimulating Charles Darwin's thinking which led to his theory of evolution.

All of the fringillids are solitary nesters, and most build open, cup-shaped nests. None are parasitic, and all defend a nesting territory. Many are migratory. Usually only the female incubates, but both sexes take care of the young.

SUBFAMILY EMBERIZINAE
(BUNTINGS AND AMERICAN SPARROWS)

This subfamily contains some 61 genera of birds that inhabit North and South America. They are basically seedeaters.

Saffron Finch
Sicalis flaveola
(Color plate 64)

This finch is native to South America, where it occurs in all countries except Chile. It has been introduced to Jamaica and the Canal Zone of Panama. The Saffron Finch inhabits gardens, cultivated lands, and brushland. Throughout its vast range, the bird is common in some areas but highly localized in others, and more common in tropical than in subtropical regions.

The details of the breeding biology of the Saffron Finch in its native range have not been studied. This species is unusual, however, in that it typically is thought to be a cavity nester. The birds build a nest of grasses, weed stems, and feathers in a natural tree cavity, in rock crevices, under the eaves of buildings, and sometimes in the abandoned dome nests of ovenbirds.

The Saffron Finch is popular among aviculturists. The birds are hardy, attractive (especially the males), and they readily nest in captivity if nesting boxes are provided. The eggs (usually five in a clutch) are said to have a grayish ground color, which is streaked and spotted with darker markings. Two or three broods per season are said to be raised in captivity.

The first mention of wild Saffron Finches in Honolulu appeared in the December 1965 issue of the *Elepaio*. Mrs. Harold Erdman saw this species in her yard on the slopes of Diamond Head during October 1965. The species has been seen in this area every year since then during the annual Christmas count of the Hawaii Audubon Society: 24 birds during December 1972, but only 6 birds in December 1978. Two Saffron Finches were reported at Bellows Field Air Force Station on December 17, 1972 (*Elepaio* 33:82). Birds were reported near Pearl Harbor during January 1975, and Diane Elliot told me that she saw two birds at Radford Terrace on April 21, 1975; three pairs at different localities near Salt Lake were seen during January 1978 (*Elepaio* 39:20).

The Saffron Finch also is established on Hawaii, at Kamuela, the Puuwaawaa ranch, Hualalai, and in the Kailua-Kona area. As many as 100 birds were seen in one day on the Puuwaawaa ranch, where it is presumed the first birds were released prior to 1966 (*Elepaio* 39:20; 39:75).

The first nest reported was found by Cindy Foursha at Radford Terrace on April 18, 1977. This nest was not built in a cavity, but was a cup-shaped nest placed 8 feet 3 inches from the ground in an Alexandrian laurel or true kamani tree *(Calophyllum inophyllum)*. The nest was constructed of twigs, weed stems, rootlets, and leaves (fig. 127). The second egg of a two-egg clutch was laid on April 26. The eggs hatched between 10:00 A.M. and 2:30 P.M. on May 9, giving an incubation period of 13 days. The background color of the shell was grayish white; reddish brown spots and splotches were scattered over the shell but were concen-

FIGURE 127. Saffron Finch nest with two eggs; Radford Terrace, Oahu. April 27, 1977.

FIGURE 128. Two nestling Saffron Finches approximately 24 hours old. May 9, 1977.

trated at the larger end of the egg. The skin of the newly hatched young was orange pink; tufts of grayish down were conspicuous on the top of the head and the dorsal spinal feather tract (fig. 128).

Yellow-faced Grassquit
Tiaris olivacea
(Color plate 65)

This finch is native to the Atlantic slope of Mexico southward through Central America to western Colombia and Venezuela; Puerto Rico, Cuba, Hispaniola, Jamaica, and other islands. Males are olive green, with a black breast and a yellow to orange-yellow eyebrow stripe and throat. Females are dull olive, paler below, with dull yellowish throat and "spectacles" around the eye. Length varies from 4.0 to 4.5 inches.

It was first reported in Hawaii when Douglas Roselle found several birds at Pacific Palisades during August 1974 (*Elepaio* 35:65). "At least 40 birds" were seen in this area on October 29, 1978 (*Elepaio* 38:106). This species also has been seen on Manana and Kipapa trails in the region of North and South Halawa valleys (*Elepaio* 39:20). Peggy H. Hodge said that she had seen this species in Lanikai during December 1974 (*Elepaio* 35:92).

Red-crested Cardinal
Paroaria coronata
(Color plate 54)

In Hawaii this species is called the Brazilian Cardinal. However, it is native not only to Brazil but also to Uruguay, Paraguay, eastern Bolivia, and northern Argentina. De Schauensee (1966) adopted *coronata* as the specific name, rather than *cucullata,* as used by Ord (1967) and others.

The Red-crested Cardinal has a brilliant red head, crest, and throat. The back, wings, and tail are ashy gray; the underparts are white. The sexes are alike. Immature birds differ from the adults in that they have a rusty brown head, crest, and throat. Length is about 7 inches.

This species was first released on Oahu in 1928, with additional releases being made during the following three years, all on Oahu (Caum 1933). Richardson and Bowles (1964) did not see any Red-crested Cardinals on Kauai during their studies in 1960, but this species is established there, although still uncommon; it has been reported at Lihue, Poipu Beach, Wailua Valley, and the Hanapepe salt ponds. Pekelo (1967) found this species on Molokai, and Lawrence T. Hirai saw single birds near Naha and in the Manele-Hulopoe Bay area of Lanai during 1976. There appear to be no records of the introduction of the Red-crested Cardinal to Maui or Hawaii, but the species has been seen in the Kona area.

The song of the Red-crested Cardinal is much softer and more melodious than that of the Cardinal; it has been described as sounding like *wheet-cheer-up,* which is repeated over and over (Yuen 1972). The birds are the first ones to sing in the morning in Honolulu. On June 7, 1972, and on March 22, 1979, I heard the first songs at 5:15 A.M. while it was still dark, although there was a bright moon in the sky. On the latter date, sunrise was at 6:35 A.M., the first light occurring at 22 minutes before sunrise; the second species I heard call was the Myna. I watched one cardinal sing while on its nest in a monkeypod tree at the Fort DeRussy parking lot on April 4, 1977. Singing subsides during July, and many birds tend to be quiet for several months; however, I have heard single birds sing sporadically on August 4 (1970), August 17 (1971), September 19 (1970), and several times during October (1976). A full resurgence of song, however, does not occur until November or December.

The Red-crested Cardinal is a common nesting bird on the Manoa campus of the University of Hawaii (annual rainfall about 41 inches), as well as in such drier areas on Leeward Oahu as at Barbers Point, at Waikiki, and in the Koko Head region around Hanauma Bay (fig. 129). We have seen flocks of Brazilian Cardinals on the campus on several occasions during the winter months. For example, October 24, 1966: 20 birds feeding on the lawn at the Maile Way entrance to the university; December 16, 1966: 16 birds feeding in very short grass in front of Edmondson Hall; December 30, 1966: 26 birds feeding in weeds and in vines on a fence between the University campus and Mid-

FIGURE 129. Kiawe habitat of the Cardinal, Red-crested Cardinal, White-eye, House Finch, and other introduced species at Hanauma Bay, Oahu. September 17, 1970. The White Tern nests in a crater lying behind and below the ridge on the left side of the picture.

Pacific Institute. Virginia B. Cleary saw a flock of more than 50 birds on the campus on December 29, 1971, and flocks of 100 birds have been reported near Iroquois Point, Oahu.

The breeding season lasts from mid-December at least into September. I have seen nests every month from January to September 6 (1976). C. Robert Eddinger saw a stub-tailed fledgling being fed by both adults on January 8, 1967; during most years, however, nests and fledglings are first found during February, which suggests that the onset of the breeding season may vary. The height of the season is from February through June. Nests are built in a variety of trees (e.g., monkeypod, shower trees, pink tecoma, paperbark, mango) often 25 or more feet above the ground. The eggs usually have a greenish-white background color, heavily covered with dark brown spots (fig. 130);

FIGURE 130. Nest and eggs of the Red-crested Cardinal; Manoa campus of the University of Hawaii. April 3, 1972.

one clutch that I saw had a light brown background that was almost completely covered with very dark brown spots (these eggs were as dark as those of the Skylark). The clutch usually consists of two or three eggs; I have seen only one nest with four eggs, and have never seen four fledglings with adults. The Red-crested Cardinal undoubtedly is multibrooded in Hawaii, but no studies of banded birds have yet been conducted. The incubation and nestling periods are unknown (fig. 131).

We do not know how long the immature birds retain their brown head feathers. I saw a pair of adults with three immature birds, each of which had some red feathers mixed with brown feathers, on November 6, 1965. On November 19, 1968, three of seven birds in a flock had completely brown heads. Four of 16 birds in a flock still had brown feathers on December 16, 1966. On December 30 of the same year, however, all 26 birds in a flock appeared to be in adult plumage. And yet, a brown-headed juvenile came to a feeder at my house on December 7, 1975; on December 10, 1976, I watched a pair feeding a brown-headed fledgling that begged as though it were still dependent on the adults for food.

C. Robert Eddinger has hand-raised several nestlings and fledglings in the Department of Zoology at the university. He fed them papaya and a mixture of Gerber's high protein cereal and egg yolks. Three young taken from a nest found on February 23, 1967, were essentially independent by March 19, although the birds still begged and followed him around in the aviary.

A fledgling captured by hand on June 19, 1966, was found to be parasitized by the eye nematode, which is known to infest many mynas in the Honolulu area. The infestation was acute in the young cardinal and seemed to impair the bird's vision. Eddinger tried to hand-raise this bird, but it died on June 27. Smith (1973a) found the gapeworm *(Syngamus trachea)* in a juvenile Red-crested Cardinal from the Diamond Head area; this was the first report of this parasite in Hawaii.

Sandra J. Guest told me of a mongoose she saw about 10 feet from the ground in a kiawe tree on the slopes of Diamond Head on February 19, 1972. Be-

FIGURE 131. Recently hatched Red-crested Cardinals showing the dense covering of blackish gray down; Manoa campus of the University of Hawaii. May 19, 1972.

tween 15 and 20 Red-crested Cardinals were flying around the mongoose and giving alarm notes. On another occasion, when H. Eddie Smith was trapping birds in the same area, a mongoose entered one of the cells in the multi-chambered trap in which a cardinal had already been caught.

Yellow-billed Cardinal
Paroaria capitata
(Color plate 66)

This cardinal is native to parts of Brazil, Paraguay, southeastern Bolivia, and northern Argentina, where it prefers a shrubby habitat in humid areas. The male and female are essentially alike in plumage pattern: the head and upper throat are crimson; the back, wings, tail, and lower throat are black; the underparts are white and there is a complete collar of white extending over the back of the neck; the bill is brownish pink; the legs and feet are brownish flesh colored. The Red-capped Cardinal *(P. gularis)* is very similar in appearance; but it lacks the white nuchal collar, has a black upper mandible and a flesh-colored lower mandible with a black tip.

The first reference to this species in Hawaii is that made by Brian A. Pedley who saw a bird in Kailua-Kona on November 23, 1973 *(Elepaio* 34:95). Reginal D. David wrote to me on July 25, 1975, saying that he also had seen this species in Kona. Collins found adults and juvenile birds near Honokohau pond on March 11, 1976. A long-time resident of Kona told Collins that he remembered having seen this species "since the time he immigrated in 1930." This species has since been found at the City of Refuge, at Opaeula and Aimakapa ponds, and at Honokohau boat harbor; as many as 20 birds were found at the latter site, and 10 at Opaeula pond *(Elepaio* 39:20).

C. Fred Zeillemaker saw an immature at Honokohau during June 1976 *(Elepaio* 37:65), and Patrick and Sheila Conant saw two brown-headed fledglings there on July 11, 1976. George C. Campbell found the first nest about 20 feet from the ground in a kiawe tree on May 3, 1977, at Honokohau harbor; an adult apparently was incubating at the time.

SUBFAMILY CARDINALINAE
(CARDINALS, GROSBEAKS, AND BUNTINGS)

The center of distribution of this New World group is tropical America, but several species range as far north as southern Canada and as far south as Argentina. Sexual dimorphism is strongly developed in most species, the plumage of the males being brilliantly colored and that of the females, dull colored. The males of some species not only incubate the eggs but also sing while on the nest.

Cardinal
Cardinalis cardinalis
(Color plate 54)

Also called the Kentucky Cardinal and the Virginia Cardinal, the several races of this species have a wide distribution extending from southern Ontario to the Gulf States and west to Colorado, and from southeastern California south to British Honduras.

The male is all red except for a patch of black feathers on the chin and surrounding the base of the bill. Females are yellowish brown, with varying amounts of red in the plumage. Both sexes are strongly crested, and both have large red conical bills. Length varies from 8 to 9 inches. Immature birds have a female-like plumage.

Cardinals were released several times on Oahu, Kauai, and Hawaii between 1929 and 1931 (Caum 1933; Berger 1975g). The species is now found on all the main islands. It is common in some lowland areas, and has moved upward into the mountains. I first saw this species at an elevation of about 6,700 feet in the Kaohe Game Management Area on Mauna Kea on November 18, 1967. On April 17, 1969, I found a singing male at an elevation of 7,500 feet in the same area.

The Cardinal is a characteristic bird in many residential areas, and it is found in a wide variety of other habitats. Richardson and Bowles (1964) found the Cardinal near sea level, in the very dry regions of the Na Pali Coast, at Kokee State Park, and in the exceedingly wet forest of the Alakai Swamp at an elevation of nearly 4,000 feet along the trail to Mt. Waialeale. I observed several Cardinals in both Milolii Valley and Naulolo Valley during early September 1969, and I have found a considerable concentration in the Barking Sands area on several occasions.

Cardinals begin their territorial songs by mid-December on Oahu, which suggests that that is the beginning of the nesting season. The birds begin to sing by dawn and I have heard them sing as early as 5:15 A.M. I observed copulation on February 19, 1967, but I have no records of nests prior to April 10 (1966); the latest nest with eggs was found on July 17 (1972). Clutch size in 11 nests from Honolulu was three or four eggs (average 3.4). The nests were built between 5 and 20 feet from the ground in a wide variety of plants: kiawe, haole koa, monkeypod, pandanus, ti, and wiliwili. A nest studied by Sandra J. Guest was built 12 feet from an active House Finch nest, 20 feet 6 inches from a Japanese White-eye nest, and 28 feet from a Myna nest. Another Cardinal nest was built 7 feet from an active White-eye nest, and a third Cardinal nest was built in a pandanus tree containing two active

House Finch nests, one with young, the other with eggs. (Figs. 132, 133.)

Cardinal eggs have a ground color varying from grayish white to greenish white, overlaid with spots and speckles in several shades of brown to violet gray. Four eggs in one clutch measured 17.8 × 25.9, 17.9 × 25.1, 18.1 × 24.7, and 18.2 × 24.5 mm. The incubation period in one nest was 12 days; the nestling period, 9 days. Young Cardinals are incapable of sustained flight when they leave the nest, and the adults try to coax them to flutter and climb into shrubs or trees. On two occasions (May 12, 1975; May 13, 1977), I watched adult male Cardinals come to a feeding tray and pick up seeds, which then were fed to a fledgling

FIGURE 132. Nest and four eggs of the Cardinal; Manoa campus of the University of Hawaii. May 3, 1972.

FIGURE 133. An egg and three nestling Cardinals less than 24 hours old; note the sparse whitish down feathers. Manoa campus of the University of Hawaii. May 13, 1972.

nearby. Fledgling Cardinals have a distinctive food call unlike any of the callnotes of the adults.

The Cardinal is a very common species in the dry, kiawe thickets in the Makena region of Maui. I found four nests there on April 26, 1964. Two of the nests held two eggs each, and two held three eggs each. On the island of Hawaii, I flushed a female from her nest in Kipuka Ki, Volcanoes National Park, on July 22, 1970; this nest was built about 20 feet from the ground in a slender mamaki *(Pipturus)* tree. In the Kawaihae region, I have found recently fledged Cardinals as early as March 24 and as late as August 11 (1974).

The interrelations of the Cardinal and the Red-crested Cardinal would make an interesting study. About 15 pairs of each species nest on the university campus (84 acres), and the two species occur together in many other areas.

Smith and Guest (1974) found Cardinals at Diamond Head infected with a nematode *(Dispharynx)* and an acanthocephalan *(Mediorhynchus)* parasite.

SUBFAMILY CARDUELINAE
(GOLDFINCHES AND ALLIES)

The 112 species of this group are primarily arboreal forest birds that are most numerous in the Northern Hemisphere, although a number of species are found in Africa and in South America. None is found as a native species in Australia or on Pacific Islands. The species are noted for having an undulating flight, and, at least during the later stages of the nestling period, for not removing the fecal sacs of the nestlings, an unusual characteristic for passerine birds. It is this behavioral trait that causes differences of opinion among taxonomists as to the placement of this group of birds.

Cardueline finches build compact, open, cup-shaped nests, and apparently defend only a small area around the nest; a few species nest in loose colonies. They are social birds, many sharing common feeding grounds during the breeding season and forming large flocks in the nonbreeding season.

Canary
Serinus canaria

The Canary is native to the Canary Islands, Madeira, and the Azores. Canaries were first imported to Europe as cage birds in the sixteenth century. Wild birds are olive, streaked with brown and black above and yellowish green below. Captive birds were bred for both color and singing ability.

Escaped domestic Canaries have not become established on any of the main islands. Bryan (1912) chronicled the establishment of the Canary on Midway Atoll. A pair was taken from Honolulu to Midway in March 1909; they were put into a breeding cage in January

1910. Ten young birds were raised, and these, together with 2 additional males brought from Honolulu, were released in July 1910. These birds began nesting in December of the same year. It was estimated that about 60 young Canaries were raised in the wild during the first breeding season.

Fisher and Baldwin (1945) counted 30 Canaries on Sand Island during May 1945, but they found none on Eastern Island. Bailey (1956) found "a few canaries" in May 1949, adding that, since his earlier visit there in 1913, "the ironwoods had grown to tall trees, probably giving the canaries safe places to nest, while the Laysan Finches, low nesting species, could not escape the rats." A flock on Sand Island contained 73 birds during July 1978 (*Elepaio* 39:76).

Yellow-fronted Canary
Serinus mozambicus
(Color plate 67)

This canary (called the Green Singing Finch in the pet store trade) has a wide distribution in Africa, from Senegal to the Ivory Coast and east to Nigeria and northern Cameroon. Ten subspecies are recognized by taxonomists. The underparts (including under tail coverts), axillary feathers, rump, cheek, and a line over the eye are yellow in the male; the yellow eyebrow line is bordered above and below by blackish feathers; the top of the head and neck are gray, changing to olive green on the back and wing coverts, the feathers have dark shaft streaks; the wings and tail are brownish, edged with olive; the eye is dark brown; the upper mandible is brown, the lower, horn-white; the legs and feet are dark brown. The adult female is more gray green on the upperparts, has a necklace of spots, and has paler yellow underparts than the male. Immature birds are much browner on the dorsal surface, and the underparts are dull yellow changing to brownish on the sides of the breast. Adults average 4.5 inches in length.

Yellow-fronted Canaries are easy to keep because of their seed diet, and aviculturists consider this species to be an ideal companion for other seedeaters, such as waxbills and Cordon-bleu. The Yellow-fronted Canary also is kept as a cage bird by the native peoples of Africa, where the birds are trapped in large numbers in double cages containing decoy birds.

In Africa the Yellow-fronted Canary inhabits village gardens, farms, fields, and bush country. The birds obtain most of their food by foraging on the ground. The female builds a very compact, cup-shaped nest of grasses and various plant fibers, and typically anchors it to a branched fork of a tree or shrub from about 4 to 40 feet above the ground. Three eggs form the usual clutch. The eggs are slightly glossy and apparently usually have a grayish ground color that is sparsely marked with fine orange-brown spots, but clutches of pure white eggs have been described.

The Yellow-fronted Canary was first reported on Oahu on June 7, 1964, when W. Michael Ord and Warren King saw one bird at Koko Head. Walter Donaghho saw one bird at the Na Laau Botanical Garden on Diamond Head on October 23, 1965, and 17 birds were seen in this area during the annual Christmas count of the Hawaii Audubon Society on January 2, 1966. The species is now a common resident in the Diamond Head–Kapiolani Park region of Waikiki; it also has been seen at Kawela Bay near the Kuilima hotel, some 30 miles from Diamond Head (*Elepaio* 38:106).

I watched a pair of Yellow-fronted Canaries feeding two well-fledged young at Kapiolani Park on May 20, 1974, and Erika Wilson saw adults with a fledgling there on October 28, 1974 (*Elepaio* 35:66). I found the first nest of the Yellow-fronted Canary at Kapiolani Park on November 22, 1976 (Berger 1977b). The nest was built 8 feet 7.5 inches from the ground in an Indian banyan tree *(Ficus benghalensis)*. The small nest, which was not symmetrical in shape, was approximately 65 mm in diameter and 50 mm in depth; the nest cup was 30 mm deep. The nest was attached to two dead banyan leaves that were wedged in a dense clump of live, drooping leaves in such a way that it was impossible to see the nest from below. The nest held one egg and one nestling that I estimated to be three or four days old. The egg measured 10.0 × 12.6 mm.

I found a second nest on December 10, 1976. This nest was placed on a branch of a pink shower tree *(Cassia grandis)* located approximately 50 yards from the first nest; it was 15 feet 2 inches from the ground and was partially saddled to the upper surface of a sloping branch about 1.5 inches in diameter (figs. 134, 135). The nest held two eggs on December 12; a third egg was laid later. A female was still incubating on December 30, but the nest apparently had been deserted by December 31; two eggs measured 10.2 × 13.1 and 10.2 × 13.9 mm.

Carol and C. J. Ralph found a nest under construction near the end of a horizontal branch of a kiawe tree at least 30 feet above the ground near the archery range in Kapiolani Park on January 16, 1977. I found another nest under construction in Kapiolani Park on February 12, 1977; the female was incubating two eggs on February 23, but this nest was also deserted at a later date. These records indicate a nesting season lasting at least from October to May.

Each of the six eggs that I found was immaculate white in color. Each of the nests was composed primarily of fine grass stems but covered on the outside with cotton.

FIGURE 134. Nest of the Yellow-fronted Canary; Kapiolani Park, Oahu. December 12, 1976.

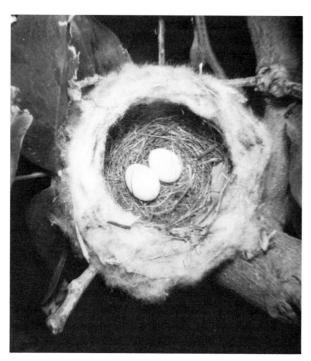

FIGURE 135. Nest and two eggs of the Yellow-fronted Canary. December 12, 1976.

Although the Yellow-fronted Canary probably was liberated on the Puuwaawaa Ranch twenty or more years ago, the first report of this species on Hawaii came in 1978 when van Riper (1978a) told of seeing a flock of 11 birds in the mamani-naio forest on Mauna Kea on December 29, 1977. Ernest Kosaka saw several

at Halepohaku (elevation 9,200 feet), and Nelson Santos saw flocks of 18 and 37 birds between Puu Kole and Puu Kaupakuhale on the following day. "Large numbers" of this canary were found on Hualalai Mountain during June 1978 by a U.S. Fish and Wildlife Service survey team (*Elepaio* 39:76).

House Finch
Carpodacus mexicanus frontalis
(Color plate 54)

The House Finch has a wide distribution in western North America from British Columbia southward into Mexico; 12 subspecies are recognized. The species also has become established in New York, Connecticut, and Massachusetts from captive birds that were released on Long Island. Caum (1933) wrote that the House Finch was introduced to Hawaii "prior to 1870, probably from San Francisco." He thought it "probably an escape from captivity." L. M. D'Albertis visited Honolulu from January 1873 until March of 1874 in order to recover from fever he had contracted in New Guinea. He collected a male House Finch during 1874, which is now in the Genoa Museum, Italy. The species often has erroneously been called the Linnet in Hawaii. Because of its fondness for ripe papaya, the bird is also known as the Papayabird.

The House Finch is a trim bird, about 5.5 inches long, with a stubby conical bill. Mainland males are brownish gray above but with a pink tinge to the back feathers and with a red rump, forehead, and superciliary line. The throat and breast are red; the gray-brown abdomen has dark stripes extending upward onto the flanks. Males in Hawaii show considerable variation, some being brightly colored like mainland males, whereas others have the red replaced by yellowish or orange-red patches. Females are described as "sparrow-like," being gray-brown above and paler and streaked below. Brush and Power (1976) studied pigmentation of House Finch feathers and noted that birds "without an adequate source of suitable carotenoids in the diet will regenerate feathers that are abnormal (usually yellow)." They found, however, no evidence of genetic geographic variation between finches from Hawaii and those in California.

The House Finch is common in cities and towns, in both wet and dry rural areas, and in the high ranch and forest lands on Maui and Hawaii. It is uncommon in the depths of the near-virgin rain forests, but it is abundant in the mamani-naio forest on Mauna Kea, as well as in partly cutover mixed ohia-koa forests.

The birds have a characteristic rapid and undulating flight, during which they utter their musical callnotes. The lengthy song has been described as "bright," "loose," and "disjointed." It is a distinctive song, unlike that of any other species in Hawaii, either native or introduced.

Despite their predilection for papaya and some other soft fruits, House Finches are primarily seedeaters, frequently also eating buds. On Mauna Kea, birds gather in large flocks to feed on pua kala or spear thistle *(Cirsium vulgare),* an introduced weed of European origin. Like many other North American cardueline species, House Finches are fond of salt, a trait presumed to be related in part to their primarily vegetarian diet.

In Honolulu some House Finches sing during late December but widespread singing usually is not heard until January. The nesting season lasts from mid-February through August. I found a nest with eggs in a small date palm in Waikiki on March 4, 1978. Hirai (1975a,b) studied the breeding biology of House Finches on the university campus from January 1972 through July 1974. He first observed nest building on February 21, 1972, and on February 10, 1973. Late nests with young were found on August 13, 1973, and August 18, 1972. He saw an adult feeding a fledgling as late as September 7. Hirai found 257 nests built in 26 different plant species. The most common nesting trees were pandanus with 41.2 percent and palms with 28.0 percent of the nests; monkeypod (7.4 percent) and fiddlewood (6.6 percent) trees also were commonly used. Nests were built from about 6 feet to 50 feet above the ground, the average being about 15 feet. The nest is built almost exclusively by the female and she may spend from 6 to 22 days before the nest is complete. The finished nest varies from being a very loose to a very compact cup. The average dimensions of 25 nests were: outer width and length, 9.5 × 12.0 cm; inner width and length, 0.6 × 6.2 cm; outer cup depth, 7.3 cm; inner cup depth, 4.2 cm; and rim thickness, from 1.0 to 4.7 cm.

Copulation follows the invitation by the female; Hirai saw no precopulatory display by the male. The eggs usually are laid before 8:00 A.M. Eggs typically are laid daily, although Hirai found five instances in which a day was skipped between eggs. House Finch eggs have a light blue background color, with black or brown-black specks or lines concentrated around the larger end of the egg (fig. 136). The average measurements of 197 eggs were: width, 13.5 mm; length, 19.1 mm; weight, 1.87 g. Clutch size averaged 4.2 eggs, and ranged from two (2 nests) to five (31 nests) eggs.

Only the female incubates the eggs, beginning after the laying of the first or second egg. The incubation period varies from 11.5 to 13.5 days, and averages 12.8 days. The egg loses 15.9 percent of its original weight before hatching. Eggs are pipped less than 24 hours before the young bird breaks out of the shell. Hatching may occur at any hour of the day or night,

FIGURE 136. Nest and eggs of the House Finch; Manoa campus of the University of Hawaii. March 19, 1972.

and the eggs in a nest hatch over a period of two or three days. The female either eats the eggshells at the nest or carries them away.

Newly hatched House Finches are helpless, blind, and nearly naked, having only some tufts of whitish down on the head and dorsal feather tracts. Both adults feed the nestlings regurgitated seeds about twice an hour. During the first third of the nestling period, the male usually feeds the female at the nest (courtship feeding), and she then feeds the young; after that the male feeds the young himself. Typically both the male and female eat the fecal sacs of the young during the early nestling period; sometimes a sac is carried away. Fecal sacs begin to accumulate on the nest rim from four to nine days after the young hatch so that the rim and sides of the nest may be completely covered with fecal sacs by the time that the birds leave the nest (fig. 137).

There is a steady increase in body weight from less than 2 g on the day of hatching to about 17 g at an age of 13 days; Hirai could not weigh the birds after that age because the young would not remain in the nest if they were disturbed. When they are ready to fledge, the young birds probably weigh about the same as the adults (19.5 g; range, 16.9 to 23.8 g). The nestling period varies from about 15 days to 19 days. The young are able to fly well when they leave the nest. Hirai wrote that the fledglings were fed by the adults for at least two weeks and that the young were independent three weeks after leaving the nest. Hirai found nesting success to be low on the university campus: 17 percent success in 1972 and 1974, and 30 percent in 1973. "Nest losses were due to: strong winds knocking eggs

FIGURE 137. Three nestling House Finches; the nest rim is fouled with the birds' fecal sacs. April 9, 1968.

and young from nests (34.7% of the total losses); predation, probably by a rat species, on eggs, young, and in six cases the nesting females (27.5%); failure of eggs to hatch because they were infertile, contained dead embryos, or were deserted (17.4%); and nestlings dying because they were inherently weak at hatching, starved to death, or became so entangled in the nest material, especially the hair used to line the cup, that they could not free themselves and were left behind when the rest of the brood fledged (20.3%)." House Sparrows also steal material from active House Finch nests and may, on occasion, kill the young.

House Finches in Hawaii not uncommonly build their nests in vegetation on the lanais of condominiums, and I have seen such nests on the eighth floor in Kahala (a nest with 4 eggs in a potted pine tree on May 2, 1973), on the twentieth floor in Kahala (a nest with 3 young in a hanging coconut planter on May 10, 1975), and on the thirty-second floor of Yacht Harbor Towers during 1976 and 1977. General and Mrs. Clarence S. Beck invited me to visit the nest at Yacht Harbor Towers on June 26, 1976, when the nest held 4 eggs. Mrs. Beck called me on March 14, 1977, to report that a female was incubating 4 eggs in another nest, and on April 18, she told me that there then were two nests (one with 4 eggs, the other with 5) on the lanai; these two nests were approximately 5 feet apart in a bougainvillea vine. Shirley Rebello wrote to tell me of a pair of House Finches that built a nest in an asparagus fern hanging on the wall of their twenty-fifth floor lanai of

Kahala Towers during April 1974; three of four eggs hatched and the young fledged.

In the mamani-naio forest on Mauna Kea, I have found nests with eggs as early as April 6 (1968) and as late as July 17 (1967). Eleven nests found there were built on horizontal branches of mamani trees; 2 nests were built in naio trees. The complete clutch was three eggs in 2 nests, four eggs in 5 nests, and five eggs in 1 nest. Although some House Finches were still incubating eggs on July 16, 1968, small flocks were roosting together. At 6:50 p.m. that day, I flushed several birds that already had gone to roost in a dense clump of naio.

Van Riper (1976) found House Finch nests in a variety of trees and shrubs on Hawaii: koa, sandalwood, kolea, Norfolk Island pine, casuarina, and pukeawe. The earliest a nest with eggs was found was on March 13 (1971); the latest, on July 14 (1972). Clutch size averaged 3.9 eggs per nest. He reported incubation periods varying from 12 to 14 days, and nestling periods varying from 15 to 19 days. Van Riper also described an abnormal House Finch nest that was more than 10 inches high; it weighed 93.5 g as compared with the average weight of 19.5 g for 12 other nests that he had weighed.

Wild birds not infrequently are injured, and Master Sergeant Marvin Parker sent me photographs of a House Finch that had lost nearly all of the upper mandible. The bird apparently was near starvation but came to a table on the lanai and actually flew up to the hand of the sergeant's wife.

Introduced seed-eating birds such as the House Finch continue to threaten the success of the much-talked-about diversified agriculture in Hawaii. The Chairman of the Board of Agriculture reported to the senate in 1972 that a study of "the bird problem in sorghum fields at Kilauea reveals that Metcalf Farms, Inc., is experiencing 30% to 50% losses due to feeding by large flocks of ricebirds and linnets. Kohala Corporation similarly reports that, because of bird predation, they were able to harvest only 10 tons of sorghum from a 30-acre planting, which was supposed to produce at least 60 tons of grains." This is a very serious loss because "of the implications it holds for the establishment of a major grain production industry on Hawaii. If the grain production industry is successful in Hawaii, it will help expand the livestock industries and eventually result in greater agricultural sufficiency for the State." A sum of $25,000 was appropriated by the legislature to attempt to control the "pestiferous wildlife." Since that time, other seed-eating birds have become established: the Warbling Silverbill on Hawaii and Maui and the Java Sparrow on Oahu.

Migratory Species and Stragglers

Several species of ducks and shorebirds are regular migrants that spend their nonbreeding season on the Hawaiian Islands. These regular migrants are indicated by asterisks in the following list.

In addition, individuals of a wide variety of species whose usual migratory flight paths do not bring them near the Hawaiian Islands have reached the islands one or more times. These birds are called stragglers, accidentals, or chance arrivals. It is assumed that most of these reach Hawaii as a result of storms and accompanying high winds. However, Rudolf Kellerman, a crewman on a Matson container ship, told me of an unidentified hawk that joined the ship near the mouth of the Columbia River in Oregon on March 25, 1977. The hawk stayed with the ship throughout the trip to Hawaii, spending most of the time on the mast but sometimes entering the hold and sometimes capturing small seabirds that skimmed the swells. The ship reached the Molokai-Oahu channel on March 31, whereupon the bird flew off toward either Mokapu, Oahu, or Molokai.

Unconfirmed or questionable sight records are not included because they add nothing of substance to the list (see Scott et al. 1978). Some species not included surely have reached one or more of the Hawaiian islands unseen by man, and it is equally certain that still other species will be recorded in the future. One also must distinguish clearly between migrants and escaped birds. For example, a Red-shouldered Hawk escaped from the Honolulu Zoo in early June 1973 and was seen in Kapiolani Park for some time after that.

No effort has been made to list all casual sight records, partly because the increased number of sightings for many species since 1965 seems to be largely related to an increase in the number of competent field observers. Dates of observations have been included for the rarer species seen on the inhabited islands through December 31, 1979.

This compilation is based on papers by Bryan (1958), Clapp and Woodward (1968), Fisher (1965), King (1967), and Sibley and McFarlane (1968); on reports in the *Elepaio;* and Atoll Research Bulletins on the Leeward Islands. The sequence of orders and families follows Van Tyne and Berger (1976).

ORDER PODICIPEDIFORMES
FAMILY PODICIPEDIDAE
(GREBES)

1. *Podiceps auritus,* Horned Grebe. Breeds in northwestern United States, Canada, and Alaska. One seen near the mouth of the Wailua River, Kauai, by S. L. Lindsey on December 26, 1976 (*Elepaio* 37:123).

2. *Podilymbus podiceps,* Pied-billed Grebe. Native to North and South America. One bird seen on a reservoir near Kilauea, Kauai, by C. Fred Zeillemaker during the period between December 14, 1974, and February 16, 1975; also November 17, 1975 (*Elepaio* 35:119; 36:115). Two at Kahuku, Oahu, and one at Hilo, Hawaii, November 1978–February 1979 (*Elepaio* 40:13).

ORDER GAVIIFORMES
FAMILY GAVIIDAE
(LOONS)

3. *Gavia arctica,* Arctic Loon. Breeds in arctic regions of North America and Eurasia. One bird seen on Salt Lake, Oahu, December 17, 1972 (*Elepaio* 33:77).

ORDER PROCELLARIIFORMES
FAMILY DIOMEDEIDAE
(ALBATROSSES)

4. *Diomedea albatrus,* Short-tailed Albatross, Stellar's Albatross. A very rare species now breeding only on Torishima in the Izu Islands. A single bird was seen at Midway Atoll during 1938–1939; one in 1940; a banded bird has returned to Midway every year since 1972; an unbanded juvenile bird stayed at Tern Island, French Frigate Shoals from November 1975 to February 1976; one at Laysan, March 28, 1976 (C. F. Zeillemaker).

FAMILY PROCELLARIIDAE
(SHEARWATERS, FULMARS, AND PETRELS)

5. *Macronectes giganteus* or *halli,* Giant Fulmar. A breeding bird on the Chatham and subantarctic islands south of New Zealand. Three sight records from Midway Atoll (King 1967).

6. *Fulmarus glacialis,* Northern Fulmar. Breeds on Aleutian, Kurile, and other northern islands. Records from Oahu, French Frigate Shoals, Midway, and Kure.

7. *Pterodroma arminjoniana heraldica,* Herald (Trinidade) Petrel. Breeds on islands of the Tuamotu, Marquesas, Tonga, and Chesterfield groups, and on Easter, Henderson, Ducie, and Oeno islands. A specimen was collected on Tern Island, French Frigate Shoals, by Roger B. Clapp on March 14, 1968.

8. *Pterodroma neglecta,* Kermadec Petrel. Breeds on islands of the Kermadec and Tuamotu groups, and on Lord Howe, Henderson, and other islands in these latitudes. One specimen was collected on Green Island, Kure Atoll, by Alexander Wetmore on April 30, 1923.

9. *Pterodroma ultima,* Murphy's Petrel. Breeds on Tuamotu, Austral, Ducie, and Oeno islands. One collected on Green Island, Kure Atoll, October 7, 1963; another on Tern Island, French Frigate Shoals, September 9, 1966.

10. *Bulweria fallax,* Jouanin's Petrel. Breeding area unknown; occurs in northwestern Indian Ocean. One collected on Lisianski Island, September 1967 (Clapp and Wirtz 1975).

11. *Puffinus carneipes,* Pale-footed Shearwater. Breeds on islands near Australia and New Zealand. Occurs at sea around the Hawaiian Islands.

12. **Puffinus griseus,* Sooty Shearwater. Breeds on islands off the coasts of Australia and New Zealand. Has been reported off Oahu, Hawaii, Laysan Island, Midway Atoll, and Kure Atoll.

13. *Puffinus assimilis,* Little or Dusky Shearwater. Breeds on the Kermadec Islands and many islands around Australia and New Zealand. One bird was collected on Sand Island, Midway Atoll, on February 18, 1963.

FAMILY HYDROBATIDAE
(STORM PETRELS)

14. *Oceanodroma leucorhoa,* Leach's Storm Petrel. Has a wide breeding range along Asian and North American coasts, south to the tropics (Ryukyu Islands and Baja California). Specimens have washed up onto the beaches of Oahu, October 26, 1964; October 31, 1966; January 5, 1967 (*Elepaio,* 25:79; *Elepaio,* 27:83); and of Green Island, Kure Atoll, May 10, 1964 (Clapp and Woodward 1968). Live birds were found on Kauai in 1977 and 1978.

ORDER PELECANIFORMES
FAMILY PHAETHONTIDAE
(TROPICBIRDS)

15. *Phaethon aethereus mesonauta,* Red-billed Tropicbird. Breeds on islands along the coasts of Central and South America. Alexander Wetmore collected an immature female at Nihoa Island on June 15, 1923. A. B. Amerson, Jr., collected a bird on East Island, French Frigate Shoals, in 1968. There are two sight records for Sand Island, Johnston Atoll, in 1957 (Clapp and Woodward 1968).

FAMILY FREGATIDAE
(FRIGATEBIRDS)

16. *Fregata ariel,* Lesser Frigatebird. Abundant in central Pacific south of Johnston Atoll. Single birds on Kure Atoll, 1967 and 1968 (Woodward 1972).

FAMILY PHALACROCORACIDAE
(CORMORANTS)

17. *Phalacrocorax pelagicus,* Pelagic Cormorant. Breeds from northern Japan along Asiatic coast to Alaska and southward to southern California. There is one record for Laysan Island and one for Midway Atoll (*Elepaio* 38:7).

ORDER CICONIIFORMES
FAMILY ARDEIDAE
(HERONS AND BITTERNS)

18. *Ardea herodias,* Great Blue Heron. Breeds in southeastern Alaska and Canada southward to southern Mexico and the West Indies. One heron was seen on Kealia Pond, Maui, by Charles G. Kaigler and Eugene Kridler on April 6, 1970.

19. *Casmerodius albus,* Great, Common, or American Egret. Breeds in mainland U.S.A. and Central and South America. Recorded on Oahu in 1944.

20. *Butorides striatus,* Green Heron. Breeds in mainland U.S.A., Central America, and northern South America. One bird seen at Kona, Hawaii, during November 1974 (*Elepaio* 35:80).

21. *Florida caerulea,* Little Blue Heron. Breeds from Massachusetts, southeastern Missouri, and central Oklahoma southward to northwestern Peru and Uruguay. A single individual has been seen on Oahu as follows (records in the *Elepaio*): September and October 1966; July 1967; September and October 1969; February and August 1970. All of these sightings probably pertain to the same bird. One bird at Waipio peninsula, Oahu, October 1976, September 1977, October 1978 (*Elepaio* 38:2; 38:102).

FAMILY THRESKIORNITHIDAE
(IBISES AND SPOONBILLS)

22. *Plegadis chihi,* White-faced Ibis. Breeds from eastern Oregon, central California east to Nebraska and south to southwestern Louisiana, Texas, and Mexico. Specimens collected on Kauai, 1872, and Molokai, 1903 (Munro 1944:133). Sight records from Kanaha Pond, Maui, 1937 (Munro 1944:133); Oahu, 1966, 1976–1979 (*Elepaio* 27:55; 38:2).

ORDER ANSERIFORMES
FAMILY ANATIDAE
(DUCKS, GEESE, AND SWANS)

23. *Anser albifrons,* White-fronted Goose. Breeds in northwestern North America and arctic Eurasia. Reported from

Hawaii, 1891; Molokai, 1895, 1978; Midway Atoll, 1962 (Fisher 1965); Hawaii, 1963.

24. *Anser caerulescens,* Snow Goose/Blue Goose. Breeds in northern Canada, Alaska, and Siberia. Reported on Maui, 1904, 1942, 1966, 1967, 1970; Oahu, 1904, 1958, 1959.

25. *Anser canagicus,* Emperor Goose. Breeds in northwest Alaska and northeast coast of Siberia. Reported from Hawaii 1903; Oahu, 1957, 1960; Kauai, 1967; Lanai, Maui, and Hawaii, 1977–1978 (*Elepaio* 39:16). Ten Emperor Geese were found on Laysan Island and Midway and Kure atolls between December 1968 and April 1969 (Clapp, Kleen, and Olsen 1969).

26. *Branta canadensis,* Canada Goose. Breeds in northwestern North America. Reported infrequently from Hawaii, Maui, Molokai, Oahu, and Midway.

27. *Branta bernicla nigricans,* Black Brant. Breeds along arctic coasts of Siberia and North America. Many records from Oahu, Molokai, Maui, and Hawaii. One bird was captured by hand on Tern Island, French Frigate Shoals, by Eugene Kridler on December 3, 1970.

28. *Anas platyrhynchos,* Mallard. Breeds in northern parts of Northern Hemisphere. Domesticated and an occasional migrant on main and Leeward islands (Bailey 1956; Fisher 1965).

29. **Anas crecca,* Green-winged Teal, Common Teal. The several subspecies have a wide distribution in North America and Eurasia. The Green-winged Teal formerly was considered a separate species (*A. carolinensis*). The females of several subspecies are indistinguishable; males are very difficult to identify when in the eclipse plumage. Hence, not all past records in the *Elepaio* are accurate. The Green-winged Teal has been seen on all main islands, on Laysan Island (1896, 1968), and Midway Atoll (1963). A Common Teal was seen repeatedly on Oahu between January 1 and March 15, 1970.

30. *Anas strepera,* Gadwall. Breeds in Northern Hemisphere. Reported on Molokai, 1902; Oahu, 1967, 1969, 1977. Eugene Kridler found the remains of a male on Tern Island, French Frigate Shoals, on December 7, 1967.

31. *Anas penelope,* European Wigeon. Breeds in Eurasia and Iceland. Reported from Hawaii and Oahu; Midway Atoll, 1965; Kure Atoll, 1964.

32. **Anas americana,* American Wigeon. Breeds in North America. Reported from main and Leeward islands; now considered a regular winter visitant.

33. **Anas acuta,* Pintail. Breeds in northern parts of Northern Hemisphere; in North America, south to Colorado, northern Arizona, and central California. A regular winter resident on the main Hawaiian islands and on Laysan Island and Midway Atoll. An adult male Pintail banded on Oahu on February 26, 1954, was recovered near Beringovaki, Russia, on May 29, 1960.

34. *Anas querquedula,* Garganey Teal. Breeds in Eurasia. Reported from Hilo, Hawaii, February and March 1961; Oahu, March 1967, 1968, 1978 (Clapp and Pyle 1968); Molokai, 1978; Midway, September 1963 (Clapp and Woodward 1968).

35. *Anas discors,* Blue-winged Teal. Breeds in North America. Reported from Maui, 1960, 1965, 1976–1979;

Oahu, 1946, 1967, 1976–1979; Molokai, 1976–1979; Kauai, 1946.

36. *Anas cyanoptera,* Cinnamon Teal. Breeds in western mainland U.S.A. and South America. A drake seen on Kauai during March and April 1975 (*Elepaio* 36:22), December 1978; Maui, 1978–1979 (*Elepaio* 40:14).

37. **Anas clypeata,* Shoveler. Breeds in northern North America and Eurasia. Reported regularly from Maui, Hawaii, Oahu, and Kauai; Laysan Island, 1966; Midway Atoll, 1963, 1964.

38. *Aythya americana,* Redhead. Breeds in western Canada and western and north-central United States. Has been reported from Midway Atoll. A female was turned over to the State Division of Fish and Game from Kailua Bay, Hawaii, in 1960; another bird was seen on Hawaii in 1961; two males, on Oahu, 1978; Kauai, 1977 (*Elepaio* 39:16); Hawaii, 1978–1979.

39. *Aythya collaris,* Ring-necked Duck. Breeds in northern North America. Reported from Maui, 1948, 1949; Oahu, 1966, 1975, 1976; Hawaii, 1978–1979.

40. *Aythya valisineria,* Canvasback. Breeds in northwestern North America. Reported from Maui, 1948, 1949, 1960, 1965; Molokai, 1964; Oahu, 1975; Hawaii, 1978.

41. *Aythya marila,* Greater Scaup. Breeds in northern North America, Iceland, Scandinavia, and northern Eurasia. There is little difference in size between the Greater Scaup (15.5 to 20 inches) and the Lesser Scaup (15.0 to 18.5 inches); the former only "averages larger" than the latter. Accurate identification of females is exceedingly difficult. Some published reports probably are inaccurate. The Greater Scaup has been reported from Kauai, Oahu, and Hawaii.

42. **Aythya affinis,* Lesser Scaup. Breeds in Alaska, western Canada, south into the western United States. A regular migrant on main islands.

43. *Aythya fuligula,* Tufted Duck. Breeds in Iceland, the Scandinavian peninsula, and northern and central Eurasia. Reported from Midway Atoll, 1959, 1963; Kure Atoll, 1963, 1964, 1965; Hawaii, 1977.

44. *Bucephala albeola,* Bufflehead. Breeds in northwestern North America. Reported occasionally from Hawaii, Maui, Oahu, Midway Atoll (1965), and Kure Atoll (1968).

45. *Clangula hyemalis,* Oldsquaw. Circumpolar breeding range. Reported on Midway Atoll, 1958.

46. *Histrionicus histrionicus,* Harlequin Duck. Breeds in eastern Siberia and northwestern North America. Reported on Laysan Island, 1906; on Midway Atoll, 1976.

47. *Melanitta perspicillata,* Surf Scoter. Breeds in northern and western Alaska and northwestern Canada. Reported from Oahu, 1959.

48. *Oxyura jamaicensis,* Ruddy Duck. Breeds in Canada and south to northern South America. Reported from Hawaii, 1952, 1966; Oahu, 1945.

49. *Lophodytes cucullatus,* Hooded Merganser. Breeds in southeastern Alaska southward into northwestern United States. Reported from Hawaii and Oahu. See *Elepaio* 37:82; 38:2; 40:15.

50. *Mergus serrator,* Red-breasted Merganser. Breeds in northern parts of Northern Hemisphere. Reported from Hawaii, Molokai, and Oahu.

ORDER FALCONIFORMES
FAMILY ACCIPITRIDAE
(HAWKS, KITES, EAGLES)

51. *Aquila chrysaetos,* Golden Eagle. Breeds in mountainous regions of the Northern Hemisphere. A single bird was first reported in Waimea Canyon, Kauai, by Gerald Swedberg on May 19, 1967; subsequent sightings have been made every year since then through 1979.

52. *Haliaeetus pelagicus,* Steller's Sea Eagle. An immature bird was photographed on Kure Atoll during February 1978; later seen at Midway Atoll (*Elepaio* 39:117).

53. *Circus cyaneus hudsonius,* Marsh Hawk. This subspecies breeds in North America. Reported from Oahu, early twentieth century and 1976 (*Elepaio* 38:2); Midway Atoll, 1964.

54. *Pandion haliaetus,* Osprey. This single species is found throughout much of the world. Seen on Oahu, 1939, 1940, 1949, 1955, 1956, 1968, 1970, 1973, 1976, 1977; Kauai, 1969; Maui, 1976–1977 (*Elepaio* 38:6); Molokai, 1973.

FAMILY FALCONIDAE
(FALCONS)

55. *Falco peregrinus,* Peregrine Falcon. Found throughout most of the world. Reported from Hawaii Volcanoes National Park, Hawaii, 1961; Oahu, 1965, 1966, 1968, 1976, 1977; Kauai, December 1975–January 1976 (*Elepaio* 37:64); Lisianski Island, 1965; Midway Atoll, 1967; Kure Atoll, 1965 (first specimen for the State; Clapp and Woodward 1968).

56. *Falco sparverius,* Kestrel. Breeds in most of North and South America. A single injured female (an escaped pet?) was reported repeatedly at Fort Shafter, Oahu, from January to March 1970.

ORDER CHARADRIIFORMES
FAMILY SCOLOPACIDAE
(WOODCOCK, SNIPE, SANDPIPERS, CURLEWS)

57. *Limosa haemastica,* Hudsonian or Black-tailed Godwit. Breeds in arctic Canada. One bird seen at Kuilima reservoir, Oahu, November 16, 1975 (*Elepaio* 37:8).

58. *Limosa lapponica baueri,* Bar-tailed Godwit. Breeds in Siberia and northern Alaska. Specimens have been collected on Oahu (1966, 1967, 1969), Laysan Island, Lisianski Island, Midway Atoll, and Kure Atoll (Clapp and Woodward 1968). Eugene Kridler saw one bird at Kanaha Pond, Maui, on October 28, 1965.

59. *Limosa fedoa,* Marbled Godwit. Breeds from central Alaska and southern Manitoba southward into North Dakota and Minnesota. One of two birds was collected on Laysan Island on October 21, 1966.

60. *Numenius phaeopus,* Whimbrel. Breeds in Arctic, circumpolar. Reported several times on Midway Atoll.

61. **Numenius tahitiensis,* Bristle-thighed Curlew. Breeds in western Alaska. A regular winter resident on the Leeward Hawaiian Chain and, in small numbers, on the main islands. Eugene Kridler saw 100 birds on Laysan Island on August 17, 1970.

62. *Tringa melanoleuca,* Greater Yellowlegs. Breeds in southern Alaska and Canada. There are sight records from

Midway Atoll and the main Hawaiian islands. The first specimen was collected on Laysan Island on October 21, 1966 (Clapp and Woodward 1968).

63. **Tringa flavipes,* Lesser Yellowlegs. Breeds in north-central Alaska and in Canada. There were four sight records from Oahu, one from Maui, and one from Midway Atoll as of 1968; numerous sightings since 1968. The first specimen was collected on Kure Atoll on August 30, 1964; birds were seen on Laysan Island on October 21, 1966, March 18, 1968, and August 13, 1970.

64. *Tringa glareola,* Wood Sandpiper. Breeds in northern Eurasia. This species was collected on Midway Atoll (1963) and Kure Atoll (1965).

65. *Catoptrophorus semipalmatus,* Willet. One seen on Oahu December 1974 (*Elepaio* 35:88); on Maui, 1976–1977 (*Elepaio* 38:6).

66. *Actitis macularia,* Spotted or Common Sandpiper. Breeds in North America. One seen on Kauai, 1975, and one at Waipio Peninsula, Oahu, 1976 (*Elepaio* 37:7).

67. *Heteroscelus brevipes,* Polynesian Tattler. Probably breeds in eastern Siberia. Also called the Gray-rumped Sandpiper, this species was collected on Eastern Island, Midway Atoll, October 30, 1964.

68. **Heteroscelus incanus,* Wandering Tattler. Breeds in Alaska and northwestern British Columbia. A regular winter resident on both the main and the Leeward islands. Some birds in nonbreeding plumage remain in Hawaii during the summer months.

69. **Arenaria interpres,* Ruddy Turnstone. Breeds in northwestern North America and northern Eurasia. This is a regular winter resident on the main Hawaiian islands and the Leeward Islands; a few birds remain throughout the summer, especially on the Leeward Islands. Eight birds banded at St. George Island, Alaska, have been captured on French Frigate Shoals; one, only four days after being banded in Alaska (Amerson 1971).

70. *Gallinago (Capella) stenura,* Pintail Snipe. Breeds from Siberia to northwestern Manchuria. A male was collected on Green Island, Kure Atoll, on January 13, 1964.

71. *Gallinago (Capella) gallinago,* Common Snipe. This species breeds in North America and Eurasia. It has been reported from Hawaii, Maui, Molokai, Oahu, Kauai, Southeast Island in Pearl and Hermes Reef, and Green Island, Kure Atoll. The report for Laysan Island (Bryan and Greenway 1944) appears to be in error (Bailey 1956).

72. *Limnodromus griseus caurinus,* Short-billed Dowitcher. This subspecies breeds in southern Alaska. The single record is of two birds seen on Sand Island, Midway Atoll, on October 30, 1964; an immature female was collected on that date.

73. *Limnodromus scolopaceus,* Long-billed Dowitcher. Breeds from northeastern Siberia to northwestern Alaska. An immature male was collected on Green Island, Kure Atoll, on October 3, 1963. Clapp and Woodward (1968) state that "from 1945 through May 1967, 15 sight records of dowitchers or long-billed dowitchers were published in the 'Elepaio.' Since none were confirmed by specimens, it is not possible to establish which of the two sibling dowitcher species the records actually comprised." Three birds on Kauai,

1975; five at Kanaha Pond, Maui, March 10, 1976 (*Elepaio* 37:65).

74. *Calidris canutus,* Red Knot. Breeds in arctic North America, east to Greenland, the New Siberian Islands, and Wrangel Island. Knots were seen on Oahu in 1961, 1968, and 1977; on Midway in 1965; and on Southeast Island, Pearl and Hermes Reef, in 1965 (the first specimen collected for the State).

75. *Calidris alba,* Sanderling. Breeds in the arctic regions; circumpolar. This is a regular winter resident on all Hawaiian islands. It occurs in late summer, fall, winter, and spring.

76. *Calidris mauri,* Western Sandpiper. Breeds in coastal areas of western and northern Alaska. There were three sight records of this species on Oahu as of 1968. Eugene Kridler saw one bird on Maui on November 16, 1970. The first specimen was collected on Green Island, Kure Atoll, on December 30, 1966.

77. *Calidris subminuta,* Long-toed Stint. Breeds on Bering Island, Komandorski Islands, Kurile Islands, and Sakhalin. One record for Midway Atoll (1967).

78. *Calidris minutilla,* Least Sandpiper. Breeds from central western Alaska eastward to Newfoundland. Least Sandpipers were reported several times on Oahu and Maui between 1963 and 1979. The first specimen was collected near Kahuku, Oahu, on March 17, 1967 (Clapp and Pyle 1968).

79. *Calidris bairdii,* Baird's Sandpiper. Breeds in northeastern Siberia and on the arctic coast of Alaska east to Greenland. The first specimens of this species collected in the central Pacific were taken on Laysan Island on September 6, 1967; another specimen was collected near Kahuku, Oahu, on August 23, 1968 (Woodward and Clapp 1969).

80. *Calidris melanotos,* Pectoral Sandpiper. Breeds on the arctic coast of Siberia and in northern North America. This species has been seen regularly on Hawaii, Maui, Oahu, Kure Atoll, and Midway Atoll. Four specimens had been collected on the main islands as of 1968, and 11 from the Leeward Islands (Clapp and Woodward 1968).

81. *Calidris acuminata,* Sharp-tailed Sandpiper. Breeds on the tundra of northern Siberia. There are many sight records for this species on the main Hawaiian islands (Munro 1944:141; Clapp and Woodward 1968; and the *Elepaio* for the years 1961–1979). Clapp and Woodward reported specimens collected on Kure Atoll, Midway Atoll, Laysan Island, and Pearl and Hermes Reef during the period from 1963 to 1966.

82. *Calidris alpina,* Dunlin. Breeds in northern America and Eurasia. This species has been reported from Oahu, Laysan Island, and Midway Atoll. Four specimens collected on Southeast Island (Pearl and Hermes Reef), Sand Island (Midway Atoll), and Green Island (Kure Atoll) were identified as *E. a. sakhalina,* a subspecies that nests in northern Siberia and winters southward through Japan to India.

83. *Tryngites subruficollis,* Buff-breasted Sandpiper. Breeds locally on coast of northern Alaska and arctic coast of Canada to Bathhurst Island. First record for the state near Kahuku, Oahu, during September 1978 (*Elepaio* 39:140).

84. *Philomachus pugnax,* Ruff. Breeds from northern Norway to southern Siberia. A specimen was collected on Green Island, Kure Atoll, on December 11, 1963. Seen on Maui, 1971; Oahu, 1977, 1978, and 1979 (*Elepaio* 38:104).

FAMILY CHARADRIIDAE
(PLOVERS)

85. *Charadrius semipalmatus,* Semipalmated Plover. Also sometimes called the Ringed Plover because of its single, dark breastband, this plover nests in arctic America. It usually migrates southward along the coast, wintering from San Francisco Bay southward. This species has been found on Oahu, Maui, Hawaii, on Midway Atoll (1967), and on Tern Island of French Frigate Shoals (1967). A specimen was collected on Oahu in 1967 (Clapp and Pyle 1968).

86. *Charadrius vociferus,* Killdeer. Breeds in North America south to Mexico. Reported from Maui prior to 1908, 1976; Oahu, 1952, 1976, 1977, 1978.

87. *Charadrius alexandrinus,* Snowy Plover. Breeds in western North America (Washington southward), Eurasia, Africa, Australia, Tasmania, and Ceylon. Reported on Oahu in 1958.

88. *Charadrius mongolus,* Mongolian Plover. Breeds in Mongolia, Kamchatka, eastern Siberia, and Commander Islands. One bird collected on Lisianski Island during 1967 (Clapp and Wirtz 1975).

89. *Eudromias morinellus,* Dotterel. Breeds in northern Eurasia. An immature female was captured in a mistnet on Green Island, Kure Atoll, on September 9, 1964.

90. *Pluvialis dominica fulva,* Pacific Golden Plover. Breeds in Siberia and arctic America. This is a common winter resident on all main Hawaiian islands, and is found from sea level to at least 10,000 feet on the mountains of Maui and Hawaii. This species also is found on all of the Leeward islands; several were seen on Necker Island in 1964 and 1967. The first migrants reach the islands in August, at which time most of the birds have some remnants of their breeding plumage, although these may be slight. Adult birds arrive several weeks before the juvenile birds. Most of the birds molt into their breeding plumage before leaving for the nesting grounds in April. Studies by personnel of the State Division of Fish and Game have shown that from 80 to 90 percent of all wintering Golden Plovers on Oahu leave for the breeding grounds by May 2. A few Golden Plovers usually can be found during the summer months, but these birds rarely attain the full breeding plumage. Johnston and McFarlane (1967) made a study of Pacific Golden Plovers that winter on Wake Island, located about 1,200 miles west of Midway Atoll. They found that, although the birds weighed more in April (an average of 153 g) than in August (133 g), the average lipid or fat storage was similar: 26.5 g in April and 22.8 g in August. Golden Plovers have been reported to fly between 60 and 70 miles per hour. Johnston and McFarlane postulate that a plover can fly 2,400 miles nonstop in 37 hours, utilizing about 18 g of fat for the required energy. They also suggest that "only a plover containing at least 18 g of lipids and weighing about 150 g will attempt the 2400-mile flight from Wake Island to the Aleutian Islands or Kamchatka Peninsula, or vice versa." They reported that plovers arriving from the north in autumn still had an average of 22 g of fat in their bodies, thus indicating

a much greater potential flight range. They stated that the fattest plovers in April "had an estimated flight range of about 6200 miles; those in August, 5900 miles; and those in December, 2500 miles." (See also *Condor* 78:144.) Studies have shown that various seeds remain viable in the intestinal tract of the plover and other shorebirds long enough to be transported several thousand miles; it has been postulated that some plant species have been transported to new areas by this method (e.g., *Science* 160, April 19,1968:321–322).

Okimoto (1975) found that the plovers are omnivorous in Hawaii, eating insects, crustaceans, snails, and various vegetable matter. He also found different populations of plovers on Oahu that have restricted home ranges, so that there is very little intraisland movement during most of the winter season. Okimoto found five kinds of internal parasites and eight kinds of external parasites; these include the first report of chiggers *(Neoschoengastia)* in Hawaii. Plovers frequently roost on the roofs of flat-topped buildings in Honolulu. Data on the breeding biology of the plover are given in *Psychologische Forschung* (1962, 26:399–470).

91. *Pluvialis squatarola,* Black-bellied Plover. Breeds from north-central Russia to northern Alaska and southwestern Baffin Island. A regular winter visitant; also reported from Laysan and Lisianski islands and from Midway and Kure atolls.

FAMILY PHALAROPODIDAE
(PHALAROPES)

92. *Phalaropus fulicarius,* Red Phalarope. Breeds circumpolarly, mainly above the Arctic Circle. This species is said to be the most abundant phalarope in the Hawaiian region, having been reported from most of the islands.

93. *Steganopus tricolor,* Wilson's Phalarope. Breeds in North America southward to the northern states. This phalarope was seen on the Waipio Peninsula, Oahu, in 1964, 1967, 1970, 1977, and 1979 (*Elepaio* 31:104); at Kanaha Pond, Maui, in August 1966 (Clapp and Pyle 1968). Two birds were seen on Kauai, August 1976 (*Elepaio* 37:65).

94. *Lobipes lobatus,* Northern Phalarope. Breeds in arctic America from Alaska to Greenland, and in the Eastern Hemisphere from Iceland to Siberia. One specimen was collected on Kauai, 1892–1893; two, on Laysan Island, March 7, 1965; one bird seen on Oahu, March 1978 (*Elepaio* 39:63).

FAMILY STERCORARIIDAE
(SKUAS AND JAEGERS)

95. *Stercorarius pomarinus,* Pomarine Jaeger or Skua. Breeds primarily north of the Arctic Circle from Greenland to Alaska and Siberia. Regularly seen over offshore waters near the main Hawaiian islands.

FAMILY LARIDAE
(GULLS, TERNS, AND NODDIES)

96. *Larus hyperboreus,* Glaucous Gull. Breeds on arctic coasts of North America and Eurasia. Specimens have been collected on Maui, Lanai, Kauai, Midway Atoll, and Kure Atoll. There are sight records for Hawaii and Oahu.

97. *Larus glaucescens,* Glaucous-winged Gull. Breeds on Komandorski and Aleutian islands and in Alaska, southward to northwestern Washington. Has been reported from Oahu, Maui, and Hawaii; the species is more common on the Leeward Islands (Sibley and McFarlane 1968).

98. *Larus schistisagus,* Slaty-backed Gull. Breeds from Kamchatka and the Komandorski Islands south through the Kurile Islands to Sakhalin and Hokkaido. An adult male in winter plumage was collected on Green Island, Kure Atoll, on March 9, 1965 (Sibley and McFarlane 1968).

99. *Larus occidentalis,* Western Gull. Breeds from northern Washington southward to western Baja California. There are several records for islets of French Frigate Shoals and Oahu.

100. *Larus argentatus,* Herring Gull. Breeds in North America south to the Great Lakes and Long Island; in Eurasia south to northern France and southern Russia; and on the Azores, Canary Islands, islands in the Mediterranean, and to the Black and Caspian seas. This species has been reported from Oahu and Maui; 12 specimens collected on the Leeward Islands were identified as *L. a. vegae,* which breeds in Siberia. Eugene Kridler saw one bird on Nihoa Island during March 1965.

101. *Larus californicus,* California Gull. Breeds in northwestern North America south to North Dakota, Utah, and Nevada. Has been reported from Hawaii (1958), Maui (1975), and Oahu (1963).

102. *Larus delawarensis,* Ring-billed Gull. Breeds in North America south to California, Michigan, and New York. Has been reported from Hawaii, Maui, Molokai, Oahu, Pearl and Hermes Reef, French Frigate Shoals, and Kure Atoll.

103. *Larus atricilla,* Laughing Gull. Breeds in North America. Eugene Kridler collected a bird on Oahu on July 26, 1968: seen on Oahu in 1977 and 1979.

104. *Larus pipixcan,* Franklin's Gull. Breeds in southern Canada and northern United States. This species has been seen at Hilo, Hawaii (May 21, 1966, by Berger), Maui, Oahu, and French Frigate Shoals; a specimen was collected from a tuna-fishing vessel about two miles from the coast of Kauai on May 30, 1958 (J. E. King 1959).

105. *Larus philadelphia,* Bonaparte's Gull. Breeds in Alaska and northwestern Canada. This species has been seen or collected on Hawaii, Maui, Oahu, Kauai, Laysan Island, and Midway Atoll.

106. *Larus ridibundus,* Black-headed Gull. Breeds in Eurasia. One record for Midway Atoll, 1976 (*Elepaio* 38:58), and Oahu, 1977 (*Elepaio* 39:18).

107. *Rissa tridactyla,* Black-legged Kittiwake. Breeds in northern Russia, Siberia, Alaska, and Greenland south to France and the British Isles. Birds have been seen, collected, or found dead on French Frigate Shoals, Laysan Island, Pearl and Hermes Reef, Midway Atoll, and Kure Atoll (*Elepaio* 40:98).

108. *Sterna hirundo,* Common Tern. Breeds in North America and Eurasia. This species is considered a "vagrant or a rare migrant" in the Hawaiian Islands by W. B. King (1967). A Common Tern banded by Frederick E. Ludwig at Alpena, Michigan, in 1960, was recovered in Honolulu on

April 25, 1961 (*Inland Bird Banding News* 49:216); the specimen is now in the Bernice P. Bishop Museum.

109. *Sterna paradisaea,* Arctic Tern. Breeds in northern North America and Eurasia. Several old (1891, 1901, 1902) records from Hawaii and Oahu. "Occurs regularly in the Central Pacific as far west as the Hawaiian Islands in moderate numbers during April and May on its northward migration" (W. B. King 1967).

110. *Sterna albifrons,* Least Tern. Breeds in North and Central America, Asia, Africa, Australia, China, Japan, and the Philippines. Reported from Oahu nearly every year during the 1970s.

111. *Sterna caspia,* Caspian Tern. Breeds locally in North America, Asia, etc. First seen on Oahu during January 1979 (*Elepaio* 40:29).

112. *Chlidonias niger,* Black Tern. Breeds in Canada and northern United States; Europe to Italy, Asia Minor, and Caspian and Aral seas. One tern was seen on the Waipio Peninsula on November 14, 1965, and a specimen was collected there on September 19, 1967 (Clapp and Pyle 1968); two terns were seen on Maui in 1965 and one, in 1978 (*Elepaio* 40:29).

FAMILY ALCIDAE
(AUKS, PUFFINS, AND MURRES)

113. *Cyclorrhynchus psittacula,* Parakeet Auklet. Breeds in Siberia, Pribilof and Aleutian islands, and Chirikof Island. Two birds were found dead on Eastern Island, Midway Atoll, in 1963 (Fisher 1965).

114. *Fratercula corniculata,* Horned Puffin. Breeds from northeastern Siberia to Alaska. About 35 dead Horned Puffins and 2 live ones were found on the Leeward Islands between January and March 1963; these were seen on Laysan Island, North Island of Pearl and Hermes Reef, Midway Atoll, and Kure Atoll (Clapp and Woodward 1968).

ORDER CORACIIFORMES
FAMILY ALCEDINIDAE
(KINGFISHERS)

115. *Megaceryle alcyon caurina,* Western Belted Kingfisher. Breeds from central Alaska south to southern California and New Mexico, east to southwestern South Dakota. A pair of these birds was found in Hakalau Gulch, north of Hilo, Hawaii, during November 1901; one bird disappeared and the other was collected (Henshaw 1902). David H. Woodside saw one Kingfisher in Waipio Valley, Hawaii, and the same or another bird in Hilo, about 1955; one near Hilo, 1978 (*Elepaio* 39:18).

ORDER PASSERIFORMES
FAMILY ALAUDIDAE
(LARKS)

116. *Alauda arvensis pekinensis,* Skylark. This subspecies breeds in northeastern Siberia, Kamchatka, and the Kurile Islands. Two birds were seen and one was collected on Green Island, Kure Atoll, on October 7, 1963 (Clapp and Woodward 1968). Fisher (1965) saw skylarks at Midway Atoll in 1961 and 1963.

FAMILY HIRUNDINIDAE
(SWALLOWS)

117. *Hirundo rustica gutteralis,* Barn Swallow. This subspecies breeds in eastern Asia south to China, Korea, and Japan. Two swallows were collected on Green Island, Kure Atoll, during September 1964; another specimen was collected on March 27, 1965. One Barn Swallow was seen on Eastern Island, Midway Atoll, during February 1964, and another, in February 1965.

FAMILY MOTACILLIDAE
(PIPITS)

118. *Anthus spinoletta japonicus,* Water Pipit. This subspecies breeds in Siberia; it migrates southward through Mongolia, Japan, and the Ryukyus. A very fat Water Pipit was collected on Green Island, Kure Atoll, on October 25, 1963.

119. *Anthus cervinus,* Red-throated Pipit. Breeds on the tundra of northern Europe and Siberia. A winter-plumaged female was shot on Green Island, Kure Atoll, on September 26, 1963.

FAMILY FRINGILLIDAE
(SPARROWS, FINCHES, BUNTINGS)

120. *Acanthis hornemanni* or *flammea,* Redpoll. One bird seen on Kure Atoll during 1977 (*Elepaio* 39:13).

121. *Passerculus sandwichensis,* Savannah Sparrow. One bird seen on Kure Atoll during 1977 (*Elepaio* 39:13).

122. *Plectrophenax nivalis townsendi,* Snow Bunting. This subspecies breeds from the Pribilof and western Aleutian islands to the western end of the Alaska Peninsula. A specimen was collected on Green Island, Kure Atoll, on March 10, 1963; one was seen on Midway Atoll during the winter of 1964–1965; another, at Kure Atoll in 1977 (*Elepaio* 39:14); one at Tern Island, French Frigate Shoals, November 1979.

Introduced and Escaped Birds
Not Known To Be Established

The information listed for the following birds is as complete as the records permit; many inconsistencies result from the absence of precise records. Also misleading are entries stating, for example, that Asian species were introduced from San Francisco (presumably from pet stores or game farms), with no further information. This list does not include birds that have been mentioned only by common name in newspapers—the "Australian Ostrich or Emu" that Mr. Taner brought to Honolulu in 1853 (*Polynesian* October 22), or the "28 little sunbirds" that Mr. Lewis brought back from Malacca in 1939 (*Honolulu Advertiser* June 7). Subspecies and color mutants are included for those birds for which accurate data are available.

One encounters many problems when dealing with the terminology for world birds because there is no single up-to-date reference. Although, in general, I have used the latest taxonomic study for each family, not all authorities agree among themselves. Consequently, in using a conservative approach in this book, I have not followed all of the latest proposed revisions.

ORDER TINAMIFORMES
FAMILY TINAMIDAE
(TINAMOUS)

1. *Nothoprocta perdicaria perdicaria,* Chilean Tinamou. Introduced to Hawaii Island from Chile in 1966 as a potential game species.

2. *Nothoprocta perdicaria sanborni,* Chilean Tinamou. Introduced to Kauai from Chile in 1966.

ORDER PELECANIFORMES
FAMILY PHALACROCORACIDAE
(CORMORANTS)

3. *Phalacrocorax carbo,* Great or Fishing Cormorant. Introduced to Lanai (Caum 1933) and Kauai (E. H. Bryan, Jr. 1958).

ORDER CICONIIFORMES
FAMILY PHOENICOPTERIDAE
(FLAMINGOS)

4. *Phoenicopterus ruber,* American Flamingo. Introduced to Kauai from Cuba in 1929.

ORDER ANSERIFORMES
FAMILY ANATIDAE
(DUCKS, GEESE, SWANS)

5. *Cygnus olor,* Mute Swan. Introduced near Hilo, Hawaii in 1920.

6. *Neochen jubatus,* Maned Goose. Introduced to Oahu in 1922.

7. *Anas platyrhynchos,* Mallard Duck. Domesticated. See also Lewin 1971 and Appendix A.

8. *Anas discors,* Blue-winged Teal. Introduced to Oahu in 1922.

ORDER GALLIFORMES
FAMILY CRACIDAE
(CURASSOWS AND GUANS)

9. *Crax rubra rubra,* Great Curassow. Introduced from Panama as a potential game bird in 1928.

10. *Penelope purpurascens aequatorialis,* Crested Guan. Introduced from Panama as a potential game bird in 1928.

11. *Ortalis cinereiceps,* Chestnut-winged Chachalaca. Introduced from Panama as a potential game bird in 1928.

FAMILY TETRAONIDAE
(GROUSE, PRAIRIE CHICKENS, AND PTARMIGANS)

12. *Pedioecetes phasianellus,* Sharp-tailed Grouse. Introduced to Hawaii in 1932.

13. *Tympanuchus cupido pinnatus,* Greater Prairie Chicken. Introduced in 1895 and before (Caum 1933).

14. *Tympanuchus pallidicinctus,* Lesser Prairie Chicken. Date of introduction unknown; was reported on Niihau (Fisher 1951; Bryan 1958).

FAMILY PHASIANIDAE
(PHEASANTS, QUAILS, PARTRIDGES, FRANCOLINS, PEACOCKS)*

15. *Oreortyx pictus palmeri,* Mountain Quail. Introduced from California in 1929 and before (Caum 1933). May be breeding on Hawaii (see Lewin 1971).

16. *Callipepla squamata castanogastris,* Chestnut-bellied Scaled Quail. Introduced in 1961.

17. *Lophortyx douglasii,* Elegant Quail, Douglas' Quail. Introduced in 1961.

18. *Lophortyx douglasii bensoni,* Benson's Quail. Introduced in 1960.

19. *Colinus virginianus,* Bobwhite. First introduced in 1906; frequently liberated during field trials.

20. *Colinus virginianus,* "Tennessee Red Quail" of aviculturists; a color phase of the Bobwhite. Introduced in 1961.

21. *Colinus virginianus ridgwayi,* Masked Bobwhite. Introduced in 1960.

22. *Cyrtonyx montezumae,* Harlequin or Mearns' Quail. Introduced in 1961.

23. *Ammoperdix grisgeogularis,* See-See Partridge. Introduced in 1959.

24. *Alectoris graeca cypriotes,* Turkish Chukar Partridge. Introduced in 1959.

25. *Francolinus pintadeanus,* Chinese Francolin. Introduced in 1961.

26. *Francolinus adspersus,* Close-barred Francolin. Introduced in 1963.

27. *Francolinus icterorhynchus,* Heuglin's Francolin. Introduced in 1961.

28. *Francolinus clappertoni sharpii,* Sharpe's Francolin. Introduced in 1958.

29. *Francolinus (Pternistis) leucoscepus,* Bare-throated Francolin. Introduced in 1958; "limited reproductive success" on the Puuwaawaa Ranch, Hawaii (Lewin 1971).

30. *Perdix perdix perdix,* Gray or Hungarian Partridge. Introduced prior to 1895 and later (Caum 1933).

31. *Coturnix pectoralis,* Pectoral Quail. Date of introduction from Australia unknown. Fisher (1951) found this species on Niihau in 1947.

32. *Coturnix (Excalfactoria) chinensis,* Painted Quail, Button Quail. First introduced from the Orient to Kauai in 1910.

33. *Rollulus roulroul,* Red-crested Wood Partridge. Introduced in 1924.

34. *Lophura (Gennaeus) nycthemerus,* Silver Pheasant. Introduced in 1865 and 1870.

35. *Gallus gallus,* Red Jungle Fowl. Introduced in 1963.

36. *Gallus sonneratii,* Gray Jungle Fowl. Introduced in 1962.

37. *Phasianus colchicus* "*tenebrosus,*" Melanistic Mutant Pheasant. Introduced in 1960; may hybridize with Ring-necked Pheasant.

38. *Phasianus colchicus colchicus,* English Black-necked Pheasant. Introduced in 1959; may hybridize with Ring-necked Pheasant.

39. *Phasianus colchicus mongolicus,* Mongolian Pheasant. Introduced in 1865 and 1880.

40. *Syrmaticus reevesii,* Reeve's Pheasant. Introduced in 1957.

41. *Syrmaticus soemmerringii,* Copper Pheasant. Introduced in 1907.

42. *Chrysolophus pictus,* Golden Pheasant. Introduced in 1865.

43. *Chrysolophus amherstiae,* Lady Amherst Pheasant. Introduced in 1932.

ORDER GRUIFORMES
FAMILY TURNICIDAE
(HEMIPODE-QUAILS)

44. *Turnix varia varia,* Painted Quail. Introduced from Australia in 1922.

FAMILY GRUIDAE
(CRANES)

45. *Grus canadensis,* Sandhill Crane. "Chance migrant or escape from captivity" (E. H. Bryan, Jr. 1958).

FAMILY RALLIDAE
(RAILS, GALLINULES, COOTS)

46. *Porphyrio porphyrio poliocephalus,* Indian Blue Gallinule. Introduced from San Francisco in 1928.

47. *Porphyrio porphyrio melanotus,* Mudhen. Introduced to Oahu "many years ago" (E. H. Bryan, Jr. 1958).

ORDER CHARADRIIFORMES
FAMILY LARIDAE
(GULLS, TERNS, AND NODDIES)

48. *Larus occidentalis,* Western Gull. "This gull has been brought to Hawaii at various times and liberated at Honolulu and Hilo, but it has always failed to persist" (Caum 1933).

49. *Larus novaehollandiae,* Silver Gull. "Several individuals escaped from the Honolulu zoo in 1924, when their cage overturned in a heavy windstorm. Although they were seen for some months thereafter flying over the harbor, they have apparently failed to survive" (Caum 1933).

ORDER COLUMBIFORMES
FAMILY COLUMBIDAE
(PIGEONS AND DOVES)*

50. *Streptopelia decaocto,* Indian Ring Dove or Collared Dove. *Streptopelia risoria* by some authors. Introduced to Kauai in 1920; to Oahu in 1928; to Hawaii in 1961 (Lewin 1971).

51. *Chalcophaps indica,* Emerald Dove or Green-winged Dove. Introduced from Singapore to Oahu in 1924.

52. *Phaps chalcoptera,* Bronze-winged Dove. Introduced from Australia to Oahu in 1922.

---

* The members of this family were introduced as potential game birds.

* Most of these species were introduced as potential game birds.

53. *Ocyphaps lophotes*, Crested Pigeon or Crested Bronzewing. Introduced from Australia to Oahu, Molokai, and Lanai in 1922. May be established on Puuwaawaa Ranch, Hawaii (Lewin 1971).

54. *Petrophassa (Lophophaps) plumifera*, White-bellied Plumed Pigeon, Plumed Bronzewing, Spinifex Pigeon. Introduced from Australia to Maui and Lanai in 1922.

55. *Petrophassa (Geophaps) smithii*, Bare-eyed Partridge Bronzewing, Squadda Pigeon. Introduced from Australia to Maui and Lanai in 1922.

56. *Geopelia cuneata*, Diamond Dove. Introduced to Oahu in 1928; to Hawaii in 1929.

57. *Geopelia striata tranquilla*, Peaceful Dove. Introduced from Australia in 1922.

58. *Geopelia humeralis*, Bar-shouldered Dove. Introduced from Australia in 1922.

59. *Leucosarcia melanoleuca*, Wonga Pigeon, also Wongawonga Pigeon. Introduced to Maui and Lanai in 1922.

60. *Zenaida (Zenaidura) macroura marginella*, Western Mourning Dove. Introduced in 1929 or 1930 (E. H. Bryan, Jr. 1958). Breeding at Puuwaawaa, Hawaii.

61. *Zenaida asiatica mearnsi*, White-winged Dove. Introduced in 1961 and 1965 (Lewin 1971).

62. *Leptotila verreauxi*, White-fronted Dove or Blue Ground Dove. Introduced to Maui in 1933.

63. *Geotrygon (Oreopeleia) montana*, Ruddy Quail-Dove, Ruddy Ground Dove. Introduced from San Francisco to Maui in 1933.

64. *Starnoenas cyanocephala*, Blue-headed Quail-Dove. Introduced in 1928.

65. *Caloenas nicobarica*, Nicobar Pigeon. Introduced from Australia to Maui in 1922; to Kauai in 1928.

66. *Gallicolumba luzonica*, Luzon Bleeding-heart Pigeon. Introduced from Philippine Islands to Kauai in 1922; to other islands, later (E. H. Bryan, Jr. 1958).

ORDER PSITTACIFORMES
FAMILY PSITTACIDAE
(PARROTS)

67. *Cacatua galerita*, Sulphur-crested White Cockatoo. Escaped from captivity on Oahu.

68. *Cacatua moluccensis*, Salmon-crested Cockatoo. Escaped from captivity on Oahu.

69. *Cacatua roseicapilla*, Galah, Rose-breasted Cockatoo. Escaped from captivity on Oahu.

70. *Ara macao*, Scarlet (Red and Blue) Macaw. Escaped from captivity on Oahu.

71. *Nandayus nendey*, Black-hooded Parakeet or Conure. Escaped from captivity on Oahu; four birds seen at Fort Shafter during May 1971 (*Elepaio* 31:118).

72. *Myiopsitta monachus*, Monk or Quaker Parakeet. Escaped from captivity on Oahu. Two seen in Kapiolani Park during December 1970 (*Elepaio* 31:76); nine birds at Kaneohe Yacht Club during April 1976.

73. *Brotogeris jugularis*, Orange-chinned Parakeet, Beebee Parakeet. Escaped from captivity on Oahu.

74. *Amazona viridigenalis*, Red-crowned Parrot (Green-checked Amazon; Mexican Redhead). Escaped from captivity on Oahu.

75. *Amazona ochrocephala*, Yellow-headed Parrot. Escaped from captivity on Oahu; reported around the base of Diamond Head in 1969 and 1970.

76. *Eclectus (Lorius) roratus*, Eclectus Parrot. Escaped from captivity on Oahu.

77. *Psittacula krameri*, Rose-ringed Parakeet. Escaped from captivity on Oahu (*Elepaio* 33:82).

78. *Agapornis roseicollis*, Peach-faced Lovebird. Escaped from captivity on Oahu; one seen in the Diamond Head area during December 1973 (*Elepaio* 34:91).

79. *Platycercus adscitus*, Pale-headed Rosella. Introduced to Maui in 1877; survived on the slopes of Haleakala at least until 1928 (Munro 1944).

80. *Melopsittacus undulatus*, Grass Parakeet, Budgerigar, Love Bird. Frequently escapes from captivity on Oahu. Woodside and I saw four birds on Diamond Head on September 11, 1970.

ORDER PASSERIFORMES
FAMILY ALAUDIDAE
(LARKS)

81. *Melanocorypha mongolica*, Mongolian Lark. Introduced to Kauai in 1898, 1904, 1914 (E. H. Bryan, Jr. 1958).

82. *Alauda arvensis japonica*, Japanese Lark. Introduced in 1934.

FAMILY GRALLINIDAE
(MUDNEST-BUILDERS)

83. *Grallina cyanoleuca*, Magpie-lark. Introduced from Australia to Oahu and Hawaii in 1922, 1929.

FAMILY TIMALIIDAE
(BABBLERS)

84. *Garrulax leucolophus*, White-crested Laughing-thrush; origin, India, Himalayas, Burma. A pair reported breeding on the slopes of Diamond Head during 1969 (*Elepaio* 30:76). This species also was seen at Foster Botanical Garden during 1972 and 1973 and at Hickam Air Force Base during 1973.

85. *Garrulax (Dryonastes) chinensis*, Black-throated Laughing-thrush. Introduced to Kauai in 1931.

FAMILY IRENIDAE
(FAIRY BLUEBIRD, IORAS)

86. *Irena puella*, Fairy Bluebird; southeast Asia. I saw one bird on the Manoa campus of the University of Hawaii on January 26, 1970. The bird killed itself by flying into a window at Kuykendall Hall the following day.

FAMILY TURDIDAE
(THRUSHES)

87. *Luscinia (Erithacus) akahige*, Japanese Red Robin, Komadori. Introduced to Oahu in 1929, 1930, 1931 (Caum 1933).

88. *Luscinia komadori komadori*, Korean Robin, Akahinga. Introduced from Japan to Oahu in 1931 and 1932 (E. H. Bryan, Jr. 1958).

FAMILY MUSCICAPIDAE
(OLD WORLD FLYCATCHERS)

89. *Muscicapa (Cyanoptila) cyanomelana,* Blue Niltava, Blue-and-White Flycatcher. Introduced from Japan to Oahu in 1929. Reported seen in 1943 and 1950 (E. H. Bryan, Jr. 1958).

90. *Rhipidura leucophrys,* Willy Wagtail, Black-and-White Fantail. Introduced from Australia to Oahu in 1926.

FAMILY STURNIDAE
(STARLINGS AND MYNAS)

91. *Sturnus (Gracula) nigricollis,* Black-collared Starling. One bird collected by State Fish and Game personnel in Kaneohe, Oahu, April 25, 1969.

92. *Leucospar rothschildi,* Rothschild's Starling; an endangered species from Bali. One bird at Ft. DeRussy during 1976 and 1978 (Berger 1977d); died 1979.

FAMILY ICTERIDAE
(BLACKBIRDS, ORIOLES, TROUPIALS, AND ALLIES)

93. *Pezites (Trupialis) militaris,* Greater Red-breasted Meadowlark, Military "Starling." Introduced to Kauai in 1931.

FAMILY PLOCEIDAE
(WEAVERBIRDS AND ALLIES)*
SUBFAMILY ESTRILDINAE (see page 206)

94. *Lagonosticta senegala,* Fire Finch; origin, West Africa.

95. *Emblema (Steganopleura) guttata,* Diamond Sparrow ("Diamond Firetail Finch" in *Elepaio* 27:73); origin, Australia.

96. *Lonchura m. malacca,* Southern Black-headed Munia; Tricolored Mannikin or Tricolored Nun in pet store trade; origin, India. First reported at Waipio Peninsula during March 1967 (*Elepaio* 27:106); numerous sightings there since then. I saw this species near the Waikiki Aquarium on several occasions during May 1970.

SUBFAMILY PLOCEINAE (see page 206)

97. *Ploceus philippinus,* Baya; origin, India, Burma, Malaya Peninsula (see *Elepaio* 26:54; and page 206).

---

* All of these species have been intentionally or accidentally released since 1965, many on the slopes of Diamond Head (*Elepaio* 30:70–75). Many of these species and others have been released at Puuwaawaa on Hawaii.

98. *Euplectes (Pyromelana) orix franciscana,* Red Bishop or Orange Bishop; erroneously called Bishop Weaver in *Elepaio* 30:70; origin, Africa. Wild birds are red to scarlet and black; captive birds molt into a black and orange plumage. Males molt into a drab eclipse plumage once each year. First reported at the foot of Diamond Head in 1964; one or more birds are seen each year in different areas: Diamond Head, Kapiolani Park, Ft. DeRussy, and Waipio Peninsula (see *Elepaio* 38:5).

99. *Euplectes afer afer,* Yellow-crowned Bishop or Napoleon Bishop; Golden Bishop in pet store trade; origin, Africa. First reported during December 1966 near Diamond Head; seen sporadically since, often with the Red Bishop.

SUBFAMILY VIDUINAE (see page 213)

100. *Hypochera chalybeata,* Senegal Combassou; origin, Africa.

FAMILY FRINGILLIDAE (see page 215)
SUBFAMILY EMBERIZINAE

101. *Gubernatrix cristata,* Yellow Cardinal, Green Cardinal; origin, Brazil, Uruguay, and Argentina. Reported on Diamond Head in 1965; Puuwaawaa in 1966.

102. *Paroaria dominicana,* Red-cowled or Pope Cardinal; origin, Brazil.

103. *Paroaria gularis,* Red-capped Cardinal; Black-throated Cardinal (*Elepaio*); origin, South America (*Elepaio* 28:101).

104. *Passerina cyanea,* Indigo Bunting; origin, North America. Imported from San Francisco to Oahu in 1934 (E. H. Bryan, Jr. 1958).

105. *Passerina leclancheri,* Leclancher's Nonpariel Bunting; origin, Mexico. Introduced to Oahu in 1941 (20 pairs), 1947 (75 pairs), 1950 (12 pairs). Birds were released in Manoa Valley, Makiki Round Top, and at Kaneohe; birds were reported breeding in Manoa Valley in 1950, but this species did not become established (*Elepaio* 13:25; E. H. Bryan, Jr. 1958). This species also was released at Olinda, Maui.

SUBFAMILY CARDUELINAE

106. *Serinus leucopygius,* White-rumped Serin or Gray Canary; Gray Singing Finch in the pet store trade; origin, Africa. First seen at Diamond Head in 1965; as many as 37 birds seen there in later years, but not seen on the Audubon Christmas counts since 1971. One seen October 23, 1977 (*Elepaio* 38:5).

Introduced Game Birds
Known To Be Established

In writing about the "decided slump" in the Hawaiian pheasant population in the 1940s, Smith (1950) commented that "we don't know enough about the Hawaiian pheasant range and its influence on this king of game birds to say very much about what caused it to hit the skids nor about how to put it back on the track to high populations. We can say further that mainland studies of the pheasant very probably will not apply to Hawaiian birds, so that leaves the field here wide open for productive research." Now, thirty years later, we are still waiting for that "productive research" on the introduced game birds. Moreover, consideration would have to be given to what has been learned about the requirements of exotic game birds on the mainland. For example, adequate amounts of calcium in the soil and plants are necessary for reproduction in mainland pheasants (Dale and DeWitt 1958). Reproduction is inhibited in California Quail by the phytoestrogens in plants that grow during dry years, whereas these substances are not present in large amounts in plants that grow during wet years. No such research has been conducted in Hawaii. Of the approximately 80 species of potential game birds that have been released in Hawaii, the following have established breeding populations. Colored illustrations of these are found in the book by Berger (1977f).

ORDER GALLIFORMES
FAMILY PHASIANIDAE

1. *Lophortyx c. californicus,* California Valley Quail. Introduced prior to 1855.

2. *Lophortyx c. brunnescens,* California Coast Quail. Introduced prior to 1855. This is an abundant species on Hawaii, Maui, Molokai, and Kauai. On Hawaii it occurs from sea level to at least 8,000 feet on Mauna Kea. The two races apparently have interbred on some islands.

3. *Lophortyx gambelii,* Gambel's Quail. Introduced to Kahoolawe in 1928; to other islands, in 1958. Now occurs on Hawaii, Lanai, and Kahoolawe.

4. *Bambusicola t. thoracica,* Chinese Bamboo Partridge. Introduced to Maui in 1959; to Hawaii in 1961. Now believed to be established in the Kula region of Maui.

5. *Alectoris chukar,* Chukar. First introduced from the Orient to Oahu in 1923; later to other islands. Now established on all main islands.

6. *Alectoris b. barbara,* Barbary Partridge. Introduced in 1958. May be established on Hawaii.

7. *Francolinus pondicerianus interpositus,* North Indian Gray Francolin. Introduced from India in 1959. Now well established on Hawaii, Maui, Molokai, and Lanai.

8. *Francolinus f. asiae,* Indian Black Francolin. Introduced from India in 1959. Well established on Hawaii, Maui, Molokai, and Kauai.

9. *Francolinus e. erckelii,* Erckel's Francolin. Native to Africa; introduced from a mainland game farm in 1967. Now established on Hawaii, Maui, Lanai, Oahu, and Molokai.

10. *Coturnix c. japonica,* Japanese Quail. Introduced from the Orient in 1921. Now found on all main islands. This is the migratory quail of the Bible. It has been introduced to 18 mainland states, but failed to become established in any.

11. *Lophura leucomelana,* White-crested Kaleej Pheasant. Native to the Himalayan foothills in India eastward into Nepal, and from southern China southward to Burma and Thailand. Introduced to the Puuwaawaa Ranch on Hawaii in 1962 (Lewin 1971). The population has spread to other parts of North Kona (Kahaluu Forest Reserve, Kaloko Mauka subdivision) and to the windward slopes of Mauna Loa (e.g., Keahou Ranch, ohia forests along Stainback Highway) and Mauna Kea.

12. *Phasianus colchicus,* Ring-necked Pheasant. Several subspecies have been introduced since 1865. Now found on all main islands.

13. *Phasianus v. versicolor,* Japanese Green Pheasant (also called Blue Pheasant). Introduced prior to 1900. Found on all main islands except Oahu; interbreeds with Ring-necked Pheasant.

14. *Pavo cristatus,* Indian Peafowl. First introduced in 1860. Occurs on all main islands except Lanai.

FAMILY NUMIDIDAE

15. *Numida meleagris galeata,* Guineafowl. Liberated from domestic stock on several islands since 1874. Established on private lands.

FAMILY MELEAGRIDIDAE

16. *Meleagris gallopavo,* Domestic Turkey. First introduced about 1815.

17. *Meleagris gallopavo intermedia,* Rio Grande Turkey. Introduced from Texas in 1962.

ORDER COLUMBIFORMES
FAMILY PTEROCLIDAE

18. *Pterocles exustus erlangeri,* Indian Sandgrouse. Introduced from India as a potential game bird in 1961. A breeding population occurs in the Waimea plains area of Hawaii.

FAMILY COLUMBIDAE

19. *Columba livia,* Rock Dove, Feral Pigeon.
20. *Streptopelia c. chinensis,* Lace-necked Dove.
21. *Geopelia s. striata,* Barred Dove.
22. *Zenaida macroura marginella,* Western Mourning Dove. Established in the North Kona region.

Literature Cited

Abou-Gabal, M., and M. Atia
1978   Study of the role of pigeons in the dissemination of *Cryptococcus neoformans* in nature. Sabouraudia 16:63–68.

Ali, Salim, and S. D. Ripley
1971   Handbook of the Birds of India and Pakistan, vol. 6, 1971, 245 pp. Oxford University Press, London.
1972   Handbook of the Birds of India and Pakistan, vol. 7, 1972, 236 pp. Oxford University Press, London.

Alicata, J. E.
1964   Parasitic Infections of Man and Animals in Hawaii. University of Hawaii College of Tropical Agriculture, Technical Bull. No. 61.
1969   Parasites of Man and Animals in Hawaii. S. Karger, Basel, Switzerland.

Allen, G. R., and A. L. Lum
1972   Seasonal abundance and daily activity of Hawaiian Stilts *(Himantopus h. knudseni)* at Paiko Lagoon, Oahu. Elepaio 32:111–117.

Amadon, Dean
1950   The Hawaiian Honeycreepers (Aves, Drepaniidae). Bull. Amer. Mus. Nat. Hist. 95:151–262.

Ambedkar, V. C.
1964   Some Indian Weaverbirds: A Contribution to Their Breeding Biology. University of Bombay, Bombay, India, 75 pp.

Amerson, A. B., Jr.
1966   *Ornithodoros capensis* (Acarina: Argasidae) infesting Sooty Tern *(Sterna fuscata)* nasal cavities. Jour. Parasitology 52:1220–1221.
1967   Incidence and transfer of Rhinonyssidae (Acarina: Megostigmata) in Sooty Terns *(Sterna fuscata)*. Jour. Med. Ent. 4:197–199.
1971   The natural history of French Frigate Shoals, Northwestern Hawaiian Islands. Atoll Research Bull. No. 150, 383 pp.

Amerson, A. B., Jr., R. B. Clapp, and W. O. Wirtz, II
1974   The natural history of Pearl and Hermes Reef, Northwestern Hawaiian Islands. Atoll Research Bull. No. 174, 306 pp.

Ashmole, M. J., and N. P. Ashmole
1967   Notes on sea-birds. 20. Notes on the breeding season and food of the Red-footed Booby *(Sula sula)* on Oahu, Hawaii. Ardea 55:265–267.

Ashmole, N. P.
1962   The Black Noddy *Anous tenuirostris* on Ascension Island. Part 1. Ibis 103b:235–273.
1963   The biology of the Wideawake or Sooty Tern *Sterna fuscata* on Ascension Island. Ibis 103b:297–364.
1965   Adaptive variation in the breeding regime of a tropical sea bird. Proc. Nat'l. Acad. Sci. 53:311–318.
1968a Breeding and molt in the White Tern *(Gygis alba)* on Christmas Island, Pacific Ocean. Condor 70:35–55.
1968b Body size, prey size, and ecological segregation in five sympatric tropical terns (Aves: Laridae). Syst. Zool. 17:292–304.

Ashmole, N. P., and M. J. Ashmole
1967   Comparative feeding ecology of sea birds of a tropical oceanic island. Peabody Mus. Nat. Hist. Bull. 24, Yale University.

Atkinson, I. A. E.
1977   A reassessment of factors, particularly *Rattus rattus* L., that influenced the decline of endemic forest birds in the Hawaiian Islands. Pacific Sci. 31:109–133.

Au, Steven, and Gerald Swedberg
1966   A progress report on the introduction of the Barn Owl *(Tyto alba pratincola)* to the island of Kauai. Elepaio 26:58–60.

Austin, O. L., Jr.
1961   Birds of the World. Golden Press, New York.

Bailey, A. M.
1956   Birds of Midway and Laysan islands. Denver Museum Pictorial No. 12.

Bailey, A. M., and R. J. Niedrach
1951   Stepping stones across the Pacific. Denver Museum Pictorial No. 3.

Baldwin, P. H.
1944   Birds of Hawaii National Park. Audubon Mag. 46:147–154.

1945a The Hawaiian Goose, its distribution and reduction in numbers. Condor 47:27–37.

1945b Fate of the Laysan Rail. Audubon Mag. 47:343–348.

1947a The life history of the Laysan Rail. Condor 49:14–21.

1947b Foods of the Hawaiian Goose. Condor 49:108–120.

1953 Annual cycle, environment and evolution in the Hawaiian honeycreepers (Aves: Drepaniidae). Univ. Calif. Publ. Zool. 52(4):285–398.

1969a The Hawaiian Hawk from 1938 to 1949. Elepaio 29:95–98.

1969b The 'Alala *(Corvus tropicus)* of western Hawaii Island. Elepaio 30:41–45.

Banko, W. E.

1968 Rediscovery of Maui Nukupuu, *Hemignathus lucidus affinis,* and sighting of Maui Parrotbill, *Pseudonestor xanthophrys,* Kipahulu Valley, Maui, Hawaii. Condor 70:265–266.

Banks, R. C., and R. C. Laybourne

1968 The Red-whiskered Bulbul in Florida. Auk 85:141.

1977 Plumage sequence and taxonomy of Laysan and Nihoa finches. Condor 79:343–348.

Bartholomew, G. A.

1966 The role of behavior in the temperature regulation of the Masked Booby. Condor 68:523–535.

Bartholomew, G. A., and T. R. Howell

1964 Experiments on nesting behaviour of Laysan and Black-footed albatrosses. Animal Behaviour 12:549–559.

Bates, G. W.

1854 Sandwich Island Notes. Harper and Brothers, New York.

Beardsley, J. W.

1962 On accidental immigration and establishment of terrestrial arthropods in Hawaii during recent years. Proc. Hawaiian Ent. Soc. 18:99–110.

Beecher, W. J.

1951 Convergence in the Coerebidae. Wilson Bull. 63:274–287.

Berger, A. J.

1966 Behavior of a captive Mockingbird. Jack-Pine Warbler 44:8–13.

1967 The incubation period of the Hawaiian Stilt. Auk 84:130.

1969a The breeding season of the Hawaii Amakihi. Occ. Pap. Bernice P. Bishop Museum 24:1–8.

1969b The nest, eggs, and young of the Elepaio. Wilson Bull. 81:333–335.

1969c Discovery of the nest of the Hawaiian Thrush. Living Bird 8:243–250.

1970a The present status of the birds of Hawaii. Pacific Sci. 24:29–42.

1970b The eggs and young of the Palila, an endangered species. Condor 72:238–240.

1971 Bird Study. Dover Publications, New York.

1974 History of the exotic birds in Hawaii. Elepaio 35:60–65, 72–80.

1975a The Hawaiian Honeycreepers. Elepaio 35:97–100, 110–118.

1975b The Warbling Silverbill, a new nesting bird in Hawaii. Pacific Sci. 29:51–54.

1975c The Mockingbird on Hawaii Island. Elepaio 35:139.

1975d The Java Sparrow in Hawaii. Elepaio 36:14–16.

1975e Red-whiskered and Red-vented Bulbuls on Oahu. Elepaio 36:16–19.

1975f The Japanese Bush Warbler on Oahu. Elepaio 36:19–21.

1975g The 1929 and 1936 "Buy-A-Bird" campaigns on Hawaii. Elepaio 36:40–44.

1975h Hawaii's dubious distinction. Defenders 50:491–496.

1976 Problems for Hawaiian bird students. Elepaio 37:14–19.

1977a Aloha means goodby. National Wildlife 28–35.

1977b Nesting of the Yellow-fronted Canary on Oahu. Elepaio 37:128.

1977c Nesting of the Japanese Bush Warbler. Elepaio 37:148.

1977d Rothschild's Starling in Waikiki. Elepaio 37:149.

1977e Nesting seasons of some introduced birds in Hawaii. Elepaio 38:35–38.

1977f The Exotic Birds of Hawaii. Island Heritage, Ltd., Norfolk Island, Australia, 50 pp.

1978a Fitness of offspring from captive populations. *In* Endangered Birds: Management Techniques for Preserving Threatened Species. S. A. Temple, ed. University of Wisconsin Press, Madison, pp. 315–320.

1978b Reintroduction of Hawaiian Geese. *In* Endangered Birds: Management Techniques for Preserving Threatened Species. S. A. Temple, ed. University of Wisconsin Press, Madison, pp. 339–344.

1980 Longevity of Hawaiian honeycreepers in captivity. Wilson Bull. 92:263–264.

Berger, A. J., C. R. Eddinger, and S. C. Frings

1969 The nest and eggs of the Anianiau. Auk 86:183–187.

Bisseru, B.

1967 Diseases of Man Acquired from His Pets. William Heinemann, London, 482 pp.

Blake, E. R., and C. Vaurie

1962 The Corvidae. *In* Peters' Check-List of Birds of the World, vol. 15, pp. 204–284. Museum of Comparative Zoology, Cambridge, Mass.

Bloxam, Andrew

1925 Diary of Andrew Bloxam. Bernice P. Bishop Museum Special Publication No. 10, Honolulu, 44 pp.

Bock, W. J.

1972 Morphology of the tongue apparatus of *Ciridops anna* (Drepanididae). Ibis 114:61–78.

Bowles, John
    1962   The Guam Edible Nest Swiftlet. Elepaio 23:14–15.
Breese, P. L.
    1959   Information on Cattle Egret, a bird new to Hawaii. Elepaio 20:33–34.
Bremer, David
    1977   Red-Vented Bulbuls roosting in a banyan tree. Elepaio 37:99.
Brigham, W. T.
    1899   Hawaiian feather work. Mem. Bernice P. Bishop Museum 1:1–81.
Brock, V. E.
    1951a   Some observations on the Laysan Duck, *Anas wyvilliana laysanensis*. Auk 68:371–372.
    1951b   Laysan Island bird census. Elepaio 12:17–18.
Brown, W. Y.
    1973   The breeding biology of Sooty Terns and Brown Noddies on Manana or Rabbit Island, Oahu, Hawaii. Ph.D. thesis, University of Hawaii, Honolulu, 233 pp.
    1974   Rabbit destruction of tern eggs. Auk 91:840–841.
    1975a   Artifactual clutch size in Sooty Terns and Brown Noddies. Wilson Bull. 87:115–116.
    1975b   Incubation shifts of Sooty Terns *Sterna fuscata* on Manana Island, Hawaii. Ibis 117:527–529.
    1975c   Longevity of the Brown Noddy. Bird-Banding 46:250–251.
    1975d   Parental feeding of young Sooty Terns (*Sterna fuscata* [L.]) and Brown Noddies (*Anous stolidus* [L.]) in Hawaii. Jour. Animal Ecology 44:731–742.
Brush, A. H., and D. M. Power
    1976   House Finch pigmentation: cartenoid metabolism and the effect of diet. Auk 93:725–739.
Bryan, E. H., Jr.
    1935   Insects from Rabbit Island. Proc. Hawaiian Ent. Soc. 9:39–43.
    1942   American Polynesia and the Hawaiian Chain. Tongg Publishing Co., Honolulu.
    1954   The Hawaiian Chain. Bishop Museum Press, Honolulu.
    1958   Check List and Summary of Hawaiian Birds. Books About Hawaii, Honolulu.
Bryan, E. H., Jr., and J. C. Greenway, Jr.
    1944   Contribution to the ornithology of the Hawaiian Islands. Bull. Mus. Comp. Zool. (Harvard) 94(2):77–142.
Bryan, L. W.
    1947   Twenty-five years of forestry work on the island of Hawaii. Hawaiian Planters' Record 51:1–80.
Bryan, W. A.
    1905a   Notes on the birds of the Waianae Mountains. Occ. Pap. Bernice P. Bishop Museum 2:229–241.
    1905b   Description of the nest and eggs of Chlorodrepanis virens (Gmel.). Occ. Pap. Bernice P. Bishop Museum 2:243–244.
    1905c   Two undescribed nests and an egg of a Hawaiian bird. Occ. Pap. Bernice P. Bishop Museum 3:251–252.
    1905d   Nest and eggs of Heterorhynchus wilsoni Roths. Occ. Pap. Bernice P. Bishop Museum 2:253–254.
    1906   Nest of the Hawaiian Hawk. Occ. Pap. Bernice P. Bishop Museum 2:274–275.
    1908   Some birds of Molokai. Occ. Pap. Bernice P. Bishop Museum 4:133–176.
    1912   The introduction and acclimatization of the yellow canary on Midway Island. Auk 29:339–342.
    1917   Description of *Telespiza ultima* from Nihoa Island. Auk 34:70–72.
Bryan, W. A., and A. Seale
    1901   Notes on the birds of Kauai. Occ. Pap. Bernice P. Bishop Museum 1:129–137.
Buxbaum, Karen
    1973   Status of the Dark-rumped Petrel on Maui, 1972. Elepaio 34:11–12.
Byrd, G. V.
    1979   Common Mynah predation on Wedge-tailed Shearwater eggs. Elepaio 39:69–70.
Byrd, G. V., and T. C. Telfer
    1979   Laysan Albatross is attempting to establish breeding colonies on Kauai. Elepaio 38:81–83.
Carpenter, F. L., and R. E. MacMillen
    1975   Pollination energetics and foraging strategies in a *Metrosideros*-honeycreeper association. Technical Report No. 63, Island Ecosystems Integrated Research Project, Honolulu, 9 pp.
    1980   Plant-pollinator interactions in Hawaii: Nectar limitation and foraging strategies in a drepanidid community. In prep.
Casey, T. L. C., and J. D. Jacobi
    1974   A new genus and species of bird from the island of Maui, Hawaii (Passeriformes: Drepanididae). Occ. Pap. Bernice P. Bishop Museum, Honolulu; 24:215–226.
Cassin, John
    1858   United States Exploring Expedition, 1838–1842. Mammalia and Ornithology, vol. 8, pp. 17–338. C. Sherman, Philadelphia.
Caum, E. L.
    1933   The exotic birds of Hawaii. Occ. Pap. Bernice P. Bishop Museum 10:1–55.
    1936   Notes on the flora and fauna of Lehua and Kaula islands. Occ. Pap. Bernice P. Bishop Museum 21:1–17.
Char, D. F. B., and L. Rosen
    1967   Eosinophilic meningitis among children in Hawaii. J. Pediatrics 70:28–35.
Clapp, R. B.
    1972   The natural history of Gardner Pinnacles, Northwestern Hawaiian Islands. Atoll Research Bull. No. 163, 25 pp.
    1976   Gray-backed Terns eat lizards. Wilson Bull. 88:354.

Clapp, R. B., and C. D. Hackman
1969   Longevity record for a breeding Great Frigate-
        bird. Bird-Banding 40:47.

Clapp, R. B., V. M. Kleen, and D. L. Olsen
1969   First records of Emperor Geese from the north-
        western Hawaiian Islands. Elepaio 30:51-52.

Clapp, R. B., and Eugene Kridler
1977   The natural history of Necker Island, Northwest-
        ern Hawaiian Islands. Atoll Research Bull. No.
        206, 102 pp.

Clapp, R. B., Eugene Kridler, and R. R. Fleet
1977   The natural history of Nihoa Island, Northwest-
        ern Hawaiian Islands. Atoll Research Bull. No.
        207, 147 pp.

Clapp, R. B., and R. L. Pyle
1968   Noteworthy records of waterbirds from Oahu.
        Elepaio 29:37-39.

Clapp, R. B., and F. C. Sibley
1966   Longevity records of some central Pacific sea-
        birds. Bird-Banding 37:193-197.

Clapp, R. B., and W. O. Wirtz, II
1975   The natural history of Lisianski Island, North-
        western Hawaiian Islands. Atoll Research Bull.
        No. 186, 196 pp.

Clapp, R. B., and P. W. Woodward
1968   New records of birds from the Hawaiian Lee-
        ward Islands. Proc. U.S. Nat'l. Mus. 124(3640):
        1-39.

Coleman, R. A.
1978   Coots prosper at Kakahaia Refuge. Elepaio 38:
        130.

Cooke, G. P.
1949   Moolelo o Molokai. A Ranch Story of Molokai.
        Honolulu Star-Bulletin Printing Co., Honolulu,
        164 pp.

Cullen, J. M., and N. P. Ashmole
1963   The Black Noddy *Anous tenuirostris* on Ascension
        Island, Part 2. Ibis 103b:423-446.

Dale, F. H., and J. B. DeWitt
1958   Calcium, phosphorus and protein levels as fac-
        tors in the distribution of the pheasant. Trans.
        23rd North American Wildlife Conference,
        Washington, pp. 291-295.

Darwin, Francis
1903   More Letters of Charles Darwin. 2 vols. J. Mur-
        ray, London.

de Schauensee, R. M.
1966   The Species of Birds of South America and Their
        Distribution. Academy of Natural Sciences, Phil-
        adelphia.

Dill, H. R., and W. A. Bryan
1912   Report of an expedition to Laysan Island in
        1911. U.S. Dept. Agri. Biol. Surv. Bull. 42.

Dixit, Dhruv
1963   Notes on a case of Redvented Bulbul *Pycnonotus
        cafer* (Linnaeus) nesting indoors. Pavo 1:19-31.

Dixon, J. D.
1973   Natural history of a small, insular population of

rabbits, *Oryctolagus cuniculus* (L.), in Hawaii. Master's
thesis, University of Hawaii, Honolulu, 87 pp.

Dole, S. B.
1869   A synopsis of the birds hitherto described from
        the Hawaiian Islands. Proc. Boston Soc. Nat.
        Hist. 12:294-309.

1879   List of birds of the Hawaiian Islands. *In* Hawai-
        ian Almanac and Annual for 1879 (compiled by
        Thos. G. Thrum), pp. 41-58.

Donaghho, Walter
1966   Indian Hill Mynah in Hawaii. Elepaio 26:110-
        111.

1967   Field Notes: Mt. Kaua, Oahu. Elepaio 28:18.

1970   Observations of the Edible Nest Swiftlet on
        Oahu. Elepaio 30:64-65.

Dorward, D. F., and N. P. Ashmole
1963   Notes on the biology of the Brown Noddy *Anous
        stolidus* on Ascension Island. Ibis 113b:447-457.

Dunmire, W. W.
1961   Birds of the National Parks in Hawaii. Hawaii
        Natural History Association.

1962   Bird populations in Hawaii Volcanoes National
        Park. Elepaio 22:65-70.

Eddinger, C. R.
1967a   A study of the breeding behavior of the mynah
        (*Acridotheres tristis* L.). Elepaio 28:1-5, 11-15.

1967b   Feeding helpers among immature White-eyes.
        Condor 69:530-531.

1969a   Experiences with hand-raising passerine birds in
        Hawaii. Avicult. Mag. 75:12-14.

1969b   The attainment of sexual maturity in the Hawai-
        ian Jungle Fowl (*Gallus gallus gallus*). Elepaio
        29:85-86.

1970a   The White-eye as an interspecific feeding helper.
        Condor 72:240.

1970b   A study of the breeding behavior of four species
        of Hawaiian Honeycreepers (Drepanididae).
        Ph.D. thesis, University of Hawaii.

1972   Discovery of the nest of the Kauai Akepa. Wilson
        Bull. 84:95-97.

Eisenmann, Eugene
1961   Observations on birds on the island of Hawaii.
        Elepaio 21:66-70.

Elder, W. H., and D. H. Woodside
1958   Biology and management of the Hawaiian
        Goose. Trans. 23rd North American Wildlife
        Conference, pp. 198-215.

Elschner, Carl
1915   The Leeward Islands of the Hawaiian group.
        Sunday Advertiser July 4-August 8, 1915.

Ely, C. A.
1971   Pelagic observations of the Japanese White-eye
        in the central Pacific. Condor 73:122-123.

Ely, C. A., and R. B. Clapp
1973   The natural history of Laysan Island, Northwest-
        ern Hawaiian Islands. Atoll Research Bull.
        No. 171, Smithsonian Institution, Washington,
        D.C., 361 pp.

Emerson, N. B.
　1895　The bird-hunters of ancient Hawaii. Thrum's Hawaiian Almanac and Annual for 1895, pp. 101–111.

Fain, Alex, and A. B. Amerson, Jr.
　1968　Two new heteromorphic deutonymphs (hypopi) *(Acarina: Hypoderidae)* from the Great Frigatebird *(Fregata minor).* Jour. Med. Ent. 5:320–324.

Fisher, H. I.
　1948a　The question of avian introductions in Hawaii. Pacific Sci. 2:59–64.

　1948b　Laysan Albatross nesting on Moku Manu islet, off Oahu. T. H. Pacific Sci. 2:66.

　1949　Populations of birds on Midway and the man-made factors affecting them. Pacific Sci. 3:103–110.

　1951　The avifauna of Niihau Island, Hawaiian Archipelago. Condor 53:31–42.

　1965　Bird records from Midway Atoll, Pacific Ocean. Condor 67:355–357.

　1966a　Airplane-albatross collisions on Midway Atoll. Condor 68:229–242.

　1966b　Midway's deadly antennas. Audubon Magazine 68 (July–August 1966):220–223.

　1966c　Aerial census of Laysan Albatrosses breeding on Midway Atoll in December 1962. Auk 83:670–673.

　1967　Body weights in Laysan Albatrosses *Diomedea immutabilis.* Ibis 109:373–382.

　1968　The "two-egg clutch" in the Laysan Albatross. Auk 85:134–136.

　1969　Eggs and egg-laying in the Laysan Albatross, *Diomedea immutabilis.* Condor 71:102–112.

　1970　The death of Midway's antennas. Audubon Magazine 72 (January 1970):62–63.

　1971　Laysan Albatross: its incubation, hatching, and associated behaviors. Living Bird 1971:19–78.

　1972　Sympatry of Laysan and Black-footed albatrosses. Auk 89:381–402.

　1973　Pollutants in North Pacific Albatrosses. Pacific Sci. 27:220–225.

　1975a　Mortality and survival in the Laysan Albatross, *Diomedea immutabilis.* Pacific Sci. 29:279–300.

　1975b　The relationship between deferred breeding and mortality in the Laysan Albatross. Auk 92:433–441.

　1975c　Longevity of the Laysan Albatross, *Diomedea immutabilis.* Bird-Banding 46:1–6.

Fisher, H. I., and P. H. Baldwin
　1945　A recent trip to Midway Islands, Pacific Ocean. Elepaio 6:11–13.

　1946　War and the birds of Midway Atoll. Condor 48:3–15.

　1947　Notes on the Red-billed Leiothrix in Hawaii. Pacific Sci. 1:45–51.

Fisher, H. I., and M. L. Fisher
　1969　The visits of Laysan Albatrosses to the breeding colony. Micronesia 5:173–221.

Fisher, J., N. Simon, and J. Vincent
　1969　Wildlife in Danger. Viking Press, New York.

Fisher, W. K.
　1906　Birds of Laysan and the Leeward Islands, Hawaiian group. Bull. U.S. Fish Commission, 23, part 3:769–807.

Friedmann, Herbert
　1960　The Parasitic Weaverbirds. U.S. Nat'l. Museum Bull. No. 223, 196 pp.

Frings, C., and S. Frings
　1965　Random jottings about Mynahs. Elepaio 26:48–49.

Frings, H., and M. Frings
　1959　Observations on salt balance and behavior of Laysan and Black-footed Albatrosses in captivity. Condor 61:305–314.

Frings, S. C.
　1968　The breeding biology of the Oahu Elepaio, *Chasiempis sandwichensis gayi.* Master's thesis, University of Hawaii.

Frohawk, F. W.
　1892　Description of a new species of rail from Laysan Island (North Pacific). Ann. Mag. Nat. Hist. 9:247–249.

Galtsoff, P. S.
　1933　Pearl and Hermes Reef, Hawaii, Hydrographical and Biological Observations. Bernice P. Bishop Museum Bull. 107.

Gould, P. J.
　1967　Nocturnal feeding of *Sterna fuscata* and *Puffinus pacificus.* Condor 69:529.

Gould, P. J., W. B. King, and G. A. Sanger
　1974　Red-tailed Tropicbird *(Phaethon rubricauda). In* Pelagic studies of seabirds in the Central and Eastern Pacific Ocean. W. B. King, ed. Smithsonian Contributions in Zoology No. 158, pp. 206–231.

Greenway, J. C., Jr.
　1958　Extinct and Vanishing Birds of the World. Special Publ. No. 13, American Commission for International Wild Life Protection, New York.

Guest, S. J.
　1973a　A reproductive biology and natural history of the Japanese White-eye *(Zosterops j. japonica)* in urban Oahu. Island Ecosystems Technical Report No. 29, Honolulu, 95 pp.

　1973b　White-eye vocal mimicry. Elepaio 34:3.

Hadden, F. C.
　1941　Midway Islands. Hawaiian Planters' Record 45:179–221.

Hamilton, R. B.
　1975　Comparative behavior of the American Avocet and the Black-necked Stilt (Recurvirostridae). Ornithological Monographs No. 17. American Ornithologists' Union, Lawrence, Kansas, 98 pp.

Hanson, C.
　1960　Easter vacation trip to Maui and Hawaii. Elepaio 20:87–88.

Hardy, D. E.
1960   Insects of Hawaii, vol. 10. University of Hawaii Press, Honolulu.

Harpham, P.
1953   Tantalus bird notes: the Shama Thrush. Elepaio 13:74–76.

Harris, M. P.
1970   The biology of an endangered species, the Dark-rumped Petrel *(Pterodroma phaeopygia)*, in the Galápagos Islands. Condor 72:76–84.

Henshaw, H. W.
1902   Belted Kingfisher in the island of Hawaii. Auk 19:199.
1902–   Complete list of the birds of the Hawaiian Posses-
1904   sions, with notes on their habits. Thrum's Hawaiian Almanac and Annual 1902:54–106; 1903: 73–117; 1904:113–145.

Hirai, L. T.
1975a   The Hawaiian House Finch. Elepaio 36:1–5.
1975b   The nesting biology of the House Finch in Honolulu, Hawaii. Western Birds 6:33–44.
1978a   Possible Dark rumped Petrel colony on Lanai, Hawaii. Elepaio 38:71–72.
1978b   Native birds of Lanai, Hawaii. Western Birds 9:71–77.

Howell, T. R., and G. A. Bartholomew
1961a   Temperature regulation in Laysan and Black-footed albatrosses. Condor 63:185–197.
1961b   Temperature regulation in nesting Bonin Island Petrels, Wedge-tailed Shearwaters, and Christmas Island Shearwaters. Auk 78:343–354.
1962a   Temperature regulation in the Red-tailed Tropic Bird and the Red-footed Booby. Condor 64:6–18.
1962b   Temperature regulation in the Sooty Tern, *Sterna fuscata*. Ibis 104:98–105.
1969   Experiments on nesting behavior of the Red-tailed Tropicbird, *Phaethon rubricauda*. Condor 71:113–119.

Howell, T. R., R. A. Paynter, Jr., and A. L. Rand
1968   Subfamily Carduelinae. *In* Peters' Check-List of Birds of the World, vol. 14, pp. 207–306. Museum of Comparative Zoology, Cambridge, Mass.

Hubbs, C. L.
1968   Black-footed Albatross banded at Midway Island, recovered off Baja California in first year. Condor 70:92.

Hull, T. G.
1963   Diseases Transmitted from Animals to Man. 5th ed. Charles C. Thomas, Springfield, Ill.

Humphrey, P. S.
1958   The trachea of the Hawaiian goose. Condor 60: 303–307.

Johnston, D. W., and R. W. McFarlane
1967   Migration and bioenergetics of flight in the Pacific Golden Plover. Condor 69:156–168.

Johnston, R. F., and R. K. Selander
1964   House Sparrows: rapid evolution of races in North America. Science 144:548–550.

Joyce, C. R., and P. Y. Nakagawa
1963   Aedes vexans nocturnus (Theobald) in Hawaii. Proc. Hawaiian Ent. Soc. 18:273–280.

Judd, C. S.
1927   The story of the forests of Hawaii. Paradise of the Pacific 40(10):9–18.

Kear, Janet, and A. J. Berger
1980   The Hawaiian Goose: An Experiment in Conservation. T. and A. D. Poyser, Ltd., London.

Keffer, M. O., editor
1976   An evaluation of the pest potential of the genus *Zosterops* (White Eyes) in California. State of California, Department of Food and Agriculture, Sacramento, 27 pp.

Kenyon, K. W., and D. W. Rice
1958   Homing of Laysan Albatrosses. Condor 60:3–6.

Kepler, C. B.
1967   Polynesian rat predation on nesting Laysan Albatrosses and other Pacific seabirds. Auk 84:426–430.
1969   Breeding biology of the Blue-faced Booby, *Sula dactylatra personata*, on Green Island, Kure Atoll. Publ. Nuttall Ornithol. Club No. 8.

Kikkawa, Jiro
1961   Social behaviour of the White-eye *Zosterops lateralis* in winter flocks. Ibis 103a:428–442.

King, J. E.
1959   Franklin Gull in the central Pacific. Condor 61:226.

King, W. B.
1967   Seabirds of the Tropical Pacific Ocean. Smithsonian Institution, Washington, D.C.
1974   Pelagic studies of seabirds in the Central and Eastern Pacific Ocean. Smithsonian Contributions to Zoology No. 158, 277 pp.

King, W. B., and P. J. Gould
1967   The status of Newell's race of the Manx Shearwater. Living Bird 6:163–186.

Kishimoto, R. A., and G. E. Baker
1969   Pathogenic and potentially pathogenic fungi isolated from beach sands and selected soils of Oahu, Hawaii. Mycologia 61:538–548.

Knudsen, A. F.
1909   The need of practical activity. Hawaiian Forester and Agriculturist 6:171–175.

Kocan, R. M., and W. Banko
1974   Trichomoniasis in the Hawaiian Barred Dove. Jour. Wildlife Diseases 10:359–360.

Kojima, Unoyo
1969   Aiea Trail, 1968 Christmas Count. Elepaio 29: 69–70.

Kridler, Eugene
1966   A recent record of the Crested Honeycreeper on Maui, Hawaii. Elepaio 26:88.

Ladd, H. S., J. I. Tracey, Jr., and M. G. Gross
1967   Drilling on Midway Atoll, Hawaii. Science 156: 1088–1094.

Lamoureux, Charles
1963   The flora and vegetation of Laysan Island. Atoll Research Bull. 97:1–14.

Laycock, George
  1966   Alien Animals: the Story of Imported Wildlife. Doubleday & Co., New York.
  1970   Trouble in paradise. Audubon Magazine May 1970:24–31.
Lewin, Victor
  1971   Exotic game birds of the Puu Waawaa Ranch, Hawaii. J. Wildlife Management 35:141–155.
Lewin, V., and J. C. Holmes
  1971   Helminths from the exotic game birds of the Puuwaawaa Ranch, Hawaii. Pacific Sci. 25:372–381.
Locke, L. N., W. O. Wirtz II, and E. E. Brown
  1965   Pox infection and a secondary cutaneous mycosis in a Red-tailed Tropicbird *(Phaethon rubricauda).* Bull. Wildlife Dis. Assoc. 1:60–61.
Lyon, H. L.
  1919   Some observations on the forest problems of Hawaii. Hawaiian Planters' Record 21:289–300.
MacMillen, R. E.
  1974   Bioenergetics of Hawaiian honeycreepers: the Amakihi *(Loxops virens)* and the Anianiau *(L. parva).* Condor 76:62–69.
MacMillen, R. E., G. C. Whittow, E. A. Christopher, and R. J. Ebisu
  1977   Oxygen consumption, evaporative water loss and body temperature in the Sooty Tern. Auk 94:72–79.
McCoy, P. C., and R. A. Gould
  1977   Alpine archeology in Hawaii. Archaeology 30:234–243.
McKeown, Sean
  1978   Hawaiian Reptiles and Amphibians. The Oriental Publishing Co., Honolulu.
Marshall, D. B.
  1964   Treasure islands—of wildlife. Audubon Magazine 66 (May–June 1964):160–165.
Mayr, Ernst
  1945   Birds of the Southwest Pacific. Macmillan Co., New York.
  1967   Family Zosteropidae. Indo-Australian taxa. *In* Peters' Check-List of Birds of the World, vol. 12, pp. 289–325. Museum of Comparative Zoology, Cambridge, Mass.
  1968   Subfamily Fringillinae. *In* Peters' Check-List of Birds of the World, vol. 14, pp. 202–206. Museum of Comparative Zoology, Cambridge, Mass.
Mayr, E., R. A. Paynter, Jr., and M. A. Traylor
  1968   Family Estrildidae. *In* Peters' Check-List of Birds of the World, vol. 14, pp. 306–390. Museum of Comparative Zoology, Cambridge, Mass.
Medway, D. G.
  1981   The contribution of Cook's third voyage to the ornithology of the Hawaiian Islands. Pacific Sci. 35 (in press).
Meyer, K. F., D. McNeill, and C. M. Wheeler
  1965   Results of a preliminary serological survey of small mammal populations for plague on the island of Hawaii. Bull. World Health Org. 33:809–815.
Miller, A. H.
  1937   Structural modifications in the Hawaiian Goose (Nesochen sandvicensis), a study in adaptive evolution. Univ. Calif. Publ. Zool. 42(1):80 pp.
Mills, Stephen
  1978   What's wrong with the Nene in Hawaii? Oryx 14:359–361.
Minette, H. P.
  1964   Leptospirosis in rodents and mongooses on the island of Hawaii. Amer. Jour. Tropical Med. and Hyg., 13:826–832.
Morrison, G. T.
  1969   Hawaiian Hawk. Elepaio 29:75–78.
Munro, G. C.
  1944   Birds of Hawaii. Bridgeway Press, Rutland, Vermont.
Murakami, L. D.
  1977   Seabirds in the city: breeding of the White Tern in lower Makiki. Elepaio 38:63–65.
Murphy, R. C.
  1936   Oceanic Birds of South America. 2 vols. Macmillan Co., New York.
Navvab Gojrati, H. A.
  1970   Epizootiological survey of avian malaria in the Hawaiian Islands. Ph.D. thesis, University of Hawaii.
Nelson, Bryan
  1968   Galapagos, Islands of Birds. William Morrow & Co., New York.
Newton, Alfred
  1897   On some new or rare birds' eggs. Proc. Zool. Soc. London 1897:890–894.
Ohashi, R. J., and M. L. Ueoka
  1977   Nests of the Red-whiskered Bulbul on Oahu. Elepaio 38:1.
Okimoto, B. F.
  1975   Parasites of the Pacific Golden Plover and their use as biological markers. Master's thesis, University of Hawaii, Honolulu, 83 pp.
Olsen, D. L.
  1971   Nesting activity of Hawaiian Stilts and Coots at Kii Pond, Kahuku. Elepaio 32:11.
Olson, S. L., and A. Wetmore
  1976   Preliminary diagnoses of two extraordinary new genera of birds from Pleistocene deposits in the Hawaiian Islands. Proc. Biological Soc. Washington 89(18):247–257.
Ord, W. M.
  1961   White Terns at Koko Head, Oahu. Elepaio 22:17–18.
  1967   Hawaii's Birds. Hawaii Audubon Society, Honolulu.
Peale, T. R.
  1848   United States Exploring Expedition, 1838–1842. Mammalia and Ornithology, vol. 8. C. Sherman, Philadelphia, Penn.

Pekelo, N., Jr.
  1963a Some notes from Molokai. Elepaio 23:64.
  1963b Nature notes from Molokai. Elepaio 24:17–18.
  1967   Letter regarding status of Molokai birds. Elepaio 27:90–91.
Perkins, R. C. L.
  1893   Notes on collecting in Kona, Hawaii. Ibis, 1893: 101–114.
  1901   An introduction to the study of the Drepanididae, a family of birds peculiar to the Hawaiian Islands. Ibis 1901:562–585.
  1903   Vertebrata (Aves). *In* Fauna Hawaiiensis. David Sharp, ed. Vol. 1, part 4:368–465. The University Press, Cambridge, England.
Peterson, R. T.
  1954   A new bird immigrant arrives. National Geographic Magazine August 1954:281–292.
Pratt, H. D.
  1977   The Black-headed Munia discovered on Kauai. Elepaio 38:18.
  1979   A systematic analysis of the endemic avifauna of the Hawaiian Islands. Ph.D. thesis, Louisiana State University, Baton Rouge, 228 pp.
Pyle, R. L.
  1976   Recent observations of birds on Oahu—May to July 1976. Elepaio 37:45–47.
Radovsky, F. J., J. M. Tenorio, P. Q. Tomich, and J. D. Jacobi.
  1975   Acari on murine rodents along an altitudinal transect on Mauna Loa, Hawaii. Technical Report No. 58, Island Ecosystems Integrated Research Project, Honolulu, 11 pp.
Rahn, H., C. V. Paganelli, I. C. T. Nisbet, and G. C. Whittow
  1976   Regulation of incubation water loss in eggs of seven species of terns. Physiological Zool. 49: 245–259.
Raikow, R. J.
  1974   Species-specific foraging behavior in some Hawaiian honeycreepers. Wilson Bull. 86:471–474.
  1976   Pelvic appendage myology of the Hawaiian honeycreepers (Drepanididae). Auk 93:774–792.
  1977a Pectoral appendage myology of the Hawaiian honeycreepers (Drepanididae). Auk 94:331–342.
  1977b The origin and evolution of the Hawaiian honeycreepers (Drepanididae). Living Bird, Cornell Laboratory of Ornithology, pp. 95–117.
  1978   Appendicular myology and relationships of the New World nine-primaried oscines (Aves: Passeriformes). Bull. No. 7. Carnegie Museum of Natural History, Pittsburgh, 43 pp.
Rice, D. W., and K. W. Kenyon
  1962a Breeding distribution, history, and populations of North Pacific albatrosses. Auk 79:365–386.
  1962b Breeding cycles and behavior of Laysan and Black-footed Albatrosses. Auk 79:517–567.
Richards, L. P., and P. H. Baldwin
  1953   Recent records of some Hawaiian honeycreepers. Condor 55:221–222.

Richards, L. P., and W. J. Bock
  1973   Functional anatomy and adaptive evolution of the feeding apparatus in the Hawaiian honeycreeper genus *Loxops* (Drepanididae). Ornithological Monographs No. 15, American Ornithologists' Union, Lawrence, Kansas, 173 pp.
Richardson, Frank
  1949   Status of native land birds on Molokai. Pacific Sci. 3:226–230.
  1954   Report on the two native passerines of Nihoa, Hawaii. Condor 56:224.
  1957   The Breeding Cycles of Hawaiian Sea Birds. Bernice P. Bishop Museum Bull. 218.
  1963   Birds of Lehua Island off Niihau, Hawaii. Elepaio 23:43–45.
Richardson, F., and J. Bowles
  1964   A Survey of the Birds of Kauai, Hawaii. Bernice P. Bishop Museum Bull. 227.
Richardson, F., and H. I. Fisher
  1950   Birds of Moku Manu and Manana islands off Oahu, Hawaii. Auk 67:285–306.
Richardson, F., and D. H. Woodside
  1954   Rediscovery of the nesting of the Dark-rumped Petrel in the Hawaiian Islands. Condor 56:323–327.
Robbins, C. S.
  1966   Birds and Aircraft on Midway Islands, 1959–1963 Investigations. Special Scientific Report, Wildlife, No. 85. Superintendent of Documents, Washington, D.C.
Rothschild, Walter
  1892   Descriptions of seven new species of birds from the Sandwich Islands. Ann. Mag. Nat. Hist. 60: 108–112.
  1893– The Avifauna of Laysan and the Neighbouring
  1900   Islands. R. H. Porter, London.
St. John, Harold
  1972   *Canavalia kauensis* (Leguminosae), a new species from the island of Hawaii . . . . Pacific Sci. 26:409–414.
  1973   List of Flowering Plants in Hawaii. Pacific Tropical Botanical Garden Memoir No. 1, Lawai, Kauai, 519 pp.
Sakai, H. F., and C. J. Ralph
  1980a Notes on the nest construction of the Hawaiian Creeper. Elepaio 40:117–119.
  1980b A study of the Hawaiian Crow *(Corvus tropicus)* in South Kona, Hawaii. Elepaio 40:133–138.
Schreiber, R. W., and D. A. Hensley
  1976   The diets of *Sula dactylatra, Sula Sula,* and *Fregata minor* on Christmas Island, Pacific Ocean. Pacific Sci. 30:241–248.
Schwartz, C. W., and E. R. Schwartz
  1949   The Game Birds in Hawaii. Board of Commissioners of Agriculture and Forestry, Honolulu, 168 pp.
  1950   The California Quail in Hawaii. Auk 67:1–38.
  1951   A survey of the Lace-necked Dove in Hawaii. Pacific Sci. 5:90–107.
  1952   The Hawaiian coot. Auk 69:446–449.

1953 Notes on the Hawaiian duck. Wilson Bull. 65: 18-25.

Scott, J. M., R. L. Pyle, and C. F. Zeillemaker
1978 Similar species of migratory waterbirds in Hawaii. Elepaio 39:1-5.

Scott, J. M., and J. L. Sincock
1977 Recent observations on the birds of the Koolau Forest Reserve, Maui. Western Birds 8:113-116.

Scott, J. M., D. H. Woodside, and T. L. Casey
1977 Observations of birds in the Molokai Forest Reserve, July 1975. Elepaio 38:25-27.

Scott, J. M., J. L. Sincock, and A. J. Berger
1980 Records of nests, eggs, nestlings, and cavity nesting of endemic passerine birds in Hawaii. Elepaio 40:163-168.

Seale, Alvin
1900 Field notes on the birds of Oahu, H. I. Occ. Pap. Bernice P. Bishop Museum 1:33-46.

Selander, R. K., and R. F. Johnston
1967 Evolution in the House Sparrow. I. Intrapopulation variation in North America. Condor 69: 217-258.

Sengupta, Sudhindranath
1968 Studies on the life of the Common Mynah, *Acridotheres tristis tristis* (Linnaeus). Proc. Zool. Soc. Calcutta 21:1-27.

Shallenberger, R. J.
1976 Avifaunal survey of North Halawa valley. Elepaio 37:40-41.
1977 Observations at the nest of a Hawaiian Hawk. Elepaio 37:74-75.

Shallenberger, R. J., and H. D. Pratt
1978 Recent observations and field identification of the Oahu Creeper. Elepaio 38:135-140.

Shallenberger, R. J., G. C. Whittow, and R. M. Smith
1974 Body temperature of the nesting Red-footed Booby *(Sula sula)*. Condor 75:476-478.

Sibley, C. G.
1970 A comparative study of the egg-white proteins of passerine birds. Peabody Mus. of Nat. Hist. Bull. 32, New Haven, Connecticut, 131 pp.

Sibley, F. C., and R. B. Clapp
1967 Distribution and dispersal of central Pacific Lesser Frigatebirds *Fregata ariel*. Ibis 109:328-337.

Sibley, F. C., and R. W. McFarlane
1968 Gulls in the central Pacific. Pacific Sci. 22: 314-321.

Sincock, J. L., and E. Kridler
1980 The extinct and endangered endemic birds of the Northwestern Hawaiian Islands. In press.

Sincock, J. L., and G. E. Swedberg
1969 Rediscovery of the nesting grounds of Newell's Manx Shearwater *(Puffinus puffinus newelli)*, with initial observations. Condor 71:69-71.

Smith, H. E.
1973a *Syngamus trachea:* a first report in Hawaii. Elepaio 33:95-96.
1973b A Rhinonyssid mite in atypical loci of estrildine finches in Hawaii. Jour. Parasitology 59:1148.

Smith, H. E., and S. J. Guest
1974 A survey of internal parasites of birds on the western slopes of Diamond Head, Oahu, Hawaii, 1972-1973. Island Ecosystems Technical Report No. 37, 18 pp.

Smith, J. D.
1950 The pheasant situation in Hawaii, 1950. Board of Commissioners of Agriculture and Forestry, Honolulu, 13 pp.

Spieth, H. T.
1966 Hawaiian honeycreeper, *Vestiaria coccinea* (Forster), feeding on lobeliad flowers, *Clermontia arborescens* (Mann) Hillebr. Amer. Naturalist, 100: 470-473.

Stanley, E. S. (13th Earl of Derby)
1834 A note on a specimen of a young Nene. London and Edinburgh Philosophical Mag. and Jour. Science 5:233-235.

Stearns, H. T.
1973 Geologic setting of the fossil goose bones found on Molokai Island, Hawaii. Occ. Pap. Bernice P. Bishop Museum 24(10):155-163.

Stonehouse, Bernard
1962a The Tropic Birds (Genus *Phaethon*) of Ascension Island. Ibis 103b:124-161.
1962b The exploitation of birds. Proc. New Zealand Ecol. Soc. 9:43-47.

Stresemann, Erwin
1950 Birds collected during Capt. James Cook's last expedition. (1776-1780). Auk 67:66-88.

Sushkin, P. P.
1929 On the systematic position of the Drepaniidae. Verhandl. VI Internatl. Ornithol. Kongress (Copenhagen), pp. 379-381.

Swedberg, G. E.
1967 The Koloa. Department of Land and Natural Resources, Honolulu.
1969 Sighting of wild Koloa on the island of Hawaii and history of a past release. Elepaio 29:87-88.

Taylor, A. L., and M. S. Collins
1979 Rediscovery and identification of the "mystery" *Garrulax* on Oahu. Elepaio 39:79-81.

Telfer, T. C.
1979 Successful Newell's Shearwater salvage on Kauai. Elepaio 39:71.

Thistle, Alan
1962 Observation on Cattle Egret—Oahu, July 1962. Elepaio 23:15.

Throp, Jack
1969 Java Ricebird. Elepaio 29:80.
1970 The Laysan Finch Bill in the Honolulu Zoo. Elepaio 31:31-34.

Tomich, P. Q.
1962 Notes on the Barn Owl in Hawaii. Elepaio 23: 16-17.
1967 Arthropoda associated with a nest of the Hawaiian Crow. Proc. Hawaiian Ent. Soc. 19:431-432.
1969 Mammals in Hawaii. Bernice P. Bishop Museum Special Publication No. 57, Honolulu, 238 pp.

1971a Notes on foods and feeding behavior of raptorial birds in Hawaii. Elepaio 31:111–114.

1971b Notes on nests and behavior of the Hawaiian Crow. Pacific Sci. 25:465–474.

Tomich, P. Q., N. Wilson, and C. H. Lamoureux
1968   Ecological factors on Manana Island, Hawaii. Pacific Sci. 22:352–368.

Udvardy, M. D. F.
1960a The Black-headed Mannikin, Lonchura malacca atricapilla, a new breeding bird on the Hawaiian Islands. Elepaio 21:15–17.

1960b Movements and concentrations of the Hawaiian Coot on the island of Oahu. Elepaio 21:20–22.

1961a The occurrence of the Mockingbird on the island of Maui. Elepaio 21:72.

1961b The Harold J. Coolidge Expedition to Laysan Island, 1961. Elepaio 22:43–47.

1963   Data on body temperature of tropical sea and water birds. Auk 80:191–194.

Vanderbilt, G., and R. M. de Schauensee
1941   Zoological results of the Vanderbilt Nihoa expedition. I. Summary of zoological explorations and the birds of Nihoa. Notulae Naturae 86: 1–14.

van der Schalie, Henry
1969   Man meddles with nature—Hawaiian style. Biologist 51:136–146.

van Riper, Charles, III
1972   Discovery of the nest of the Maui Creeper. Elepaio 32:100–102.

1973a A comparison of different nesting locations of the Chinese Thrush in Hawaii. Elepaio 33:91–92.

1973b The nesting of the Apapane in lava caves on the island of Hawaii. Wilson Bull. 85:238–240.

1974a Unusual uses of Ricebird's nests in Hawaii. Elepaio 35:5.

1974b An albinistic Elepaio from Hawaii. Auk 91:841.

1975   Parasites of the Hawaii Amakihi *(Loxops virens virens)*. Technical Report No. 62, Island Ecosystems Integrated Research Project, Honolulu, 25 pp.

1976   Aspects of House Finch breeding biology in Hawaii. Condor 78:224–229.

1977   The use of sheep wool in nest construction by Hawaiian birds. Auk 94:646–651.

1978a Discovery of the Yellow-fronted Canary on Mauna Kea, Hawaii. Elepaio 38:99–100.

1978b The breeding biology of the Amakihi *(Loxops virens)* and Palila *(Psittirostra bailleui)* on Mauna Kea, Hawaii. Ph.D. thesis, University of Hawaii, Honolulu, 166 pp.

van Riper, C., III, J. M. Scott, and D. M. Woodside
1978   Distribution and abundance patterns of the Palila on Mauna Kea, Hawaii. Auk 95:518–527.

van Riper, C., III, S. G. van Riper, and A. J. Berger
1979   The Red-whiskered Bulbul in Hawaii. Wilson Bull., 91:323–328.

Van Tyne, J., and A. J. Berger
1976   Fundamentals of Ornithology. 2nd ed. John Wiley & Sons, New York, 808 pp.

Walker, R. L.
1967a A brief history of exotic game bird and mammal introductions into Hawaii, with a look to the future. Proc. 47th Annual Conference of the Western Assoc. of State Game and Fish Commissioners, Honolulu, pp. 94–112.

1967b Indian Hill Mynah, Cattle Egret, and Red-vented Bulbul. Elepaio 28:23–24.

1969   Field notes, 1958–1962: Hawaiian Hawk. Elepaio 30:17.

Wallace, G. D., D. Awai, A. Oda, R. E. Kissling, and W. B. Quisenberry
1964   Arthropod-borne virus survey on the island of Oahu, Hawaii. Hawaii Medical Jour. 23:364–368.

Ward, W. V.
1964   The songs of the Apapane. Living Bird 3:97–117.

Warner, R. E.
1960   A forest dies on Mauna Kea. Pacific Discovery 13(1):6–14.

1961   Hawaii's birds—birth and death of an island biota. Pacific Discovery 14(5):6–14.

1963   Recent history of the Laysan Duck. Condor 65: 3–23.

1968   The role of introduced diseases in the extinction of the endemic Hawaiian avifauna. Condor 70: 101–120.

Watling, Dick
1978   Observations on the naturalised distribution of the Red-vented Bulbul in the Pacific. Notornis 25:109–117.

Weller, M. W.
1969   Potential dangers of exotic waterfowl introductions. Wildfowl 20:55–58.

Wetmore, Alexander
1924   A warbler from Nihoa. Condor 26:177–178.

1925   Bird life among lava rock and coral sand. National Geographic Magazine 48(July 1925):76–108.

1943   An extinct goose from the island of Hawaii. Condor 45:146–148.

Whittow, G. C.
1976   The Red-footed Boobies of Oahu. Sea Frontiers 22:131–135.

Wilson, Erika
1975   Longevity of Pacific seabirds. Elepaio 35:124–126.

Wilson, S. B.
1888   On *Chloridops*, a new generic form of *Fringillidae* from the island of Hawaii. Proc. Zool. Soc. London, 1888:218.

1890a On some of the birds of the Sandwich Islands. Ibis 1890:170–196.

1890b On a new finch from Midway Island, North Pacific. Ibis 1890:339–341.

Wilson, S. B., and A. H. Evans
1890– Aves Hawaiienses: The Birds of the Sandwich
1899   Islands. R. H. Porter, London.

Wodzicki, Kazimierz
1965   The status of some exotic vertebrates in the ecolo-

gy of New Zealand. *In* The Genetics of Coloniz-
ing Species. Academic Press, New York.

Woodward, P. W.
   1972   The natural history of Kure Atoll, Northwestern
Hawaiian Islands. Atoll Research Bull. No. 164,
318 pp.

Woodward, P. W., and R. B. Clapp
   1969   First records of Baird's Sandpiper from the central Pacific. Elepaio 30:25.

Yocum, C. F.
   1967   Ecology of feral goats in Haleakala National

Park, Maui, Hawaii. Amer. Midl. Naturalist 77:
418–451.

Yuen, H. J.
   1972   Agonistic behavior of the Red Crested Cardinal.
Elepaio 33:55–61.

Zeillemaker, C. F.
   1975   Field notes from Kauai. Elepaio 36:22.

Zeillemaker, C. F., and C. J. Ralph
   1977   First breeding record of Laysan Albatross on
Kauai. Elepaio 38:51–53.

Index